Pro Android 2

Sayed Y. Hashimi
Satya Komatineni
Dave MacLean

Apress®

Pro Android 2

ISBN-13 (pbk): 978-1-4302-2659-8

ISBN-13 (electronic): 978-1-4302-2660-4

Printed and bound in the United States of America (POD)

Trademarked names may appear in this book. Rather than use a trademark symbol with every occurrence of a trademarked name, we use the names only in an editorial fashion and to the benefit of the trademark owner, with no intention of infringement of the trademark.

President and Publisher: Paul Manning
Lead Editor: Steve Anglin
Development Editor: Douglas Pundick
Technical Reviewer: Vikram Goyal
Editorial Board: Clay Andres, Steve Anglin, Mark Beckner, Ewan Buckingham, Gary Cornell, Jonathan Gennick, Jonathan Hassell, Michelle Lowman, Matthew Moodie, Duncan Parkes, Jeffrey Pepper, Frank Pohlmann, Douglas Pundick, Ben Renow-Clarke, Dominic Shakeshaft, Matt Wade, Tom Welsh
Coordinating Editor: Fran Parnell
Copy Editor: Elizabeth Berry
Compositor: MacPS, LLC
Indexer: BIM Indexing & Proofreading Services
Artist: April Milne
Cover Designer: Anna Ishchenko

Distributed to the book trade worldwide by Springer-Verlag New York, Inc., 233 Spring Street, 6th Floor, New York, NY 10013. Phone 1-800-SPRINGER, fax 201-348-4505, e-mail orders-ny@springer-sbm.com, or visit www.springeronline.com.

For information on translations, please e-mail rights@apress.com, or visit www.apress.com.

Apress and friends of ED books may be purchased in bulk for academic, corporate, or promotional use. eBook versions and licenses are also available for most titles. For more information, reference our Special Bulk Sales–eBook Licensing web page at www.apress.com/info/bulksales.

The information in this book is distributed on an "as is" basis, without warranty. Although every precaution has been taken in the preparation of this work, neither the author(s) nor Apress shall have any liability to any person or entity with respect to any loss or damage caused or alleged to be caused directly or indirectly by the information contained in this work.

The source code for this book is available to readers at www.apress.com. You will need to answer questions pertaining to this book in order to successfully download the code.

To my son, Sayed-Adieb.

—Sayed Y. Hashimi

To my beautiful wife, AnnMarie, for her spirit; to Ashley, for her undaunting hope; to Nikolas, for his kindness; to Kavitha, for being smart, witty, and fabulous; to Narayan, for sheer cuteness; and to all my extended family in India and the USA for their love.

—Satya Komatineni

To my wife, Rosie, and my son, Mike, for their support; I couldn't have done this without them. And to Max, for spending so much time at my feet keeping me company.

—Dave MacLean

Contents at a Glance

Contents

Chapter 15: Exploring Text to Speech and Translate APIs 563

Chapter 16: Touchscreens 591

Chapter 17: Titanium Mobile: A WebKit-Based Approach
to Android Development 627

Chapter 18: Working with Android Market... 661

About the Authors

Sayed Y. Hashimi was born in Afghanistan and now resides in Jacksonville, Florida. His expertise spans the fields of health care, financials, logistics, and service-oriented architecture. In his professional career, Sayed has developed large-scale distributed applications with a variety of programming languages and platforms, including C/C++, MFC, J2EE, and .NET. He has published articles in major software journals and has written several other popular Apress titles. Sayed holds a master's degree in engineering from the University of Florida. You can reach Sayed by visiting www.sayedhashimi.com.

Satya Komatineni (www.satyakomatineni.com) has over 20 years of programming experience working with small and large corporations. Satya has published over 30 articles around web development using Java, .NET, and database technologies. He is a frequent speaker at industry conferences on innovative technologies and a regular contributor to the weblogs on java.net. He is the author of AspireWeb (www.activeintellect.com/aspire), a simplified open source tool for Java web development, and the creator of Aspire Knowledge Central (www.knowledgefolders.com), an open source personal Web OS with a focus on individual productivity and publishing. Satya is also a contributing member to a number of Small Business Innovation Research Programs (SBIR). He received a bachelor's degree in Electrical Engineering from Andhra University, Visakhapatnam, and a master's degree in Electrical Engineering from the Indian Institute of Technology, New Delhi.

Dave MacLean is a software engineer and architect currently living and working in Jacksonville, Florida. Since 1980, he has programmed in many languages, developing systems ranging from robot automation systems to data warehousing, web self-service applications to EDI transaction processors. Dave has worked for Sun Microsystems, IBM, Trimble Navigation, General Motors, and several small companies. He graduated from the University of Waterloo in Canada with a degree in Systems Design Engineering. Please visit us at our website http://www.androidbook.com.

About the Technical Reviewer

 **Vikram Goyal** is a software developer living in Brisbane, Australia who has taken some time off to enjoy life with his kids. You can contact him at vikram@craftbits.com.

Acknowledgments

Writing this book took effort not only on the part of the authors, but also from some of the very talented staff at Apress, as well as the technical reviewer. Therefore, we would like to thank Steve Anglin, Douglas Pundick, Fran Parnell, Elizabeth Berry, and Brigid Duffy from Apress. We would also like to extend our appreciation to the technical reviewer, Vikram Goyal, for the work he did on the book. His commentary and corrections were invaluable. Finally, the authors are deeply grateful to their families for accommodating prolonged irresponsibility.

Foreword

Think. Code. Write. Rinse and repeat ad infinitum. This is the mantra of a technical writer. Technology changes so quickly that by the time an author has finished the last sentence, it is time to rewrite it. As a technical reader, you are probably well aware of this fact, and yet you have taken the time to purchase this book and read it. Not only that, but you are even taking the time to read this foreword. This means you are not just a fly-by-night coder, but somebody who wants to know the technology behind the technology. Well done, and congratulations on making this investment. Let me validate your decision to buy this book.

This is the best book on the market for learning about Android. It has so many chapters crammed with Android goodness that you will thank yourself many times over for making the decision to buy it. I am the technical reviewer of this book and, frankly, I wish there had been more for me to edit—the authors did such a good job, I was left with hardly anything to correct. (I did, however, curse them several times for the volume of content they managed to fit in a single book, which increased my workload several times over, right up to the last minute.) But my loss is your gain: this book covers everything you could possibly need to know about Android. Just take a look at the table of contents.

Tradition requires that I talk a little about Android itself, the subject of this book. Of course you probably already know something about Android—the operating system from Google that Google hopes will rival iPhone for market domination—which is why you are holding this book in your hands. Android, as a technology, has matured beyond its initial stab in the dark and now, with the recent announcement of NexusOne, the Android-based phone from Google, it is a force to contend with. The year 2010 will be the year of the dogfight between Google and Apple for mobile phone domination. There is room for both technologies to co-exist, but with Google's massive presence on the Web, people at Apple will be on edge.

With the massive market for Android in mind, you have taken the first two steps: a) You have chosen to develop for Android, and b) You have chosen the best book on the market to learn about Android. Now take the final step: turn the page and begin to cram your mind full of Android goodness.

Vikram Goyal
vikram@craftbits.com
www.craftbits.com
January 2010
Brisbane, Australia

Chapter 1

Introducing the Android Computing Platform

Computing continues to become more "personal," increasingly accessible anytime, anywhere. At the forefront of this development are handheld devices that are transforming into computing platforms. Mobile phones are no longer just for talking— they have been capable of carrying data and video for some time. Significantly, the mobile device is becoming so capable of general-purpose computing that it's destined to become the next PC (Personal Computer). It is also anticipated that even a number of traditional PC manufacturers such as ASUS, HP, and Dell will be producing devices of various form factors based on the Android OS. The battle lines between operating systems, computing platforms, programming languages, and development frameworks are being shifted and reapplied to mobile devices.

We are also expecting a surge in mobile programming in the IT industry as more and more IT applications start to offer mobile counterparts. To help you profit from this trend, we'll show you how to use Java to write programs for devices that run on Google's Android Platform (http://developer.android.com/index.html), an open source platform for mobile development. We are excited about Android because it is an advanced platform that introduces a number of new paradigms in framework design (even with the limitations of a mobile platform).

In this chapter, we'll provide an overview of Android and its SDK, give a brief overview of key packages, introduce what we are going to cover in each chapter briefly, show you how to take advantage of Android source code, and highlight the benefits of programming for the Android Platform.

A New Platform for a New Personal Computer

The fact that hitherto dedicated devices such as mobile phones can now count themselves among other venerable general-computing platforms is great news for programmers (see Figure 1–1). This new trend makes mobile devices accessible through general-purpose computing languages, which increases the range and market share for mobile applications.

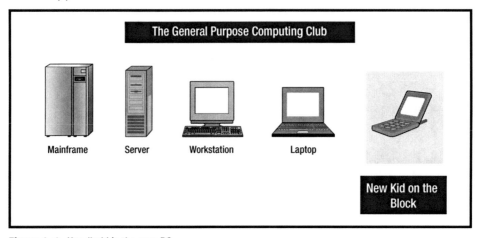

Figure 1–1. *Handheld is the new PC.*

The Android Platform embraces the idea of general-purpose computing for handheld devices. It is a comprehensive platform that features a Linux-based operating system stack for managing devices, memory, and processes. Android's libraries cover telephony, video, graphics, UI programming, and a number of other aspects of the device.

NOTE: Although built for mobile devices, the Android platform exhibits the characteristics of a full-featured desktop framework. Google makes this framework available to Java programmers through a Software Development Kit (SDK) called the Android SDK. When you are working with the Android SDK, you rarely feel that you are writing to a mobile device because you have access to most of the class libraries that you use on a desktop or a server—including a relational database.

The Android SDK supports most of the Java Platform, Standard Edition (Java SE) except for the Abstract Window Toolkit (AWT) and Swing. In place of AWT and Swing, Android SDK has its own *extensive modern UI framework*. Because you're programming your applications in Java, you could expect that you need a Java Virtual Machine (JVM) that is responsible for interpreting the runtime Java byte code. A JVM typically provides the necessary optimization to help Java reach performance levels comparable to compiled languages such as C and C++. Android offers its own optimized JVM to run the compiled Java class files in order to counter the handheld device limitations such as memory, processor speed, and power. This virtual machine is called the Dalvik VM, which we'll explore in a later section "Delving into the Dalvik VM."

The familiarity and simplicity of the Java programming language coupled with Android's extensive class library makes Android a compelling platform to write programs for.

Figure 1–2 provides an overview of the Android software stack. (We'll provide further details in the section "Understanding the Android Software Stack.")

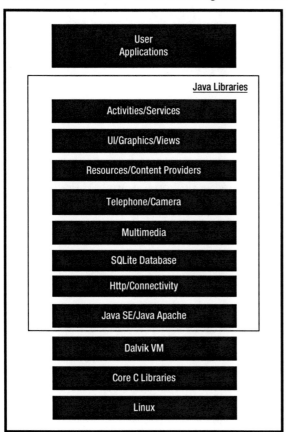

Figure 1–2. *High-level view of the Android software stack*

History of Android

Let us look at how Android arrived on the Mobile OS landscape. Mobile phones use a variety of operating systems such as Symbian OS, Microsoft's Windows Mobile, Mobile Linux, iPhone OS (based on Mac OS X), Moblin (from Intel), and many other proprietary OSs. So far no single OS has become the de facto standard. The available APIs and environments for developing mobile applications are too restrictive and seem to fall behind when compared to desktop frameworks. This is where Google comes in. The Android platform promised openness, affordability, open source code, and a high-end development framework.

Google acquired the startup company Android Inc. in 2005 to start the development of the Android Platform (see Figure 1–3). The key players at Android Inc. included Andy Rubin, Rich Miner, Nick Sears, and Chris White.

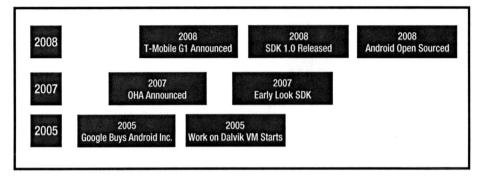

Figure 1–3. *Android timeline*

In late 2007, a group of industry leaders came together around the Android Platform to form the Open Handset Alliance (http://www.openhandsetalliance.com). Some of the alliance's prominent members are as follows:

- Sprint Nextel
- T-Mobile
- Motorola
- Samsung
- Sony Ericsson
- Toshiba
- Vodafone
- Google
- Intel
- Texas Instruments

Part of the alliance's goal is to innovate rapidly and respond better to consumer needs, and its first key outcome was the Android Platform. Android was designed to serve the needs of mobile operators, handset manufacturers, and application developers. The members have committed to release significant intellectual property through the open source Apache License, Version 2.0.

> **NOTE:** Handset manufacturers do not need to pay any licensing fees to load Android on their handsets or devices.

The Android SDK was first issued as an "early look" release in November 2007. In September 2008, T-Mobile announced the availability of T-Mobile G1, the first smartphone based on the Android platform. A few days after that, Google announced the availability of Android SDK Release Candidate 1.0. In October 2008, Google made the source code of the Android platform available under Apache's open source license.

When Android was released, one of its key architectural goals was to allow applications to interact with one another and reuse components from one another. This reuse not only applies to services, but also to data and the user interface (UI). As a result, the Android platform has a number of architectural features that keep this openness a reality. We'll delve into some of these features in Chapter 3.

Android has also attracted an early following because of its fully developed features to exploit the cloud-computing model offered by web resources and to enhance that experience with local data stores on the handset itself. Android's support for a relational database on the handset also played a part in early adoption.

In late 2008 Google released a handheld device called Android Dev Phone 1 that was capable of running Android applications without being tied to any cell phone provider network. The goal of this device (at an approximate cost of $400.00) was to allow developers to experiment with a real device that could run the Android OS without any contracts. At around the same time, Google also released a bug fix, version 1.1 of the OS, that is solely based on version 1.0. In releases 1.0 and 1.1 Android did not support soft keyboards, requiring the devices to carry physical keys. Android fixed this issue by releasing the 1.5 SDK in April 2009, along with a number of other features, such as advanced media-recording capabilities, widgets, and live folders. (We cover live folders in Chapter 12 and widgets in Chapter 13.)

In September 2009 came release 1.6 of the Android OS and, within a month, Android 2.0 followed, facilitating a flood of Android devices in time for the 2009 Christmas season. This release has introduced advanced search capabilities and text to speech. (We cover text to speech in Chapter 15. We cover Android search in Chapter 14.) This release has also introduced gestures and multi-touch. These topics are covered in Chapter 16.

With support for HTML 5, Android 2.0 introduces interesting possibilities for using HTML. These new programming possibilities are covered in Chapter 17, where we discuss Titanium Mobile. More and more Android-based applications are introduced every day, as well as new types of independent online application stores. These application stores, along with the Google-operated online Android Market, are covered in Chapter 18. In Chapter 19 we will analyze how well-positioned Android is in the mobile space.

Delving into the Dalvik VM

As part of Android, Google has spent a lot of time thinking about optimizing designs for low-powered handheld devices. Handheld devices lag behind their desktop counterparts in memory and speed by eight to ten years. They also have limited power for computation; a handheld device's total RAM might be as little as 64MB, and its available space for applications might be as little as 20MB.

NOTE: The T-Mobile G1 phone, released in late 2008, comes with 192MB of RAM, a 1GB SD card, and a 528 MHz Qualcomm MSM7201A processor. Motorola Droid, released in late 2009, comes with 256MB of RAM, a 16GB microSD card, and a 550 MHz Arm Cortex Processor. Compare that to the lowest-priced Dell laptop, which comes with a 2.1 GHz dual-core processor and 4GB of RAM.

The performance requirements on handsets are severe as a result, requiring handset designers to optimize everything. If you look at the list of packages in Android, you'll see that they are full-featured and extensive. According to Google, these system libraries might use as much as 10 to 20MB, even with their optimized JVM.

These issues led Google to revisit the standard JVM implementation in many respects. (The key figure in Google's implementation of this JVM is Dan Bornstein, who wrote the Dalvik VM—Dalvik is the name of a town in Iceland.) First, the Dalvik VM takes the generated Java class files and combines them into one or more Dalvik Executable (.dex) files. It reuses duplicate information from multiple class files, effectively reducing the space requirement (uncompressed) by half from a traditional .jar file. For example, the .dex file of the web browser app in Android is about 200K, whereas the equivalent uncompressed .jar version is about 500K. The .dex file of the alarm clock app is about 50K, and roughly twice that size in its . jar version.

Second, Google has fine-tuned the garbage collection in the Dalvik VM, but it has chosen to omit a just-in-time (JIT) compiler, in early releases. The 2.0 codebase seem to have the necessary sources for a JIT compiler but is not enabled in the final release. It is anticipated that it will be part of future releases. The company can justify this choice because many of Android's core libraries, including the graphics libraries, are implemented in C and C++. For example, the Java graphics APIs are actually thin wrapper classes around the native code using the Java Native Interface (JNI). Similarly, Android provides an optimized C-based native library to access the SQLite database, but this library is encapsulated in a higher-level Java API. Because most of the core code is in C and C++, Google reasoned that the impact of JIT compilation would not be significant.

Finally, the Dalvik VM uses a different kind of assembly-code generation, in which it uses registers as the primary units of data storage instead of the stack. Google is hoping to accomplish 30 percent fewer instructions as a result. We should point out that the final executable code in Android, as a result of the Dalvik VM, is based not on Java byte code but on .dex files instead. This means you cannot directly execute Java byte code; you have to start with Java class files and then convert them to linkable .dex files.

This performance paranoia extends into the rest of the Android SDK. For example, the Android SDK uses XML extensively to define UI layouts. However, all of this XML is compiled to binary files before these binary files become resident on the devices. Android provides special mechanisms to use this XML data. While we are on the subject of Android's design considerations, we should answer this question: How would one compare and contrast Android to Java Platform, Micro Edition (Java ME)?

Comparing Android and Java ME

As you have already seen, Android has taken a comprehensive, dedicated, and focused approach to its mobile platform efforts that go beyond a simple JVM-based solution. The Android Platform comes with everything you need in a single package: the OS, device drivers, core libraries, JNI, optimized Dalvik VM, and the Java development environment. Developers can be assured that when they develop new applications, all key libraries will be available on the device.

This comprehensive approach differs from other mobile efforts such as Java ME. Let us offer a brief overview of Java ME before comparing the two approaches. Figure 1–4 shows the availability of Java for various computing configurations. Java Platform, Standard Edition (Java SE) is suitable for desktop and workstation configurations. Java Platform, Enterprise Edition (Java EE) is designed for server configurations.

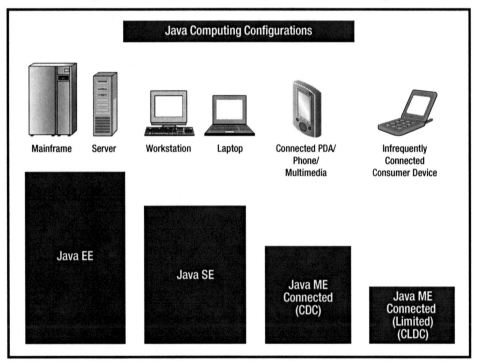

Figure 1–4. *Java computing configurations*

Java Platform, Micro Edition (Java ME) is an edition of Java that is pared down for smaller devices. Two configuration sets are available for Java ME. The first configuration is called the Connected Device Configuration (CDC). Java ME for CDC involves a pared-down version of Java SE with fewer packages, fewer classes within those packages, and even fewer fields and methods within those classes. For appliances and devices that are further constrained, Java defines a configuration called Connected Limited Device Configuration (CLDC). The available APIs for various Java configurations are contrasted in Figure 1–5.

Any optional packages that are installed on top of the base CDC and CLDC APIs are treated as "profiles" that are standardized using the JSR process. Each defined profile makes an additional set of APIs available to the developer.

CAUTION: Both CLDC and CDC might support some Java APIs outside Java SE, and their classes might not start with the `java.*` namespace. As a consequence, if you have a Java program that runs on your desktop, there are no guarantees that it will run on devices supporting only micro editions.

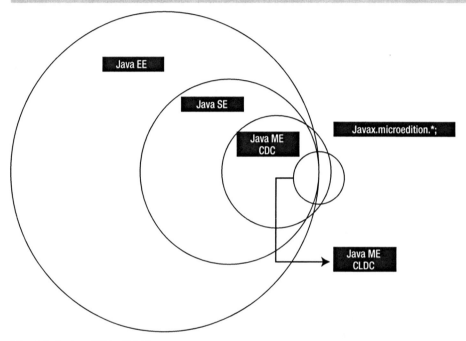

Figure 1–5. *Java API availability*

The CLDC Java platform is hosted on a specialized and greatly reduced JVM called the K Virtual Machine (KVM), which is capable of running on devices whose memory is as low as 128K. (The K in KVM stands for kilobytes.) CLDC can run additional APIs under MIDP (Mobile Information Device Profile) 2.0. This API includes a number of packages under `javax.microedition.*`. The key packages are MIDlets (simple applications), a UI package called LCDUI, gaming, and media.

The CDC configuration APIs include the `java.awt` API, the `java.net` API, and more security APIs, in addition to the CLDC configuration APIs. The additional profiles available on top of CDC make the `javax.microedition.xlet` API available to application programmers (Xlets represent applications in the CDC configuration). On top of a CDC configuration you'll find about ten more optional packages that you can run, including Bluetooth, Media API, OpenGL for Embedded Systems (OpenGL ES), Java API for XML Processing (JAXP), JAXP-RPC, Java 2D, Swing, Java Remote Method Invocation (Java

RMI), Java Database Connectivity (JDBC), and Java API. Overall, the Java ME specification includes more than 20 JSRs. It is also expected that JavaFX (http://javafx.com) will play an increasing role in the mobile space for Java.

> **NOTE:** JavaFX is a new user interface effort from Sun to dramatically improve applet-like functionality in browsers. It offers a declarative UI programming model that is also friendlier to designers.

Now that you have a background on Java ME, let's look at how it compares to Android.

- *Multiple device configurations*: Java ME addresses two classes of micro devices and offers standardized and distinct solutions for each. Android, on the other hand, applies to just one model. It won't run on low-end devices unless or until the configurations of those devices improve.

- *Ease of understanding*: Because Android is geared toward only one device model, it's easier to understand than Java ME. Java ME has multiple UI models for each configuration, depending on the features supported by the device: MIDlets, Xlets, the AWT, and Swing. The JSRs for each Java ME specification are harder to follow. They take longer to mature, and finding implementations for them can be difficult.

- *Responsiveness*: The Dalvik VM is expected to be more optimized and more responsive compared to the standard JVM supported on a similarly configured device. You can compare the Dalvik VM to the KVM, but the KVM addresses a lower-level device with much less memory.

- *Java compatibility*: Because of the Dalvik VM, Android runs .dex byte code instead of Java byte code. This should not be a major concern as long as Java is compiled to standard Java class files. Only runtime interpretation of Java byte code is not possible.

- *Adoption*: There is widespread support for Java ME on mobile devices because most mobile phones support it. But the uniformity, cost, and ease of development in Android are compelling reasons for Java developers to program for it.

- *Java SE support*: Compared to the support for Java SE in CDC, the Android support for Java SE is a bit more complete, except for the AWT and Swing. As we mentioned earlier, Android has its own UI approach instead. In fact, Android's declarative UI resembles more advanced UI platforms such as Microsoft Silverlight and Sun's JavaFX.

Understanding the Android Software Stack

So far we've covered Android's history and its optimization features including the Dalvik VM, and we've hinted at the Java programming stack available. In this section, we would like to cover the development aspect of Android. Figure 1–6 is a good place to start this discussion.

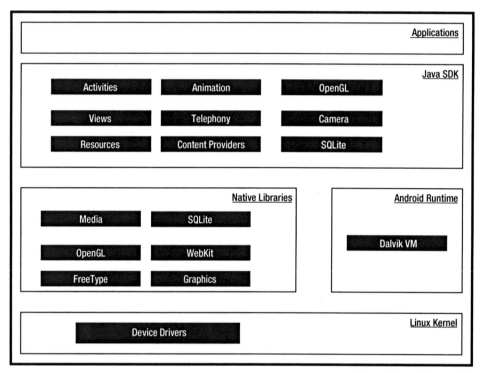

Figure 1–6. *Detailed Android SDK software stack*

At the core of the Android Platform is Linux kernel version 2.6.29, responsible for device drivers, resource access, power management, and other OS duties. The supplied device drivers include Display, Camera, Keypad, WiFi, Flash Memory, Audio, and IPC (inter-process communication). Although the core is Linux, the majority—if not all—of the applications on an Android device such as the T-Mobile G1 or Motorola Droid are developed in Java and run through the Dalvik VM.

Sitting at the next level, on top of the kernel, are a number of C/C++ libraries such as OpenGL, WebKit, FreeType, Secure Sockets Layer (SSL), the C runtime library (libc), SQLite, and Media. The system C library based on Berkeley Software Distribution (BSD) is tuned (to roughly half its original size) for embedded Linux-based devices. The media libraries are based on PacketVideo's (http://www.packetvideo.com/) OpenCORE. These libraries are responsible for recording and playback of audio and video formats. A library called Surface Manager controls access to the display system and supports 2D and 3D.

The WebKit library is responsible for browser support; it is the same library that supports Google Chrome and Apple's Safari. The FreeType library is responsible for font support. SQLite (http://www.sqlite.org/) is a relational database that is available on the device itself. SQLite is also an independent open source effort for relational databases and not directly tied to Android. You can acquire and use tools meant for SQLite for Android databases as well.

Most of the application framework accesses these core libraries through the Dalvik VM, the gateway to the Android Platform. As we indicated in the previous sections, Dalvik is optimized to run multiple instances of VMs. As Java applications access these core libraries, each application gets its own VM instance.

The Android Java API's main libraries include telephony, resources, locations, UI, content providers (data), and package managers (installation, security, and so on). Programmers develop end-user applications on top of this Java API. Some examples of end-user applications on the device include Home, Contacts, Phone, Browser, and so on.

Android also supports a custom Google 2D graphics library called Skia, which is written in C and C++. Skia also forms the core of the Google Chrome browser. The 3D APIs in Android, however, are based on an implementation of OpenGL ES from the Khronos group (http://www.khronos.org). OpenGL ES contains subsets of OpenGL that are targeted toward embedded systems.

From a media perspective, the Android Platform supports the most common formats for audio, video, and images. From a wireless perspective, Android has APIs to support Bluetooth, EDGE, 3G, WiFi, and Global System for Mobile Communication (GSM) telephony, depending on the hardware.

Developing an End-User Application with the Android SDK

In this section, we'll introduce you to the high-level Android Java APIs that you'll use to develop end-user applications on Android. We will briefly talk about the Android emulator, Android foundational components, UI programming, services, media, telephony, animation, and OpenGL. We will also show you some code snippets.

Android Emulator

Android SDK ships with an Eclipse plug-in called Android Development Tools (ADT). You will use this Integrated Development Environment (IDE) tool for developing, debugging, and testing your Java applications. (We'll cover ADT in depth in Chapter 2.) You can also use the Android SDK without using ADT; you'd use command-line tools instead. Both approaches support an emulator that you can use to run, debug, and test your applications. You will not even need the real device for 90 percent of your application development. The full-featured Android emulator mimics most of the device features.

The emulator limitations include USB connections, camera and video capture, headphones, battery simulation, and Bluetooth.

The Android emulator accomplishes its work through an open source "processor emulator" technology called QEMU (http://bellard.org/qemu/) developed by Fabrice Bellard. This is the same technology that allows emulation of one operating system on top of another, irrespective of the processor. QEMU allows emulation at the CPU level.

With the Android emulator, the processor is based on ARM (Advanced RISC Machine). ARM is a 32-bit microprocessor architecture based on RISC (Reduced Instruction Set Computer), in which design simplicity and speed is achieved through a reduced number of instructions in an instruction set. The emulator runs the Android version of Linux on this simulated processor.

> **NOTE:** Many high-end graphics and scientific workstations from HP and Sun are based on advanced RISC processors.

ARM is widely used in handhelds and other embedded electronics where lower power consumption is important. Much of the mobile market uses processors based on this architecture. For example, Apple Newton was based on the ARM6 processor. Devices such as the iPod, Nintendo DS, and Game Boy Advance run on ARM architecture version 4 with approximately 30,000 transistors. Compared to that, the Pentium classic contains 3,200,000 (3. 2 million) transistors.

You can find more details about the emulator in the Android SDK documentation at http://developer.android.com/guide/developing/tools/emulator.html.

The Android UI

Android uses a UI framework that resembles other desktop-based, full-featured UI frameworks. In fact, it's more modern and more asynchronous in nature. The Android UI is essentially a fourth-generation UI framework, if you consider the traditional C-based Microsoft Windows API the first generation and the C++-based MFC (Microsoft Foundation Classes) the second generation. The Java-based Swing UI framework would be the third generation, introducing design flexibility far beyond that offered by MFC. The Android UI, JavaFX, Microsoft Silverlight, and Mozilla XML User Interface Language (XUL) fall under this new type of fourth-generation UI framework, in which the UI is declarative and independently themed.

> **NOTE:** In Android, you program using a modern user interface paradigm even though the device you're programming for happens to be a handheld.

Programming in the Android UI involves declaring the interface in XML files. You then load these XML view definitions as windows in your UI application. Even menus in your application are loaded from XML files. Screens or windows in Android are often referred to as *activities*, which comprise multiple views that a user needs in order to accomplish a logical unit of action. *Views* are Android's basic UI building blocks, and you can further combine them to form composite views called *view groups*. Views internally use the familiar concepts of canvases, painting, and user interaction. An activity hosting these composite views, which include views and view groups, is the logical replaceable UI component in Android.

One of the Android framework's key concepts is the lifecycle management of activity windows. Protocols are put in place so that Android can manage state as users hide, restore, stop, and close activity windows. You will get a feel for these basic ideas in Chapter 2, along with an introduction to setting up the Android development environment.

The Android Foundational Components

The Android UI framework, along with other parts of Android, relies on a new concept called an *intent*. An intent is an amalgamation of ideas such as windowing messages, actions, publish-and-subscribe models, inter-process communications, and application registries. Here is an example of using the Intent class to invoke or start a web browser:

```
public static void invokeWebBrowser(Activity activity)
{
    Intent intent = new Intent(Intent.ACTION_VIEW);
    intent.setData(Uri.parse("http://www.google.com"));
    activity.startActivity(intent);
}
```

In this example, through an intent, we are asking Android to start a suitable window to display the content of a web site. Depending on the list of browsers that are installed on the device, Android will choose a suitable one to display the site. You will learn more about intents in Chapter 3.

Android also has extensive support for *resources*, which include familiar elements and files such as strings and bitmaps, as well as some not-so-familiar items such as XML-based view definitions. The framework makes use of resources in a novel way to make their usage easy, intuitive, and convenient. Here is an example where resource IDs are automatically generated for resources defined in XML files:

```
public final class R {
    public static final class attr { }
    public static final class drawable {
        public static final int myanimation=0x7f020001;
        public static final int numbers19=0x7f02000e;
    }

    public static final class id {
        public static final int textViewId1=0x7f080003;
    }
    public static final class layout {
        public static final int frame_animations_layout=0x7f030001;
        public static final int main=0x7f030002;
    }
```

```
    public static final class string {
        public static final int hello=0x7f070000;
    }
}
```

Each auto-generated ID in this class corresponds to either an element in an XML file or a whole file itself. Wherever you would like to use those XML definitions, you will use these generated IDs instead. This indirection helps a great deal when it comes to localization. (Chapter 3 covers the R.java file and resources in more detail.)

Another new concept in Android is the *content provider*. A content provider is an abstraction on a data source that makes it look like an emitter and consumer of RESTful services. The underlying SQLite database makes this facility of content providers a powerful tool for application developers. (In Chapter 3, we'll discuss how intents, resources, and content providers promote openness in the Android Platform.)

Advanced UI Concepts

We have already pointed out that XML plays a critical role in describing the Android UI. Let's look at an example of how XML does this for a simple layout containing a text view:

```xml
<?xml version="1.0" encoding="utf-8"?>
<LinearLayout xmlns:android=http://schemas.android.com/apk/res/android>
<TextView android:id="@+id/textViewId"
    android:layout_width="fill_parent"
    android:layout_height="wrap_content"
    android:text="@string/hello"
    />
</LinearLayout>
```

You will use an ID generated for this XML file to load this layout into an activity window. (We'll cover this process further in Chapter 4.) Android also provides extensive support for menus, from standard menus to context menus. You'll find it convenient to work with menus in Android because they are also loaded as XML files and because resource IDs for those menus are auto-generated. Here's how you would declare menus in an XML file:

```xml
<menu xmlns:android="http://schemas.android.com/apk/res/android">
    <!-- This group uses the default category. -->
    <group android:id="@+id/menuGroup_Main">
        <item android:id="@+id/menu_clear"
            android:orderInCategory="10"
            android:title="clear" />
        <item android:id="@+id/menu_show_browser"
            android:orderInCategory="5"
            android:title="show browser" />
    </group>
</menu>
```

Although Android supports dialogs, all dialogs in Android are asynchronous. These asynchronous dialogs present a special challenge to developers accustomed to the synchronous modal dialogs in some windowing frameworks. We'll address menus and dialogs more extensively in Chapter 5, where we'll also provide a number of mechanisms to deal with asynchronous-dialog protocols.

Android also offers support for animation as part of its UI stack based on views and drawable objects. Android supports two kinds of animation: tweening animation and frame-by-frame animation. *Tweening* is a term in animation that refers to the drawings that are *in between* the key drawings. You accomplish this with computers by changing the intermediate values at regular intervals and redrawing the surface. Frame-by-frame animation occurs when a series of frames is drawn one after the other at regular intervals. Android enables both animation approaches through animation callbacks, interpolators, and transformation matrices. Moreover, Android allows you to define these animations in an XML resource file. Check out this example, in which a series of numbered images is played in frame-by-frame animation:

```
<animation-list xmlns:android="http://schemas.android.com/apk/res/android"
        android:oneshot="false">
  <item android:drawable="@drawable/numbers11" android:duration="50" />
  ......
  <item android:drawable="@drawable/numbers19" android:duration="50" />
</animation-list>
```

The underlying graphics libraries support the standard transformation matrices, allowing scaling, movement, and rotation. A Camera object in the graphics library provides support for depth and projection, which allows 3D-like simulation on a 2D surface. (We'll explore animation further in Chapter 6.)

Android also supports 3D graphics through its implementation of the OpenGL ES 1.0 standard. OpenGL ES, like OpenGL, is a C-based flat API. The Android SDK, because it's a Java-based programming API, needs to use Java binding to access the OpenGL ES. Java ME has already defined this binding through Java Specification Request (JSR) 239 for OpenGL ES, and Android uses the same Java binding for OpenGL ES in its implementation. If you are not familiar with OpenGL programming, the learning curve is steep. But we've reviewed the basics here, so you'll be ready to start programming in OpenGL for Android when you complete Chapter 10.

Android has a number of new ideas that revolve around *information at your fingertips* using the home page. The first of these ideas is *live folders*. Using live folders you can publish a collection of items as a folder on the home page. The contents of this collection change as the underlying data changes. This changing data could be either on the device or from the Internet. (We will cover live folders in Chapter 12.)

The second home page–based idea is the *home screen widget*. Home screen widgets are used to paint information on the home page using a UI widget. This information can change at regular intervals. An example could be the number of e-mail messages in your e-mail store. We describe home screen widgets in Chapter 13.

Integrated Android Search is the third home page–based idea. Using integrated search you can search for content both on the device and also across the Internet. Android search goes beyond search and allows you to fire off commands through the search control. We cover Android search in Chapter 14.

Android also supports gestures based on finger movement on the device. Android allows you to record any random motion on the screen as a named gesture. This gesture can then be used by applications to indicate specific actions. We cover touchscreens and gestures in Chapter 16.

Outside of the Android SDK, there are a number of independent innovations taking place to make development exciting and easy. Some examples are XML/VM, PhoneGap, and Titanium. Titanium allows you to use HTML technologies to program the WebKit-based Android browser. This is a very fluid and exciting approach to UI development, which we cover in Chapter 17.

Android Service Components

Security is a fundamental part of the Android Platform. In Android, security spans all phases of the application lifecycle—from design-time policy considerations to runtime boundary checks. Location-based service is another of the more exciting components of the Android SDK. This portion of the SDK provides application developers APIs to display and manipulate maps, as well as obtain real-time device-location information. We'll cover these ideas in detail in Chapter 7.

In Chapter 8, we'll show you how to build and consume services in Android, specifically HTTP services. This chapter will also cover inter-process communication (communication between applications on the same device).

Here is an example of an HttpPost in Android:

```
InputStream is = this.getAssets().open("data.xml");
HttpClient httpClient = new DefaultHttpClient();
HttpPost postRequest = new HttpPost("http://192.178.10.131/WS2/Upload.aspx");

byte[] data = IOUtils.toByteArray(is);

InputStreamBody isb = new InputStreamBody(
                new ByteArrayInputStream(data),"uploadedFile");
StringBody sb1 = new StringBody("someTextGoesHere");
StringBody sb2 = new StringBody("someTextGoesHere too");

MultipartEntity multipartContent = new MultipartEntity();
multipartContent.addPart("uploadedFile", isb);
multipartContent.addPart("one", sb1);
multipartContent.addPart("two", sb2);

postRequest.setEntity(multipartContent);
HttpResponse res =httpClient.execute(postRequest);
res.getEntity().getContent().close();
```

Android Media and Telephony Components

Android has APIs that cover audio, video, and telephony components. Here is a quick example of how to play an audio file from an Internet URL:

```
private void playAudio(String url)throws Exception
{
    mediaPlayer = new MediaPlayer();
    mediaPlayer.setDataSource(internetUrl);
    mediaPlayer.prepare();
    mediaPlayer.start();
}
```

And here's an example of playing an audio file from the local device:

```
private void playLocalAudio()throws Exception
{
    //The file is located in the /res/raw directory and called "music_file.mp3"
    mediaPlayer = MediaPlayer.create(this, R.raw.music_file);
    mediaPlayer.start();
}
```

We'll cover these audio and video APIs extensively in Chapter 9. The chapter will also address the following aspects of the telephony API:

- Sending and receiving Short Message Service (SMS) messages

- Monitoring SMS messages

- Managing SMS folders

- Placing and receiving phone calls

Here is an example of sending an SMS message:

```
private void sendSmsMessage(String address,String message)throws Exception
{
    SmsManager smsMgr = SmsManager.getDefault();
    smsMgr.sendTextMessage(address, null, message, null, null);
}
```

Prior to the 1.5 release you could record audio but not video. Both audio and video recording are accommodated in release 1.5 through MediaRecorder. Chapter 9 also covers voice recognition, along with the input-method framework (IMF), which allows a variety of inputs to be interpreted as text while typing into text controls. The input methods include keyboard, voice, pen device, mouse, and so forth. This framework was originally designed as part of Java API 1.4; you can read more about it at the following Java site:

```
http://java.sun.com/j2se/1.4.2/docs/guide/imf/overview.html
```

Starting with Android 2.0, Android includes the Pico Text To Speech engine. Android provides a very simple interface to read text as speech. The code is as simple as

```
TextToSpeech mTTS;
....
mTTS.speak(sometextString, TextToSpeech.QUEUE_ADD);
...
 mTTS.setOnUtteranceCompletedListener(this);
....
mTTS.stop();
....
mTTS.shutdown();
```

```
...
mTTS.synthesizeToFile(...)
```

Some other methods in this space include

```
playEarcon
playSilence
setLanguage
setPitch
setSpeechRate
isSpeaking
```

You will learn all about these in Chapter 15.

Last but not least, Android ties all these concepts into an application by creating a single XML file that defines what an application package is. This file is called the application's manifest file (AndroidManifest.xml). Here is an example:

```xml
<?xml version="1.0" encoding="utf-8"?>
<manifest xmlns:android="http://schemas.android.com/apk/res/android"
    package="com.ai.android.HelloWorld"
    android:versionCode="1"
    android:versionName="1.0.0">
  <application android:icon="@drawable/icon" android:label="@string/app_name">
    <activity android:name=".HelloWorld"
          android:label="@string/app_name">
      <intent-filter>
        <action android:name="android.intent.action.MAIN" />
        <category android:name="android.intent.category.LAUNCHER" />
      </intent-filter>
    </activity>
  </application>
</manifest>
```

The Android manifest file is where activities are defined, where services and content providers are registered, and where permissions are declared. Details about the manifest file will emerge throughout the book as we develop each idea.

Android Java Packages

One way to get a quick snapshot of the Android Platform is to look at the structure of Java packages. Because Android deviates from the standard JDK distribution, it is important to know what is supported and what is not. Here's a brief description of the important packages that are included in the Android SDK:

- *android.app*: Implements the Application model for Android. Primary classes include Application, representing the start and stop semantics, as well as a number of activity-related classes, controls, dialogs, alerts, and notifications.

- *android.bluetooth*: Provides a number of classes to work with Bluetooth functionality. The main classes include `BluetoothAdapter`, `BluetoothDevice`, `BluetoothSocket`, `BluetoothServerSocket`, and `BluetoothClass`. You can use `BluetoothAdapter` to control the locally installed Bluetooth adapter. For example, you can enable it, disable it, and start the discovery process. The `BluetoothDevice` represents the remote Bluetooth device that you are connecting with. The two Bluetooth sockets are used to establish communication between the devices. A Bluetooth class represents the type of Bluetooth device you are connecting to.

- *android.content*: Implements the concepts of content providers. Content providers abstract out data access from data stores. This package also implements the central ideas around intents and Android Uniform Resource Identifiers (URIs).

- *android.content.pm*: Implements Package Manager–related classes. A package manager knows about permissions, installed packages, installed providers, installed services, installed components such as activities, and installed applications.

- *android.content.res*: Provides access to resource files both structured and unstructured. The primary classes are `AssetManager` (for unstructured resources) and `Resources`.

- *android.database*: Implements the idea of an abstract database. The primary interface is the `Cursor` interface.

- *android.database.sqlite*: Implements the concepts from the android.database package using SQLite as the physical database. Primary classes are `SQLiteCursor`, `SQLiteDatabase`, `SQLiteQuery`, `SQLiteQueryBuilder`, and `SQLiteStatement`. However, most of your interaction is going to be with classes from the abstract android.database package.

- *android.gesture*: This package houses all the classes and interfaces necessary to work with user-defined gestures. Primary classes are `Gesture`, `GestureLibrary`, `GestureOverlayView`, `GestureStore`, `GestureStroke`, `GesturePoint`. A `Gesture` is a collection of `GestureStrokes` and `GesturePoints`. Gestures are collected in a `GestureLibrary`. Gesture libraries are stored in a `GestureStore`. Gestures are named so that they can be identified as actions.

- *android.graphics*: Contains the classes `Bitmap`, `Canvas`, `Camera`, `Color`, `Matrix`, `Movie`, `Paint`, `Path`, `Rasterizer`, `Shader`, `SweepGradient`, and `TypeFace`.

- *android.graphics.drawable*: Implements drawing protocols and background images, and allows animation of drawable objects.

- *android.graphics.drawable.shapes*: Implements shapes including ArcShape, OvalShape, PathShape, RectShape, and RoundRectShape.

- *android.hardware*: Implements the physical Camera-related classes. The Camera represents the hardware camera, whereas android.graphics.Camera represents a graphical concept that's not related to a physical camera at all.

- *android.location*: Contains the classes Address, GeoCoder, Location, LocationManager, and LocationProvider. The Address class represents the simplified XAL (Extensible Address Language). GeoCoder allows you to get a latitude/longitude coordinate given an address, and vice versa. Location represents the latitude/longitude.

- *android.media*: Contains the classes MediaPlayer, MediaRecorder, Ringtone, AudioManager, and FaceDetector. MediaPlayer, which supports streaming, is used to play audio and video. MediaRecorder is used to record audio and video. The Ringtone class is used to play short sound snippets that could serve as ringtones and notifications. AudioManager is responsible for volume controls. You can use FaceDetector to detect people's faces in a bitmap.

- *android.net*: Implements the basic socket-level network APIs. Primary classes include Uri, ConnectivityManager, LocalSocket, and LocalServerSocket. It is also worth noting here that Android supports HTTPS at the browser level and also at the network level. Android also supports JavaScript in its browser.

- *android.net.wifi*: Manages WiFi connectivity. Primary classes include WifiManager and WifiConfiguration. WifiManager is responsible for listing the configured networks and the currently active WiFi network.

- *android.opengl*: Contains utility classes surrounding OpenGL ES operations. The primary classes of OpenGL ES are implemented in a different set of packages borrowed from JSR 239. These packages are javax.microedition.khronos.opengles, javax.microedition.khronos.egl, and javax.microedition.khronos.nio. These packages are thin wrappers around the Khronos implementation of OpenGL ES in C and C++.

- *android.os*: Represents the OS services accessible through the Java programming language. Some important classes include BatteryManager, Binder, FileObserver, Handler, Looper, and PowerManager. Binder is a class that allows interprocess communication. FileObserver keeps tabs on changes to files. You use Handler classes to run tasks on the message thread, and Looper to run a message thread.

- *android.preference*: Allows applications the ability to have users manage their preferences for that application in a uniform way. The primary classes are PreferenceActivity, PreferenceScreen, and various Preference-derived classes such as CheckBoxPreference and SharedPreferences.

- *android.provider*: Comprises a set of prebuilt content providers adhering to the android.content.ContentProvider interface. The content providers include Contacts, MediaStore, Browser, and Settings. This set of interfaces and classes stores the metadata for the underlying data structures.

- *android.sax*: Contains an efficient set of Simple API for XML (SAX) parsing utility classes. Primary classes include Element, RootElement, and a number of ElementListener interfaces.

- *android.speech*: Contains constants for use with speech recognition. This package is available only in releases 1.5 and later.

- *android.speech.tts*: Provides support for converting text to speech. The primary class is TextToSpeech. You will be able to take text and ask an instance of this class to queue the text to be spoken. You have access to a number of callbacks to monitor when the speech has finished, for example. Android uses the Pico TTS (Text to Speech) engine from SVOX.

- *android.telephony*: Contains the classes CellLocation, PhoneNumberUtils, and TelephonyManager. A TelephonyManager lets you determine cell location, phone number, network operator name, network type, phone type, and Subscriber Identity Module (SIM) serial number.

- *android.telephony.gsm*: Allows you to gather cell location based on cell towers and also hosts classes responsible for SMS messaging. This package is called GSM because Global System for Mobile Communication is the technology that originally defined the SMS data-messaging standard.

- *android.telephony.cdma*: Provides support for CDMA telephony.

- *android.text*: Contains text-processing classes.

- *android.text.method*: Provides classes for entering text input for a variety of controls.

- *android.text.style*: Provides a number of styling mechanisms for a span of text.

- *android.utils*: Contains the classes Log, DebugUtils, TimeUtils, and Xml.

- *android.view*: Contains the classes Menu, View, ViewGroup, and a series of listeners and callbacks.

- *android.view.animation*: Provides support for tweening animation. The main classes include Animation, a series of interpolators for animation, and a set of specific animator classes that include AlphaAnimation, ScaleAnimation, TranslationAnimation, and RotationAnimation.

- *android.view.inputmethod*: Implements the input-method framework architecture. This package is available only in releases 1.5 and later.

- *android.webkit*: Contains classes representing the web browser. The primary classes include WebView, CacheManager, and CookieManager.

- *android.widget*: Contains all of the UI controls usually derived from the View class. Primary widgets include Button, Checkbox, Chronometer, AnalogClock, DatePicker, DigitalClock, EditText, ListView, FrameLayout, GridView, ImageButton, MediaController, ProgressBar, RadioButton, RadioGroup, RatingButton, Scroller, ScrollView, Spinner, TabWidget, TextView, TimePicker, VideoView, and ZoomButton.

- *com.google.android.maps*: Contains the classes MapView, MapController, and MapActivity, essentially classes required to work with Google maps.

These are some of the critical Android-specific packages. From this list you can see the depth of the Android core platform.

NOTE: In all, the Android Java API contains more than 40 packages and more than 700 classes.

In addition, Android provides a number of packages in the java.* namespace. These include awt.font, io, lang, lang.annotation, lang.ref, lang.reflect, math, net, nio, nio.channels, nio.channels.spi, nio.charset, security, security.acl, security.cert, security.interfaces, security.spec, sql, text, util, util.concurrent, util.concurrent.atomic, util.concurrent.locks, util.jar, util.logging, util.prefs, util.regex, and util.zip. Android comes with these packages from the javax namespace: crypto, crypto.spec, microedition.khronos.egl, microedition.khronos.opengles, net, net.ssl, security.auth, security.auth.callback, security.auth.login, security.auth.x500, security.cert, sql, xml, and xmlparsers. In addition to these, it contains a lot of packages from org.apache.http.* as well as org.json, org.w3c.dom, org.xml.sax, org.xml.sax.ext, org.xml.sax.helpers, org.xmlpull.v1, and org.xmlpull.v1.sax2. Together, these numerous packages provide a rich computing platform to write applications for handheld devices.

Taking Advantage of Android Source Code

In the early releases of Android, documentation was a bit wanting in places. Android source code could be used to fill the gaps.

The details of the Android source distribution are published at http://source.android.com. The code was made available as open source around October 2008 (read the announcement at http://source.android.com/posts/opensource). One of the Open Handset Alliance's goals was to make Android a free and fully customizable mobile platform. The announcement strongly suggests that the Android platform is a fully capable mobile computing platform with no gaps. The open source model allows contributions from public communities.

As indicated, Android is a platform and not just one project. You can see the scope and the number of projects at http://source.android.com/projects.

The source code for Android and all its projects is managed by the Git source code control system. Git (http://git.or.cz/) is an open-source source-control system designed to handle large and small projects with speed and convenience. The Linux kernel and Ruby on Rails projects also rely on Git for version control. The complete list of Android projects in the Git repository appears at http://android.git.kernel.org/.

You can download any of these projects using the tools provided by Git and described at the product's web site. Some of the primary projects include Dalvik, frameworks/base (the android.jar file), the Linux kernel, and a number of external libraries such as Apache HTTP libraries (apache-http). The core Android applications are also hosted here. Some of these core applications include: AlarmClock, Browser, Calculator, Calendar, Camera, Contacts, Email, GoogleSearch, HTML Viewer, IM, Launcher, Mms, Music, PackageInstaller, Phone, Settings, SoundRecorder, Stk, Sync, Updater, and VoiceDialer.

The Android projects also include the Provider projects. *Provider projects* are like databases in Android that wrap their data into RESTful services. These projects are CalendarProvider, ContactsProvider, DownloadProvider, DrmProvider, GoogleContactsProvider, GoogleSubscribedFeedsProvider, ImProvider, MediaProvider, SettingsProvider, Subscribed FeedsProvider, and TelephonyProvider.

As a programmer, you will be most interested in the source code that makes up the android.jar file. (If you'd rather download the entire platform and build it yourself, refer to the documentation available at http://source.android.com/download.) You can download the source for this .jar file by typing in the following URL: http://git.source.android.com/?p=platform/frameworks/base.git;a=snapshot;h=HEAD ;sf=tgz.

This is a general-purpose URL you can use to download Git projects. On Windows, you can unzip this file using pkzip. Although you can download and unzip the source, it might be more convenient to just look at these files online, if you don't need to debug the source code through your IDE. Git also allows you to do this. For example, you can

browse through android.jar source files by visiting this URL:
http://android.git.kernel.org/?p=platform/frameworks/base.git;a=summary.

However, you have to do some work after you visit this page. Pick grep from the drop-down list and enter some text in the search box. Click one of the resulting file names to open that source file in your browser. This facility is convenient for a quick look-up of source code.

At times, the file you are looking for might not be in the frameworks/base directory or project. In that case, you need to find the list of projects and search each one step by step. The URL for this list is here: http://android.git.kernel.org/.

You cannot grep across all projects, so you will need to know which project belongs to which facility in Android. For example, the graphics-related libraries in the Skia project are available here:
http://android.git.kernel.org/?p=platform/external/skia.git;a=summary.

The SkMatrix.cpp file contains the source code for a transformational matrix, which is useful in animation:
http://android.git.kernel.org/?p=platform/external/skia.git;a=blob;f=src/core/SkMatrix.cpp.

Summary

In this chapter, we wanted to pique your curiosity about Android. You learned that Android programming is done in Java and that the Open Handset Alliance is propelling the Android effort. You saw how handhelds are becoming general-purpose computing devices, and you got an overview of the Dalvik VM, which makes it possible to run a complex framework on a constrained handset.

You also saw how Android's approach compares to that of Java ME. You explored Android's software stack and got a taste of its programming concepts, which we'll cover in subsequent chapters. You saw some sample code and learned where to find and download Android source code.

We hope this chapter has convinced you that you can program productively for the Android platform without hurdles. We welcome you to journey through the rest of the book for an in-depth understanding of the Android SDK.

Chapter 2

Getting Your Feet Wet

In the last chapter, we provided an overview of Android's history and hinted at concepts we'll cover in the rest of the book. At this point, you're probably eager to get your hands on some code. We'll start by showing you what you need to start building applications with the Android Software Development Kit (SDK) and help you set up your development environment. Next, we'll baby-step you through a "Hello World!" application and dissect a slightly larger application after that. Then we'll explain the Android application lifecycle and end with a brief discussion about debugging your applications with Android Virtual Devices (AVDs).

To build applications for Android, you'll need the Java SE Development Kit (JDK), the Android SDK, and a development environment. Strictly speaking, you can develop your applications using a primitive text editor, but for the purposes of this book, we'll use the commonly available Eclipse IDE. The Android SDK requires JDK 5 or higher (we used JDK 6 for the examples) and Eclipse 3.3 or higher (we used Eclipse 3.5, or Galileo). For this book, we used Android SDK 2.0.

Finally, to make your life easier, you'll want to use Android Development Tools (ADT). ADT is an Eclipse plug-in that supports building Android applications with the Eclipse IDE. In fact, we built all the examples in this book using the Eclipse IDE with the ADT tool.

Setting Up Your Environment

To build Android applications, you need to establish a development environment. In this section, we are going to walk you through downloading JDK 6, the Eclipse IDE, the Android SDK, and Android Development Tools (ADT). We'll also help you configure Eclipse to build Android applications.

The Android SDK is compatible with Windows (Windows XP, Windows Vista, and Windows 7), Mac OS X (Intel only), and Linux (Intel only). In this chapter, we'll show you how to set up your environment for all of these platforms (for Linux, we only cover the Ubuntu variant). We will not specifically address any platform differences in other chapters.

Downloading JDK 6

The first thing you'll need is the Java SE Development Kit. The Android SDK requires JDK 5 or higher; we developed the examples using JDK 6. For Windows, download JDK 6 from the Sun web site (http://java.sun.com/javase/downloads/) and install it. You only need the Java SE Development Kit (JDK), not the bundles. For Mac OS X, download the JDK from the Apple web site (http://developer.apple.com/java/download/), select the appropriate file for your particular version of Mac OS, and install it. To install the JDK for Linux, open a terminal window and type the following:

```
sudo apt-get install sun-java6-jdk
```

This will install the JDK as well as any dependencies such as the Java Runtime Environment (JRE).

Next, set the JAVA_HOME environment variable to point to the JDK install folder. On a Windows XP machine, you can do this by going to Start ➤ My Computer, right-click to get Properties, choose the Advanced tab, and click Environment Variables. Click New to add the variable, or Edit to fix it if it already exists. The value of JAVA_HOME will be something like C:\Program Files\Java\jdk1.6.0_16. For Windows Vista and Windows 7, the steps to get to the Environment Variables screen are a little different; go to Start ➤ Computer, right-click to get Properties, click the link for "Advanced system settings" and click Environment Variables. After that, follow the same instructions as for Windows XP to change the JAVA_HOME environment variable. For Mac OS X, you set JAVA_HOME in your .profile in your HOME directory. Edit or create your .profile file and add a line that looks like this:

```
export JAVA_HOME=path_to_JDK_directory
```

where path_to_JDK_directory is probably /Library/Java/Home. For Linux, edit your .profile file and add a line like the one for Mac OS X above, except that your path is probably something like /usr/lib/jvm/java-6-sun.

Downloading Eclipse 3.5

Once the JDK is installed, you can download the Eclipse IDE for Java Developers. (You don't need the edition for Java EE; it works, but it's much larger and includes things we won't need for this book.) The examples in this book use Eclipse 3.5 (on a Windows environment). You can download all versions of Eclipse from http://www.eclipse.org/downloads/. The Eclipse distribution is a .zip file that can be extracted just about anywhere. The simplest place to extract to on Windows is C:\ which results in a C:\eclipse folder where you'll find eclipse.exe. For Mac OS X you can extract to Applications, and on Linux to your HOME directory. The Eclipse executable is in the eclipse folder for all platforms.

When you first start up Eclipse, it will ask you for a location for the workspace. To make things easy, you can choose a simple location such as C:\android. If you share the computer with others, you should put your workspace folder somewhere underneath your HOME folder.

Downloading the Android SDK

To build applications for Android, you need the Android SDK. The SDK includes an emulator so you don't need a mobile device with the Android OS to develop Android applications. In fact, we developed the examples in this book on a Windows XP machine.

You can download the Android SDK from `http://developer.android.com/sdk`. The Android SDK ships as a .zip file, similar to the way Eclipse is distributed, so you need to unzip it to an appropriate location. For Windows, unzip the file to a convenient location (we used our C: drive), after which you should have a folder called something like `C:\android-sdk-windows` which will contain the files as shown in Figure 2–1. For Mac OS X and Linux you can unzip the file to your HOME directory.

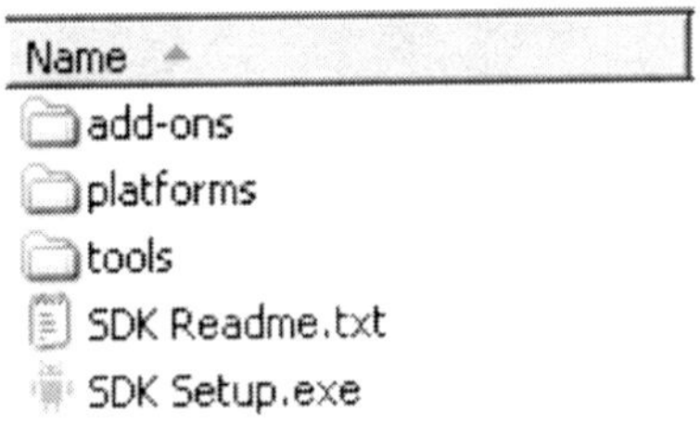

```
Name  ▲

 add-ons
 platforms
 tools
 SDK Readme.txt
 SDK Setup.exe
```

Figure 2–1. *Contents of the Android SDK*

The Android SDK comes with a tools directory that you'll want to have in your PATH. Let's add it now or, if you're upgrading, let's make sure it's correct. While we're there, we'll also add our JDK bin directory which will make life easier later. For Windows, get back to your Environment Variables window as we described above. Edit the PATH variable and add a semi-colon (;) on the end followed by the path to the Android SDK tools folder, followed by another semi-colon and then %JAVA_HOME%\bin. Click OK when done. For Mac OS X and Linux, edit your .profile file and add the Android SDK tools directory path to your PATH variable, as well as the $JAVA_HOME/bin directory. Something like the following would work:

```
export PATH=$PATH:$HOME/android-sdk-linux_x86/tools:$JAVA_HOME/bin
```

Later in this book there will be times when you need to execute a command-line utility program. These programs will be part of the JDK or will be part of the Android SDK. By having these directories in our PATH we will not need to specify the full pathnames in order to execute them, but we will need to start up a "tools window" in order to run them. We'll refer to this tools window in later chapters. The easiest way to create a tools window in Windows is to click Start ➤ Run, type in cmd, and click OK. For Mac OS X, choose Terminal from your Applications folder in Finder or from the Dock if it's there. For Linux, choose Terminal from the Applications ➤ Accessories menu.

One last thing, while we're talking about the differences between platforms: you may need to know the IP address of your workstation later on. To do this in Windows, launch a tools window and enter the command ipconfig. The results will contain an entry for

IPv4 (or something like that), with your IP address listed next to it. An IP address looks something like this: 192.168.1.25. For Mac OS X and Linux, launch a tools window and use the command `ifconfig`. You'll find your IP address next to a label called "inet addr". You might see a network connection called "localhost" or "lo". The IP address for this network connection is 127.0.0.1. This is a special network connection used by the operating system and is not the same as your workstation's IP address. Look for a different number for your workstation's IP address.

Installing Android Development Tools (ADT)

Now you need to install ADT, an Eclipse plug-in that helps you build Android applications. Specifically, ADT integrates with Eclipse to provide facilities for you to create, test, and debug Android applications. You'll need to use the Install New Software facility within Eclipse to perform the installation. If you are upgrading ADT, see the instructions following these installation instructions. To get started, launch the Eclipse IDE and follow these steps:

1. Select the Help menu item and choose the Install New Software… option. This was called "Software Updates" in previous versions of Eclipse.

2. Select the "Work with" field, type in `https://dl-ssl.google.com/android/eclipse/` and press Return. Eclipse will contact the site and populate the list as shown in Figure 2–2.

3. You should see an entry named Developer Tools with two child nodes: Android DDMS and Android Development Tools. Select the parent node Developer Tools, make sure the child nodes are also selected, and click the Next button. The versions that you see will likely be newer than these, and that's okay.

4. Eclipse now asks you to verify the two tools to install. Click Next again.

5. You will be asked to review the licenses for ADT as well as for the tools required to install ADT. Review the licenses, click "I accept…", and then click the Finish button.

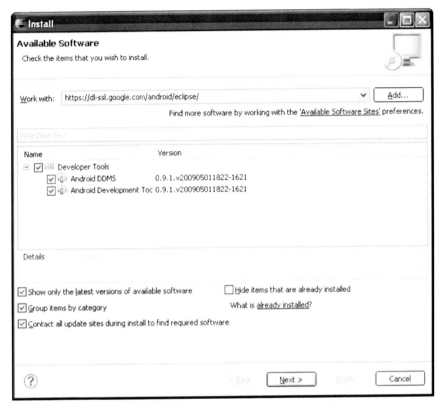

Figure 2-2. *Installing ADT using the Install New Software feature in Eclipse*

Eclipse will then download ADT and install it. You'll need to restart Eclipse for the new plug-in to show up in the IDE.

If you already have an older version of ADT in Eclipse, go to the Eclipse Help menu and choose Check for Updates. You should see the new version of ADT and be able to follow the installation instructions above, picking up at step 3.

The final step to get ADT functional inside of Eclipse is to point it to the Android SDK. Select the Window menu and choose Preferences. (On Mac OS X, Preferences is under the Eclipse menu.) In the Preferences dialog box, select the Android node and set the SDK Location field to the path of the Android SDK (see Figure 2-3), then click the Apply button. Note that you might see a dialog box asking if you want to send usage statistics to Google concerning the Android SDK. That decision is up to you. Click OK to close the Preferences window.

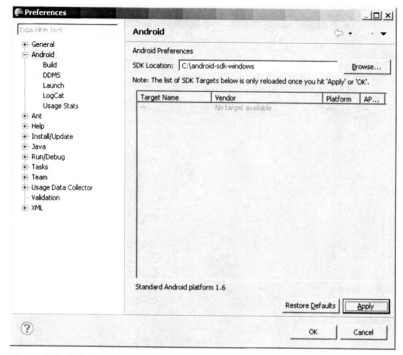

Figure 2–3. *Pointing ADT to the Android SDK*

When you first install the Android SDK it does not come with any platform versions. If it did you would see them in the Android Preferences window as shown in Figure 2–3 after setting the SDK Location. Installing platforms is pretty easy. Within Eclipse, go to Window ➤ Android SDK and AVD Manager, choose Available Packages, choose the `https://dl-ssl.google.com/android/repository/repository.xml` source, then select the platforms and add-ons that you want (e.g., Android 2.0). See Figure 2–4.

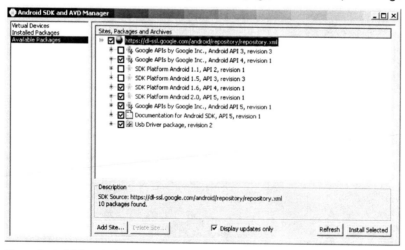

Figure 2–4. *Adding platforms to the Android SDK*

Click Install Selected. You will need to click Accept for each item that you're installing, then click Install Accepted. ADT will then download your packages and platforms to make them available in Eclipse. The Google APIs are add-ons for developing applications using Google Maps. You can always see the installed platforms by clicking Installed Packages on the left-hand side of this window.

You are almost ready for your first Android application—but first, we must briefly discuss the fundamental concepts of Android applications.

Learning the Fundamental Components

Every application framework has some key components that developers need to understand before they can begin to write applications based on the framework. For example, you would need to understand JavaServer Pages (JSP) and servlets in order to write Java 2 Platform, Enterprise Edition (J2EE) applications. Similarly, you need to understand activities, views, intents, content providers, services, and the `AndroidManifest.xml` file when you build applications for Android. We will briefly cover these fundamental concepts here and we'll discuss them in more detail throughout the book.

View

Views are user interface (UI) elements that form the basic building blocks of a user interface. Views are hierarchical and they know how to draw themselves. A view could be a button or a label or a text field, or lots of other UI elements. If you're familiar with views in J2EE and Swing then you'll understand views in Android.

Activity

An activity is a user interface concept. An activity usually represents a single screen in your application. It generally contains one or more views, but it doesn't have to. Moreover, other concepts in Android could better represent a viewless activity (as you'll see in the "Service" section shortly).

Intent

An intent generically defines an "intention" to do some work. Intents encapsulate several concepts, so the best approach to understanding them is to see examples of their use. You can use intents to perform the following tasks:

- Broadcast a message
- Start a service
- Launch an activity
- Display a web page or a list of contacts
- Dial a phone number or answer a phone call

Intents are not always initiated by your application—they're also used by the system to notify your application of specific events (such as the arrival of a text message).

Intents can be explicit or implicit. If you simply say that you want to display a URL, the system will decide what component will fulfill the intention. You can also provide specific information about what should handle the intention. Intents loosely couple the action and action handler.

Content Provider

Data sharing among mobile applications on a device is common. Therefore, Android defines a standard mechanism for applications to share data (such as a list of contacts) without exposing the underlying storage, structure, and implementation. Through content providers, you can expose your data and have your applications use data from other applications.

Service

Services in Android resemble services you see in Windows or other platforms—they're background processes that can potentially run for a long time. Android defines two types of services: local services and remote services. Local services are components that are only accessible by the application that is hosting the service. Conversely, remote services are services that are meant to be accessed remotely by other applications running on the device.

An example of a service is a component that is used by an e-mail application to poll for new messages. This kind of service might be a local service if the service is not used by other applications running on the device. If several applications use the service, then it would be implemented as a remote service. The difference, as you'll see in Chapter 8, is in startService() vs. bindService().

You can use existing services and also write your own services by extending the Service class.

AndroidManifest.xml

AndroidManifest.xml, which is similar to the web.xml file in the J2EE world, defines the contents and behavior of your application. For example, it lists your application's activities and services, along with the permissions the application needs to run.

Android Virtual Devices

An Android Virtual Device (AVD) allows developers to test their applications without hooking up an actual Android phone. AVDs can be created in various configurations to emulate different types of real phones.

Hello World!

Now you're ready to build your first Android application. You'll start by building a simple "Hello World!" program. Create the skeleton of the application by following these steps:

1. Launch Eclipse and select File ➤ New ➤ Project. In the New Project dialog box, select Android and then click Next. You will then see the New Android Project dialog box, as shown in Figure 2–5. Eclipse might have added "Android Project" to the New menu so you can use that if it's there. There's also a New Android Project button on the toolbar which you can use.

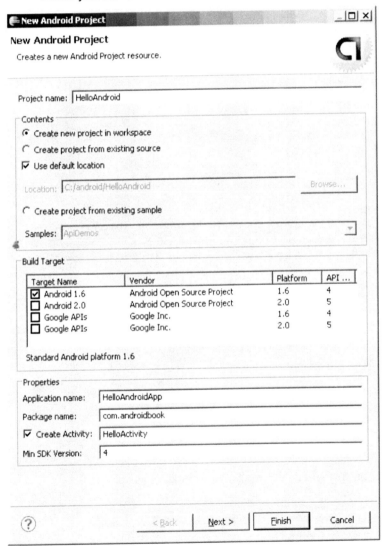

Figure 2–5. *Using the New Project Wizard to create an Android application*

2. As shown in Figure 2–5, enter **HelloAndroid** as the project name, **HelloAndroidApp** as the application name, **com.androidbook** as the package name, and **HelloActivity** as the Create Activity name. Note that for a real application, you'll want to use a meaningful application name because it will appear in the application's title bar. Also note that the default location for the project will be derived from the Eclipse workspace location. In this case, your Eclipse workspace is c:\android, and the New Project Wizard appends the name of the new application to the workspace location to come up with c:\android\HelloAndroid\. Finally, the Min SDK Version value of 4 tells Android that your application requires Android 1.6 or newer.

3. Click the Finish button, which tells ADT to generate the project skeleton for you. For now, open the HelloActivity.java file under the src folder and modify the onCreate() method as follows:

```
/** Called when the activity is first created. */
  @Override
  public void onCreate(Bundle savedInstanceState) {
      super.onCreate(savedInstanceState);
      /** create a TextView and write Hello World! */
      TextView tv = new TextView(this);
      tv.setText("Hello World!");
      /** set the content view to the TextView */
      setContentView(tv);
  }
```

Eclipse should automatically add an import statement for android.widget.TextView. You might need to click the "+" sign next to the first import statement to see them all. If the import statement doesn't get added automatically, be sure to add it yourself. Save the HelloActivity.java file.

To run the application, you'll need to create an Eclipse launch configuration, and you'll need a virtual device on which to run. We're going to quickly take you through these steps and come back later to more details about Android Virtual Devices (AVDs). Create the Eclipse launch configuration by following these steps:

1. Select Run ➤ Run Configurations.

2. In the Run Configurations dialog box, double-click Android Application in the left pane. The wizard will insert a new configuration named New Configuration.

3. Rename the configuration **RunHelloWorld**.

4. Click the Browse... button and select the HelloAndroid project.

5. Under Launch Action, select Launch and select com.androidbook.HelloActivity from the drop-down list. The dialog should appear as shown in Figure 2–6.

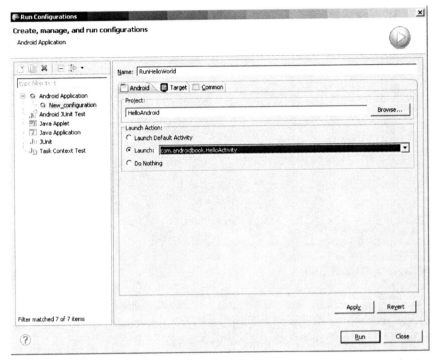

Figure 2–6. *Configuring an Eclipse launch configuration to run the "Hello World!" application*

6. Click Apply and then Run. You're almost there. Eclipse is ready to run your application, but it needs a device on which to run. As shown in Figure 2–7, you will be warned that no compatible targets were found and asked if you'd like to create one. Click Yes.

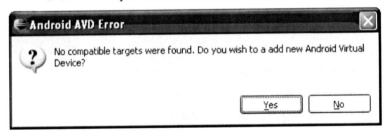

Figure 2–7. *Eclipse warning about targets and asking for a new AVD*

7. You'll be presented with a window that shows the existing AVDs. (See Figure 2–8.) Note that this is the same window we saw earlier in Figure 2–4.You'll need to add one suitable for your new application. Click the New button.

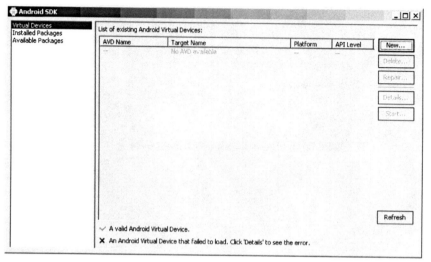

Figure 2–8. *The existing Android Virtual Devices*

8.   Fill in the Create AVD form as shown in Figure 2–9. Set Name to DefaultAVD, choose Android 2.0 - API Level 5 for the Target, set SD Card to 32 (for 32MB) and leave the default HVGA for Skin. Click Create AVD. Eclipse will confirm the successful creation of your AVD. Close the Android SDK window by clicking OK.

NOTE: We're choosing a newer version of the SDK for our Android Virtual Device, but our application could also run on an older one. This is okay because AVDs with newer SDKs can run applications that require older SDKs. The opposite, of course, would not be true: an application that requires a newer SDK won't run on an AVD with an older SDK.

9.   Finally, select your new AVD from the bottom list. Note that you may need to click the Refresh button for any new AVDs to show up in the list. Click the OK button.

10.   Eclipse will now launch the emulator with your very first Android app!

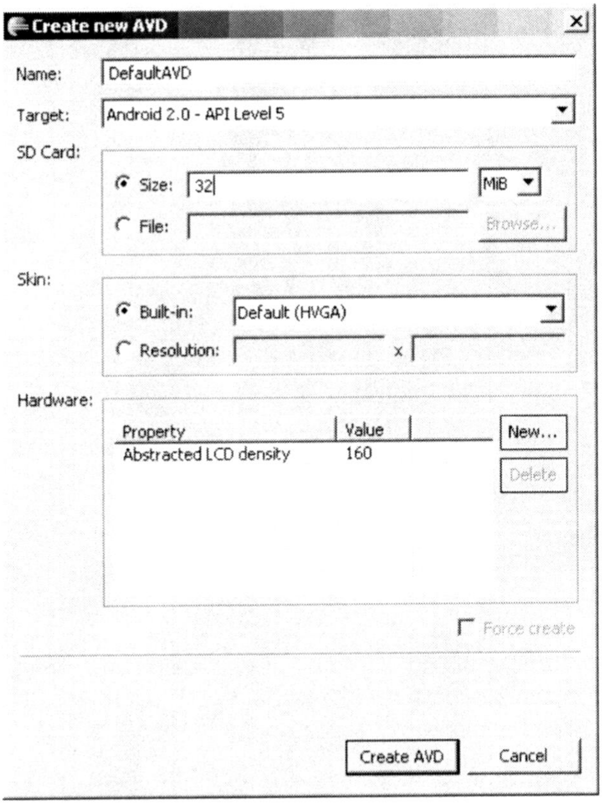

Figure 2–9. *Configuring an Android Virtual Device*

NOTE: It might take the emulator a minute to emulate the device-bootup process. After starting up, you should see HelloAndroidApp running in the emulator, as shown in Figure 2–10. In addition, be aware that the emulator starts other applications in the background during the startup process, so you might see a warning or error message from time to time. If you see an error message, you can generally dismiss it to allow the emulator to go to the next step in the startup process. For example, if you run the emulator and see a message like "application abc is not responding," you can either wait for the application to start or simply ask the emulator to forcefully close the application. Generally, you should wait and let the emulator start up cleanly.

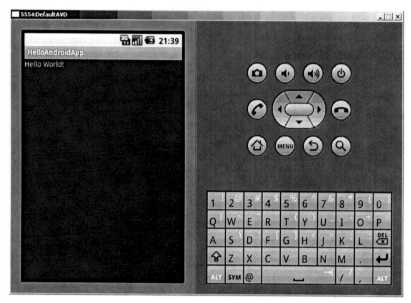

Figure 2–10. *HelloAndroidApp running in the emulator*

Now you know how to create a new Android application and run it in the emulator. Next, we'll look more closely at Android Virtual Devices, followed by a deeper dive into an Android application's artifacts and structure.

Android Virtual Devices

An Android Virtual Device (AVD) represents a device configuration. For example, you could have an AVD representing an older Android device running version 1.5 of the SDK with a 32MB SD card. The idea is that you create AVDs you are going to support and then point the emulator to one of those AVDs when developing and testing your application. Specifying (and changing) which AVD to use is very easy and makes testing with various configurations a snap. Earlier you saw how to create an AVD using Eclipse. You can make more AVDs in Eclipse by going to Window ➤ Android SDK and AVD Manager and clicking Virtual Devices on the left-hand side. You can also create AVDs using the command line. Here's how.

To create an AVD, you'll use a batch file named android under the tools directory (c:\android-sdk-windows\tools\). android allows you to create a new AVD and manage existing AVDs. For example, you can view existing AVDs, move AVDs, and so on. You can see the options available for using android by running android -help. For now, let's just create an AVD.

By default, AVDs are stored under your HOME directory (all platforms) in a folder called .android\AVD. If you created an AVD for "Hello World!" above then you will find it here. If you want to store or manipulate AVDs somewhere else, you can do that too. For this example, let's create a folder where the AVD image will be stored, such as c:\avd\. The next step is to run the android file to create the AVD. Open a tools window and type the following command (using an appropriate path to store the AVD files for your workstation, and using an appropriate value for the t argument based on what older SDK platform you installed):

```
android create avd -n OlderAVD -t 2 -c 32M -p C:\AVD\OlderAVD\
```

The parameters passed to the batch file are listed in Table 2–1.

Table 2–1. *Parameters Passed to the android.bat Tool*

Argument/Command	Description
create avd	Tells the tool to create an AVD.
n	The name of the AVD.
t	The target runtime. Use 1 to specify Android 1.1, 2 for Android 1.5, 3 for Android 1.6, etc.
c	Size of the SD card in bytes. Use K or M for kilobytes and megabytes.
p	The path to the generated AVD. This is optional.

Executing the preceding command will generate an AVD; you should see output similar to what's shown in Figure 2–11. Note that when you run the create avd command, you are asked if you want to create a custom hardware profile. Answer no to this question for now, but know that answering yes will then prompt you for lots of options for your AVD, such as screen size, presence of a camera, and so on.

Figure 2–11. *Creating an AVD yields this android.bat output.*

Even though you specified an alternate location for OlderAVD using the android.bat program, there is an OlderAVD.ini file under your HOME directory's .android/AVD folder. This is a good thing because if you go back into Eclipse, and select Window ➤ Android SDK and AVD Manager, you will see all of your AVDs, and you can access any of them when running your Android applications within Eclipse.

Take another look back at Figure 2–5. For our "Hello World!" application we chose to use Android 1.6 which set Min SDK Version to 4. If you select Android 1.5 (assuming you installed it), the Min SDK Version is set to 3. For Android 2.0, the Min SDK Version is set to 5.

Also be aware that selecting the Google APIs in the SDK Target list will include mapping functionality in your application, while selecting Android 1.5 or later will not. In the previous versions of the SDK prior to 1.5, the mapping classes were included with `android.jar`, but they've since been moved to a separate .jar file called `maps.jar`. When you select Google APIs, your Min SDK Version is defaulted to 5 (for Android 2.0) or 4 (for Android 1.6), and so on, and the ADT plug-in will include the `maps.jar` file in your project. In other words, if you are building an application that is using the mapping-related classes, you'll want to set your SDK Target to Google APIs. Note that you still need to add the maps uses-library (`<uses-library android:name="com.google.android.maps" />`) entry to your `AndroidManifest.xml` file. We'll cover that in more detail in Chapter 7.

Exploring the Structure of an Android Application

Although the size and complexity of Android applications can vary greatly, their structures will be similar. Figure 2–12 shows the structure of the "Hello World!" app you just built.

Figure 2–12. *The structure of the "Hello World!" application*

Android applications have some artifacts that are required and some that are optional. Table 2–2 summarizes the elements of an Android application.

Table 2–2. *The Artifacts of an Android Application*

Artifact	Description	Required?
AndroidManifest.xml	The Android application descriptor file. This file defines the activities, content providers, services, and intent receivers of the application. You can also use this file to declaratively define permissions required by the application, as well as grant specific permissions to other applications using the services of the application. Moreover, the file can contain instrumentation detail that you can use to test the application or another application.	Yes
src	A folder containing all of the source code of the application.	Yes
assets	An arbitrary collection of folders and files.	No
res	A folder containing the resources of the application. This is the parent folder of drawable, anim, layout, menu, values, xml, and raw.	Yes
drawable	A folder containing the images or image-descriptor files used by the application.	No
anim	A folder containing the XML-descriptor files that describe the animations used by the application.	No
layout	A folder containing views of the application. You should create your application's views by using XML descriptors rather than coding them.	No
menu	A folder containing XML-descriptor files for menus in the application.	No
values	A folder containing other resources used by the application. All the resources in the folder are also defined with XML descriptors. Examples of resources included in this folder include strings, styles, and colors.	No
xml	A folder containing additional XML files used by the application.	No
raw	A folder containing additional data—possibly non-XML data—that is required by the application.	No

As you can see from Table 2–2, an Android application is primarily made up of three pieces: the application descriptor, a collection of various resources, and the application's source code. If you put aside the AndroidManifest.xml file for a moment, you can view an Android app in this simple way: you have some business logic implemented in code, and everything else is a resource. This basic structure resembles the basic structure of a J2EE app, where the resources correlate to JSPs, the business logic correlates to servlets, and the AndroidManifest.xml file correlates to the web.xml file.

You can also compare J2EE's development model to Android's development model. In J2EE, the philosophy of building views is to build them using markup language. Android has also adopted this approach, although the markup in Android is XML. You benefit from this approach because you don't have to hard-code your application's views; you can modify the look and feel of the application by editing the markup.

It is also worth noting a few constraints regarding resources. First, Android supports only a linear list of files within the predefined folders under res. For example, it does not support nested folders under the layout folder (or the other folders under res). Second, there are some similarities between the assets folder and the raw folder under res. Both folders can contain raw files, but the files within raw are considered resources and the files within assets are not. So the files within raw will be localized, accessible through resource IDs, and so on. But the contents of the assets folder are considered general-purpose contents, to be used without resource constraints and support. Note that because the contents of the assets folder are not considered resources, you can put an arbitrary hierarchy of folders and files within it. (We'll talk a lot more about resources in Chapter 3.)

> **NOTE:** You might have noticed that XML is used quite heavily with Android. We all know that XML is a bloated data format, so this begs the question, does it make sense to rely on XML when you know your target is going to be a device with limited resources? It turns out that the XML we create during development is actually compiled down to binary using the Android Asset Packaging Tool (AAPT). Therefore, when your application is installed on a device, the files on the device are stored as binary. When the file is needed at runtime, the file is read in its binary form and is not transformed back into XML. This gives us the benefits of both worlds—we get to work with XML and don't have to worry about taking up valuable resources on the device.

Analyzing the Notepad Application

Not only have you learned how to create a new Android application and run it in the emulator, but you should also have a feel for the artifacts of an Android application. Next, we are going to look at the Notepad application that ships with the Android SDK. Notepad's complexity falls between that of the "Hello World!" app and a full-blown Android application, so analyzing its components will give you some realistic insight into Android development.

Loading and Running the Notepad Application

In this section, we'll show you how to load the Notepad application into the Eclipse IDE and run it in the emulator. Before we start, you should know that the Notepad application implements several use cases. For example, the user can create a new note, edit an existing note, delete a note, view the list of created notes, and so on. When the user launches the application, there aren't any saved notes yet, so the user sees an empty note list. If the user presses the Menu key, the application presents him with a list of actions, one of which allows him to add a new note. After he adds the note, he can edit or delete the note by selecting the corresponding menu option.

Follow these steps to load the Notepad sample into the Eclipse IDE:

1. Start Eclipse.

2. Go to File ➤ New ➤ Project.

3. In the New Project dialog, select Android ➤ Android Project.

4. In the New Android Project dialog, type in **NotesList** for the Project name, select "Create project from existing sample", then select a Build Target of Android 2.0 and in the Samples menu scroll down to the Notepad application. Note that the Notepad application is located in the `platforms\android-2.0\samples` folder of the Android SDK which you downloaded earlier. After you choose Notepad, the dialog reads the `AndroidManifest.xml` file and prepopulates the remaining fields in the New Android Project dialog box. (See Figure 2–13.)

5. Click the Finish button.

You should now see the NotesList application in your Eclipse IDE. If you see any Problems reported in Eclipse for this project, try using the Clean option from the Project menu in Eclipse to clear them. To run the application, you can create a launch configuration (as you did for the "Hello World!" application), or you can simply right-click the project, choose Run As, and select Android Application. This will launch the emulator and install the application on it. After the emulator has completed loading (you'll see the date and time displayed in the center of the emulator's screen), press the Menu button to view the Notepad application. Play around with the application for a few minutes to become familiar with it.

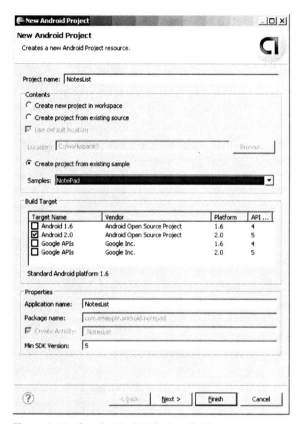

Figure 2–13. *Creating the NotePad application*

Dissecting the Application

Now let's study the contents of the application (see Figure 2–14).

As you can see, the application contains several .java files, a few .png images, three views (under the layout folder), and the AndroidManifest.xml file. If this were a command-line application, you would start looking for the class with the Main method. So what's the equivalent of a Main method in Android?

Android defines an entry-point activity, also called the top-level activity. If you look in the AndroidManifest.xml file, you'll find one provider and three activities. The NotesList activity defines an intent-filter for the action android.intent.action.MAIN and for the category android.intent.category.LAUNCHER. When an Android application is asked to run, the host loads the application and reads the AndroidManifest.xml file. It then looks for, and starts, an activity or activities with an intent-filter that has the MAIN action with a category of LAUNCHER, as shown here:

```
<intent-filter>
    <action android:name="android.intent.action.MAIN" />
    <category android:name="android.intent.category.LAUNCHER" />
</intent-filter>
```

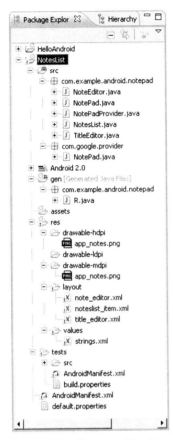

Figure 2–14. *Contents of the Notepad application*

After the host finds the activity it wants to run, it must resolve the defined activity to an actual class. It does this by combining the root package name and the activity name, which in this case is com.example.android.notepad.NotesList (see Listing 2–1).

Listing 2–1. *The AndroidManfiest.xml File*

```
<manifest xmlns:android="http://schemas.android.com/apk/res/android"
    package="com.example.android.notepad"
>
    <application android:icon="@drawable/app_notes"
        android:label="@string/app_name"
    >
        <provider android:name="NotePadProvider"
            android:authorities="com.google.provider.NotePad"
        />
        <activity android:name="NotesList" android:label="@string/title_notes_list">
            <intent-filter>
                <action android:name="android.intent.action.MAIN" />
                <category android:name="android.intent.category.LAUNCHER" />
            </intent-filter>
            <intent-filter>
                <action android:name="android.intent.action.VIEW" />
```

```
            <action android:name="android.intent.action.EDIT" />
            <action android:name="android.intent.action.PICK" />
            <category android:name="android.intent.category.DEFAULT" />
            <data android:mimeType="vnd.android.cursor.dir/vnd.google.note" />
        </intent-filter>
        <intent-filter>
            <action android:name="android.intent.action.GET_CONTENT" />
            <category android:name="android.intent.category.DEFAULT" />
            <data android:mimeType="vnd.android.cursor.item/vnd.google.note" />
        </intent-filter>
    </activity>
...
</manfiest>
```

The application's root package name is defined as an attribute of the `<manifest>` element in the `AndroidManifest.xml` file, and each activity has a name attribute.

Once the entry-point activity is determined, the host starts the activity and the `onCreate()` method is called. Let's have a look at `NotesList.onCreate()`, shown in Listing 2–2.

Listing 2–2. *The onCreate Method*

```java
public class NotesList extends ListActivity {
  @Override
  protected void onCreate(Bundle savedInstanceState) {
        super.onCreate(savedInstanceState);

        setDefaultKeyMode(DEFAULT_KEYS_SHORTCUT);
        Intent intent = getIntent();
        if (intent.getData() == null) {
            intent.setData(Notes.CONTENT_URI);
        }

        getListView().setOnCreateContextMenuListener(this);

        Cursor cursor = managedQuery(getIntent().getData(),
  PROJECTION, null, null,
                    Notes.DEFAULT_SORT_ORDER);

        SimpleCursorAdapter adapter = new SimpleCursorAdapter(this,
  R.layout.noteslist_item, cursor, new String[] { Notes.TITLE },
  new int[] { android.R.id.text1 });
        setListAdapter(adapter);
  }
}
```

Activities in Android are usually started with an intent, and one activity can start another activity. The `onCreate()` method checks whether the current activity's intent has data (notes). If not, it sets the URI to retrieve the data on the intent. In Chapter 3 we'll show that Android accesses data through content providers that operate on URIs. In this case, the URI provides enough information to retrieve data from a database. The constant `Notes.CONTENT_URI` is defined as a `static final` in `Notepad.java`:

```java
public static final Uri CONTENT_URI =
        Uri.parse("content://" + AUTHORITY + "/notes");
```

The `Notes` class is an inner class of the `Notepad` class. For now, know that the preceding URI tells the content provider to get all of the notes. If the URI looked something like this:

```
public static final Uri CONTENT_URI =
    Uri.parse("content://" + AUTHORITY + "/notes/11");
```

then the consuming content provider would return the note with an ID equal to 11. We will discuss content providers and URIs in depth in Chapter 3.

The `NotesList` class extends the `ListActivity` class, which knows how to display list-oriented data. The items in the list are managed by an internal `ListView` (a UI component), which displays the notes in the list. After setting the URI on the activity's intent, the activity registers to build the context menu for notes. If you've played with the application, you probably noticed that context-sensitive menu items are displayed depending on your selection. For example, if you select an existing note, the application displays "Edit note" and "Edit title." Similarly, if you don't select a note, the application shows you the "Add note" option.

Next, we see the activity execute a managed query and get a cursor for the result. A managed query means that Android will manage the returned cursor. As part of managing the cursor, if the application has to be unloaded or reloaded, neither the application nor the activity has to worry about positioning the cursor, loading it, or unloading it. The parameters to `managedQuery()`, shown in Table 2–3, are interesting.

Table 2–3. *Parameters to Activity.managedQuery()*

Parameter	Data Type	Description
URI	Uri	URI of the content provider
projection	String[]	The column to return (column names)
selection	String	Optional where clause
selectionArgs	String[]	The arguments to the selection, if the query contains ?s
sortOrder	String	Sort order to be used on the result set

We will discuss `managedQuery()` and its sibling `query()` later in this section and also in Chapter 3. For now, realize that a query in Android returns tabular data. The `projection` parameter allows you to define the columns you are interested in. You can also reduce the overall result set and sort the result set using a SQL order-by clause (such as `asc` or `desc`). Also note that an Android query must return a column named `_ID` to support retrieving an individual record. Moreover, you must know the type of data returned by the content provider—whether a column contains a `string`, `int`, `binary`, or the like.

After the query is executed, the returned cursor is passed to the constructor of `SimpleCursorAdapter`, which adapts records in the dataset to items in the user interface (`ListView`). Look closely at the parameters passed to the constructor of `SimpleCursorAdapter`:

```
    SimpleCursorAdapter adapter =
  new SimpleCursorAdapter(this, R.layout.noteslist_item,
  cursor, new String[] { Notes.TITLE }, new int[] { android.R.id.text1 });
```

Specifically, look at the second parameter: an identifier to the view that represents the items in the `ListView`. As you'll see in Chapter 3, Android provides an auto-generated utility class that provides references to the resources in your project. This utility class is called the R class because its name is `R.java`. When you compile your project, the AAPT generates the R class for you from the resources defined within your `res` folder. For example, you could put all your string resources into the `values` folder and the AAPT will generate a `public static` identifier for each string. Android supports this generically for all of your resources. For example, in the constructor of `SimpleCursorAdapter`, the `NotesList` activity passes in the identifier of the view that displays an item from the notes list. The benefit of this utility class is that you don't have to hard-code your resources and you get compile-time reference checking. In other words, if a resource is deleted, the R class will lose the reference and any code referring to the resource will not compile.

Let's look at another important concept in Android that we alluded to earlier: the `onListItemClick()` method of `NotesList` (see Listing 2–3).

Listing 2–3. *The onListItemClick Method*

```
@Override
    protected void onListItemClick(ListView l, View v, int position, long id) {
        Uri uri = ContentUris.withAppendedId(getIntent().getData(), id);

        String action = getIntent().getAction();
        if (Intent.ACTION_PICK.equals(action) ||
  Intent.ACTION_GET_CONTENT.equals(action)) {
            setResult(RESULT_OK, new Intent().setData(uri));
        } else {
            startActivity(new Intent(Intent.ACTION_EDIT, uri));
        }
    }
```

The `onListItemClick()` method is called when a user selects a note in the UI. The method demonstrates that one activity can start another activity. When a note is selected, the method creates a URI by taking the base URI and appending the selected note's ID to it. The URI is then passed to `startActivity()` with a new intent. `startActivity()` is one way to start an activity: it starts an activity but doesn't report on the results of the activity after it completes. Another way to start an activity is to use `startActivityForResult()`. With this method, you can start another activity and register a callback to be used when the activity completes. For example, you'll want to use `startActivityForResult()` to start an activity to select a contact because you want that contact after the activity completes.

At this point, you might be wondering about user interaction with respect to activities. For example, if the running activity starts another activity, and *that* activity starts an activity (and so on), then what activity can the user work with? Can she manipulate all the activities simultaneously, or is she restricted to a single activity? Actually, activities have a defined lifecycle. They're maintained on an activity stack, with the running activity at the top. If the running activity starts another activity, the first running activity moves down the stack and the new activity is placed on the top. Activities lower in the stack can be in a "paused" or "stopped" state. A paused activity is partially or fully visible to the user; a stopped activity is not visible to the user. The system can kill paused or stopped activities if it deems that resources are needed elsewhere.

Let's move on to data persistence now. The notes that a user creates are saved to an actual database on the device. Specifically, the Notepad application's backing store is a SQLite database. The managedQuery() method that we discussed earlier eventually resolves to data in a database, via a content provider. Let's examine how the URI, passed to managedQuery(), results in the execution of a query against a SQLite database. Recall that the URI passed to managedQuery() looks like this:

```
public static final Uri CONTENT_URI =
Uri.parse("content://" + AUTHORITY + "/notes");
```

Content URIs always have this form: content://, followed by the authority, followed by a general segment (context-specific). Because the URI doesn't contain the actual data, it somehow results in the execution of code that produces data. What is this connection? How is the URI reference resolved to code that produces data? Is the URI an HTTP service or a web service? Actually, the URI, or the authority portion of the URI, is configured in the AndroidManifest.xml file as a content provider:

```
<provider android:name="NotePadProvider"
    android:authorities="com.google.provider.NotePad"/>
```

When Android sees a URI that needs to be resolved, it pulls out the authority portion of it and looks up the ContentProvider class configured for the authority. In the Notepad application, the AndroidManifest.xml file contains a class called NotePadProvider configured for the com.google.provider.NotePad authority. Listing 2–4 shows a small portion of the class.

Listing 2–4. *The NotePadProvider Class*

```
public class NotePadProvider extends ContentProvider
{

    @Override
    public Cursor query(Uri uri, String[] projection, String selection,
  String[] selectionArgs,String sortOrder) {}

    @Override
    public Uri insert(Uri uri, ContentValues initialValues) {}

    @Override
    public int update(Uri uri, ContentValues values, String where,
String[] whereArgs) {}

    @Override
    public int delete(Uri uri, String where, String[] whereArgs) {}

    @Override
    public String getType(Uri uri) {}

    @Override
```

```
public boolean onCreate() {}


private static class DatabaseHelper extends SQLiteOpenHelper {}

@Override
    public void onCreate(SQLiteDatabase db) {}

    @Override
    public void onUpgrade(SQLiteDatabase db,
int oldVersion, int newVersion) {
        //...
    }
  }
}
```

The NotePadProvider class extends the ContentProvider class. The ContentProvider class defines six abstract methods, four of which are CRUD (Create, Read, Update, Delete) operations. The other two abstract methods are onCreate() and getType(). onCreate() is called when the content provider is created for the first time. getType() provides the MIME type for the result set (you'll see how MIME types work when you read Chapter 3).

The other interesting thing about the NotePadProvider class is the internal DatabaseHelper class, which extends the SQLiteOpenHelper class. Together, the two classes take care of initializing the Notepad database, opening and closing it, and performing other database tasks. Interestingly, the DatabaseHelper class is just a few lines of custom code (see Listing 2–5), while the Android implementation of SQLiteOpenHelper does most of the heavy lifting.

Listing 2–5. *The DatabaseHelper Class*

```
 private static class DatabaseHelper extends SQLiteOpenHelper {

        DatabaseHelper(Context context) {
            super(context, DATABASE_NAME, null, DATABASE_VERSION);
        }

        @Override
        public void onCreate(SQLiteDatabase db) {
            db.execSQL("CREATE TABLE " + NOTES_TABLE_NAME + " ("
                    + Notes._ID + " INTEGER PRIMARY KEY,"
                    + Notes.TITLE + " TEXT,"
                    + Notes.NOTE + " TEXT,"
                    + Notes.CREATED_DATE + " INTEGER,"
                    + Notes.MODIFIED_DATE + " INTEGER"
                    + ");");
        }

        //…
 }
```

As shown in Listing 2–5, the onCreate() method creates the Notepad table. Notice that the class's constructor calls the superclass's constructor with the name of the table. The superclass will call the onCreate() method only if the table does not exist in the database. Also notice that one of the columns in the Notepad table is the _ID column we discussed in the section "Dissecting the Application."

Now let's look at one of the CRUD operations: the insert() method (see Listing 2–6).

Listing 2–6. *The insert() Method*

```
//...
SQLiteDatabase db = mOpenHelper.getWritableDatabase();
        long rowId = db.insert(NOTES_TABLE_NAME, Notes.NOTE, values);
        if (rowId > 0) {
            Uri noteUri = ContentUris.withAppendedId(
NotePad.Notes.CONTENT_URI, rowId);
            getContext().getContentResolver().notifyChange(noteUri, null);
            return noteUri;
        }
```

The insert() method uses its internal DatabaseHelper instance to access the database and then inserts a notes record. The returned row ID is then appended to the URI and a new URI is returned to the caller.

At this point, you should be familiar with how an Android application is laid out. You should be able to navigate your way around Notepad, as well as some of the other samples in the Android SDK. You should be able to run the samples and play with them. Now let's look at the overall lifecycle of an Android application.

Examining the Application Lifecycle

The lifecycle of an Android application is strictly managed by the system, based on the user's needs, available resources, and so on. A user might want to launch a web browser, for example, but the system ultimately decides whether to start the application. Although the system is the ultimate manager, it adheres to some defined and logical guidelines to determine whether an application can be loaded, paused, or stopped. If the user is currently working with an activity, the system will give high priority to that application. Conversely, if an activity is not visible and the system determines that an application must be shut down to free up resources, it will shut down the lower-priority application.

Contrast this with the lifecycle of web-based J2EE applications. J2EE apps are loosely managed by the container they run in. For example, a J2EE container can remove an application from memory if it sits idle for a predetermined time period. But the container generally won't move applications in and out of memory based on load and/or available resources. A J2EE container will generally have sufficient resources to run lots of applications at the same time. With Android, resources are more limited so Android must have more control and power over applications.

> **NOTE:** Android runs each application in a separate process, each of which hosts its own virtual machine. This provides a protected-memory environment. Moreover, by isolating applications to an individual process, the system can control which application deserves higher priority. For example, a background process that's doing a CPU-intensive task cannot block an incoming phone call.

The concept of application lifecycle is logical, but a fundamental aspect of Android applications complicates matters. Specifically, the Android application architecture is component- and integration-oriented. This allows a rich user experience, seamless reuse, and easy application integration, but creates a complex task for the application-lifecycle manager.

Let's consider a typical scenario. A user is talking to someone on the phone and needs to open an e-mail message to answer a question. She goes to the home screen, opens the mail application, opens the e-mail message, clicks a link in the e-mail, and answers her friend's question by reading a stock quote from a web page. This scenario would require four applications: the home application, a talk application, an e-mail application, and a browser application. As the user navigates from one application to the next, her experience is seamless. In the background, however, the system is saving and restoring application state. For instance, when the user clicks the link in the e-mail message, the system saves metadata on the running e-mail message activity before starting the browser-application activity to launch a URL. In fact, the system saves metadata on any activity before starting another so that it can come back to the activity (when the user backtracks, for example). If memory becomes an issue, the system will have to shut down a process running an activity and resume it as necessary.

Android is sensitive to the lifecycle of an application and its components. Therefore, you'll need to understand and handle lifecycle events in order to build a stable application. The processes running your Android application and its components go through various lifecycle events, and Android provides callbacks that you can implement to handle state changes. For starters, you'll want to become familiar with the various lifecycle callbacks for an activity (see Listing 2–7).

Listing 2–7. *Lifecycle Methods of an Activity*

```
protected void onCreate(Bundle savedInstanceState);
protected void onStart();

protected void onRestart();
protected void onResume();
protected void onPause();
protected void onStop();
protected void onDestroy();
```

Listing 2–7 shows the list of lifecycle methods that Android calls during the life of an activity. It's important to understand when each of the methods is called by the system to ensure that you implement a stable application. Note that you do not need to react to all of these methods. If you do, however, be sure to call the superclass versions as well. Figure 2–15 shows the transitions between states.

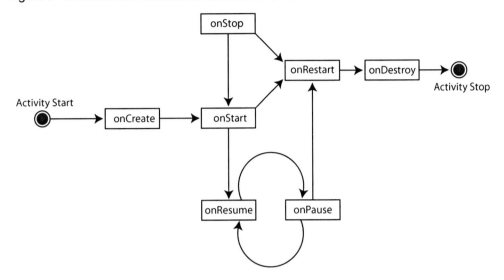

Figure 2–15. *State transitions of an activity*

The system can start and stop your activities based on what else is happening. Android calls the onCreate() method when the activity is freshly created. onCreate() is always followed by a call to onStart(), but onStart() is not always preceded by a call to onCreate() because onStart() can be called if your application was stopped (from onStop()). When onStart()is called, your activity is not visible to the user, but it's about to be. onResume() is called after onStart(), just when the activity is in the foreground and accessible to the user. At this point, the user is interacting with your activity.

 When the user decides to move to another activity, the system will call your activity's onPause() method. From onPause(), you can expect either onResume() or onStop() to be called. onResume() is called, for example, if the user brings your activity back to the foreground. onStop()is called if your activity becomes invisible to the user. If your activity is brought back to the foreground, after a call to onStop(), then onRestart() will be called. If your activity sits on the activity stack but is not visible to the user, and the system decides to kill your activity, onDestroy() will be called.

The state model described for an activity appears complex, but you are not required to deal with every possible scenario. In fact, you will mostly handle onCreate() and onPause(). You will handle onCreate() to create the user interface for your activity. In this method, you will bind data to your widgets and wire up any event handlers for your UI components. In onPause(), you will want to persist critical data to your application's data store. It's the last safe method that will get called before the system kills your application. onStop() and onDestroy() are not guaranteed to be called, so don't rely on these methods for critical logic.

The takeaway from this discussion? The system manages your application, and it can start, stop, or resume an application component at any time. Although the system controls your components, they don't run in complete isolation with respect to your application. In other words, if the system starts an activity in your application, you can count on an application context in your activity. For example, it's not uncommon to have global variables shared among the activities in your application. You can share a global variable by writing an extension of the android.app.Application class and then initializing the global variable in the onCreate()method (see Listing 2–8). Activities and other components in your application can then access these references with confidence when they are executing.

Listing 2–8. *An Extension of the Application Class*

```
public class MyApplication extends Application
{
    // global variable
    private static final String myGlobalVariable;

    @Override
    public void onCreate()
    {
        super.onCreate();
        //... initialize global variables here
        myGlobalVariable = loadCacheData();
    }

    public static String getMyGlobalVariable() {
        return myGlobalVariable;
    }

}
```

In the next section, we'll give you some armor to help you develop Android applications: we will discuss debugging.

Debugging Your App

After you write a few lines of code for your first application, you'll start wondering if it's possible to have a debug session while you interact with your application in the emulator. The Android SDK includes a host of tools that you can use for debugging purposes. These tools are integrated with the Eclipse IDE (see Figure 2–16).

One of the tools that you'll use throughout your Android development is LogCat. This tool displays the log messages that you emit using android.util.Log, exceptions, System.out.println, and so on. While System.out.println works and the messages show up in the LogCat window, to log messages from your application, you'll want to use the android.util.Log class. This class defines the familiar informational, warning, and error methods which you can filter within the LogCat window to see just what you want to see. A sample of a Log command is:

```
Log.v("string TAG", "This is my message to write to the log");
```

The SDK also includes a file-explorer tool that you can use to view, drag and drop files on the device, even if the device is an emulator.

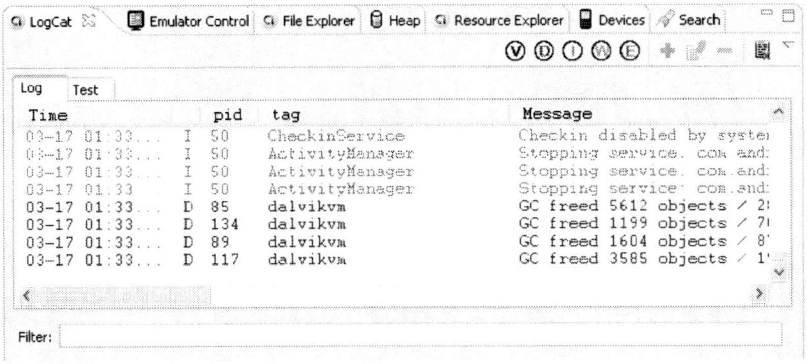

Figure 2–16. *Debugging tools that you can use while building Android applications*

You can view the tools by selecting the Debug perspective in Eclipse. You can also launch each tool in the Java perspective by going to Window ➤ Show View ➤ Other ➤ Android.

You can also get detailed tracing information of your Android application by using the `android.os.Debug` class, which provides a start-tracing method (`Debug.startMethodTracing()`) and a stop-tracing method (`Debug.stopMethodTracing()`). Android will create a trace file on the device (or emulator). You can then copy the trace file to your workstation and view the tracer output using the traceview tool included in the Android SDK tools directory. We will introduce the other tools throughout the book.

Summary

In this chapter, we showed you how to set up your development environment for building Android applications. We discussed some of the basic building blocks of the Android APIs, and introduced views, activities, intents, content providers, and services. We then analyzed the Notepad application in terms of the aforementioned building blocks and application components. Next, we talked about the importance of the Android application lifecycle. Finally, we briefly mentioned some of the Android SDK's debugging tools that integrate with the Eclipse IDE.

And so begins the foundation of your Android development. The next chapter will discuss content providers, resources, and intents in great detail.

Chapter 3

Using Resources, Content Providers, and Intents

In Chapter 2, we gave you an overview of an Android application and a quick look at some of its underlying concepts. You also learned about the Android SDK, the Eclipse ADT (Eclipse Android Development Tool) and how to run your applications on emulators identified by AVDs (Android Virtual Devices).

In this chapter, we'll follow that introduction with an in-depth look at Android SDK fundamentals and cover resources, content providers, and intents. These three concepts are fundamental to understanding Android programming and should place you on a solid foundation for the material in subsequent chapters.

Android depends on resources for defining UI components in a declarative manner. This declarative approach is not that dissimilar to how HTML uses declarative tags to define its UI. In this sense Android is quite forward thinking in its approach to UI development. Android further allows these resources to be localized. In the "Understanding Resources" section we will cover the variety of resources that are available in Android and how to use them.

Android uses a concept called *content providers* for abstracting data into services. This idea of content providers makes data sources look like REST-enabled data providers, such as web sites.

Just as web sites are responsible for telling browsers the type of data that is available at a given URL, a content provider is also responsible for describing the data that it returns for each service it provides. Much like web sites, these data services are exposed as URIs. In the section "Understanding Content Providers" we will explore this idea in detail and show you how to create a sample content provider.

NOTE: REST stands for REpresentational State Transfer. It is a very confounding name for a simple concept which, as web users, everyone is quite familiar with. When you type a URL in a web browser and the web server responds with HTML back, you have essentially performed a REST-based "query" operation on the web server. Similarly, when you update some content using a web form, you have done a REST-based "update" on the web server (or site) and changed the state of the web server. REST is also usually contrasted with (SOAP—Simple Object Access Protocol) Web Services. You can read more about REST at the following Wikipedia entry: http://en.wikipedia.org/wiki/Representational_State_Transfer.

Android introduced a concept called *intents* to invoke UI components (components in general) and to share data between them. In the section on intents you will learn what intents are and how to use them to discover and invoke UI programs called Activities. You will also learn the connection between intents, data, URIs, and content providers. In the process you will learn how intents form the basis of flexibility and reuse in Android.

In all, this chapter will give you the foundation you need to go further into Android programming.

Understanding Resources

Resources play a central part in Android architecture. In this section you'll learn that resources are declarative, and that Android creates resource IDs for convenient use in your Java programs. You'll also see how the R.java source file mediates the generation and usage of these resource IDs. Then you'll learn how to define resources in XML files, reuse resources in other resource XML definitions, and reuse resources in Java programs. In addition to these XML-based resources, we will cover two other types of resources: *raw resources* and *assets*.

A resource in Android is a file (like a music file) or a value (like the title of a dialog box) that is bound to an executable application. These files and values are bound to the executable in such a way that you can change them without recompiling and redeploying the application. Resources play a part in many, if not all, familiar UI frameworks.

Familiar examples of resources include strings, colors, and bitmaps. Instead of hard-coding strings in an application, for example, you can use their IDs instead. This indirection lets you change the text of the string resource without changing the source code.

Let's start this discussion of resources with a very common resource: a string.

String Resources

Android allows you to define multiple strings in one or more XML resource files. These XML files containing string-resource definitions reside in the /res/values subdirectory. The names of the XML files are arbitrary, although you will commonly see the file name as strings.xml. Listing 3–1 shows an example of a string-resource file.

Listing 3–1. *Example strings.xml File*

```
<?xml version="1.0" encoding="utf-8"?>
<resources>
    <string name="hello">hello</string>
    <string name="app_name">hello appname</string>
</resources>
```

When this file is created or updated, the Eclipse ADT plug-in will automatically create or update a Java class in your application's root package called R.java with unique IDs for the two string resources specified.

Notice the placement of this R.java file below. We have given a high level directory structure for a project like, say, "MyProject."

```
\MyProject
    \src
            \com\mycompany\android\my-root-package
            \com\mycompany\android\my-root-package\another-package
    \gen
            \com\mycompany\android\my-root-package\
            \com\mycompany\android\my-root-package\R.java
    \assets
    \res
    \AndroidManifest.xml
.....etc
```

> **NOTE:** Regardless of the number of resource files, there is only one R.java file.

For the string-resource file in Listing 3–1, the updated R.java file would have these entries:

```
package com.mycompany.android.my-root-package;
public final class R {
    ...other entries depending on your project and application

    public static final class string
    {
        ...other entries depending on your project and application

        public static final int hello=0x7f040000;
        public static final int app_name=0x7f040001;

        ...other entries depending on your project and application
    }
    ...other entries depending on your project and application
}
```

Notice, first, how R.java defines a top level class in the root package: public static final class R. Within that outer class of R, Android defines an inner class, namely, static final class string. R.java creates this inner static class as a namespace to hold string-resource IDs.

The two static final ints defined with variable names hello and app_name are the resource IDs that represent the corresponding string resources. You could use these resource IDs anywhere in the source code through the following code structure:

```
R.string.hello
```

Note that these generated IDs point to ints rather than strings. Most methods that take strings also take these resource identifiers as inputs. Android will resolve those ints to strings where needed.

It is merely a convention that most sample applications define all strings in one strings.xml file. Android takes any number of arbitrary files as long as the structure of the XML file looks like Listing 3–1 and the file resides in the /res/values subdirectory.

The structure of this file is easy to follow. You have the root node of <resources> followed by one or more of its child elements of <string>. Each <string> element or node has a property called name that will end up as the id attribute in R.java.

To see that multiple string-resource files are allowed in this subdirectory, you can place another file with the following content in the same subdirectory and call it strings1.xml:

```
<?xml version="1.0" encoding="utf-8"?>
<resources>
    <string name="hello1">hello 1</string>
    <string name="app_name1">hello appname 1</string>
</resources>
```

The Eclipse ADT plug-in will validate the uniqueness of these IDs at compile time and place them in R.java as two additional constants: R.string.hello1 and R.string.app_name1.

Layout Resources

In Android, the view for a screen is often loaded from an XML file as a resource. These XML files are called layout resources. A *layout resource* is an essential key resource used in Android UI programming. Consider this code segment for a sample Android activity:

```java
public class HelloWorldActivity extends Activity
{
    @Override
    public void onCreate(Bundle savedInstanceState)
    {
        super.onCreate(savedInstanceState);
        setContentView(R.layout.main);
        TextView tv = (TextView)this.findViewById(R.id.text1);
        tv.setText("Try this text instead");
    }
}
```

```
        ........
}
```

The line `setContentView(R.layout.main)` points out that there is a static class called `R.layout`, and within that class there is a constant called `main` (an integer) pointing to a View defined by an XML layout-resource file. The name of the XML file would be `main.xml`, which needs to be placed in the resources' layout subdirectory. In other words, this statement would expect the programmer to create the file `/res/layout/main.xml` and place the necessary layout definition in that file. The contents of the `main.xml` layout file could look like Listing 3–2.

Listing 3–2. *Example main.xml Layout File*

```xml
<?xml version="1.0" encoding="utf-8"?>
<LinearLayout xmlns:android="http://schemas.android.com/apk/res/android"
    android:orientation="vertical"
    android:layout_width="fill_parent"
    android:layout_height="fill_parent"
    >
<TextView     android:id="@+id/text1"
    android:layout_width="fill_parent"
    android:layout_height="wrap_content"
    android:text="@string/hello"
    />
 <Button      android:id="@+id/b1"
    android:layout_width="fill_parent"
    android:layout_height="wrap_content"
    android:text="@+string/hello"
    />
</LinearLayout>
```

The layout file in Listing 3–2 defines a root node called `LinearLayout`, which contains a `TextView` followed by a `Button`. A `LinearLayout` lays out its children vertically or horizontally—vertically, in this example.

You will need to define a separate layout file for each screen. More accurately, each layout needs a dedicated file. If you are painting two screens, you will likely need two layout files such as `/res/layout/screen1_layout.xml` and `/res/layout/screen2_layout.xml`.

> **NOTE:** Each file in the `/res/layout/` subdirectory generates a unique constant based on the name of the file (extension excluded). With layouts, what matters is the number of files; with string resources, what matters is the number of individual string resources *inside* the files.

For example, if you have two files under `/res/layout/` called `file1.xml` and `file2.xml`, you'll have the following entries in `R.java`:

```java
public static final class layout {
    .... any other files
      public static final int file1=0x7f030000;
      public static final int file2=0x7f030001;
}
```

The views defined in these layout files such as a TextView (see Listing 3–2) are accessible in Java code through their resource IDs generated in R.java:

```
TextView tv = (TextView)this.findViewById(R.id.text1);
tv.setText("Try this text instead");
```

In this example, you locate the TextView by using the findViewById method of the Activity class. The constant R.id.text1 corresponds to the ID defined for the TextView. The id for the TextView in the layout file is as follows:

```
<TextView android:id="@+id/text1"
..
</TextView>
```

The attribute value for the id attribute indicates that a constant called text1 will be used to uniquely identify this view among other views hosted by that activity. The plus sign (+) in @+id/text1 means that the ID text1 will be created if it doesn't exist already. There is more to this resource ID syntax. We'll talk about that next.

Resource-Reference Syntax

Irrespective of the type of resource (String and Layout are the two we have covered so far), all Android resources are identified (or referenced) by their id in Java source code. The syntax you use to allocate an id to a resource in the XML file is called *resource-reference syntax*. The id attribute syntax in the previous example @+id/text1 has the following formal structure:

@[package:]type/name

The type corresponds to one of the resource-type namespaces available in R.java, some of which are:

- R.drawable
- R.id
- R.layout
- R.string
- R.attr

The corresponding types in XML resource-reference syntax are as follows:

- drawable
- id
- layout
- string
- attr

The name part in the resource reference @[package:]type/name is the name given to the resource; it also gets represented as an int constant in R.java.

If you don't specify any "package" in the syntax @[package:]type/name then the pair type/name will be resolved based on local resources and the application's local R.java package.

If you specify android:type/name, the reference ID will be resolved using the package android and specifically through the android.R.java file. You can use any Java package name in place of the package placeholder to locate the right R.java file to resolve the reference. Based on this information, let's analyze a few examples:

```
<TextView  android:id="text">
// Compile error, as id will not take raw text strings

<TextView  android:id="@text">
// wrong syntax. It is missing a type name
// you will get an error "No Resource type specified

<TextView  android:id="@id/text">
//Error: No Resource found that matches id "text"
//Unless you have taken care to define "text" as an ID before

<TextView  android:id="@android:id/text">
// Error: Resource is not public
// indicating that there is no such id in android.R.id
// Of course this would be valid if Android R.java were to define
// an id with this name

<TextView  android:id="@+id/text">
//Success: Creates an id called "text" in the local package's R.java
```

Defining Your Own Resource IDs for Later Use

The general pattern for allocating an id is either to create a new one or to use the one created by the Android package. However, it is possible to create ids beforehand and use them later in your own packages.

The line <TextView android:id="@+id/text"> in the preceding code segment indicates that an id named text is going to be used if one already exists. If the id doesn't exist, then a new one is going to be created. So when might an id such as text already exist in R.java for it to be reused?

You might be inclined to put a constant like R.id.text in R.java, but R.java is not editable. Even if it were, it gets regenerated every time something gets changed, added, or deleted in the /res/* subdirectory.

The solution is to use a resource tag called item to define an id without attaching to any particular resource. Here is an example:

```
<resources>
<item type="id" name="text"/>
</resources>
```

The type refers to the type of resource—an id in this case. Once this id is in place, the following View definition would work:

```
<TextView android:id="@id/text">
..
</TextView>
```

Compiled and Noncompiled Android Resources

So far we have given you an idea of resources by talking about String resources and layout resources. We have covered the resource reference syntax, especially in the context of a layout resource. Let us now talk about another key aspect of android resources, where most resources are compiled into binary files before being deployed, and some are not, and are left in their raw form.

Android supports resources primarily through two types of files: *XML files* and *raw files* (examples of which include images, audio and video). Even within XML files, you have seen that in some cases the resources are defined as values inside an XML file (Strings, for example) and sometimes an XML file as a whole is a resource (a layout resource file to quote).

As a further distinction within the set of XML files, you'll find two types: one gets compiled into binary format, and the other gets copied as-is to the device. The examples you have seen so far—the string-resource XML files and the layout-resource XML files—get compiled into binary format before becoming part of the installable package. These XML files have predefined formats where XML nodes are translated to IDs.

You can also choose some XML files to have their own free format structure and not get interpreted and have resource IDs generated. However, you do want them compiled to binary formats and also have the comfort of localization. To do this, you can place these XML files in the `/res/xml/` subdirectory to have them compiled into binary format. In this case, you would use Android-supplied XML readers to read the XML nodes.

But if you place files, including XML files, in the `/res/raw/` directory instead, they don't get compiled into binary format. You must use explicit stream-based APIs to read these files. Audio and video files fall into this category.

> **NOTE:** It is worth noting that because the `raw` directory is part of the `/res/*` hierarchy, even these raw audio and video files can take advantage of localization like all other resources.

As we mentioned in Table 2-1 in the previous chapter, resource files are housed in various subdirectories based on their type. Here are some important subdirectories in the `/res` folder and the types of resources they host:

- `anim`: Compiled animation files
- `drawable`: Bitmaps
- `layout`: UI/view definitions
- `values`: Arrays, colors, dimensions, strings, and styles

■ xml: Compiled arbitrary XML files

■ raw: Noncompiled raw files

The resource compiler in the Android Asset Packaging Tool (AAPT) compiles all the resources except the raw resources and places them all into the final .apk file. This file, which contains the Android application's code and resources, correlates to Java's .jar file ("apk" stands for "Android Package"). The .apk file is what gets installed onto the device.

> **NOTE:** Although the XML resource parser allows resource names such as hello-string, you will see a compile-time error in R.java. You can fix this by renaming your resource to hello_string (replacing the dash with an underscore).

Enumerating Key Android Resources

Now that we've been through the basics of resources, we'll enumerate some of the other key resources that Android supports, their XML representations, and the way they're used in Java code. (You can use this section as a quick reference as you write resource files for each resource.) To start with, take a quick glance at the types of resources and what they are used for (see Table 3–1).

Table 3–1. *Types of Resources*

Resource Type	Location	Description
Colors	/res/values/any-file	Represents color identifiers pointing to color codes. These Resource ids are exposed in R.java as R.color.*. The XML node in the file is /resources/color.
Strings	/res/values/any-file	Represents string resources. String resources allow java formatted strings and raw html in addition to simple strings. These Resource ids are exposed in R.java as R.string.*. The XML node in the file is /resources/string.
Dimensions	/res/values/any-file	Represents dimensions or sizes of various elements or views in Android. Supports pixels, inches, millimeters, density independent pixels, and scale independent pixels. These Resource ids are exposed in R.java as R.dimen.* . The XML node in the file is /resources/dimen.

Resource Type	Location	Description
Images	`/res/drawable/multiple-files`	Represents image resources. Supported images include .jpg, .gif, .png etc. Each image is in a separate file and gets its own id based on the file name. These Resource ids are exposed in `R.java` as `R.drawable.*`. The image support also includes an image type called a stretchable image that allows portions of an image to stretch while other portions of that image stay static.
Color Drawables	`/res/values/any-file` also `/res/drawable/multiple-files`	Represents rectangles of colors to be used as view backgrounds or general drawables like bitmaps. This can be used in lieu of specifying a single colored bitmap as a background. In Java, this will be equivalent to creating a colored rectangle and setting it as a background for a view. The `<drawable>` value tag in the values subdirectory supports this. These Resource ids are exposed in `R.java` as `R.drawable.*`. The XML node in the file is `/resources/drawable`. Android also supports rounded rectangles and gradient rectangles through xml files placed in `/res/drawable` with the root xml tag of `<shape>`. These Resource ids are also exposed in `R.java` as `R.drawable.*`. Each file name in this case translates to a unique drawable id.
Arbitrary XML files	`/res/xml/*.xml`	Android allows arbitrary XML files as resources. These files will be compiled by aapt compiler. These Resource ids are exposed in `R.java` as `R.xml.*`.
Arbitrary Raw Resources	`/res/raw/*.*`	Android allows arbitrary **non-compiled** binary or text files under this directory. Each file gets a unique Resource id. These Resource ids are exposed in `R.java` as `R.raw.*`.
Arbitrary Raw Assets	`/assets/*.*/*.*`	Android allows arbitrary files in arbitrary sub directories starting at `/assets` subdirectory. These are not really resources but just raw files. This directory unlike the `/res` resources subdirectory allows an arbitrary depth of subdirectories. These files do not generate any Resource ids. You have to use relative pathname starting at and excluding `/assets`.

Each of the resources specified in this table is further elaborated in the following sections with XML and java code snippets.

NOTE: Looking at the nature of ID generation, it appears—although we haven't seen it officially stated anywhere—that there are IDs generated based on filenames if those XML files are anywhere but in the `res/values` subdirectory. If they are in the values subdirectory, only the contents of the files are looked at to generate the IDs.

Color Resources

As you can with string resources, you can use reference identifiers to indirectly reference colors as well. Doing this enables Android to localize colors and apply themes. Once you've defined and identified colors in resource files, you can access them in Java code through their IDs. Whereas string-resource IDs are available under the *<your-package>*.R.string namespace, the color IDs are available under the *<your-package>*.R.color namespace.

Android also defines a base set of colors in its own resource files. These IDs, by extension, are accessible through the Android android.R.color namespace. Check out this URL to learn the color constants available in the android.R.color namespace:

http://code.google.com/android/reference/android/R.color.html

See Listing 3–3 for some examples of specifying color in an XML resource file.

Listing 3–3. *XML Syntax for Defining Color Resources*

```
<resources>
    <color name="red">#f00</color>
    <color name="blue">#0000ff</color>
    <color name="green">#f0f0</color>
    <color name="main_back_ground_color">#ffffff00</color>
</resources>
```

The entries in Listing 3–3 need to be in a file residing in the /res/values subdirectory. The name of the file is arbitrary, meaning the file name can be anything you choose. Android will read all the files and then process them and look for individual nodes such as "resources" and "color" to figure out individual IDs.

Listing 3–4 shows an example of using a color resource in Java code.

Listing 3–4. *Color Resources in Java code*

```
int mainBackGroundColor
    = activity.getResources.getColor(R.color.main_back_ground_color);
```

Listing 3–5 shows how you would use a color resource in a view definition.

Listing 3–5. *Using Colors in View Definitions*

```
<TextView android:layout_width="fill_parent"
        android:layout_height="wrap_content"
        android:textColor="@color/ red"
        android:text="Sample Text to Show Red Color"/>
```

More on String Resources

We covered string resources briefly when we introduced resources at the beginning of this chapter. Let us revisit them in order to provide some more detail. We will show you how to define and use HTML strings, as well as how to substitute variables in string resources.

> **NOTE:** Most UI frameworks allow string resources. However, unlike other UI frameworks, Android offers the ability to quickly associate IDs with string resources through `R.java`. So using strings as resources is that much easier in Android.

We'll start by showing how you can define normal strings, quoted strings, HTML strings, and substitutable strings in an XML resource file (see Listing 3–6).

Listing 3–6. *XML Syntax for Defining String Resources*

```
<resources>
    <string name="simple_string">simple string</string>
    <string name="quoted_string">"quoted'string"</string>
    <string name="double_quoted_string">\"double quotes\"</string>
    <string name="java_format_string">
            hello %2$s java format string. %1$s again
    </string>
    <string name="tagged_string">
        Hello <b><i>Slanted Android</i></b>, You are bold.
    </string>
</resources>
```

This XML string-resource file needs to be in the /res/values subdirectory. The name of the file is arbitrary.

Notice how quoted strings need to be either escaped or placed in alternate quotes. The string definitions also allow standard Java string-formatting sequences.

Android also allows child XML elements such as <b>, <i>, and other simple text-formatting HTML within the <string> node. You can use this compound HTML string to style the text before painting in a text view.

The Java examples in Listing 3–7 illustrate each usage.

Listing 3–7. *Using String Resources in Java Code*

```
//Read a simple string and set it in a text view
String simpleString = activity.getString(R.string.simple_string);
textView.setText(simpleString);

//Read a quoted string and set it in a text view
String quotedString = activity.getString(R.string.quoted_string);
textView.setText(quotedString);

//Read a double quoted string and set it in a text view
String doubleQuotedString = activity.getString(R.string.double_quoted_string);
textView.setText(doubleQuotedString);
```

```
//Read a Java format string
String javaFormatString = activity.getString(R.string.java_format_string);
//Convert the formatted string by passing in arguments
String substitutedString = String.format(javaFormatString, "Hello" , "Android");
//set the output in a text view
textView.setText(substitutedString);

//Read an html string from the resource and set it in a text view
String htmlTaggedString = activity.getString(R.string.tagged_string);
//Convert it to a text span so that it can be set in a text view
//android.text.Html class allows painting of "html" strings
//This is strictly an Android class and does not support all html tags
Spanned textSpan = android.text.Html.fromHtml(htmlTaggedString);
//Set it in a text view
textView.setText(textSpan);
```

Once you've defined the strings as resources, you can set them directly on a view such as TextView in the XML layout definition for that TextView. Listing 3–8 shows an example where an HTML string is set as the text content of a TextView.

Listing 3–8. *Using String Resources in XML*

```
<TextView android:layout_width="fill_parent"
          android:layout_height="wrap_content"
          android:textAlign="center"
          android:text="@string/tagged_string"/>
```

TextView automatically realizes that this string is an HTML string, and honors its formatting accordingly. This is nice because you can quickly set attractive text in your views as part of the layout.

Dimension Resources

Pixels, inches, and points are all examples of dimensions that can play a part in XML layouts or Java code. You can use these dimension resources to style and localize Android UIs without changing the source code.

Listing 3–9 shows how you can use dimension resources in XML.

Listing 3–9. *XML Syntax for Defining Dimension Resources*

```
<resources>
    <dimen name="mysize_in_pixels">1px</dimen>
    <dimen name="mysize_in_dp">5dp</dimen>
    <dimen name="medium_size">100sp</dimen>
</resources>
```

You can specify the dimensions in any of the following units:

- *px*: Pixels

- *in*: Inches

- *mm*: Millimeters

- *pt*: Points

- *dp*: Density-independent pixels based on a 160-dpi (pixel density per inch) screen (dimensions adjust to screen density)

- *sp*: Scale-independent pixels (dimensions that allow for user sizing; helpful for use in fonts)

In Java, you need to access your Resources object instance to retrieve a dimension. You can do this by calling getResources on an activity object (see Listing 3–10). Once you have the Resources object, you can ask it to locate the dimension using the dimension id. (Again, see Listing 3–10.)

Listing 3–10. *Using Dimension Resources in Java Code*

```
float dimen = activity.getResources().getDimension(R.dimen.mysize_in_pixels);
```

NOTE: The Java method call uses Dimension (full word) whereas the R.java namespace uses the shortened version dimen to represent "dimension."

As in Java, the resource reference for a dimension in XML uses dimen as opposed to the full word "dimension" (see Listing 3–11).

Listing 3–11. *Using Dimension Resources in XML*

```
<TextView android:layout_width="fill_parent"
          android:layout_height="wrap_content"
          android:textSize="@dimen/medium_size"/>
```

Image Resources

Android generates resource IDs for image files placed in the /res/drawable subdirectory. The supported image types include .gif, .jpg, and .png. Each image file in this directory generates a unique ID from its base file name. If the image file name is sample_image.jpg, for example, then the resource ID generated will be R.drawable.sample_image.

CAUTION: You'll get an error if you have two file names with the same base file name. Also, subdirectories underneath /res/drawable will be ignored. Any files placed under those subdirectories will not be read.

You can reference these images available in /res/drawable in other XML layout definitions, as shown in Listing 3–12.

Listing 3–12. *Using Image Resources in XML*

```
<Button
      android:id="@+id/button1"
      android:layout_width="fill_parent"
      android:layout_height="wrap_content"
      android:text="Dial"
      android:background="@drawable/sample_image"
/>
```

You can also retrieve the image programmatically using Java and set it yourself against a UI object like a button (see Listing 3–13).

Listing 3–13. *Using Image Resources in Java*

```
//Call getDrawable to get the image
BitmapDrawable d = activity.getResources().getDrawable(R.drawable.sample_image);

//You can use the drawable then to set the background
button.setBackgroundDrawable(d);

//or you can set the background directly from the Resource Id
button.setBackgroundResource(R.drawable.icon);
```

> **NOTE:** These background methods go all the way back to the View class. As a result, most of the UI controls have this background support.

Android also supports a special type of image called a *stretchable* image. This is a kind of .png where parts of the image can be specified as static and stretchable. Android provides a tool called the Draw 9-patch tool to specify these regions. (You can read more about it at http://developer.android.com/guide/developing/tools/draw9patch.html.)

Once the .png image is made available, you can use it as any other image. It comes in handy when used as a background for buttons where the button has to stretch itself to accommodate the text.

Color-Drawable Resources

In Android, an image is one type of a drawable resource. Android supports another drawable resource called a color-drawable resource; it's essentially a colored rectangle.

> **CAUTION:** The Android documentation seems to suggest that rounded corners are possible. But we were not successful in doing that. We have presented an alternate approach to do that below instead. The documentation also suggests that the instantiated Java class is PaintDrawable, but the code returns a ColorDrawable.

To define one of these color rectangles, you define an XML element by the node name of drawable in any XML file in the /res/values subdirectory. Listing 3–14 shows a couple of color-drawable resource examples.

Listing 3–14. *XML Syntax for Defining Color-Drawable Resources*

```
<resources>
    <drawable name="red_rectangle">#f00</drawable>
    <drawable name="blue_rectangle">#0000ff</drawable>
    <drawable name="green_rectangle">#f0f0</drawable>
</resources>
```

Listings 3–15 and 3–16 show how you can use a color-drawable resource in Java and XML, respectively.

Listing 3–15. *Using Color-Drawable Resources in Java Code*

```
// Get a drawable
ColorDrawble redDrawable =
(ColorDrawable)
activity.getResources().getDrawable(R.drawable.red_rectangle);

//Set it as a background to a text view
textView.setBackground(redDrawable);
```

Listing 3–16. *Using Color-Drawable Resources in XML Code*

```
<TextView android:layout_width="fill_parent"
          android:layout_height="wrap_content"
          android:textAlign="center"
          android:background="@drawable/red_rectangle"/>
```

To achieve the rounded corners in your Drawable, you can use the currently undocumented <shape> tag. However, this tag needs to reside in a file by itself in the /res/drawable directory. Listing 3–17 shows how you can use the <shape> tag to define a rounded rectangle in a file called /res/drawable/my_rounded_rectangle.xml.

Listing 3–17. *Defining a Rounded Rectangle*

```
<shape xmlns:android="http://schemas.android.com/apk/res/android">
    <solid android:color="#f0600000"/>
    <stroke android:width="3dp" color="#ffff8080"/>
    <corners android:radius="13dp" />
    <padding android:left="10dp" android:top="10dp"
        android:right="10dp" android:bottom="10dp" />
</shape>
```

You can then use this drawable resource as a background of the previous text-view example:

```
// Get a drawable
GradientDrawable roundedRectangle =
(GradientDrawable)
activity.getResources().getDrawable(R.drawable.red_rectnagle);

//Set it as a background to a text view
textView.setBackground(roundedRectangle);
```

> **NOTE:** It is not necessary to cast the returned base Drawable to a GradientDrawable, but it was done to show you that this <shape> tag becomes a GradientDrawable. This information is important because you can look up the Java API documentation for this class to know the XML tags it defines.
>
> In the end, a bitmap image in the drawable subdirectory will resolve to a BitmapDrawable class. A "drawable" resource value, such as one of the above rectangles, resolves to a ColorDrawable. An XML file with a shape tag in it resolves to a "GradientDrawable".

Working with Arbitrary XML Resource Files

Android also allows arbitrary XML files as resources. This approach extends the three usual "resource" advantages to arbitrary XML files. First, it provides a quick way to reference these files based on their generated resource IDs. Second, the approach allows you to localize these resource XML files. Third, you can compile and store these XML files on the device efficiently.

XML files that need to be read in this fashion are stored under the /res/xml subdirectory. Here is an example XML file called /res/xml/test.xml:

```
<rootelem1>
    <subelem1>
        Hello World from an xml sub element
    </subelem1>
</rootelem1>
```

As it does with other Android XML resource files, the AAPT will compile this XML file before placing it in the application package. You will need to use an instance of XmlPullParser if you want to parse these files. You can get an instance of the XmlPullParser implementation using this code from any context (including activity):

```
Resources res = activity.getResources();
XmlResourceParser xpp = res.getXml(R.xml.test);
```

The returned XmlResourceParser is an instance of XmlPullParser, and it also implements java.util.AttributeSet. Listing 3–18 shows a more complete code snippet that reads the test.xml file.

Listing 3–18. *Using XmlPullParser*

```
private String getEventsFromAnXMLFile(Activity activity)
throws XmlPullParserException, IOException
{
    StringBuffer sb = new StringBuffer();
    Resources res = activity.getResources();
    XmlResourceParser xpp = res.getXml(R.xml.test);

    xpp.next();
    int eventType = xpp.getEventType();
    while (eventType != XmlPullParser.END_DOCUMENT)
    {
        if(eventType == XmlPullParser.START_DOCUMENT)
        {
            sb.append("******Start document");
        }
        else if(eventType == XmlPullParser.START_TAG)
        {
            sb.append("\nStart tag "+xpp.getName());
        }
        else if(eventType == XmlPullParser.END_TAG)
        {
            sb.append("\nEnd tag "+xpp.getName());
        }
        else if(eventType == XmlPullParser.TEXT)
        {
```

```
        sb.append("\nText "+xpp.getText());
    }
    eventType = xpp.next();
}//eof-while
sb.append("\n******End document");
return sb.toString();
}//eof-function
```

In Listing 3–18, you can see how to get XmlPullParser, how to use XmlPullParser to navigate the XML elements in the XML document, and how to use additional methods of XmlPullParser to access the details of the XML elements. If you want to run this code, you must create an XML file as shown earlier and call the getEventsFromAnXMLFile function from any menu item or button click. It will return a string, which you can print out to the log stream using the Log.d debug method.

Working with Raw Resources

Android also allows raw files in addition to arbitrary XML files. These raw resources, placed in /res/raw, are raw file resources such as audio, video, or text files that require localization or references through resource IDs. Unlike the XML files placed in /res/xml, these files are not compiled, but moved to the application package as they are. However, each file will have an identifier generated in R.java. If you were to place a text file at /res/raw/test.txt, you would be able to read that file using the code in Listing 3–19.

Listing 3–19. *Reading a Raw Resource*

```
String getStringFromRawFile(Activity activity)
    throws IOException
    {
        Resources r = activity.getResources();
        InputStream is = r.openRawResource(R.raw.test);
        String myText = convertStreamToString(is);
        is.close();
        return myText;
    }

    String convertStreamToString(InputStream is)
    throws IOException
    {
        ByteArrayOutputStream baos = new ByteArrayOutputStream();
        int i = is.read();
        while (i != -1)
        {
            baos.write(i);
            i = is.read();
        }
        return baos.toString();
    }
```

CAUTION: File names with duplicate base names generate a build error in the Eclipse ADT plug-in. This is the case for all resource IDs generated for resources that are based on files.

Working with Assets

Android offers one more directory where you can keep files to be included in the package: /assets. It's at the same level as /res, meaning it's not part of the /res subdirectories. The files in /assets do not generate IDs in R.java; you must specify the file path to read them. The file path is a relative path starting at /assets. You will use the AssetManager class to access these files:

```
//Note: Exceptions are not shown in the code
String getStringFromAssetFile(Activity activity)
{
    AssetManager am = activity.getAssets();
    InputStream is = am.open("test.txt");
    String s = convertStreamToString(is);
    is.close();
    return s;
}
```

Reviewing the Resources Directory Structure

In summary, here is a quick look at the overall resources directory structure:

```
/res/values/strings.xml
            /colors.xml
            /dimens.xml
            /attrs.xml
            /styles.xml
    /drawable/*.png
             /*.jpg
             /*.gif
             /*.9.png
    /anim/*.xml
    /layout/*.xml
    /raw/*.*
    /xml/*.xml
/assets/*.*/*.*
```

> **NOTE:** Because it's not under the /res directory, only the /assets directory can contain an arbitrary list of subdirectories. Every other directory can only have files at the level of that directory and no deeper. This is how R.java generates identifiers for those files.

Let us conclude this section by quickly enumerating what you have learned about resources so far. You know the types of resources supported in Android and you know how to create these resources in XML files. You know how resource IDs are generated and how to use them in Java code. You also learned that resource ID generation is a convenient scheme that simplifies resource usage in Android. Finally, you learned how to work with raw resources and assets. With that, we will now turn our attention to content providers, and you will learn to work with data on Android.

Understanding Content Providers

So, what is a content provider? A content provider is a wrapper around data. Android allows you to expose data sources (or data providers) through a REST (Representational State Transfer)-like abstraction called a *content provider*. A SQLite database on an Android device is an example of a data source that you can encapsulate into a content provider. To retrieve data from a content provider or save data into a content provider, you will need to use a set of REST-like URIs. For example, if you were to retrieve a set of books from a content provider that is an encapsulation of a book database, you would need to use a URI like this:

```
content://com.android.book.BookProvider/books
```

To retrieve a specific book from the book database (book 23), you would need to use a URI like this:

```
content://com.android.book.BookProvider/books/23
```

You will see in this section how these URIs translate to underlying database-access mechanisms. Any application on the device can make use of these URIs to access and manipulate data. As a consequence, content providers play a significant role in sharing data between applications.

Strictly speaking, though, the content providers' responsibilities comprise more of an encapsulation mechanism than a data-access mechanism. You'll need an actual data-access mechanism such as SQLite or network access to get to the underlying data sources. So, content-provider abstraction is required only if you want to share data externally or between applications. For internal data access, an application can use any data storage/access mechanism that it deems suitable, such as the following:

- *Preferences*: A set of key/value pairs that you can persist to store application preferences

- *Files*: Files internal to applications, which you can store on a removable storage medium

- *SQLite*: SQLite databases, each of which is private to the package that creates that database

- *Network*: A mechanism that lets you retrieve or store data externally through the Internet

NOTE: Despite the number of data-access mechanisms allowed in Android, this chapter focuses on SQLite and the content-provider abstraction because content providers form the basis of data sharing, which is much more common in the Android framework compared to other UI frameworks. We'll cover the network approach in Chapter 8 and the preferences mechanism in Chapter 11.

As we go through this section, we will show you the content providers that come with Android and how to explore them. We will discuss in detail the structure of content URIs and how these URIs are linked with MIME types. After covering these content-provider concepts in detail, we will show you how to build a content provider from scratch that encapsulates a simple book database.

Exploring Android's Built-in Providers

Android comes with a number of built-in content providers, which are documented in the SDK's android.provider Java package. You can view the list of these providers here:

```
http://developer.android.com//reference/android/provider/package-summary.html
```

Here are a few of the providers listed on that documentation page:

```
Browser
CallLog
Contacts
    People
    Phones
    Photos
    Groups
MediaStore
    Audio
        Albums
        Artists
        Genres
        Playlists
    Images
        Thumbnails
    Video
Settings
```

> **NOTE:** The list of providers may vary slightly, depending on the release of Android you are working with. The purpose of this list is to give you an idea of what is available, and not to serve as a definitive reference.

The top-level items are databases and the lower-level items are tables. So Browser, CallLog, Contacts, MediaStore, and Settings are individual SQLite databases encapsulated as providers. These SQLite databases typically have an extension of .db and are accessible only from the implementation package. Any access outside that package must go through the content-provider interface.

Exploring Databases on the Emulator and Available Devices

Because many content providers in Android use SQLite databases (http://www.sqlite.org/), you can use tools provided both by Android and by SQLite to examine the databases. Many of these tools reside in the `\android-sdk-install-directory\tools` subdirectory.

> **NOTE:** Refer to Chapter 2 for information on locating the "tools" directory and invoking a command window for different operating systems. This chapter, like most of the remaining chapters, gives examples primarily on Windows platforms. As you go through this section, in which we use a number of command-line tools, you can focus on the name of the executable or the batch file and not pay as much attention to the directory the tool is in. We covered how to set the path for the tools directory on various platforms in Chapter 2.

One of the tools is a remote shell on the device that allows you to execute a command-line SQLite tool against a specified database. You'll see in this section how to use this command-line utility to examine the built-in Android databases.

Android uses another command-line tool called Android Debug Bridge (adb), which is available as

```
tools\adb.exe
```

adb is a special tool in the Android toolkit that most other tools go through to get to the device. However, you must have an emulator running or an Android device connected for adb to work. You can find out whether you have running devices or emulators by typing this at the command line:

```
adb devices
```

If the emulator is not running, you can start the emulator by typing this at the command line:

```
\tools\emulator.exe @avdname
```

The argument @avdname is the name of an AVD (Android Virtual Device). (We covered the need for android virtual devices and how to create them in Chapter 2.) To find out what virtual devices you already have you can run the following command:

```
\tools\android    list    avd
```

This command will list the available AVD. If you have developed and run any Android applications through Eclipse ADT then you will have configured at least one virtual device. The above command will list at least that one virtual device.

Here is an example output of that list command. (Depending on where your tools directory is and also depending on the Android release, the following printout may vary as to the path or release numbers, such as `i:\android`.)

```
I:\android\tools>android list avd
Available Android Virtual Devices:
    Name: avd
    Path: I:\android\tools\..\avds\avd3
  Target: Google APIs (Google Inc.)
        Based on Android 1.5 (API level 3)
    Skin: HVGA
```

```
  Sdcard: 32M
---------
    Name: titanium
    Path: C:\Documents and Settings\Satya\.android\avd\titanium.avd
  Target: Android 1.5 (API level 3)
    Skin: HVGA
```

As indicated, AVDs are covered in detail in Chapter 2.

You can also start the emulator through the Eclipse ADT plug-in. This automatically happens when you choose a program to run or debug in the emulator. Once the emulator is up and running, you can test again for a list of running devices by typing this:

```
\tools\adb.exe devices
```

Now you should see a printout that looks like this:

List of devices attached

emulator-5554 device

You can see the many options and commands that you can run with adb by typing this at the command line:

```
adb help
```

You can also visit the following URL for many of the runtime options for adb: `http://developer.android.com/guide/developing/tools/adb.html`.

You can use adb to open a shell on the connected device by typing this:

```
\tools\adb.exe shell
```

> **NOTE:** This shell is essentially a Unix ash, albeit with a limited command set. You can do ls, for example, but find, grep, and awk are not available in the shell.

You can see the available command set in the shell by typing this at the shell prompt:

```
#ls    /system/bin
```

The # sign is the prompt for the shell. For brevity, we will omit this prompt in some of the following examples. The preceding line brings up the following commands listed in Table 3–2. (Please note that we have shown these commands only as a demonstration and not for completeness. This list may be somewhat different depending on the release of Android SDK you are running.)

Table 3–2. *Available Shell Command Set*

dumpcrash	sh	date
am	hciattach	dd
dumpstate	sdptool	cmp
input	logcat	cat
itr	servicemanager	dmesg
monkey	dbus-daemon	df
pm	debug_tool	getevent
svc	flash_image	getprop
ssltest	installd	hd
debuggerd	dvz	id
dhcpcd	hostapd	ifconfig
hostapd_cli	htclogkernel	insmod
fillup	mountd	ioctl
linker	qemud	kill
logwrapper	radiooptions	ln
telnetd	toolbox	log
iftop	hcid	lsmod
mkdosfs	route	ls
mount	setprop	mkdir
mv	sleep	dumpsys
notify	setconsole	service
netstat	smd	playmp3
printenv	stop	sdutil
reboot	top	rild
ps	start	dalvikvm
renice	umount	dexopt
rm	vmstat	surfaceflinger
rmdir	wipe	app_process
rmmod	watchprops	mediaserver
sendevent	sync	system_server
schedtop	netcfg	
ping	Chmod	

To see a list of root-level directories and files, you can type the following in the shell:

```
ls    -l
```

You'll need to access this directory to see the list of databases:

```
ls    /data/data
```

This directory contains the list of installed packages on the device. Let's look at an example by exploring the com.android.providers.contacts package:

```
ls    /data/data/com.android.providers.contacts/databases
```

This will list a database file called contacts.db, which is a SQLite database.

> **NOTE:** We also should tell you that, in Android, databases may be created when they are accessed the first time. This means you may not see this file if you have never accessed the "contacts" application.

If there were a find command in the included ash, you could look at all the *.db files. But there is no good way to do this with ls alone. The nearest thing you can do is this:

```
ls -R /data/data/*/databases
```

With this command you will notice that the Android distribution has the following databases (again, a bit of caution; depending on your release, this list may vary):

```
alarms.db
contacts.db
downloads.db
internal.db
settings.db
mmssms.db
telephony.db
```

You can invoke sqlite3 on one of these databases inside the adb shell by typing this:

```
#sqlite3   /data/data/com.android.providers.contacts/databases/contacts.db
```

You can exit sqlite3 by typing this:

```
sqlite>.exit
```

Notice that the prompt for adb is # and the prompt for sqlite3 is sqlite>. You can read about the various sqlite3 commands by visiting http://www.sqlite.org/sqlite.html. However, we will list a few important commands here so that you don't have to make a trip to the web. You can see a list of tables by typing

```
sqlite> .tables
```

This command is a shortcut for

```
SELECT name FROM sqlite_master
WHERE type IN ('table','view') AND name NOT LIKE 'sqlite_%'
UNION ALL
SELECT name FROM sqlite_temp_master
WHERE type IN ('table','view')
ORDER BY 1
```

As you probably guessed, the table sqlite_master is a master table that keeps track of tables and views in the database. The following command line prints out a create statement for a table called people in contacts.db:

```
.schema people
```

This is one way to get at the column names of a table in SQLite. This will also print out the column data types. While working with content providers, you should note these column types because access methods depend on them.

However, it is pretty tedious to manually parse through this long create statement just to learn the column names and their types. Luckily, there is a workaround: you can pull contacts.db down to your local box and then examine the database using any number of GUI tools for SQLite version 3. You can issue the following command from your OS command prompt to pull down the contacts.db file:

```
adb pull  /data/data/com.android.providers.contacts/databases/contacts.db ↩
c:/somelocaldir/contacts.db
```

We used a free download of Sqliteman (http://sqliteman.com/), a GUI tool for SQLite databases, which seemed to work fine. We experienced a few crashes, but otherwise found the tool completely usable for exploring Android SQLite databases.

Quick SQLite Primer

The following sample SQL statements could help you navigate through the SQLite databases quickly:

```
//Set the column headers to show in the tool
sqlite>.headers on

//select all rows from a table
select * from table1;

//count the number of rows in a table
select count(*) from table1;

//select a specific set of columns
select col1, col2 from table1;

//Select distinct values in a column
select distinct col1 from table1;

//counting the distinct values
select count(col1) from (select distinct col1  from table1);

//group by
select count(*), col1 from table1 group by col1;

//regular inner join
select * from table1 t1, table2 t2
where t1.col1 = t2.col1;

//left outer join
//Give me everything in t1 even though there are no rows in t2
select * from table t1 left outer join table2 t2
on t1.col1 = t2.col1
where ....
```

Architecture of Content Providers

You now know how to explore existing content providers through Android and SQLite tools. Next, we'll examine some of the architectural elements of content providers and how these content providers relate to other data-access abstractions in the industry.

Overall, the content-provider approach has parallels to the following industry abstractions:

- Web sites
- REST
- Web services
- Stored procedures

Let's first explore the similarities content of providers to web sites. Each content provider on a device registers itself like a web site with a string (akin to a domain name, but called an *authority*). This uniquely identifiable string forms the basis of a set of URIs that this content provider can offer. This is not unlike how a web site with a domain offers a number of URLs to expose its documents or content in general.

This authority registration occurs in the AndroidManifest.xml. Here are two examples of how you may register providers in AndroidManifest.xml:

```
<provider android:name="SomeProvider"
        android:authorities="com.your-company.SomeProvider" />

<provider android:name="NotePadProvider"
    android:authorities="com.google.provider.NotePad"
/>
```

An authority is like a domain name for that content provider. Given the preceding authority registration, these providers will honor URLs starting with that authority prefix:

```
content://com.your-company.SomeProvider/
content://com.google.provider.NotePad/
```

You see that "content providers", like a web site, has a base domain name that acts as a starting URL.

> **NOTE:** It must be noted that the providers offered by Android may not carry a fully qualified authority name. It is recommended at the moment only for third-party content providers. This is why you sometimes see that content providers are referenced with a simple word such as "contacts" as opposed to "com.google.android.contacts" (in the case of a third-party provider).

Content providers also provide REST-like URLs to retrieve or manipulate data. For the preceding registration, the URI to identify a directory or a collection of notes in the NotePadProvider database is

```
content://com.google.provider.NotePad/Notes
```

The URI to identify a specific note is

```
content://com.google.provider.NotePad/Notes/#
```

where # is the id of a particular note. Here are some additional examples of URIs that some data providers accept:

```
content://media/internal/images
content://media/external/images
content://contacts/people/
content://contacts/people/23
```

Notice here how these providers' "media" (content://media) and "contacts" (content://contacts) don't have a fully qualified structure. This is because these are not third-party providers and controlled by Android.

Content providers exhibit characteristics of web services as well. A content provider, through its URIs, exposes internal data as a service. However, the output from the URL of a content provider is not typed data, as is the case for a SOAP-based web-service call. This output is more like a result set coming from a JDBC statement. Even there the similarities to JDBC are conceptual. We don't want to give the impression that this is the same as a ResultSet.

The caller is expected to know the structure of the rows and columns that are returned. Also, as you will see in this chapter's "Structure of Android MIME Types" section, a content provider has a built-in mechanism that allows you to determine the Multipurpose Internet Mail Extensions (MIME) type of the data represented by this URI.

In addition to resembling web sites, REST, and web services, a content provider's URIs also resemble the names of stored procedures in a database. Stored procedures present service-based access to the underlying relational data. URIs are similar to stored procedures because URI calls against a content provider return a cursor. However, content providers differ from stored procedures in that the input to a service call in a content provider is typically embedded in the URI itself.

We've provided these comparisons to give you an idea of the broader scope of content providers.

Structure of Android Content URIs

We compared a content provider to a web site because it responds to incoming URIs. So, to retrieve data from a content provider, all you have to do is invoke a URI. The retrieved data in the case of a content provider, however, is in the form of a set of rows and columns represented by an Android cursor object. In this context, we'll examine the structure of the URIs that you could use to retrieve data.

Content URIs in Android look similar to HTTP URIs, except that they start with content and have this general form:

```
content://*/*/*
```

or

```
content://authority-name/path-segment1/path-segment2/etc…
```

Here's an example URI that identifies a note numbered 23 in a database of notes:

```
content://com.google.provider.NotePad/notes/23
```

After `content:`, the URI contains a unique identifier for the authority, which is used to locate the provider in the provider registry. In the preceding example, `com.google.provider.NotePad` is the authority portion of the URI.

`/notes/23` is the path section of the URI that is specific to each provider. The `notes` and `23` portions of the path section are called path segments. It is the responsibility of the provider to document and interpret the path section and path segments of the URIs.

The developer of the content provider usually does this by declaring constants in a Java class or a Java interface in that provider's implementation Java package. Furthermore, the first portion of the path might point to a collection of objects. For example, `/notes` indicates a collection or a directory of notes, whereas `/23` points to a specific note item.

Given this URI, a provider is expected to retrieve rows that the URI identifies. The provider is also expected to alter content at this URI using any of the state-change methods: insert, update, or delete.

Structure of Android MIME Types

Just as a web site returns a MIME type for a given URL (this allows browsers to invoke the right program to view the content), a content provider has an added responsibility to return the MIME type for a given URI. This allows flexibility of viewing data. Knowing what kind of data it is, you may have more than one program that knows how to handle that data. For example if you have a text file on your hard drive, there are many editors that can display that text file. Depending on the OS, it may even give you an option of which editor to pick.

MIME types work in Android similarly to how they work in HTTP. You ask a provider for the MIME type of a given URI that it supports, and the provider returns a two-part string identifying its MIME type according to the standard web MIME conventions. You can find the MIME-type standard here:

```
http://tools.ietf.org/html/rfc2046
```

According to the MIME-type specification, a MIME type has two parts: a type and a subtype. Here are some examples of well-known MIME-type pairs:

```
text/html
text/css
text/xml
text/vnd.curl
application/pdf
application/rtf
application/vnd.ms-excel
```

You can see a complete list of registered types and subtypes at the Internet Assigned Numbers Authority (IANA) web site:

```
http://www.iana.org/assignments/media-types/
```

The primary registered content types are

```
application
audio
example
image
message
model
multipart
text
video
```

Each of these primary types has subtypes. But if a vendor has proprietary data formats, the subtype name begins with vnd. For example, Microsoft Excel spreadsheets are identified by the subtype vnd.ms-excel, whereas pdf is considered a nonvendor standard and is represented as such without any vendor-specific prefix.

Some subtypes start with x-; these are nonstandard subtypes that don't have to be registered. They're considered private values that are bilaterally defined between two collaborating agents. Here are a few examples:

```
application/x-tar
audio/x-aiff
video/x-msvideo
```

Android follows a similar convention to define MIME types. The vnd in Android MIME types indicates that these types and subtypes are nonstandard, vendor-specific forms. To provide uniqueness, Android further demarcates the types and subtypes with multiple parts similar to a domain spec. Furthermore, the Android MIME type for each content type has two forms: one for a specific record, and one for multiple records.

For a single record, the MIME type looks like this:

```
vnd.android.cursor.item/vnd.yourcompanyname.contenttype
```

For a collection of records or rows, the MIME type looks like this:

```
vnd.android.cursor.dir/vnd.yourcompanyname.contenttype
```

Here are a couple of examples:

```
//One single note
vnd.android.cursor.item/vnd.google.note

//A collection or a directory of notes
vnd.android.cursor.dir/vnd.google.note
```

> **NOTE:** The implication here is that Android natively recognizes a "directory" of items and a "single" item. As a programmer, your flexibility is only limited to the sub type. For example, things like list controls rely on what is returned from a cursor as one of these MIME "main" types.

MIME types are extensively used in Android, especially in intents, where the system figures out what activity to invoke based on the MIME type of data. MIME types are invariably derived from their URIs through content providers. You need to keep three things in mind when you work with MIME types:

- The type and subtype need to be unique for what they represent. The type is pretty much decided for you, as pointed out. It is primarily a directory of items or a single item. In the context of Android, these may not be as open as you might think.

- Type and subtype need to be preceded with vnd if they are not standard (which is usually the case when you talk about specific records).

- They are typically namespaced for your specific need.

To reiterate this point, the primary MIME typefor a collection of items returned through an Android cursor should always be vnd.android.cursor.dir, and the primary MIME type of a single item retrieved through an Android cursor should be vnd.android.cursor.item. You have more wiggle room when it comes to the subtype, as in vnd.google.note; after the vnd. part, you are free to subtype it with anything you'd like.

Reading Data Using URIs

Now you know that to retrieve data from a content provider you need to use URIs supplied by that content provider. Because the URIs defined by a content provider are unique to that provider, it is important that these URIs are documented and available to programmers to see and then call. The providers that come with Android do this by defining constants representing these URI strings.

Consider these three URIs defined by helper classes in the Android SDK:

```
MediaStore.Images.Media.INTERNAL_CONTENT_URI
MediaStore.Images.Media.EXTERNAL_CONTENT_URI
Contacts.People.CONTENT_URI
```

The equivalent textual URI strings would be as follows:

```
content://media/internal/images
content://media/external/images
content://contacts/people/
```

The MediaStore provider defines two URIs and the Contacts provider defines one URI. If you notice, these constants are defined using a hierarchical scheme. For example the content URI example for the contacts is pointed out as Contacts.People.CONTENT_URI. This is because the databases of contacts may have a lot of tables to represent the entitities of a Contact. People is one of the tables or a collection. Each primary entity of a database may carry its own content URI, however, all rooted at the base authority name (such as contacts://contacts in the case of contacts provider).

> **NOTE:** In the reference Contacts.People.CONTENT_URI, Contacts is a java package and People is the interface within that package.

Given these URIs, the code to retrieve a single row of people from the contacts provider looks like this:

```
Uri peopleBaseUri = Contacts.People.CONTENT_URI;
Uri myPersonUri = peopleBaseUri.withAppendedId(Contacts.People.CONTENT_URI, 23);

//Query for this record.
//managedQuery is a method on Activity class
Cursor cur = managedQuery(myPersonUri, null, null, null);
```

Notice how the Contacts.People.CONTENT_URI is predefined as a constant in the People class. In this example, the code takes the root URI, adds a specific person ID to it, and makes a call to the managedQuery method.

As part of the query against this URI, it is possible to specify a sort order, the columns to select, and a where clause. These additional parameters are set to null in this example.

> **NOTE:** A content provider should list which columns it supports by implementing a set of interfaces or by listing the column names as constants. However, the class or interface that defines constants for columns should also make the column types clear through a column naming convention, or comments or documentation, as there is no formal way to indicate the type of a column through constants.

Listing 3–20 shows how to retrieve a cursor with a specific list of columns from the People table of the contacts content provider, based on the previous example.

Listing 3–20. *Retrieving a Cursor from a Content Provider*

```
// An array specifying which columns to return.
string[] projection = new string[] {
    People._ID,
    People.NAME,
    People.NUMBER,
};

// Get the base URI for People table in Contacts Content Provider.
// ie. content://contacts/people/
Uri mContactsUri = Contacts.People.CONTENT_URI;

// Best way to retrieve a query; returns a managed query.
Cursor managedCursor = managedQuery( mContactsUri,
                    projection, //Which columns to return.
                    null,       // WHERE clause
                    Contacts.People.NAME + " ASC"); // Order-by clause.
```

Notice how a `projection` is merely an array of strings representing column names. So unless you know what these columns are, you'll find it difficult to create a `projection`. You should look for these column names in the same class that provides the URI, in this case the `People` class. Let's look at the other column names defined in this class:

```
CUSTOM_RINGTONE
DISPLAY_NAME
LAST_TIME_CONTACTED
NAME
NOTES
PHOTO_VERSION
SEND_TO_VOICE_MAIL
STARRED
TIMES_CONTACTED
```

You can discover more about each of these columns by looking at the SDK documentation for the `android.provider.Contacts.PeopleColumns` class, available at this URL:

```
http://code.google.com/android/reference/android/provider/↩
Contacts.PeopleColumns.html
```

As alluded to earlier, a database like `contacts` contains several tables, each of which is represented by a class or an interface to describe its columns and their types. Let's take a look at the package `android.providers.Contacts`, documented at the following URL:

```
http://code.google.com/android/reference/android/provider/Contacts.html
```

You will see that this package has the following nested classes or interfaces:

```
ContactMethods
Extensions
Groups
Organizations
People
Phones
Photos
Settings
```

Each of these classes represents a table name in the `contacts.db` database, and each table is responsible for describing its own URI structure. Plus, a corresponding `Columns` interface is defined for each class to identify the column names, such as `PeopleColumns`.

Let's revisit the `cursor` that is returned: it contains zero or more records. Column names, order, and type are provider specific. However, every row returned has a default column called `_id` representing a unique ID for that row.

Using the Cursor

Before you access one, you should know a few things about an Android cursor:

- A cursor is a collection of rows.

- You need to use `moveToFirst()` because the cursor is positioned before the first row.

- You need to know the column names.

- You need to know the column types.

- All field-access methods are based on column number, so you must convert the column name to a column number first.

- The cursor is a random cursor (you can move forward and backward, and you can jump).

- Because the cursor is a random cursor, you can ask it for a row count.

An Android cursor has a number of methods that allow you to navigate through it. Listing 3–21 shows you how to check if a cursor is empty, and how to walk through the cursor row by row when it is not empty.

Listing 3–21. *Navigating Through a Cursor Using a while Loop*

```
if (cur.moveToFirst() == false)
{
   //no rows empty cursor
   return;
}

//The cursor is already pointing to the first row
//let's access a few columns
int nameColumnIndex = cur.getColumnIndex(People.NAME);
String name = cur.getString(nameColumnIndex);

//let's now see how we can loop through a cursor

while(cur.moveToNext())
{
   //cursor moved successfully
   //access fields
}
```

The assumption at the beginning of Listing 3–21 is that the cursor has been positioned before the first row. To position the cursor on the first row, we use the moveToFirst() method on the cursor object. This method returns false if the cursor is empty. We then use the moveToNext() method repetitively to walk through the cursor.

To help you learn where the cursor is, Android provides the following methods:

```
isBeforeFirst()
isAfterLast()
isClosed()
```

Using these methods, you can also use a for loop as in Listing 3–22 to navigate through the cursor instead of the while loop used in Listing 3–21.

Listing 3–22. *Navigating Through a Cursor Using a for Loop*

```
for(cur.moveToFirst();!cur.isAfterLast();cur.moveToNext())
{
    int nameColumn = cur.getColumnIndex(People.NAME);
    int phoneColumn = cur.getColumnIndex(People.NUMBER);
```

```
    String name = cur.getString(nameColumn);
    String phoneNumber = cur.getString(phoneColumn);
}
```

To find the number of rows in a cursor, Android provides a method on the cursor object called getCount().

Working with the where Clause

Content providers offer two ways of passing a where clause:

- Through the URI

- Through the combination of a string clause and a set of replaceable string-array arguments

We will cover both of these approaches through some sample code.

Passing a where Clause Through a URI

Imagine you want to retrieve a note whose ID is 23 from the Google notes database. You'd use the code in Listing 3–23 to retrieve a cursor containing one row corresponding to row 23 in the notes table.

Listing 3–23. *Passing SQL WHERE Clauses Through the URI*

```
Activity someActivity;
//..initialize someActivity
String noteUri = "content://com.google.provider.NotePad/notes/23";
Cursor managedCursor = someActivity.managedQuery( noteUri,
                projection, //Which columns to return.
                null,        // WHERE clause
                null); // Order-by clause.
```

We left the where clause argument of the managedQuery method null because, in this case, we assumed that the note provider is smart enough to figure out the id of the book we wanted. This id is embedded in the URI itself. In a sense, we used the URI as a vehicle to pass the where clause. This becomes apparent when you notice how the notes provider implements the corresponding query method. Here is a code snippet from that query method:

```
//Retrieve a note id from the incoming uri that looks like
//content://.../notes/23
int noteId = uri.getPathSegments().get(1);

//ask a query builder to build a query
//specify a table name
queryBuilder.setTables(NOTES_TABLE_NAME);

//use the noteid to put a where clause
queryBuilder.appendWhere(Notes._ID + "=" + );
```

Notice how the id of a note is extracted from the URI. The Uri class representing the incoming argument uri has a method to extract the portions of a URI after the root content://com.google.provider.NotePad. These portions are called path segments; they're strings between / separators such as /seg1/seg3/seg4/ and they're indexed by their positions. For the URI here, the first path segment would be 23. We then used this ID of 23 to append to the where clause specified to the QueryBuilder class. In the end, the equivalent select statement would be

```
select * from notes where _id = 23
```

> **NOTE:** The classes Uri and UriMatcher are used to identify URIs and extract parameters from them. (We'll cover UriMatcher further in the section "Using UriMatcher to Figure Out the URIs.") SQLiteQueryBuilder is a helper class in android.database.sqlite that allows you to construct SQL queries to be executed by SQLiteDatabase on a SQLite database instance.

Using Explicit WHERE Clauses

Now that you have seen how to use a URI to send in a where clause, consider the other method by which Android lets us send a list of explicit columns and their corresponding values as a where clause. To explore this, let's take another look at the managedQuery method of the Activity class that we used in Listing 3–23. Here's its signature:

```
public final Cursor managedQuery(Uri uri,
    String[] projection,
    String selection,
    String[] selectionArgs,
    String sortOrder)
```

Notice the argument named selection, which is of type String. This selection string represents a filter (a where clause, essentially) declaring which rows to return, formatted as a SQL WHERE clause (excluding the WHERE itself). Passing null will return all rows for the given URI. In the selection string you can include ?s, which will be replaced by the values from selectionArgs in the order that they appear in the selection. The values will be bound as Strings.

Because you have two ways of specifying a where clause, you might find it difficult to determine how a provider has used these where clauses and which where clause takes precedence if both where clauses are utilized.

For example, you can query for a note whose ID is 23 using either of these two methods:

```
//URI method
managedQuery("content://com.google.provider.NotePad/notes/23"
,null
,null
,null
,null);
```

or

```
//explicit where clause
managedQuery("content://com.google.provider.NotePad/notes"
```

```
,null
,"_id=?"
,new String[] {23}
,null);
```

The convention is to use where clauses through URIs where applicable and use the explicit option as a special case.

Inserting Records

So far we have talked about how to retrieve data from content providers using URIs. Now let us turn our attention to inserts, updates, and deletes. Let us start with `insert` first.

Android uses a class called `android.content.ContentValues` to hold the values for a single record, which is to be inserted. `ContentValues` is a dictionary of key/value pairs, much like column names and their values. You insert records by first populating a record into `ContentValues` and then asking `android.content.ContentResolver` to insert that record using a URI.

> **NOTE:** You need to locate `ContentResolver` because at this level of abstraction, you are not asking a database to insert a record; instead, you are asking to insert a record into a provider identified by a URI. `ContentResolver getCount()` is responsible for resolving the URI reference to the right provider and then passing on the `ContentValues` object to that specific provider.

Here is an example of populating a single row of notes in `ContentValues` in preparation for an insert:

```
ContentValues values = new ContentValues();
values.put("title", "New note");
values.put("note","This is a new note");

//values object is now ready to be inserted
```

Although we have hard-coded the column names, you can use constants defined in your Notepad application instead. You can get a reference to `ContentResolver` by asking the Activity class:

```
ContentResolver contentResolver = activity.getContentResolver();
```

Now all you need is a URI to tell `ContentResolver` to insert the row. These URIs are defined in a class corresponding to the `Notes` table. In the Notepad example, this URI is

```
Notepad.Notes.CONTENT_URI
```

We can take this URI and the `ContentValues` we have, and make a call to insert the row:

```
Uri uri = contentResolver.insert(Notepad.Notes.CONTENT_URI, values);
```

This call returns a URI pointing to the newly inserted record. This returned URI would match the following structure:

```
Notepad.Notes.CONTENT_URI/new_id
```

Adding a File to a Content Provider

Occasionally, you might need to store a file in a database. The usual approach is to save the file to disk and then update the record in the database that points to the corresponding file name.

Android takes this protocol and automates it by defining a specific procedure for saving and retrieving these files. Android uses a convention where a reference to the file name is saved in a record with a reserved column name of _data.

When a record is inserted into that table, Android returns the URI to the caller. Once you save the record using this mechanism, you also need to follow it up by saving the file in that location. To do this, Android allows ContentResolver to take the Uri of the database record and return a writable output stream. Behind the scenes, Android allocates an internal file and stores the reference to that file name in the _data field.

If you were to extend the Notepad example to store an image for a given note, you could create an additional column called _data and run an insert first to get a URI back. The following code demonstrates this part of the protocol:

```
ContentValues values = new ContentValues();
values.put("title", "New note");
values.put("note","This is a new note");

//Use a content resolver to insert the record
ContentResolver contentResolver = activity.getContentResolver();
Uri newUri = contentResolver.insert(Notepad.Notes.CONTENT_URI, values);
```

Once you have the URI of the record, the following code asks the ContentResolver to get a reference to the file output stream:

```
….
//Use the content resolver to get an output stream directly
//ContentResolver hides the access to the _data field where
//it stores the real file reference.
OutputStream outStream = activity.getContentResolver().openOutputStream(newUri);
someSourceBitmap.compress(Bitmap.CompressFormat.JPEG, 50, outStream);
outStream.close();
```

The code then uses that output stream to write to.

Updates and Deletes

So far we have talked about queries and inserts; updates and deletes are fairly straightforward. Performing an update is similar to performing an insert, in which changed column values are passed through a ContentValues object. Here is the signature of an update method on the ContentResolver object:

```
int numberOfRowsUpdated =
activity.getContentResolver().update(
    Uri uri,
```

```
    ContentValues values,
    String whereClause,
    String[] selectionArgs )
```

The whereClause argument will constrain the update to the pertinent rows. Similarly, the signature for the delete method is

```
int numberOfRowsDeleted =
activity.getContentResolver().delete(
    Uri uri,
    String whereClause,
    String[] selectionArgs )
```

Clearly a delete method will not require the ContentValues argument because you will not need to specify the columns you want when you are deleting a record.

Almost all the calls from managedQuery and ContentResolver are directed eventually to the provider class. Knowing how a provider implements each of these methods gives us enough clues as to how those methods are used by a client. In the next section, we'll cover the implementation from scratch of an example content provider called BookProvider.

Implementing Content Providers

We've discussed how to interact with a content provider for data needs, but haven't yet discussed how to write a content provider. To write a content provider, you have to extend android.content.ContentProvider and implement the following key methods:

```
query
insert
update
delete
getType
```

However, to make these methods work, you'll have to set up a number of things before implementing them. We will illustrate all the details of a content-provider implementation by describing the steps you'll need to take:

1. Plan your database, URIs, column names, and so on, and create a metadata class that defines constants for all of these metadata elements.

2. Extend the abstract class ContentProvider.

3. Implement these methods: query, insert, update, delete, and getType.

4. Register the provider in the manifest file.

Planning a Database

To explore this topic, we'll create a database that contains a collection of books. The book database contains only one table called books, and its columns are name, isbn, and author. You'll define this sort of relevant metadata in a Java class. This metadata-bearing Java class BookProviderMetaData is shown in Listing 3–24. Some key elements of this metadata class are highlighted.

Listing 3–24. *Defining Metadata for Your Database: The BookProviderMetaData Class*

```java
public class BookProviderMetaData
{
    public static final String AUTHORITY = "com.androidbook.provider.BookProvider";

    public static final String DATABASE_NAME = "book.db";
    public static final int DATABASE_VERSION = 1;
    public static final String BOOKS_TABLE_NAME = "books";

    private BookProviderMetaData() {}

    //inner class describing BookTable
    public static final class BookTableMetaData implements BaseColumns
    {
        private BookTableMetaData() {}
        public static final String TABLE_NAME = "books";

        //uri and MIME type definitions
        public static final Uri CONTENT_URI =
                        Uri.parse("content://" + AUTHORITY + "/books");

        public static final String CONTENT_TYPE =
                        "vnd.android.cursor.dir/vnd.androidbook.book";

        public static final String CONTENT_ITEM_TYPE =
                        "vnd.android.cursor.item/vnd.androidbook.book";

        public static final String DEFAULT_SORT_ORDER = "modified DESC";

        //Additional Columns start here.
        //string type
        public static final String BOOK_NAME = "name";

        //string type
        public static final String BOOK_ISBN = "isbn";

        //string type
        public static final String BOOK_AUTHOR = "author";

        //Integer from System.currentTimeMillis()
        public static final String CREATED_DATE = "created";

        //Integer from System.currentTimeMillis()
        public static final String MODIFIED_DATE = "modified";
    }
}
```

This BookProviderMetaData class starts by defining its authority to be com.androidbook.provider.BookProvider. We are going to use this string to register the provider in the Android manifest file. This string forms the front part of the URIs intended for this provider.

This class then proceeds to define its one table (books) as an inner BookTableMetaData class. The BookTableMetaData class then defines a URI for identifying a collection of books. Given the authority in the previous paragraph, the URI for a collection of books will look like this:

```
content://com.androidbook.provider.BookProvider/books
```

This URI is indicated by the constant

```
BookProviderMetaData.BookTableMetaData.CONTENT_URI
```

The BookTableMetaData class then proceeds to define the MIME types for a collection of books and a single book. The provider implementation will use these constants to return the MIME types for the incoming URIs.

BookTableMetaData then defines the set of columns: name, isbn, author, created (creation date), and modified (last-updated date).

> **NOTE:** You should point out your columns' data types through comments in the code.

The metadata class BookTableMetaData also inherits from the BaseColumns class that provides the standard _id field, which represents the row ID. With these metadata definitions in hand, we're ready to tackle the provider implementation.

Extending ContentProvider

Implementing our BookProvider sample content provider involves extending the ContentProvider class and overriding onCreate() to create the database and then implement the query, insert, update, delete, and getType methods. This section covers the setup and creation of the database, while the following sections deal with each of the individual methods: query, insert, update, delete, and getType.

A query method requires the set of columns it needs to return. This is similar to a select clause that requires column names along with their as counterparts (sometimes called synonyms). Android uses a map object that it calls a projection map to represent these column names and their synonyms. We will need to set up this map so we can use it later in the query-method implementation. In the code for the provider implementation (see Listing 3–25), you will see this done up front.

Most of the methods we'll be implementing take a URI as an input. Although all the URIs that this content provider is able to respond to start with the same pattern, the tail ends of the URIs will be different—just like a web site. Each URI, although it starts the same, must be different to identify different data or documents. Let us illustrate this with an example:

```
Uri1: content://com.androidbook.provider.BookProvider/books
Uri2: content://com.androidbook.provider.BookProvider/books/12
```

See how the Book Provider needs to distinguish each of these URIs. This is a simple case. If our book provider had been housing more objects rather than just books, then there would be more URIs to identify those objects.

The provider implementation needs a mechanism to distinguish one URI from the other; Android uses a class called UriMatcher for this work. So we need to set up this object with all our URI variations. You will see this code in Listing 3–25 after the segment that creates a projection map. We'll further explain the UriMatcher class in the section "Using UriMatcher to Figure Out the URIs," but for now, know that the code shown here allows the content provider to identify one URI vs. the other.

And finally, the code in Listing 3–25 overrides the onCreate() method to facilitate the database creation. We have demarcated the code with highlighted comments to reflect the three areas we have talked about here:

- Setting up a column projection
- Setting up the UriMatcher
- Creating the database

Listing 3–25. *Implementing the BookProvider Content Provider*

```
public class BookProvider extends ContentProvider
{
    //Create a Projection Map for Columns
    //Projection maps are similar to "as" construct in an sql
    //statement whereby you can rename the
    //columns.
    private static HashMap<String, String> sBooksProjectionMap;
    static
    {
        sBooksProjectionMap = new HashMap<String, String>();
        sBooksProjectionMap.put(BookTableMetaData._ID, BookTableMetaData._ID);

        //name, isbn, author
        sBooksProjectionMap.put(BookTableMetaData.BOOK_NAME
                                        , BookTableMetaData.BOOK_NAME);
        sBooksProjectionMap.put(BookTableMetaData.BOOK_ISBN
                                        , BookTableMetaData.BOOK_ISBN);
        sBooksProjectionMap.put(BookTableMetaData.BOOK_AUTHOR
                                        , BookTableMetaData.BOOK_AUTHOR);

        //created date, modified date
        sBooksProjectionMap.put(BookTableMetaData.CREATED_DATE
                                        , BookTableMetaData.CREATED_DATE);
        sBooksProjectionMap.put(BookTableMetaData.MODIFIED_DATE
                                        , BookTableMetaData.MODIFIED_DATE);
    }

    //Provide a mechanism to identify all the incoming uri patterns.
    private static final UriMatcher sUriMatcher;
    private static final int INCOMING_BOOK_COLLECTION_URI_INDICATOR = 1;
    private static final int INCOMING_SINGLE_BOOK_URI_INDICATOR = 2;
    static {
        sUriMatcher = new UriMatcher(UriMatcher.NO_MATCH);
```

```
        sUriMatcher.addURI(BookProviderMetaData.AUTHORITY
                        , "books"
                        , INCOMING_BOOK_COLLECTION_URI_INDICATOR);

        sUriMatcher.addURI(BookProviderMetaData.AUTHORITY
                        , "books/#",
                        INCOMING_SINGLE_BOOK_URI_INDICATOR);

    }
// Deal with OnCreate call back

    private DatabaseHelper mOpenHelper;

    @Override
    public boolean onCreate() {
        mOpenHelper = new DatabaseHelper(getContext());
        return true;
    }

    private static class DatabaseHelper extends SQLiteOpenHelper {

        DatabaseHelper(Context context) {
            super(context, BookProviderMetaData.DATABASE_NAME, null
                    , BookProviderMetaData.DATABASE_VERSION);
        }

//Create the database
        @Override
        public void onCreate(SQLiteDatabase db) {
            db.execSQL("CREATE TABLE " + BookTableMetaData.TABLE_NAME + " ("
                    + BookProviderMetaData.BookTableMetaData._ID
                    + " INTEGER PRIMARY KEY,"
                    + BookTableMetaData.BOOK_NAME + " TEXT,"
                    + BookTableMetaData.BOOK_ISBN + " TEXT,"
                    + BookTableMetaData.BOOK_AUTHOR + " TEXT,"
                    + BookTableMetaData.CREATED_DATE + " INTEGER,"
                    + BookTableMetaData.MODIFIED_DATE + " INTEGER"
                    + ");");
        }
//Deal with version changes
        @Override
        public void onUpgrade(SQLiteDatabase db, int oldVersion, int newVersion) {
            Log.w(TAG, "Upgrading database from version " + oldVersion + " to "
                    + newVersion + ", which will destroy all old data");
            db.execSQL("DROP TABLE IF EXISTS " + BookTableMetaData.TABLE_NAME);
            onCreate(db);
        }
    }
```

Fulfilling MIME-Type Contracts

The BookProvider content provider must also implement the getType() method to return a MIME type for a given URI. This method, like many other methods of a content provider, is overloaded with respect to the incoming URI. As a result, the first responsibility of the getType() method is to distinguish the type of the URI. Is it a collection of books, or a single book?

As we pointed out in the previous section, we will use the UriMatcher to decipher this URI type. Depending on this URI, the BookTableMetaData class has defined the MIME-type constants to return for each URI. Without further ado, we present the complete code for the getType() method implementation in Listing 3–26.

Listing 3–26. *The getType() Method Implementation*

```
@Override
public String getType(Uri uri) {
    switch (sUriMatcher.match(uri)) {
    case INCOMING_BOOK_COLLECTION_URI_INDICATOR:
        return BookTableMetaData.CONTENT_TYPE;

    case INCOMING_SINGLE_BOOK_URI_INDICATOR:
        return BookTableMetaData.CONTENT_ITEM_TYPE;

    default:
        throw new IllegalArgumentException("Unknown URI " + uri);
    }
}
```

Implementing the Query Method

The query method in a content provider is responsible for returning a collection of rows depending on an incoming URI and a where clause.

Like the other methods, the query method uses UriMatcher to identify the URI type. If the URI type is a single-item type, the method retrieves the book ID from the incoming URI like this:

1. It extracts the path segments using getPathSegments().

2. It indexes into the URI to get the first path segment, which happens to be the book ID.

The query method then uses the projections that we created in Listing 3–25 to identify the return columns. In the end, query returns the cursor to the caller. Throughout this process, the query method uses the SQLiteQueryBuilder object to formulate and execute the query (see Listing 3–27).

Listing 3–27. *The query() Method Implementation*

```
@Override
public Cursor query(Uri uri, String[] projection, String selection
                        , String[] selectionArgs, String sortOrder)
{
    SQLiteQueryBuilder qb = new SQLiteQueryBuilder();

    switch (sUriMatcher.match(uri))
    {
        case INCOMING_BOOK_COLLECTION_URI_INDICATOR:
        qb.setTables(BookTableMetaData.TABLE_NAME);
```

```
    qb.setProjectionMap(sBooksProjectionMap);
    break;

    case INCOMING_SINGLE_BOOK_URI_INDICATOR:
    qb.setTables(BookTableMetaData.TABLE_NAME);
    qb.setProjectionMap(sBooksProjectionMap);
    qb.appendWhere(BookTableMetaData._ID + "="
                            + uri.getPathSegments().get(1));
    break;

    default:
    throw new IllegalArgumentException("Unknown URI " + uri);
}

// If no sort order is specified use the default
String orderBy;
if (TextUtils.isEmpty(sortOrder)) {
    orderBy = BookTableMetaData.DEFAULT_SORT_ORDER;
} else {
    orderBy = sortOrder;
}

// Get the database and run the query
SQLiteDatabase db =
        mOpenHelper.getReadableDatabase();
Cursor c = qb.query(db, projection, selection,
                    selectionArgs, null, null, orderBy);
int i = c.getCount();

// Tell the cursor what uri to watch,
// so it knows when its source data changes
c.setNotificationUri(getContext().getContentResolver(), uri);
return c;
}
```

Implementing an Insert Method

The insert method in a content provider is responsible for inserting a record into the underlying database and then returning a URI that points to the newly created record.

Like the other methods, insert uses UriMatcher to identify the URI type. The code first checks whether the URI indicates the proper collection-type URI. If not, the code throws an exception (see Listing 3–28).

The code then validates the optional and mandatory column parameters. The code can substitute default values for some columns if they are missing.

Next, the code uses a SQLiteDatabase object to insert the new record and returns the newly inserted ID. In the end, the code constructs the new URI using the returned ID from the database.

Listing 3–28. *The insert() Method Implementation*

```
@Override
public Uri insert(Uri uri, ContentValues values) {
    // Validate the requested uri
```

```
        if (sUriMatcher.match(uri) != INCOMING_BOOK_COLLECTION_URI_INDICATOR) {
            throw new IllegalArgumentException("Unknown URI " + uri);
        }

        Long now = Long.valueOf(System.currentTimeMillis());

        //validate input fields
        // Make sure that the fields are all set
        if (values.containsKey(BookTableMetaData.CREATED_DATE) == false) {
            values.put(BookTableMetaData.CREATED_DATE, now);
        }

        if (values.containsKey(BookTableMetaData.MODIFIED_DATE) == false) {
            values.put(BookTableMetaData.MODIFIED_DATE, now);
        }

        if (values.containsKey(BookTableMetaData.BOOK_NAME) == false) {
            throw new SQLException(
                "Failed to insert row because Book Name is needed " + uri);
        }

        if (values.containsKey(BookTableMetaData.BOOK_ISBN) == false) {
            values.put(BookTableMetaData.BOOK_ISBN, "Unknown ISBN");
        }
        if (values.containsKey(BookTableMetaData.BOOK_AUTHOR) == false) {
            values.put(BookTableMetaData.BOOK_ISBN, "Unknown Author");
        }

        SQLiteDatabase db = mOpenHelper.getWritableDatabase();
        long rowId = db.insert(BookTableMetaData.TABLE_NAME
                                , BookTableMetaData.BOOK_NAME, values);
        if (rowId > 0) {
            Uri insertedBookUri = ContentUris.withAppendedId(
                                    BookTableMetaData.CONTENT_URI, rowId);
            getContext().getContentResolver().notifyChange(insertedBookUri, null);
            return insertedBookUri;
        }

        throw new SQLException("Failed to insert row into " + uri);
    }
```

Implementing an Update Method

The update method in a content provider is responsible for updating a record based on
the column values passed in, as well as the where clause that is passed in. The update
method then returns the number of rows updated in the process.

Like the other methods, update uses UriMatcher to identify the URI type. If the URI type
is a collection, the where clause is passed through so it can affect as many records as
possible. If the URI type is a single-record type, then the book ID is extracted from the
URI and specified as an additional where clause. In the end, the code returns the number
of records updated (see Listing 3–29). Chapter 12 fully explains the implications of this
notifyChange method. Also notice how this notifyChange method enables you to
announce to the world that the data at that URI has changed. Potentially, you can do the

same in the insert method by saying that the "..../books" has changed when a record is inserted.

Listing 3–29. *The update() Method Implementation*

```
@Override
public int update(Uri uri, ContentValues values, String where, String[] whereArgs)
{
        SQLiteDatabase db = mOpenHelper.getWritableDatabase();
        int count;
        switch (sUriMatcher.match(uri)) {
        case INCOMING_BOOK_COLLECTION_URI_INDICATOR:
            count = db.update(BookTableMetaData.TABLE_NAME,
                                                values, where, whereArgs);
            break;

        case INCOMING_SINGLE_BOOK_URI_INDICATOR:
            String rowId = uri.getPathSegments().get(1);
            count = db.update(BookTableMetaData.TABLE_NAME
                , values
                , BookTableMetaData._ID + "=" + rowId
                + (!TextUtils.isEmpty(where) ? " AND (" + where + ')' : "")
                , whereArgs);
            break;

        default:
            throw new IllegalArgumentException("Unknown URI " + uri);
        }

        getContext().getContentResolver().notifyChange(uri, null);
        return count;
    }
```

Implementing a Delete Method

The delete method in a content provider is responsible for deleting a record based on the where clause that is passed in. The delete method then returns the number of rows deleted in the process.

Like the other methods, delete uses UriMatcher to identify the URI type. If the URI type is a collection type, the where clause is passed through so you can delete as many records as possible. If the where clause is null, all records will be deleted. If the URI type is a single-record type, the book ID is extracted from the URI and specified as an additional where clause. In the end, the code returns the number of records deleted (see Listing 3–30).

Listing 3–30. *The delete() Method Implementation*

```
    @Override
    public int delete(Uri uri, String where, String[] whereArgs) {
        SQLiteDatabase db = mOpenHelper.getWritableDatabase();
        int count;
        switch (sUriMatcher.match(uri)) {
        case INCOMING_BOOK_COLLECTION_URI_INDICATOR:
            count = db.delete(BookTableMetaData.TABLE_NAME, where, whereArgs);
```

```
        break;

    case INCOMING_SINGLE_BOOK_URI_INDICATOR:
        String rowId = uri.getPathSegments().get(1);
        count = db.delete(BookTableMetaData.TABLE_NAME
          , BookTableMetaData._ID + "=" + rowId
          + (!TextUtils.isEmpty(where) ? " AND (" + where + ')' : "")
          , whereArgs);
        break;

    default:
        throw new IllegalArgumentException("Unknown URI " + uri);
    }
    getContext().getContentResolver().notifyChange(uri, null);
    return count;
}
```

Using UriMatcher to Figure Out the URIs

We've mentioned the UriMatcher class several times now; let's look into it. Almost all methods in a content provider are overloaded with respect to the URI. For example, the same query() method is called whether you want to retrieve a single book or a list of multiple books. It is up to the method to know which type of URI is being requested. Android's UriMatcher utility class helps you identify the URI types.

Here's how it works: you tell an instance of UriMatcher what kind of URI patterns to expect. You will also associate a unique number with each pattern. Once these patterns are registered, you can then ask UriMatcher if the incoming URI matches a certain pattern.

As we've mentioned, our BookProvider content provider has two URI patterns: one for a collection of books, and one for a single book. The code in Listing 3–31 registers both these patterns using UriMatcher. It allocates 1 for a collection of books and a 2 for a single book (the URI patterns themselves are defined in the metadata for the books table).

Listing 3–31. *Registering URI Patterns with UriMatcher*

```
    private static final UriMatcher sUriMatcher;
    //define ids for each uri type
    private static final int INCOMING_BOOK_COLLECTION_URI_INDICATOR = 1;
    private static final int INCOMING_SINGLE_BOOK_URI_INDICATOR = 2;

    static {
        sUriMatcher = new UriMatcher(UriMatcher.NO_MATCH);
        //Register pattern for the books
        sUriMatcher.addURI(BookProviderMetaData.AUTHORITY
                        , "books"
                        , INCOMING_BOOK_COLLECTION_URI_INDICATOR);
        //Register pattern for a single book
        sUriMatcher.addURI(BookProviderMetaData.AUTHORITY
                        , "books/#",
                        INCOMING_SINGLE_BOOK_URI_INDICATOR);
```

```
    }
```

Now that this registration is in place, you can see how UriMatcher plays a part in the query-method implementation:

```
switch (sUriMatcher.match(uri)) {
    case INCOMING_BOOK_COLLECTION_URI_INDICATOR:

    ......

    case INCOMING_SINGLE_BOOK_URI_INDICATOR:

    ......

    default:
        throw new IllegalArgumentException("Unknown URI " + uri);
}
```

Notice how the match method returns the same number that was registered earlier. The constructor of UriMatcher takes an integer to use for the root URI. UriMatcher returns this number if there are neither path segments nor authorities on the URL. UriMatcher also returns NO_MATCH when the patterns don't match. You can construct a UriMatcher with no root-matching code; in that case, Android initializes UriMatcher to NO_MATCH internally. So you could have written the code in Listing 3–31 as follows instead:

```
  static {
        sUriMatcher = new UriMatcher();
        sUriMatcher.addURI(BookProviderMetaData.AUTHORITY
                        , "books"
                        , INCOMING_BOOK_COLLECTION_URI_INDICATOR);

        sUriMatcher.addURI(BookProviderMetaData.AUTHORITY
                        , "books/#",
                        INCOMING_SINGLE_BOOK_URI_INDICATOR);
}
```

Using Projection Maps

A content provider acts like an intermediary between an abstract set of columns and a real set of columns in a database, yet these column sets might differ. While constructing queries, you must map between the where-clause columns that a client specifies and the real database columns. You set up this *projection map* with the help of the SQLiteQueryBuilder class.

Here is what the Android SDK documentation says about the mapping method public void setProjectionMap(Map columnMap) available on the QueryBuilder class:

Sets the projection map for the query. The projection map maps from column names that the caller passes into query to database column names. This is useful for renaming columns as well as disambiguating column names when doing joins. For example you could map "name" to "people.name". If a projection map is set it must contain all column names the user may request, even if the key and value are the same.

Here is how our BookProvider content provider sets up the projection map:

```
sBooksProjectionMap = new HashMap<String, String>();
```

```
sBooksProjectionMap.put(BookTableMetaData._ID, BookTableMetaData._ID);

//name, isbn, author
sBooksProjectionMap.put(BookTableMetaData.BOOK_NAME
                                        , BookTableMetaData.BOOK_NAME);
sBooksProjectionMap.put(BookTableMetaData.BOOK_ISBN
                                        , BookTableMetaData.BOOK_ISBN);
sBooksProjectionMap.put(BookTableMetaData.BOOK_AUTHOR
                                        , BookTableMetaData.BOOK_AUTHOR);

//created date, modified date
sBooksProjectionMap.put(BookTableMetaData.CREATED_DATE
                                        , BookTableMetaData.CREATED_DATE);
sBooksProjectionMap.put(BookTableMetaData.MODIFIED_DATE
                                        , BookTableMetaData.MODIFIED_DATE);
```

And then the query builder uses the variable sBooksProjectionMap like this:

```
queryBuilder.setTables(NOTES_TABLE_NAME);
queryBuilder.setProjectionMap(sNotesProjectionMap);
```

Registering the Provider

Finally, you must register the content provider in the Android.Manifest.xml file using this tag structure:

```
<provider android:name="BooksProvider"
    android:authorities=" com.androidbook.provider.BookProvider "/>
```

This concludes our discussion about content providers. In this section, you learned the nature of content URIs and MIME types, and how to use SQLite to construct your providers that respond to URIs. Once your underlying data is exposed in this manner, any application on the Android Platform can take advantage of it. This ability to access and update data using URIs, irrespective of the process boundaries, falls right in step with the current service-centric, cloud-computing landscape that we described in Chapter 1. In the next section, we will cover intents, which get tied to content providers through URIs and MIME types. What you have learned in this section is going to be very helpful in understanding intents.

Understanding Intents

Android folds multiple ideas into the concept of an *intent*. You can use intents to invoke other applications from your application. You can use intents to invoke internal or external components from your application. You can use intents to raise events so that others can respond in a manner similar to a publish-and subscribe model. However, what gets invoked based on an intent action also depends on what the payload of the intent is. So what on earth are these intents?

NOTE: What are intents? The shortest answer may be that an intent is an action with its associated data payload.

At the simplest level, an intent is an action that you can tell Android to invoke. The action Android invokes depends on what is registered for that action. Imagine you've written the following activity:

```
public class BasicViewActivity extends Activity
{
    @Override
    public void onCreate(Bundle savedInstanceState)
    {
        super.onCreate(savedInstanceState);
        setContentView(R.layout.some-view);
    }
}//eof-class
```

Android allows you to register this activity in its manifest file, making it available for other applications to invoke. The registration looks like this:

```
<activity android:name="BasicViewActivity"
          android:label="Basic View Tests">
  <intent-filter>
    <action android:name="com.androidbook.intent.action.ShowBasicView"/>
    <category android:name="android.intent.category.DEFAULT" />
  </intent-filter>
</activity>
```

The registration here not only involves an activity, but also an action that you can use to invoke that activity. The activity designer usually chooses a name for the action and specifies that action as part of an intent-filter for this activity. As we go through the rest of the chapter, you will have a chance to learn more about these intent-filters.

Now that you have specified the activity and its registration against an action, you can use an intent to invoke this `BasicViewActivity`:

```
public static invokeMyApplication(Activity parentActivity)
{
    String actionName= " com.androidbook.intent.action.ShowBasicView ";
    Intent intent = new Intent(actionName);
    parentActivity.startActivity(intent);
}
```

NOTE: The general convention for an action name is *<your-package-name>*.intent.action.*YOUR_ACTION_NAME*.

Available Intents in Android

Now that you have a basic understanding of intents, you can give them a test run by invoking one of the prefabricated applications that comes with Android (see Listing 3–32).

The page at `http://developer.android.com/guide/appendix/g-app-intents.html` documents the available applications and the intents that invoke them. Please note, however, that this list may change depending on the Android release; it is presented here to enhance your understanding. The set of predefined applications could include the following:

- A browser application to open a browser window

- An application to call a telephone number

- An application to present a phone dialer so the user can enter the numbers and make the call through the UI

- A mapping application to show the map of the world at a given latitude/longitude coordinate

- A detailed mapping application that can show Google street views

Here now is the code to exercise these applications through their published intents.

Listing 3–32. *Exercising Android's Prefabricated Applications*

```
public class IntentsUtils
{
    public static void invokeWebBrowser(Activity activity)
    {
        Intent intent = new Intent(Intent.ACTION_VIEW);
        intent.setData(Uri.parse("http://www.google.com"));
        activity.startActivity(intent);
    }
    public static void invokeWebSearch(Activity activity)
    {
        Intent intent = new Intent(Intent.ACTION_WEB_SEARCH);
        intent.setData(Uri.parse("http://www.google.com"));
        activity.startActivity(intent);
    }
    public static void dial(Activity activity)
    {
        Intent intent = new Intent(Intent.ACTION_DIAL);
        activity.startActivity(intent);
    }

    public static void call(Activity activity)
    {
        Intent intent = new Intent(Intent.ACTION_CALL);
        intent.setData(Uri.parse("tel:555-555-5555"));
        activity.startActivity(intent);
    }
    public static void showMapAtLatLong(Activity activity)
    {
        Intent intent = new Intent(Intent.ACTION_VIEW);
        //geo:lat,long?z=zoomlevel&q=question-string
        intent.setData(Uri.parse("geo:0,0?z=4&q=business+near+city"));
        activity.startActivity(intent);
    }

    public static void tryOneOfThese(Activity activity)
```

```
    {
        IntentsUtils.call(activity);
    }
}
```

You will be able to exercise this code as long you have a simple activity with a simple view (like the one in the previous section) and a menu item to invoke tryOneOfThese(activity). Creating a simple menu is easy (see Listing 3–33).

Listing 3–33. *A Test Harness to Create a Simple Menu*

```
public class HelloWorld extends Activity
{
    public void onCreate(Bundle savedInstanceState)    {
        super.onCreate(savedInstanceState);

        TextView tv = new TextView(this);
        tv.setText("Hello, Android. Say hello");
        setContentView(tv);
        registerMenu(this.getTextView());
    }
    @Override
    public boolean onCreateOptionsMenu(Menu menu)    {
        super.onCreateOptionsMenu(menu);
        int base=Menu.FIRST; // value is 1
        MenuItem item1 = menu.add(base,base,base,"Test");
        return true;
    }

    @Override
    public boolean onOptionsItemSelected(MenuItem item)    {
        if (item.getItemId() == 1)        {
            IntentUtils.tryOneOfThese(this);
        }
        else {
            return super.onOptionsItemSelected(item);
        }
        return true;
    }
}
```

NOTE: See Chapter 2 for instructions on how to make an Android project out of these files, as well as how to compile and run it. You can also read the early parts of Chapter 5 to see more sample code relating to menus.

Intents and Data URIs

So far, we've covered the simplest of the intents, where all we need is the name of an action. The ACTION_DIAL activity in Listing 3–32 is one of these; to invoke the dialer, all we need is the dialer's action and nothing else:

```
public static void dial(Activity activity)
{
    Intent intent = new Intent(Intent.ACTION_DIAL);
    activity.startActivity(intent);
}
```

Unlike ACTION_DIAL, the intent ACTION_CALL that is used to make a call to a given phone number takes an additional parameter called Data. This parameter points to a URI, which in turn points to the phone number:

```
public static void call(Activity activity)
{
    Intent intent = new Intent(Intent.ACTION_CALL);
    intent.setData(Uri.parse("tel:555-555-5555"));
    activity.startActivity(intent);
}
```

The action portion of an intent is a string or a string constant, usually prefixed by the Java package name. The data portion is always a string representing a URI. The format of this URI could be specific to each activity that is invoked by that action. In this case, the CALL action decides what kind of data URI it would expect. From the URI it extracts the telephone number.

> **NOTE:** The invoked activity can also use the URI as a pointer to a data source, extract the data from the data source, and use that data instead. This would be the case for media such as audio, video, and images.

Generic Actions

The actions Intent.ACTION_CALL and Intent.ACTION_DIAL could easily lead us to the wrong assumption that there is a one-to-one relationship between an action and what it invokes. To disprove this, let us extract a counterexample from the IntentUtils code in Listing 3–32:

```
public static void invokeWebBrowser(Activity activity)
{
    Intent intent = new Intent(Intent.ACTION_VIEW);
    intent.setData(Uri.parse("http://www.google.com"));
    activity.startActivity(intent);
}
```

Note that the action is simply stated as ACTION_VIEW. How does Android know which activity to invoke in response to such a generic action name? In these cases, Android relies more heavily on the nature of the URI. Android looks at the scheme of the URI, which happens to be http, and questions all the registered activities to see which ones understand this scheme. Out of these, it inquires which ones can handle the VIEW and then invokes that activity. For this to work, the browser activity should have registered a VIEW intent against the data scheme of http. That intent declaration might look like this in the manifest file:

```
<activity…..>
    <intent-filter>
        <action android:name="android.intent.action.VIEW" />
        <data android:scheme="http"/>
        <data android:scheme="https"/>
</intent-filter>
</activity>
```

You can learn more about the data options by looking at the XML definition for the data element at http://code.google.com/android/reference/android/R.styleable.html#AndroidManifestData. The child elements or attributes of data XML node include these:

```
host
mimeType
path
pathPattern
pathPrefix
port
scheme
```

mimeType is one attribute you'll see used often. For example, the following intent-filter for the activity that displays a list of notes indicates the MIME type as a directory of notes:

```
<intent-filter>
    <action android:name="android.intent.action.VIEW" />
    <data android:mimeType="vnd.android.cursor.dir/vnd.google.note" />
</intent-filter>
```

The screen that displays a single note, on the other hand, declares its intent-filter using a MIME type indicating a single note item:

```
<intent-filter>
    <action android:name="android.intent.action.VIEW" />
    <data android:mimeType="vnd.android.cursor.item/vnd.google.note" />
</intent-filter>
```

Using Extra Information

In addition to its primary attributes of action and data, an intent can include additional attributes called *extras*. An extra can provide more information to the component that receives the intent. The extra data is in the form of key/value pairs: the key name should start with the package name, and the value can be any fundamental data type or arbitrary object as long as it implements the android.os.Parcelable interface. This extra information is represented by an Android class called android.os.Bundle.

The following two methods on an Intent class provide access to the extra Bundle:

```
//Get the Bundle from an Intent
Bundle extraBundle = intent.getExtras();

// Place a bundle in an intent
Bundle anotherBundle = new Bundle();

//populate the bundle with key/value pairs
...
```

```
//set the bundle on the Intent
intent.putExtras(anotherBundle);
```

getExtras is straightforward: it returns the Bundle that the intent has. putExtras checks whether the intent currently has a bundle. If the intent already has a bundle, putExtras transfers the additional keys and values from the new bundle to the existing bundle. If the bundle doesn't exist, putExtras will create one and copy the key/value pairs from the new bundle to the created bundle.

> **NOTE:** putExtras replicates the incoming bundle rather than referencing it. So if you were to change the incoming bundle, you wouldn't be changing the bundle inside the intent.

You can use a number of methods to add fundamental types to the bundle. Here are some of the methods that add simple data types to the extra data:

```
putExtra(String name, boolean value);
putExtra(String name, int value);
putExtra(String name, double value);
putExtra(String name, String value);
```

And here are some not-so-simple extras:

```
//simple array support
putExtra(String name, int[] values);
putExtra(String name, float[] values);

//Serializable objects
putExtra(String name, Serializable value);

//Parcelable support
putExtra(String name, Parcelable value);

//Add another bundle at a given key
//Bundles in bundles
putExtra(String name, Bundle value);

//Add bundles from another intent
//copy of bundles
putExtra(String name, Intent anotherIntent);

//Explicit Array List support
putIntegerArrayListExtra(String name, ArrayList arrayList);
putParcelableArrayListExtra(String name, ArrayList arrayList);
putStringArrayListExtra(String name, ArrayList arrayList);
```

On the receiving side, equivalent methods starting with get retrieve information from the extra bundle based on key names.

The Intent class defines extra key strings that go with certain actions. You can discover a number of these extra-information key constants at http://code.google.com/android/reference/android/content/Intent.html#EXTRA_ALARM_COUNT.

Let us consider a couple of example extras that involve sending e-mails:

EXTRA_EMAIL: You will use this string key to hold a set of e-mail addresses. The value of the key is android.intent.extra.EMAIL. It should point to a string array of textual e-mail addresses.

EXTRA_SUBJECT: You will use this key to hold the subject of an e-mail message. The value of the key is android.intent.extra.SUBJECT. The key should point to a string of subject.

Using Components to Directly Invoke an Activity

You've seen a couple of ways to start an activity using intents. You saw an explicit action start an activity, and you saw a generic action start an activity with the help of a data URI. Android also provides a more direct way to start an activity: you can specify the activity's ComponentName, which is an abstraction around an object's package name and class name. There are a number of methods available on the Intent class to specify a component:

```
setComponent(ComponentName name);
setClassName(String packageName, String classNameInThatPackage);
setClassName(Context context, String classNameInThatContext);
setClass(Context context, Class classObjectInThatContext);
```

Ultimately, they are all shortcuts for calling one method:

```
setComponent(ComponentName name);
```

ComponentName wraps a package name and a class name together. For example, the following code invokes the contacts activity that ships with the emulator:

```
Intent intent = new Intent();
intent.setComponent(new ComponentName(
    "com.android.contacts"
    ,"com.android.contacts.DialContactsEntryActivity");
startActivity(intent)
```

Notice that the package name and the class name are fully qualified, and are used in turn to construct the ComponentName before passing to the Intent class.

You can also use the class name directly without constructing a ComponentName. Consider the BasicViewActivity code snippet again:

```
public class BasicViewActivity extends Activity
{
    @Override
    public void onCreate(Bundle savedInstanceState)
    {
        super.onCreate(savedInstanceState);
        setContentView(R.layout.some-view);
    }
}//eof-class
```

Given this, you can use the following code to start this activity:

```
Intent directIntent = new Intent(activity, BasicViewActivity.class);
activity.start(directIntent);
```

If you want any type of intent to start an activity, however, you should register the activity in the Android.Manifest.xml file like this:

```
<activity android:name="BasicViewActivity"
          android:label="Test Activity">
```

No intent-filters are necessary for invoking an activity directly through its class name or component name.

Best Practice for Component Designers

If you look at the design for the contacts application in Android, you will notice some patterns for designing with intents. To make intents known to the clients of this application, the contacts application defines them in three classes in a package called android.provider.contacts. These three classes are as follows:

```
contacts.Intents
contacts.Intents.Insert //nested class
contacts.Intents.UI //nested class
```

The top-level class contacts.Intents defines the primary intents that the contacts application will respond to and the events that the app generates as it does its work.

The nested class contacts.Intents.Insert defines the supporting intents and other constants to insert new records. The contacts.Intents.UI nested class defines a number of ways to invoke the UI. The intents also clarify the extra information needed to invoke them, including key names and their expected value types.

As you design your own content providers and activities that act upon those content providers, you might want to follow this pattern for making intents explicit by defining constants for them in interfaces or classes.

Understanding Intent Categories

You can classify activities into categories so you can search for them based on a category name. For example, during startup Android looks for activities whose category (also known as a tag) is marked as CATEGORY_LAUNCHER. It then picks up these activity names and icons and places them on the home screen to launch.

Here's another example: Android looks for an activity tagged as CATEGORY_HOME to show the home screen during startup. Similarly, CATEGORY_GADGET marks an activity as suitable for embedding or reuse inside another activity.

The format of the string for a category like CATEGORY_LAUNCHER follows the category definition convention:

```
android.intent.category.LAUNCHER
```

You will need to know these text strings for category definitions because activities register their categories in the AndroidManifest.xml file as part of their activity-filter definitions. Here is an example:

```
<activity android:name=".HelloWorld"
        android:label="@string/app_name">
    <intent-filter>
        <action android:name="android.intent.action.MAIN" />
        <category android:name="android.intent.category.LAUNCHER" />
    </intent-filter>
</activity>
```

NOTE: Activities might have certain capabilities that restrict them or enable them, such as whether you can embed them in a parent activity. These types of activity characteristics are declared through categories.

Let us take a quick look at some predefined Android categories and how you use them (see Table 3–3).

Table 3–3. *Activity Categories and Their Descriptions*

Category Name	Description
CATEGORY_DEFAULT	An activity can declare itself as a DEFAULT activity to operate on a certain aspect of data such as type, scheme, and so on.
CATEGORY_BROWSABLE	An activity can declare itself as BROWSABLE by promising the browser that it will not violate browser-security considerations when started.
CATEGORY_TAB	An activity of this type is embeddable in a tabbed parent activity.
CATEGORY_ALTERNATIVE	An activity can declare itself as an ALTERNATIVE activity for a certain type of data that you are viewing. These items normally show up as part of the options menu when you are looking at that document. For example, print view is considered an alternative to regular view.
CATEGORY_SELECTED_ALTERNATIVE	An activity can declare itself as an ALTERNATIVE activity for a certain type of data. This is similar to listing a series of possible editors for a text document or an HTML document.
CATEGORY_LAUNCHER	Assigning this category to an activity will allow it to be listed on the launcher screen.
CATEGORY_HOME	An activity of this type will be the home screen. Typically, there should be only one activity of this type. If there are more, the system will prompt you to pick one.
CATEGORY_PREFERENCE	This activity identifies an activity as a preference activity, so it will be shown as part of the preferences screen.
CATEGORY_GADGET	An activity of this type is embeddable in a parent activity.
CATEGORY_TEST	A test activity.
CATEGORY_EMBED	This category has been superseded by the GADGET category, but it's been kept for backward compatibility.

You can read the details of these activity categories at the following Android SDK URL for the Intent class: http://code.google.com/android/reference/android/content/Intent.html#CATEGORY_A LTERNATIVE.

When you use an intent to start an activity, you can specify the kind of activity to choose by specifying a category. Or you can search for activities that match a certain category. Here is an example to retrieve a set of main activities that match the category of CATEGORY_SAMPLE_CODE:

```
Intent mainIntent = new Intent(Intent.ACTION_MAIN, null);
mainIntent.addCategory(Intent.CATEGORY_SAMPLE_CODE);
PackageManager pm = getPackageManager();
List<ResolveInfo> list = pm.queryIntentActivities(mainIntent, 0);
```

PackageManager is a key class that allows you to discover activities that match certain intents without invoking them. You can cycle through the received activities and invoke them as you see fit, based on the ResolveInfo API.

Following the same logic, you can also get a list of all launchable applications by populating an intent with a category of CATEGORY_LAUNCHER:

```
//Get me all launchable applications
Intent mainIntent = new Intent(Intent.ACTION_MAIN, null);
mainIntent.addCategory(Intent.CATEGORY_LAUNCHER);
List mApps = getPackageManager().queryIntentActivities(mainIntent, 0);
```

In fact, we can do better. Let's start an activity based on the preceding intent category CATEGORY_LAUNCHER:

```
public static void invokeAMainApp(Activity activity)
{
   Intent mainIntent = new Intent(Intent.ACTION_MAIN, null);
   mainIntent.addCategory(Intent.CATEGORY_LAUNCHER);
   activity.startActivity(mainIntent);
}
```

More than one activity will match the intent, so which activity will Android pick? To resolve this, Android presents a "Complete action using" dialog that lists all the possible activities so you can choose one to run.

Here is another example of using an intent to go to a home page:

```
//Go to home screen
Intent mainIntent = new Intent(Intent.ACTION_MAIN, null);
mainIntent.addCategory(Intent.CATEGORY_HOME);
startActivity(mainIntent);
```

If you don't want to use Android's default home page, you can write your own and declare that activity to be of category HOME. In that case, the preceding code will give you an option to open your home activity because more than one home activity is registered now:

```
//Replace the home screen with yours
<intent-filter>
    <action android:value="android.intent.action.MAIN" />
    <category android:value="android.intent.category.HOME"/>
    <category android:value="android.intent.category.DEFAULT" />
</intent-filter>
```

The Rules for Resolving Intents to Their Components

So far, we have discussed a number of aspects about intents. To recap, we talked about actions, data URIs, extra data, and finally, categories. Given these aspects, Android uses the following algorithm to resolve the intents to activities.

At the top of the hierarchy, with an air of exclusivity, is the component name attached to an intent. If this is set, then every other aspect or attribute of the intent is ignored and that component is chosen for execution.

Android then looks at the action attribute of the intent. If the intent indicates an action, then the target activity must list that action as part of its intent-filter. If no other attributes are specified, then Android invokes this activity. If there are multiple activities, Android will present the activity chooser.

Android then looks at the data portion of the intent. If the intent specifies a data URI, the type is retrieved from this URI via ContentProvider.getType() if it is not already supplied in the intent. The target activity must indicate through an intent-filter that it can handle data of this type. If the data URI is not a content URI or the data type is not specified, then the URI scheme is taken into account. The target activity should indicate that it could handle the URIs of this type of scheme.

Android then looks at the category. Android will only pick activities matching that category. As a result, if the intent category is specified, then the target activity should declare this category in its intent-filter.

Exercising the ACTION_PICK

So far we have exercised intents or actions that mainly invoke another activity without expecting any results back. Now let's look at an action that is a bit more involved, in that it returns a value after being invoked. ACTION_PICK is one such generic action.

The idea of ACTION_PICK is to start an activity that displays a list of items. The activity then should allow a user to pick one item from that list. Once the user picks the item, the activity should return the URI of the picked item to the caller. This allows reuse of the UI's functionality to select items of a certain type.

You should indicate the collection of items to choose from using a MIME type that points to an Android content cursor. The actual MIME type of this URI should look similar to the following:

```
vnd.android.cursor.dir/vnd.google.note
```

It is the responsibility of the activity to retrieve the data from the content provider based on the URI. This is also the reason that data should be encapsulated into content providers where possible.

For all actions that return data like this, we cannot use `startActivity()` because `startActivity()` does not return any result. `startActivity()` cannot return a result because it opens the new activity as a modal dialog in a separate thread and leaves the main thread for attending events. In other words, `startActivity()` is an asynchronous call with no callbacks to indicate what happened in the invoked activity. But if you want to return data, you can use a variation on `startActivity()` called `startActivityForResult()`, which comes with a callback.

Let us look at the signature of the `startActivityForResult()` method from the Activity class:

```
public void startActivityForResult(Intent intent, int requestCode)
```

This method launches an activity from which you would like a result. When this activity exits, the source activity's `onActivityResult()` method will be called with the given `requestCode`. The signature of this callback method is

```
protected void onActivityResult(int requestCode, int resultCode, Intent data)
```

The `requestCode` is what you passed in to the `startActivityForResult()` method. The `resultCode` can be `RESULT_OK`, `RESULT_CANCELED`, or a custom code. The custom codes should start at `RESULT_FIRST_USER`. The Intent parameter contains any additional data that the invoked activity wants to return. In the case of `ACTION_PICK`, the returned data in the intent points to the data URI of a single item (see Listing 3–34).

Listing 3–34. *Returning Data After Invoking an Action*

```
public static void invokePick(Activity activity)
{
  Intent pickIntent = new Intent(Intent.ACTION_PICK);
  int requestCode = 1;
  pickIntent.setData(Uri.parse(
    "content://com.google.provider.NotePad/notes"));
  activity.startActivityForResult(pickIntent, requestCode);
}

protected void onActivityResult(int requestCode
    ,int resultCode
    ,Intent outputIntent)
{
  super.onActivityResult(requestCode, resultCode, outputIntent);
  parseResult(this, requestCode, resultCode, outputIntent);
}
public static void parseResult(Activity activity
    , int requestCode
    , int resultCode
```

```
, Intent outputIntent)
{
    if (requestCode != 1)
    {
     Log.d("Test", "Some one else called this. not us");
            return;
    }
    if (resultCode != Activity.RESULT_OK)
    {
      Log.d("Result code is not ok:" + resultCode);
            return;
    }
    Log.d("Test", "Result code is ok:" + resultCode);
    Uri selectedUri = outputIntent.getData();
    Log.d("Test", "The output uri:" + selectedUri.toString());

    //Proceed to display the note
    outputIntent.setAction(Intent.VIEW);
    startActivity(outputIntent);
}
```

The constants RESULT_OK, RESULT_CANCEL, and RESULT_FIRST_USER are all defined in the Activity class. The numerical values of these constants are

```
RESULT_OK = -1;
RESULT_CANCEL = 0;
RESULT_FIRST_USER = 1;
```

To make this work, the implementer should have code that explicitly addresses the needs of a PICK. Let's look at how this is done in the Google sample Notepad application. When the item is selected in the list of items, the intent that invoked the activity is checked to see whether it's a PICK intent. If it is, the data URI is set in a new intent and returned through setResult():

```
@Override
protected void onListItemClick(ListView l, View v, int position, long id) {
    Uri uri = ContentUris.withAppendedId(getIntent().getData(), id);

    String action = getIntent().getAction();
    if (Intent.ACTION_PICK.equals(action) ||
            Intent.ACTION_GET_CONTENT.equals(action))
    {
        // The caller is waiting for us to return a note selected by
        // the user.  They have clicked on one, so return it now.
        setResult(RESULT_OK, new Intent().setData(uri));
    } else {
        // Launch activity to view/edit the currently selected item
        startActivity(new Intent(Intent.ACTION_EDIT, uri));
    }
}
```

Exercising the GET_CONTENT Action

ACTION_GET_CONTENT is similar to ACTION_PICK. In the case of ACTION_PICK, you are specifying a URI that points to a collection of items such as a collection of notes. You will expect the action to pick one of the notes and return it to the caller. In the case of ACTION_GET_CONTENT, you indicate to Android that you need an item of a particular MIME type. Android searches for either activities that can create one of those items or activities that can choose from an existing set of items that satisfy that MIME type.

Using ACTION_GET_CONTENT, you can pick a note from a collection of notes supported by the Notepad application using the following code:

```
public static void invokeGetContent(Activity activity)
{
    Intent pickIntent = new Intent(Intent.ACTION_GET_CONTENT);
    int requestCode = 2;
    pickIntent.setType("vnd.android.cursor.item/vnd.google.note");
    activity.startActivityForResult(pickIntent, requestCode);
}
```

Notice how the intent type is set to the MIME type of a single note. Contrast this with the ACTION_PICK code in the following snippet, where the input is a data URI:

```
public static void invokePick(Activity activity)
{
  Intent pickIntent = new Intent(Intent.ACTION_PICK);
  int requestCode = 1;
  pickIntent.setData(Uri.parse(
     "content://com.google.provider.NotePad/notes"));
  activity.startActivityForResult(pickIntent, requestCode);
}
```

For an activity to respond to ACTION_GET_CONTENT, the activity has to register an intent-filter indicating that the activity can provide an item of that MIME type. Here is how the SDK's Notepad application accomplishes this:

```
<activity android:name="NotesList" android:label="@string/title_notes_list">
......
<intent-filter>
    <action android:name="android.intent.action.GET_CONTENT" />
    <category android:name="android.intent.category.DEFAULT" />
    <data android:mimeType="vnd.android.cursor.item/vnd.google.note" />
      </intent-filter>
....
</activity>
```

The rest of the code for responding to onActivityResult() is identical to the previous ACTION_PICK example. If there are multiple activities that can return the same MIME type, Android will show you the chooser dialog to let you pick an activity. The default chooser might not allow you to pick a different title, however. To address this restriction, Android provides the createChooser method on the Intent class that lets you use a specialized chooser whose title can be changed. Here is an example of how to invoke such a chooser:

```
//start with your target Intent type you want to pick
Intent intent  = new Intent();
intent.setType(…);
Intent chooserIntent = Intent.createChooser(intent, "Hello use this title");
activity.startActivityForResult(chooserIntent);
```

Further Resources for This Chapter

Here are some useful links to further strengthen your understanding of this chapter:

Read this URL to see the most current list of resources supported by Android:

`http://developer.android.com/guide/topics/resources/available-resources.html`

Read this URL to understand the localization aspects using Resources:

`http://developer.android.com/guide/topics/resources/resources-i18n.html`

The following Resources API is handy to retrieve Resources explicitly where needed:

`http://developer.android.com/reference/android/content/res/Resources.html`

You can read about Android documentation on Content Providers here:

`http://developer.android.com/guide/topics/providers/content-providers.html`

Here is the API description for a ContentProvider. You can learn about ContentProvider contracts here:

`http://developer.android.com/reference/android/content/ContentProvider.html`

This URL is useful for understanding UriMatcher:

`http://developer.android.com/reference/android/content/UriMatcher.html`

This URL will help you to read data from a content provider or a database directly:

`http://developer.android.com/reference/android/database/Cursor.html`

Here is the home page of SQLite:

`http://www.sqlite.org/sqlite.html`

Here is an overview of intents from Android:

`http://developer.android.com/reference/android/content/Intent.html`

Here is a list of intents to invoke Google applications:

`http://developer.android.com/guide/appendix/g-app-intents.html`

Here is some information that is useful when you register intent filters:

`http://developer.android.com/reference/android/content/IntentFilter.html`

Here is an effort on the web to collect open intents from all vendors:

`http://www.openintents.org/`

Summary

In this chapter we covered the Android SDK's three key concepts: resources, content providers, and intents.

In the section on resources, you learned how to create resources in XML files and use their resource IDs in programming.

In the section about content providers, you learned how to work with URIs and MIME types, along with how to encapsulate data access in a content provider. You also learned the basics of creating and using a SQLite database, which should work well even if you use it without a content-provider abstraction.

The third section showed you how to use intents to start other activities in a number of ways. Now you know how intents pave the way for plug-and-play and accomplish reuse at the UI level. With a good grasp of these three concepts, you should find it easier to understand the Android SDK and Android UI programming in general.

Chapter 4

Building User Interfaces and Using Controls

Thus far, we have covered the fundamentals of Android but have not touched the user interface (UI). In this chapter, we are going to discuss user interfaces and controls. We will begin by discussing the general philosophy of UI development in Android, then we'll describe the common UI controls that ship with the Android SDK. We will also discuss layout managers and view adapters. We will conclude by discussing the Hierarchy Viewer tool—a tool used to debug and optimize Android UIs.

UI Development in Android

UI development in Android is fun. It's fun because the unattractive features in some other platforms are absent from Android. Swing, for example, has to support desktop applications as well as Java applets. The Java Foundation Classes (JFC) contains so much functionality that it's frustrating to use and difficult to navigate. JavaServer Faces (JSF) is another example. JSF, a common framework used to build web applications, is actually built on top of JavaServer Pages (JSP) and servlets. So you have to know all of the underlying frameworks before you can begin working with JSF.

Fortunately, this type of baggage carried by other platforms does not exist in Android. With Android, we have a simple framework with a limited set of out-of-the-box controls. The available screen area is generally limited. This, combined with the fact that the user usually wants to do one specific action, allows us to easily build a good user interface to deliver a good user experience.

The Android SDK ships with a host of controls that you can use to build user interfaces for your application. Similar to other SDKs, the Android SDK provides text fields, buttons, lists, grids, and so on. In addition, Android provides a collection of controls that are appropriate for mobile devices.

At the heart of the common controls are two classes: `android.view.View` and `android.view.ViewGroup`. As the name of the first class suggests, the View class represents a general-purpose View object. The common controls in Android ultimately extend the View class. ViewGroup is also a view, but contains other views too. ViewGroup is the base class for a list of layout classes. Android, like Swing, uses the concept of layouts to manage how controls are laid out within a container view. Using layouts, as we'll see, makes it easy for us to control the position and orientation of the controls in our user interfaces.

You can choose from several approaches to build user interfaces in Android. You can construct user interfaces entirely in code. You can also define user interfaces in XML. You can even combine the two—define the user interface in XML and then refer to it, and modify it, in code. To demonstrate this, we are going to build a simple user interface using each of these three approaches.

Before we get started, let's define some nomenclature. In this book and other Android literature, you will find the terms *view*, *control*, *widget*, *container*, and *layout* in discussions regarding UI development. If you are new to Android programming or UI development in general, you might not be familiar with these terms. We'll briefly describe them before we get started (see Table 4–1).

Table 4–1. *UI Nomenclature*

Term	Description
View, Widget, Control	Each of these represents a user interface element. Examples include a button, a grid, a list, a window, a dialog box, and so on. The terms "view," "widget," and "control" are used interchangeably in this chapter.
Container	This is a view used to contain other views. For example, a grid can be considered a container because it contains cells, each of which is a view.
Layout	This is an XML file used to describe a view.

Figure 4–1 shows a screenshot of the application that we are going to build. Next to the screenshot is the layout hierarchy of the controls and containers in the application.

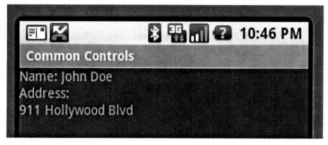 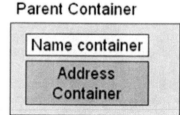

Figure 4–1. *The user interface and layout of an activity*

We will refer to this layout hierarchy as we discuss the sample programs. For now, know that the application has one activity. The user interface for the activity is composed of three containers: a container that contains a person's name, a container that contains the address, and an outer parent container for the child containers.

The first example, Listing 4–1, demonstrates how to build the user interface entirely in code. To try this out, create a new Android project with an activity named **MainActivity** and then copy the code from Listing 4–1 into your MainActivity class.

Listing 4–1. *Creating a Simple User Interface Entirely in Code*

```
package pro.android;
import android.app.Activity;
import android.os.Bundle;
import android.view.ViewGroup.LayoutParams;
import android.widget.LinearLayout;
import android.widget.TextView;
public class MainActivity extends Activity
{
    private LinearLayout nameContainer;

    private LinearLayout addressContainer;

    private LinearLayout parentContainer;


    /** Called when the activity is first created. */
    @Override
    public void onCreate(Bundle savedInstanceState)
    {
        super.onCreate(savedInstanceState);

        createNameContainer();

        createAddressContainer();

        createParentContainer();

        setContentView(parentContainer);

    }

    private void createNameContainer()
    {
        nameContainer = new LinearLayout(this);

        nameContainer.setLayoutParams(new LayoutParams(LayoutParams.FILL_PARENT,
                LayoutParams.WRAP_CONTENT));
        nameContainer.setOrientation(LinearLayout.HORIZONTAL);

        TextView nameLbl = new TextView(this);

        nameLbl.setText("Name: ");
        nameContainer.addView(nameLbl);

        TextView nameValueLbl = new TextView(this);
        nameValueLbl.setText("John Doe");

        nameContainer.addView(nameValueLbl);
    }

    private void createAddressContainer()
```

```
        {
            addressContainer = new LinearLayout(this);

            addressContainer.setLayoutParams(new LayoutParams(LayoutParams.FILL_PARENT,
                    LayoutParams.WRAP_CONTENT));
            addressContainer.setOrientation(LinearLayout.VERTICAL);

            TextView addrLbl = new TextView(this);

            addrLbl.setText("Address:");

            TextView addrValueLbl = new TextView(this);

            addrValueLbl.setText("911 Hollywood Blvd");

            addressContainer.addView(addrLbl);
            addressContainer.addView(addrValueLbl);

        }

        private void createParentContainer()
        {
            parentContainer = new LinearLayout(this);

            parentContainer.setLayoutParams(new LayoutParams(LayoutParams.FILL_PARENT,
                    LayoutParams.FILL_PARENT));
            parentContainer.setOrientation(LinearLayout.VERTICAL);

            parentContainer.addView(nameContainer);
            parentContainer.addView(addressContainer);
        }
    }
```

As shown in Listing 4–1, the activity contains three LinearLayout objects. As we mentioned earlier, layout objects contain logic to position objects within a portion of the screen. A LinearLayout, for example, knows how to lay out controls either vertically or horizontally. Layout objects can contain any type of view—even other layouts.

The nameContainer object contains two TextView controls: one for the label Name: and the other to hold the actual name (i.e., John Doe). The addressContainer also contains two TextView controls. The difference between the two containers is that the nameContainer is laid out horizontally and the addressContainer is laid out vertically. Both of these containers live within the parentContainer, which is the root view of the activity. After the containers have been built, the activity sets the content of the view to the root view by calling setContentView(parentContainer). When it comes time to render the user interface of the activity, the root view is called to render itself. The root view then calls its children to render themselves, and the child controls call their children, and so on, until the entire user interface is rendered.

As shown in Listing 4–1, we have several LinearLayout controls. In fact, two of them are laid out vertically and one is laid out horizontally. The nameContainer is laid out horizontally. This means the two TextView controls appear side by side horizontally. The addressContainer is laid out vertically, which means that the two TextView controls are stacked one on top of the other. The parentContainer is also laid out vertically, which is why the nameContainer appears above the addressContainer. Note a subtle difference between the two vertically laid-out containers, addressContainer and parentContainer: parentContainer is set to take up the entire width and height of the screen.

```
parentContainer.setLayoutParams(new LayoutParams(LayoutParams.FILL_PARENT,
    LayoutParams.FILL_PARENT));
```

And addressContainer wraps its content vertically:

```
addressContainer.setLayoutParams(new LayoutParams(LayoutParams.FILL_PARENT,
    LayoutParams.WRAP_CONTENT));
```

Now let's build the same user interface in XML (see Listing 4–2). Recall from Chapter 3 that XML layout files are stored under the resources (/res/) directory within a folder called layout. To try out this example, create a new Android project in Eclipse. By default, you will get an XML layout file named main.xml, located under the res/layout folder. Double-click main.xml to see the contents. Eclipse will display a visual editor for your layout file. You probably have a string at the top of the view that says "Hello World, MainActivity!" or something like that. Click the main.xml tab at the bottom of the view to see the XML of the main.xml file. This reveals a LinearLayout and a TextView control. Using either the Layout or main.xml tab, or both, re-create Listing 4–2 in the main.xml file. Save it.

Listing 4–2. *Creating a User Interface Entirely in XML*

```xml
<?xml version="1.0" encoding="utf-8"?>
<LinearLayout xmlns:android="http://schemas.android.com/apk/res/android"
    android:orientation="vertical" android:layout_width="fill_parent"
    android:layout_height="fill_parent">
    <!-- NAME CONTAINER -->
    <LinearLayout xmlns:android="http://schemas.android.com/apk/res/android"
        android:orientation="horizontal" android:layout_width="fill_parent"
        android:layout_height="wrap_content">

        <TextView  android:layout_width="wrap_content"
        android:layout_height="wrap_content" android:text="Name:" />

        <TextView android:layout_width="wrap_content"
        android:layout_height="wrap_content" android:text="John Doe" />

    </LinearLayout>

    <!-- ADDRESS CONTAINER -->
    <LinearLayout xmlns:android="http://schemas.android.com/apk/res/android"
        android:orientation="vertical" android:layout_width="fill_parent"
        android:layout_height="wrap_content">

        <TextView android:layout_width="fill_parent"
        android:layout_height="wrap_content" android:text="Address:" />

        <TextView android:layout_width="fill_parent"
        android:layout_height="wrap_content" android:text="911 Hollywood Blvd." />
    </LinearLayout>

</LinearLayout>
```

Under your new project's src directory, there is a default .java file containing an Activity class definition. Double-click that file to see its contents. Notice the statement setContentView(R.layout.main). The XML snippet shown in Listing 4–2, combined with a call to setContentView(R.layout.main), will render the same user interface as before when we generated it completely in code. The XML file is self-explanatory, but note that we have three container views defined. The first LinearLayout is the equivalent of our parent container. This container sets its orientation to vertical by setting the corresponding property like this: android:orientation="vertical". The parent container contains two LinearLayout containers, which represent the nameContainer and addressContainer.

Listing 4–2 is a contrived example. Notably, it doesn't make any sense to hard-code the values of the TextView controls in the XML layout. Ideally, we should design our user interfaces in XML and then reference the controls from code. This approach enables us to bind dynamic data to the controls defined at design time. In fact, this is the recommended approach.

Listing 4–3 shows the same user interface with slightly different XML. This XML assigns IDs to the TextView controls so that we can refer to them in code.

Listing 4–3. *Creating a User Interface in XML with IDs*

```xml
<?xml version="1.0" encoding="utf-8"?>
<LinearLayout xmlns:android="http://schemas.android.com/apk/res/android"
    android:orientation="vertical" android:layout_width="fill_parent"
    android:layout_height="fill_parent">
    <!-- NAME CONTAINER -->
    <LinearLayout xmlns:android="http://schemas.android.com/apk/res/android"
        android:orientation="horizontal" android:layout_width="fill_parent"
        android:layout_height="wrap_content">

        <TextView android:id="@+id/nameText" android:layout_width="wrap_content"
        android:layout_height="wrap_content" android:text="@+string/name_text" />

        <TextView android:id="@+id/nameValueText"
        android:layout_width="wrap_content"
        android:layout_height="wrap_content" />

    </LinearLayout>

    <!-- ADDRESS CONTAINER -->
    <LinearLayout xmlns:android="http://schemas.android.com/apk/res/android"
        android:orientation="vertical" android:layout_width="fill_parent"
        android:layout_height="wrap_content">

        <TextView android:id="@+id/addrText" android:layout_width="fill_parent"
        android:layout_height="wrap_content" android:text="@+string/addr_text" />

        <TextView android:id="@+id/addrValueText"
        android:layout_width="fill_parent"
        android:layout_height="wrap_content" />
    </LinearLayout>

</LinearLayout>
```

The code in Listing 4–4 demonstrates how you can obtain references to the controls defined in the XML to set their properties.

Listing 4–4. *Referring to Controls in Resources at Runtime*

```
setContentView(R.layout.main);

TextView nameValue = (TextView)findViewById(R.id.nameValueText);
nameValue.setText("John Doe");
TextView addrValue = (TextView)findViewById(R.id.addrValueText);
addrValue.setText("911 Hollywood Blvd.");
```

The code in Listing 4–4 is straightforward, but note that we load the resource (by calling setContentView(R.layout.main)) before calling findViewById()—we cannot get references to views if they have not been loaded yet.

Understanding Android's Common Controls

We will now start our discussion of the common controls in the Android SDK. We'll start with text controls and then discuss buttons, check boxes, radio buttons, lists, grids, date and time controls, and a map-view control. We will also talk about layout controls. Finally, we will conclude the chapter by showing you how to write your own custom controls.

Text Controls

Text controls are likely to be the first type of control that you'll work with in Android. Android has a complete, but not overwhelming, set of text controls. In this section, we are going to discuss the TextView, EditText, AutoCompleteTextView, and MultiCompleteTextView controls. Figure 4–2 shows the controls in action.

TextView

The TextView control knows how to display text but does not allow editing. This might lead you to conclude that the control is essentially a dummy label. Not true. The TextView control has a few interesting properties that make it very handy. If you know that the content of the TextView is going to contain a web URL, for example, you can set the autoLink property to web and the control will find and highlight the URL. Moreover, when the user clicks the TextView, the system will take care of launching the browser with the URL.

Actually, a more interesting use of TextView comes via the android.text.util.Linkify class (see Listing 4–5).

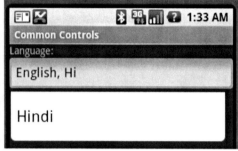

Figure 4–2. *Text controls in Android*

Listing 4–5. *Using the Linkify Class with a TextView*

```
TextView tv =(TextView)this.findViewById(R.id.cctvex);
tv.setText("Please visit my website, http://www.sayedhashimi.com
or email me at sayed@sayedhashimi.com.");
Linkify.addLinks(tv, Linkify.ALL);
```

As shown, you can pass a TextView to the Linkify class to find and add links to the content of the TextView. In our example, we call the addLinks() method of Linkify, passing the TextView and a mask indicating what types of links that Linkify should look for. Linkify can create links for text that looks like a phone number, an e-mail address, a web URL, or a map address. Passing Linkify.ALL tells the class to "linkify" all of these link types. Clicking a link will cause the default intent to be called for that action. For example, clicking a web URL will launch the browser with the URL. Clicking a phone number will launch the phone dialer, and so on. The Linkify class can perform this work right out of the box. You can also have the class linkify other content (such as a name) by giving it a regular expression along with the content-provider URI.

EditText

The EditText control is a subclass of TextView. As suggested by the name, the EditText control allows for text editing. EditText is not as powerful as the text-editing controls that you find in JFC, for example, but users of Android-based devices probably won't type documents—they'll type a couple paragraphs at most. Therefore, the class has limited but appropriate functionality. For example, you can set the autoText property to have the control correct common misspellings. You can use the `capitalize` property to have the control capitalize words, the beginning of sentences, and so on. You can set the `phoneNumber` property if you need to accept a phone number. You can also set the `password` property if you need a password field.

The default behavior of the `EditText` control is to display text on one line and expand as needed. In other words, if the user types past the first line, another line will appear, and so on. You can, however, force the user to a single line by setting the `singleLine` property to `true`. In this case, the user will have to continue typing on the same line.

Software programming for mobile devices is all about helping the user make a decision quickly. Thus, a common task is to highlight or style a portion of the `EditText`'s content. You can do this statically or dynamically. Statically, you can apply markup directly to the strings in your string resources (`<string name="styledText"><i>Static</i> style in an <b>EditText</b>.</string>`) and then reference it in your XML or from code. Note that you can use only the following HTML tags with string resources: `<i>`, `<b>`, and `<u>`.

Styling an `EditText` control's content programmatically requires a little additional work but allows for much more flexibility (see Listing 4–6).

Listing 4–6. *Applying Styles to the Content of an EditText Dynamically*

```
EditText et =(EditText)this.findViewById(R.id.cctvex5);
et.setText("Styling the content of an editText dynamically");
Spannable spn = et.getText();
spn.setSpan(new BackgroundColorSpan(Color.RED), 0, 7,
Spannable.SPAN_EXCLUSIVE_EXCLUSIVE);
spn.setSpan(new StyleSpan(android.graphics.Typeface.BOLD_ITALIC)
, 0, 7, Spannable.SPAN_EXCLUSIVE_EXCLUSIVE);
```

As shown in Listing 4–6, you can get the content of the `EditText` (as a `Spannable` object) and then set styles to portions of the text. The code in the listing sets the text styling to bold and italics and sets the background to red. You are not limited to bold, italics, and underline as before. You can use superscript, subscript, strikethrough and others.

AutoCompleteTextView

The `AutoCompleteTextView` control is a `TextView` with auto-complete functionality. In other words, as the user types in the `TextView`, the control can display suggestions for the user to select. Listing 4–7 demonstrates the `AutoCompleteTextView` control.

Listing 4–7. *Using an AutoCompleteTextView Control*

```
AutoCompleteTextView actv = (AutoCompleteTextView) this.findViewById(R.id.ccactv);

ArrayAdapter<String> aa = new ArrayAdapter<String>(this,
            android.R.layout.simple_dropdown_item_1line,
new String[] {"English", "Hebrew", "Hindi", "Spanish", "German", "Greek" });

actv.setAdapter(aa);
```

The AutoCompleteTextView control shown in Listing 4–7 suggests a language to the user. For example, if the user types **en**, the control suggests English. If the user types **gr**, the control recommends Greek, and so on.

If you have used a suggestion control or a similar auto-complete control, then you know that controls like this have two parts: a text-view control and a control that displays the suggestion(s). That's the general concept. To use a control like this, you have to create the control, create the list of suggestions, tell the control the list of suggestions, and possibly tell the control how to display the suggestions. Alternatively, you could create a second control for the suggestions and then associate the two controls.

Android has made this simple, as is evident from Listing 4–7. To use an AutoCompleteTextView, you can define the control in your layout file and then reference it in your activity. You then create an adapter class that holds the suggestions and define the ID of the control that will show the suggestion (in this case, a simple list item). In Listing 4–7, the second parameter to the ArrayAdapter tells the adapter to use a simple list item to show the suggestion. The final step is to associate the adapter with the AutoCompleteTextView, which you do using the setAdapter() method.

MultiAutoCompleteTextView

If you have played with the AutoCompleteTextView control, then you know that the control offers suggestions only for the *entire* text in the text view. In other words, if you type a sentence, you don't get suggestions for each word. That's where MultiAutoCompleteTextView comes in. You can use the MultiAutoCompleteTextView to provide suggestions as the user types. For example, Figure 4–2 shows that the user typed the word **English** followed by a comma, and then **Hi**, at which point the control suggested **Hindi**. If the user were to continue, the control would offer additional suggestions.

Using the MultiAutoCompleteTextView is like using the AutoCompleteTextView. The difference is that you have to tell the control where to start suggesting again. For example, in Figure 4–2, you can see that the control can offer suggestions at the beginning of the sentence and after it sees a comma. The MultiAutoCompleteTextView control requires that you give it a tokenizer that can parse the sentence and tell it whether to start suggesting again. Listing 4–8 demonstrates using the MultiAutoCompleteTextView control.

Listing 4–8. *Using the MultiAutoCompleteTextView Control*

```
MultiAutoCompleteTextView mactv = (MultiAutoCompleteTextView) this
            .findViewById(R.id.ccmactv);
ArrayAdapter<String> aa2 = new ArrayAdapter<String>(this,
            android.R.layout.simple_dropdown_item_1line,
new String[] {"English", "Hebrew", "Hindi", "Spanish", "German", "Greek" });

mactv.setAdapter(aa2);

mactv.setTokenizer(new MultiAutoCompleteTextView.CommaTokenizer());
```

The only significant difference between Listing 4–7 and Listing 4–8 is the use of `MultiAutoCompleteTextView` and the call to the `setTokenizer()` method. Because of the `CommaTokenizer` in this case, after a comma (,) is typed into the `EditText` field, the field will again make suggestions using the array of strings. Any other characters typed in will not trigger the field to make suggestions. So even if you were to type "French Spani" the partial word "Spani" would not trigger the suggestion because it did not follow a comma.

Button Controls

Buttons are common in any widget toolkit, and Android is no exception. Android offers the typical set of buttons as well as a few extras. In this section, we will discuss three types of button controls: the basic button, the image button, and the toggle button. Figure 4–3 shows a UI with these controls. The button at the top is the basic button, the middle button is an image button, and the last one is a toggle button.

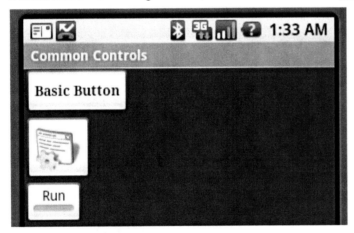

Figure 4–3. *Android button controls*

Let's get started with the basic button.

The Button Control

The basic button class in Android is `android.widget.Button`. There's not much to this type of button, beyond how you use it to handle click events (see Listing 4–9).

Listing 4–9. *Handling Click Events on a Button*

```
<Button android:id="@+id/ccbtn1"
    android:text="@+string/basicBtnLabel"
    android:typeface="serif" android:textStyle="bold"
    android:layout_width="fill_parent"
    android:layout_height="wrap_content" />

Button btn = (Button)this.findViewById(R.id.ccbtn1);
btn.setOnClickListener(new OnClickListener()
```

```
{
    public void onClick(View v)
    {
        Intent intent = getButtonIntent();
        intent.setAction("some intent data");
        setResult(RESULT_OK, intent);
        finish();
    }
});
```

Listing 4–9 shows how to register for a button-click event. You register for the on-click event by calling the setOnClickListener() method with an OnClickListener. In Listing 4–9, an anonymous listener is created on the fly to handle click events for btn. When the button is clicked, the onClick() method of the listener is called.

Since Android SDK 1.6, there is an easier way to set up a click handler for your button or buttons. In the XML for a Button, you specify an attribute like this:

android:onClick="myClickHandler"

with a corresponding button handler method in your activity class like this:

```
public void myClickHandler(View target) {
    switch(target.getId()) {
    case R.id.ccbtn1:
    ...
```

The handler method is called with target set to the View object representing the button that was pressed. Notice how the switch statement in the click handler method uses the resource IDs of the buttons to select the logic to run. Using this method means you won't have to explicitly create each Button object in your code, and you can reuse the same method across multiple buttons; in general, it makes things easier to understand and maintain. This works with the other button types as well.

The ImageButton Control

Android provides an image button via android.widget.ImageButton. Using an image button is similar to using the basic button (see Listing 4–10).

Listing 4–10. *Using an ImageButton*

```
<ImageButton android:id="@+id/imageBtn"
    android:layout_width="wrap_content"
    android:layout_height="wrap_content" />
```

```
ImageButton btn = (ImageButton)this.findViewById(R.id.imageBtn);
btn.setImageResource(R.drawable.icon);
```

You can set the button's image dynamically by calling setImageResource() or modifying the XML layout file (by setting the android:src property to the image ID), as shown in Listing 4–11.

Listing 4-11. *Setting the ImageButton Image via XML*

```
<ImageButton android:id="@+id/imageBtn"
    android:src="@drawable/btnImage"
    android:layout_width="wrap_content"
    android:layout_height="wrap_content" />
```

The ToggleButton Control

The `ToggleButton`, like a check box or a radio button, is a two-state button. This button can be in either the On state or the Off state. As shown in Figure 4–3, the `ToggleButton`'s default behavior is to show a green bar when in the On state, and a grayed-out bar when in the Off state. Moreover, the default behavior also sets the button's text to "On" when it's in the On state and "Off" when it's in the Off state.

Listing 4–12 shows an example.

Listing 4-12. *The Android ToggleButton*

```
<ToggleButton android:id="@+id/cctglBtn"
        android:layout_width="wrap_content"
        android:layout_height="wrap_content"
        android:text="Toggle Button"/>
```

You can modify the text for the `ToggleButton` if On/Off is not appropriate for your application. For example, if you have a background process that you want to start and stop via a `ToggleButton`, you could set the button's text to Run and Stop by using `android:textOn` and `android:textOff` properties (see Listing 4–13). Because `ToggleButtons` have on and off text as separate attributes, the `android:text` attribute of a `ToggleButton` is not really used. It's available because it has been inherited (from `TextView`, actually), but in this case you don't need to use it.

Listing 4-13. *Setting the ToggleButton's Label*

```
<ToggleButton android:id="@+id/cctglBtn"
        android:layout_width="wrap_content"
        android:layout_height="wrap_content"
        android:textOn="Run"
        android:textOff="Stop"
        android:text="Toggle Button"/>
```

The CheckBox Control

A check-box control plays a part in virtually all widget toolkits. HTML, JFC, and JSF all support the concept of a check box. The check-box control is a two-state button that allows the user to toggle its state.

In Android, you can create a check box by creating an instance of `android.widget.CheckBox`. See Listing 4–14 and Figure 4–4.

Listing 4-14. *Creating Check Boxes*

```
<LinearLayout xmlns:android="http://schemas.android.com/apk/res/android"
        android:orientation="vertical" android:layout_width="fill_parent"
        android:layout_height="fill_parent">
```

```
<CheckBox android:text="Chicken"
android:layout_width="wrap_content" android:layout_height="wrap_content" />

<CheckBox android:text="Fish"
android:layout_width="wrap_content" android:layout_height="wrap_content" />

<CheckBox android:text="Steak"
android:layout_width="wrap_content" android:layout_height="wrap_content" />

</LinearLayout>
```

Figure 4–4. *Using the CheckBox control*

You manage the state of a check box by calling setChecked() or toggle(). You can obtain the state by calling isChecked().

If you need to implement specific logic when a check box is checked or unchecked, you can register for the on-checked event by calling setOnCheckedChangeListener() with an implementation of the OnCheckedChangeListener interface. You'll then have to implement the onCheckedChanged() method, which will be called when the check box is checked or unchecked.

The RadioButton Control

Radio-button controls are an integral part of any UI toolkit. A radio button gives the user several choices and forces her to select a single item. To enforce this single-selection model, radio buttons generally belong to a group and each group is forced to have only one item selected at a time.

To create a group of radio buttons in Android, first create a RadioGroup and then populate the group with radio buttons. Listing 4–15 and Figure 4–5 show an example.

Listing 4–15. *Using Android Radio-Button Widgets*

```
<LinearLayout xmlns:android="http://schemas.android.com/apk/res/android"
        android:orientation="vertical" android:layout_width="fill_parent"
```

```
            android:layout_height="fill_parent">

<RadioGroup      android:id="@+id/rBtnGrp" android:layout_width="wrap_content"
          android:layout_height="wrap_content"
          android:orientation="vertical" >

<RadioButton      android:id="@+id/chRBtn" android:text="Chicken"
          android:layout_width="wrap_content"
          android:layout_height="wrap_content"/>

<RadioButton   android:id="@+id/fishRBtn" android:text="Fish"
          android:layout_width="wrap_content"
          android:layout_height="wrap_content"/>

<RadioButton android:id="@+id/stkRBtn" android:text="Steak"
          android:layout_width="wrap_content"
          android:layout_height="wrap_content"/>

</RadioGroup>

</LinearLayout>
```

In Android, you implement a radio group using android.widget.RadioGroup and a radio button using android.widget.RadioButton.

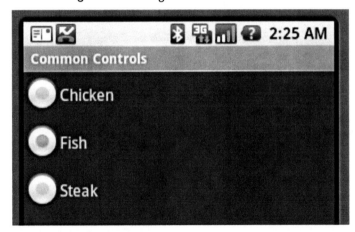

Figure 4–5. *Using radio buttons*

Note that the radio buttons within the radio group are, by default, unchecked to begin with, although you can set one to checked in the XML definition. To set one of the radio buttons to the checked state programmatically, you can obtain a reference to the radio button and call setChecked():

```
RadioButton rbtn = (RadioButton)this.findViewById(R.id.stkRBtn);
rbtn.setChecked(true);
```

You can also use the toggle() method to toggle the state of the radio button. As with the CheckBox control, you will be notified of on-checked or on-unchecked events if you call the setOnCheckedChangeListener() with an implementation of the OnCheckedChangeListener interface.

Realize that RadioGroup can also contain views other than the radio button. For example, Listing 4–16 adds a TextView after the last radio button. Also note that a radio button lies outside the radio group.

Listing 4–16. *A Radio Group with More Than Just Radio Buttons*

```
<LinearLayout xmlns:android="http://schemas.android.com/apk/res/android"
        android:orientation="vertical"
        android:layout_width="fill_parent"
        android:layout_height="fill_parent">

<RadioButton android:id="@+id/anotherRadBtn"
        android:text="Outside"
        android:layout_width="wrap_content"
        android:layout_height="wrap_content"/>
<RadioGroup android:id="@+id/rdGrp"
        android:layout_width="wrap_content"
        android:layout_height="wrap_content">
<RadioButton android:id="@+id/chRBtn"
        android:text="Chicken"
        android:layout_width="wrap_content"
        android:layout_height="wrap_content"/>
<RadioButton android:id="@+id/fishRBtn"
        android:text="Fish"
        android:layout_width="wrap_content"
        android:layout_height="wrap_content"/>
<RadioButton android:id="@+id/stkRBtn"
        android:text="Steak"
        android:layout_width="wrap_content"
        android:layout_height="wrap_content"/>

<TextView android:text="My Favorite"
        android:layout_width="wrap_content"
        android:layout_height="wrap_content"/>
</RadioGroup>

</LinearLayout>
```

Listing 4–16 shows that you can have non-RadioButton controls inside a radio group. Moreover, you should know that the radio group can enforce single-selection only on the radio buttons within its own container. That is, the radio button with ID anotherRadBtn will not be affected by the radio group shown in Listing 4–16 because it is not one of the group's children.

Also know that you can manipulate the RadioGroup programmatically. For example, you can obtain a reference to a radio group programmatically and add a radio button (or other type of control):

```
RadioGroup rdgrp = (RadioGroup)findViewById(R.id.rdGrp);
RadioButton newRadioBtn = new RadioButton(this);
newRadioBtn.setText("Pork");
rdgrp.addView(newRadioBtn);
```

Finally, once a user has checked a radio button within a radio group, the user cannot uncheck it by clicking it again. The only way to clear all radio buttons within a radio group is to call the clearCheck() method on the RadioGroup programmatically.

List Controls

The Android SDK offers several list controls. Figure 4–6 shows a `ListView` control that we'll discuss in this section.

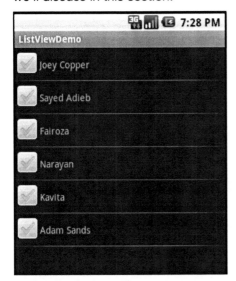

Figure 4–6. *Using the ListView control*

The `ListView` control displays a list of items vertically. You generally use a `ListView` by writing a new activity that extends `android.app.ListActivity`. `ListActivity` contains a `ListView`, and you set the data for the `ListView` by calling the `setListAdapter()` method. For this exercise, we will fill the entire screen with the `ListView` so we don't even need to specify a `ListView` in our main layout XML file. But we do need to provide a layout for each row. Listing 4–17 demonstrates the layout file for our row, plus the Java code for our `ListActivity`.

Listing 4–17. *Adding Items to a ListView*

```xml
<?xml version="1.0" encoding="utf-8"?>
<!-- This file is at /res/layout/list_item.xml -->
<LinearLayout xmlns:android="http://schemas.android.com/apk/res/android"
    android:orientation="horizontal"
    android:layout_width="wrap_content"
    android:layout_height="wrap_content">

<CheckBox xmlns:android="http://schemas.android.com/apk/res/android"
    android:id="@+id/row_chbox"
    android:layout_width="wrap_content"
    android:layout_height="wrap_content"
/>

<TextView android:id="@+id/row_tv" android:layout_width="wrap_content"
    android:layout_height="wrap_content"
/>
</LinearLayout>
```

```
public class ListDemoActivity extends ListActivity
{
    private SimpleCursorAdapter adapter;

    @Override
    protected void onCreate(Bundle savedInstanceState)
    {
        super.onCreate(savedInstanceState);
        Cursor c = getContentResolver().query(People.CONTENT_URI,
 null, null, null, null);
        startManagingCursor(c);
        String[] cols = new String[]{People.NAME};
        int[] names = new int[]{R.id.row_tv};
        adapter = new SimpleCursorAdapter(this,R.layout.list_item,c,cols,names);
        this.setListAdapter(adapter);
    }
}
```

Listing 4–17 creates a ListView control populated with the list of contacts on the device. To the left of each contact is a check-box control. As we stated earlier, the usage pattern is to extend ListActivity and then set the list's adapter by calling setListAdapter() on the activity. In our example, we query the device for the list of contacts and then create a projection to select only the names of the contacts—a projection defines the columns that we are interested in. We then map a name to a TextView control. Next, we create a cursor adapter and set the list's adapter. The adapter class has the smarts to take the rows in the data source and pull out the name of each contact to populate the user interface.

There's one more thing we need to do to make this work. Because this demonstration is accessing the phone's contacts database, we need to ask permission to do so. This security topic will be covered in more detail in Chapter 7 so, for now, we'll just walk you through getting our ListView to show up. Double-click the AndroidManifest.xml file for this project, then click the Permissions tab. Click the Add... button, choose Uses Permission, and click OK. Scroll down the Name list until you get to android.permission.READ_CONTACTS. Your Eclipse window should look like Figure 4–7. Then save the AndroidManifest.xml file. Now you can run this application in the emulator. You might need to add some contacts using the Contacts application before any names will show up in this example application.

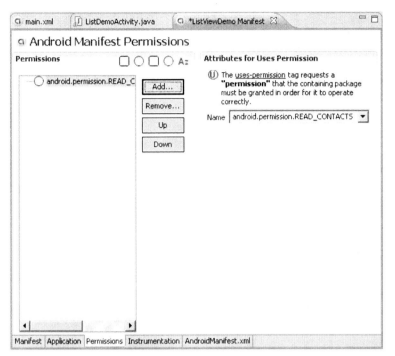

Figure 4–7. *Modifying AndroidManifest.xml so our application will run*

You'll notice that the onCreate() method does not set the content view of the activity. Instead, because the base class ListActivity contains a ListView already, it just needs to provide the data for the ListView. If you want additional controls in your layout, you can provide a layout XML file, put in a ListView, and add other desired controls.

For example, you could add a button below the ListView in the UI to submit an action on the selected items, as shown in Figure 4–8.

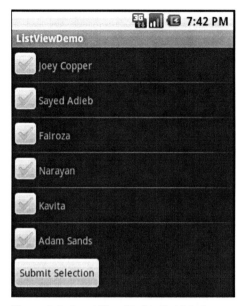

Figure 4–8. *An additional button that lets the user submit the selected item(s)*

The layout XML file for this example is broken up into two files. The first contains the user interface definition of the activity—the ListView and the button (see Figure 4–8 and Listing 4–18).

Listing 4–18. *Overriding the ListView Referenced by ListActivity*

```xml
<?xml version="1.0" encoding="utf-8"?>
<!-- This file is at /res/layout/list.xml -->
<LinearLayout xmlns:android="http://schemas.android.com/apk/res/android"
    android:orientation="vertical"
    android:layout_width="fill_parent"
    android:layout_height="wrap_content">

    <ListView android:id="@android:id/list"
            android:layout_width="fill_parent"
            android:layout_height="0dip"
            android:layout_weight="1"
            android:stackFromBottom="true"
            android:transcriptMode="normal"/>

    <Button android:layout_width="wrap_content"
        android:layout_height="wrap_content" android:text="Submit Selection" />

</LinearLayout>
```

The second file contains the definition of the items in the list, which is the same as the definition in Listing 4–17. The activity implementation would then look like Listing 4–19.

Listing 4–19. *Setting the Content View of the ListActivity*

```java
public class ListDemoActivity extends ListActivity
{
    private SimpleCursorAdapter adapter;
```

```
    @Override
    protected void onCreate(Bundle savedInstanceState)
    {
        super.onCreate(savedInstanceState);

        setContentView(R.layout.list);

        Cursor c = getContentResolver().query(People.CONTENT_URI,
null, null, null, null);
        startManagingCursor(c);

        String[] cols = new String[]{People.NAME};
        int[] names = new int[]{R.id.row_tv};
        adapter = new SimpleCursorAdapter(this,R.layout.list_item,c,cols,names);
        this.setListAdapter(adapter);
    }
}
```

Listing 4–19 shows that the activity calls `setContentView()` to set the user interface for the activity. It also sets the layout file for the items in the list when it creates the adapter (we'll talk more about adapters in the "Understanding Adapters" section toward the end of this chapter).

Grid Controls

Most widget toolkits offer one or more grid-based controls. Android has a `GridView` control that can display data in the form of a grid. Note that although we use the term "data" here, the contents of the grid can be text, images, and so on.

The `GridView` control displays information in a grid. The usage pattern for the `GridView` is to define the grid in the XML layout (see Listing 4–20), and then bind the data to the grid using an `android.widget.ListAdapter`. Don't forget to add the uses-permission tag to the `AndroidManifest.xml` file to make this example work.

Listing 4–20. *Definition of a GridView in an XML Layout and Associated Java Code*

```
<?xml version="1.0" encoding="utf-8"?>
<!-- This file is at /res/layout/gridview.xml -->
<GridView xmlns:android="http://schemas.android.com/apk/res/android"
    android:id="@+id/dataGrid"
    android:layout_width="fill_parent"
    android:layout_height="fill_parent"
    android:padding="10px"
    android:verticalSpacing="10px"
    android:horizontalSpacing="10px"
    android:numColumns="auto_fit"
    android:columnWidth="100px"
    android:stretchMode="columnWidth"
    android:gravity="center"
/>

    protected void onCreate(Bundle savedInstanceState) {
            super.onCreate(savedInstanceState);
```

```
        setContentView(R.layout.gridview);
        GridView gv = (GridView)this.findViewById(R.id.dataGrid);

        Cursor c = getContentResolver().query(People.CONTENT_URI,
null, null, null, null);
        startManagingCursor(c);

        String[] cols = new String[]{People.NAME};
        int[] names = new int[]{android.R.id.text1};

        SimpleCursorAdapter adapter = new SimpleCursorAdapter(this,
            android.R.layout.simple_list_item_1 ,c,cols,names);

        gv.setAdapter(adapter);

    }
```

Listing 4–20 defines a simple GridView in an XML layout. The grid is then loaded into the activity's content view. The generated UI is shown in Figure 4–9.

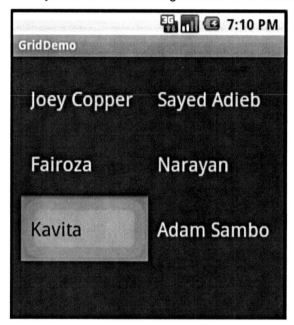

Figure 4–9. *A GridView populated with contact information*

The grid shown in Figure 4–9 displays the names of the contacts on the device. We have decided to show a TextView with the contact names, but you could easily generate a grid filled with images and the like. In fact, we've used another shortcut in this example. Instead of creating our own layout file for the grid items, we've taken advantage of predefined layouts in Android. Notice the prefix on the resources for the grid item layout and the grid item field is android:. Instead of looking in our local /res directory, Android looks in its own. You can browse to this folder by navigating to the Android SDK folder and looking under `platforms/<android-version>/data/res/layout`. You'll find `simple_list_item_1.xml` there and can see inside that it defines a simple `TextView` whose `android:id` is `@android:id/text1`. That's why we specified `android.R.id.text1` for the names ID for the cursor adapter.

The interesting thing about the `GridView` is that the adapter used by the grid is a `ListAdapter`. Lists are generally one-dimensional, whereas grids are two-dimensional. What we can conclude, then, is that the grid actually displays list-oriented data. In fact, if you call `getSelection()`, you get back an integer representing the index of the selected item. Likewise, to set a selection in the grid, you call `setSelection()` with the index of the item you want selected.

Date and Time Controls

Date and time controls are quite common in many widget toolkits. Android offers several date- and time-based controls, some of which we'll discuss in this section. Specifically, we are going to introduce the `DatePicker`, the `TimePicker`, the `AnalogClock`, and the `DigitalClock` controls.

The DatePicker and TimePicker Controls

As the names suggest, you use the `DatePicker` control to select a date and the `TimePicker` control to pick a time. Listing 4–21 and Figure 4–10 show examples of these controls.

Listing 4–21. The DatePicker and TimePicker Controls in XML

```
<LinearLayout xmlns:android="http://schemas.android.com/apk/res/android"
        android:orientation="vertical"
        android:layout_width="fill_parent"
        android:layout_height="fill_parent">

    <DatePicker android:id="@+id/datePicker"
    android:layout_width="wrap_content" android:layout_height="wrap_content" />

    <TimePicker android:id="@+id/timePicker"
    android:layout_width="wrap_content" android:layout_height="wrap_content" />

</LinearLayout>
```

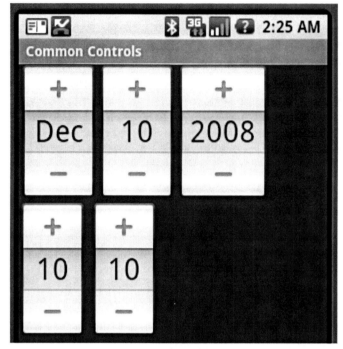

Figure 4–10. *The DatePicker and TimePicker UIs*

If you look at the XML layout, you can see that defining these controls is quite easy. The user interface, however, looks a bit overdone. Both controls seem oversized, but for a mobile device, you can't argue with the look and feel.

As with any other control in the Android toolkit, you can access the controls programmatically to initialize them or to retrieve data from them. For example, you can initialize these controls as shown in Listing 4–22.

Listing 4–22. *Initializing the DatePicker and TimePicker with Date and Time, Respectively*

```
protected void onCreate(Bundle savedInstanceState) {
    super.onCreate(savedInstanceState);

    setContentView(R.layout.datetime);

    DatePicker dp = (DatePicker)this.findViewById(R.id.datePicker);
    dp.init(2008, 11, 10, null);

    TimePicker tp = (TimePicker)this.findViewById(R.id.timePicker);
    tp.setIs24HourView(true);
    tp.setCurrentHour(new Integer(10));
    tp.setCurrentMinute(new Integer(10));
}
```

Listing 4–22 sets the date on the DatePicker to November 10, 2008. Similarly, the number of hours and minutes is set to 10. Note also that the control supports 24–hour view. If you do not set values for these controls, the default values will be the current date and time as known to the device.

Finally, note that Android offers versions of these controls as modal windows, such as `DatePickerDialog` and `TimePickerDialog`. These controls are useful if you want to display the control to the user and force the user to make a selection. We'll cover dialogs in more detail in Chapter 5.

The AnalogClock and DigitalClock Controls

Android also offers an AnalogClock and a DigitalClock (see Figure 4–11).

Figure 4–11. *Using the AnalogClock and DigitalClock*

As shown, the analog clock in Android is a two-handed clock, with one hand for the hour indicator and the other hand for the minute indicator. The digital clock supports seconds in addition to hours and minutes.

These two controls are not that interesting because they don't let you modify the date or time. In other words, they are merely clocks whose only capability is to display the current time. Thus, if you want to change the date or time, you'll need to stick to the `DatePicker`/`TimePicker` or `DatePickerDialog`/`TimePickerDialog`.

Other Interesting Controls in Android

The controls that we have discussed so far are fundamental to any Android application. In addition to these, Android also offers a few other interesting controls. We'll briefly introduce these other controls in this section.

The MapView Control

The com.google.android.maps.MapView control can display a map. You can instantiate this control either via XML layout or code, but the activity that uses it must extend MapActivity. MapActivity takes care of multithreading requests to load a map, perform caching, and so on.

Listing 4–23 shows an example instantiation of a MapView.

Listing 4–23. *Creating a MapView Control via XML Layout*

```xml
<LinearLayout xmlns:android="http://schemas.android.com/apk/res/android"
        android:orientation="vertical" android:layout_width="fill_parent"
        android:layout_height="fill_parent">

    <com.google.android.maps.MapView
        android:layout_width="fill_parent"
        android:layout_height="fill_parent"
        android:enabled="true"
        android:clickable="true"
        android:apiKey="myAPIKey"
        />

</LinearLayout>
```

We'll discuss the MapView control in detail in Chapter 7, when we discuss location-based services. This is also where you'll learn how to obtain your own mapping API key.

The Gallery Control

The Gallery control is a horizontally scrollable list control that always focuses at the center of the list. This control generally functions as a photo gallery in touch mode. You can instantiate a Gallery either via XML layout or code:

```xml
<Gallery
    android:id="@+id/galleryCtrl"
    android:layout_width="fill_parent"
    android:layout_height="wrap_content"
/>
```

Using the Gallery control is similar to using a list control. That is to say, you get a reference to the gallery, then call the setAdapter() method to populate data, then register for on-selected events.

The Spinner Control

The Spinner control is like a dropdown menu. You can instantiate a Spinner either via XML layout or code:

```xml
<Spinner
    android:id="@+id/spinner"
    android:layout_width="wrap_content"
    android:layout_height="wrap_content"
/>
```

Using the Spinner control is also similar to using a list control. That is to say, you get a reference to the spinner, then call the setAdapter() method to populate data, then register for on-selected events. We'll use Spinner as an example in the section later in this chapter called "Getting to Know ArrayAdapter".

This concludes our discussion of the Android control set. As we mentioned in the beginning of the chapter, building user interfaces in Android requires you to master two things: the control set and the layout managers. In the next section, we are going to discuss the Android layout managers.

Understanding Layout Managers

Like Swing, Android offers a collection of view classes that act as containers for views. These container classes are called layouts (or layout managers), and each implements a specific strategy to manage the size and position of its children. For example, the LinearLayout class lays out its children either horizontally or vertically, one after the other.

The layout managers that ship with the Android SDK are defined in Table 4–2.

Table 4–2. *Android Layout Managers*

Layout Manager	Description
LinearLayout	Organizes its children either horizontally or vertically
TableLayout	Organizes its children in tabular form
RelativeLayout	Organizes its children relative to one another or to the parent
FrameLayout	Allows you to dynamically change the control(s) in the layout

We will discuss these layout managers in the sections that follow. There used to be a layout manager called AbsoluteLayout, but it has been deprecated and will not be covered in this book.

The LinearLayout Layout Manager

The LinearLayout is the most basic layout. This layout manager organizes its children either horizontally or vertically based on the value of the orientation property. Listing 4–24 shows a LinearLayout with horizontal configuration.

Listing 4–24. *A LinearLayout with Horizontal Configuration*

```
<LinearLayout xmlns:android="http://schemas.android.com/apk/res/android"
    android:orientation="horizontal"
    android:layout_width="fill_parent"
    android:layout_height="wrap_content">

    <!-- add children here-->
```

```
</LinearLayout>
```

You can create a vertically-oriented `LinearLayout` by setting the value of `orientation` to vertical.

Understanding Weight and Gravity

The `orientation` attribute is the first important attribute recognized by the `LinearLayout` layout manager. Other important properties that can affect size and position of child controls include *weight* and *gravity*. You use weight to assign size importance to a control relative to the other controls in the container. Suppose a container has three controls: one has a weight of 1 (the highest possible value), while the others have a weight of 0. In this case, the control whose weight equals 1 will consume the empty space in the container. Gravity is essentially alignment. For example, if you want to align a label's text to the right, you would set its gravity to `right`. There are quite a few possible values for gravity, including `left`, `center`, `right`, `top`, `bottom`, `center_vertical`, `clip_horizontal`, and still others. See the reference pages for details on these and the other values of gravity.

> **NOTE:** Layout managers extend `android.widget.ViewGroup`, as do many control-based container classes such as `ListView`. Although the layout managers and control-based containers extend the same class, the layout-manager classes strictly deal with the sizing and position of controls and not user interaction with child controls. For example, compare the `LinearLayout` to the `ListView` control. On the screen, they look similar in that both can organize children vertically. But the `ListView` control provides APIs for the user to make selections, while the `LinearLayout` does not. In other words, the control-based container (`ListView`) supports user interaction with the items in the container, whereas the layout manager (`LinearLayout`) addresses sizing and positioning only.

Now let's look at an example involving the weight and gravity properties (see Figure 4–12).

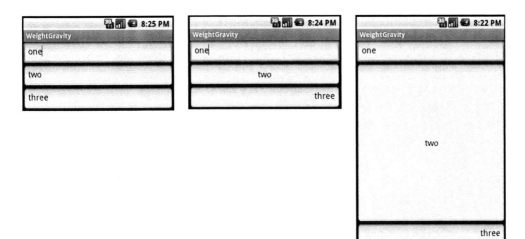

Figure 4–12. *Using the LinearLayout layout manager*

Figure 4–12 shows three user interfaces that utilize LinearLayout, with different weight and gravity settings. The UI on the left uses the default settings for weight and gravity. The XML layout for this first user interface is shown in Listing 4–25.

Listing 4–25. *Three Text Fields Arranged Vertically in a LinearLayout, Using Default Values for Weight and Gravity*

```
<LinearLayout xmlns:android="http://schemas.android.com/apk/res/android"
    android:orientation="vertical" android:layout_width="fill_parent"
    android:layout_height="fill_parent">

    <EditText android:layout_width="fill_parent"
        android:layout_height="wrap_content"
        android:text="one"/>
    <EditText android:layout_width="fill_parent"
        android:layout_height="wrap_content"
        android:text="two"/>
    <EditText android:layout_width="fill_parent"
        android:layout_height="wrap_content"
        android:text="three"/>
</LinearLayout>
```

The user interface in the center of Figure 4–12 uses the default value for weight but sets android:gravity for the controls in the container to left, center, and right, respectively. The last example sets the android:layout_weight attribute of the center component to 1.0 and leaves the others to the default value of 0.0 (see Listing 4–26). By setting the weight attribute to 1.0 for the middle component and leaving the weight attributes for the other two components at 0.0, we are specifying that the center component should take up all the remaining white space in the container and that the other two components should remain at their ideal size.

Similarly, if you want two of the three controls in the container to share the remaining white space among them, you would set the weight to 1.0 for those two and leave the third one at 0.0. Finally, if you want the three components to share the space equally, you'd set all of their weight values to 1.0. Doing this would expand each text field equally.

Listing 4–26. *LinearLayout with Weight Configurations*

```
<LinearLayout xmlns:android="http://schemas.android.com/apk/res/android"
    android:orientation="vertical" android:layout_width="fill_parent"
    android:layout_height="fill_parent">

    <EditText android:layout_width="fill_parent" android:layout_weight="0.0"
    android:layout_height="wrap_content" android:text="one"
    android:gravity="left"/>

    <EditText android:layout_width="fill_parent" android:layout_weight="1.0"
    android:layout_height="wrap_content" android:text="two"
    android:gravity="center"/>

    <EditText android:layout_width="fill_parent" android:layout_weight="0.0"
    android:layout_height="wrap_content" android:text="three"
    android:gravity="right"
    />
</LinearLayout>
```

android:gravity vs. android:layout_gravity

Note that Android defines two similar gravity attributes: android:gravity and android:layout_gravity. Here's the difference: android:gravity is a setting used by the view, whereas android:layout_gravity is used by the container (android.view.ViewGroup). For example, you can set android:gravity to center to have the text in the EditText centered within the control. Similarly, you can align an EditText to the far right of a LinearLayout (the container) by setting android:layout_gravity="right". See Figure 4–13 and Listing 4–27.

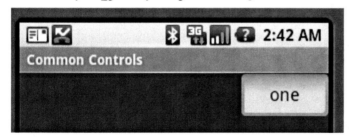

Figure 4–13. *Applying gravity settings*

Listing 4–27. *Understanding the Difference Between android:gravity and android:layout_gravity*

```
<LinearLayout xmlns:android="http://schemas.android.com/apk/res/android"
    android:orientation="vertical" android:layout_width="fill_parent"
    android:layout_height="fill_parent">

    <EditText android:layout_width="wrap_content" android:gravity="center"
    android:layout_height="wrap_content" android:text="one"
 android:layout_gravity="right"/>
</LinearLayout>
```

As shown in Figure 4–13, the text is centered within the EditText and the EditText itself is aligned to the right of the LinearLayout.

The TableLayout Layout Manager

The TableLayout layout manager is an extension of LinearLayout. This layout manager structures its child controls into rows and columns. Listing 4–28 shows an example.

Listing 4–28. *A Simple TableLayout*

```
<TableLayout xmlns:android="http://schemas.android.com/apk/res/android"
        android:layout_width="fill_parent"
        android:layout_height="fill_parent">

    <TableRow>
        <TextView android:layout_width="wrap_content"
        android:layout_height="wrap_content" android:text="First Name:"/>

        <EditText android:layout_width="wrap_content"
        android:layout_height="wrap_content" android:text="Barack"/>

    </TableRow>

    <TableRow>
        <TextView android:layout_width="wrap_content"
        android:layout_height="wrap_content" android:text="Last Name:"/>

        <EditText android:layout_width="wrap_content"
        android:layout_height="wrap_content" android:text="Obama"/>

    </TableRow>

</TableLayout>
```

To use a TableLayout, you create an instance of TableLayout and then place TableRow elements within it. TableRow elements then contain the controls of the table. The user interface for Listing 4–28 is shown in Figure 4–14.

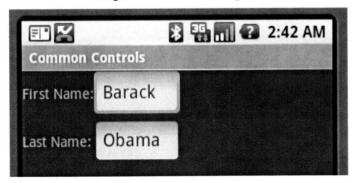

Figure 4–14. *The TableLayout layout manager*

Because the contents of a TableLayout are defined by rows as opposed to columns, Android determines the number of columns in the table by finding the row with the most cells. For example, Listing 4–29 creates a table with two rows where one row has two cells and the other has three cells (see Figure 4–15). In this case, Android creates a table with two rows and three columns. The last column of the first row is an empty cell.

Listing 4–29. *An Irregular Table Definition*

```xml
<TableLayout xmlns:android="http://schemas.android.com/apk/res/android"
        android:layout_width="fill_parent"
        android:layout_height="fill_parent">

    <TableRow>
        <TextView android:layout_width="wrap_content"
        android:layout_height="wrap_content" android:text="First Name:"/>

        <EditText android:layout_width="wrap_content"
        android:layout_height="wrap_content" android:text="Barack"/>

    </TableRow>

    <TableRow>
        <TextView android:layout_width="wrap_content"
        android:layout_height="wrap_content" android:text="Last Name:"/>

        <EditText android:layout_width="wrap_content"
        android:layout_height="wrap_content" android:text="Hussein"/>

        <EditText android:layout_width="wrap_content"
        android:layout_height="wrap_content" android:text="Obama"/>

    </TableRow>

</TableLayout>
```

Figure 4–15. *An irregular TableLayout*

In Listings 4–28 and 4–29, we populated the TableLayout with TableRow elements. Although this is the usual pattern, you can place any android.widget.View as a child of the table. For example, Listing 4–30 creates a table where the first row is an EditText (see also Figure 4–16).

Listing 4–30. *Using an EditText Instead of a TableRow*

```
<TableLayout xmlns:android="http://schemas.android.com/apk/res/android"
        android:layout_width="fill_parent"
        android:layout_height="fill_parent"
        android:stretchColumns="0,1,2">

<EditText
    android:text="Full Name:"/>

    <TableRow>
        <TextView android:layout_width="wrap_content"
        android:layout_height="wrap_content" android:text="Barack"/>


        <TextView android:layout_width="wrap_content"
        android:layout_height="wrap_content" android:text="Hussein"/>


        <TextView android:layout_width="wrap_content"
        android:layout_height="wrap_content" android:text="Obama"/>

    </TableRow>

</TableLayout>
```

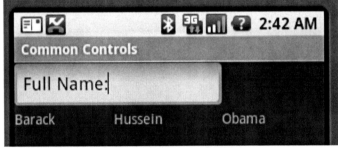

Figure 4–16. *An EditText as a child of a TableLayout*

The user interface for Listing 4–30 is shown in Figure 4–16. Notice that the EditText takes up the entire width of the screen, even though we have not specified this in the XML layout. That's because children of TableLayout always span the entire row. In other words, children of TableLayout cannot specify android:layout_width="wrap_content" — they are forced to accept fill_parent. They can, however, set android:layout_height.

Because the content of a table is not always known at design time, TableLayout offers several attributes that can help you control the layout of a table. For example, Listing 4–30 sets the android:stretchColumns property on the TableLayout to "0,1,2". This gives a hint to the TableLayout that columns 0, 1, and 2 can be stretched if required, based on the contents of the table.

Similarly, you can set android:shrinkColumns to wrap the content of a column or columns if other columns require more space. You can also set android:collapseColumns to make columns invisible. Note that columns are identified with a zero-based indexing scheme.

TableLayout also offers android:layout_span. You can use this property to have a cell span multiple columns. This field is similar to the HTML colspan property.

At times, you might also need to provide spacing within the contents of a cell or a control. The Android SDK supports this via android:padding and its siblings. android:padding lets you control the space between a view's outer boundary and its content (see Listing 4–31).

Listing 4–31. *Using android:padding*

```
<LinearLayout xmlns:android="http://schemas.android.com/apk/res/android"
    android:orientation="vertical" android:layout_width="fill_parent"
    android:layout_height="fill_parent">

    <EditText android:layout_width="wrap_content"
    android:layout_height="wrap_content" android:text="one"
    android:padding="40px" />
</LinearLayout>
```

Listing 4–31 sets the padding to 40px. This creates 40 pixels of white space between the EditText control's outer boundary and the text displayed within it. Figure 4–17 shows the same EditText with two different padding values. The UI on the left does not set any padding, while the one on the right sets android:padding="40px".

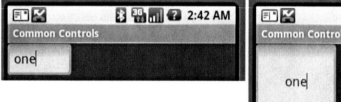 

Figure 4–17. *Utilizing padding*

android:padding sets the padding for all sides: left, right, top, and bottom. You can control the padding for each side by using android:leftPadding, android:rightPadding, android:topPadding, and android:bottomPadding.

Android also defines android:layout_margin, which is similar to android:padding. In fact, android:padding/android:layout_margin is analogous to android:gravity/android:layout_gravity. That is, one is for a view, while the other is for a container.

Finally, the padding value is always set as a dimension type. Android supports the following dimension types:

- *Pixels*: Abbreviated as px. This dimension represents physical pixels on the screen.

- *Inches*: Abbreviated as in.

- *Millimeters*: Abbreviated as mm.

- *Points*: Abbreviated as pt. A pt is equal to 1/72 of an inch.

- *Density-independent pixels*: Abbreviated as dip or dp. This dimension type uses a 160-dp screen as a frame of reference, and then maps that to the actual screen. For example, a screen with a 160-pixel width would map 1 dip to 1 pixel.

- *Scale-independent pixels*: Abbreviated as sp. Generally used with font types. This dimension type will take the user's preferences and font size into account to determine actual size.

Note that the preceding dimension types are not specific to padding—any Android field that accepts a dimension value (such as android:layout_width or android:layout_height) can accept these types.

The RelativeLayout Layout Manager

Another interesting layout manager is the RelativeLayout. As the name suggests, this layout manager implements a policy where the controls in the container are laid out relative to either the container or another control in the container. Listing 4–32 and Figure 4–18 show an example.

Listing 4–32. *Using a RelativeLayout Layout Manager*

```
<RelativeLayout xmlns:android="http://schemas.android.com/apk/res/android"
        android:layout_width="fill_parent"
        android:layout_height="wrap_content">

<TextView android:id="@+id/userNameLbl"
        android:layout_width="fill_parent"
        android:layout_height="wrap_content"
        android:text="Username: "
        android:layout_alignParentTop="true" />

<EditText android:id="@+id/userNameText"
        android:layout_width="fill_parent"
        android:layout_height="wrap_content"
     android:layout_below="@id/userNameLbl" />

<TextView android:id="@+id/pwdLbl"
        android:layout_width="fill_parent"
        android:layout_height="wrap_content"
        android:layout_below="@id/userNameText"
         android:text="Password: " />

<EditText android:id="@+id/pwdText"
        android:layout_width="fill_parent"
```

```
            android:layout_height="wrap_content"
        android:layout_below="@id/pwdLbl" />

<TextView android:id="@+id/pwdHintLbl"
        android:layout_width="fill_parent"
        android:layout_height="wrap_content"
        android:layout_below="@id/pwdText"
          android:text="Password Criteria... " />

<TextView android:id="@+id/disclaimerLbl"
        android:layout_width="fill_parent"
        android:layout_height="wrap_content"
        android:layout_alignParentBottom="true"
          android:text="Use at your own risk... " />

</RelativeLayout>
```

Figure 4–18. *A UI laid out using the RelativeLayout layout manager*

As shown, the user interface looks like a simple login form. The username label is pinned to the top of the container because we set android:layout_alignParentTop to true. Similarly, the username input field is positioned below the username label because we set android:layout_below. The password label appears below the username label, the password input field appears below the password label, and the disclaimer label is pinned to the bottom of the container because we set android:layout_alignParentBottom to true.

Besides these three layout attributes, you can also specify layout_above, layout_toRightOf, layout_toLeftOf, layout_centerInParent, and several more. Working with RelativeLayout is fun due to its simplicity. In fact, once you start using it, it'll become your favorite layout manager—you'll find yourself going back to it over and over again.

The FrameLayout Layout Manager

The layout managers that we've discussed implement various layout strategies. In other words, each one has a specific way that it positions and orients its children on the screen. With these layout managers, you can have many controls on the screen at one time, each taking up a portion of the screen. Android also offers a layout manager that is mainly used to display a single item. This layout manager is called the FrameLayout layout manager. You mainly use this utility layout class to dynamically display a single view, but you can populate it with many items, setting one to visible while the others are invisible. Listing 4–33 demonstrates using a FrameLayout.

Listing 4–33. *Populating a FrameLayout*

```xml
<?xml version="1.0" encoding="utf-8"?>
<FrameLayout xmlns:android="http://schemas.android.com/apk/res/android"
    android:id="@+id/frmLayout"
    android:layout_width="fill_parent"
    android:layout_height="fill_parent">

    <ImageView
       android:id="@+id/oneImgView" android:src="@drawable/one"
       android:scaleType="fitCenter"
       android:layout_width="fill_parent"
       android:layout_height="fill_parent"/>
    <ImageView
       android:id="@+id/twoImgView" android:src="@drawable/two"
       android:scaleType="fitCenter"
       android:layout_width="fill_parent"
       android:layout_height="fill_parent"
       android:visibility="gone" />

</FrameLayout>

@Override
protected void onCreate(Bundle savedInstanceState) {
    super.onCreate(savedInstanceState);

    setContentView(R.layout.frame);
```

```
    ImageView one = (ImageView)this.findViewById(R.id.oneImgView);
    ImageView two = (ImageView)this.findViewById(R.id.twoImgView);

    one.setOnClickListener(new OnClickListener(){

        @Override
        public void onClick(View view) {
            ImageView two = (ImageView)FramelayoutActivity.this.
    findViewById(R.id.twoImgView);

            two.setVisibility(View.VISIBLE);

            view.setVisibility(View.GONE);
        }});

    two.setOnClickListener(new OnClickListener(){

        @Override
        public void onClick(View view) {
            ImageView one = (ImageView)FramelayoutActivity.
    this.findViewById(R.id.oneImgView);

            one.setVisibility(View.VISIBLE);

            view.setVisibility(View.GONE);
        }});
}
```

Listing 4–33 shows the layout file as well as the onCreate() method of the activity. The idea of the demonstration is to load two ImageView objects in the FrameLayout, with only one of the ImageView objects visible at a time. In the UI, when the user clicks the visible image, we hide one image and show the other one.

Look at Listing 4–33 more closely now, starting with the layout. You can see that we define a FrameLayout with two ImageView objects (an ImageView is a control that knows how to display images). Notice that the second ImageView's visibility is set to gone, making the control invisible. Now look at the onCreate() method. In the onCreate() method, we register listeners to click events on the ImageView objects. In the click handler, we hide one ImageView and show the other one.

As we said earlier, you generally use the FrameLayout when you need to dynamically set the content of a view to a single control. Although this is the general practice, the control will accept many children, as we demonstrated. Listing 4–33 adds two controls to the layout but has one of the controls visible at a time. The FrameLayout, however, does not force you to have only one control visible at a time. If you add many controls to the layout, the FrameLayout will simply stack the controls, one on top of the other, with the last one on top. This can create an interesting UI. For example, Figure 4–19 shows a FrameLayout with two ImageView objects that are visible. You can see that the controls are stacked, and that the top one is partially covering the image behind it.

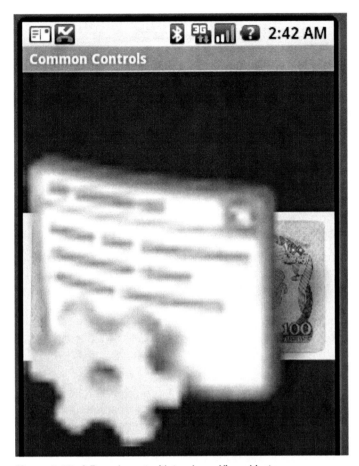

Figure 4–19. *A FrameLayout with two ImageView objects*

Another interesting aspect of the FrameLayout is that if you add more than one control to the layout, the size of the layout is computed as the size of the largest item in the container. In Figure 4–19, the top image is actually much smaller than the image behind it, but because the size of the layout is computed based on the largest control, the image on top is stretched.

Also note that if you put many controls inside a FrameLayout with one or more of them invisible to start, you might want to consider using setConsiderGoneChildrenWhenMeasuring(). Because the largest child dictates the layout size, you'll have a problem if the largest child is invisible to begin with. That is, when it becomes visible, it will be only partially visible. To ensure that all items get rendered properly, call setConsiderGoneChildrenWhenMeasuring() and pass it a value of true.

Customizing Layout for Various Device Configurations

By now you know very well that Android offers a host of layout managers that help you build user interfaces. If you've played around with the layout managers we've discussed, then you know that you can combine the layout managers in various ways to obtain the look and feel you want. Even with all the layout managers, building UIs—and getting them right—can be a challenge. This is especially true for mobile devices. Users and manufacturers of mobile devices are getting more and more sophisticated, and that makes the developer's job even more challenging.

One of the challenges is building a UI for an application that displays in various screen configurations. For example, what would your UI look like if your application were displayed in portrait vs. landscape mode? If you haven't run into this yet, your mind is probably racing right now, wondering how to deal with this common scenario. Interestingly, and thankfully, Android provides some support for this use case.

Here's how it works: Android will find and load layouts from specific folders based on the configuration of the device. A device can be in one of three configurations: portrait, landscape, or square. To provide different layouts for the various configurations, you have to create specific folders for each configuration from which Android will load the appropriate layout. As you know, the default layout folder is located at res/layout. To support the portrait display, create a folder called res/layout-port. For landscape, create a folder called res/layout-land. And for square, create one called res/layout-square.

A good question at this point is, "With these three folders, do I need the default layout folder (res/layout)?" Generally, yes. Realize that Android's resource-resolution logic looks in the configuration-specific directory first. If Android doesn't find a resource there, it goes to the default layout directory. Therefore, you can place default-layout definitions in res/layout and the customized versions in the configuration-specific folders.

Note that the Android SDK does not offer any APIs for you to programmatically specify which configuration to load—the system simply selects the folder based on the configuration of the device. You can, however, set the orientation of the device in code, for example, using the following:

```
import android.content.pm.ActivityInfo;
...
setRequestedOrientation(ActivityInfo.SCREEN_ORIENTATION_LANDSCAPE);
```

This forces your application to appear on the device in landscape mode. Go ahead and try it out in one of your earlier projects. Add the code to your onCreate() method of an Activity, run it in the emulator and see your application sideways.

The layout is not the only resource that is configuration-driven, and there are other qualifiers of the device configuration that are taken into account when finding the resource to use. The entire contents of the res folder can have variations for each configuration. For example, to have different drawables loaded per configuration, create folders for drawable-port, drawable-land, and drawable-square. But it gets even more powerful than that. The complete list of qualifiers that can be used when finding resources is shown in Table 4–3.

Table 4–3. *Qualifiers for Resources*

Qualifier	Description
MCC and MNC	Mobile country code and mobile network code
Language and region	Two-letter language code, could add 'r' and two-letter region code
screen dimensions	Gives rough idea of screen size; values: small, normal, large
wider/taller screens	Related to aspect ratio; values: long, notlong
screen orientation	Values: land, port, square
screen pixel density	Values: ldpi, mdpi, hdpi, nodpi corresponding to 120, 160, 240
touchscreen type	Values: finger, notouch, stylus
keyboard	State of the keyboard. Values: keysexposed, keyshidden, keyssoft
text input	Values: nokeys, qwerty, 12key (numeric)
non-touchscreen navigation	Values: dpad, nonav, trackball, wheel
SDK version	Values: v4 (SDK 1.6), v5 (SDK 2.0), etc.

For more details on these qualifiers, please refer to this Android web page:

```
http://developer.android.com/guide/topics/resources/resources-i18n.html#table2
```

These qualifiers can be used in many combinations to get whatever behavior you desire. A resource directory name would use zero or one of each of these qualifier values, separated by dashes, in order. For example, this is technically a valid drawable resource directory name (although not recommended):

```
drawable-mcc310-en-rUS-large-long-port-mdpi-stylus-keyssoft-qwerty-dpad-v3
```

but so are these:

```
drawable-en-rUS-land (images for English in US in landscape mode)
values-fr   (strings in French)
```

Regardless of how many qualifiers you're using for resources in your application, remember that in your code, you still only refer to the resource as R.resource_type.name without any qualifiers, For example, if you have lots of different variations of your layout file main.xml in several different qualified resource directories, your code will still refer to R.layout.main. Android takes care of finding the appropriate main.xml for you.

Understanding Adapters

Adapters have several responsibilities, as we'll see, but generally speaking, they make binding data to a control easier and more flexible. Adapters in Android are employed for widgets that extend `android.widget.AdapterView`. Classes that extend `AdapterView` include `ListView`, `GridView`, `Spinner`, and `Gallery` (see Figure 4–20). `AdapterView` itself actually extends `android.widget.ViewGroup`, which means that `ListView`, `GridView`, and so on are container controls. In other words, they display a collection of child controls.

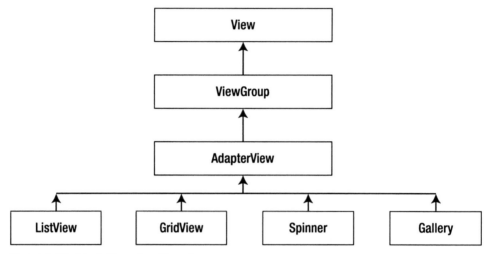

Figure 4–20. *AdapterView class hierarchy*

The purpose of an adapter is to provide the child views for the container. It takes the data and metadata about the view to construct each child view. Let's see how this works by examining the `SimpleCursorAdapter`.

Getting to Know SimpleCursorAdapter

The SimpleCursorAdapter, which we've used many times already, is depicted in Figure 4–21.

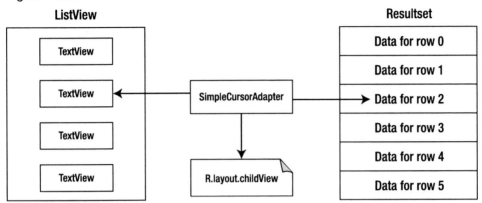

Figure 4–21. *The SimpleCursorAdapter*

The constructor of SimpleCursorAdapter looks like this: SimpleCursorAdapter(Context context, int layout, Cursor c, String[] from, int[] to). This adapter converts a row in the cursor to a child view for the container control. The definition of the child view is defined in an XML resource (layout parameter). Note that because a row in the cursor might have many columns, you tell the SimpleCursorAdapter which columns you want to select from the row by specifying an array of column names (using the from parameter).

Similarly, because each column you select is mapped to a TextView, you must specify the IDs in the to parameter. There's a one-to-one mapping between the column that you select and a TextView that displays the data in the column, so the from and to parameters must be the same size.

Figure 4–21 reveals some flexibility in using adapters. Because the container control operates on an adapter, you can substitute various types of adapters based on your data and child view. For example, if you are not going to populate an AdapterView from the database, you don't have to use the SimpleCursorAdapter. You can opt for an even "simpler" adapter—the ArrayAdapter.

Getting to Know ArrayAdapter

The ArrayAdapter is the simplest of the adapters in Android. It specifically targets list controls and assumes that TextView controls represent the list items (the child views). Creating a new ArrayAdapter generally looks like this:

```
ArrayAdapter<String> adapter = new ArrayAdapter<String>(
this,android.R.layout.simple_list_item_1,
new string[]{"sayed","satya"});
```

The constructor in the preceding code creates an `ArrayAdapter` where the `TextView` controls' data is represented by strings. Note that `android.R.layout.simple_list_item_1` points to a `TextView` defined by the Android SDK.

`ArrayAdapter` provides a handy method that you can use, if the data for the list comes from a resource file. Listing 4–34 shows an example.

Listing 4–34. *Creating an ArrayAdapter from a String-Resource File*

```
Spinner s2 = (Spinner) findViewById(R.id.spinner2);

adapter = ArrayAdapter.createFromResource(this,
R.array.planets,android.R.layout.simple_spinner_item);

adapter.setDropDownViewResource(android.R.layout.simple_spinner_dropdown_item);

s2.setAdapter(adapter);


<string-array name="planets">
    <item>Mercury</item>
    <item>Venus</item>
    <item>Earth</item>
    <item>Mars</item>
    <item>Jupiter</item>
    <item>Saturn</item>
    <item>Uranus</item>
    <item>Neptune</item>
</string-array>
```

Listing 4–34 shows that `ArrayAdapter` has a utility method called `createFromResource()` that can create an `ArrayAdapter` whose data source is defined in a string-resource file. Using this method allows you not only to externalize the contents of the list to an XML file, but also to use localized versions.

Creating Custom Adapters

Adapters in Android are easy to use, but they have some limitations. To address this, Android provides an abstract class called `BaseAdapter` that you can extend if you need a custom adapter. The adapters that ship with the SDK all extend this base adapter. Thus, if you are looking to extend an adapter, you could consider the following adapters:

- `ArrayAdapter<T>`: This is an adapter on top of a generic array of arbitrary objects. It's meant to be used with a `ListView`.

- `CursorAdapter`: This adapter, also meant to be used in a `ListView`, provides data to the list via a cursor.

- `SimpleAdapter`: As the name suggests, this adapter is a simple adapter. It is generally used to populate a list with static data (possibly from resources).

- ResourceCursorAdapter: This adapter extends CursorAdapter and knows how to create views from resources.

- SimpleCursorAdapter: This adapter extends ResourceCursorAdapter and creates TextView/ImageView views from the columns in the cursor. The views are defined in resources.

This concludes our discussion about building UIs. In the next section, we are going to introduce you to the Hierarchy Viewer tool. This tool will help you debug and optimize your user interfaces.

Debugging and Optimizing Layouts with the Hierarchy Viewer

The Android SDK ships with a host of tools that you can use to make your development life a lot easier. Because we are on the topic of user interface development, it makes sense for us to discuss the Hierarchy Viewer tool. This tool, shown in Figure 4–22, allows you to debug your user interfaces from a layout perspective.

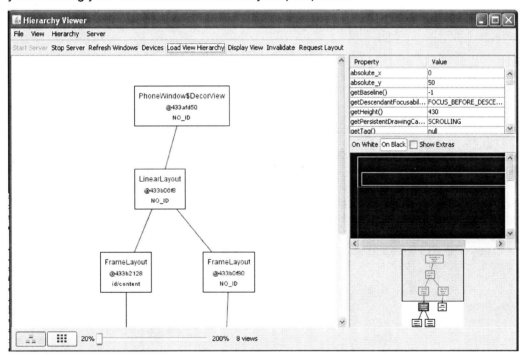

Figure 4–22. *The layout view of the Hierarchy Viewer tool*

As shown in Figure 4–22, the Hierarchy Viewer shows the hierarchy of views in the form of a tree. The idea is this: you load a layout into the tool and then inspect the layout to (1) determine possible layout problems, and/or (2) try to optimize the layout so that you minimize the number of views (for performance reasons).

To debug your UIs, run your application in the emulator and browse to the UI that you want to debug. Then go to the Android SDK /tools directory to start the Hierarchy Viewer tool. On a Windows installation, you'll see a batch file called hierarchyviewer.bat in the /tools directory. When you run the batch file, you'll see the Hierarchy Viewer's Devices screen (see Figure 4–23).

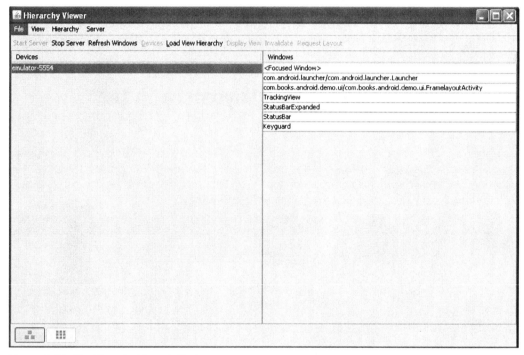

Figure 4–23. *The Hierarchy Viewer's Devices screen*

The Devices screen's left pane displays the set of devices (emulators, in this case) running on the machine. When you select a device, the list of windows in the selected device appears in the right pane. To view the hierarchy of views for a particular window, select that window from the right pane (typically the fully qualified name of your activity prefixed with the application's package name), then click the Load View Hierarchy button.

In the View Hierarchy screen, you'll see that window's hierarchy of views in the left pane (see Figure 4–22). When you select a view element in the left pane, you can see the properties of that element in the properties view to the right and you can see the location of the view, relative to the other views, in the wire-frame pane to the right. The selected view will be highlighted with a red border. By seeing all of the views in use, a developer can hopefully find ways to reduce the number of views and thereby make the application perform faster,

Figure 4–22 shows two buttons in the lower left corner of the Hierarchy Viewer tool. The left button displays the Tree view that we explained earlier. The right button displays the current layout in Pixel Perfect view. This view is interesting in that you get a pixel-by-pixel representation of your layouts. (See Figure 4–24.) There are several items of interest on this screen. On the left-hand side is a navigator view of all of the window's components. If you click one of the components, it will be highlighted with a red border in the middle view. The cross-hairs in the middle view allow you to direct what shows up in the view on the right-hand side (the loupe; a *loupe* is a small magnifier used by jewelers and watchmakers). The zoom control allows you to zoom in even closer in the loupe. The loupe also shows the exact location of the selected pixel in (x, y) coordinates as well as the color value of that pixel.

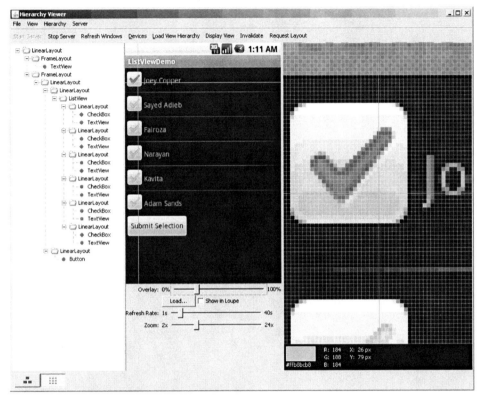

Figure 4–24. *Pixel Perfect mode of the Hierarchy Viewer*

The last very interesting feature of this screen is the Load button and the Overlay slider. You can load an image file behind the displayed screen to compare that image file (perhaps a mockup of the screen you're developing) and use the Overlay slider to make it more or less visible. The image comes in anchored to the lower-left corner. By default, the image is not shown in the loupe, but selecting the check box will make it show up in the loupe. With tools like these, you have a vast amount of control over the look and feel of your application.

Summary

At this point, you should have a good overview of the controls that are available in the Android SDK. You should also be familiar with Android's layout managers, as well as its adapters. Given a potential screen requirement, you should be able to quickly identify the controls and layout managers that you'll use to build the screen.

In the next chapter, we'll take user interface development further—we are going to discuss menus and dialogs.

Chapter 5

Working with Menus and Dialogs

In Chapter 3, we introduced you to resources, content providers, and intents—the foundations of the Android SDK. Then we covered UI controls and layouts in Chapter 4. In this chapter, we'll show you how to work with Android menus and dialogs.

The Android SDK offers extensive support for menus and dialogs. In this chapter, you'll learn to work with several of the menu types that Android supports: regular menus, submenus, context menus, icon menus, secondary menus, and alternative menus.

In Android, menus are represented as resources. As resources, the Android SDK allows you to load menus from XML files, like other resources. Android generates resource IDs for each of the loaded menu items. We will cover these XML menu resources in detail in this chapter. We will also show you how to take advantage of auto-generated resource IDs for all types of menu items.

We will then turn our attention to dialogs. Dialogs in Android are asynchronous, which provides flexibility. If you are accustomed to a programming framework where dialogs could be synchronous (such as Microsoft Windows), you might find asynchronous dialogs a bit unintuitive to use. After giving you the basics of creating and using Android dialogs, we will provide an intuitive abstraction that will make working with asynchronous dialogs easier.

Understanding Android Menus

Whether you've worked with Swing in Java, with Windows Presentation Foundation (WPF) in Windows, or with any other UI framework, you've no doubt worked with menus. In addition to providing comprehensive support for menus, Android presents some new menu patterns such as XML menus and alternative menus.

We will start this chapter by describing the basic classes involved in the Android menu framework. In the process, you will learn how to create menus and menu items, and how to respond to menu items. The key class in Android menu support is `android.view.Menu`. Every activity in Android is associated with a menu object of this type, which can contain a number of menu items and submenus. Menu items are represented by `android.view.MenuItem` and submenus are represented by `android.view.SubMenu`. These relationships are graphically represented in Figure 5–1. Strictly speaking, this is not a class diagram, but a structural diagram designed to help you visualize the relationships between the various menu-related classes and functions.

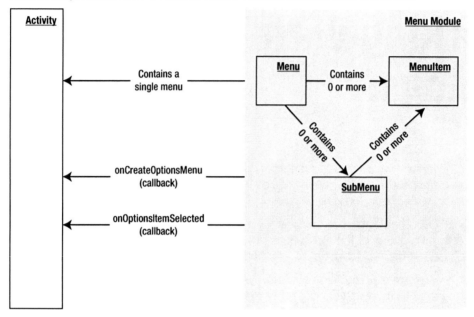

Figure 5–1. *Structure of Android menu classes*

You can group menu items together by assigning each one a group ID, which is merely an attribute. Multiple menu items that carry the same group ID are considered part of the same group. In addition to carrying a group ID, a menu item also carries a name (title), a menu-item ID, and a sort-order ID (or number). You use the sort-order IDs to specify the order of menu items within a menu. For example, if one menu item carries a sort-order number of 4 and another menu item carries a sort-order number of 6, then the first menu item will appear above the second menu item in the menu.

Some of these order-number ranges are reserved for certain kinds of menus. Secondary menu items, which are considered less important than others, start at 0x30000 and are defined by the constant `Menu.CATEGORY_SECONDARY`. Other types of menu categories—such as system menus, alternative menus, and container menus—have different order-number ranges. System menu items start at 0x20000 and are defined by the constant `Menu.CATEGORY_SYSTEM`. Alternative menu items start at 0x40000 and are defined by the constant `Menu.CATEGORY_ALTERNATIVE`. Container menu items start at 0x10000 and are defined by the constant `Menu.CATEGORY_CONTAINER`. By looking at the values for these constants, you can see the order in which they'll appear in the menu. (We'll discuss these various types of menu items in the "Working with Other Menu Types" section.)

Figure 5–1 also shows two callback methods that you can use to create and respond to menu items: onCreateOptionsMenu and onOptionsItemSelected. We will cover these in the next few subsections.

Creating a Menu

In the Android SDK, you don't need to create a menu object from scratch. Because an activity is associated with a single menu, Android creates this single menu for that activity and passes it to the onCreateOptionsMenu callback method of the activity class. (As the name of the method indicates, menus in Android are also known as *options menus*.) This method allows you to populate the single passed-in menu with a set of menu items (see Listing 5–1).

Listing 5–1. *Signature for the onCreateOptionsMenu Method*

```
@Override
public boolean onCreateOptionsMenu(Menu menu)
{
    // populate menu items
    …..
    ...return true;
}
```

Once the menu items are populated, the code should return true to make the menu visible. If this method returns false, the menu is invisible. The code in Listing 5–2 shows how to add three menu items using a single group ID along with incremental menu-item IDs and sort-order IDs.

Listing 5–2. *Adding Menu Items*

```
@Override
public boolean onCreateOptionsMenu(Menu menu)
{
    //call the base class to include system menus
    super.onCreateOptionsMenu(menu);

    menu.add(0          // Group
          ,1                      // item id
          ,0                      //order
          ,"append");     // title

    menu.add(0,2,1,"item2");
    menu.add(0,3,2,"clear");

    //It is important to return true to see the menu
    return true;
}
```

You should also call the base-class implementation of this method to give the system an opportunity to populate the menu with system menu items. To keep these system menu items separate from other kinds of menu items, Android adds them starting at 0x20000. (As we mentioned before, the constant Menu.CATEGORY_SYSTEM defines the starting ID for these system menu items.)

The first parameter required for adding a menu item is the group ID (an integer). The second parameter is the menu-item ID, which is sent back to the callback function when that menu item is chosen. The third argument represents the sort-order ID.

The last argument is the name or title of the menu item. Instead of free text, you can use a string resource through the R.java constants file. The group ID, menu-item ID, and sort-order ID are all optional; you can use Menu.NONE if you don't want to specify any of those.

Working with Menu Groups

Now let us show you how to work with menu groups. Listing 5–3 shows how you would add two groups of menus: Group 1 and Group 2.

Listing 5–3. *Using Group IDs to Create Menu Groups*

```
@Override
public boolean onCreateOptionsMenu(Menu menu)
{
    //Group 1
    int group1 = 1;
    menu.add(group1,1,1,"g1.item1");
    menu.add(group1,2,2,"g1.item2");

    //Group 2
    int group2 = 2;
    menu.add(group2,3,3,"g2.item1");
    menu.add(group2,4,4,"g2.item2");

    return true; // it is important to return true
}
```

Notice how the menu-item IDs and the sort-order IDs are independent of the groups. So what good is a group, then? Well, Android provides a set of methods that are based on group ids. You can manipulate a group's menu items using these methods:

```
removeGroup(id)
setGroupCheckable(id, checkable, exclusive)
setGroupEnabled(id,boolean enabled)
setGroupVisible(id,visible)
```

removeGroup removes all menu items from that group, given the group ID. You can enable or disable menu items in a given group using the setGroupEnabled method. Similarly, you can control the visibility of a group of menu items using setGroupVisible.

setGroupCheckable is a bit interesting. You can use this method to show a check mark on a menu item when that menu item is selected. When applied to a group, it will enable this functionality for all menu items within that group. If this method's exclusive flag is set, then only one menu item within that group is allowed to go into a checked state. The other menu items will remain unchecked.

You now know how to populate an activity's main menu with a set of menu items and group them according to their nature. Next, we will show you how to respond to these menu items.

Responding to Menu Items

There are multiple ways of responding to menu-item clicks in Android. You can use the onOptionsItemSelected method of the activity class, you can use stand-alone listeners, or you can use intents. We will cover each of these techniques in this section.

Responding to Menu Items Through onOptionsItemSelected

When a menu item is clicked, Android calls the onOptionsItemSelected callback method on the Activity class (see Listing 5–4).

Listing 5–4. *Signature and Body of the onOptionsItemSelected Method*

```
@Override
public boolean onOptionsItemSelected(MenuItem item)
{
    switch(item.getItemId()) {
        .....
    }
    //for items handled
    return true;

    //for the rest
    ...return super.onOptionsItemSelected(item);
}
```

The key pattern here is to examine the menu-item ID through the getItemId() method of the MenuItem class and do what's necessary. If onOptionsItemSelected() handles a menu item, it returns true. The menu event will not be further propagated. For the menu-item callbacks that onOptionsItemSelected() doesn't deal with, onOptionsItemSelected() should call the parent method through super.onOptionsItemSelected. The default implementation of the onOptionsItemSelected() method returns false so that the "normal" processing can take place. Normal processing includes alternative means of invoking responses for a menu click.

Responding to Menu Items Through Listeners

You usually respond to menus by overriding onOptionsItemSelected; this is the recommended technique for better performance. However, a menu item allows you to register a listener that could be used as a callback.

This approach is a two-step process. In the first step, you implement the OnMenuClickListener interface. Then you take an instance of this implementation and pass it to the menu item. When the menu item is clicked, the menu item will call the onMenuItemClick() method of the OnMenuClickListener interface (see Listing 5–5).

Listing 5–5. *Using a Listener as a Callback for a Menu-Item Click*

```
//Step 1
public class MyResponse implements OnMenuClickListener
{
```

```
        //some local variable to work on
        //...
        //Some constructors
        @override
        boolean onMenuItemClick(MenuItem item)
        {
            //do your thing
            return true;
        }
    }
}

//Step 2
MyResponse myResponse = new MyResponse(...);
menuItem.setOnMenuItemClickListener(myResponse);
...
```

The onMenuItemClick method is called when the menu item has been invoked. This code executes right when the menu item is clicked, even before the onOptionsItemSelected method is called. If onMenuItemClick returns true, no other callbacks will be executed—including the onOptionsItemSelected callback method. This means that the listener code takes precedence over the onOptionsItemSelected method.

Using an Intent to Respond to Menu Items

You can also associate a menu item with an intent by using the MenuItem's method setIntent(intent). By default, a menu item has no intent associated with it. But when an intent *is* associated with a menu item, and nothing else handles the menu item, then the default behavior is to invoke the intent using startActivity(intent). For this to work, all the handlers—especially the onOptionsItemSelected method—should call the parent class's onOptionsItemSelected() method for those items that are not handled. Or you could look at it this way: the system gives onOptionsItemSelected an opportunity to handle menu items first (followed by the listener, of course).

If you don't override the onOptionsItemSelected method, then the base class in the Android framework will do what's necessary to invoke the intent on the menu item. But if you do override this method and you're not interested in this menu item, then you must call the parent method, which in turn facilitates the intent invocation. So here's the bottom line: either don't override the onOptionsItemSelected method, or override it and invoke the parent for the menu items that you are not handling.

Creating a Test Harness for Testing Menus

That's pretty straightforward so far. You have learned how to create menus and how to respond to them through various callbacks. Now we'll show you a sample activity to exercise these menu APIs that you have already learned.

The goal of this exercise is to create a simple activity with a text view in it. The text view will act like a debugger. As we invoke menus, we will write out the invoked menu-item name and menu-item ID to this text view. The finished Menus application will look like the one shown in Figure 5–2.

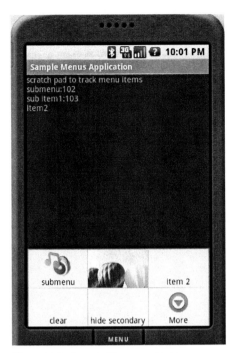

Figure 5-2. *Sample Menus application*

Figure 5-2 shows two things of interest: the menu and the text view. The menu appears at the bottom. You will not see it, though, when you start the application; you must click the Menu button on the emulator or the device in order to see the menu. The second point of interest is the text view that lists the debug messages near the top of the screen. As you click through the available menu items, the test harness logs the menu-item names in the text view. If you click the "clear" menu item, the program clears the text view.

> **NOTE:** Figure 5-2 does not necessarily represent the beginning state of the sample application. We have presented it here to illustrate the menu types that we'll cover in this chapter.

Follow these steps to implement the test harness:

1. Create an XML layout file that contains the text view.

2. Create an `Activity` class that hosts the layout defined in step 1.

3. Set up the menu.

4. Add some regular menu items to the menu.

5. Add some secondary menu items to the menu.

6. Respond to the menu items.

7. Modify the AndroidManifest.xml file to show the application's proper title.

We will cover each of these steps in the following sections and provide the necessary source code to assemble the test harness.

Creating an XML Layout

Step 1 involves creating a simple XML layout file with a text view in it (see Listing 5–6). You could load this file into an activity during its startup.

Listing 5–6. *XML Layout File for the Test Harness*

```
<?xml version="1.0" encoding="utf-8"?>
<LinearLayout xmlns:android="http://schemas.android.com/apk/res/android"
    android:orientation="vertical"
    android:layout_width="fill_parent"
    android:layout_height="fill_parent"
    >
<TextView android:id="@+id/textViewId"
    android:layout_width="fill_parent"
    android:layout_height="wrap_content"
    android:text="Debugging Scratch Pad"
    />
</LinearLayout>
```

Creating an Activity

Step 2 dictates that you create an activity, which is also a simple process. Assuming that the layout file in step 1 is available at \res\layout\main.xml, you can use that file through its resource ID to populate the activity's view (see Listing 5–7).

Listing 5–7. *Menu Test Harness Activity Class*

```
public class SampleMenusActivity extends Activity {

    //Initialize this in onCreateOptions
    Menu myMenu = null;

    @Override
    public void onCreate(Bundle savedInstanceState) {
        super.onCreate(savedInstanceState);

        setContentView(R.layout.main);
    }
```

For brevity, we have not included the import statements. In Eclipse, you can automatically populate the import statements by pulling up the context menu in the editor and selecting Source ~TRA Organize Imports.

Setting Up the Menu

Now that you have a view and an activity, you can move on to step 3: overriding the onCreateOptionsMenu and setting up the menu programmatically (see Listing 5–8).

Listing 5–8. *Setting Up the Menu Programatically*

```
@Override
public boolean onCreateOptionsMenu(Menu menu)
{
    //call the parent to attach any system level menus
    super.onCreateOptionsMenu(menu);

    this.myMenu = menu;

    //add a few normal menus
    addRegularMenuItems(menu);

    //add a few secondary menus
    add5SecondaryMenuItems(menu);

    //it must return true to show the menu
    //if it is false menu won't show
    return true;
}
```

The code in Listing 5–8 first calls the parent onCreateOptionsMenu to give the parent an opportunity to add any system-level menus.

> **NOTE:** In all releases of the Android SDK so far, this method, onCreateOptionsMenu, does not add new menu items. However, a future release might, so it is a good practice to call the parent.

The code then remembers the Menu object in order to manipulate it later for demonstration purposes. After that, the code proceeds to add a few regular menu items and a few secondary menu items.

Adding Regular Menu Items

Now for step 4: adding a few regular menu items to the menu. The code for addRegularMenuItems appears in Listing 5–9.

Listing 5–9. *The addRegularMenuItems Function*

```
private void addRegularMenuItems(Menu menu)
{
    int base=Menu.FIRST; // value is 1

    menu.add(base,base,base,"append");
    menu.add(base,base+1,base+1,"item 2");
    menu.add(base,base+2,base+2,"clear");

    menu.add(base,base+3,base+3,"hide secondary");
```

```
        menu.add(base,base+4,base+4,"show secondary");

        menu.add(base,base+5,base+5,"enable secondary");
        menu.add(base,base+6,base+6,"disable secondary");

        menu.add(base,base+7,base+7,"check secondary");
        menu.add(base,base+8,base+8,"uncheck secondary");
    }
```

The Menu class defines a few convenience constants, one of which is Menu.FIRST. You can use this as a baseline number for menu IDs and other menu-related sequential numbers. Notice how you can peg the group ID at base and increment only the sort-order ID and menu-item ID. In addition, the code adds a few specific menu items such as "hide secondary," "enable secondary," and others to demonstrate some of the menu concepts.

Adding Secondary Menu Items

Let us now add a few secondary menu items to perform step 5 (see Listing 5–10). Secondary menu items, as mentioned earlier, start at 0x30000 and are defined by the constant Menu.CATEGORY_SECONDARY. Their sort-order IDs are higher than regular menu items, so they appear after the regular menu items in a menu. Note that the sort order is the only thing that distinguishes a secondary menu item from a regular menu item. In all other aspects, a secondary menu item works and behaves like any other menu item.

Listing 5–10. *Adding Secondary Menu Items*

```
    private void add5SecondaryMenuItems(Menu menu)
    {
        //Secondary items are shown just like everything else
        int base=Menu.CATEGORY_SECONDARY;

        menu.add(base,base+1,base+1,"sec. item 1");
        menu.add(base,base+2,base+2,"sec. item 2");
        menu.add(base,base+3,base+3,"sec. item 3");
        menu.add(base,base+3,base+3,"sec. item 4");
        menu.add(base,base+4,base+4,"sec. item 5");
    }
```

Responding to Menu-Item Clicks

Now that the menus are set up, we move on to step 6: responding to them. When a menu item is clicked, Android calls the onOptionsItemSelected callback method of the Activity class by passing a reference to the clicked menu item. You then use the getItemId() method on the MenuItem to see which item it is.

It is not uncommon to see either a switch statement or a series of if and else statements calling various functions in response to menu items. Listing 5–11 shows this standard pattern of responding to menu items in the onOptionsItemSelected callback method. (You will learn a slightly better way of doing the same thing in the "Loading

Menus Through XML Files" section, where you will have symbolic names for these menu-item IDs.)

Listing 5–11. *Responding to Menu-Item Clicks*

```
@Override
public boolean onOptionsItemSelected(MenuItem item)     {
    if (item.getItemId() == 1)        {
        appendText("\nhello");
    }
    else if (item.getItemId() == 2)        {
        appendText("\nitem2");
    }
    else if (item.getItemId() == 3)        {
        emptyText();
    }
    else if (item.getItemId() == 4)        {
        //hide secondary
        this.appendMenuItemText(item);
        this.myMenu.setGroupVisible(Menu.CATEGORY_SECONDARY,false);
    }
    else if (item.getItemId() == 5)        {
        //show secondary
        this.appendMenuItemText(item);
        this.myMenu.setGroupVisible(Menu.CATEGORY_SECONDARY,true);
    }
    else if (item.getItemId() == 6)        {
        //enable secondary
        this.appendMenuItemText(item);
        this.myMenu.setGroupEnabled(Menu.CATEGORY_SECONDARY,true);
    }
    else if (item.getItemId() == 7)        {
        //disable secondary
        this.appendMenuItemText(item);
        this.myMenu.setGroupEnabled(Menu.CATEGORY_SECONDARY,false);
    }
    else if (item.getItemId() == 8)        {
        //check secondary
        this.appendMenuItemText(item);
        myMenu.setGroupCheckable(Menu.CATEGORY_SECONDARY,true,false);
    }
    else if (item.getItemId() == 9)        {
        //uncheck secondary
        this.appendMenuItemText(item);
        myMenu.setGroupCheckable(Menu.CATEGORY_SECONDARY,false,false);
    }
    else        {
        this.appendMenuItemText(item);
    }
    //should return true if the menu item
    //is handled
    return true;
}
```

Listing 5–11 also exercises operations on menus at the group level; calls to these methods are highlighted in bold. The code also logs the details about the clicked menu item to the TextView. Listing 5–12 shows some utility functions to write to the TextView. Notice an additional method on a MenuItem to get its title.

Listing 5–12. *Utility Functions to Write to the Debug TextView*

```
//Given a string of text append it to the TextView
    private void appendText(String text)     {
        TextView tv = (TextView)this.findViewById(R.id.textViewId);
        tv.setText(tv.getText() + text);
    }

//Given a menu item append its title to the TextView
    private void appendMenuItemText(MenuItem menuItem)     {
        String title = menuItem.getTitle().toString();
        TextView tv = (TextView)this.findViewById(R.id.textViewId);
        tv.setText(tv.getText() + "\n" + title);
    }
//Empty the TextView of its contents
    private void emptyText()     {
        TextView tv = (TextView)this.findViewById(R.id.textViewId);
        tv.setText("");
    }
```

Tweaking the AndroidManifest.xml File

Your final step in the process to create the test harness is to update the application's AndroidManifest.xml file. This file, which is automatically created for you when you create a new project, is available in your project's root directory.

This is the place where you register the Activity class (such as SampleMenusActivity) and where you specify a title for the activity. We called this activity "Sample Menus Application," as shown in Figure 5–2. See this entry highlighted in Listing 5–13.

Listing 5–13. *The AndroidManifest.xml File for the Test Harness*

```
<?xml version="1.0" encoding="utf-8"?>
<manifest xmlns:android="http://schemas.android.com/apk/res/android"
    package="your-package-name-goes-here "
    android:versionCode="1"
    android:versionName="1.0.0">
    <application android:icon="@drawable/icon" android:label="Sample Menus">
        <activity android:name=".SampleMenusActivity"
                android:label="Sample Menus Application">
            <intent-filter>
                <action android:name="android.intent.action.MAIN" />
                <category android:name="android.intent.category.LAUNCHER" />
            </intent-filter>
        </activity>
    </application>
</manifest>
```

Using the code we've provided, you should be able to quickly construct this test harness for experimenting with menus. We showed you how to create a simple activity initialized with a text view, and then how to populate and respond to menus. Most menus follow this basic yet functional pattern. You can use Figure 5–2 as a guide for what kind of UI to expect when you are done with the exercise. But as we pointed out, what you see might not exactly match the figure because we haven't yet shown you how to add the icon menus. Your UI might differ even after you add the icon menus, because your images might differ from the images we used.

Working with Other Menu Types

So far we've covered some of the simpler, although quite functional, menu types. As you walk through the SDK, you will see that Android also supports icon menus, submenus, context menus, and alternative menus. Out of these, alternative menus are unique to Android. We will cover all of these menu types in this section.

Expanded Menus

Recall from Figure 5–2 that the sample application displays a menu item called "More" at the bottom-right corner of the menu. We didn't show you how to add this menu item in any of the sample code, so where does it come from?

If an application has more menu items than it can display on the main screen, Android shows the More menu item to allow the user to see the rest. This menu, called an *expanded menu*, shows up automatically when there are too many menu items to display in the limited amount of space. But the expanded menu has a limitation: it cannot accommodate icons. Users who click More will see a resultant menu that omits icons.

Working with Icon Menus

Now that we've hinted at icon menus, let's talk about them in more detail. Android supports not only text, but also images or icons as part of its menu repertoire. You can use icons to represent your menu items instead of and in addition to text. But note a few limitations when it comes to using icon menus. First, as you saw in the previous paragraph, you can't use icon menus for expanded menus. Second, icon menu items do not support menu-item check marks. Third, if the text in an icon menu item is too long, it will be truncated after a certain number of characters, depending on the size of the display. (This last limitation applies to text-based menu items also.)

Creating an icon menu item is straightforward. You create a regular text-based menu item as before, then you use the `setIcon` method on the `MenuItem` class to set the image. You'll need to use the image's resource ID, so you must generate it first by placing the image or icon in the `/res/drawable` directory. For example, if the icon's file name is `balloons`, then the resource ID will be `R.drawable.balloons`.

Here is some sample code that demonstrates this:

```
//add a menu item and remember it so that you can use it
//subsequently to set the icon on it.
MenuItem item8 = menu.add(base,base+8,base+8,"uncheck secondary");
item8.setIcon(R.drawable.balloons);
```

As you add menu items to the menu, you rarely need to keep a local variable returned by the menu.add method. But in this case, you need to remember the returned object so you can add the icon to the menu item. The code in this example also demonstrates that the type returned by the menu.add method is MenuItem.

The icon will show as long as the menu item is displayed on the main application screen. If it's displayed as part of the expanded menu, the icon will not show, just the text. The menu item displaying an image of balloons in Figure 5–2 is an example of an icon menu item.

Working with Submenus

Let's take a look at Android's submenus now. Figure 5–1 points out the structural relationship of a SubMenu to a Menu and a MenuItem. A Menu object can have multiple SubMenu objects. Each SubMenu object is added to the Menu object through a call to the Menu.addSubMenu method (see Listing 5–14). You add menu items to a submenu the same way that you add menu items to a menu. This is because SubMenu is also derived from a Menu object. However, you cannot add additional submenus to a submenu.

Listing 5–14. *Adding Submenus*

```
private void addSubMenu(Menu menu)
{
    //Secondary items are shown just like everything else
    int base=Menu.FIRST + 100;
    SubMenu sm = menu.addSubMenu(base,base+1,Menu.NONE,"submenu");
    sm.add(base,base+2,base+2,"sub item1");
    sm.add(base,base+3,base+3, "sub item2");
    sm.add(base,base+4,base+4, "sub item3");

     //submenu item icons are not supported
    item1.setIcon(R.drawable.icon48x48_2);

    //the following is ok however
    sm.setIcon(R.drawable.icon48x48_1);

    //This will result in runtime exception
     //sm.addSubMenu("try this");
}
```

> **NOTE:** A SubMenu, as a subclass of the Menu object, continues to carry the addSubMenu method. The compiler won't complain if you add a submenu to another submenu, but you'll get a runtime exception if you try to do it.

The Android SDK documentation also suggests that submenus do not support icon menu items. When you add an icon to a menu item and then add that menu item to a submenu, the menu item will ignore that icon, even if you don't see a compile-time or runtime error. However, the submenu itself can have an icon.

Provisioning for System Menus

Most Windows applications come with menus such as File, Edit, View, Open, Close, and Exit. These menus are called system menus. The Android SDK suggests that the system could insert a similar set of menus when an options menu is created. However, current releases of the Android SDK do not populate any of these menus as part of the menu-creation process. It is conceivable that these system menus might be implemented in a subsequent release. The documentation suggests that programmers make provisions in their code so that they can accommodate these system menus when they become available. You do this by calling the onCreateOptionsMenu method of the parent, which allows the system to add system menus to a group identified by the constant CATEGORY_SYSTEM.

Working with Context Menus

Users of desktop programs are no doubt familiar with context menus. In Windows applications, for example, you can access a context menu by right-clicking a UI element. Android supports the same idea of context menus through an action called a *long click*. A long click is a mouse click held down slightly longer than usual on any Android view.

On handheld devices such as cell phones, mouse clicks are implemented in a number of ways, depending on the navigation mechanism. If your phone has a wheel to move the cursor, a press of the wheel would serve as the mouse click. Or if the device has a touch pad, then a tap or a press would be equivalent to a mouse click. Or you might have a set of arrow buttons for movement and a selection button in the middle; clicking that button would be equivalent to clicking the mouse. Regardless of how a mouse click is implemented on your device, if you hold the mouse click a bit longer you will realize the long click.

A context menu differs structurally from the standard options menu that we've been discussing (see Figure 5–3). Context menus have some nuances that options menus don't have.

Figure 5–3 shows that a context menu is represented as a ContextMenu class in the Android menu architecture. Just like a Menu, a ContextMenu can contain a number of menu items. You will use the same set of Menu methods to add menu items to the context menu. The biggest difference between a Menu and a ContextMenu boils down to the ownership of the menu in question. An activity owns a regular options menu, whereas a view owns a context menu. This is to be expected because the long clicks that activate context menus apply to the *view* being clicked. So an activity can have only one options menu but many context menus. Because an activity can contain multiple views, and each view can have its own context menu, an activity can have as many context menus as there are views.

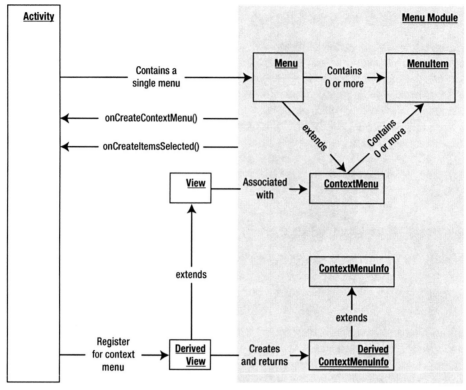

Figure 5–3. *Activities, views, and context menus*

Although a context menu is owned by a view, the method to populate context menus resides in the `Activity` class. This method is called `activity.onCreateContextMenu()`, and its role resembles that of the `activity.onCreateOptionsMenu()` method. This callback method also carries with it the view for which the context menu items are to be populated.

There is one more notable wrinkle to the context menu. Whereas the `onCreateOptionsMenu()` method is automatically called for every activity, this is not the case with `onCreateContextMenu()`. A view in an activity does not *have* to own a context menu. You can have three views in your activity, for example, but perhaps you want to enable context menus for only one view and not the others. If you want a particular view to own a context menu, you must register that view with its activity specifically for the purpose of owning a context menu. You do this through the `activity.registerForContextMenu(view)` method, which we'll discuss in the section "Registering a View for a Context Menu."

Now note the `ContextMenuInfo` class shown in Figure 5–3. An object of this type is passed to the `onCreateContextMenu` method. This is one way for the view to pass additional information to this method. For a view to do this, it needs to override the `getContextViewInfo()` method and return a derived class of `ContextMenuInfo` with additional methods to represent the additional information. You might want to look at the source code for `android.view.View` to fully understand this interaction.

> **NOTE:** Per the Android SDK documentation, context menus do not support shortcuts, icons, or submenus.

Now that you know the general structure of the context menus, let's look at some sample code that demonstrates each of the steps to implement a context menu:

1. Register a view for a context menu in an activity's `onCreate()` method.

2. Populate the context menu using `onCreateContextMenu()`. You must complete step 1 before this callback method is invoked by Android.

3. Respond to context-menu clicks.

Registering a View for a Context Menu

The first step in implementing a context menu is to register a view for the context menu in an activity's `onCreate()` method. If you were to use the menu test harness introduced in this chapter, you could register the `TextView` for a context menu in that test harness by using the code in Listing 5–15. You would first find the `TextView` and then call `registerForContextMenu` on the activity using the `TextView` as an argument. This will set up the `TextView` for context menus.

Listing 5–15. *Registering a TextView for a Context Menu*

```
@Override
public void onCreate(Bundle savedInstanceState) {
    super.onCreate(savedInstanceState);
    setContentView(R.layout.main);

    TextView tv = (TextView)this.findViewById(R.id.textViewId);
    registerForContextMenu(this.getTextView());
}
```

Populating a Context Menu

Once a view like the `TextView` in this example is registered for context menus, Android will call the `onCreateContextMenu()` method with this view as the argument. This is where you can populate the context menu items for that context menu. The `onCreateContextMenu()` callback method provides three arguments to work with.

The first argument is a preconstructed `ContextMenu` object, the second is the view (such as the `TextView`) that generated the callback, and the third is the `ContextMenuInfo` class that we covered briefly while discussing Figure 5–3. For a lot of simple cases, you can just ignore the `ContextMenuInfo` object. However, some views might pass extra information through this object. In those cases, you will need to cast the

ContextMenuInfo class to a subclass and then use the additional methods to retrieve the additional information.

Some examples of classes derived from ContextMenuInfo include AdapterContextMenuInfo and ExpandableContextMenuInfo. Views that are tied to database cursors in Android use the AdapterContextMenuInfo class to pass the row ID within that view for which the context menu is being displayed. In a sense, you can use this class to further clarify the object underneath the mouse click, even within a given view.

Listing 5–16 demonstrates the onCreateContextMenu() method.

Listing 5–16. *The onCreateContextMenu() Method*

```
@Override
public void onCreateContextMenu(ContextMenu menu, View v, ContextMenuInfo menuInfo)
{
        menu.setHeaderTitle("Sample Context Menu");
        menu.add(200, 200, 200, "item1");
}
```

Responding to Context Menu Items

The third step in our implementation of a context menu is responding to context-menu clicks. The mechanism of responding to context menus is similar to the mechanism of responding to options menus. Android provides a callback method similar to onOptionsItemSelected() called onContextItemSelected(). This method, like its counterpart, is also available on the Activity class. Listing 5–17 demonstrates onContextItemSelected().

Listing 5–17. *Responding to Context Menus*

```
@Override
 public boolean onContextItemSelected(MenuItem item)
{
     if (item.itemId() = some-menu-item-id)
     {
        //handle this menu item
return true;
     }
… other exception processing
}
```

Working with Alternative Menus

So far you have learned to create and work with menus, submenus, and context menus. Android introduces a new concept called *alternative menus*, which allow alternative menu items to be part of menus, submenus, and context menus. Alternative menus allow multiple applications on Android to use one another. These alternative menus are part of the Android inter-application communication or usage framework.

Specifically, alternative menus allow one application to include menus from another application. When the alternative menus are chosen, the target application or activity will be launched with a URL to the data needed by that activity. The invoked activity will then use the data URL from the intent that is passed. To understand alternative menus well, you must first understand content providers, content URIs, content MIME types, and intents (see Chapter 3).

The general idea here is this: imagine you are writing a screen to display some data. Most likely, this screen will be an activity. On this activity, you will have an options menu that allows you to manipulate or work with the data in a number of ways. Also assume for a moment that you are working with a document or a note that is identified by a URI and a corresponding MIME type. What you want to do as a programmer is anticipate that the device will eventually contain more programs that will know how to work with this data or display this data. You want to give this new set of programs an opportunity to display their menu items as part of the menu that you are constructing for this activity.

To attach alternative menu items to a menu, follow these steps while setting up the menu in the onCreateOptionsMenu method:

1. Create an intent whose data URI is set to the data URI that you are showing at the moment.

2. Set the category of the intent as CATEGORY_ALTERNATIVE.

3. Search for activities that allow operations on data supported by this type of URI.

4. Add intents that can invoke those activities as menu items to the menu.

These steps tell us a lot about the nature of Android applications, so we'll examine each one. As we know now, attaching the alternative menu items to the menu happens in the onCreateOptionsMenu method:

```
@Override public boolean onCreateOptionsMenu(Menu menu)
{
}
```

Let us now figure out what code makes up this function. We first need to know the URI for the data we might be working on in this activity. You can get the URI like this:

```
this.getIntent().getData()
```

This works because the Activity class has a method called getIntent() that returns the data URI for which this activity is invoked. This invoked activity might be the main activity invoked by the main menu; in that case, it might not have an intent and the getIntent()method will return null. In your code, you will have to guard against this situation.

Our goal now is to find out the other programs that know how to work with this kind of data. We do this search using an intent as an argument. Here's the code to construct that intent:

```
Intent criteriaIntent = new Intent(null, getIntent().getData());
```

```
intent.addCategory(Intent.CATEGORY_ALTERNATIVE);
```

Once we construct the intent, we will also add a category of actions that we are interested in. Specifically, we are interested only in activities that can be invoked as part of an alternative menu. We are ready now to tell the Menu object to search for matching activities and add them as menu options (see Listing 5–18).

Listing 5–18. *Populating a Menu with Alternative Menu Items*

```
// Search for, and populate the menu with matching Activities.
menu.addIntentOptions(
    Menu.CATEGORY_ALTERNATIVE,    // Group
    Menu.CATEGORY_ALTERNATIVE,    // Any unique IDs we might care to add.
    Menu.CATEGORY_ALTERNATIVE,    // order
    getComponentName(),           // Name of the class displaying
                                  // the menu--here, it's this class.
    null,                         // No specifics.
    criteriaIntent,               // Previously created intent that
                                  // describes our requirements.
    0,                            // No flags.
    null);                        // returned menu items
```

Before going through this code line by line, we'll explain what we mean by the term matching activities. A *matching activity* is an activity that's capable of handling a URI that it has been given. Activities typically register this information in their manifest files using URIs, actions, and categories. Android provides a mechanism that lets you use an Intent object to look for the matching activities given these attributes.

Now let's look closely at Listing 5–18. The method addIntentOptions on the Menu class is responsible for looking up the activities that match an intent's URI and category attributes. Then the method adds these activities to the menu under the right group with the appropriate menu-item IDs and sort-order IDs. The first three arguments deal with this aspect of the method's responsibility. In Listing 5–18, we start off with the Menu.CATEGORY_ALTERNATIVE as the group under which the new menu items will be added. We also use this same constant as the starting point for the menu-item IDs and sort-order IDs.

The next argument points to the fully qualified component name of the activity that this menu is part of. The code uses a helper method called getComponentName(); we will leave it as an exercise for the reader to get a component name from the class and package names. This component name is needed because when a new menu item is added, that menu item will need to invoke the target activity. To do that, the system needs the source activity that started the target activity. The next argument is an array of intents that you should use as a filter on the returned intents.

The next argument points to criteriaIntent, which we just constructed. This is the search criteria we want to use. The argument after that is a flag such as Menu.FLAG_APPEND_TO_GROUP to indicate whether to append to the set of existing menu items in this group or replace them. The default value is 0, which indicates that the menu items in the menu group should be replaced.

The last argument in Listing 5–18 is an array of menu items that are added. You could use these added menu-item references if you want to manipulate them in some manner after adding them.

All of this is well and good. But a few questions remain unanswered. For example, what will be the names of the added menu items? The Android documentation is quite silent about this. So we snooped around the source code to see what this function is actually doing behind the scenes.

As it turns out, the Menu class is only an interface, so we can't see any implementation source code for it. (Refer to Chapter 1 to see how to get to Android's source code.) The class that implements the Menu interface is called MenuBuilder. Listing 5–19 shows the source code of a relevant method, addIntentOptions, from the MenuBuilder class. (We're providing the code for your reference; we won't explain it line by line.)

Listing 5–19. *MenuBuilder.addIntentOptions Method*

```
public int addIntentOptions(int group, int id, int categoryOrder,
                        ComponentName caller,
                        Intent[] specifics,
                        Intent intent, int flags,
                        MenuItem[] outSpecificItems)
{
    PackageManager pm = mContext.getPackageManager();
    final List<ResolveInfo> lri =
            pm.queryIntentActivityOptions(caller, specifics, intent, 0);
    final int N = lri != null ? lri.size() : 0;

    if ((flags & FLAG_APPEND_TO_GROUP) == 0) {
        removeGroup(group);
    }

    for (int i=0; i<N; i++) {
        final ResolveInfo ri = lri.get(i);
        Intent rintent = new Intent(
            ri.specificIndex < 0 ? intent : specifics[ri.specificIndex]);
        rintent.setComponent(new ComponentName(
                ri.activityInfo.applicationInfo.packageName,
                ri.activityInfo.name));
        final MenuItem item = add(group, id, categoryOrder, ri.loadLabel(pm));
        item.setIntent(rintent);
        if (outSpecificItems != null && ri.specificIndex >= 0) {
            outSpecificItems[ri.specificIndex] = item;
        }
    }
    return N;
}
```

Note the line in Listing 5–19 highlighted in bold; this portion of the code constructs a menu item. The code delegates the work of figuring out a menu title to the ResolveInfo class. The source code of the ResolveInfo class shows us that the intent-filter that declared this intent should have a title associated with it. Here is an example:

```
<intent-filter android:label="Menu Title ">
    ......
    <category android:name="android.intent.category.ALTERNATE" />
```

```
        <data android:mimeType="some type data" />
</intent-filter>
```

The `label` value of the intent-filter ends up serving as the menu name. You can go through the Android Notepad example to see this behavior.

Working with Menus in Response to Changing Data

So far we've talked about static menus; you set them up once, and they don't change dynamically according to what's onscreen. If you want to create dynamic menus, use the `onPrepareOptionsMenu` method that Android provides. This method resembles `onCreateOptionsMenu` except that it gets called every time a menu is invoked. You should use `onPrepareOptionsMenu`, for example, if you want to disable some menus or menu groups based on the data you are displaying. You might want to keep this in mind as you design your menu functionality.

We need to cover one more important aspect of menus before moving on to dialogs. Android supports the creation of menus using XML files. The next high-level topic is dedicated to exploring this XML menu support in Android.

Loading Menus Through XML Files

Up until this point, we've created all our menus programmatically. This is not the most convenient way to create menus because for every menu you have to provide several IDs and define constants for each of those IDs. You'll no doubt find this tedious.

Instead, you can define menus through XML files; you can do this in Android because menus are also resources. The XML approach to menu creation offers several advantages, such as the ability to name the menus, order them automatically, give them IDs, and so on. You can also get localization support for the menu text.

Follow these steps to work with XML-based menus:

1. Define an XML file with menu tags.

2. Place the file in the `/res/menu` subdirectory. The name of the file is arbitrary, and you can have as many files as you want. Android automatically generates a resource ID for this menu file.

3. Use the resource ID for the menu file to load the XML file into the menu.

4. Respond to the menu items using the resource IDs generated for each menu item.

We will talk about each of these steps and provide corresponding code snippets in the following sections.

Structure of an XML Menu Resource File

First, we'll look at an XML file with menu definitions (see Listing 5–20). All menu files start with the same high-level menu tag followed by a series of group tags. Each of these group tags corresponds to the menu-item group we talked about at the beginning of the chapter. You can specify an ID for the group using the @+id approach. Each menu group will have a series of menu items with their menu-item IDs tied to symbolic names. You can refer to the Android SDK documentation for all the possible arguments for these XML tags.

Listing 5–20. *An XML File with Menu Definitions*

```
<menu xmlns:android="http://schemas.android.com/apk/res/android">
    <!-- This group uses the default category. -->
    <group android:id="@+id/menuGroup_Main">

        <item android:id="@+id/menu_testPick"
            android:orderInCategory="5"
            android:title="Test Pick" />
        <item android:id="@+id/menu_testGetContent"
            android:orderInCategory="5"
            android:title="Test Get Content" />
        <item android:id="@+id/menu_clear"
            android:orderInCategory="10"
            android:title="clear" />
        <item android:id="@+id/menu_dial"
            android:orderInCategory="7"
            android:title="dial" />
        <item android:id="@+id/menu_test"
            android:orderInCategory="4"
            android:title="@+string/test" />
        <item android:id="@+id/menu_show_browser"
            android:orderInCategory="5"
            android:title="show browser" />
    </group>
</menu>
```

The menu XML file in Listing 5–20 has one group. Based on the resource ID definition @+id/menuGroup_main, this group will be automatically assigned a resource ID called menuGroup_main in the R.java resource ID file. Similarly, all the child menu items are allocated menu-item IDs based on their symbolic resource ID definitions in this XML file.

Inflating XML Menu Resource Files

Let us assume that the name of this XML file is my_menu.xml. You will need to place this file in the /res/menu subdirectory. Placing the file in /res/menu automatically generates a resource ID called R.menu.my_menu.

Now let's look at how you can use this menu resource ID to populate the options menu. Android provides a class called android.view.MenuInflater to populate Menu objects from XML files. We will use an instance of this MenuInflater to make use of the R.menu.my_menu resource ID to populate a menu object:

```
@Override
public boolean onCreateOptionsMenu(Menu menu)
{
    MenuInflater inflater = getMenuInflater(); //from activity
    inflater.inflate(R.menu.my_menu, menu);

    //It is important to return true to see the menu
    return true;

}
```

In this code, we first get the `MenuInflater` from the `Activity` class and then tell it to inflate the menu XML file into the menu directly.

Responding to XML-Based Menu Items

You haven't yet seen the specific advantage of this approach—it becomes apparent when you start responding to the menu items. You respond to XML menu items the way you respond to menus created programmatically, but with a small difference. As before, you handle the menu items in the `onOptionsItemSelected` callback method. But this time, you will have some help from Android's resources (see Chapter 3 for details on resources). As we mentioned in the section "Structure of an XML Menu Resource File," Android not only generates a resource ID for the XML file, but also generates the necessary menu-item IDs to help you distinguish between the menu items. This is an advantage in terms of responding to the menu items because you don't have to explicitly create and manage their menu-item IDs.

To further elaborate on this, in the case of XML menus you don't have to define constants for these IDs and you don't have to worry about their uniqueness because resource ID generation takes care of that. The following code illustrates this:

```
private void onOptionsItemSelected (MenuItem item)
{
    this.appendMenuItemText(item);
    if (item.getItemId() == R.id.menu_clear)
    {
        this.emptyText();
    }
    else if (item.getItemId() == R.id.menu_dial)
    {
        this.dial();
    }
    else if (item.getItemId() == R.id.menu_testPick)
    {
        IntentsUtils.invokePick(this);
    }
    else if (item.getItemId() == R.id.menu_testGetContent)
    {
        IntentsUtils.invokeGetContent(this);
    }
    else if (item.getItemId() == R.id.menu_show_browser)
    {
```

```
            IntentsUtils.tryOneOfThese(this);
    }
}
```

Notice how the menu-item names from the XML menu resource file have automatically generated menu-item IDs in the R.id space.

A Brief Introduction to Additional XML Menu Tags

As you construct your XML files, you will need to know the various XML tags that are possible. You can quickly get this information by examining the API demos that come with the Android SDK. These Android API demos include a series of menus that help you explore all aspects of Android programming. If you look at the /res/menu subdirectory, you will find a number of XML menu samples. We'll briefly cover some key tags here.

Group Category Tag

In an XML file, you can specify the category of a group by using the menuCategory tag:

```
<group android:id="@+id/some_group_id "
       android:menuCategory="secondary">
```

Checkable Behavior Tags

You can use the checkableBehavior tag to control checkable behavior at a group level:

```
<group android:id="@+id/noncheckable_group"
       android:checkableBehavior="none">
```

You can use the checked tag to control checkable behavior at an item level:

```
<item android:id=".."
      android:title="…"
      android:checked="true" />
```

Tags to Simulate a Submenu

A submenu is represented as a menu element under a menu item:

```
 <item android:title="All without group">
       <menu>
                   <item…>
       </menu>
 </item>
```

Menu Icon Tag

You can use the icon tag to associate an image with a menu item:

```
 <item android:id=".. "
```

```
android:icon="@drawable/some-file" />
```

Menu Enabling/Disabling Tag

You can enable and disable a menu item using the `enabled` tag:

```
<item android:id=".. "
      android:enabled="true"
      android:icon="@drawable/some-file" />
```

Menu Item Shortcuts

You can set a shortcut for a menu item using the `alphabeticShortcut` tag:

```
<item android:id="… "
      android:alphabeticShortcut="a"
    …
  </item>
```

Menu Visibility

You can control a menu item's visibility using the `visible` flag:

```
<item android:id="… "
      android:visible="true"
    …
</item>
```

By now, we have covered options menus, submenus, icon menus, context menus, and alternative menus. We also covered the means and advantages of using XML menus. Now let's turn our attention to Android's support for dialogs.

Using Dialogs in Android

If you are coming from an environment where dialogs are synchronous (especially modal dialogs), you might need to think differently when you work with Android dialogs. Dialogs in Android are asynchronous. This asynchronicity is a bit counterintuitive for modal dialogs; it's as if the front of your brain is having a conversation with someone, while the back of your brain is thinking about something else. However, the "split-brain" model isn't that bad when it comes to computers. This asynchronous approach does increase the handheld's responsiveness.

Not only are Android dialogs asynchronous, but they are also *managed*; that is, they are reused between multiple invocations. This design arose from the need to optimize memory and performance as dialogs are created, shown, and dismantled.

In the following sections we will cover these aspects of Android dialogs in depth. We'll review the need for basic dialogs such as alert dialogs, and show you how to create and use them. We will then show you how to work with *prompt* dialogs—dialogs that ask the user for input and return that input to the program. We will also show you how to load your own view layouts into dialogs.

We will then address the managed nature of Android dialogs by exploring the protocol to create dialogs using callback functions in an activity. Finally, we will take the managed-dialog protocol that Android uses and abstract it out to make the asynchronous managed dialogs as seamless as possible. This abstraction might prove helpful to you in itself, and it will also give us an opportunity to explain the behind-the-scenes dialog architecture.

Designing an Alert Dialog

We will begin our exploration with alert dialogs. *Alert* dialogs commonly contain simple messages about validating forms or debugging. Consider the following debug example that you often find in HTML pages:

```
if (validate(field1) == false)
{
    //indicate that formatting is not valid through an alert dialog
    showAlert("What you have entered in field1 doesn't match required format");
    //set focus to the field
    //..and continue
}
```

You would likely program this dialog in JavaScript through the `alert` JavaScript function, which displays a simple synchronous dialog box containing a message and an OK button. After the user clicks the OK button, the flow of the program continues. This dialog is considered modal as well as synchronous because the next line of code will not be executed until the `alert` function returns.

This type of alert dialog proves useful for debugging. But Android offers no such direct function or dialog. Instead, it supports an alert-dialog builder, a general-purpose facility for constructing and working with alert dialogs. So you can build an alert dialog yourself using the `android.app.AlertDialog.Builder` class. You can use this builder class to construct dialogs that allow users to perform the following tasks:

- Read a message and respond with Yes or No
- Pick an item from a list
- Pick multiple items from a list
- View the progress of an application
- Choose an option from a set of options
- Respond to a prompt before continuing the program

We will show you how to build one of these dialogs and invoke that dialog from a menu item. This approach, which applies to any of these dialogs, consists of these steps:

1. Construct a `Builder` object.

2. Set parameters for the display such as the number of buttons, the list of items, and so on.

3. Set the callback methods for the buttons.

4. Tell the `Builder` to build the dialog. The type of dialog that's built depends on what you've set on the `Builder` object.

5. Use `dialog.show()` to show the dialog.

Listing 5–21 shows the code that implements these steps.

Listing 5–21. *Building and Displaying an Alert Dialog*

```
public class Alerts
{
    public static void showAlert(String message, Context ctx)
    {
        //Create a builder
        AlertDialog.Builder builder = new AlertDialog.Builder(ctx);
        builder.setTitle("Alert Window");

        //add buttons and listener
        PromptListener pl = new EmptyListener();
        builder.setPositiveButton("OK", pl);

        //Create the dialog
        AlertDialog ad = builder.create();

        //show
        ad.show();
    }
}

public class EmptyListener
implements android.content.DialogInterface.OnClickListener {
    public void onClick(DialogInterface v, int buttonId)
    {
    }
}
```

You can invoke the code in Listing 5–21 by creating a menu item in your test harness and responding to it using this code:

```
if (item.getItemId() == R.id.menu_simple_alert)
{
    Alerts.showAlert("Simple Sample Alert", this);
}
```

The result will look like the screen shown in Figure 5–4.

Figure 5–4. *A simple alert dialog*

The code for this simple alert dialog is straightforward (see Listing 5–21 and the code snippet that appears after it). Even the listener part is easy to understand. Essentially, we have nothing to perform when the button is clicked. We just created an empty listener to register against the OK button. The only odd part is that you don't use a new to create the dialog; instead, you set parameters and ask the alert-dialog builder to create it.

Designing a Prompt Dialog

Now that you've successfully created a simple alert dialog, let's tackle an alert dialog that's a little more complex: the prompt dialog. Another JavaScript staple, the prompt dialog shows the user a hint or question and asks for input via an edit box. The prompt dialog returns that string to the program so it can continue. This will be a good example to study because it features a number of facilities provided by the Builder class and also allows us to examine the synchronous, asynchronous, modal, and nonmodal nature of Android dialogs.

Here are the steps you need to take in order to create a prompt dialog:

1. Come up with a layout view for your prompt dialog.

2. Load the layout into a View class.

3. Construct a Builder object.

4. Set the view in the Builder object.

5. Set the buttons along with their callbacks to capture the entered text.

6. Create the dialog using the alert-dialog builder.

7. Show the dialog.

Now we'll show you the code for each step.

XML Layout File for the Prompt Dialog

When we show the prompt dialog, we need to show a prompt TextView followed by an edit box where a user can type a reply. Listing 5–22 contains the XML layout file for the prompt dialog. If you call this file prompt_layout.xml, then you need to place it in the /res/layout subdirectory to produce a resource ID called R.layout.prompt_layout.

Listing 5–22. *The prompt_layout.xml File*

```
<LinearLayout xmlns:android="http://schemas.android.com/apk/res/android"
    android:layout_width="fill_parent"
    android:layout_height="wrap_content"
    android:orientation="vertical">

    <TextView
        android:id="@+id/promptmessage"
        android:layout_height="wrap_content"
        android:layout_width="wrap_content"
        android:layout_marginLeft="20dip"
        android:layout_marginRight="20dip"
        android:text="Your text goes here"
        android:gravity="left"
        android:textAppearance="?android:attr/textAppearanceMedium" />

    <EditText
        android:id="@+id/editText_prompt"
        android:layout_height="wrap_content"
        android:layout_width="fill_parent"
        android:layout_marginLeft="20dip"
        android:layout_marginRight="20dip"
        android:scrollHorizontally="true"
        android:autoText="false"
        android:capitalize="none"
        android:gravity="fill_horizontal"
        android:textAppearance="?android:attr/textAppearanceMedium" />

</LinearLayout>
```

Setting Up an Alert-Dialog Builder with a User View

Let's combine steps 2 through 4 from our instructions to create a prompt dialog: loading the XML view and setting it up in the alert-dialog builder. Android provides a class called android.view.LayoutInflater to create a View object from an XML layout definition file. We will use an instance of the LayoutInflater to populate the view for our dialog based on the XML layout file (see Listing 5–23).

Listing 5-23. *Inflating a Layout into a Dialog*

```
LayoutInflater li = LayoutInflater.from(ctx);
View view = li.inflate(R.layout.promptdialog, null);

//get a builder and set the view
AlertDialog.Builder builder = new AlertDialog.Builder(ctx);
builder.setTitle("Prompt");
builder.setView(view);
```

In Listing 5-23, we get the LayoutInflater using the static method LayoutInflater.from(ctx) and then use the LayoutInflater object to inflate the XML to create a View object. We then configure an alert-dialog builder with a title and the view that we just created.

Setting Up Buttons and Listeners

We now move on to step 5: setting up buttons. You need to provide OK and Cancel buttons so the user can respond to the prompt. If the user clicks Cancel, then the program doesn't need to read any text for the prompt. If the user clicks OK, the program gets the value from the text and passes it back to the activity.

To set up these buttons, you need a listener to respond to these callbacks. We will give you the code for the listener in the "Prompt Dialog Listener" section, but first examine the button setup in Listing 5-24.

Listing 5-24. *Setting Up OK and Cancel Buttons*

```
//add buttons and listener
PromptListener pl = new PromptListener(view,ctx);
builder.setPositiveButton("OK", pl);
builder.setNegativeButton("Cancel", pl);
```

The code in Listing 5-24 assumes that the name of the listener class is PromptListener. We have registered this listener against each button.

Creating and Showing the Prompt Dialog

Finally, we finish up with steps 6 and 7: creating and showing the prompt dialog. That's easy to do once you have the alert-dialog builder (see Listing 5-25).

Listing 5-25. *Telling the Alert-Dialog Builder to Create the Dialog*

```
//get the dialog
AlertDialog ad = builder.create();
ad.show();

//return the prompt
return pl.getPromptReply();
```

The last line uses the listener to return the reply for the prompt. Now, as promised, we'll show you the code for the PromptListener class.

Prompt Dialog Listener

The prompt dialog interacts with an activity through a listener callback class called PromptListener. The class has one callback method called onClick, and the button ID that is passed to onClick identifies what type of button is clicked. The rest of the code is easy to follow (see Listing 5–26). When the user enters text and clicks the OK button, the value of the text is transferred to the promptReply field. Otherwise, the value stays null.

Listing 5–26. *PromptListener, the Listener Callback Class*

```
public class PromptListener
implements android.content.DialogInterface.OnClickListener
{
  // local variable to return the prompt reply value
  private String promptReply = null;

  //Keep a variable for the view to retrieve the prompt value
  View promptDialogView = null;

 //Take in the view in the constructor
   public PromptListener(View inDialogView)   {
        promptDialogView = inDialogView;
   }

//Call back method from dialogs
   public void onClick(DialogInterface v, int buttonId)   {
        if (buttonId == DialogInterface.BUTTON1)     {
            //ok button
            promptReply = getPromptText();
      }
      else    {
         //cancel button
         promptValue = null;
      }
   }

  //Just an access method for what is in the edit box
   private String getPromptText()   {
       EditText et = (EditText)
       promptDialogView.findViewById(R.id.promptEditTextControlId);
       return et.getText().toString();
   }
   public String getPromptReply() { return promptReply; }
}
```

Putting It All Together

Now that we have explained each piece of code that goes into a prompt dialog, we'll present it in one place so you can use it to test the dialog (see Listing 5–27). We have excluded the PromptListener class because it appears separately in Listing 5–26.

Listing 5–27. *Code to Test the Prompt Dialog*

```
public class Alerts
{
   public static String prompt(String message, Context ctx)
```

```
{
    //load some kind of a view
    LayoutInflater li = LayoutInflater.from(ctx);
    View view = li.inflate(R.layout.promptdialog, null);

    //get a builder and set the view
    AlertDialog.Builder builder = new AlertDialog.Builder(ctx);
    builder.setTitle("Prompt");
    builder.setView(view);

    //add buttons and listener
    PromptListener pl = new PromptListener(view,ctx);
    builder.setPositiveButton("OK", pl);
    builder.setNegativeButton("Cancel", pl);

    //get the dialog
    AlertDialog ad = builder.create();

    //show
    ad.show();

    return pl.getPromptReply();
  }
}
```

You can invoke the code in Listing 5–27 by creating a menu item in the test harness described at the beginning of this chapter and responding to that menu item using this code:

```
if (item.getItemId() == R.id.menu_simple_alert)
{
    String  reply = Alerts.showPrompt("Your text goes here", this);
}
```

The result should look like the screen shown in Figure 5–5.

Figure 5–5. *A simple prompt dialog*

After writing all this code, however, you will notice that the prompt dialog always returns null even if the user enters text into it. As it turns out, in the following code the show() method will invoke the dialog asynchronously:

```
ad.show() //dialog.show
return pl.getPromptReply(); // listener.getpromptReply()
```

This means the getPromptReply() method gets called for the prompt value before the user has time to enter text and click the OK button. This fallacy takes us to the heart of the nature of Android dialogs.

The Nature of Dialogs in Android

As we've mentioned, displaying dialogs in Android is an asynchronous process. Once a dialog is shown, the main thread that invoked the dialog returns and continues to process the rest of the code. This doesn't mean that the dialog isn't *modal*. The dialog is still modal. The mouse clicks apply only to the dialog, while the parent activity goes back to its message loop.

On some windowing systems, modal dialogs behave a bit differently. The caller is blocked until the user provides a response through the dialog. (This block can be a virtual block instead of a real block.) On the Windows operating system, the message-dispatching thread starts dispatching to the dialog and suspends dispatching to the parent window. When the dialog closes, the thread returns to the parent window. This makes the call synchronous.

Such an approach might not work for a handheld device, where unexpected events on the device are more frequent and the main thread needs to respond to those events. To accomplish this level of responsiveness, Android returns the main thread to its message loop right away.

The implication of this model is that you cannot have a simple dialog where you ask for a response and wait for it before moving on. In fact, your programming model for dialogs must differ in its incorporation of callbacks.

Rearchitecting the Prompt Dialog

Let us revisit the problematic code in the previous prompt-dialog implementation:

```
if (item.getItemId() == R.id.menu_simple_alert)
{
    String  reply = Alerts.showPrompt("Your text goes here", this);
}
```

As we have proven, the value of the string variable reply will be null, because the prompt dialog initiated by Alerts.showPrompt() is incapable of returning a value on the same thread. The only way you can accomplish this is to have the activity implement the callback method directly and not rely on the PromptListener class. You do this in the Activity class by implementing the OnClickListener:

```
public class SampleActivity extends Activity
implements android.content.DialogInterface.OnClickListener
{
...... other code

if (item.getItemId() == R.id.menu_simple_alert)
{
    Alerts.showPrompt("Your text goes here", this);
}
.....
public void onClick(DialogInterface v, int buttonId)
{
        //figure out a way here to read the reply string from the dialog
}
```

As you can see from this onClick callback method, you can correctly read the variables from the instantiated dialog because the user will have closed the dialog by the time this method is called.

It is perfectly legitimate to use dialogs this way. However, Android provides a supplemental mechanism to optimize performance by introducing *managed dialogs*—dialogs that are reused between multiple invocations. You'll still need to use callbacks when you work with managed dialogs, though. In fact, everything you've learned in implementing the prompt dialog will help you work with managed dialogs and understand the motivation behind them.

Working with Managed Dialogs

Android follows a managed-dialog protocol to promote the reuse of previously created dialog instances rather than creating new dialogs in response to actions. In this section, we will talk about the details of the managed-dialog protocol and show you how to implement the alert dialog as a managed dialog. However, in our view, the managed-dialog protocol makes using dialogs tedious. We will subsequently develop a small framework to abstract out most of this protocol to make it easier to work with managed dialogs.

Understanding the Managed-Dialog Protocol

The primary goal of the managed-dialog protocol is to reuse a dialog if it's invoked a second time, or subsequently. It is similar to using object pools in Java. The managed-dialog protocol consists of these steps:

1. Assign a unique ID to each dialog you want to create and use. Suppose one of the dialogs is tagged as 1.

2. Tell Android to show a dialog called 1.

3. Android checks whether the current activity already has a dialog tagged as 1. If the dialog exists, Android shows it without re-creating it. Android calls the onPrepareDialog() function before showing the dialog, for cleanup purposes.

4. If the dialog doesn't exist, Android calls the onCreateDialog method by passing the dialog ID (1, in this case).

5. You, as the programmer, need to override the onCreateDialog method. You must create the dialog using the alert-dialog builder and return it. But before creating the dialog, your code needs to determine which dialog ID needs to be created. You'll need a switch statement to figure this out.

6. Android shows the dialog.

7. The dialog calls the callbacks when its buttons are clicked.

Let's now use this protocol to re-implement our non-managed alert dialog as a managed alert dialog.

Recasting the Non-Managed Dialog As a Managed Dialog

We will follow each of the steps laid out to re-implement the alert dialog. Let's start by defining a unique ID for this dialog in the context of a given activity:

```
//unique dialog id
private static final int DIALOG_ALERT_ID = 1;
```

That is simple enough. We have just created an ID to represent a dialog to orchestrate the callbacks. This ID will allow us to do the following in response to a menu item:

```
 if (item.getItemId() == R.id.menu_simple_alert)
{
     showDialog(this.DIALOG_ALERT_ID);
}
```

The Android SDK method showDialog triggers a call to the onCreateDialog() method. Android is smart enough not to call onCreateDialog() multiple times. When this method is called, we need to create the dialog and return it to Android. Android then keeps the created dialog internally for reuse purposes. Here is the sample code to create the dialog based on a unique ID:

```
@Override
protected Dialog onCreateDialog(int id) {
    switch (id) {
        case DIALOG_ALERT_ID:
            return createAlertDialog();
    }
    return null;
}

private Dialog createAlertDialog()
{
    AlertDialog.Builder builder = new AlertDialog.Builder(this);
    builder.setTitle("Alert");
    builder.setMessage("some message");
    EmptyOnClickListener emptyListener = new EmptyOnClickListener();
    builder.setPositiveButton("Ok", emptyListener );
    AlertDialog ad = builder.create();
    return ad;
}
```

Notice how onCreateDialog() has to figure out the incoming ID to identify a matching dialog. createAlertDialog() itself is kept in a separate function and parallels the alert-dialog creation described in the previous sections. This code also uses the same EmptyOnClickListener that was used when we worked with the alert dialog.

Because the dialog is created only once, you need a mechanism if you want to change something in the dialog every time you show it. You do this through the onPrepareDialog() callback method:

```
@Override
protected void onPrepareDialog(int id, Dialog dialog) {
    switch (id) {
    case DIALOG_ALERT_ID:
        prepareAlertDialog(dialog);
    }
}

private void prepareAlertDialog(Dialog d)       {
    AlertDialog ad = (AlertDialog)d;
    //change something about this dialog
```

```
    }
```

With this code in place, showDialog(1) will work. Even if you were to invoke this method multiple times, your onCreateMethod would get called only once. You can follow the same protocol to redo the prompt dialog.

So responding to dialog callbacks is work, but the managed-dialog protocol adds even more work. After looking at the managed-dialog protocol, we got the idea to abstract out the protocol and rearrange it in such a way that it accomplishes two goals:

- Moving the dialog identification and creation out of the activity class

- Concentrating the dialog creation and response in a dedicated dialog class

In the next subsection, we will go through the design of this framework and then use it to re-create both the alert and prompt dialogs.

Simplifying the Managed-Dialog Protocol

As you've probably noticed, working with managed-alert dialogs can become quite messy and can pollute the mainline code. If we abstract out this protocol into a simpler protocol, the new protocol could look like this:

1. Create an instance of a dialog you want by using new and keeping it as a local variable. Call this dialog1.

2. Show the dialog using dialog1.show().

3. Implement one method in the activity called dialogFinished().

4. In the dialogFinished() method, read attributes from dialog1 such as dialog1.getValue1().

Under this scheme, showing a managed alert dialog will look like this:

```
....class MyActivity ....
{
   //new dialog
   ManagedAlertDialog  mad = new ManagedAlertDialog("message", ..., .. );

   ....some menu method
   if (item.getItemId() == R.id.menu_simple_alert)
   {
      //show dialog
      mad.show();
   }
   ....
   //access the mad dialog for internals if you want
   dialogFinsihed()
   {
      ....
      //use values from dialog
      mad.getA();
```

```
        mad.getB();
    }
}
```

We think this is a far simpler model to work with dialogs. You don't have to remember IDs, you don't have to pollute the mainline code with dialog creation, and you can use derived dialog objects directly to access values.

The principle of this abstraction is as follows. As a first step, we abstract out the creation of a dialog and the preparation of that dialog into a class that identifies a base dialog. We call this interface `IDialogProtocol`. This dialog also has a `show()` method on it directly. These dialogs are collected and kept in a registry in the base class for an activity, and they use their IDs as keys. The base activity will demultiplex the `onCreate`, `onPrepare`, and `onClick` calls based on their IDs and reroute them to the dialog class. This architecture is further illustrated in Figure 5–6.

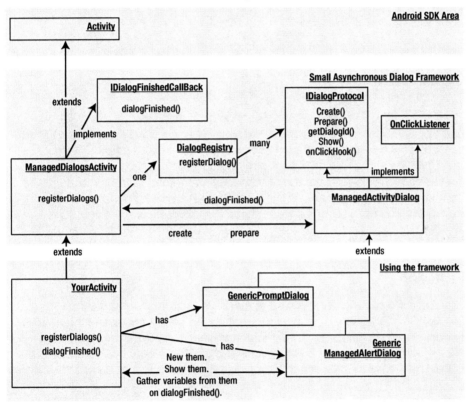

Figure 5–6. *A simple managed-dialog framework*

Listing 5–28 illustrates the utility of this framework.

Listing 5–28. *The Abstraction of the Managed-Dialog Protocol*

```
public class MainActivity extends ManagedDialogsActivity
{
    //dialog 1
```

```
    private GenericManagedAlertDialog gmad =
        new GenericManagedAlertDialog(this,1,"InitialValue");

    //dialog 2
    private GenericPromptDialog gmpd =
        new GenericPromptDialog(this,2,"InitialValue");

    //menu items to start the dialogs
    else if (item.getItemId() == R.id.menu_simple_alert)
    {
        gmad.show();
    }
    else if (item.getItemId() == R.id.menu_simple_prompt)
    {
        gmpd.show();
    }

    //dealing with call backs
    public void dialogFinished(ManagedActivityDialog dialog, int buttonId)
    {
        if (dialog.getDialogId() == gmpd.getDialogId())
        {
            String replyString = gmpd.getReplyString();
        }
    }
}
```

To make use of this framework, you start by extending ManagedDialogsActivity. Then you instantiate the dialogs you need, each of which derives from ManagedActivityDialog. In a menu-item response, you can simply do a show() on these dialogs. The dialogs themselves take the necessary parameters up front in order to be created and shown. Although we are passing a dialog ID, we don't need to remember those IDs anymore. You could even abstract these IDs out completely if you'd like.

Now we'll explore each of the classes shown in Figure 5–6.

IDialogProtocol

The IDialogProtocol interface defines what it means to be a managed dialog. Responsibilities of a managed dialog include creating the dialog and preparing it every time it is shown. It also makes sense to delegate the show functionality to the dialog itself. A dialog also must recognize button clicks and call the respective parent of the dialog closure. The following interface code represents these ideas as a set of functions:

```
public interface IDialogProtocol
{
    public Dialog create();
    public void prepare(Dialog dialog);
    public int getDialogId();
    public void show();
    public void onClickHook(int buttonId);
}
```

ManagedActivityDialog

The abstract class ManagedActivityDialog provides the common implementation for all
the dialog classes wanting to implement the IDialogProtocol interface. It leaves the
create and prepare functions to be overridden by the base classes, but provides
implementations for the rest of the IDialogProtocol methods. ManagedActivityDialog
also informs the parent activity that the dialog has finished after responding to a button-
click event. It uses the template-hook pattern and allows the derived classes to
specialize the hook method onClickHook. This class is also responsible for redirecting
the show() method to the parent activity, thereby providing a more natural
implementation for show(). You should use the ManagedActivityDialog class as the
base class for all your new dialogs (see Listing 5–29).

Listing 5–29. *The ManagedActivityDialog Class*

```
public abstract class ManagedActivityDialog implements IDialogProtocol
    ,android.content.DialogInterface.OnClickListener

{
    private ManagedDialogsActivity mActivity;
    private int mDialogId;
    public ManagedActivityDialog(ManagedDialogsActivity a, int dialogId)
    {
        mActivity = a;
        mDialogId = dialogId;
    }
    public int getDialogId()
    {
        return mDialogId;
    }
    public void show()
    {
        mActivity.showDialog(mDialogId);
    }
    public void onClick(DialogInterface v, int buttonId)
    {
        onClickHook(buttonId);
        this.mActivity.dialogFinished(this, buttonId);
    }
}
```

DialogRegistry

The DialogRegistry class is responsible for two things. It keeps a mapping between the
dialog IDs and the actual dialog (factory) instances. It also translates the generic
onCreate and onPrepare calls to the specific dialogs using the ID-to-object mapping. The
ManagedDialogsActivity uses the DialogRegistry class as a repository to register new
dialogs (see Listing 5–30).

Listing 5–30. *The DialogRegistry Class*

```
public class DialogRegistry
{
    SparseArray<IDialogProtocol> idsToDialogs
```

```
                                                   = new SparseArray();

    public void registerDialog(IDialogProtocol dialog)
    {
        idsToDialogs.put(dialog.getDialogId(),dialog);
    }

    public Dialog create(int id)
    {
        IDialogProtocol dp = idsToDialogs.get(id);
        if (dp == null) return null;

        return dp.create();
    }
    public void prepare(Dialog dialog, int id)
    {
        IDialogProtocol dp = idsToDialogs.get(id);
        if (dp == null)
        {
            throw new RuntimeException("Dialog id is not registered:" + id);
        }
        dp.prepare(dialog);
    }
}
```

ManagedDialogsActivity

The ManagedDialogsActivity class acts as a base class for your activities that support managed dialogs. It keeps a single instance of DialogRegistry to keep track of the managed dialogs identified by the IDialogProtocol interface. It allows the derived activities to register their dialogs through the registerDialogs() function. As shown in Figure 5–6, it is also responsible for transferring the create and prepare semantics to the respective dialog instance by locating that dialog instance in the dialog registry. Finally, it provides the callback method dialogFinished for each dialog in the dialog registry (see Listing 5–31).

Listing 5–31. *The ManagedDialogsActivity Class*

```
public class ManagedDialogsActivity extends Activity
            implements IDialogFinishedCallBack
{
    //A registry for managed dialogs
    private DialogRegistry dr = new DialogRegistry();

    public void onCreate(Bundle savedInstanceState) {
        super.onCreate(savedInstanceState);
        this.registerDialogs();
    }

    protected void registerDialogs()
    {
        // does nothing
        // have the derived classes override this method
        // to register their dialogs
        // example:
```

```
        // registerDialog(this.DIALOG_ALERT_ID_3, gmad);

    }
    public void registerDialog(IDialogProtocol dialog)
    {
        this.dr.registerDialog(dialog);
    }

    @Override
    protected Dialog onCreateDialog(int id) {
            return this.dr.create(id);
    }
    @Override
    protected void onPrepareDialog(int id, Dialog dialog) {
            this.dr.prepare(dialog, id);
    }

    public void dialogFinished(ManagedActivityDialog dialog, int buttonId)
    {
        //nothing to do
        //have derived classes override this
    }
}
```

IDialogFinishedCallBack

The IDialogFinishedCallBack interface allows the ManagedActivityDialog class to tell
the parent activity that the dialog has finished and that the parent activity can call
methods on the dialog to retrieve parameters. Usually a ManagedDialogsActivity
implements this interface and acts as a parent activity to the ManagedActivityDialog
(see Listing 5–32).

Listing 5–32. *The IDialogFinishedCallBack Interface*

```
public interface IDialogFinishedCallBack
{
        public static int OK_BUTTON = -1;
        public static int CANCEL_BUTTON = -2;
        public void dialogFinished(ManagedActivityDialog dialog, int buttonId);
}
```

GenericManagedAlertDialog

GenericManagedAlertDialog is the alert-dialog implementation; it extends
ManagedActivityDialog. This class is responsible for creating the actual alert dialog
using the alert-dialog builder. It also carries all the information it needs as local variables.
Because GenericManagedAlertDialog implements a simple alert dialog, it does nothing
in the onClickHook method. The key thing to note is that when you use this approach,
GenericManagedAlertDialog encapsulates all pertinent information in one place (see
Listing 5–33). That keeps the mainline code in the activity squeaky clean.

Listing 5–33. *The GenericManagedAlertDialog Class*

```
public class GenericManagedAlertDialog extends ManagedActivityDialog
{
    private String alertMessage = null;
    private Context ctx = null;
    public GenericManagedAlertDialog(ManagedDialogsActivity inActivity,
                                     int dialogId,
                                     String initialMessage)
    {
        super(inActivity,dialogId);
        alertMessage = initialMessage;
        ctx = inActivity;
    }
    public Dialog create()
    {
        AlertDialog.Builder builder = new AlertDialog.Builder(ctx);
        builder.setTitle("Alert");
        builder.setMessage(alertMessage);
        builder.setPositiveButton("Ok", this );
        AlertDialog ad = builder.create();
        return ad;
    }

    public void prepare(Dialog dialog)
    {
        AlertDialog ad = (AlertDialog)dialog;
        ad.setMessage(alertMessage);
    }
    public void setAlertMessage(String inAlertMessage)
    {
        alertMessage = inAlertMessage;
    }
    public void onClickHook(int buttonId)
    {
        //nothing to do
        //no local variables to set
    }
}
```

GenericPromptDialog

The GenericPromptDialog class encapsulates all the needs of a prompt dialog by extending the ManagedActivityDialog class and providing the necessary create and prepare methods (see Listing 5–34). You can also see that it saves the reply text in a local variable so that the parent activity can get to it in the dialogFinished callback method.

Listing 5–34. *The GenericPromptDialog Class*

```
public class GenericPromptDialog extends ManagedActivityDialog
{
    private String mPromptMessage = null;
    private View promptView = null;
    String promptValue = null;
```

```
private Context ctx = null;
public GenericPromptDialog(ManagedDialogsActivity inActivity,
        int dialogId,
        String promptMessage)
{
    super(inActivity,dialogId);
    mPromptMessage = promptMessage;
    ctx = inActivity;
}
public Dialog create()
{
    LayoutInflater li = LayoutInflater.from(ctx);
    promptView = li.inflate(R.layout.promptdialog, null);
    AlertDialog.Builder builder = new AlertDialog.Builder(ctx);
    builder.setTitle("prompt");
    builder.setView(promptView);
    builder.setPositiveButton("OK", this);
    builder.setNegativeButton("Cancel", this);
    AlertDialog ad = builder.create();
    return ad;
}

public void prepare(Dialog dialog)
{
    //nothing for now
}
public void onClickHook(int buttonId)
{
    if (buttonId == DialogInterface.BUTTON1)
    {
        //ok button
        String promptValue = getEnteredText();
    }
}
private String getEnteredText()
{
    EditText et =
        (EditText)
        promptView.findViewById(R.id.editText_prompt);
    String enteredText = et.getText().toString();
    Log.d("xx",enteredText);
    return enteredText;
}
}
```

Summary

In this chapter we have given you a thorough understanding of Android menus and dialogs, which are key components of UI programming. You learned how to work with the various kinds of menus available in Android. You also saw how to work with menus more effectively by using XML menu resources.

We presented a test harness for the menus, which you'll find useful not only for testing menus, but also for testing other programs you end up writing. Menus provide a simple way to invoke and test new functionality.

You also saw that dialogs present a special challenge in Android. We showed you the implications of asynchronous dialogs and presented an abstraction to simplify the managed dialogs.

The knowledge you gained in this chapter and in Chapter 5 should give you a good foundation for writing your own complex UI programs. This foundation should also serve you well in preparation for the next chapter on animation.

Chapter 6

Unveiling 2D Animation

The previous chapters gave you a broad introduction to UI programming in Android. In this chapter, we would like to further strengthen your ability to create intuitive and appealing applications on the Android Platform by covering the animation capabilities of the Android SDK. If our experience is any guide, animation puts a lot of creativity at the hands of a programmer.

Animation is a process by which an object on a screen changes its color, position, size, or orientation over time. Android supports three types of animation: *frame-by-frame animation*, which occurs when a series of frames is drawn one after the other at regular intervals; *layout animation*, in which you animate views inside a container view such as lists and tables; and *view animation*, in which you animate any general-purpose view. The latter two types fall into the category of *tweening animation*, which involves the drawings in between the key drawings. The idea is that knowing the beginning state and ending state of a drawing allows an artist to vary certain aspect of the drawing in time. This varying aspect could be color, position, size, etc. With computers, you accomplish this kind of animation by changing the intermediate values at regular intervals and redrawing the surface. We will cover each type of animation using working examples and in-depth analysis.

Frame-by-frame animation is the simplest of the three animation types, so we'll cover that one in this chapter's first section. We'll show you how it works, how to tell a story, and how to use the `AnimationDrawable` class to execute the frames at a certain refresh rate. We will present an example, with screenshots and code, in which you'll animate an image of a ball moving along the circumference of a circle.

In the second section, we'll cover layout animation, which is more involved than frame-by-frame animation but still easier than view animation. We will talk about scale animation (changing size), translate animation (changing position), rotate animation (changing orientation), and alpha animation (changing a color gradient). We will show you how to declare these animations in an XML file and associate the animation IDs with a container view such as a list box. As an example, you'll apply a variety of animation transformations to a series of text items in a list box. We will also cover interpolators, which define an animation's rate of change, and animation sets, which contain an aggregated set of individual animations.

In the last section on view animation, we will cover animating a view by changing the transformation matrices. You'll need a good understanding of transformation matrices to grasp the material in this section, so we'll provide several examples to illustrate their use. Android also introduces the idea of a Camera to simulate 3D-like viewing capabilities by projecting a 2D view moving in 3D space. This section will illustrate these ideas by taking a ListView and rotating it in 3D space.

Frame-by-Frame Animation

Frame-by-frame animation is the simple process of showing a series of images in succession at quick intervals so that the final effect is that of an object moving. This is how movie or film projectors work. We'll explore an example in which we'll design an image and save that image as a number of distinct images, where each one differs from the other slightly. Then we will take the collection of those images and run them through the sample code to simulate animation.

Planning for Frame-by-Frame Animation

Before you start writing code, you first need to plan the animation sequence using a series of drawings. As an example of this planning exercise, Figure 6–1 shows a set of same-sized circles with a colored ball on each of the circles placed at a different position. You can take a series of these pictures showing the circle at the same size and position with the colored ball at different points along the circle's border. Once you save seven or eight of these frames, you can use animation to suggest that the colored ball is moving around the circle.

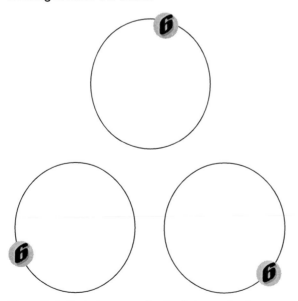

Figure 6–1. *Designing your animation before coding it*

Give the image a base name of colored-ball. Then you can store eight of these images in the /res/drawable subdirectory so that you can access them using their resource IDs. The name of each image will have the pattern colored-ballN, where N is the digit representing the image number. When you have finished with the animation, you want it to look like Figure 6–2.

Figure 6–2. *Frame-by-frame animation test harness*

The primary area in this activity is used by the animation view. We have included a button to start and stop the animation to observe its behavior. We have also included a debug scratch pad at the top, so you can write any significant events to it as you experiment with this program. Let us see now how we could create the layout for such an activity.

Creating the Activity

Start by creating the basic XML layout file in the /res/layout subdirectory (see Listing 6–1).

Listing 6–1. *XML Layout File for the Frame Animation Example*

```
<?xml version="1.0" encoding="utf-8"?>
<!-filename: /res/layout/frame_animations_layout.xml -->
<LinearLayout xmlns:android="http://schemas.android.com/apk/res/android"
    android:orientation="vertical"
    android:layout_width="fill_parent"
    android:layout_height="fill_parent"
    >
<TextView android:id="@+id/textViewId1"
    android:layout_width="fill_parent"
    android:layout_height="wrap_content"
```

```
        android:text="Debug Scratch Pad"
        />
    <Button
        android:id="@+id/startFAButtonId"
        android:layout_width="fill_parent"
        android:layout_height="wrap_content"
        android:text="Start Animation"
    />
    <ImageView
            android:id="@+id/animationImage"
            android:layout_width="fill_parent"
            android:layout_height="wrap_content"
            />
</LinearLayout>
```

The first control is the debug-scratch text control, which is a simple TextView. You then add a button to start and stop the animation. The last view is the ImageView, where you will play the animation. Once you have the layout, create an activity to load this view (see Listing 6–2).

Listing 6–2. *Activity to Load the ImageView*

```
public class FrameAnimationActivity extends Activity
{
    @Override
    public void onCreate(Bundle savedInstanceState)
    {
        super.onCreate(savedInstanceState);
        setContentView(R.layout.frame_animations_layout);
    }
}
```

You will be able to run this activity from any menu item you might have in your current application by executing the following code:

```
Intent intent = new Intent(inActivity,FrameAnimationActivity.class);
inActivity.startActivity(intent);
```

At this point, you will see an activity that looks like the one in Figure 6–3.

Adding Animation to the Activity

Now that you have the activity and layout in place, we'll show you how to add animation to this sample. In Android, you accomplish frame-by-frame animation through a class in the graphics package called AnimationDrawable. You can tell from its name that it is like any other drawable that can work as a background for any view. For example the background bitmaps are represented as Drawables. This class AnimationDrawable, in addition to being a Drawable, can take a list of other Drawable resources (like images) and render them at specified intervals. This class is really a thin wrapper around the animation support provided by the basic Drawable class.

Figure 6–3. *Frame-by-frame animation activity*

TIP: The `Drawable` class enables animation by asking its container or view to invoke a `Runnable` class that essentially redraws the `Drawable` using a different set of parameters. Note that you don't need to know these internal implementation details to use the `AnimationDrawable` class. But if your needs are more complex, you can look at the `AnimationDrawable` source code for guidance in writing your own animation protocols.

To make use of the `AnimationDrawable` class, start with a set of `Drawable` resources placed in the `/res/drawable` subdirectory. An example would be a set of images placed in the /res/drawable subdirectory. In our case these will be the eight similar, but slightly different, images that we talked about in the "Planning for Frame-by-Frame Animation" section. You will then construct an XML file that defines the list of frames (see Listing 6–3). This XML file will need to be placed in the /res/drawable subdirectory as well.

Listing 6–3. *XML File Defining the List of Frames to Be Animated*

```
<animation-list xmlns:android="http://schemas.android.com/apk/res/android"
android:oneshot="false">
    <item android:drawable="@drawable/colored_ball1" android:duration="50" />
    <item android:drawable="@drawable/colored_ball2" android:duration="50" />
    <item android:drawable="@drawable/colored_ball3" android:duration="50" />
    <item android:drawable="@drawable/colored_ball4" android:duration="50" />
    <item android:drawable="@drawable/colored_ball5" android:duration="50" />
    <item android:drawable="@drawable/colored_ball6" android:duration="50" />
    <item android:drawable="@drawable/colored_ball7" android:duration="50" />
    <item android:drawable="@drawable/colored_ball8" android:duration="50" />
</animation-list>
```

Each frame points to one of the colored-ball images you have assembled through their resource IDs. The animation-list tag essentially gets converted into an AnimationDrawable object representing the collection of images. You will then need to set this Drawable as a background resource for our ImageView in the sample. Assuming that the file name for this XML file is frame_animation.xml and that it resides in the /res/drawable subdirectory, you can use the following code to set the AnimationDrawable as the background of the ImageView:

```
view.setBackGroundResource(Resource.drawable.frame_animation);
```

With this code, Android realizes that the resource ID Resource.drawable.frame_animation is an XML resource and accordingly constructs a suitable AnimationDrawable Java object for it before setting it as the background. Once this is set, you can access this AnimationDrawable object by doing a get on the view object like this:

```
Object  backgroundObject = view.getBackground();
AnimationDrawable ad = (AnimationDrawable)backgroundObject;
```

Once you have the AnimationDrawable, you can use the start() and stop() methods of this object to start and stop the animation. Here are two other important methods on this object:

```
setOneShot();
addFrame(drawable, duration);
```

The setOneShot() method runs the animation once and then stops. The addFrame() method adds a new frame using a Drawable object and sets its display duration. The functionality of the addFrame() method resembles that of the XML tag android:drawable.

Put this all together to get the complete code for our frame-by-frame animation test harness (see Listing 6–4).

Listing 6–4. *Complete Code for the Frame-by-Frame Animation Test Harness*

```
public class FrameAnimationActivity extends Activity {
    @Override
    public void onCreate(Bundle savedInstanceState)
    {
        super.onCreate(savedInstanceState);
        setContentView(R.layout.frame_animations_layout);
        this.setupButton();
    }

    private void setupButton()
    {
        Button b = (Button)this.findViewById(R.id.startFAButtonId);
        b.setOnClickListener(
            new Button.OnClickListener(){
                public void onClick(View v)
                {
                    parentButtonClicked(v);
                }
            });
    }
    private void parentButtonClicked(View v)
```

```
{
    animate();
}
private void animate()
{
    ImageView imgView =
        (ImageView)findViewById(R.id.animationImage);
    imgView.setVisibility(ImageView.VISIBLE);
    imgView.setBackgroundResource(R.drawable.frame_animation);

    AnimationDrawable frameAnimation =
        (AnimationDrawable) imgView.getBackground();

    if (frameAnimation.isRunning())
    {
        frameAnimation.stop();
    }
    else
    {
        frameAnimation.stop();
        frameAnimation.start();
    }
}
}//eof-class
```

The animate() method locates the ImageView in the current activity and sets its background to the AnimationDrawable identified by the resource R.drawable.frame_animation. The code then retrieves this object and performs the animation. The Start/Stop button is set up such that if the animation is running, clicking the button will stop it; if the animation is in a stopped state, clicking the button will start it.

Note that if you set the OneShot parameter of the animation list to true, then the animation will stop after executing once. However, there is no clear-cut way to know when that happens. Although the animation ends when it plays the last picture, you have no callback telling you when it finishes. Because of this, there isn't a direct way to invoke another action in response to the completed animation.

That drawback aside, you can bring great visual effects to bear by drawing a number of images in succession through the simple process of frame-by-frame animation.

Layout Animation

As you have seen, frame-by-frame animation is a quick and dirty way to add visual effects to your Android applications. Layout animation is almost as simple. You'll use layout animation with the ListView and GridView, which are the two most commonly-used controls in Android. Specifically, you'll use layout animation to add visual effects to the way each item in a ListView or GridView is displayed. In fact, you can use this type of animation on all controls derived from a ViewGroup.

As we pointed out at the beginning of this chapter, layout animation works by applying *tweening* principles to each view that is part of the layout being animated. Tweening, as mentioned earlier, is a process in which a number of the view's properties are changed at regular intervals. Every view in Android has a transformation matrix that maps the view to the screen. By changing this matrix in a number of ways, you can accomplish scaling, rotation, and movement (translation) of the view. By changing the transparency of the view from 0 to 1, for example, you can accomplish what is called an *alpha* animation.

In this section, we will offer a simple test harness to learn, test, and experiment with layout-animation capabilities. We will show you how to attach a tweening animation to a `ListView`. We will also introduce and explain the idea of interpolators and their role in animation. The SDK documentation on interpolators is a bit vague, so we will clarify interpolator behavior by showing you relevant source code. We will also cover something called a `LayoutAnimationController` that mediates between an animation and a `ViewGroup`.

Basic Tweening Animation Types

Before we design the test harness to apply the various tweening animations, we'll give you some detail on the basic types of tweening animation:

   ▓ *Scale animation*: You use this type of animation to make a view smaller or larger either on the x axis or on the y axis. You can also specify the pivot point around which you want the animation to take place.

   ▓ *Rotate animation*: You use this to rotate a view around a pivot point by a certain number of degrees.

   ▓ *Translate animation*: You use this to move a view along the x axis or the y axis.

   ▓ *Alpha animation*: You use this to change the transparency of a view.

All of the parameter values associated with these animations have a from and a to flavor because you must specify the starting values and ending values for when the animation starts and ends. Each animation also allows duration as an argument and a time interpolator as an argument. We'll cover interpolators at the end of this section on layout animation, but for now, know that interpolators determine the rate of change of the animated argument during animation.

You'll define these animations as XML files in the /res/anim subdirectory. You will see this amply illustrated in the test harness, but Listing 6–5 shows a quick sample to cement your understanding of how these animations are described.

Listing 6–5. *A Scale Animation Defined in an XML File at* /res/anim/scale.xml

```
<set xmlns:android="http://schemas.android.com/apk/res/android"
    android:interpolator="@android:anim/accelerate_interpolator">
    <scale
        android:fromXScale="1"
        android:toXScale="1"
        android:fromYScale="0.1"
        android:toYScale="1.0"
        android:duration="500"
```

```
        android:pivotX="50%"
        android:pivotY="50%"
        android:startOffset="100" />
</set>
```

Once you have this file, you can associate this animation with a layout; this means that each view in the layout will go through this animation. The test harness goes through this process in much more detail, as you'll see shortly.

> **NOTE:** This is a good place to point out that each of these animations is represented as a Java class in the android.view.animation package. The Java documentation for each of these classes describes not only its Java methods, but also the allowed XML arguments for each type of animation.

Now that you have enough background on animation types to understand layout animation, let's proceed to the design of the layout-animation test harness.

Planning the Layout-Animation Test Harness

You can test all the layout-animation concepts we've covered using a simple ListView set in an activity. Once you have a ListView, you can attach an animation to it so that each list item will go through that animation.

Assume you have a scale animation that makes a view grow from 0 to its original size on the y axis. You can attach that animation to a ListView. When this happens, the ListView will animate each item in that list using this animation. You can set some additional parameters that extend the basic animation, such as animating the list from top to bottom or from bottom to top. You specify these parameters through an intermediate class that acts as a mediator between the individual animation and the list.

You can define both the individual animation and the mediator in XML files in the /res/anim subdirectory. Once you have the mediator XML file, you can use that file as an input to the ListView in its own XML layout definition. This will become clear to you when you see the code listings we'll provide in the rest of this section. Once you have this basic setup working, you can start altering the individual animations to see how they impact the ListView display.

Our examples will cover scale animation, translate animation, rotate animation, alpha animation, and a combination of translate and alpha animation. If this high-level plan seems a bit vague, just hang tight; by the end of this section, you will know what we are talking about.

Before we embark on this exercise, you should see what the ListView will look like after the animation completes (see Figure 6–4).

Figure 6-4. *The ListView we will animate*

Creating the Activity and the ListView

Start by creating an XML layout for the ListView in Figure 6–4 so you can load that
layout in a basic activity. Listing 6–6 contains a simple layout with a ListView in it. You
will need to place this file in the /res/layout subdirectory. Assuming the file name is
list_layout.xml, your complete file will reside in /res/layout/list_layout.xml.

Listing 6-6. *XML Layout File Defining the ListView*

```xml
<?xml version="1.0" encoding="utf-8"?>
<!-- filename: /res/layout/list_layout.xml -->
<LinearLayout xmlns:android="http://schemas.android.com/apk/res/android"
    android:orientation="vertical"
    android:layout_width="fill_parent"
    android:layout_height="fill_parent"
    >

    <ListView
        android:id="@+id/list_view_id"
        android:layout_width="fill_parent"
        android:layout_height="fill_parent"
        />
</LinearLayout>
```

Listing 6–6 shows a simple LinearLayout with a single ListView in it. However, we
should mention one point about the ListView definition. If you happen to work through
the Notepad examples and other Android examples, you'll see that the ID for a ListView

is usually specified as @android:id/list. As we discussed in Chapter 3, the resource reference @android:id/list points to an ID that is predefined in the android namespace. The question is, when do we use this android:id vs. our own ID such as @+id/list_view_id?

You will need to use @android:id/list only if the activity is a ListActivity. A ListActivity assumes that a ListView identified by this predetermined ID is available for loading. In this case, you're using a general-purpose activity rather than a ListActivity, and you are going to explicitly populate the ListView yourself. As a result, there are no restrictions on the kind of ID you can allocate to represent this ListView. However, you do have the option of also using @android:id/list because it doesn't conflict with anything as there is no ListActivity in sight.

This surely is a digression, but it's worth noting as you create your own ListViews outside a ListActivity. Now that you have the layout needed for the activity, you can write the code for the activity to load this layout file so you can generate your UI (see Listing 6–7).

Listing 6–7. *Code for the Layout-Animation Activity*

```
public class LayoutAnimationActivity extends Activity
{
    @Override
    public void onCreate(Bundle savedInstanceState)
    {
        super.onCreate(savedInstanceState);
        setContentView(R.layout.list_layout);
        setupListView();
    }
    private void setupListView()
    {
        String[] listItems = new String[] {
            "Item 1", "Item 2", "Item 3",
            "Item 4", "Item 5", "Item 6",
        };

        ArrayAdapter listItemAdapter =
            new ArrayAdapter(this
                    ,android.R.layout.simple_list_item_1
                    ,listItems);
        ListView lv = (ListView)this.findViewById(R.id.list_view_id);
        lv.setAdapter(listItemAdapter);
    }
}
```

Some of the code in Listing 6–7 is obvious, and some is not. The first part of the code simply loads the view based on the generated layout ID R.layout.list_layout. Our goal is to take the ListView from this layout and populate it with six text items. These text items are loaded up into an array. You'll need to set a data adapter into a ListView so that the ListView can show those items.

To create the necessary adapter, you will need to specify how each item will be laid out when the list is displayed. You specify the layout by using a predefined layout in the base Android framework. In this example, this layout is specified as

```
android.R.layout.simple_list_item_1
```

The other possible view layouts for these items include

```
simple_list_item_2
simple_list_item_checked
simple_list_item_multiple_choice
simple_list_item_single_choice
```

You can refer to the Android documentation to see how each of these layouts look and behave. You can now invoke this activity from any menu item in your application using the following code:

```
Intent intent = new Intent(inActivity,LayoutAnimationActivity.class);
inActivity.startActivity(intent);
```

However, as with any other activity invocation, you will need to register the LayoutAnimationActivity in the AndroidManifest.xml file for the preceding intent invocation to work. Here is the code for it:

```
<activity android:name=". LayoutAnimationActivity"
        android:label="View Animation Test Activity"/>
```

Animating the ListView

Now that you have the test harness ready (see Listings 6–6 and 6–7), you'll learn how to apply scale animation to this ListView. Take a look at how this scale animation is defined in an XML file (see Listing 6–8).

Listing 6–8. *Defining Scale Animation in an XML File*

```
<set xmlns:android="http://schemas.android.com/apk/res/android"
android:interpolator="@android:anim/accelerate_interpolator">
   <scale
        android:fromXScale="1"
        android:toXScale="1"
        android:fromYScale="0.1"
        android:toYScale="1.0"
        android:duration="500"
        android:pivotX="50%"
        android:pivotY="50%"
        android:startOffset="100" />
</set>
```

These animation-definition files reside in the /res/anim subdirectory. Let's break down these XML attributes into plain English. The from and to scales point to the starting and ending magnification factors. Here, the magnification starts at 1 and stays at 1 on the x axis. This means the list items will not grow or shrink on the x axis. On the y axis, however, the magnification starts at 0.1 and grows to 1.0. In other words, the object being animated starts at one-tenth of its normal size and then grows to reach its normal size. The scaling operation will take 500 milliseconds to complete. The center of action is halfway (50%) in both x and y directions. The startOffset value refers to the number of milliseconds to wait before starting the animation.

The parent node of scale animation points to an animation set that could allow more than one animation to be in effect. We will cover one of those examples as well. But for now, there is only one animation in this set.

Name this file scale.xml and place it in the /res/anim subdirectory. You are not yet ready to set this animation XML as an argument to the ListView; the ListView first requires another XML file that acts as a mediator between itself and the animation set. The XML file that describes that mediation is shown in Listing 6–9.

Listing 6–9. *Definition for a Layout-Controller XML File*

```
<layoutAnimation xmlns:android="http://schemas.android.com/apk/res/android"
        android:delay="30%"
        android:animationOrder="reverse"
        android:animation="@anim/scale" />
```

You will also need to place this XML file in the /res/anim subdirectory. For our example, assume that the file name is list_layout_controller. Once you look at this definition, you can see why this intermediate file is necessary. This XML file specifies that the animation in the list should proceed in reverse, and that the animation for each item should start with a 30 percent delay with respect to the total animation duration. This XML file also refers to the individual animation file, scale.xml. Also notice that instead of the file name, the code uses the resource reference @anim/scale.

Now that you have the necessary XML input files, we'll show you how to update the ListView XML definition to include this animation XML as an argument. First, review the XML files you have so far:

```
// individual scale animation
/res/anim/scale.xml

// the animation mediator file
/res/anim/list_layout_controller.xml

// the activity view layout file
/res/layout/list_layout.xml
```

With these files in place, you need to modify the XML layout file list_layout.xml to have the ListView point to the list_layout_controller.xml file (see Listing 6–10).

Listing 6–10. *The Updated Code for the* list_layout.xml *File*

```
<?xml version="1.0" encoding="utf-8"?>
<LinearLayout xmlns:android="http://schemas.android.com/apk/res/android"
    android:orientation="vertical"
    android:layout_width="fill_parent"
    android:layout_height="fill_parent"
    >
    <ListView
        android:id="@+id/list_view_id"
        android:persistentDrawingCache="animation|scrolling"
        android:layout_width="fill_parent"
        android:layout_height="fill_parent"
        android:layoutAnimation="@anim/list_layout_controller" />
        />
</LinearLayout>
```

The changed lines are highlighted in bold. android:layoutAnimation is the key tag, which points to the mediating XML file that defines the layout controller using the XML tag layoutAnimation (see Listing 6–9). The layoutAnimation tag, in turn, points to the individual animation, which in this case is the scale animation defined in scale.xml. Android also recommends setting the persistentDrawingCache tag to optimize for animation and scrolling. Refer to the Android SDK documentation for more details on this tag.

When you update the list_layout.xml file as shown in Listing 6–10, Eclipse's ADT plug-in will automatically recompile the package taking this change into account. If you were to run the application now, you would see the scale animation take effect on the individual items. We have set the duration to 500 milliseconds so that you can observe the scale change clearly as each item is drawn.

Now you're in a position to experiment with different animation types. You'll try alpha animation next. To do this, create a file called /res/anim/alpha.xml and populate it with the content from Listing 6–11.

Listing 6–11. *The alpha.xml File to Test Alpha Animation*

```
<alpha xmlns:android="http://schemas.android.com/apk/res/android"
       android:interpolator="@android:anim/accelerate_interpolator"
       android:fromAlpha="0.0" android:toAlpha="1.0" android:duration="1000" />
```

Alpha animation is responsible for controlling the fading of color. In this example, you are asking the alpha animation to go from invisible to full color in 1000 milliseconds, or 1 second. Make sure the duration is 1 second or longer; otherwise, the color change is hard to notice.

Every time you want to change the animation of an individual item like this, you will need to change the mediator XML file (see Listing 6–9) to point to this new animation file. Here is how to change the animation from scale animation to alpha animation:

```
<layoutAnimation xmlns:android="http://schemas.android.com/apk/res/android"
       android:delay="30%"
       android:animationOrder="reverse"
       android:animation="@anim/alpha" />
```

The changed line in the layoutAnimation XML file is highlighted. Let us now try an animation that combines a change in position with a change in color gradient. Listing 6–12 shows the sample XML for this animation.

Listing 6–12. *Combining Translate and Alpha Animations Through an Animation Set*

```
<set xmlns:android="http://schemas.android.com/apk/res/android"
android:interpolator="@android:anim/accelerate_interpolator">
    <translate android:fromYDelta="-100%" android:toYDelta="0"
android:duration="500" />
    <alpha android:fromAlpha="0.0" android:toAlpha="1.0"
android:duration="500" />
</set>
```

Notice how we have specified two animations in the animation set. The translate animation will move the text from top to bottom in its currently allocated display space. The alpha animation will change the color gradient from invisible to visible as the text item descends into its slot. The duration setting of 500 will allow the user to perceive the change in a comfortable fashion. Of course, you will have to change the layoutAnimation mediator XML file again with a reference to this file name. Assuming the file name for this combined animation is /res/anim/translate-alpha.xml, your layoutAnimation XML file will look like this:

```
<layoutAnimation xmlns:android="http://schemas.android.com/apk/res/android"
        android:delay="30%"
        android:animationOrder="reverse"
        android:animation="@anim/translate-alpha" />
```

Let us see now how to use rotate animation (see Listing 6–13).

Listing 6–13. *Rotate Animation XML File*

```
<rotate xmlns:android="http://schemas.android.com/apk/res/android"
        android:interpolator="@android:anim/accelerate_interpolator"
        android:fromDegrees="0.0"
        android:toDegrees="360"
        android:pivotX="50%"
        android:pivotY="50%"
        android:duration="500" />
```

The code in Listing 6–13 will spin each text item in the list one full circle around the midpoint of the text item. The duration of 500 milliseconds is a good amount of time for the user to perceive the rotation. As before, to see this effect you must change the layout-controller XML file and the ListView XML layout file and then rerun the application.

Now we've covered the basic concepts in layout animation, where we start with a simple animation file and associate it with a ListView through an intermediate layoutAnimation XML file. That's all you need to do to see the animated effects. However, we need to talk about one more thing with regard to layout animation: interpolators.

Using Interpolators

Interpolators tell an animation how a certain property, such as a color gradient, changes over time. Will it change in a linear fashion, or in an exponential fashion? Will it start quickly, but slow down toward the end? Consider the alpha animation that we introduced in Listing 6–11:

```
<alpha xmlns:android="http://schemas.android.com/apk/res/android"
        android:interpolator="@android:anim/accelerate_interpolator"
        android:fromAlpha="0.0" android:toAlpha="1.0" android:duration="1000" />
```

The animation identifies the interpolator it wants to use—the accelerate_interpolator, in this case. There is a corresponding Java object that defines this interpolator. Also, note that we've specified this interpolator as a resource reference. This means there must be a file corresponding to the anim/accelerate_interpolator that describes what this Java object looks like and what additional parameters it might take. That indeed is the case. Look at the XML file definition for @android:anim/accelerate_interpolator:

```
<accelerateInterpolator
```

```
    xmlns:android="http://schemas.android.com/apk/res/android"
    factor="1" />
```

You can see this XML file in the following subdirectory within the Android package:

```
/res/anim/accelerate_interpolator.xml
```

The accelerateInterpolator XML tag corresponds to a Java object with this name:

```
android.view.animation.AccelerateInterpolator
```

You can look up the Java documentation for this class to see what XML tags are available. This interpolator's goal is to provide a multiplication factor given a time interval based on a hyperbolic curve. The source code for the interpolator illustrates this:

```
public float getInterpolation(float input)
{
    if (mFactor == 1.0f)
    {
        return (float)(input * input);
    }
    else
    {
        return (float)Math.pow(input, 2 * mFactor);
    }
}
```

Every interpolator implements this getInterpolation method differently. In this case, if the interpolator is set up so that the factor is 1.0, it will return the square of the factor. Otherwise, it will return a power of the input that is further scaled by the factor. So if the factor is 1.5, then you will see a cubic function instead of a square function.

The supported interpolators include

```
AccelerateDecelerateInterpolator
AccelerateInterpolator
CycleInterpolator
DecelerateInterpolator
LinearInterpolator
AnticipateInterpolator
AnticipateOvershootInterpolator
BounceInterpolator
OvershootInterpolator
```

To see how flexible these interpolators can be, take a quick look at the BounceInterpolator which bounces the object (that is, moves it back and forth) towards the end of the following animation:

```
public class BounceInterpolator implements Interpolator {
    private static float bounce(float t) {
        return t * t * 8.0f;
    }

    public float getInterpolation(float t) {
        t *= 1.1226f;
        if (t < 0.3535f) return bounce(t);
        else if (t < 0.7408f) return bounce(t - 0.54719f) + 0.7f;
        else if (t < 0.9644f) return bounce(t - 0.8526f) + 0.9f;
```

```
              else return bounce(t - 1.0435f) + 0.95f;
        }
  }
```

You can find the behavior of these interpolators described at the following URL:

`http://developer.android.com/reference/android/view/animation/package-summary.html`

The Java documentation for each of these classes also points out the XML tags available to control them. However, the description of what each interpolator does is hard to figure out from the documentation. The best approach is to try it out in an example and see the effect produced. You can also use this URL to search the online source code:

`http://android.git.kernel.org/?p=platform%2Fframeworks%2Fbase.git&a=search&h=HEAD&st=gre p&s=BounceInterpolator`

This concludes our section on layout animation. We will now move to the third section on view animation, in which we'll discuss animating a view programmatically.

View Animation

Now that you're familiar with frame-by-frame animation and layout animation, you're ready to tackle view animation—the most complex of the three animation types. View animation allows you to animate any arbitrary view by manipulating the transformation matrix that is in place for displaying the view.

We will start this section by giving you a brief introduction to view animation. We will then show you the code for a test harness to experiment with view animation, followed by a few view-animation examples. Then we'll explain how you can use the Camera object in association with view animation. (This Camera has nothing to do with the physical camera on the device; it's purely a graphics concept.) Finally, we'll give you an in-depth look at working with transformation matrices.

Understanding View Animation

When a view is displayed on a presentation surface in Android, it goes through a transformation matrix. In graphics applications, you use transformation matrices to transform a view in some way. The process involves taking the input set of pixel coordinates and color combinations and translating them into a new set of pixel coordinates and color combinations. At the end of a transformation, you will see an altered picture in terms of size, position, orientation, or color.

You can achieve all of these transformations mathematically by taking the input set of coordinates and multiplying them in some manner using a transformation matrix to arrive at a new set of coordinates. By changing the transformation matrix, you can impact how a view will look. A matrix that *doesn't* change the view when you multiply it is called an *identity matrix*. You typically start with an identity matrix and apply a series of transformations involving size, position, and orientation. You then take the final matrix and use that matrix to draw the view.

Android exposes the transformation matrix for a view by allowing you to register an animation object with that view. The animation object will have a callback that lets it obtain the current matrix for a view and change it in some manner to arrive at a new view. We will go through this process now.

Let's start by planning an example for animating a view. You'll begin with an activity where you'll place a ListView with a few items, similar to the way you began the example in the "Layout Animation" section. You will then create a button at the top of the screen to start the ListView animation when clicked (see Figure 6–5). Both the button and the ListView appear, but nothing has been animated yet. You'll use the button to trigger the animation.

When you click the Start Animation button in this example, you want the view to start small in the middle of the screen and gradually become bigger until it consumes all the space that is allocated for it. We'll show you how to write the code to make this happen. Listing 6–14 shows the XML layout file that you can use for the activity.

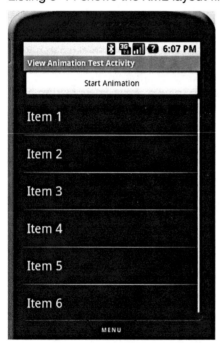

Figure 6–5. *The view-animation activity*

Listing 6–14. *XML Layout File for the View-Animation Activity*

```xml
<?xml version="1.0" encoding="utf-8"?>
<!-- This file is at /res/layout/list_layout.xml -->
<LinearLayout xmlns:android="http://schemas.android.com/apk/res/android"
    android:orientation="vertical"
    android:layout_width="fill_parent"
    android:layout_height="fill_parent"
    >
<Button
```

```
    android:id="@+id/btn_animate"
     android:layout_width="fill_parent"
     android:layout_height="wrap_content"
     android:text="Start Animation"
/>
<ListView
     android:id="@+id/list_view_id"
     android:persistentDrawingCache="animation|scrolling"
     android:layout_width="fill_parent"
     android:layout_height="fill_parent"
 />
</LinearLayout>
```

Notice that the file location and the file name are embedded at the top of the XML file for your reference. This layout has two parts: the first is the button named btn_animate to animate a view, and the second is the ListView, which is named list_view_id.

Now that you have the layout for the activity, you can create the activity to show the view and set up the Start Animation button (see Listing 6–15).

Listing 6–15. *Code for the View-Animation Activity, Before Animation*

```
public class ViewAnimationActivity extends Activity {

    @Override
    public void onCreate(Bundle savedInstanceState)
    {
        super.onCreate(savedInstanceState);
        setContentView(R.layout.list_layout);
        setupListView();
        this.setupButton();
    }
    private void setupListView()
    {
        String[] listItems = new String[] {
            "Item 1", "Item 2", "Item 3",
            "Item 4", "Item 5", "Item 6",
        };

        ArrayAdapter listItemAdapter =
            new ArrayAdapter(this
                    ,android.R.layout.simple_list_item_1
                    ,listItems);
        ListView lv = (ListView)this.findViewById(R.id.list_view_id);
        lv.setAdapter(listItemAdapter);
    }
    private void setupButton()
    {
        Button b = (Button)this.findViewById(R.id.btn_animate);
        b.setOnClickListener(
            new Button.OnClickListener(){
              public void onClick(View v)
              {
                  //animateListView();
              }
            });
    }
}
```

The code for the view-animation activity in Listing 6–15 closely resembles the code for the layout-animation activity in Listing 6–7. We have similarly loaded the view and set up the ListView to contain six text items. We've set up the button in such a way that it would call animateListView() when clicked. But for now, comment out that part until you get this basic example running.

You can invoke this activity as soon as you register it in the AndroidManifest.xml file:

```
<activity android:name=".ViewAnimationActivity"
        android:label="View Animation Test Activity">
```

Once this registration is in place, you can invoke this view-animation activity from any menu item in your application by executing the following code:

```
Intent intent = new Intent(this, ViewAnimationActivity.class);
startActivity(intent);
```

When you run this program, you will see the UI as laid out in Figure 6–5.

Adding Animation

Our aim in this example is to add animation to the ListView shown in Figure 6–5. To do that, you need a class that derives from android.view.animation.Animation. You then need to override the applyTransformation method to modify the transformation matrix. Call this derived class ViewAnimation. Once you have the ViewAnimation class, you can do something like this on the ListView class:

```
ListView lv = (ListView)this.findViewById(R.id.list_view_id);
lv.startAnimation(new ViewAnimation());
```

Let us go ahead and show you the source code for ViewAnimation and discuss the kind of animation we want to accomplish (see Listing 6–16).

Listing 6–16. *Code for the ViewAnimation Class*

```
public class ViewAnimation extends Animation
{
    public ViewAnimation2(){}

    @Override
    public void initialize(int width, int height, int parentWidth,
                                            int parentHeight)
    {
        super.initialize(width, height, parentWidth, parentHeight);
        setDuration(2500);
        setFillAfter(true);
        setInterpolator(new LinearInterpolator());
    }
    @Override
    protected void applyTransformation(float interpolatedTime, Transformation t)
    {
        final Matrix matrix = t.getMatrix();
        matrix.setScale(interpolatedTime, interpolatedTime);
    }
}
```

The `initialize` method is a callback method that tells us about the dimensions of the view. This is also a place to initialize any animation parameters you might have. In this example, we have set the duration to be 2500 milliseconds (2.5 seconds). We have also specified that we want the animation effect to remain intact after the animation completes by setting `FillAfter` to `true`. Plus, we've indicated that the interpolator is a linear interpolator, meaning that the animation changes in a gradual manner from start to finish. All of these properties come from the base `android.view.animation. Animation` class.

The main part of the animation occurs in the `applyTransformation` method. The Android framework will call this method again and again to simulate animation. Every time Android calls the method, `interpolatedTime` has a different value. This parameter changes from 0 to 1 depending on where you are in the 2.5-second duration that you set during initialization. When `interpolatedTime` is 1, you are at the end of the animation.

Our goal, then, is to change the transformation matrix that is available through the transformation object called t in the `applyTransformation` method. You will first get the matrix and change something about it. When the view gets painted, the new matrix will take effect. You can find the kinds of methods available on the `Matrix` object by looking up the API documentation for `android.graphics.Matrix`:

http://developer.android.com/reference/android/graphics/Matrix.html

In Listing 6–16, here is the code that changes the matrix:

```
matrix.setScale(interpolatedTime, interpolatedTime);
```

The `setScale` method takes two parameters: the scaling factor in the x direction and the scaling factor in the y direction. Because the `interpolatedTime` goes between 0 and 1, you can use that value directly as the scaling factor. So when you start the animation, the scaling factor is 0 in both x and y directions. Halfway through the animation, this value will be 0.5 in both x and y directions. At the end of the animation, the view will be at its full size because the scaling factor will be 1 in both x and y directions. The end result of this animation is that the `ListView` starts out tiny and grows into full size.

Listing 6–17 shows the complete source code for the `ViewAnimationActivity` that includes the animation.

Listing 6–17. *Code for the View-Animation Activity, Including Animation*

```
public class ViewAnimationActivity extends Activity {

    @Override
    public void onCreate(Bundle savedInstanceState)
    {
        super.onCreate(savedInstanceState);
        setContentView(R.layout.list_layout);
        setupListView();
        this.setupButton();
    }
    private void setupListView()
    {
        String[] listItems = new String[] {
                "Item 1", "Item 2", "Item 3",
```

```
                    "Item 4", "Item 5", "Item 6",
            };

            ArrayAdapter listItemAdapter =
                new ArrayAdapter(this
                        ,android.R.layout.simple_list_item_1
                        ,listItems);
            ListView lv = (ListView)this.findViewById(R.id.list_view_id);
            lv.setAdapter(listItemAdapter);
        }
        private void setupButton()
        {
            Button b = (Button)this.findViewById(R.id.btn_animate);
            b.setOnClickListener(
                new Button.OnClickListener(){
                    public void onClick(View v)
                    {
                        animateListView();
                    }
                });
        }
        private void animateListView()
        {
            ListView lv = (ListView)this.findViewById(R.id.list_view_id);
            lv.startAnimation(new ViewAnimation());
        }
    }
```

When you run the code in Listing 6–17, you will notice something odd. Instead of uniformly growing larger from the middle of the screen, the ListView grows larger from the top-left corner. The reason is that the origin for the matrix operations is at the top-left corner. To get the desired effect, you first have to move the whole view so that the view's center matches the animation center (top-left). Then you apply the matrix and move the view back to the previous center.

Here's the code for doing this:

```
        final Matrix matrix = t.getMatrix();
        matrix.setScale(interpolatedTime, interpolatedTime);
        matrix.preTranslate(-centerX, -centerY);
        matrix.postTranslate(centerX, centerY);
```

The preTranslate and postTranslate methods set up a matrix before the scale operation and after the scale operation. This is equivalent to making three matrix transformations in tandem. The code

```
        matrix.setScale(interpolatedTime, interpolatedTime);
        matrix.preTranslate(-centerX, -centerY);
        matrix.postTranslate(centerX, centerY);
```

is equivalent to

```
move to a different center
scale it
move to the original center
```

Here is the code for the transformation method that will give us the desired effect:

```
protected void applyTransformation(float interpolatedTime, Transformation t)
{
        final Matrix matrix = t.getMatrix();
        matrix.setScale(interpolatedTime, interpolatedTime);
        matrix.preTranslate(-centerX, -centerY);
        matrix.postTranslate(centerX, centerY);
}
```

You will see this pattern of pre and post applied again and again. You can also accomplish this result using other methods on the Matrix class, but this technique is the most common—plus, it's succinct. We will, however, cover these other methods toward the end of this section.

More important, the Matrix class allows you not only to scale a view, but also to move it around through translate methods and change its orientation through rotate methods. You can experiment with these methods and see what the resulting animation looks like. In fact, the animations presented in the preceding "Layout Animation" section are all implemented internally using the methods on this Matrix class.

Using Camera to Provide Depth Perception in 2D

The graphics package in Android provides another animation-related—or more accurately, transformation-related—class called Camera. You can use this class to provide depth perception by projecting a 2D image moving in 3D space onto a 2D surface. For example, you can take our ListView and move it back from the screen by 10 pixels along the z axis and rotate it by 30 degrees around the y axis. Here is an example of manipulating the matrix using a Camera:

```
...
Camera camera = new Camera();
..
protected void applyTransformation(float interpolatedTime, Transformation t)
{
    final Matrix matrix = t.getMatrix();
    camera.save();
    camera.translate(0.0f, 0.0f, (1300 - 1300.0f * interpolatedTime));
    camera.rotateY(360 * interpolatedTime);
    camera.getMatrix(matrix);

    matrix.preTranslate(-centerX, -centerY);
    matrix.postTranslate(centerX, centerY);
    camera.restore();
}
```

This code animates the ListView by first placing the view 1300 pixels back on the z axis and then bringing it back to the plane where the z coordinate is 0. While doing this, the code also rotates the view from 0 degrees to 360 degrees around the y axis. Let's see how the code relates to this behavior by looking at the following method:

```
camera.translate(0.0f, 0.0f, (1300 - 1300.0f * interpolatedTime));
```

This method tells the camera object to translate the view such that when interpolatedTime is 0 (at the beginning of the animation), the z value will be 1300. As the animation progresses, the z value will get smaller and smaller until the end, when the `interpolatedTime` becomes 1 and the z value becomes 0.

The method `camera.rotateY(360 * interpolatedTime)` takes advantage of 3D rotation around an axis by the `camera`. At the beginning of the animation, this value will be 0. At the end of the animation, it will be 360.

The method `camera.getMatrix(matrix)` takes the operations performed on the `Camera` so far and imposes those operations on the matrix that is passed in. Once the code does that, the `matrix` has the translations it needs to get the end effect of having a `Camera`. Now the `Camera` is out of the picture (no pun intended) because the matrix has all the operations embedded in it. Then you do the `pre` and `post` on the matrix to shift the center and bring it back. At the end, you set the `Camera` to its original state that was saved earlier.

When you plug this code into our example, you will see the `ListView` arriving from the center of the view in a spinning manner toward the front of the screen, as we intended when we planned our animation.

As part of our discussion about view animation, we showed you how to animate any view by extending an `Animation` class and then applying it to a view. In addition to letting you manipulate matrices (both directly and through a `Camera` class), the `Animation` class lets you detect various stages in an animation. We will cover this next.

Exploring the AnimationListener Class

Android uses a listener interface called `AnimationListener` to monitor animation events (see Listing 6–18). You can listen to these animation events by implementing the `AnimationListener` interface and setting that implementation against the `Animation` class implementation.

Listing 6–18. *An Implementation of the* `AnimationListener` *Interface*

```
public class ViewAnimationListener
implements Animation.AnimationListener {

    private ViewAnimationListener(){}

    public void onAnimationStart(Animation animation)
    {
        Log.d("Animation Example", "onAnimationStart");
    }
    public void onAnimationEnd(Animation animation)
    {
        Log.d("Animation Example", "onAnimationEnd");
    }
    public void onAnimationRepeat(Animation animation)
    {
        Log.d("Animation Example", "onAnimationRepeat");
    }
}
```

The ViewAnimationListener class just logs messages. You can update the animateListView method in the view-animation example (see Listing 6–17) to take the animation listener into account:

```
private void animateListView()
{
   ListView lv = (ListView)this.findViewById(R.id.list_view_id);
   ViewAnimation animation = new ViewAnimation();
   animation.setAnimationListener(new ViewAnimationListener()):
   lv.startAnimation(animation);
}
```

Some Notes on Transformation Matrices

As you have seen in this chapter, matrices are key to transforming views and animations. We will now briefly explore some key methods of the Matrix class. These are the primary operations on a matrix:

```
matrix.reset();
matrix.setScale();
matrix.setTranslate()
matrix.setRotate();
matrix.setSkew();
```

The first operation resets a matrix to an identity matrix, which causes no change to the view when applied. setScale is responsible for changing size, setTranslate is responsible for changing position to simulate movement, and setRotate is responsible for changing orientation. setSkew is responsible for distorting a view.

You can concatenate matrices or multiply them together to compound the effect of individual transformations. Consider the following example, where m1, m2, and m3 are identity matrices:

```
m1.setScale();
m2.setTranlate()
m3.concat(m1,m2)
```

Transforming a view by m1 and then transforming the resulting view with m2 is equivalent to transforming the same view by m3. Note that set methods replace the previous transformations, and that m3.concat(m1,m2) is different from m3.concat(m2,m1).

You have already seen the pattern used by preTranslate and postTranslate methods to affect matrix transformation. In fact, pre and post methods are not unique to translate, and you have versions of pre and post for every one of the set transformation methods. Ultimately, a preTranslate such as m1.preTranslate(m2) is equivalent to

```
m1.concat(m2,m1)
```

In a similar manner, the method m1.postTranslate(m2) is equivalent to

```
m1.concat(m1,m2)
```

By extension, the code

```
matrix.setScale(interpolatedTime, interpolatedTime);
```

```
matrix.preTranslate(-centerX, -centerY);
matrix.postTranslate(centerX, centerY);
```

is equivalent to

```
Matrix matrixPreTranslate = new Matrix();
matrixPreTranslate.setTranslate(-centerX, -centerY);

Matrix matrixPostTranslate = new Matrix();
matrixPostTranslate.setTranslate(cetnerX, centerY);

matrix.concat(matrixPreTranslate,matrix);
matrix.postTranslate(matrix,matrixpostTranslate);
```

Summary

In this chapter, we showed you a fun way to enhance your UI programs by extending them with animation capabilities. We covered all major types of animation supported by Android, including frame-by-frame animation, layout animation, and view animation. We also covered supplemental animation concepts such as interpolators and transformation matrices.

Now that you have this background, we encourage you to go through the API samples that come with the Android SDK to examine the sample XML definitions for a variety of animations. We will also return to animation briefly in Chapter 10, when you'll see how to draw and animate using OpenGL.

But now we will turn our attention to services in Android. We'll cover location-based services and security in Chapter 7, and HTTP-related services in Chapter 8.

Exploring Security and Location-Based Services

In this chapter, we are going to talk about Android's application-security model and location-based services. Although the two topics are disparate, you need to understand security prior to working with location-based services.

The first part of the chapter discusses security, which is a fundamental part of the Android Platform. In Android, security spans all phases of the application lifecycle—from design-time policy considerations to runtime boundary checks. You'll learn Android's security architecture and understand how to design secure applications.

The second part of the chapter concerns location-based services. Location-based services comprise one of the more exciting pieces of the Android SDK. This portion of the SDK provides APIs to let application developers display and manipulate maps, obtain real-time device-location information, and take advantage of other exciting features. After you read this section of the book, you'll definitely be convinced that Android is truly amazing.

Let's get started with the Android security model.

Understanding the Android Security Model

Security in Android spans the deployment and execution of the application. With respect to deployment, Android applications have to be signed with a digital certificate in order for you to install them onto a device. With respect to execution, Android runs each application within a separate process, each of which has a unique and permanent user ID (assigned at install time). This places a boundary around the process and prevents one application from having direct access to another's data. Moreover, Android defines a declarative permission model that protects sensitive features (such as the contact list).

In the next several sections, we are going to discuss these topics. But before we get started, let's provide an overview of some of the security concepts that we'll refer to later.

Overview of Security Concepts

As we said earlier, Android requires that applications be signed with a digital certificate. One of the benefits of this requirement is that an application cannot be updated with a version that was not published by the original author. If we publish an application, for example, then you cannot update our application with your version (unless, of course, you somehow obtain our certificate and the password associated with it). That said, what does it mean for an application to be signed? And what is the process of signing an application?

You sign an application with a digital certificate. A *digital certificate* is an artifact that contains information about you, such as your company name, address, and so on. A few important attributes of a digital certificate include its signature and public/private key. A public/private key is also called a *key pair*. Note that although you use digital certificates here to sign .apk files, you can also use them for other purposes (such as encrypted communication). You can obtain a digital certificate from a trusted certificate authority (CA) and you can also generate one yourself using tools such as the keytool, which we'll discuss shortly. Digital certificates are stored in keystores. A *keystore* contains a list of digital certificates, each of which has an alias that you can use to refer to it in the keystore.

Signing an Android application requires three things: a digital certificate, an .apk file, and a utility that knows how to apply the signature of the digital certificate to the .apk file. As you'll see, we use a free utility that is part of the Java Development Kit (JDK) distribution called the jarsigner. This utility is a command-line tool that knows how to sign a .jar file with a digital certificate.

Now let's move on and talk about how you can sign an .apk file with a digital certificate.

Signing Applications for Deployment

To install an Android application onto a device, you first need to sign the Android package (.apk file) with the digital signature of a certificate. The certificate, however, can be self-signed—you do not need to purchase a certificate from a certificate authority such as VeriSign.

Signing your application for deployment involves three steps. The first step is to generate a certificate using the keytool (or a similar tool). The second step involves using the jarsigner tool (or a similar tool) to sign the .apk file with the signature of the generated certificate. The third step aligns portions of your application on memory boundaries for more efficient memory usage when running on a device. Note that during development, the ADT plug-in for Eclipse takes care of signing your .apk file and doing the memory alignment, before deploying onto the emulator. Moreover, the default certificate used for signing during development cannot be used for production deployment onto a real device.

Generating a Self-Signed Certificate Using the Keytool

The keytool utility manages a database of private keys and their corresponding X.509 certificates (a standard for digital certificates). This utility ships with the JDK and resides under the JDK bin directory. If you followed the instructions in Chapter 2 regarding changing your PATH, the JDK bin directory should already be in your PATH.

In this section, we'll show you how to generate a keystore with a single entry, which you'll later use to sign an Android .apk file. To generate a keystore entry, do the following:

1. Create a folder to hold the keystore, for example c:\android\release\.

2. Open a tools window and execute the keytool utility with the parameters shown in Listing 7–1. (See Chapter 2 for details of what we mean by a "tools window.")

Listing 7–1. *Generating a Keystore Entry Using the Keytool*

```
keytool -genkey -v -keystore "FULL PATH OF release.keystore FILE FROM STEP 1"
-alias androidbook -storepass paxxword -keypass paxxword -keyalg RSA
-validity 14000
```

All of the arguments passed to the keytool are summarized in Table 7–1.

Table 7–1. *Arguments Passed to the Keytool*

Argument	Description
genkey	Tells the keytool to generate a public/private key pair.
v	Tells the keytool to emit verbose output during key generation.
keystore	Path to the keystore database (in this case, a file).
alias	A unique name for the keystore entry. The alias is used later to refer to the keystore entry.
storepass	The password for the keystore.
keypass	The password used to access the private key.
keyalg	The algorithm.
validity	The validity period.

The keytool will prompt you for the passwords listed in Table 7–1 if you do not provide them on the command line. If you are not the sole user of your computer, it would be safer to not specify -storepass and -keypass on the command line, but rather type them in when prompted by the keytool. The command in Listing 7–1 will generate a keystore database file in your keystore folder. The database will be a file named release.keystore. The validity of the entry will be 14,000 days (or approximately 38 years)—which is a long time from now. You should understand the reason for this. The Android documentation recommends that you specify a validity period long enough to surpass the entire lifespan of the application, which will include many updates to the application. It recommends that the validity be at least 25 years. Moreover, if you plan to publish the application on Android Market (http://www.android.com/market/), your certificate will need to be valid through at least October 22, 2033. Android Market checks each application when uploaded to make sure it will be valid at least until then.

Going back to the keytool, the argument alias is a unique name given to the entry in the keystore database; you can use this name later to refer to the entry. When you run the keytool command in Listing 7–1, keytool will ask you a few questions (see Figure 7–1) and then generate the keystore database and entry.

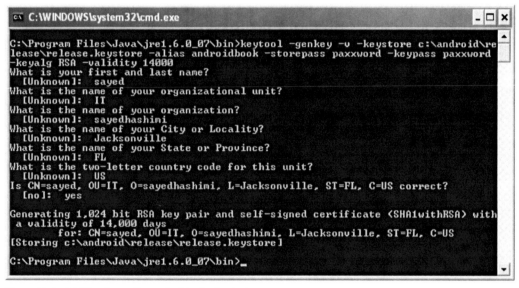

Figure 7–1. *Additional questions asked by the keytool*

Now you have a digital certificate that you can use to sign your .apk file. To sign an .apk file with the certificate, you use the jarsigner tool. Here's how to do that.

Using the Jarsigner Tool to Sign the .apk File

The keytool in the previous section created a digital certificate, which is one of the parameters for the jarsigner tool. The other parameter for jarsigner is the actual Android package to be signed. To generate an Android package, you need to use the

Export Unsigned Application Package utility in the ADT plug-in for Eclipse. You access the utility by right-clicking an Android project in Eclipse, selecting Android Tools, and then selecting Export Unsigned Application Package. Running the Export Unsigned Application Package utility will generate an .apk file that will not be signed with the debug certificate. To see how this works, run the Export Unsigned Application Package utility on one of your Android projects and store the generated .apk file somewhere. For this example, we'll use the keystore folder we created earlier, and generate an apk file called `c:\android\release\myapp.apk`.

With the .apk file and the keystore entry, run the `jarsigner` tool to sign the .apk file (see Listing 7–2). Use the full pathnames to your keystore file and .apk file as appropriate when you run this.

Listing 7–2. *Using Jarsigner to Sign the .apk File*

```
jarsigner -keystore "PATH TO YOUR release.keystore FILE" -storepass paxxword
-keypass paxxword  "PATH TO YOUR APK FILE" androidbook
```

To sign the .apk file, you pass the location of the keystore, the keystore password, the private-key password, the path to the .apk file, and the alias for the keystore entry. The `jarsigner` will then sign the .apk file with the signature from the keystore entry. To run the `jarsigner` tool, you will need to either open a tools window (as explained in Chapter 2), or open a command or Terminal window and either navigate to the JDK `bin` directory or ensure that your JDK `bin` directory is on the system path.

As we pointed out earlier, Android requires that an application be signed with a digital signature to prevent a malicious programmer from updating your application with his version. For this to work, Android requires that updates to an application be signed with the same signature as the original. If you sign the application with a different signature, Android treats them as two different applications.

Aligning Your Application with zipalign

You want your application to be as memory efficient as possible when running on a device. If your application contains uncompressed data (perhaps certain image types or data files) at runtime, Android can map this data straight into memory using the `mmap()` call. In order for this to work, though, the data must be aligned on a 4-byte memory boundary. The CPUs in Android devices are 32-bit processors, and 32 bits equals 4 bytes. The `mmap()` call makes the data in your .apk file look like memory, but if the data is not aligned on a 4-byte boundary then it can't do that and extra copying of data must occur at runtime. The `zipalign` tool, found in the Android SDK tools directory, looks through your application and moves slightly any uncompressed data not already on a 4-byte memory boundary to a 4-byte memory boundary. You may see the file size of your application increase slightly but not significantly. To perform an alignment on your .apk file, use this command in a tools window (see also Figure 7–2):

```
zipalign -v 4 infile.apk outfile.apk
```

Note that `zipalign` performs a verification of the alignment when you create your aligned file. If you need to overwrite an existing outfile.apk file you can use the –f option. Also, to verify that an existing file is properly aligned, use `zipalign` the following way:

```
zipalign -c -v 4 filename.apk
```

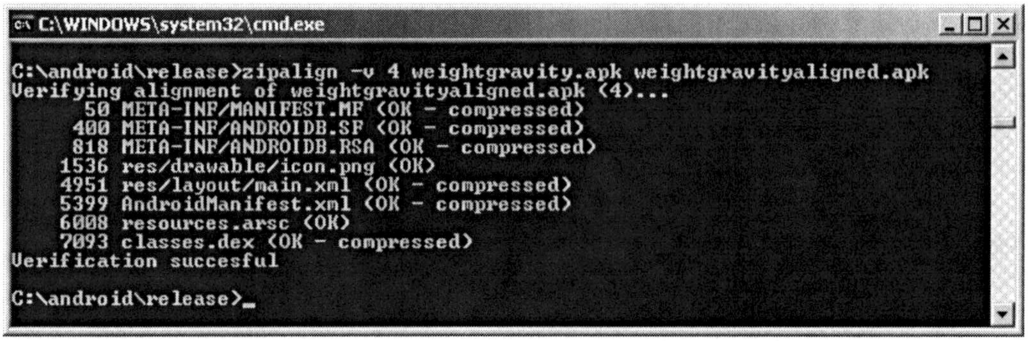

Figure 7–2. *Using zipalign*

It is very important that you align *after* signing, otherwise, signing could cause things to go back out of alignment. This does not mean your application would crash, but it could use more memory than it needs to.

Once you have signed and aligned an .apk file, you can install it onto the emulator manually using the adb tool. As an exercise, start the emulator. One way to do this, which we haven't discussed yet, is to go to the Window menu of Eclipse and select Android SDK and AVD Manager. A window will be displayed showing your available AVDs. Select the one you want to use for your emulator and click on the Start… button. The emulator will start without copying over any of your development projects from Eclipse. Now open a tools window, and then run the adb tool with the `install` command:

```
adb install "PATH TO APK FILE GOES HERE"
```

This may fail for a couple of reasons, but the most likely are that the debug version of your application was already installed on the emulator, giving you a certificate error, or the release version of your application was already installed on the emulator, giving you an already exists error. In the first case, you can uninstall the debug application with this command:

```
adb uninstall packagename
```

Note that the argument to uninstall is the application's package name and not the .apk filename. The package name is defined in the AndroidManifest.xml file of the installed application. For the second case, you can use this command, where –r says to reinstall the application while keeping its data on the device (or emulator):

```
adb install -r "PATH TO APK FILE GOES HERE"
```

Now let's see how signing affects the process of updating an application.

Installing Updates to an Application and Signing

Earlier, we mentioned that a certificate has an expiration date and that Google recommends you set expiration dates far into the future, to account for a lot of application updates. That said, what happens if the certificate does expire? Would Android still run the application? Fortunately, yes—Android tests the certificate's expiration only at install time. Once your application is installed, it will continue to run even if the certificate expires.

But what about updates? Unfortunately, you will not be able to update the application once the certificate expires. In other words, as Google suggests, you need to make sure the life of the certificate is long enough to support the entire life of the application. If a certificate does expire, Android will not install an update to the application. The only choice left will be for you to create another application—an application with a different package name—and sign it with a new certificate. So as you can see, it is critical for you to consider the expiration date of the certificate when you generate it.

Now that you understand security with respect to deployment and installation, let's move on to runtime security in Android.

Performing Runtime Security Checks

Runtime security in Android happens at the process level and at the operation level. At the process level, Android prevents one application from directly accessing another application's data. It does this by running each application within a different process and under a unique and permanent user ID. At the operational level, Android defines a list of protected features and resources. In order for your application to access this information, you have to add one or more permission requests to your `AndroidManifest.xml` file. You can also define custom permissions with your application.

In the sections that follow, we will talk about process-boundary security and how to declare and use predefined permissions. We will also discuss creating custom permissions and enforcing them within your application. Let's start by dissecting Android security at the process boundary.

Understanding Security at the Process Boundary

Unlike your desktop environment, where most of the applications run under the same user ID, each Android application generally runs under its own unique ID. By running each application under a different ID, Android creates an isolation boundary around each process. This prevents one application from directly accessing another application's data.

Although each process has a boundary around it, data sharing between applications is obviously possible, but has to be explicit. In other words, to get data from another application, you have to go through the components of that application. For example, you can query a content provider of another application, you can invoke an activity in another application, or—as you'll see in Chapter 8—you can communicate with a service of another application. All of these facilities provide methods for you to share information between applications, but they do so in an explicit manner because you don't access the underlying database, files, and so on.

Android's security at the process boundary is clear and simple. Things get interesting when we start talking about protecting resources (such as contact data), features (such as the device's camera), and our own components. To provide this protection, Android defines a permission scheme. Let's dissect that now.

Declaring and Using Permissions

Android defines a permission scheme meant to protect resources and features on the device. For example, applications, by default, cannot access the contacts list, make phone calls, and so on. To protect the user from malicious applications, Android requires applications to request permissions if they need to use a protected feature or resource. As you'll see shortly, permission requests go in the manifest file. At install time, the APK installer either grants or denies the requested permissions based on the signature of the .apk file and/or feedback from the user. If a permission is not granted, any attempt to execute or access the associated feature will result in a permission failure.

Table 7–2 shows some commonly-used features and the permissions they require. Note that you are not yet familiar with all the features listed, but you will learn about them later (either in this chapter or in subsequent chapters).

Table 7–2. *Features and Resources, and the Permissions They Require*

Feature/Resource	Required Permission	Description
Camera	`android.permission.CAMERA`	Enables you to access the device's camera.
Internet	`android.permission.INTERNET`	Enables you to make a network connection.
User's Contact Data	`android.permission.READ_CONTACTS` `android.permission.WRITE_CONTACTS`	Enables you to read from or write to the user's contact data.
User's Calendar Data	`android.permission.READ_CALENDAR` `android.permission.WRITE_CALENDAR`	Enables you to read from or write to the user's calendar data.
Record Audio	`android.permission.RECORD_AUDIO`	Enables you to record audio.

Feature/Resource	Required Permission	Description
GPS Location Information	android.permission.ACCESS_FINE_LOCATION	Enables you to access fine-grained location information. This includes GPS location information.
WiFi Location Information	android.permission.ACCESS_COARSE_LOCATION	Enables you to access coarse-grained location information. This includes WiFi location information.
Battery Information	android.permission.BATTERY_STATS	Enables you to obtain battery-state information.
Bluetooth	android.permission.BLUETOOTH	Enables you to connect to paired Bluetooth devices.

For a complete list of permissions, see the following URL:

```
http://developer.android.com/reference/android/Manifest.permission.html
```

Application developers can request permissions by adding entries to the AndroidManifest.xml file. For example, Listing 7–3 asks to access the camera on the device, to read the list of contacts, and to read the calendar.

Listing 7–3. *Permissions in AndroidManifest.xml*

```
<manifest …  >
    <application>
       …
    </application>
    <uses-permission android:name="android.permission.CAMERA" />
    <uses-permission android:name="android.permission.READ_CONTACTS"/>
    <uses-permission android:name="android.permission.READ_CALENDAR" />
</manifest>
```

Note that you can either hand-code permissions in the AndroidManifest.xml file or use the manifest editor. The manifest editor is wired up to launch when you open (double-click) the manifest file. The manifest editor contains a drop-down list that has all of the permissions preloaded to prevent you from making a mistake. As shown in Figure 7–3, you can access the permissions list by selecting the Permissions tab in the manifest editor.

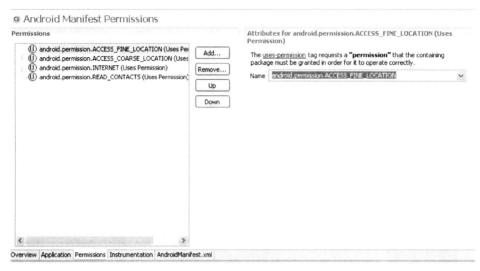

Figure 7–3. *The Android manifest editor tool in Eclipse*

You now know that Android defines a set of permissions that protects a set of features and resources. Similarly, you can define, and enforce, custom permissions with your application. Let's see how that works.

Understanding and Using Custom Permissions

Android allows you to define custom permissions with your application. For example, if you wanted to prevent certain users from starting one of the activities in your application, you could do that by defining a custom permission. To use custom permissions, you first declare them in your `AndroidManifest.xml` file. Once you've defined a permission, you can then refer to it as part of your component definition. We'll show you how this works.

Let's create an application containing an activity that not everyone is allowed to start. Instead, to start the activity, a user must have a specific permission. Once you have the application with a privileged activity, you can write a client that knows how to call the activity.

First, create the project with the custom permission and activity. Open the Eclipse IDE and select New ➤ New Project ➤ Android Project. This will open the New Android Project dialog box. Enter **CustomPermission** as the project name, select the "Create new project in workspace" radio button, and mark the "Use default location" check box. Enter **Custom Permission** as the application name, **com.cust.perm** as the package name, **CustPermMainActivity** as the activity name, and select a Build Target. Click the Finish button to create the project. The generated project will have the activity you just created, which will serve as the default (main) activity. Let's also create a so-called *privileged activity*—an activity that requires a special permission. In the Eclipse IDE, go to the `com.cust.perm` package, create a class named **PrivActivity** whose superclass is `android.app.Activity`, and copy the code shown in Listing 7–4.

Listing 7–4. *The PrivActivity Class*

```
package com.cust.perm;

import android.app.Activity;
import android.os.Bundle;
import android.view.ViewGroup.LayoutParams;
import android.widget.LinearLayout;
import android.widget.TextView;


public class PrivActivity extends Activity
{

    @Override
    public void onCreate(Bundle savedInstanceState) {
        super.onCreate(savedInstanceState);
        LinearLayout view = new LinearLayout(this);

        view.setLayoutParams(new LayoutParams(
                LayoutParams.FILL_PARENT, LayoutParams.WRAP_CONTENT));
        view.setOrientation(LinearLayout.HORIZONTAL);

        TextView nameLbl = new TextView(this);

        nameLbl.setText("Hello from PrivActivity");
        view.addView(nameLbl);

        setContentView(view);

    }
}
```

As you can see, `PrivActivity` does not do anything miraculous. We just want to show you how to protect this activity with a permission and then call it from a client. If the client succeeds, then you'll see the text "Hello from PrivActivity" on the screen. Now that you have an activity you want to protect, you can create the permission for it.

To create a custom permission, you have to define it in the `AndroidManifest.xml` file. The easiest way to do this is to use the manifest editor. Double-click the `AndroidManifest.xml` file and then select the Permissions tab. In the Permissions window, click the Add button, choose Permission, and then click the OK button. The manifest editor will create an empty new permission for you. Populate the new permission by setting its attributes as shown in Figure 7–4. Fill in the fields on the right-hand side, and if the label on the left-hand side still says just "Permission", click it and it should update with the name from the right-hand side.

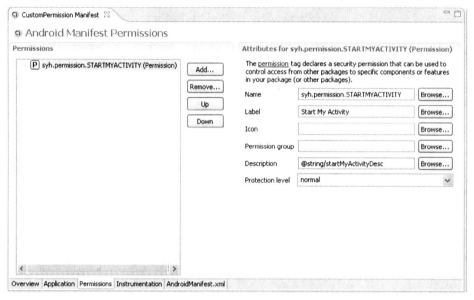

Figure 7–4. *Declaring a custom permission using the manifest editor*

As shown in Figure 7–4, a permission has a name, a label, an icon, a permission group, a description, and a protection level. Table 7–3 defines these properties.

Table 7–3. *Attributes of a Permission*

Attribute	Required?	Description
android:name	Yes	Name of the permission. You should generally follow the Android naming scheme (*.permission.*).
android:protectionLevel	Yes	Defines the "potential for risk" associated with the permission. Must be one of the following values: normal dangerous signature signatureOrSystem Depending on the protection level, the system might take different action when determining whether to grant the permission or not. normal signals that the permission is low-risk and will not harm the system, the user, or other applications. dangerous signals that the permission is high-risk, and that the system will likely require input from the user before granting this permission. signature tells Android that the permission should be granted only to applications that have been signed with the same digital signature as the application that declared the permission. signatureOrSystem tells Android to grant the permission to applications with the same signature or to the Android package classes. This protection level is for very special cases involving multiple vendors needing to share features through the system image.

Attribute	Required?	Description
android:permissionGroup	No	You can place permissions into a group, but for custom permissions you should avoid setting this property. If you really want to set this property, use this instead: `android.permission-group.SYSTEM_TOOLS`
android:label	No	Although it's not required, use this property to provide a short description of the permission.
android:description	No	Although it's not required, you should use this property to provide a more useful description of what the permission is for and what it protects.
android:icon	No	Permissions can be associated with an icon out of your resources (such as `@drawable/myicon`).

Now you have a custom permission. Next, you want to tell the system that the PrivActivity activity should be launched only by applications that have the `syh.permission.STARTMYACTIVITY` permission. You can set a required permission on an activity by adding the `android:permission` attribute to the activity definition in the AndroidManifest.xml file. For you to be able to launch the activity, you'll also need to add an intent-filter to the activity. Update your AndroidManifest.xml file with the content from Listing 7–6.

Listing 7–6. *The AndroidManifest.xml File for the Custom-Permission Project*

```xml
<?xml version="1.0" encoding="utf-8"?>
<manifest xmlns:android="http://schemas.android.com/apk/res/android"
        package="com.cust.perm"
        android:versionCode="1"
        android:versionName="1.0.0">
    <application android:icon="@drawable/icon" android:label="@string/app_name">
        <activity android:name=".CustPermMainActivity"
                android:label="@string/app_name">
            <intent-filter>
                <action android:name="android.intent.action.MAIN" />
                <category android:name="android.intent.category.LAUNCHER" />
            </intent-filter>
        </activity>
    <activity android:name="PrivActivity"
android:permission="syh.permission.STARTMYACTIVITY">
        <intent-filter>
                <action android:name="android.intent.action.MAIN" />
                <category android:name="android.intent.category.LAUNCHER" />
        </intent-filter>
    </activity>
</application>

<permission
android:protectionLevel="normal"
android:label="Start My Activity"
android:description="@string/startMyActivityDesc"
android:name="syh.permission.STARTMYACTIVITY"></permission>

    <uses-sdk android:minSdkVersion="2" />
```

```
</manifest>
```

Listing 7–6 requires that you add a string constant named `startMyActivityDesc` to your string resources. To ensure compilation of Listing 7–6, add the following string resource to the `res/values/strings.xml` file:

```
<string name="startMyActivityDesc">Allows starting my activity</string>
```

Now run the project in the emulator. Although the main activity does not do anything, you want the application installed on the emulator before you write a client for the privileged activity.

Let's write a client for the activity. In the Eclipse IDE, click New ➤ Project ➤ Android Project. Enter **ClientOfCustomPermission** as the project name, select the "Create new project in workspace" radio button, and mark the "Use default location" check box. Set the application name to **Client Of Custom Permission**, the package name to **com.client.cust.perm**, the activity name to **ClientCustPermMainActivity**, and select a Build Target. Click the Finish button to create the project.

Next, you want to write an activity that displays a button you can click to call the privileged activity. Copy the layout shown in Listing 7–7 to the `main.xml` file in the project you just created.

Listing 7–7. *Main.xml File for the Client Project*

```xml
<?xml version="1.0" encoding="utf-8"?>
<LinearLayout xmlns:android="http://schemas.android.com/apk/res/android"
    android:orientation="vertical"
    android:layout_width="fill_parent"
    android:layout_height="fill_parent"
    >
    <Button android:id="@+id/btn"
    android:text="Launch PrivActivity"
    android:layout_width="wrap_content"
    android:layout_height="wrap_content" />
</LinearLayout>
```

As you can see, the XML layout file defines a single button whose text reads "Launch PrivActivity." Now let's write an activity that will handle the button-click event and launch the privileged activity. Copy the code from Listing 7–8 to your `ClientCustPermMainActivity` class.

Listing 7–8. *The Modified ClientCustPermMainActivity Activity*

```java
package com.client.cust.perm;
// This file is ClientCustPermMainActivity.java

import android.app.Activity;
import android.content.Intent;
import android.os.Bundle;
import android.view.View;
import android.view.View.OnClickListener;
import android.widget.Button;

public class ClientCustPermMainActivity extends Activity {
    @Override
    public void onCreate(Bundle savedInstanceState) {
```

```
super.onCreate(savedInstanceState);
setContentView(R.layout.main);

Button btn = (Button)findViewById(R.id.btn);
btn.setOnClickListener(new OnClickListener(){

    @Override
    public void onClick(View arg0) {

        Intent intent = new Intent();

        intent.setClassName("com.cust.perm","com.cust.perm.PrivActivity");
        startActivity(intent);
    }});

    }
}
```

As shown in Listing 7–8, you obtain a reference to the button defined in the `main.xml` file and then wire up the on-click listener. When the button is invoked, you create a new intent, and then set the class name of the activity you want to launch. In this case, you want to launch `com.cust.perm.PrivActivity` in the `com.cust.perm` package.

The only thing missing at this point is a `uses-permission` entry, which you add into the manifest file to tell the Android runtime that you need the `syh.permission.STARTMYACTIVITY` to run. Replace your client project's manifest file with that shown in Listing 7–9.

Listing 7–9. *The Client Manifest File*

```xml
<?xml version="1.0" encoding="utf-8"?>
<manifest xmlns:android="http://schemas.android.com/apk/res/android"
    package="com.client.cust.perm"
    android:versionCode="1"
    android:versionName="1.0.0">
    <application android:icon="@drawable/icon" android:label="@string/app_name">
        <activity android:name=".ClientCustPermMainActivity"
                android:label="@string/app_name">
            <intent-filter>
                <action android:name="android.intent.action.MAIN" />
                <category android:name="android.intent.category.LAUNCHER" />
            </intent-filter>
        </activity>

    </application>

    <uses-permission android:name="syh.permission.STARTMYACTIVITY"></uses-permission>
    <uses-sdk android:minSdkVersion="2" />
</manifest>
```

As shown in Listing 7–9, we added a `uses-permission` entry to request the custom permission required to start the `PrivActivity` we implemented in the custom-permission project.

With that, you should be able to deploy the client project to the emulator and then select the Launch PrivActivity button. When the button is invoked, you should see the text "Hello from PrivActivity."

After you successfully call the privileged activity, remove the `uses-permission` entry from your client project's manifest file and redeploy the project to the emulator. Once it's deployed, confirm that you get an error when you invoke the button to launch the privileged activity. Note that LogCat will display a permission-denial exception.

Now you know how custom permissions work in Android. Obviously, custom permissions are not limited to activities. In fact, you can apply both predefined and custom permissions to Android's other types of components as well. We'll explore an important one next: URI permissions.

Understanding and Using URI Permissions

Content providers (discussed in Chapter 3) often need to control access at a finer level than all or nothing. Fortunately, Android provides a mechanism for this. Think about e-mail attachments. The attachment may need to be read by another activity to display it. But the other activity should not get access to all of the e-mail data, and does not need access even to all attachments. This is where URI permissions come in.

When invoking another activity and passing a URI, your application can specify that it is granting permissions to the URI being passed. This is done with the `grantUriPermission()` method and passing either the `Intent.FLAG_GRANT_READ_URI_PERMISSION` or `Intent.FLAG_GRANT_WRITE_URI_PERMISSION` flag as an argument.

Working with Location-Based Services

The location-based services facility in Android sits on two pillars: the mapping APIs and the location APIs. Each of these APIs is isolated with respect to its own package. For example, the mapping package is `com.google.android.maps` and the location package is `android.location`. The mapping APIs in Android provide facilities for you to display a map and manipulate it. For example, you can zoom and pan, you can change the map mode (from satellite view to street view, for example), you can add custom data to the map, and so on. The other end of the spectrum is Global Positioning System (GPS) data and real-time location data, both of which are handled by the location package.

These APIs reach across the Internet to invoke services from Google servers. Therefore you will need to have Internet connectivity for these to work. In addition, Google has Terms of Service that you will agree to before you can develop applications with these Android Maps API services. Read the terms carefully; Google places some restrictions on what you can do with the service data. For example, you can use location information for users' personal use, but certain commercial uses are restricted, as are applications involving automated control of vehicles. The terms will be presented to you when you sign up for a map-api key.

In this section, we'll go through each of these packages. We'll start with the mapping APIs and show you how to use maps with your applications. As you'll see, mapping in Android boils down to using the `MapView` UI control and the `MapActivity` class in addition to the mapping APIs, which integrate with Google Maps. We will also show you how to place custom data onto the maps that you display. After talking about maps, we'll delve into location-based services, which extend the mapping concepts. We will show you how to use the Android `Geocoder` class and the `LocationManager` service. We will also touch on threading issues that surface when you use these APIs.

Understanding the Mapping Package

As we mentioned, the mapping APIs comprise one of the components of Android's location-based services. The mapping package contains everything you'll need to display a map on the screen, handle user interaction with the map (such as zooming), display custom data on top of the map, and so on. The first step to working with this package is to display a map. To do that, you'll use the `MapView` view class. Using this class, however, requires some prep work. Specifically, before you can use the `MapView`, you'll need to get a map-api key from Google. The *map-api key* enables Android to interact with Google Maps services to obtain map data. Here's how to obtain a map-api key.

Obtaining a map-api Key from Google

The first thing to understand about the map-api key is that you'll need two keys: one for development with the emulator, and another for production (on the device). The reason for this is that the certificate used to obtain the map-api key will differ between development and production (as we discussed in the first part of this chapter).

For example, during development, the ADT plug-in generates the .apk file and deploys it to the emulator. Because the .apk file must be signed with a certificate, the ADT plug-in uses the debug certificate during development. For production deployment, you'll likely use a self-signed certificate to sign your .apk file. The good news is that you can obtain a map-api key for development and one for production, and swap the keys before exporting the production build.

To obtain a map-api key, you need the certificate that you'll use to sign your application. (Recall that in the development phase, the ADT plug-in uses a debug certificate to sign your application for you prior to deployment onto the emulator.) So you'll get the MD5 fingerprint of your certificate, then you'll enter it on Google's web site to generate an associated map-api key.

First you must locate your debug certificate, which is generated and maintained by Eclipse. You can find the exact location using the Eclipse IDE. From Eclipse's Preferences menu, go to Android ➤ Build. The debug certificate's location will be displayed in the "Default debug keystore" field, as shown in Figure 7–5. (See Chapter 2 if you have trouble finding the Preferences menu.)

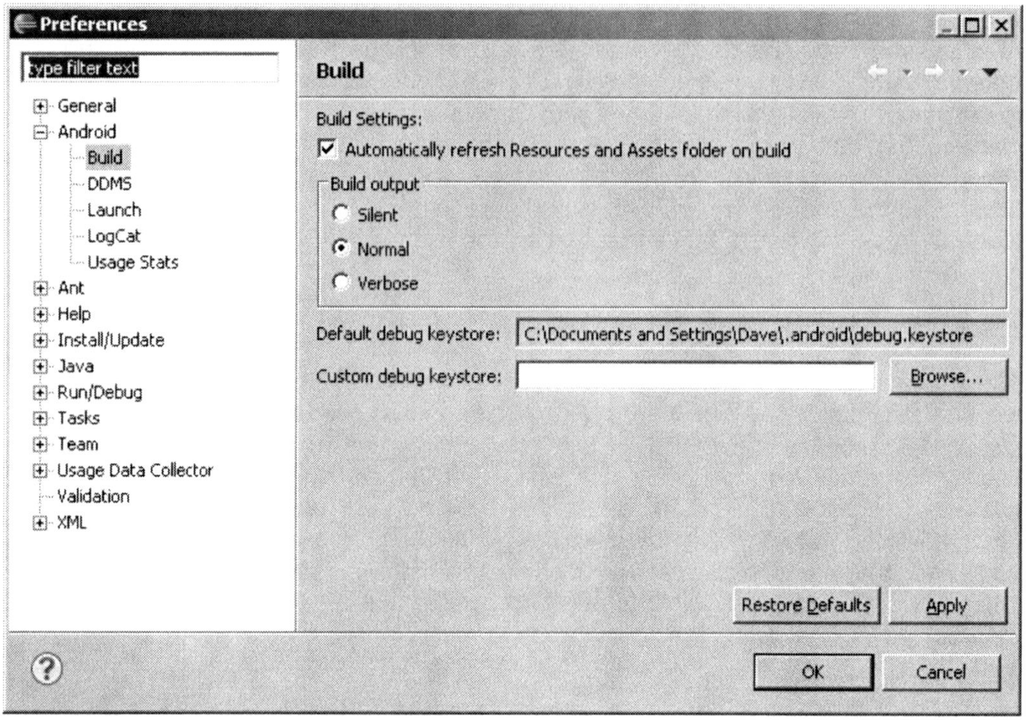

Figure 7–5. *The debug certificate's location*

To extract the MD5 fingerprint, you can run the keytool with the -list option, as shown in Listing 7–10.

Listing 7–10. *Using the Keytool to Obtain the MD5 Fingerprint of the Debug Certificate*

```
keytool -list -alias androiddebugkey -keystore
"FULL PATH OF YOUR debug.keystore FILE" -storepass android -keypass android
```

Note that the alias of the debug store is androiddebugkey. Similarly, the keystore password is android and the private-key password is also android. When you run the command in Listing 7–10, the keytool provides the fingerprint (see Figure 7–6).

Figure 7–6. *The keytool output for the list option (actual fingerprint smudged on purpose)*

Now paste your certificate's MD5 fingerprint in the appropriate field on this Google site:

http://code.google.com/android/maps-api-signup.html

Read through the Terms of Service. If you agree to the terms, click the Generate API Key button to get a corresponding map-api key from the Google Maps service. The map-api key is active immediately, so you can start using it to obtain map data from Google. Note that you will need a Google account to obtain a map-api key—when you try to generate the map-api key, you will be prompted to log in to your Google account.

Now let's start playing with maps.

Understanding MapView and MapActivity

A lot of the mapping technology in Android relies on the `MapView` UI control and an extension of `android.app.Activity` called `MapActivity`. The `MapView` and `MapActivity` classes take care of the heavy lifting when it comes to displaying and manipulating a map in Android. One of the things that you'll have to remember about these two classes is that they have to work together. Specifically, in order to use a `MapView`, you need to instantiate it within a `MapActivity`. In addition, when instantiating a `MapView`, you need to supply the map-api key. If you instantiate a `MapView` using an XML layout, you need to set the `android:apiKey` property. If you create a `MapView` programmatically, you have to pass the map-api key to the `MapView` constructor. Finally, because the underlying data for the map comes from Google Maps, your application will need permission to access the Internet. This means you need at least the following permission request in your `AndroidManifest. xml` file:

```
<uses-permission android:name="android.permission.INTERNET" />
```

In fact, whenever you use location-based services (maps, GPS, and so on), you will likely need to include three permissions in your `AndroidManifest.xml` file. The other two are `android.permission.ACCESS_COARSE_LOCATION` and `android.permission.ACCESS_FINE_LOCATION`. Listing 7–11 shows in bold the entries required in AndroidManifest.xml to make a map application work.

Listing 7–11. *Tags needed in AndroidManifest.xml for a map application*

```xml
<?xml version="1.0" encoding="utf-8"?>
<manifest xmlns:android="http://schemas.android.com/apk/res/android"
    package="com.androidbook"
    android:versionCode="1"
    android:versionName="1.0">
    <application android:icon="@drawable/icon" android:label="@string/app_name">
        <uses-library android:name="com.google.android.maps" />
        <activity android:name=".MapViewDemoActivity"
                android:label="@string/app_name">
            <intent-filter>
                <action android:name="android.intent.action.MAIN" />
                <category android:name="android.intent.category.LAUNCHER" />
            </intent-filter>
        </activity>
    </application>
    <uses-permission android:name="android.permission.ACCESS_FINE_LOCATION" />
    <uses-permission android:name="android.permission.ACCESS_COARSE_LOCATION" />
    <uses-permission android:name="android.permission.INTERNET"/>
    <uses-sdk android:minSdkVersion="3" />
```

```
</manifest>
```

Recall from Table 7–2 that `android.permission.ACCESS_FINE_LOCATION` allows you to obtain "fine" location data such as GPS data. `android.permission.ACCESS_COARSE_LOCATION` allows you to obtain "coarse" location data, which includes cell tower and WiFi location information.

There's another modification you need to make to the AndroidManifest.xml file. The definition of your map application needs to reference a mapping library. (This line was also included in Listing 7–11.) With the prerequisites out of the way, have a look at Figure 7–7.

Figure 7–7. *A MapView control in street-view mode*

Figure 7–7 shows an application that displays a map in street-view mode. The application also demonstrates how you can zoom in, zoom out, and change the map's view mode. The XML layout is shown in Listing 7–12.

Listing 7–12. *XML Layout of MapView Demo*

```xml
<?xml version="1.0" encoding="utf-8"?>
<!-- This file is /res/layout/mapview.xml -->
<LinearLayout xmlns:android="http://schemas.android.com/apk/res/android"
    android:orientation="vertical" android:layout_width="fill_parent"
    android:layout_height="fill_parent">

    <LinearLayout xmlns:android="http://schemas.android.com/apk/res/android"
        android:orientation="horizontal" android:layout_width="fill_parent"
        android:layout_height="wrap_content">

        <Button android:id="@+id/zoomin" android:layout_width="wrap_content"
            android:layout_height="wrap_content" android:text="+"
            android:onClick="myClickHandler" android:padding="12px" />
```

```
        <Button android:id="@+id/zoomout" android:layout_width="wrap_content"
            android:layout_height="wrap_content" android:text="-"
            android:onClick="myClickHandler" android:padding="12px" />

        <Button android:id="@+id/sat" android:layout_width="wrap_content"
            android:layout_height="wrap_content" android:text="Satellite"
            android:onClick="myClickHandler" android:padding="8px" />

        <Button android:id="@+id/street" android:layout_width="wrap_content"
            android:layout_height="wrap_content" android:text="Street"
            android:onClick="myClickHandler" android:padding="8px" />

        <Button android:id="@+id/traffic" android:layout_width="wrap_content"
            android:layout_height="wrap_content" android:text="Traffic"
            android:onClick="myClickHandler" android:padding="8px" />

        <Button android:id="@+id/normal" android:layout_width="wrap_content"
            android:layout_height="wrap_content" android:text="Normal"
            android:onClick="myClickHandler" android:padding="8px" />

    </LinearLayout>

    <com.google.android.maps.MapView
        android:id="@+id/mapview" android:layout_width="fill_parent"
        android:layout_height="wrap_content" android:clickable="true"
        android:apiKey="YOUR MAP API KEY GOES HERE" />

</LinearLayout>
```

As shown in Listing 7–12, a parent LinearLayout contains a child LinearLayout and a MapView. The child LinearLayout contains the buttons shown at the top of Figure 7–7. Also note that you need to update the MapView control's android:apiKey value with the value of your own map-api key.

The code for our sample mapping application is shown in Listing 7–13.

Listing 7–13. *The MapActivity Extension Class That Loads the XML Layout*

```
// This file is MapViewDemoActivity.java
import android.os.Bundle;
import android.view.View;

import com.google.android.maps.MapActivity;
import com.google.android.maps.MapView;

public class MapViewDemoActivity extends MapActivity
{
    private MapView mapView;

    @Override
    protected void onCreate(Bundle savedInstanceState) {
        super.onCreate(savedInstanceState);
        setContentView(R.layout.mapview);

        mapView = (MapView)findViewById(R.id.mapview);
    }
```

```
        public void myClickHandler(View target) {
            switch(target.getId()) {
            case R.id.zoomin:
                mapView.getController().zoomIn();
                break;
            case R.id.zoomout:
                mapView.getController().zoomOut();
                break;
            case R.id.sat:
                mapView.setSatellite(true);
                break;
            case R.id.street:
                mapView.setStreetView(true);
                break;
            case R.id.traffic:
                mapView.setTraffic(true);
                break;
            case R.id.normal:
                mapView.setSatellite(false);
                mapView.setStreetView(false);
                mapView.setTraffic(false);
                break;
            }
        }

        @Override
        protected boolean isLocationDisplayed() {
            return false;
        }

        @Override
        protected boolean isRouteDisplayed() {
            return false;
        }
    }
```

As shown in Listing 7–13, displaying the MapView using onCreate() is no different from displaying any other control. That is, you set the content view of the UI to a layout file that contains the MapView, and that takes care of it. Surprisingly, supporting zoom features is also fairly easy. To zoom in or zoom out, you use the MapController class of the MapView. Do this by calling mapView.getController() and then calling the approproiate zoomIn() or zoomOut() method. Zooming this way produces a one-level zoom; users need to repeat the action to increase the amount of magnification or reduction.

You'll also find it straightforward to offer the ability to change view modes. The MapView supports several modes: map, street view, satellite, and traffic. Map is the default mode. Street view mode places a layer on top of the map that puts blue outlines on roads for which street-level images are available for viewing. These images were taken from cameras mounted on trucks that drove around the streets. Note, however, that the MapView control does not display street view images. To view those street-level images you will need a separate view control. This will be covered in greater detail in Chapter 16. Satellite mode shows aerial photographs of the map so you can see the actual tops of buildings, trees, roads, and so on. Traffic mode shows traffic information on the map with colored lines to represent traffic that is moving well as opposed to traffic that is backed up. Note that traffic mode is supported on a limited number of major highways. To change modes, you must call the appropriate setter method with `true`. In some cases, setting one mode will turn off another. For example, you can't have street view mode on at the same time as traffic mode, so setting traffic mode on turns street view mode off automatically. To turn off a mode, set that mode to `false`.

> **NOTE:** You may find that setting street view mode or traffic mode on doesn't appear to do anything. If you move the map just a little after setting one of these modes, you will see the map update with the appropriate information.

To make the map move sideways, set the attribute `android:clickable="true"` for the MapView in XML—otherwise, you will only be able to zoom in and out, not laterally. You can also set this in code using the `setClickable(true)` method call on your `mapView`.

One more thing to mention from this example are the two methods `isLocationDisplayed()` and `isRouteDisplayed()`. These methods are required by the Google Terms of Service. Your application is obligated to respond with `true` or `false` to indicate to the map server whether or not the current device location is being displayed, or if any route information is being displayed such as driving directions.

You'll probably agree that the amount of code required to display a map and to implement zoom and mode changes is minimal with Android (see Listing 7–13). However, there's an even easier way to implement zoom controls. Take a look at the XML layout and code shown in Listing 7–14.

Listing 7–14. *Zooming Made Easier*

```xml
<?xml version="1.0" encoding="utf-8"?>
<!-- This file is /res/layout/mapview.xml -->
<RelativeLayout xmlns:android="http://schemas.android.com/apk/res/android"
        android:orientation="vertical" android:layout_width="fill_parent"
        android:layout_height="fill_parent">

    <com.google.android.maps.MapView android:id="@+id/mapview"
            android:layout_width="fill_parent"
            android:layout_height="wrap_content"
            android:clickable="true"
            android:apiKey="YOUR MAP API KEY GOES HERE"
            />
</RelativeLayout>
```

```java
public class MapViewDemoActivity extends MapActivity
{
    private MapView mapView;
    @Override
    protected void onCreate(Bundle savedInstanceState) {
        super.onCreate(savedInstanceState);

        setContentView(R.layout.mapview);

        mapView = (MapView)findViewById(R.id.mapview);
```

```
        mapView.setBuiltInZoomControls(true);
    }

    @Override
    protected boolean isLocationDisplayed() {
        return false;
    }

    @Override
    protected boolean isRouteDisplayed() {
        return false;
    }
}
```

The difference between Listing 7–14 and Listing 7–13 is that we changed the XML layout for our view to use RelativeLayout. We removed all the zoom controls and view-mode controls. The magic in this example is in the code and not the layout. The MapView already has controls that allow you to zoom in and out. All you have to do is turn them on using the setBuiltInZoomControls() method. Figure 7–8 shows the MapView's default zoom controls.

Figure 7–8. *The MapView's built-in zoom controls*

Now let's learn how to add custom data to the map.

Using Overlays

Google Maps provides a facility that allows you to place custom data on top of the map. You can see an example of this if you search for pizza restaurants in your area: Google Maps places pushpins, or balloon markers, to indicate each location. The way Google

Maps provides this facility is by allowing you to add a layer on top of the map. Android provides several classes that help you to add layers to a map. The key class for this type of functionality is `Overlay`, but you can use an extension of this class called `ItemizedOverlay`. Listing 7–15 shows an example.

Listing 7–15. *Marking Up a Map Using ItemizedOverlay*

```java
import java.util.ArrayList;
import java.util.List;

import android.graphics.Canvas;
import android.graphics.drawable.Drawable;
import android.os.Bundle;
import android.widget.LinearLayout;

import com.google.android.maps.GeoPoint;
import com.google.android.maps.ItemizedOverlay;
import com.google.android.maps.MapActivity;
import com.google.android.maps.MapView;
import com.google.android.maps.OverlayItem;

public class MappingOverlayActivity extends MapActivity {
    private MapView mapView;

    @Override
    protected void onCreate(Bundle savedInstanceState) {
        super.onCreate(savedInstanceState);

        setContentView(R.layout.mapview);

        mapView = (MapView) findViewById(R.id.mapview);

        mapView.setBuiltInZoomControls(true);

        mapView.setClickable(true);

        Drawable marker=getResources().getDrawable(R.drawable.mapmarker);
        marker.setBounds(0, 0, marker.getIntrinsicWidth(),
                                marker.getIntrinsicHeight());

        InterestingLocations funPlaces = new InterestingLocations(marker);
        mapView.getOverlays().add(funPlaces);

        GeoPoint pt = funPlaces.getCenter();      // get the first-ranked point
        mapView.getController().setCenter(pt);
        mapView.getController().setZoom(15);
    }

    @Override
    protected boolean isLocationDisplayed() {
        return false;
    }

    @Override
    protected boolean isRouteDisplayed() {
        return false;
    }

    class InterestingLocations extends ItemizedOverlay {
        private List<OverlayItem> locations = new ArrayList<OverlayItem>();
```

```
        private Drawable marker;

        public InterestingLocations(Drawable marker)
        {
            super(marker);
            this.marker=marker;
            // create locations of interest
            GeoPoint disneyMagicKingdom = new
GeoPoint((int)(28.418971*1000000),(int)(-81.581436*1000000));
            GeoPoint disneySevenLagoon = new
GeoPoint((int)(28.410067*1000000),(int)(-81.583699*1000000));

            locations.add(new OverlayItem(disneyMagicKingdom ,
"Magic Kingdom", "Magic Kingdom"));
            locations.add(new OverlayItem(disneySevenLagoon ,
"Seven Lagoon", "Seven Lagoon"));

            populate();
        }

        @Override
        public void draw(Canvas canvas, MapView mapView, boolean shadow) {
            super.draw(canvas, mapView, shadow);

            boundCenterBottom(marker);
        }

        @Override
        protected OverlayItem createItem(int i) {
            return locations.get(i);
        }

        @Override
        public int size() {
            return locations.size();
        }

    }
}
```

Listing 7–15 demonstrates how you can overlay markers onto a map. The example places two markers: one at Disney's Magic Kingdom and another at Disney's Seven Seas Lagoon (both near Orlando, Florida; see Figure 7–9).

> **NOTE:** In order to run this demo, you'll need to get a drawable to serve as your map marker. This image file must be saved into your /res/drawable folder so that the resource ID reference in the getDrawable() call matches the filename you choose for your image file. For the overlay, you also need to define where the anchor point is for your marker—that is, exactly where on your marker you want to attach to the point of interest on the map. For our example, we call boundCenterBottom() within the draw() method. This defines the anchor point as the middle of the bottom edge of our marker. The other method for defining the anchor point is

boundCenter() which chooses the very center of the drawable as where the point on the map should be.

In order for you to add markers onto a map, you have to create and add an extension of com.google.android.maps.Overlay to the map. The Overlay class itself cannot be instantiated, so you'll have to extend it or use one of the extensions. In our example, we have implemented InterestingLocations, which extends ItemizedOverlay, which in turn extends Overlay. The Overlay class defines the contract for an overlay, and ItemizedOverlay is a handy implementation that makes it easy for you to create a list of locations that can be marked on a map.

The general usage pattern is to extend the ItemizedOverlay class and add your "items"—interesting locations—in the constructor. After you instantiate your points of interest, you call the populate() method of ItemizedOverlay. The populate() method is a utility that caches the OverlayItem(s). Internally, the class calls the size() method to determine the number of overlay items, and then enters a loop, calling createItem(i) for each item. In the createItem method, you return the already-created item given the index in the array.

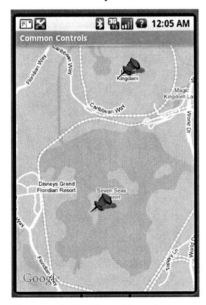

Figure 7–9. *MapView with markers*

As you can see from Listing 7–15, you simply create the points and call populate() to show markers on a map. The Overlay contract manages the rest. To make it all work, the onCreate() method of the activity creates the InterestingLocations instance, passing in the Drawable that's used for the markers. Then onCreate() adds the InterestingLocations instance to the overlay collection (mapView.getOverlays().add()).

Now that the overlay is associated to our map, we still need to move into the right position in order to actually see the markers in the display. To do this we need to set the center of the displayed map to a point. We choose the first point from the overlay to use as our new center. The getCenter() method of the overlay returns the first point (not the center point, as you might expect). The setCenter() method of the mapview's controller sets the center of what's displayed. The setZoom() method sets how high we are above the map. For this demo we chose a zoom level of 15 for convenience. We could have iterated through the items in the overlap to determine the outer bounds, then calculated an appropriate zoom level so all markers appear at the same time.

Another interesting aspect of Listing 7–15 is the creation of the OverlayItem(s). In order to create an OverlayItem, you need an object of type GeoPoint. The GeoPoint class represents a location by its latitude and longitude, in micro degrees. In our example, we obtained the latitude and longitude of Magic Kingdom and Seven Seas Lagoon using geocoding sites on the Web. (As you'll see shortly, you can use geocoding to convert an address to a latitude/longitude pair, for example.) We then converted the latitude and longitude to micro degrees—the APIs operate on micro degrees—by multiplying by 1,000,000 and then performing a cast to an integer.

So far, we've shown how to place markers on a map. But overlays are not restricted to showing pushpins or balloons. They can be used to do other things. For example, we could show animations of products moving across maps, or we could show symbols such as weather fronts or thunderstorms.

All in all, you'll agree that placing markers on a map couldn't be easier. Or could it? We don't have a database of latitude/longitude pairs, but we're guessing that we'll need to somehow create one or more GeoPoints using a real address. That's when you can use the Geocoder, which is part of the location package that we'll discuss next.

Understanding the Location Package

The android.location package provides facilities for location-based services. In this section, we are going to discuss two important pieces of this package: the Geocoder class and the LocationManager service. We'll start with Geocoder.

Geocoding with Android

If you are going to do anything practical with maps, you'll likely have to convert an address (or location) to a latitude/longitude pair. This concept is known as *geocoding*, and the android.location.Geocoder class provides this facility. In fact, the Geocoder class provides both forward and backward conversion—it can take an address and return a latitude/longitude pair, and it can translate a latitude/longitude pair into a list of addresses. The class provides the following methods:

- List<Address>   getFromLocation(double latitude, double longitude, int maxResults)

- List<Address>   getFromLocationName(String locationName, int maxResults, double lowerLeftLatitude, double lowerLeftLongitude, double upperRightLatitude, double upperRightLongitude)

- List<Address> getFromLocationName(String locationName, int maxResults)

It turns out that computing an address is not an exact science, due to the various ways a location can be described. For example, the getFromLocationName() methods can take the name of a place, the physical address, an airport code, or simply a well-known name for the location. Thus, the methods provide a list of addresses and not a single address. Because the methods return a list, you are encouraged to limit the result set by providing a value for maxResults that ranges between 1 and 5. Now let's see an example.

Listing 7–16 shows the XML layout and corresponding code for the user interface shown in Figure 7–10. To run the example, you'll need to update the listing with your own map-api key.

Listing 7–16. *Working with the Android Geocoder Class*

```xml
<?xml version="1.0" encoding="utf-8"?>
<!-- This file is /res/layout/geocode.xml -->
<RelativeLayout xmlns:android="http://schemas.android.com/apk/res/android"
        android:layout_width="fill_parent"
        android:layout_height="fill_parent">

        <LinearLayout android:layout_width="fill_parent"
            android:layout_alignParentBottom="true"
            android:layout_height="wrap_content" android:orientation="vertical" >

            <EditText android:layout_width="fill_parent" android:id="@+id/location"
            android:layout_height="wrap_content" android:text="White House"/>

            <Button android:id="@+id/geocodeBtn"
                android:layout_width="wrap_content"
                android:layout_height="wrap_content" android:text="Find Location"/>
        </LinearLayout>

        <com.google.android.maps.MapView
                android:id="@+id/geoMap" android:clickable="true"
                android:layout_width="fill_parent"
                android:layout_height="320px"
                android:apiKey="YOUR MAP API KEY GOES HERE"
                />

</RelativeLayout>

import java.io.IOException;
import java.util.List;

import android.location.Address;
import android.location.Geocoder;
import android.os.Bundle;
import android.view.View;
import android.view.View.OnClickListener;
import android.widget.Button;
import android.widget.EditText;

import com.google.android.maps.GeoPoint;
```

```java
import com.google.android.maps.MapActivity;
import com.google.android.maps.MapView;

public class GeocodingDemoActivity extends MapActivity
{
    Geocoder geocoder = null;
    MapView mapView = null;

    @Override
    protected boolean isLocationDisplayed() {
        return false;
    }

    @Override
    protected boolean isRouteDisplayed() {
        return false;
    }

    @Override
    protected void onCreate(Bundle savedInstanceState)
    {
        super.onCreate(savedInstanceState);

        setContentView(R.layout.geocode);
        mapView = (MapView)findViewById(R.id.geoMap);
        mapView.setBuiltInZoomControls(true);

        // lat/long of Jacksonville, FL
        int lat = (int)(30.334954*1000000);
        int lng = (int)(-81.5625*1000000);
        GeoPoint pt = new GeoPoint(lat,lng);
        mapView.getController().setZoom(10);
        mapView.getController().setCenter(pt);

        Button geoBtn =(Button)findViewById(R.id.geocodeBtn);

        geocoder = new Geocoder(this);

        geoBtn.setOnClickListener(new OnClickListener(){

        @Override
        public void onClick(View arg0) {
            try {
                EditText loc = (EditText)findViewById(R.id.location);
                String locationName = loc.getText().toString();

                List<Address> addressList =
geocoder.getFromLocationName(locationName, 5);
                if(addressList!=null && addressList.size()>0)
                {
                    int lat = (int)(addressList.get(0).getLatitude()*1000000);
                    int lng = (int)(addressList.get(0).getLongitude()*1000000);

                    GeoPoint pt = new GeoPoint(lat,lng);
                    mapView.getController().setZoom(15);
                    mapView.getController().setCenter(pt);
                }
```

```
            } catch (IOException e) {
                e.printStackTrace();
            }
        }});

    }
}
```

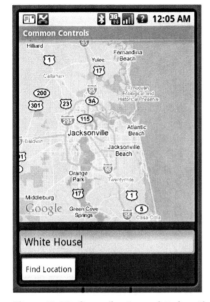

Figure 7-10. *Geocoding to a point given the location name*

To demonstrate the uses of geocoding in Android, type the name of the location, or its address, in the EditText field and then click the Find Location button. To find the address of a location, call the getFromLocationName() method of Geocoder. The location can be an address or a well-known name such as "White House." Geocoding can be a timely operation, so we recommend that you limit the results to five, as the Android documentation suggests. The call to getFromLocationName() returns a list of addresses. The sample application takes the list of addresses and processes the first one if any were found. Every address has a latitude and longitude, which you use to create a GeoPoint. You then get the map controller and navigate to the point. The zoom level can be set to an integer between 1 and 21, inclusive. As you move from 1 toward 21, the zoom level increases by a factor of 2.

You should understand a few points with respect to geocoding. First, a returned address is not always an exact address. Obviously, because the returned list of addresses depends on the accuracy of the input, you need to make every effort to provide an accurate location name to the Geocoder. Second, whenever possible, set the maxResults parameter to a value between 1 and 5. Finally, you should seriously consider doing the geocoding operation in a different thread from the UI thread. There are two reasons for this. The first is obvious: the operation is time-consuming and you don't want the UI to hang while you do the geocoding. The second reason is that with a mobile device, you always need to assume that the network connection can be lost and that the connection is weak. Therefore, you need to handle input/output (I/O) exceptions and timeouts appropriately. Once you have computed the addresses, you can post the results to the UI thread. Let's investigate this a bit more.

Geocoding with Background Threads

Using background threads to handle time-consuming operations is very common. The general pattern is to handle a UI event (such as a button click) to initiate a timely operation. From the event handler, you create a new thread to execute the work, and then you start the new thread. The UI thread then returns to the user interface to handle the interaction with the user, while the background thread works. After the background thread completes, a part of the UI might have to be updated or the user might have to be notified. The background thread does not update the UI directly; instead, the background thread notifies the UI thread to update itself. Listing 7–17 demonstrates this idea using geocoding. We'll use the same geocode.xml file as before. We can also use the same AndroidManifest.xml file as before.

Listing 7–17. *Geocoding in a Separate Thread*

```
import java.io.IOException;
import java.util.List;

import android.app.AlertDialog;
import android.app.Dialog;
import android.app.ProgressDialog;
import android.location.Address;
import android.location.Geocoder;
import android.os.Bundle;
import android.os.Handler;
import android.os.Message;
import android.view.View;
import android.view.View.OnClickListener;
import android.widget.Button;
import android.widget.EditText;

import com.google.android.maps.GeoPoint;
import com.google.android.maps.MapActivity;
import com.google.android.maps.MapView;
public class GeocodingDemoActivity extends MapActivity
{
    Geocoder geocoder = null;
    MapView mapView = null;
    ProgressDialog progDialog=null;
    List<Address> addressList=null;

    @Override
    protected boolean isLocationDisplayed() {
        return false;
    }

    @Override
    protected boolean isRouteDisplayed() {
        return false;
```

```java
    }

    @Override
    protected void onCreate(Bundle savedInstanceState) {
        super.onCreate(savedInstanceState);

        setContentView(R.layout.geocode);
        mapView = (MapView)findViewById(R.id.geoMap);
        mapView.setBuiltInZoomControls(true);

        // lat/long of Jacksonville, FL
        int lat = (int)(30.334954*1000000);
        int lng = (int)(-81.5625*1000000);
        GeoPoint pt = new GeoPoint(lat,lng);
        mapView.getController().setZoom(10);
        mapView.getController().setCenter(pt);

        Button geoBtn =(Button)findViewById(R.id.geocodeBtn);

        geocoder = new Geocoder(this);

        geoBtn.setOnClickListener(new OnClickListener(){

            @Override
            public void onClick(View view) {
                EditText loc = (EditText)findViewById(R.id.location);
                String locationName = loc.getText().toString();

                progDialog =
ProgressDialog.show(GeocodingDemoActivity.this,
"Processing...", "Finding Location...", true, false);

                findLocation(locationName);
        }});

    }

    private void findLocation(final String locationName)
    {
        Thread thrd = new Thread()
        {
            public void run()
            {
                try {
                    // do backgrond work
                    addressList = geocoder.getFromLocationName(locationName, 5);
                    //send message to handler to process results
                    uiCallback.sendEmptyMessage(0);

                } catch (IOException e) {
                    e.printStackTrace();
                }
            }
        };
        thrd.start();
    }
    // ui thread callback handler
```

```
        private Handler uiCallback = new Handler()
        {
            @Override
            public void handleMessage(Message msg)
            {
                progDialog.dismiss();

                if(addressList!=null && addressList.size()>0)
                {
                    int lat = (int)(addressList.get(0).getLatitude()*1000000);
                    int lng = (int)(addressList.get(0).getLongitude()*1000000);
                    GeoPoint pt = new GeoPoint(lat,lng);
                    mapView.getController().setZoom(15);
                    mapView.getController().setCenter(pt);
                }
                else
                {
                    Dialog foundNothingDlg = new
AlertDialog.Builder(GeocodingDemoActivity.this)
                        .setIcon(0)
                        .setTitle("Failed to Find Location")
                        .setPositiveButton("Ok", null)
                        .setMessage("Location Not Found...")
                        .create();
                    foundNothingDlg.show();
                }
            }
        };
}
```

Listing 7–17 is a modified version of the example in Listing 7–16. The difference is that now, in the onClick() method, you display a progress dialog and call findLocation() (see Figure 7–11). findLocation() then creates a new thread and calls the start() method, which ultimately results in a call to the thread's run() method. In the run() method, you use the Geocoder class to search for the location. When the search is done, you must post the message to something that knows how to interact with the UI thread, because you need to update the map. Android provides the android.os.Handler class for this purpose. From the background thread, call the uiCallback.sendEmptyMessage(0) to have the UI thread process the results from the search. In our case, we don't need to actually send any content in the message since the data is being shared through the addressList. The code calls the handler's callback, which dismisses the dialog, then looks at the addressList returned by the Geocoder. The callback then updates the map with the result or displays an alert dialog to indicate that the search returned nothing. The UI for this example is shown in Figure 7–11.

Figure 7–11. *Showing a progress window during long operations*

Understanding the LocationManager Service

The LocationManager service is one of the key services offered by the android.location package. This service provides two things: a mechanism for you to obtain the device's geographical location, and a facility for you to be notified (via an intent) when the device enters a specified geographical location.

In this section, you are going to learn how the LocationManager service works. To use the service, you must first obtain a reference to it. Listing 7–18 shows the usage pattern for the LocationManager service.

Listing 7–18. *Using the LocationManager Service*

```java
import java.util.List;

import android.app.Activity;
import android.content.Context;
import android.location.Location;
import android.location.LocationManager;
import android.os.Bundle;

public class LocationManagerDemoActivity extends Activity
{
    @Override
    protected void onCreate(Bundle savedInstanceState)
    {
        super.onCreate(savedInstanceState);
        LocationManager locMgr =
                (LocationManager)this.getSystemService(Context.LOCATION_SERVICE);
        Location loc = locMgr.getLastKnownLocation(LocationManager.GPS_PROVIDER);
```

```
        List<String> providerList = locMgr.getAllProviders();

    }
}
```

The LocationManager service is a system-level service. System-level services are services that you obtain from the context using the service name; you don't instantiate them directly. The android.app.Activity class provides a utility method called getSystemService() that you can use to obtain a system-level service. As shown in Listing 7–18, you call getSystemService() and pass in the name of the service you want—in this case, Context.LOCATION_SERVICE.

The LocationManager service provides geographical location details by using location providers. Currently, there are two types of location providers: GPS and Network. GPS providers use a Global Positioning System to obtain location information, whereas network providers use cell-phone towers or WiFi networks to obtain location information. The LocationManager class can provide the device's last-known location (which is probably close to the current location) via the getLastKnownLocation() method. Location information is obtained from a provider, so the method takes as a parameter the name of the provider you want to use. Valid values for provider names are LocationManager.GPS_PROVIDER and LocationManager.NETWORK_PROVIDER. Calling getLastKnownLocation() returns an android.location.Location instance. The Location class provides the location's latitude and longitude, the time the location was computed, and possibly the device's altitude, speed, and bearing.

Because the LocationManager operates on providers, the class provides APIs to obtain providers. For example, you can get all of the providers by calling getAllProviders(). You can obtain a specific provider by calling getProvider(), passing the name of the provider as an argument (such as LocationManager.GPS_PROVIDER).

To that end, the gotcha with using the LocationManager services occurs at development time—LocationManager needs location information and the emulator doesn't really have access to GPS or cell towers. So in order for you to develop with the LocationManager service, you (sort of) tell the emulator about your location. For example, you can ask the LocationManager to notify you if the device is near a location. To test something like this with the emulator, you would have to send the emulator periodic updates on your location; the emulator would then play that information back to the application. Listing 7–19 shows an example.

Listing 7–19. *Registering for Location Updates*

```
import android.app.Activity;
import android.content.Context;
import android.location.Location;
import android.location.LocationListener;
import android.location.LocationManager;
import android.os.Bundle;
import android.widget.Toast;

public class LocationUpdateDemoActivity extends Activity
{
```

```
    @Override
    public void onCreate(Bundle savedInstanceState)
    {
        super.onCreate(savedInstanceState);

        LocationManager locMgr = (LocationManager)
getSystemService(Context.LOCATION_SERVICE);

        LocationListener locListener = new LocationListener()
        {

            public void  onLocationChanged(Location location)
            {
                    if (location != null)
                    {
                            Toast.makeText(getBaseContext(),
                                "New location latitude [" +
location.getLatitude() +
                                "] longitude [" + location.getLongitude()+"]",
                                Toast.LENGTH_SHORT).show();
                    }
            }

            public void  onProviderDisabled(String provider)
            {
            }

            public void  onProviderEnabled(String provider)
            {
            }

            public void  onStatusChanged(String provider,
int status, Bundle extras)
            {
            }

        };

        locMgr.requestLocationUpdates(
            LocationManager.GPS_PROVIDER,
            0,          // minTime in ms
            0,          // minDistance in meters
            locListener);
    }
}
```

As we said, one of the primary uses of the LocationManager service is to receive
notifications of the device's location. Listing 7–19 demonstrates how you can register
a listener to receive location-update events. To register a listener, you call the
requestLocationUpdates() method, passing the provider type as one of the
parameters. When the location changes, the LocationManager calls the
onLocationChanged() method of the listener with the new Location. In our example,
we set the minTime and minDistance to zero. This tells the LocationManager to send
us updates as often as possible. These are not desired settings in real life but we use
them here to make the demos run better. (In real life, you would not want the hardware

trying to figure out our current position so often, as this drains the battery.) Set these values appropriately for the situation, trying to minimize how often you truly need to be notified of a change in position.

A new tool was introduced to you in Listing 7–19: the Toast widget. This is a handy device that allows you to briefly display a small pop-up view to the user. It appears to hover over the existing view, then goes away by itself. You can lengthen how long it hovers by using LENGTH_LONG instead of LENGTH_SHORT.

To test this in the emulator, you can use the Dalvik Debug Monitor Service (DDMS) interface that ships with the ADT plug-in for Eclipse. The DDMS UI provides a screen for you to send the emulator a new location (see Figure 7–12).

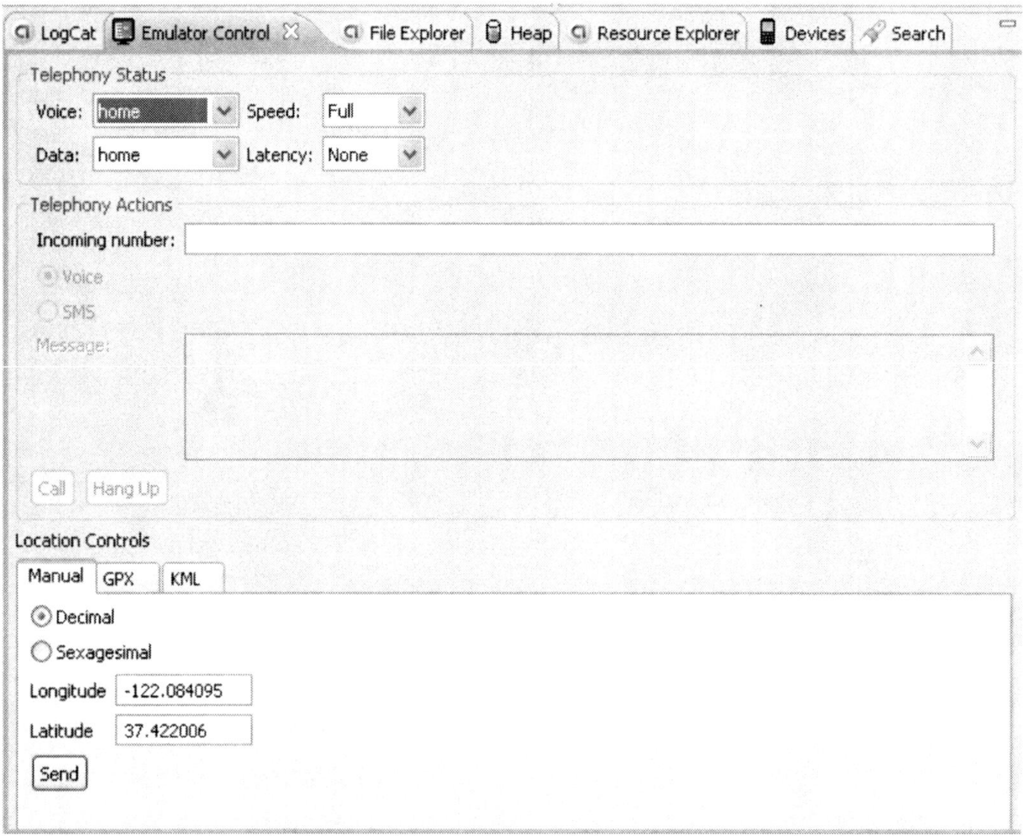

Figure 7–12. *Using the DDMS UI in Eclipse to send location data to the emulator*

As shown in Figure 7–12, the Manual tab in the DDMS user interface allows you to send a new GPS location (latitude/longitude pair) to the emulator. Sending a new location will fire the onLocationChanged() method on the listener, which will result in a message to the user conveying the new location.

You can send location data to the emulator using several other techniques, as shown in the DDMS user interface (see Figure 7–12). For example, the DDMS interface allows you to submit a GPS Exchange Format (GPX) file or a Keyhole Markup Language (KML) file. You can obtain sample GPX files from these sites:

- `http://www.topografix.com/gpx_resources.asp`
- `http://tramper.co.nz/?view=gpxFiles`
- `http://www.gpxchange.com/`

Similarly, you can use the following KML resources to obtain or create KML files:

- `http://bbs.keyhole.com/`
- `http://code.google.com/apis/kml/documentation/kml_tut.html`

NOTE: Some sites provide KMZ files. These are zipped KML files, so simply unzip them to get to the KML file. Some KML files need to have their XML namespace values altered in order to play properly in DDMS. If you have trouble with a particular KML file, make sure it has this: `<kml xmlns="http://earth.google.com/kml/2.x">`.

You can upload a GPX or KML file to the emulator and set the speed at which the emulator will play back the file (see Figure 7–13). The emulator will then send location updates to your application based on the configured speed. As Figure 7–13 shows, a GPX file contains points, shown in the top part, and paths, shown in the bottom part. You can't play a point but when you click on a point it will be sent to the emulator. You click on a path and then the Play button will be enabled so you can play the points.

NOTE: There have been reports that not all GPX files are understandable by the Emulator Control. If you attempt to load a GPX file and nothing happens, try a different file from a different source.

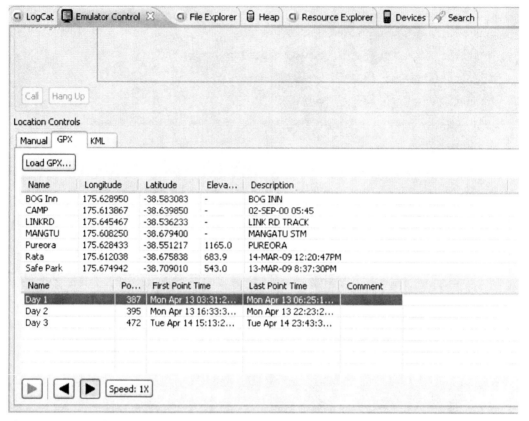

Figure 7–13. *Uploading GPX and KML files to the emulator for playback*

Using MyLocationOverlay

A common use for GPS and maps is to show the user where they are. Fortunately, Android makes this easy to do by supplying a special overlay called MyLocationOverlay. By adding this overlay to your MapView, you can quite easily add a blinking blue dot to your map showing where the LocationManager service says you are.

For this example, we're going to combine a bunch of concepts together into one application. Create a new Android project and call it MyLocationDemo with a main activity called MyLocationDemoActivity. Choose a Build Target of Google APIs. Using Listing 7–20, update the main.xml and MyLocationDemoActivity.java files.

Listing 7–20. *Using MyLocationOverlay*

```
<?xml version="1.0" encoding="utf-8"?>
<!-- This file is /res/layout/main.xml -->
<RelativeLayout xmlns:android="http://schemas.android.com/apk/res/android"
        android:layout_width="fill_parent"
        android:layout_height="fill_parent">

    <com.google.android.maps.MapView
```

```
            android:id="@+id/geoMap" android:clickable="true"
            android:layout_width="fill_parent"
            android:layout_height="fill_parent"
            android:apiKey="YOUR MAP API KEY GOES HERE"
            />

</RelativeLayout>


import com.google.android.maps.MapActivity;
import com.google.android.maps.MapController;
import com.google.android.maps.MapView;
import com.google.android.maps.MyLocationOverlay;

import android.os.Bundle;

public class MyLocationDemoActivity extends MapActivity {

    MapView mapView = null;
    MapController mapController = null;
    MyLocationOverlay whereAmI = null;

    @Override
    protected boolean isLocationDisplayed() {
        return whereAmI.isMyLocationEnabled();
    }

    @Override
    protected boolean isRouteDisplayed() {
        return false;
    }

    /** Called when the activity is first created. */
    @Override
    public void onCreate(Bundle savedInstanceState) {
        super.onCreate(savedInstanceState);
        setContentView(R.layout.main);

        mapView = (MapView)findViewById(R.id.geoMap);
        mapView.setBuiltInZoomControls(true);

        mapController = mapView.getController();
        mapController.setZoom(15);

        whereAmI = new MyLocationOverlay(this, mapView);
        mapView.getOverlays().add(whereAmI);
        mapView.postInvalidate();
    }

    @Override
    public void onResume()
    {
        super.onResume();
        whereAmI.enableMyLocation();
        whereAmI.runOnFirstFix(new Runnable() {
            public void run() {
                mapController.setCenter(whereAmI.getMyLocation());
```

```
                      }
            });
        }

        @Override
        public void onPause()
        {
            super.onPause();
            whereAmI.disableMyLocation();
        }
    }
```

Make sure you change the superclass from `Activity` to `MapActivity` and include the corresponding import. You'll also need to update the `AndroidManifest.xml` file to include the appropriate uses-permission and the uses-library tags, which were introduced before. Notice that in this example, `isLocationDisplayed()` will return true if we are now showing the current location of the device on a map.

Once you launch this application in the emulator, you need to start sending it location updates before it gets very interesting. To do this, go to the DDMS Emulator Control view in Eclipse as described earlier in this section. You need to find a sample GPX file from somewhere on the Internet. The sites listed earlier for GPX files have lots of them. Just pick one and download it to your workstation. Then load it into the Emulator Control using the Load GPX button on the GPX tab under Location Controls. Select a path from the bottom list, and click on the play button (the green arrow). Notice the Speed button also. This should start sending a stream of location updates to the emulator, which will be picked up by your application. Click on the Speed button to make the updates happen more often.

The code above is very straightforward. After setting up the basics of a `MapView`, turning on the zoom controls and zooming in close, we create the `MyLocationOverlay` overlay. We add the new overlay to the `MapView` then call `postInvalidate()` on the `MapView` so the new overlay will appear on the screen. Without this last call, the overlay will be created but it will not show up.

Remember that our application will call `onResume()` even when it's just starting up, as well as after waking up. Therefore, we want to enable location tracking in `onResume()`, and disable it in `onPause()`. No sense in draining the battery with location requests if we're not going to be around to consume them. But in addition to enabling location requests in `onResume()`, we also want to jump to where we're at right now. The `MyLocationOverlay` class has a helpful method for this: `runOnFirstFix()`. This method allows us to set up code that will run as soon as we have a location at all. This could be immediately, because we've got a last location, or it could be later when we get something from either the `GPS_PROVIDER` or the `NETWORK_PROVIDER`. So when we have a fix, we center on it. After that, we don't need to do anything ourselves because the `MyLocationOverlay` is getting location updates and putting the blinking blue dot where that location is.

You should notice that you are able to zoom in and out while the location updates are occurring, and you can even pan away from the current location. This could be a good thing or a bad thing depending on your point of view. If you pan away and don't remember where you are, it will be difficult to find yourself again unless you zoom way out and look for the blue dot.

If you want the current location to always be displayed near the center of the screen, we need to make sure we keep animating to the current location, and to do that we'll add location updates to our activity. For the next version of this exercise we'll reuse everything in our MyLocationDemo project except for the MyLocationDemoActivity.java file. The new version of MyLocationDemoActivity.java is shown in Listing 7–21.

Listing 7–21. *Using MyLocationOverlay and Keeping Our Location in View*

```java
import com.google.android.maps.GeoPoint;
import com.google.android.maps.MapActivity;
import com.google.android.maps.MapView;
import com.google.android.maps.MyLocationOverlay;

import android.content.Context;
import android.location.Location;
import android.location.LocationListener;
import android.location.LocationManager;
import android.os.Bundle;
import android.widget.Toast;

public class MyLocationDemoActivity extends MapActivity {

    MapView mapView = null;
    MyLocationOverlay whereAmI = null;
    LocationManager locMgr = null;
    LocationListener locListener = null;

    @Override
    protected boolean isLocationDisplayed() {
        return whereAmI.isMyLocationEnabled();
    }

    @Override
    protected boolean isRouteDisplayed() {
        return false;
    }

    /** Called when the activity is first created. */
    @Override
    public void onCreate(Bundle savedInstanceState)
    {
        super.onCreate(savedInstanceState);
        setContentView(R.layout.main);

        mapView = (MapView)findViewById(R.id.geoMap);
        mapView.setBuiltInZoomControls(true);
        mapView.getController().setZoom(15);

        whereAmI = new MyLocationOverlay(this, mapView);
        mapView.getOverlays().add(whereAmI);
        mapView.postInvalidate();

        locMgr = (LocationManager)getSystemService(Context.LOCATION_SERVICE);
```

```
        locListener = new LocationListener()
        {
            public void  onLocationChanged(Location location)
            {
                showLocation(location);
            }

            public void  onProviderDisabled(String provider)
            {
            }

            public void  onProviderEnabled(String provider)
            {
            }

            public void  onStatusChanged(String provider,
                int status, Bundle extras)
            {
            }
        };
    }

    @Override
    public void onResume()
    {
        super.onResume();
        Location lastLoc = locMgr.getLastKnownLocation(LocationManager.GPS_PROVIDER);
        showLocation(lastLoc);
        locMgr.requestLocationUpdates(
            LocationManager.GPS_PROVIDER,
            0,              // minTime in ms
            0,              // minDistance in meters
            locListener);
        whereAmI.enableMyLocation();
        whereAmI.runOnFirstFix(new Runnable() {
            public void run() {
                mapView.getController().setCenter(whereAmI.getMyLocation());
            }
        });
    }

    @Override
    public void onPause()
    {
        super.onPause();
        locMgr.removeUpdates(locListener);
        whereAmI.disableMyLocation();
    }

    private void showLocation(Location location) {
        if (location != null)
        {
            double lat = location.getLatitude();
            double lng = location.getLongitude();
            GeoPoint myLocation = new GeoPoint(
                (int)(lat*1000000),
                (int)(lng*1000000));
```

```
            Toast.makeText(getBaseContext(),
                "New location latitude [" +
                lat + "] longitude [" + lng +"]",
                Toast.LENGTH_SHORT).show();
            mapView.getController().animateTo(myLocation);
        }
    }
}
```

This time we've added a `LocationListener` of our own, so as `MyLocationOverlay` gets updates from the location providers, we're getting updates from the `GPS_PROVIDER` too. Since we will be getting the same updates, we'll be in sync. In our callback we're calling our `showLocation()` method, which moves our map so our current location is always in view.

Within the `onResume()` method, we're using more than we need to; the extra calls are strictly for demonstration purposes. For example, the `getLastKnownLocation()` call will return either null if there is no last known location, or a Location object. We turn around and call `showLocation()` with this value. This would be fine if we have a valid location but won't do anything if we don't. We're also calling `runOnFirstFix()` in this method, which does almost the same thing. If we have a known location, we go to it immediately. The difference is that if we don't have a last known location, this part sets up a `Runnable` to center our map on our current location as soon as it is known. Go ahead and run this in the emulator and then send it new locations through the Emulator Control. Note that in this demonstration, we're also using Toast to show the points we're moving to. Finally, note again that the values passed for minTime and minDistance (both zero) are not realistic values for a production application. We do not want location updates as fast as we can get them because that would likely drain our battery very quickly.

Summary

In this chapter, we discussed two important parts of the Android SDK: the application-security model and location-based services.

With respect to security, you learned that Android requires all applications to be signed with a digital signature. We discussed ensuring build-time security with the emulator and Eclipse, as well as signing an Android package for release. We also talked about runtime security—you learned that the Android installer requests the permissions your application needs at install time. We also showed you how to define the permissions required by your application, as well as how to sign the .apk file for deployment.

With respect to location-based services, we talked at length about using the `MapView` control and the `MapActivity` class. We started with the basics of the map and then showed you how to utilize overlays to place markers on maps. We even showed you how to geocode and handle geocoding in background threads. We talked about the `LocationManager` class, which provides detailed location information through providers. Last, we showed you how to display the current location of the device on a map.

In the next chapter, we'll talk about building and consuming services in Android.

Chapter 8

Building and Consuming Services

The Android Platform provides a complete software stack. This means you get an operating system and middleware, as well as working applications (such as a phone dialer). Alongside all of this, you have an SDK that you can use to write applications for the platform. Thus far, we've seen that we can build applications that directly interact with the user through a user interface. We have not, however, discussed background services or the possibilities of building components that run in the background.

In this chapter, we are going to focus on building and consuming services in Android. First we'll discuss consuming HTTP services, then we'll discuss interprocess communication—that is, communication between applications on the same device.

Consuming HTTP Services

Android applications and mobile applications in general are small apps with a lot of functionality. One of the ways that mobile apps deliver such rich functionality on such a small device is that they pull information from various sources. For example, the T-Mobile G1 comes with the Maps application, which provides seemingly sophisticated mapping functionality. We, however, know that the application is integrated with Google Maps and other services, which provide most of the sophistication.

That said, it is likely that the applications you write will also leverage information from other applications. A common integration strategy is to use HTTP. For example, you might have a Java servlet available on the Internet that provides services you want to leverage from one of your Android applications. How do you do that with Android? Interestingly, the Android SDK ships with Apache's `HttpClient` (http://hc.apache.org/httpclient-3.x/), which is universally used within the J2EE space. The Android SDK ships with a version of the `HttpClient` that has been modified for Android, but the APIs are very similar to the APIs in the J2EE version.

The Apache HttpClient is a comprehensive HTTP client. Although it offers full support for the HTTP protocol, you will likely utilize HTTP GET and POST. In this section, we will discuss using the HttpClient to make HTTP GET and HTTP POST calls.

Using the HttpClient for HTTP GET Requests

Here's the general pattern for using the HttpClient:

1. Create an HttpClient (or get an existing reference).

2. Instantiate a new HTTP method, such as PostMethod or GetMethod.

3. Set HTTP parameter names/values.

4. Execute the HTTP call using the HttpClient.

5. Process the HTTP response.

Listing 8–1 shows how to execute an HTTP GET using the HttpClient.

> **NOTE:** Because the code attempts to use the Internet, you will need to add android.permission.INTERNET to your manifest file when making HTTP calls using the HttpClient.

Listing 8–1. *Using the HttpClient to Get an HTTP GET Request*

```java
import java.io.BufferedReader;
import java.io.IOException;
import java.io.InputStreamReader;
import java.net.URI;

import org.apache.http.HttpResponse;
import org.apache.http.client.HttpClient;
import org.apache.http.client.methods.HttpGet;
import org.apache.http.impl.client.DefaultHttpClient;

public class TestHttpGet {

    public void executeHttpGet() throws Exception {
    BufferedReader in = null;
    try {
        HttpClient client = new DefaultHttpClient();
        HttpGet request = new HttpGet();
        request.setURI(new URI("http://code.google.com/android/"));
        HttpResponse response = client.execute(request);
        in = new BufferedReader
(new InputStreamReader(response.getEntity()
            .getContent()));

        StringBuffer sb = new StringBuffer("");
        String line = "";
        String NL = System.getProperty("line.separator");
        while ((line = in.readLine()) != null) {
```

```
            sb.append(line + NL);
        }
        in.close();

        String page = sb.toString();
        System.out.println(page);
    } finally {
        if (in != null) {
            try {
                in.close();
            } catch (IOException e) {
                e.printStackTrace();
            }
        }
    }
}
}
```

The HttpClient provides abstractions for the various HTTP request types, such as HttpGet, HttpPost, and so on. Listing 8–1 uses the HttpClient to get the contents of the http://code.google.com/android/ URL. The actual HTTP request is executed with the call to client.execute(). After executing the request, the code reads the entire response into a string object. Note that the BufferedReader is closed in the finally block, which also closes the underlying HTTP connection.

Realize that the class in Listing 8–1 does not extend android.app.Activity. In other words, you don't need to be within the context of an activity to use HttpClient — because HttpClient is packaged with Android, you can use it from within the context of an Android component (such as an activity) or use it as part of a standalone class.

The code in Listing 8–1 executes an HTTP request without passing any HTTP parameters to the server. You can pass name/value parameters as part of the request by appending name/value pairs to the URL, as shown in Listing 8–2.

Listing 8–2. *Adding Parameters to an HTTP GET Request*

```
HttpGet method = new HttpGet("http://somehost/WS2/Upload.aspx?one=valueGoesHere");
client.execute(method);
```

When you execute an HTTP GET, the parameters (names and values) of the request are passed as part of the URL. Passing parameters this way has some limitations. Namely, the length of a URL should be kept below 2,048 characters. Instead of using HTTP GET, you can use HTTP POST. The POST method is more flexible and passes parameters as part of the request body.

Using the HttpClient for HTTP POST Requests

Making an HTTP POST call is very similar to making an HTTP GET call (see Listing 8–3).

Listing 8–3. *Making an HTTP POST Request with the HttpClient*

```
import java.util.ArrayList;
import java.util.List;

import org.apache.http.HttpResponse;
```

```
import org.apache.http.NameValuePair;
import org.apache.http.client.HttpClient;
import org.apache.http.client.entity.UrlEncodedFormEntity;
import org.apache.http.client.methods.HttpPost;
import org.apache.http.impl.client.DefaultHttpClient;
import org.apache.http.message.BasicNameValuePair;

public class TestHttpPost
{
    public String executeHttpPost() throws Exception {
        BufferedReader in = null;
        try {
            HttpClient client = new DefaultHttpClient();
            HttpPost request = new HttpPost(
                    "http://somewebsite/WS2/Upload.aspx");

            List<NameValuePair> postParameters = new ArrayList<NameValuePair>();
            postParameters.add(new BasicNameValuePair("one", "valueGoesHere"));
            UrlEncodedFormEntity formEntity = new UrlEncodedFormEntity(
                    postParameters);

            request.setEntity(formEntity);
            HttpResponse response = client.execute(request);
            in = new BufferedReader(new InputStreamReader(response.getEntity()
                    .getContent()));

            StringBuffer sb = new StringBuffer("");
            String line = "";
            String NL = System.getProperty("line.separator");
            while ((line = in.readLine()) != null) {
                sb.append(line + NL);
            }
            in.close();

            String result = sb.toString();
            return result;
        } finally {
            if (in != null) {
                try {
                    in.close();
                } catch (IOException e) {
                    e.printStackTrace();
                }
            }
        }
    }
}
```

To make an HTTP POST call with the HttpClient, you have to call the execute() method of the HttpClient with an instance of HttpPost. When making HTTP POST calls, you generally pass URL-encoded name/value form parameters as part of the HTTP request. To do this with the HttpClient, you have to create a list that contains instances of NameValuePair objects and then wrap that list with a UrlEncodedFormEntity object. The NameValuePair wraps a name/value combination and the UrlEncodedFormEntity class knows how to encode a list of NameValuePair objects suitable for HTTP calls (generally

POST calls). After you create a `UrlEncodedFormEntity`, you can set the entity type of the `HttpPost` to the `UrlEncodedFormEntity` and then execute the request.

In Listing 8–3, we created an `HttpClient` and then instantiated the `HttpPost` with the URL of the HTTP endpoint. Next, we will create a list of `NameValuePair` objects and populate that with a single name/value parameter. We set the name of the parameter to one and the value of the parameter to `valueGoesHere`. We then create a `UrlEncodedFormEntity` instance, passing the list of `NameValuePairobjects` to its constructor. Finally, we call the `setEntity()` method of the POST request and then execute the request using the `HttpClient` instance.

HTTP POST is actually much more powerful than this. With an HTTP POST, we can pass simple name/value parameters, as shown in Listing 8–3, as well as complex parameters such as files. HTTP POST supports another request-body format known as a *multipart POST*. With this type of POST, you can send name/value parameters as before, along with arbitrary files. Unfortunately, the version of `HttpClient` shipped with Android does not directly support multipart POST. To do multipart POST calls, you need to get three additional Apache open source projects: Apache Commons IO, Mime4j, and HttpMime. You can download these projects from the following web sites:

- *Commons IO*: http://commons.apache.org/io/

- *Mime4j*: http://james.apache.org/mime4j/

- *HttpMime*: http://hc.apache.org/httpcomponents-client/httpmime/index.html

Alternatively, you can visit this site to download all of the required .jar files to do multipart POST with Android:

http://www.apress.com/book/view/1430226595

Listing 8–4 demonstrates a multipart POST using Android.

Listing 8–4. *Making a Multipart POST Call*

```java
import java.io.ByteArrayInputStream;
import java.io.InputStream;

import org.apache.commons.io.IOUtils;
import org.apache.http.HttpResponse;
import org.apache.http.client.HttpClient;
import org.apache.http.client.methods.HttpPost;
import org.apache.http.entity.mime.MultipartEntity;
import org.apache.http.entity.mime.content.InputStreamBody;
import org.apache.http.entity.mime.content.StringBody;
import org.apache.http.impl.client.DefaultHttpClient;

import android.app.Activity;

public class TestMultipartPost extends Activity
{
    public void executeMultipartPost()throws Exception
    {
```

```
        try {
            InputStream is = this.getAssets().open("data.xml");
            HttpClient httpClient = new DefaultHttpClient();
            HttpPost postRequest =
             new HttpPost("http://192.178.10.131/WS2/Upload.aspx");

            byte[] data = IOUtils.toByteArray(is);

            InputStreamBody isb = new InputStreamBody(new
ByteArrayInputStream(data),"uploadedFile");
            StringBody sb1 = new StringBody("someTextGoesHere");
            StringBody sb2 = new StringBody("someTextGoesHere too");

            MultipartEntity multipartContent = new MultipartEntity();
            multipartContent.addPart("uploadedFile", isb);
            multipartContent.addPart("one", sb1);
            multipartContent.addPart("two", sb2);

            postRequest.setEntity(multipartContent);
            HttpResponse res =httpClient.execute(postRequest);
            res.getEntity().getContent().close();
        } catch (Throwable e)
        {
            // handle exception here
        }
    }
}
```

NOTE: The multipart example uses several .jar files that are not included as part of the Android runtime. To ensure that the .jar files will be packaged as part of your .apk file, you need to add them as external .jar files in Eclipse. To do this, right-click your project in Eclipse, select Properties, choose Java Class Path, select the Libraries tab, and then select Add External JARs.

Following these steps will make the .jar files available during compile time as well as runtime.

To execute a multipart POST, you need to create an HttpPost and call its setEntity() method with a MultipartEntity instance (rather than the UrlEncodedFormEntity we created for the name/value parameter form post). MultipartEntity represents the body of a multipart POST request. As shown, you create an instance of a MultipartEntity and then call the addPart() method with each part. Listing 8–4 adds three parts to the request: two string parts and an XML file.

Finally, if you are building an application that requires you to pass a multipart POST to a web resource, you'll likely have to debug the solution using a dummy implementation of the service on your local workstation. When you're running applications on your local workstation, you can access the local machine by using localhost or IP address 127.0.0.1. With Android applications, however, you will not be able to use localhost (or 127.0.0.1) because the emulator will be its own localhost. To refer to your development workstation from the application running in the emulator, you'll have to use your workstation's IP address. (Refer back to Chapter 2 if you need help figuring out what your workstation's IP address is.) You will need to modify Listing 8–4 by substituting the IP address with the IP address of your workstation.

But what about SOAP? There are lots of SOAP-based web services on the Internet, but to date, Google has not provided direct support in Android for calling SOAP web services. Google instead prefers REST-like web services, seemingly to reduce the amount of computing required on the client device. However, the tradeoff is that the developer must do more work to send data and to parse the returned data. Ideally, you will have some options for how you can interact with your web services. Some developers have used the kSOAP2 developer kit to build SOAP clients for Android. We won't be covering that approach, but it's out there if you're interested (http://ksoap2.sourceforge.net/).

Dealing with Exceptions

Dealing with exceptions is part of any program, but software that makes use of external services (such as HTTP services) must pay additional attention to exceptions because the potential for errors is magnified. There are several types of exceptions that you can expect while making use of HTTP services. These are transport exceptions, protocol exceptions, and timeouts. You should understand when these exceptions could occur.

Transport exceptions can occur due to a number of reasons, but the most likely scenario with a mobile device is poor network connectivity. Protocol exceptions are exceptions at the HTTP protocol layer. These include authentication errors, invalid cookies, and so on. You can expect to see protocol exceptions if, for example, you have to supply login credentials as part of your HTTP request but fail to do so. Timeouts, with respect to HTTP calls, come in two flavors: connection timeouts and socket timeouts. A connection timeout can occur if the HttpClient is not able to connect to the HTTP server—if, for example, the URL is not correct or the server is not available. A socket timeout can occur if the HttpClient fails to receive a response within a defined time period. In other words, the HttpClient was able to connect to the server, but the server failed to return a response within the allocated time limit.

Now that you understand the types of exceptions that might occur, how do you deal with them? Fortunately, the HttpClient is a robust framework that takes most of the burden off your shoulders. In fact, the only exception types that you'll have to worry about are the ones that you'll be able to manage easily. The HttpClient takes care of transport exceptions by detecting transport issues and retrying requests (which works very well with this type of exception). Protocol exceptions are exceptions that can generally be flushed out during development. Timeouts are the ones that you'll have to deal with. A simple and effective approach to dealing with both types of timeouts—connection timeouts and socket timeouts—is to wrap the execute() method of your HTTP request with a try/catch and then retry if a failure occurs. This is demonstrated in Listing 8–5.

Listing 8–5. *Implementing a Simple Retry Technique to Deal with Timeouts*

```
import java.io.BufferedReader;
import java.io.IOException;
```

```java
import java.io.InputStreamReader;
import java.net.URI;

import org.apache.http.HttpResponse;
import org.apache.http.client.HttpClient;
import org.apache.http.client.methods.HttpGet;
import org.apache.http.impl.client.DefaultHttpClient;

public class TestHttpGet {

    public String executeHttpGetWithRetry() throws Exception {
        int retry = 3;

        int count = 0;
        while (count < retry) {
            count += 1;
            try {
                String response = executeHttpGet();
                /**
                 * if we get here, that means we were successful and we can
                 * stop.
                 */
                return response;
            } catch (Exception e) {
                /**
                 * if we have exhausted our retry limit
                 */
                if (count < retry) {
                /**
                 * we have retries remaining, so log the message and go
                 * again.
                 */
                System.out.println(e.getMessage());
                } else {
                    System.out.println("could not succeed with retry...");
                    throw e;
                }
            }
        }
        return null;
    }

    public String executeHttpGet() throws Exception {
        BufferedReader in = null;
        try {
            HttpClient client = new DefaultHttpClient();
            HttpGet request = new HttpGet();
            request.setURI(new URI("http://code.google.com/android/"));
            HttpResponse response = client.execute(request);
            in = new BufferedReader(new InputStreamReader(response.getEntity()
                    .getContent()));

            StringBuffer sb = new StringBuffer("");
            String line = "";
            String NL = System.getProperty("line.separator");
            while ((line = in.readLine()) != null) {
                sb.append(line + NL);
```

```
        }
        in.close();

        String result = sb.toString();
        return result;
    } finally {
        if (in != null) {
            try {
                in.close();
            } catch (IOException e) {
                e.printStackTrace();
            }
        }
    }
  }
}
```

The code in Listing 8–5 shows how you can implement a simple retry technique to recover from timeouts when making HTTP calls. The listing shows two methods: one that executes an HTTP GET (executeHttpGet()), and another that wraps this method with the retry logic (executeHttpGetWithRetry()). The logic is very simple. We set the number of retries we want to attempt to 3, and then we enter a while loop. Within the loop, we execute the request. Note that the request is wrapped with a try/catch block, and in the catch block we check whether we have exhausted the number of retry attempts.

When using the HttpClient as part of a real-world application, you need to pay some attention to multithreading issues that might come up. Let's delve into these now.

Addressing Multithreading Issues

The examples we've shown so far created a new HttpClient for each request. In practice, however, you should create one HttpClient for the entire application and use that for all of your HTTP communication. With one HttpClient servicing all of your HTTP requests, you should also pay attention to multithreading issues that could surface if you make simultaneous requests through the same HttpClient. Fortunately, the HttpClient provides facilities that make this easy—all you have to do is create the DefaultHttpClient using a ThreadSafeClientConnManager, as shown in Listing 8–6.

Listing 8–6. *Creating an HttpClient for Multithreading Purposes*

```java
// ApplicationEx.java
import org.apache.http.HttpVersion;
import org.apache.http.client.HttpClient;
import org.apache.http.conn.ClientConnectionManager;
import org.apache.http.conn.scheme.PlainSocketFactory;
import org.apache.http.conn.scheme.Scheme;
import org.apache.http.conn.scheme.SchemeRegistry;
import org.apache.http.conn.ssl.SSLSocketFactory;
import org.apache.http.impl.client.DefaultHttpClient;
import org.apache.http.impl.conn.tsccm.ThreadSafeClientConnManager;
import org.apache.http.params.BasicHttpParams;
import org.apache.http.params.HttpParams;
import org.apache.http.params.HttpProtocolParams;
```

```java
import org.apache.http.protocol.HTTP;

import android.app.Application;
import android.util.Log;

public class ApplicationEx extends Application
{
    private static final String TAG = "ApplicationEx";
    private HttpClient httpClient;

    @Override
    public void onCreate()
    {
        super.onCreate();

        httpClient = createHttpClient();

    }

    @Override
    public void onLowMemory()
    {
        super.onLowMemory();
        shutdownHttpClient();
    }

    @Override
    public void onTerminate()
    {
        super.onTerminate();
        shutdownHttpClient();
    }


    private HttpClient createHttpClient()
    {
        Log.d(TAG,"createHttpClient()...");
        HttpParams params = new BasicHttpParams();
        HttpProtocolParams.setVersion(params, HttpVersion.HTTP_1_1);
        HttpProtocolParams.setContentCharset(params, HTTP.DEFAULT_CONTENT_CHARSET);
        HttpProtocolParams.setUseExpectContinue(params, true);


        SchemeRegistry schReg = new SchemeRegistry();
        schReg.register(new Scheme("http",
      PlainSocketFactory.getSocketFactory(), 80));
        schReg.register(new Scheme("https",
      SSLSocketFactory.getSocketFactory(), 443));
        ClientConnectionManager conMgr = new
          ThreadSafeClientConnManager(params,schReg);

        return new DefaultHttpClient(conMgr, params);
    }

    public HttpClient getHttpClient() {
        return httpClient;
    }
```

```
    private void shutdownHttpClient()
    {
        if(httpClient!=null && httpClient.getConnectionManager()!=null)
        {
            httpClient.getConnectionManager().shutdown();
        }
    }
}

// HttpActivity.java

import java.net.URI;

import org.apache.http.HttpResponse;
import org.apache.http.client.HttpClient;
import org.apache.http.client.methods.HttpGet;
import org.apache.http.util.EntityUtils;

import android.app.Activity;
import android.os.Bundle;
import android.util.Log;

public class HttpActivity extends Activity
{
    /** Called when the activity is first created. */
    @Override
    public void onCreate(Bundle savedInstanceState)
    {
        super.onCreate(savedInstanceState);

        Log.d("ServicesDemoActivity", "a debug statement");
        getHttpContent();
    }
    public void getHttpContent()
    {
        try {
            ApplicationEx app = (ApplicationEx)this.getApplication();
            HttpClient client = app.getHttpClient();
            HttpGet request = new HttpGet();
            request.setURI(new URI("http://www.google.com/"));
            HttpResponse response = client.execute(request);

            String page=EntityUtils.toString(response.getEntity());
            System.out.println(page);
        }
        catch (Exception e)
        {
            e.printStackTrace();
        }
    }
}
```

Note that when you override or extend the default application object, you also have to modify the application node in the AndroidManifest.xml file by setting the android:name attribute like this:

```
    <application android:icon="@drawable/icon"
android:label="@string/app_name"
android:name="ApplicationEx">
```

If your application needs to make more than a few HTTP calls, you should create an HttpClient that services all of your HTTP requests. One way to do this is to take advantage of the fact that each Android application has an associated application object. By default, if you don't define a custom application object, Android uses android.app.Application. Here's the interesting thing about the application object: there will always be exactly one application object for your application and all of your components can access it (using the global context object).

For example, from an activity class, you can call getApplication() to get the application object for your application. The idea here is that because the application is a singleton and always available, we can extend that class and create our HttpClient there. We then provide an accessor method for all of the components in our application to get the HttpClient. This is what we have done in Listing 8–6. First notice that we have two classes defined in the listing (each should be placed in a separate Java file). One is our custom application object, and the other is a typical component—an activity class. In the ApplicationEx class we extend android.app.Application and then create our HttpClient in the onCreate() method. The class then provides an accessor method for components to obtain a reference to the client. In the HttpActivity class, we get a reference to the global application object and cast that to our ApplicationEx class. We then call the getHttpClient() method and use that to make an HTTP call.

Now take a look at the createHttpClient() method of ApplicationEx. This method is responsible for creating our singleton HttpClient. Notice that when we instantiate the DefaultHttpClient(), we pass in a ClientConnectionManager. The ClientConnectionManager is responsible for managing HTTP connections for the HttpClient. Because we want to use a single HttpClient for all of the HTTP requests, we create a ThreadSafeClientConnManager.

> **NOTE:** When you are finished with the connection manager, you should call the shutdown() method on it as demonstrated in Listing 8–6.

This concludes our discussion of using HTTP services with the HttpClient. In the sections that follow, we will turn our focus to another interesting part of the Android Platform: writing background/long-running services. Although not immediately obvious, the processes of making HTTP calls and writing Android services are linked in that you will do a lot of integration from within Android services. Take, for example, a simple mail-client application. On an Android device, this type of application will likely be composed of two pieces: one that will provide the UI to the user, and another to poll for mail messages. The polling will likely have to be done within a background service. The component that polls for new messages will be an Android service, which will in turn use the HttpClient to perform the work.

Now, let's get on with writing services.

Doing Interprocess Communication

Android supports the concept of services. Services are components that run in the background, without a user interface. You can think of these components as Windows services or Unix services. Similar to these types of services, Android services are always available but don't have to be actively doing something.

Android supports two types of services: *local services* and *remote services*. A local service is a service that is not accessible from other applications running on the device. Generally, these types of services simply support the application that is hosting the service. A remote service is accessible from other applications in addition to the application hosting the service. Remote services define themselves to clients using Android Interface Definition Language (AIDL).

Let's begin our exploration of services by writing a simple service.

Creating a Simple Service

To build a service, you extend the abstract class `android.app.Service` and put a service-configuration entry in your application's manifest file. Listing 8–7 shows an example.

Listing 8–7. *A Simple Android Service Definition*

```
import android.app.Service;
public class TestService1 extends Service
{
    private static final String TAG = "TestService1";

    @Override
    public void onCreate() {
        Log.d(TAG, "onCreate");
        super.onCreate();
    }

    @Override
    public IBinder onBind(Intent intent) {
        Log.d(TAG, "onBind");
        return null;
    }
}

// service definition entry: must go in the AndroidManifest.xml file as
// a child of <application>.
<service android:name="TestService1"></service>
```

The service in Listing 8–7 isn't meant for practical use, but it serves our purpose of showing how a service is defined. To create a service, you write a class that extends `android.app.Service` and implements the `onBind()` method. You then put a service-definition entry in your `AndroidManifest.xml` file. That is how you implement a service. The next obvious question, then, is this: how do you call the service? The answer depends on the service's client and requires a bit more discussion of services.

Understanding Services in Android

We can gain more insight into the concept of a service by looking at the public methods of android.app.Service (see Listing 8–8).

Listing 8–8. *The Public Methods of a Service*

```
Application  getApplication();
abstract IBinder  onBind(Intent intent);
void onConfigurationChanged(Configuration newConfig);
void     onCreate();
void     onDestroy();
void     onLowMemory();
void     onRebind(Intent intent);
void     onStart(Intent intent, int startId);
boolean  onUnbind(Intent intent);
final void     setForeground(boolean isForeground);
final void     stopSelf();
final void     stopSelf(int startId);
final boolean  stopSelfResult(int startId);
```

The getApplication() method returns the application that implements the service. The onBind() method provides an interface for external applications running on the same device to talk to the service. onConfigurationChanged() allows the service to reconfigure itself if the device configuration changes.

The system calls onCreate() when the service is first created, but before calling onStart(). This process, which resembles the process for creating an activity, provides a way for the service to perform one-time initialization at startup. (See the "Examining the Application Lifecycle" section of Chapter 2 for details on creating an activity.) For example, if you create a background thread, do so in the onCreate() method and make sure to stop the thread in onDestroy(). The system calls onCreate(), then calls onStart(), then calls onDestroy() when the service is being shut down. The onDestroy() method provides a mechanism for the service to do final cleanup prior to shutting down.

Note that onStart(), onCreate(), and onDestroy() are called by the system; you should not call them directly. Moreover, if you override any of the on*() methods in your service class, be sure to call the superclass's version from yours. The various versions of stopSelf() provide a mechanism for the application to stop the service. A client can also call Context.stopService() to stop a service. We will talk about these methods and the others in the "Understanding Local Services" section.

Android supports the concept of a service for two reasons. First, to allow you to implement background tasks easily; second, to allow you to do interprocess communication between applications running on the same device. These two reasons correspond to the two types of services that Android supports: local services and remote services. An example of the first case might be a local service implemented as part of the e-mail application that we mentioned earlier. The service would poll the mail server for new messages and notify the user when new mail arrives. An example of the second case might be a router application. Suppose you have several applications running on a device and you need a service to accept messages and route them to various destinations. Rather than repeat the logic in every application, you could write a remote router service and have the applications talk to the service.

There are some important differences between local services and remote services. Specifically, if a service is strictly used by the components in the same process (to run background tasks), then the clients must start the service by calling `Context.startService()`. This type of service is a local service because its purpose is, generally, to run background tasks for the application that is hosting the service. If the service supports the `onBind()` method, it's a remote service that can be called via interprocess communication (`Context.bindService()`). We also call remote services *AIDL-supporting services* because clients communicate with the service using AIDL.

Although the interface of `android.app.Service` supports both local and remote services, it's not a good idea to provide one implementation of a service to support both types. The reason for this is that each type of service has a predefined lifecycle; mixing the two, although allowed, can cause errors.

Now we can begin a detailed examination of the two types of services. We will start by talking about local services and then discuss remote services (AIDL-supporting services). As mentioned before, local services are services that are called only by the application that hosts them. Remote services are services that support a Remote Procedure Call (RPC) mechanism. These services allow external clients, on the same device, to connect to the service and use its facilities.

NOTE: The second type of service in Android is known by several names: remote service, AIDL-supporting service, AIDL service, external service, and RPC service. These terms all refer to the same type of service—one that's meant to be accessed remotely by other applications running on the device.

Understanding Local Services

Local services are services that are started via `Context.startService()`. Once started, these types of services will continue to run until a client calls `Context.stopService()` on the service or the service itself calls `stopSelf()`. Note that when `Context.startService()` is called, the system will instantiate the service and call the service's `onStart()` method. Keep in mind that calling `Context.startService()` after the service has been started (that is, while it's running) will not result in another instance of the service, but doing so will invoke the service's `onStart()` method. Here are a couple of examples of local services:

- A service to retrieve data over the network (such as the Internet) based on a timer (to either upload or download information)

- A task-executor service that lets your application's activities submit jobs and queue them for processing

Listing 8–9 demonstrates a local service by implementing a service that executes background tasks. The listing contains all of the artifacts required to create and consume the service: BackgroundService.java, the service itself; MainActivity.java, an activity class to call the service; and main.xml, a layout file for the activity.

Listing 8–9. *Implementing a Local Service*

```java
// BackgroundService.java

import android.app.Notification;
import android.app.NotificationManager;
import android.app.PendingIntent;
import android.app.Service;
import android.content.Intent;
import android.os.IBinder;

public class BackgroundService extends Service
{
    private NotificationManager notificationMgr;

    @Override
    public void onCreate() {
        super.onCreate();

        notificationMgr =(NotificationManager)getSystemService(
        NOTIFICATION_SERVICE);

        displayNotificationMessage("starting Background Service");

        Thread thr = new Thread(null, new ServiceWorker(), "BackgroundService");
        thr.start();

    }

    class ServiceWorker implements Runnable
    {
        public void run() {
            // do background processing here...

            // stop the service when done...
            // BackgroundService.this.stopSelf();
        }
    }

    @Override
    public void onDestroy()
    {
        displayNotificationMessage("stopping Background Service");
        super.onDestroy();

    }

    @Override
    public void onStart(Intent intent, int startId) {
        super.onStart(intent, startId);

    }
```

```java
    @Override
    public IBinder onBind(Intent intent) {
        return null;
    }

    private void displayNotificationMessage(String message)
    {

        Notification notification = new Notification(R.drawable.note,
message,System.currentTimeMillis());

        PendingIntent contentIntent =
PendingIntent.getActivity(this, 0, new Intent(this, MainActivity.class), 0);

        notification.setLatestEventInfo(this, "Background Service",message,
contentIntent);

        notificationMgr.notify(R.id.app_notification_id, notification);
    }
}

// MainActivity.java

import android.app.Activity;
import android.content.Intent;
import android.os.Bundle;
import android.util.Log;
import android.view.View;
import android.view.View.OnClickListener;
import android.widget.Button;

public class MainActivity extends Activity
{
    private static final String TAG = "MainActivity";


    @Override
    public void onCreate(Bundle savedInstanceState)
    {
        super.onCreate(savedInstanceState);
        setContentView(R.layout.main);

        Log.d(TAG, "starting service");

        Button bindBtn = (Button)findViewById(R.id.bindBtn);
        bindBtn.setOnClickListener(new OnClickListener(){

            @Override
            public void onClick(View arg0) {
                startService(new Intent(MainActivity.this,
                        BackgroundService.class));
            }});

        Button unbindBtn = (Button)findViewById(R.id.unbindBtn);
        unbindBtn.setOnClickListener(new OnClickListener(){
```

```
            @Override
            public void onClick(View arg0) {
                stopService(new Intent(MainActivity.this,
                        BackgroundService.class));
            }});

    }
}

<?xml version="1.0" encoding="utf-8"?>
<!-- This file is /res/layout/main.xml -->
<LinearLayout xmlns:android="http://schemas.android.com/apk/res/android"
    android:orientation="vertical"
    android:layout_width="fill_parent"
    android:layout_height="fill_parent"
    >
<Button  android:id="@+id/bindBtn"
    android:layout_width="wrap_content"
    android:layout_height="wrap_content"
    android:text="Bind"
    />

    <Button android:id="@+id/unbindBtn"
    android:layout_width="wrap_content"
    android:layout_height="wrap_content"
    android:text="UnBind"
    />
</LinearLayout>
```

To run the example, you need to create the BackgroundService.java service, the
MainActivity.java activity class, and the main.xml layout file. You'll also need to create
an icon named note and place it within your project's drawable folder. You need an
application-level unique ID (integer) for the notification manager. You can create a
unique ID by adding an item ID to your string resources file at /res/values/strings.xml.
The unique ID is passed to the notification manager when you call the notify() method.
In our example, we use the following:

```
<item type="id" name="app_notification_id"/>
```

Finally, you need to add a <service android:name="BackgroundService"/> tag to the
AndroidManifest.xml file, as a child of <application>.

Note that Listing 8–9 uses an activity to interface with the service, but any component in
your application can use the service. This includes other services, activities, generic
classes, and so on. The example creates a user interface with two buttons, labeled Bind
and UnBind. Clicking the Bind button will start the service by calling startService();
clicking UnBind will stop the service by calling stopService(). Now let's talk about the
meat of the example: the BackgroundService.

The BackgroundService is a typical example of a service that is used by the components
of the application that is hosting the service. In other words, the application that is
running the service is also the only consumer. Because the service does not support
clients from outside its process, the service is a local service. And because it's a local
service as opposed to a remote service, it returns null in the bind() method. Therefore,

the only way to bind to this service is to call `Context.startService()`. The critical methods of a local service are `onCreate()`, `onStart()`, `stop*()`, and `onDestroy()`.

In the `onCreate()` method of the `BackgroundService`, we create a thread that does the service's heavy lifting. We need the application's main thread to deal with user interface activities, so we delegate the service's work to a secondary thread. Also note that we create and start the thread in `onCreate()` rather than `onStart()`. We do this because `onCreate()` is called only once, and we want the thread to be created only once during the life of the service. `onStart()` can be called more than once, so it doesn't suit our needs here. We don't do anything useful in the implementation of the thread's `run()` method, but this would be the place to make an HTTP call, query a database, and so on.

The `BackgroundService` also uses the `NotificationManager` class to send notifications to the user when the service is started and stopped. This is one way for a local service to communicate information back to the user. To send notifications to the user, you obtain the notification manager by calling `getSystemService(NOTIFICATION_SERVICE)`. Messages from the notification manager appear in the status bar.

This concludes our discussion of local services. Let's dissect AIDL services—the more complicated type of service.

Understanding AIDL Services

In the previous section, we showed you how to write an Android service that is consumed by the application that hosts the service. Now we are going to show you how to build a service that can be consumed by other processes via Remote Procedure Call (RPC). As with many other RPC-based solutions, in Android you need an Interface Definition Language (IDL) to define the interface that will be exposed to clients. In the Android world, this IDL is called Android Interface Definition Language, or AIDL. To build a remote service, you do the following:

1. Write an AIDL file that defines your interface to clients. The AIDL file uses Java syntax and has an .aidl extension. Use the same package name as the package for your Android Project.

2. Add the AIDL file to your Eclipse project under the src directory. The Android Eclipse plug-in will call the AIDL compiler to generate a Java interface from the AIDL file (the AIDL compiler is called as part of the build process).

3. Implement a service and return the interface from the `onBind()` method.

4. Add the service configuration to your `AndroidManifest.xml` file. The sections that follow show you how to execute each step.

Defining a Service Interface in AIDL

To demonstrate an example of a remote service, we are going to write a stock-quoter service. This service will provide a method that takes a ticker symbol and returns the stock value. To write a remote service in Android, the first step is to define the service interface definition in an AIDL file. Listing 8–10 shows the AIDL definition of IStockQuoteService.

Listing 8–10. *The AIDL Definition of the Stock-Quoter Service*

```
// This file is IStockQuoteService.aidl
package com.androidbook.stockquoteservice;
interface IStockQuoteService
{
        double getQuote(String ticker);
}
```

The IStockQuoteService accepts the stock-ticker symbol as a string and returns the current stock value as a double. When you create the AIDL file, the Android Eclipse plug-in runs the AIDL compiler to process your AIDL file (as part of the build process). If your AIDL file compiles successfully, the compiler generates a Java interface suitable for RPC communication. Note that the generated file will be in the package named in your AIDL file—com.androidbook.stockquoteservice, in this case.

Listing 8–11 shows the generated Java file for our IStockQuoteService interface. The generated file will be put into the gen folder of our Eclipse project.

Listing 8–11. *The Compiler-Generated Java File*

```
   /*
 * This file is auto-generated.  DO NOT MODIFY.
 * Original file: C:\\android\\StockQuoteService\\src\\com\\androidbook\\↩
stockquoteservice\\IStockQuoteService.aidl
 */
package com.androidbook.stockquoteservice;
import java.lang.String;
import android.os.RemoteException;
import android.os.IBinder;
import android.os.IInterface;
import android.os.Binder;
import android.os.Parcel;
public interface IStockQuoteService extends android.os.IInterface
{
/** Local-side IPC implementation stub class. */
public static abstract class Stub extends android.os.Binder implements ↩
com.androidbook.stockquoteservice.IStockQuoteService
{
private static final java.lang.String DESCRIPTOR = ↩
"com.androidbook.stockquoteservice.IStockQuoteService";
/** Construct the stub at attach it to the interface. */
public Stub()
{
this.attachInterface(this, DESCRIPTOR);
}
/**
 * Cast an IBinder object into an IStockQuoteService interface,
```

```java
 * generating a proxy if needed.
 */
public static com.androidbook.stockquoteservice.IStockQuoteService ⤸
asInterface(android.os.IBinder obj)
{
if ((obj==null)) {
return null;
}
android.os.IInterface iin = (android.os.IInterface)obj.queryLocalInterface(DESCRIPTOR);
if (((iin!=null)&&(iin instanceof
com.androidbook.stockquoteservice.IStockQuoteService))) {
return ((com.androidbook.stockquoteservice.IStockQuoteService)iin);
}
return ((com.androidbook.stockquoteservice.IStockQuoteService)iin);
}
return new com.androidbook.stockquoteservice.IStockQuoteService.Stub.Proxy(obj);
}
public android.os.IBinder asBinder()
{
return this;
}
@Override public boolean onTransact(int code, android.os.Parcel data,⤸
     android.os.Parcel reply, int flags) throws android.os.RemoteException
{
switch (code)
{
case INTERFACE_TRANSACTION:
{
reply.writeString(DESCRIPTOR);
return true;
}
case TRANSACTION_getQuote:
{
data.enforceInterface(DESCRIPTOR);
java.lang.String _arg0;
_arg0 = data.readString();
double _result = this.getQuote(_arg0);
reply.writeNoException();
reply.writeDouble(_result);
return true;
}
}
return super.onTransact(code, data, reply, flags);
}
private static class Proxy implements
com.androidbook.stockquoteservice.IStockQuoteService
{
private android.os.IBinder mRemote;
Proxy(android.os.IBinder remote)
{
mRemote = remote;
}
public android.os.IBinder asBinder()
{
return mRemote;
}
public java.lang.String getInterfaceDescriptor()
```

```
{
return DESCRIPTOR;
}
public double getQuote(java.lang.String ticker) throws android.os.RemoteException
{
android.os.Parcel _data = android.os.Parcel.obtain();
android.os.Parcel _reply = android.os.Parcel.obtain();
double _result;
try {
_data.writeInterfaceToken(DESCRIPTOR);
_data.writeString(ticker);
mRemote.transact(Stub.TRANSACTION_getQuote, _data, _reply, 0);
_reply.readException();
_result = _reply.readDouble();
}
finally {
_reply.recycle();
_data.recycle();
}
return _result;
}
}
static final int TRANSACTION_getQuote = (IBinder.FIRST_CALL_TRANSACTION + 0);
}
public double getQuote(java.lang.String ticker) throws android.os.RemoteException;
}
```

Note the following important points regarding the generated classes:

- The interface we defined in the AIDL file is implemented as an interface in the generated code (that is, there is an interface named IStockQuoteService).

- A static final abstract class named Stub extends android.os.Binder and implements IStockQuoteService. Note that the class is an abstract class.

- An inner class named Proxy implements the IStockQuoteService that proxies the Stub class.

- The AIDL file must reside in the package where the generated files are supposed to be (as specified in the AIDL file's package declaration).

Now let's move on and implement the AIDL interface in a service class.

Implementing an AIDL Interface

In the previous section, we defined an AIDL file for a stock-quoter service and generated the binding file. Now we are going to provide an implementation of that service. To implement the service's interface, we need to write a class that extends android.app.Service and implements the IStockQuoteService interface. The class we are going to write we'll call StockQuoteService. To expose the service to clients, our StockQuoteService will need to provide an implementation of the onBind() method, and we'll need to add some configuration information to the AndroidManifest.xml file. Listing 8–12 shows an implementation of the IStockQuoteService interface.

Listing 8–12. *The IStockQuoteService Service Implementation*

```java
// StockQuoteService.java
import android.app.Service;
import android.content.Intent;
import android.os.IBinder;
import android.os.RemoteException;
import android.util.Log;

public class StockQuoteService extends Service
{
    private static final String TAG = "StockQuoteService";
    public class StockQuoteServiceImpl extends IStockQuoteService.Stub
    {
        @Override
        public double getQuote(String ticker) throws RemoteException
        {
            Log.v(TAG, "getQuote() called for " + ticker);
            return 20.0;
        }
    }

    @Override
    public void onCreate() {
        super.onCreate();
        Log.v(TAG, "onCreate() called");
    }

    @Override
    public void onDestroy()
    {
        super.onDestroy();
        Log.v(TAG, "onDestroy() called");
    }

    @Override
    public void onStart(Intent intent, int startId) {
        super.onStart(intent, startId);
        Log.v(TAG, "onStart() called");
    }

    @Override
    public IBinder onBind(Intent intent)
    {
        Log.v(TAG, "onBind() called");
        return new StockQuoteServiceImpl();
    }
}
```

The StockQuoteService.java class in Listing 8–12 resembles the local BackgroundService we created earlier, but without the NotificationManager. The important difference is that we now implement the onBind() method. Recall that the Stub class generated from the AIDL file was an abstract class and that it implemented the IStockQuoteService interface. In our implementation of the service, we have an inner class that extends the Stub class called StockQuoteServiceImpl. This class serves as the remote-service implementation, and an instance of this class is returned from the onBind() method. With that, we have a functional AIDL service, although external clients cannot connect to it yet.

To expose the service to clients, we need to add a service declaration in the AndroidManifest.xml file, and this time, we need an intent-filter to expose the service. Listing 8–13 shows the service declaration for the StockQuoteService. The <service> tag is a child of the <application> tag.

Listing 8–13. *Manifest Declaration for the IStockQuoteService*

```
<service android:name="StockQuoteService">
    <intent-filter>
        <action android:name="com.androidbook.stockquoteservice.IStockQuoteService"
/>
    </intent-filter>
</service>
```

As with all services, we define the service we want to expose with a <service> tag. For an AIDL service, we also need to add an <intent-filter> with an <action> entry for the service interface we want to expose.

With this in place, we have everything we need to deploy the service. Let's now look at how we would call the service from another application (on the same device, of course).

Calling the Service from a Client Application

When a client talks to a service, there must be a protocol or contract between the two. With Android, the contract is AIDL. So the first step in consuming a service is to take the service's AIDL file and copy it to your client project. When you copy the AIDL file to the client project, the AIDL compiler creates the same interface-definition file that was created when the service was implemented (in the service-implementation project). This exposes to the client all of the methods, parameters, and return types on the service. Let's create a new project and copy the AIDL file.

1. Create a new Android project named **StockQuoteClient**. Use a different package name, such as com.androidbook.stockquoteclient. Use MainActivity for the Create Activity field.

2. Create a new Java package in this project named **com.androidbook.stockquoteservice** in the src directory.

3. Copy the IStockQuoteService.aidl file from the StockQuoteService project to this new package. Note that after you copy the file to the project, the AIDL compiler will generate the associated Java file.

The service interface that you regenerate serves as the contract between the client and the service. The next step is to get a reference to the service so we can call the getQuote() method. With remote services, we have to call the bindService() method rather than the startService() method. Listing 8–14 shows an activity class that acts as a client of the `IStockQuoteService` service. The listing also contains the layout file for the activity.

To follow along, copy the XML contents from Listing 8–14 to the `/res/layout/main.xml` file, and copy the Java contents from Listing 8–14 to the `MainActivity.java` file. Realize that the package name of the activity is not that important—you can put the activity in any package you'd like. However, the AIDL artifacts that you create are package-sensitive because the AIDL compiler generates code from the contents of the AIDL file.

Listing 8–14. *A Client of the IStockQuoteService Service*

```xml
<?xml version="1.0" encoding="utf-8"?>
<!-- This file is /res/layout/main.xml -->
<LinearLayout xmlns:android="http://schemas.android.com/apk/res/android"
    android:orientation="vertical"
    android:layout_width="fill_parent"
    android:layout_height="fill_parent"
    >
<Button  android:id="@+id/bindBtn"
    android:layout_width="wrap_content"
    android:layout_height="wrap_content"
    android:text="Bind"
    />

    <Button android:id="@+id/callBtn"
    android:layout_width="wrap_content"
    android:layout_height="wrap_content"
    android:text="Call Again"
    />

    <Button android:id="@+id/unbindBtn"
    android:layout_width="wrap_content"
    android:layout_height="wrap_content"
    android:text="UnBind"
    />
</LinearLayout>


// This file is MainActivity.java
import com.androidbook.stockquoteservice.IStockQuoteService;

import android.app.Activity;
import android.content.ComponentName;
import android.content.Context;
import android.content.Intent;
import android.content.ServiceConnection;
import android.os.Bundle;
import android.os.IBinder;
import android.os.RemoteException;
import android.util.Log;
import android.view.View;
import android.view.View.OnClickListener;
import android.widget.Button;
import android.widget.Toast;

public class MainActivity extends Activity {
```

```java
    protected static final String TAG = "StockQuoteClient";
    private IStockQuoteService stockService = null;

    private Button bindBtn;
    private Button callBtn;
    private Button unbindBtn;

    /** Called when the activity is first created. */
    @Override
    public void onCreate(Bundle savedInstanceState) {
        super.onCreate(savedInstanceState);
        setContentView(R.layout.main);

        bindBtn = (Button)findViewById(R.id.bindBtn);
        bindBtn.setOnClickListener(new OnClickListener(){

            @Override
            public void onClick(View view) {
                bindService(new Intent(IStockQuoteService.class
                        .getName()),
                            serConn, Context.BIND_AUTO_CREATE);
                bindBtn.setEnabled(false);
                callBtn.setEnabled(true);
                unbindBtn.setEnabled(true);
        }});

        callBtn = (Button)findViewById(R.id.callBtn);
        callBtn.setOnClickListener(new OnClickListener(){

            @Override
            public void onClick(View view) {
                callService();
        }});
        callBtn.setEnabled(false);

        unbindBtn = (Button)findViewById(R.id.unbindBtn);
        unbindBtn.setOnClickListener(new OnClickListener(){

            @Override
            public void onClick(View view) {
                unbindService(serConn);
                bindBtn.setEnabled(true);
                callBtn.setEnabled(false);
                unbindBtn.setEnabled(false);
        }});
        unbindBtn.setEnabled(false);
    }

    private void callService() {
        try {
            double val = stockService.getQuote("SYH");
            Toast.makeText(MainActivity.this, "Value from service is "+val,
Toast.LENGTH_SHORT).show();
        } catch (RemoteException ee) {
            Log.e("MainActivity", ee.getMessage(), ee);
        }
    }
```

```
        private ServiceConnection serConn = new ServiceConnection() {

            @Override
            public void onServiceConnected(ComponentName name, IBinder service)
            {
                Log.v(TAG, "onServiceConnected() called");
                stockService = IStockQuoteService.Stub.asInterface(service);
                callService();
            }

            @Override
            public void onServiceDisconnected(ComponentName name) {
                Log.v(TAG, "onServiceDisconnected() called");
                stockService = null;
            }
        };
}
```

The activity wires up the OnClickListeners for three buttons: Bind, Call Again, and UnBind. When the user clicks the Bind button, the activity calls the bindService() method. Similarly, when the user clicks UnBind, the activity calls the unbindService() method. Notice that three parameters are passed to the bindService() method: the name of the AIDL service, a ServiceConnection instance, and a flag to autocreate the service.

With an AIDL service, you need to provide an implementation of the ServiceConnection interface. This interface defines two methods: one called by the system when a connection to the service has been established, and one called when the connection to the service has been destroyed. In our activity implementation, we define a private anonymous member that implements the ServiceConnection for the IStockQuoteService. When we call the bindService() method, we pass in the reference to this member. When the connection to the service is established, we obtain a reference to the IStockQuoteService using the Stub and then call the getQuote() method from our callService() method.

Note that the bindService() call is an asynchronous call. It is asynchronous because the process or service might not be running and thus might have to be created or started. Because bindService() is asynchronous, the platform provides the ServiceConnection callback so we know when the service has been started and when the service is no longer available.

Now you know how to create and consume an AIDL interface. Before we move on and complicate matters further, let's review what it takes to build a simple local service vs. an AIDL service. A local service is a service that does not support onBind()—it returns null from onBind(). This type of service is accessible only to the components of the application that is hosting the service. You call local services by calling startService().

On the other hand, an AIDL service is a service that can be consumed both by components within the same process and by those that exist in other applications. This type of service defines a contract between itself and its clients in an AIDL file. The service implements the AIDL contract, and clients bind to the AIDL definition. The service implements the contract by returning an implementation of the AIDL interface from the onBind() method. Clients bind to an AIDL service by calling bindService() and they disconnect from the service by calling unbindService().

In our service examples thus far, we have strictly dealt with passing simple Java primitive types. Android services actually support passing complex types, too. This is very useful, especially for AIDL services, because you might have an open-ended number of parameters that you want to pass to a service, and it's unreasonable to pass them all as simple primitives. It makes more sense to package them as complex types and then pass them to the service.

Let's see how we can pass complex types to services.

Passing Complex Types to Services

Passing complex types to and from services requires more work than passing Java primitive types. Before embarking on this work, you should get an idea of AIDL's support for nonprimitive types:

- AIDL supports String and CharSequence.

- AIDL allows you to pass other AIDL interfaces, but you need to have an import statement for each AIDL interface you reference (even if the referenced AIDL interface is in the same package).

- AIDL allows you to pass complex types that implement the android.os.Parcelable interface. You need to have an import statement in your AIDL file for these types.

- AIDL supports java.util.List and java.util.Map, with a few restrictions. The allowable data types for the items in the collection include Java primitive, String, CharSequence, or android.os.Parcelable. You do not need import statements for List or Map, but you do need them for the Parcelables.

- Nonprimitive types, other than String, require a directional indicator. Directional indicators include in, out, and inout. in means the value is set by the client, out means the value is set by the service, and inout means both the client and service set the value.

The Parcelable interface tells the Android runtime how to serialize and deserialize objects during the marshalling and unmarshalling process. Listing 8–15 shows a Person class that implements the Parcelable interface.

Listing 8–15. *Implementing the Parcelable Interface*

```
// This file is Person.java
package com.syh;
import android.os.Parcel;
import android.os.Parcelable;

public class Person implements Parcelable {
    private int age;
```

```java
    private String name;
    public static final Parcelable.Creator<Person> CREATOR =
new Parcelable.Creator<Person>() {
        public Person createFromParcel(Parcel in) {
            return new Person(in);
        }

        public Person[] newArray(int size) {
            return new Person[size];
        }
    };

    public Person() {
    }

    private Person(Parcel in) {
        readFromParcel(in);
    }

    @Override
    public int describeContents() {
        return 0;
    }

    @Override
    public void writeToParcel(Parcel out, int flags) {
        out.writeInt(age);
        out.writeString(name);
    }

    public void readFromParcel(Parcel in) {
        age = in.readInt();
        name = in.readString();
    }

    public int getAge() {
        return age;
    }

    public void setAge(int age) {
        this.age = age;
    }

    public String getName() {
        return name;
    }

    public void setName(String name) {
        this.name = name;
    }
}
```

To get started on implementing this, create a new Android Project in Eclipse called StockQuoteService2. Set Create Activity to MainActivity and use a package of com.syh. Then add the Person.java file above to the com.syh package of our new project.

The `Parcelable` interface defines the contract for hydration and dehydration of objects during the marshalling/unmarshalling process. Underlying the `Parcelable` interface is the `Parcel` container object. The `Parcel` class is a fast serialization/deserialization mechanism specially designed for interprocess communication within Android. The class provides methods that you use to flatten your members to the container and to expand the members back from the container. To properly implement an object for interprocess communication, we have to do the following:

1. Implement the `Parcelable` interface. This means that you implement `writeToParcel()` and `readFromParcel()`. The write method will write the object to the parcel and the read method will read the object from the parcel. Note that the order in which you write properties must be the same as the order in which you read them.

2. Add a `static final` property to the class with the name `CREATOR`. The property needs to implement the `android.os.Parcelable.Creator<T>` interface.

3. Provide a constructor for the `Parcelable` that knows how to create the object from the `Parcel`.

4. Define a `Parcelable` class in an .aidl file that matches the .java file containing the complex type. The AIDL compiler will look for this file when compiling your AIDL files. An example of a `Person.aidl` file is shown in Listing 8–16. This file should be in the same place as `Person.java`.

> **NOTE:** Seeing `Parcelable` might have triggered the question, why is Android not using the built-in Java serialization mechanism? It turns out that the Android team came to the conclusion that the serialization in Java is far too slow to satisfy Android's interprocess-communication requirements. So the team built the `Parcelable` solution. The `Parcelable` approach requires that you explicitly serialize the members of your class, but in the end, you get a much faster serialization of your objects.
>
> Also realize that Android provides two mechanisms that allow you to pass data to another process. The first is to pass a bundle to an activity using an intent, and the second is to pass a `Parcelable` to a service. These two mechanisms are not interchangeable and should not be confused. That is, the `Parcelable` is not meant to be passed to an activity. If you want to start an activity and pass it some data, use a bundle. `Parcelable` is meant to be used only as part of an AIDL definition.

Listing 8–16. *An Example of Person.aidl File*

```
package com.syh;
parcelable com.syh.Person
```

You will need an .aidl file for each Parcelable in your project. In this case, we have just one Parcelable, which is Person.

Now let's use the Person class in a remote service. To keep things simple, we will modify our IStockQuoteService to take an input parameter of type Person. The idea is that clients will pass a Person to the service to tell the service who is requesting the quote. The new IStockQuoteService.aidl looks like Listing 8–17.

Listing 8–17. *Passing Parcelables to Services*

```
package com.syh;
import com.syh.Person;

interface IStockQuoteService
{
    String getQuote(in String ticker,in Person requester);
}
```

The getQuote() method now accepts two parameters: the stock's ticker symbol and a Person object to specify who is making the request. Note that we have directional indicators on the parameters because the parameters are nonprimitive types, and that we have an import statement for the Person class. The Person class is also in the same package as the service definition (com.syh).

The service implementation now looks like Listing 8–18.

Listing 8–18. *The StockQuoteService2 Implementation*

```
<?xml version="1.0" encoding="utf-8"?>
<!-- This file is /res/layout/main.xml -->
<LinearLayout xmlns:android="http://schemas.android.com/apk/res/android"
    android:orientation="vertical"
    android:layout_width="fill_parent"
    android:layout_height="fill_parent"
    >
<TextView
    android:layout_width="fill_parent"
    android:layout_height="wrap_content"
    android:text="This is where the service would ask for help."
    />
</LinearLayout>


package com.syh;
// This file is StockQuoteService2.java

import android.app.Notification;
import android.app.NotificationManager;
import android.app.PendingIntent;
import android.app.Service;
import android.content.Intent;
import android.os.IBinder;
import android.os.RemoteException;

public class StockQuoteService2 extends Service
{
    private NotificationManager notificationMgr;
```

```java
public class StockQuoteServiceImpl extends IStockQuoteService.Stub
{

    @Override
    public String getQuote(String ticker, Person requester)
            throws RemoteException {
        return "Hello "+requester.getName()+"! Quote for "+ticker+" is 20.0";
    }

}

@Override
public void onCreate() {
    super.onCreate();

    notificationMgr =
(NotificationManager)getSystemService(NOTIFICATION_SERVICE);

    displayNotificationMessage("onCreate() called in StockQuoteService2");
}
@Override
public void onDestroy()
{
    displayNotificationMessage("onDestroy() called in StockQuoteService2");
    super.onDestroy();
}

@Override
public void onStart(Intent intent, int startId) {
    super.onStart(intent, startId);
}

@Override
public IBinder onBind(Intent intent)
{
    displayNotificationMessage("onBind() called in StockQuoteService2");
    return new StockQuoteServiceImpl();
}

private void displayNotificationMessage(String message)
{
    Notification notification = new Notification(R.drawable.note,
message,System.currentTimeMillis());

    PendingIntent contentIntent =
PendingIntent.getActivity(this, 0, new Intent(this, MainActivity.class), 0);

    notification.setLatestEventInfo(this, "StockQuoteService2",message,
contentIntent);

    notificationMgr.notify(R.id.app_notification_id, notification);
    }
}
```

The differences between this implementation and the previous one are that we brought
back the Notifications, and we now return the stock value as a string and not a double.

The string returned to the user contains the name of the requester from the `Person` object, which demonstrates that we read the value sent from the client and that the `Person` object was passed correctly to the service.

There are a few other things that need to be done to make this work:

1. Add a `note` image file to the `/res/drawable` directory.

2. Add a new `<item type="id" name="app_notification_id"/>` tag to the `/res/values/strings.xml` file

3. We need to modify the application in the `AndroidManifest.xml` file as shown in Listing 8–19.

Listing 8–19. *Modified <application> in AndroidManifest.xml File for StockQuoteService2*

```xml
<application android:icon="@drawable/icon" android:label="@string/app_name">
    <activity android:name=".MainActivity"
                android:label="@string/app_name">
        <intent-filter>
            <action android:name="android.intent.action.MAIN" />
        </intent-filter>
    </activity>
    <service android:name="StockQuoteService2">
        <intent-filter>
            <action android:name="com.syh.IStockQuoteService" />
        </intent-filter>
    </service>
</application>
```

Last, we'll use the default `MainActivity.java` file that simply displays a basic layout with a simple message. Now that we have our service implementation, let's create a new Android project called StockQuoteClient2. Use `com.sayed` for the package and `MainActivity` for the activity name. To implement a client that passes the `Person` object to the service, we need to copy everything that the client needs from the service project to the client project. In our previous example, all we needed was the `IStockQuoteService.aidl` file. Now we also need to copy the `Person.java` and `Person.aidl` files because the `Person` object is now part of the interface. After you copy the three files to the client project, modify `main.xml` and `MainActivity.java` according to Listing 8–20.

Listing 8–20. *Calling the Service with a Parcelable*

```xml
<?xml version="1.0" encoding="utf-8"?>
<!-- This file is /res/layout/main.xml -->
<LinearLayout xmlns:android="http://schemas.android.com/apk/res/android"
    android:orientation="vertical"
    android:layout_width="fill_parent"
    android:layout_height="fill_parent"
    >
<Button  android:id="@+id/bindBtn"
    android:layout_width="wrap_content"
    android:layout_height="wrap_content"
    android:text="Bind"
    />
```

```
            <Button android:id="@+id/callBtn"
            android:layout_width="wrap_content"
            android:layout_height="wrap_content"
            android:text="Call Again"
            />

            <Button android:id="@+id/unbindBtn"
            android:layout_width="wrap_content"
            android:layout_height="wrap_content"
            android:text="UnBind"
            />
</LinearLayout>

package com.sayed;
// This file is MainActivity.java

import com.syh.IStockQuoteService;
import com.syh.Person;

import android.app.Activity;
import android.content.ComponentName;
import android.content.Context;
import android.content.Intent;
import android.content.ServiceConnection;
import android.os.Bundle;
import android.os.IBinder;
import android.os.RemoteException;
import android.util.Log;
import android.view.View;
import android.view.View.OnClickListener;
import android.widget.Button;
import android.widget.Toast;

public class MainActivity extends Activity {

    protected static final String TAG = "StockQuoteClient2";
    private IStockQuoteService stockService = null;

    private Button bindBtn = null;
    private Button callBtn = null;
    private Button unbindBtn = null;

    /** Called when the activity is first created. */
    @Override
    public void onCreate(Bundle savedInstanceState) {
        super.onCreate(savedInstanceState);
        setContentView(R.layout.main);

        bindBtn = (Button)findViewById(R.id.bindBtn);
        bindBtn.setOnClickListener(new OnClickListener(){

            @Override
            public void onClick(View view) {
                bindService(new Intent(IStockQuoteService.class
                        .getName()),
                            serConn, Context.BIND_AUTO_CREATE);
                bindBtn.setEnabled(false);
```

```java
                callBtn.setEnabled(true);
                unbindBtn.setEnabled(true);
        }});

        callBtn = (Button)findViewById(R.id.callBtn);
        callBtn.setOnClickListener(new OnClickListener(){

            @Override
            public void onClick(View view) {
                callService();
        }});
        callBtn.setEnabled(false);

        unbindBtn = (Button)findViewById(R.id.unbindBtn);
        unbindBtn.setOnClickListener(new OnClickListener(){

            @Override
            public void onClick(View view) {
                unbindService(serConn);
                bindBtn.setEnabled(true);
                callBtn.setEnabled(false);
                unbindBtn.setEnabled(false);
        }});
        unbindBtn.setEnabled(false);
    }

    private void callService() {
        try {
            Person person = new Person();
            person.setAge(33);
            person.setName("Sayed");
            String response = stockService.getQuote("GOOG", person);
            Toast.makeText(MainActivity.this, "Value from service is "+response,
Toast.LENGTH_SHORT).show();
        } catch (RemoteException ee) {
            Log.e("MainActivity", ee.getMessage(), ee);
        }
    }

    private ServiceConnection serConn = new ServiceConnection() {

        @Override
        public void onServiceConnected(ComponentName name, IBinder service)
        {
            Log.v(TAG, "onServiceConnected() called");
            stockService = IStockQuoteService.Stub.asInterface(service);
            callService();
        }

        @Override
        public void onServiceDisconnected(ComponentName name) {
            Log.v(TAG, "onServiceDisconnected() called");
            stockService = null;
        }
    };
}
```

This is now ready to run. Remember to send over the service to the emulator before you send over the client to run. Let's take a look at what we've got. The onServiceConnected() method is where we know our service is running, so we call the callService() method. As shown, we create a new Person object and set its Age and Name properties. We then execute the service and display the result from the service call. The result looks like Figure 8–1.

> Value from service Is: Hello Sayed!
> Quote for GOOG Is 20.0

Figure 8–1. *Result from calling the service with a Parcelable*

Notice that when the service is called you get a notification in the status bar. This is coming from the service itself. We briefly touched on Notifications earlier as a way for a service to communicate to the user. Normally, services are in the background and do not display any sort of UI. But what if a service needs to interact with the user? While tempting to think that a service can invoke an activity, a service should *never* invoke an activity directly. A service should instead create a notification, and the notification should be how the user gets to the desired activity. This was shown in our last exercise. We defined a simple layout and activity implementation for our service. When we created the notification within the service, we set the activity in the notification. The user can click on the notification and it will take the user to our activity that is part of this service. This will allow the user to interact with the service.

Notifications are saved so that you can get to them by pulling up the Menu on the Android Home page and clicking on Notifications. A user can also drag down from the notification icon in the status bar to see them. Note the use of the setLatestEventInfo() method call and the fact that we reuse the same ID for every message. This combination means that we are updating the one and only notification every time, rather than creating new notification entries. Therefore, if you go to the Notifications screen in Android after clicking on Bind, Call Again, and Unbind a few times, you will only see one message in Notifications, and it will be the last one sent by the BackgroundService. If we used different IDs we could have multiple notification messages, and we could update each one separately. Notifications can also be set with additional user "prompts" such as sound, lights and/or vibration.

It is also useful to see the artifacts of the service project and the client that calls it (see Figure 8–2).

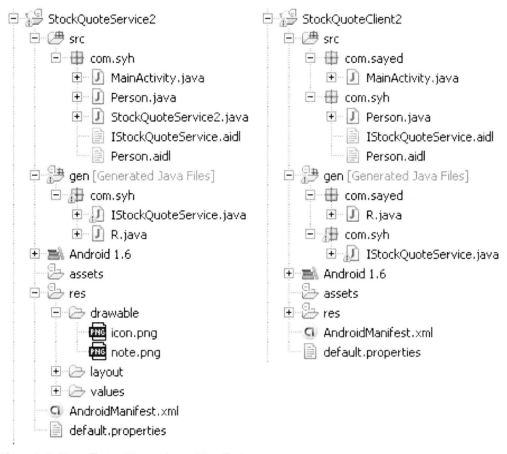

Figure 8–2. *The artifacts of the service and the client*

Figure 8–2 shows the Eclipse project artifacts for the service (left) and the client (right). Note that the contract between the client and the service consists of the AIDL artifacts and the `Parcelable` objects exchanged between the two parties. This is the reason that we see `IStockQuoteService.aidl`, `Person.java`, and `Person.aidl` on both sides. Because the AIDL complier generates the Java interface, stub, proxy, and so on from the AIDL artifacts, the build process creates the `IStockQuoteService.java` file on the client side when we copy the contract artifacts to the client project.

Now we know how to exchange complex types between services and clients. Let's briefly touch on another important aspect of calling services: synchronous vs. asynchronous service invocation.

All of the calls that you make on services are synchronous. This brings up the obvious question, do you need to implement all of your service calls in a worker thread? Not necessarily. On most other platforms, it's common for a client to use a service that is a complete black box, so the client would have to take appropriate precautions when making service calls. With Android, you will likely know what is in the service (generally because you wrote the service yourself), so you can make an informed decision. If you know that the method you are calling is doing a lot of heavy lifting, then you should consider using a secondary thread to make the call. If you are sure that the method does not have any bottlenecks, then you can safely make the call on the UI thread. If you conclude that it's best to make the service call within a worker thread, you can create the thread from the `onServiceConnected()` method of `ServiceConnection` and then call the service. You can then communicate the result to the UI thread.

Summary

This chapter was all about services. We talked about consuming external HTTP services using the Apache `HttpClient` and about writing background services. With regard to using the `HttpClient`, we showed you how to do HTTP GET calls and HTTP POST calls. We also showed you how to do multipart POSTs.

The second part of the chapter dealt with writing services in Android. Specifically, we talked about writing local services and remote services. We said that local services are services that are consumed by the components (such as activities) in the same process as the service. Remote services are services whose clients are outside the process hosting the services.

In the next chapter, we are going to discuss multimedia and telephony support in Android.

Chapter 9

Using the Media Framework and Telephony APIs

Now we are going to explore two very interesting portions of the Android SDK: media and telephony. In our media discussion in the first part of the chapter, we will show you how to play and record audio and video. In our telephony discussion in the second part of the chapter, we will show you how to send and receive Short Message Service (SMS) messages. We will also touch on several other interesting aspects of the telephony APIs in Android.

Let's begin by talking about the media APIs.

Using the Media APIs

Android supports playing audio and video content under the android.media package. In this section, we are going to explore the media APIs from this package.

At the heart of the android.media package is the android.media.MediaPlayer class. The MediaPlayer class is responsible for playing both audio and video content. The content for this class can come from the following sources:

- *Web*: You can play content from the Web via a URL.

- *.apk file*: You can play content that is packaged as part of your .apk file. You can package the media content as a resource or as an asset (within the assets folder).

- *Secure Digital (SD) card*: You can play content that resides on the device's SD card.

The MediaPlayer is capable of decoding quite a few different content formats, including 3GPP (.3gp), MP3 (.mp3), MIDI (.mid and others), PCM/WAVE (.wav), and MPEG-4 (.mp4). For a complete list of supported media formats, go here:

`http://developer.android.com/guide/appendix/media-formats.html`

Understanding and Using SD Cards

Before we get to creating and using our different types of media, let's understand how to work with SD cards, the third source of content for the MediaPlayer. SD cards are used in Android phones for storing lots of user data, usually media content such as pictures, audio, and video. They are basically pluggable memory chips that keep their data even when they lose power. On a real phone, the SD card plugs into a memory slot and is accessible to the device. You can have multiple cards, switching among them with your device, and you can use them across different devices. Fortunately for us, the Android emulator can simulate SD cards, using space on your workstation's hard drive as if it were a plug-in SD card.

When you created your first Android Virtual Device (AVD) in Chapter 2, you specified a size for an SD card, which made it available to your application when you ran it in the emulator. If you look inside the AVD directory that was created, you will see a file called `sdcard.img` with the file size you specified. We didn't use the SD card then but we'll be using it in this chapter. As a developer, once you have an SD card, you can use the Android tools within Eclipse to push media files (or any other files) to the SD card. You can also use the `adb` utility (Android Debug Bridge) to push or pull files to and from an SD card. The `adb` utility is located in the tools subdirectory of the Android SDK; it is easy to get to from a tools window, as described in Chapter 2.

You already know how to get an SD card by creating an AVD. And, of course, you could create lots of AVDs that are the same except for the size of the SD card. Here's the other way to go. The Android SDK tools bundle contains a utility called `mksdcard` that can create an SD card image. Actually, the utility creates a formatted file that is used as an SD card. To use this utility, first find or create a folder for the image file, at `c:\Android\sdcard\`, for example. Then open a tools window and run a command like the following, using an appropriate path to the SD card image file:

`mksdcard 256M c:\Android\sdcard\sdcard.img`

This example command creates an SD card image at `c:\Android\sdcard\` with a file name of `sdcard.img`. The size of the SD card will be 256MB. To specify other sizes you can use K for kilobytes, but G doesn't work yet for gigabytes, so you'll need to specify multiples of 1024M to get gigabyte sizes. You can also simply specify an integer value representing the total number of bytes. Also note that the Android emulator won't work with SD card sizes below 8MB.

The Android Development Tools (ADT) in Eclipse offers a way to specify extra command-line arguments when launching the emulator. To find the field for the emulator options, go to the Preferences window of Eclipse, then choose Android ➤ Launch. In theory, you could add `-sdcard "PATH_TO_YOUR_SD_CARD_IMAGE_FILE"` here and it would override the SD card file path for your AVD. But this hasn't worked for a few Android releases now, and you always get the SD card image file that was created along with the AVD. The most reliable way to use a separate SD card with your AVD is to launch the emulator from the command line and specify the SD card image to use there. From within a tools window the following command launches a named AVD but uses the specified SD card image file instead of the SD card image file that was created with the AVD:

```
emulator -avd AVDName -sdcard "PATH_TO_YOUR_SD_CARD_IMAGE_FILE"
```

When your SD card is first created, there are no files on it. You can add files by using the File Explorer tool in Eclipse. Start the emulator and wait until the emulator initializes. Then go to either the Java, Debug, or DDMS perspectives in Eclipse and look for the File Explorer tab as shown in Figure 9–1.

Name	Size	Date	Time	Permissions	Info
⊞ 📂 data		2008-09-22	20:44	drwxrwx--x	
⊟ 📂 sdcard		1970-01-01	00:00	d---rwxrwx	
⊞ 📂 download		2008-11-26	23:55	d---rwxrwx	
📄 movie.mp4	466888	2009-03-28	15:02	----rw-rw-	
📄 recordoutput.3gpp	5572	2008-12-31	18:47	----rw-rw-	
⊞ 📂 system		2008-09-22	20:41	drwxr-xr-x	

Figure 9–1. *The File Explorer view*

If the File Explorer is not shown, you can bring it up by going to Window ➤ Show View ➤ Other ➤ Android and selecting File Explorer. Alternatively, you can show the Dalvik Debug Monitor Service (DDMS) perspective by going to Window ➤ Open Perspective ➤ Other ➤ DDMS, which will show all of the views shown in Figure 9–2.

Figure 9–2. *Enabling Android views*

To push a file onto the SD card, select the sdcard folder in the File Explorer and choose the button with the right-facing arrow (at the top-right corner) pointing into what looks like a phone. This launches a dialog box that lets you select a file. Select the file that you want to upload to the SD card. The button next to it looks like a left arrow pointing into a floppy disk. Choose this button for pulling a file from the device onto your workstation, after selecting the file you want to pull from within the File Explorer.

Realize that if the File Explorer displays an empty view, you either don't have the emulator running, Eclipse has disconnected from the emulator, or the project that you are running in the emulator is not selected under the Devices tab shown in Figure 9–1.

The other way to move files onto and off of the SD card is to use the adb utility. To try this, open a tools window, then type a command such as this:

```
adb push c:\path_to_my_file\filename /sdcard/newfile
```

This will push a file from your workstation to the SD card. Note that the device uses forward slashes to separate directories. Use whatever directory separator character is appropriate for your workstation for the file that's being pushed, and use an appropriate path for the file on your workstation. Conversely, the following command will pull a file from the SD card to your workstation:

```
adb pull /sdcard/devicefile c:\path_to_where_its_going\filename
```

One of the nice features of this command is that it will create directories as needed, in either direction (push or pull), to get the file to the desired destination. Unfortunately, you cannot use adb to copy multiple files at the same time. You must do each file separately.

You may have noticed a directory on the SD card called DCIM. This is the Digital Camera Images directory. It's an industry standard to put a DCIM directory within the root directory of an SD card that's used for digital images. It's also an industry standard to put a directory underneath DCIM that represents a camera, in the format 123ABCDE, meaning three digits followed by five alpha characters. The emulator creates a directory called 100ANDRO under DCIM, but makers of digital cameras, and Android phone makers, can call this directory whatever they want. The emulator also has, as do some Android phones, a directory called Camera under the DCIM directory, but this isn't compliant with the standard. Nevertheless, you may find image files under Camera and you may find them under 100ANDRO, or you may find some other directory under DCIM where image files are stored.

And finally a word about security. With the introduction of Android SDK 1.6, you need to add this permission to your manifest file in order for your application to be able to write to the SD card:

```
<uses-permission android:name="android.permission.WRITE_EXTERNAL_STORAGE" />
```

However, applications written for the older Android SDKs are not required to request this permission. That means that if your application's minSdkVersion is less than 4 (corresponding to Android SDK 1.6), you do not need to add this tag to your AndroidManifest.xml file, even if you're running on a device that supports a newer Android SDK. Therefore, when you are creating an application, if you choose a Build Target of Android 1.6 or newer (i.e., minSdkVersion of 4 or higher) and you want to be able to write to the SD card, make sure you add the tag above to your manifest file. If your Build Target is Android 1.5 or older you do not need this tag. Now that you know the basics of SD cards, let's get into audio.

Playing Audio Content

To get started, we'll show you how to build a simple application that plays an MP3 file located on the Web (see Figure 9–3). After that, we will talk about using the setDataSource() method of the MediaPlayer class to play content from the .apk file or the SD card. We will conclude our media discussion by talking about some of the shortfalls of the media APIs.

Figure 9–3 shows the user interface for our first example. This application will demonstrate some of the fundamental uses of the MediaPlayer class, such as starting, pausing, and restarting the media file. Look at the layout for the application's user interface.

Figure 9–3. *The user interface for the media application*

The user interface consists of a LinearLayout with three buttons (see Listing 9–1): one to start the player, one to pause the player, and one to restart the player. The code and layout file for the application are shown in Listing 9–1.

Listing 9–1. *The Layout and Code for the Media Application*

```xml
<?xml version="1.0" encoding="utf-8"?>
<!-- This file is /res/layout/main.xml -->
<LinearLayout xmlns:android="http://schemas.android.com/apk/res/android"
    android:orientation="vertical"
    android:layout_width="fill_parent"
    android:layout_height="fill_parent"
    >
<Button android:id="@+id/startPlayerBtn"
    android:layout_width="fill_parent"
    android:layout_height="wrap_content"
```

```
            android:text="Start Playing Audio"
            />

    <Button android:id="@+id/restartPlayerBtn"
        android:layout_width="fill_parent"
        android:layout_height="wrap_content"
        android:text="Restart Player"
        />

    <Button android:id="@+id/pausePlayerBtn"
        android:layout_width="fill_parent"
        android:layout_height="wrap_content"
        android:text="Pause Player"
        />
</LinearLayout>


import android.app.Activity;
import android.media.MediaPlayer;
import android.os.Bundle;
import android.view.View;
import android.view.View.OnClickListener;
import android.widget.Button;

public class MainActivity extends Activity
{
    static final String AUDIO_PATH =
"http://www.androidbook.com/akc/filestorage/android/documentfiles/3389/play.mp3";

    private MediaPlayer mediaPlayer;
    private int playbackPosition=0;

    /** Called when the activity is first created. */
    @Override
    public void onCreate(Bundle savedInstanceState) {
        super.onCreate(savedInstanceState);
        setContentView(R.layout.main);

        Button startPlayerBtn = (Button)findViewById(R.id.startPlayerBtn);
        Button pausePlayerBtn = (Button)findViewById(R.id.pausePlayerBtn);
        Button restartPlayerBtn = (Button)findViewById(R.id.restartPlayerBtn);

        startPlayerBtn.setOnClickListener(new OnClickListener(){

            @Override
            public void onClick(View view)
            {
                try {
                    playAudio(AUDIO_PATH);
//                    playLocalAudio();
//                    playLocalAudio_UsingDescriptor();
                } catch (Exception e) {
                    e.printStackTrace();
                }
            }});

        pausePlayerBtn.setOnClickListener(new OnClickListener(){
```

```java
            @Override
            public void onClick(View view)
            {
                if(mediaPlayer!=null)
                {
                    playbackPosition = mediaPlayer.getCurrentPosition();
                    mediaPlayer.pause();
                }
            }});

    restartPlayerBtn.setOnClickListener(new OnClickListener(){

            @Override
            public void onClick(View view)
            {
                if(mediaPlayer!=null && !mediaPlayer.isPlaying())
                {
                    mediaPlayer.seekTo(playbackPosition);
                    mediaPlayer.start();
                }
            }});
    }

    private void playAudio(String url)throws Exception
    {
        killMediaPlayer();

        mediaPlayer = new MediaPlayer();
        mediaPlayer.setDataSource(url);
        mediaPlayer.prepare();
        mediaPlayer.start();
    }

    @Override
    protected void onDestroy()
    {
        super.onDestroy();
        killMediaPlayer();
    }
    private void killMediaPlayer()
    {
        if(mediaPlayer!=null)
        {
            try
            {
                mediaPlayer.release();
            }
            catch(Exception e)
            {
                e.printStackTrace();
            }
        }
    }
}
```

Realize that in this scenario you are playing an MP3 file from a web address. Therefore, you will need to add `android.permission.INTERNET` to your manifest file. The code in Listing 9–1 shows that the `MainActivity` class contains three members: a `final` string that points to the URL of the MP3 file, a `MediaPlayer` instance, and an integer member called `playbackPosition`. You can see from the `onCreate()` method that the code wires up the click listeners for the three buttons. In the button-click handler for the Start Playing Audio button, the `playAudio()` method is called. In the `playAudio()` method, a new instance of the `MediaPlayer` is created and the data source of the player is set to the URL of the MP3 file. The `prepare()` method of the player is then called to prepare the media player for playback, and then the `start()` method is called to start playback.

Now look at the button-click handlers for the Pause Player and Restart Player buttons. You can see that when the Pause Player button is selected, you get the current position of the player by calling `getCurrentPosition()`. You then pause the player by calling `pause()`. When the player has to be restarted, you call `seekTo()`, passing in the position obtained from `getCurrentPosition()`, and then call `start()`.

The `MediaPlayer` class also contains a `stop()` method. Note that if you stop the player by calling `stop()`, you need to call `prepare()` before calling `start()` again. Conversely, if you call `pause()`, you can call `start()` again without having to prepare the player. Also, be sure to call the `release()` method of the media player once you are done using it. In this example, you do this as part of the `killMediaPlayer()` method.

The example in Listing 9–1 shows you how to play an audio file located on the Web. The `MediaPlayer` class also supports playing media local to your .apk file. Listing 9–2 shows how to reference and play back a file from the `/res/raw` folder of your .apk file. Go ahead and add the `raw` folder under `/res` if it's not already there in the Eclipse project. Then copy the mp3 file of your choice into `/res/raw` with the file name `music_file.mp3`.

Listing 9–2. *Using the MediaPlayer to Play Back a File Local to Your Application*

```
private void playLocalAudio()throws Exception
{
    mediaPlayer = MediaPlayer.create(this, R.raw.music_file);
    mediaPlayer.start();
}
```

If you need to include an audio or video file with your application, you should place the file in the `/res/raw` folder. You can then get a `MediaPlayer` instance for the resource by passing in the resource ID of the media file; you do this by calling the static `create()` method, as shown in Listing 9–2. Note that the `MediaPlayer` class also provides static `create()` methods that you can use to get a `MediaPlayer` rather than instantiating one yourself. For example, in Listing 9–2 you call the `create()` method, but you could instead call the constructor `MediaPlayer(Context context,int resourceId)`. Using the static `create()` methods is preferable because they hide the creation of the `MediaPlayer`. However, as you will see shortly, at times you will not have a choice between these two options—you will have to instantiate the default constructor because media content cannot be located via a resource ID or a URL.

Understanding the setDataSource Method

In Listing 9–2, we called the `create()` method to load the audio file from a raw resource. With this approach, you don't need to call `setDataSource()`. Alternatively, if you instantiate the `MediaPlayer` yourself using the default constructor, or if your media content is not accessible through a resource ID or a URL, you'll need to call `setDataSource()`.

The `setDataSource()` method has overloaded versions that you can use to customize the data source for your specific needs. For example, Listing 9–3 shows how you can load an audio file from a raw resource using a `FileDescriptor`.

Listing 9–3. *Setting the MediaPlayer's Data Source Using a FileDescriptor*

```
private void playLocalAudio_UsingDescriptor() throws Exception {

    AssetFileDescriptor fileDesc = getResources().openRawResourceFd(
            R.raw.music_file);
    if (fileDesc != null) {

        mediaPlayer = new MediaPlayer();
        mediaPlayer.setDataSource(fileDesc.getFileDescriptor(), fileDesc
                .getStartOffset(), fileDesc.getLength());

        fileDesc.close();

        mediaPlayer.prepare();
        mediaPlayer.start();
    }
}
```

The code in Listing 9–3 assumes that it's within the context of an activity. As shown, you call the `getResources()` method to get the application's resources and then use the `openRawResourceFd()` method to get a file descriptor for an audio file within the `/res/raw` folder. You then call the `setDataSource()` method using the `AssetFileDescriptor`, the starting position to begin playback, and the ending position. You can also use this version of `setDataSource()` if you want to play back a specific portion of an audio file. If you always want to play the entire file, you can call the simpler version of `setDataSource(FileDescriptor desc)`, which does not require the initial offset and length.

Using one of the `setDataSource()` methods with the `FileDescriptor` can also be handy if you want to feed a media file located within your application's `/data` directory. For security reasons, the media player does not have access to an application's `/data` directory, but your application can open the file and then feed the (opened) `FileDescriptor` to `setDataSource()`. Realize that the application's `/data` directory resides in the set of files and folders under `/data/data/`APP_PACKAGE_NAME`/`. You can get access to this directory by calling the appropriate method from the `Context` class, rather than hard-coding the path. For example, you can call `getFilesDir()` on `Context` to get the current application's files directory. Currently, this path looks like the following: `/data/data/`APP_PACKAGE_NAME`/files`. Similarly, you can call `getCacheDir()` to get the application's cache directory. Your application will have read and write permission on the contents of these folders, so you can create files dynamically and feed them to the player. Finally, if you use `FileDescriptor`, as shown in Listing 9–3, be sure to close the handle after calling `setDataSource()`.

Observe that an application's `/data` directory differs greatly from its `/res/raw` folder. The `/res/raw` folder is physically part of the .apk file, and it is static—that is, you cannot modify the .apk file dynamically. The contents of the `/data` directory, on the other hand, are dynamic.

We have one more source for audio content to talk about: the SD card. Earlier we showed you how to put content onto the SD card. Using it with MediaPlayer is pretty easy. In our example above, we used `setDataSource()` to access content on the Internet by passing in a URL for an MP3 file. If you've got an audio file on your SD card, you can use the same `setDataSource()` method but instead pass it the path to your audio file on the SD card. For example, if you put an MP3 file under `/sdcard` called `music_file.mp3`, you could modify the `AUDIO_PATH` variable to be `"/sdcard/music_file.mp3"` and it would play, like so:

```
static final String AUDIO_PATH = "/sdcard/music_file.mp3";
```

This concludes our discussion about playing audio content. Now we'll turn our attention to playing video. As you will see, referencing video content is similar to referencing audio content.

Playing Video Content

In this section, we are going to discuss video playback using the Android SDK. Specifically, we will discuss playing a video from a web server and playing one from an SD card. As you can imagine, video playback is a bit more involved than audio playback. Fortunately, the Android SDK provides some additional abstractions that do most of the heavy lifting.

Playing video requires more effort than playing audio since there's a visual component to take care of in addition to the audio. To take some of the pain away, Android provides a specialized view control called `android.widget.VideoView` that encapsulates creating and initializing the `MediaPlayer`. To play video, you create a `VideoView` widget and set that as the content of the UI. You then set the path or URI of the video and fire the `start()` method. Listing 9–4 demonstrates video playback in Android.

Listing 9–4. *Playing a Video Using the Media APIs*

```xml
<?xml version="1.0" encoding="utf-8"?>
<!-- This file is /res/layout/main.xml -->
<LinearLayout
 android:layout_width="fill_parent" android:layout_height="fill_parent"
 xmlns:android="http://schemas.android.com/apk/res/android">

    <VideoView
        android:id="@+id/videoView"
        android:layout_width="200px"
        android:layout_height="200px" />
```

```
</LinearLayout>

import android.app.Activity;
import android.net.Uri;
import android.os.Bundle;
import android.widget.MediaController;
import android.widget.VideoView;

public class MainActivity extends Activity {
    /** Called when the activity is first created. */
    @Override
    protected void onCreate(Bundle savedInstanceState) {
        super.onCreate(savedInstanceState);
        this.setContentView(R.layout.main);

        VideoView videoView = (VideoView)this.findViewById(R.id.videoView);
        MediaController mc = new MediaController(this);
        videoView.setMediaController(mc);
        videoView.setVideoURI(Uri.parse(
            "http://www.androidbook.com/akc/filestorage/android/documentfiles/
             3389/movie.mp4"));
        // videoView.setVideoPath("/sdcard/movie.mp4");
        videoView.requestFocus();
        videoView.start();
    }
}
```

The example in Listing 9–4 demonstrates video playback of a file located on the Web at
http://www.androidbook.com/akc/filestorage/android/documentfiles/3389/movie.mp4,
which means the application running the code will need to request the
android.permission.INTERNET permission. All of the playback functionality is hidden
behind the VideoView class. In fact, all you have to do is feed the video content to the
video player. The user interface of the application is shown in Figure 9–4.

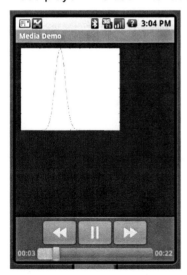

Figure 9–4. *The video-playback UI with media controls enabled*

When this application runs, you will see the button controls along the bottom of the screen for about three seconds, and then they disappear. You get them back by clicking anywhere within the video frame. When we were doing playback of audio content, we only needed to display the button controls to start, pause, and restart the audio. We did not need a view component for the audio itself. With video, of course, we need button controls as well as something to view the video in. For this example, we're using a VideoView component to display the video content. But instead of creating our own button controls (which we could still do if we wanted to), we create a MediaController that provides the buttons for us. As shown in Figure 9–4 and Listing 9–4, you set the VideoView's media controller by calling setMediaController() to enable the play, pause, and seek-to controls. If you want to manipulate the video programmatically with your own buttons, you can call the start(), pause(), stopPlayback(), and seekTo() methods.

Keep in mind that we're still using a MediaPlayer in this example—we just don't see it. You can in fact "play" videos directly in MediaPlayer. If you go back to the example from Listing 9–1, put a movie file on your SD card, and plug in the movie's file path in AUDIO_PATH, you will find that it plays the audio quite nicely even though you can't see the video.

While MediaPlayer has a setDataSource() method, VideoView does not. VideoView instead uses the setVideoPath() or setVideoURI() methods. Assuming you put a movie file onto your SD card, you change the code from Listing 9–4 to comment out the setVideoURI() call and uncomment the setVideoPath() call, adjusting the path to the movie file as necessary. When you run the application again, you will now hear *and see* the video in the VideoView. Technically, we could have called setVideoURI() with the following to get the same effect as setVideoPath(), being careful to include three forward slashes in the file URI between file: and sdcard:

```
videoView.setVideoURI(Uri.parse("file:///sdcard/movie.mp4"));
```

Understanding the MediaPlayer Oddities

In general, the MediaPlayer is very systematic, so you need to call operations in a specific order to initialize a media player properly and prepare it for playback. This list summarizes some of the oddities of using the media APIs:

- Once you set the data source of a MediaPlayer, you cannot easily change it to another one—you'll have to create a new MediaPlayer or call the reset() method to reinitialize the state of the player.

- After you call prepare(), you can call getCurrentPosition(), getDuration(), and isPlaying() to get the current state of the player. You can also call the setLooping() and setVolume() methods after the call to prepare().

- After you call start(), you can call pause(), stop(), and seekTo().

■ Every MediaPlayer creates a new thread, so be sure to call the release() method when you are done with the media player. The VideoView takes care of this in the case of video playback, but you'll have to do it manually if you decide to use MediaPlayer instead of VideoView.

Now let's explore recording media.

Exploring Audio Recording

The Android media framework supports recording audio. You record audio using the android.media.MediaRecorder class. In this section, we'll show you how to build an application that records audio content and then plays the content back. The user interface of the application is shown in Figure 9–5.

Figure 9–5. *The user interface of the audio-recorder example*

As shown in Figure 9–5, the application contains four buttons: two to control recording, and two to start and stop playback of the recorded content. Listing 9–5 shows the layout file and activity class for the UI.

Listing 9–5. *Media Recording and Playback in Android*

```xml
<?xml version="1.0" encoding="utf-8"?>
<!-- This file is /res/layout/record.xml -->
<LinearLayout xmlns:android="http://schemas.android.com/apk/res/android"
    android:orientation="vertical"
    android:layout_width="fill_parent"
    android:layout_height="fill_parent"
    >
    <Button android:id="@+id/bgnBtn" android:layout_width="fill_parent"
    android:layout_height="wrap_content" android:text="Begin Recording"/>
```

```xml
        <Button android:id="@+id/stpBtn" android:layout_width="fill_parent"
    android:layout_height="wrap_content" android:text="Stop Recording"/>

        <Button android:id=
"@+id/playRecordingBtn" android:layout_width="fill_parent"
    android:layout_height="wrap_content" android:text="Play Recording"/>

        <Button android:id=
"@+id/stpPlayingRecordingBtn" android:layout_width="fill_parent"
    android:layout_height="wrap_content" android:text="Stop Playing Recording"/>

    </LinearLayout>
```

```java
// RecorderActivity.java
import java.io.File;
import android.app.Activity;
import android.media.MediaPlayer;
import android.media.MediaRecorder;
import android.os.Bundle;
import android.view.View;
import android.view.View.OnClickListener;
import android.widget.Button;
public class RecorderActivity extends Activity {
    private MediaPlayer mediaPlayer;
    private MediaRecorder recorder;
    private static final String OUTPUT_FILE= "/sdcard/recordoutput.3gpp";

    @Override
    protected void onCreate(Bundle savedInstanceState) {
        super.onCreate(savedInstanceState);

        setContentView(R.layout.record);

        Button startBtn = (Button) findViewById(R.id.bgnBtn);

        Button endBtn = (Button) findViewById(R.id.stpBtn);

        Button playRecordingBtn = (Button) findViewById(R.id.playRecordingBtn);

        Button stpPlayingRecordingBtn =
(Button) findViewById(R.id.stpPlayingRecordingBtn);

        startBtn.setOnClickListener(new OnClickListener() {

            @Override
            public void onClick(View view) {
                try {
                    beginRecording();
                } catch (Exception e) {
                    e.printStackTrace();
                }
            }
        });

        endBtn.setOnClickListener(new OnClickListener() {
```

```
        @Override
        public void onClick(View view) {
            try {
                stopRecording();
            } catch (Exception e) {
                e.printStackTrace();
            }
        }
    });

    playRecordingBtn.setOnClickListener(new OnClickListener() {

        @Override
        public void onClick(View view) {
            try {
                playRecording();
            } catch (Exception e) {
                e.printStackTrace();
            }
        }
    });

    stpPlayingRecordingBtn.setOnClickListener(new OnClickListener() {

        @Override
        public void onClick(View view) {
            try {
                stopPlayingRecording();
            } catch (Exception e) {
                e.printStackTrace();
            }
        }
    });
}

private void beginRecording() throws Exception {
    killMediaRecorder();

    File outFile = new File(OUTPUT_FILE);

    if(outFile.exists())
    {
        outFile.delete();
    }
    recorder = new MediaRecorder();
    recorder.setAudioSource(MediaRecorder.AudioSource.MIC);
    recorder.setOutputFormat(MediaRecorder.OutputFormat.THREE_GPP);
    recorder.setAudioEncoder(MediaRecorder.AudioEncoder.AMR_NB);
    recorder.setOutputFile(OUTPUT_FILE);
    recorder.prepare();
    recorder.start();

}

private void stopRecording() throws Exception {
    if (recorder != null) {
        recorder.stop();
```

```
        }
    }

    private void killMediaRecorder() {
        if (recorder != null) {
            recorder.release();
        }
    }

    private void killMediaPlayer() {
        if (mediaPlayer != null) {
            try {
                mediaPlayer.release();
            } catch (Exception e) {
                e.printStackTrace();
            }
        }
    }

    private void playRecording() throws Exception {
        killMediaPlayer();

        mediaPlayer = new MediaPlayer();
        mediaPlayer.setDataSource(OUTPUT_FILE);

        mediaPlayer.prepare();
        mediaPlayer.start();
    }
    private void stopPlayingRecording() throws Exception {
        if(mediaPlayer!=null)
        {
            mediaPlayer.stop();
        }
    }

    @Override
    protected void onDestroy() {
        super.onDestroy();

        killMediaRecorder();
        killMediaPlayer();
    }

}
```

Before we jump into Listing 9–5, realize that in order to record audio, you'll need to add the following permission to your manifest file:

```
<uses-permission android:name="android.permission.RECORD_AUDIO" />
```

As discussed earlier in the section on SD cards, if your application's minSdkVersion is 4 or higher, you will also need to add a uses-permission tag for "android.permission.WRITE_EXTERNAL_STORAGE". Finally, if you are going to try this out with the emulator, you'll need to provide a microphone input on your workstation.

If you look at the onCreate() method in Listing 9–5, you'll see that the on-click event handlers are wired up for the four buttons. The beginRecording() method handles recording. To record audio, you must create an instance of `MediaRecorder` and set the audio source, output format, audio encoder, and output file. Up until Android SDK 1.6, the only supported audio source was the microphone. Since Android SDK 1.6, there are three more audio sources available, all related to phone calls. You can record the entire call (`MediaRecorder.AudioSource.VOICE_CALL`), the uplink side only (`MediaRecorder.AudioSource.VOICE_UPLINK`), or the downlink side only (`MediaRecorder.AudioSource.VOICE_DOWNLINK`). The uplink side of a call would be the voice of the phone's user. The downlink side of the call would be sounds coming from the other end of the call. The only supported output format for audio is 3rd Generation Partnership Project (3GPP). You must set the encoder to `AMR_NB`, which signifies the Adaptive Multi-Rate (AMR) narrowband audio codec, as this is the only supported audio encoder. The recorded audio in our example is written to the SD card at `/sdcard/recordoutput.3gpp`. Note that Listing 9–5 assumes that you've created an SD card image and that you've pointed the emulator to the SD card. If you have not done this, refer to the section "Understanding and Using SD Cards" for details on setting this up.

There are some additional methods to the `MediaRecorder` that you might find useful. In order to limit the length and size of audio recordings, the methods `setMaxDuration(int length_in_ms)` and `setMaxFileSize(long length_in_bytes)` can be used. You would set the maximum length of the recording, in milliseconds, or the maximum length of the recording file, in bytes, to stop recording when these limits are reached. These were both introduced with Android 1.5 so they are available on some older phones.

Note that the current media APIs do not support streaming. For example, if you record audio, you cannot access the audio stream during the recording process (for analysis purposes, for example). Instead, you have to write the audio content to a file first and then work with it. Future releases of the Android SDK will likely support audio streaming. One way that you might try to work around this is to write the audio to a file, and read the file with another thread or application as it's being written.

Exploring Video Recording

Since the introduction of Android SDK 1.5, you can capture video using the media framework. This works in a similar way to recording audio and, in fact, recorded video usually includes an audio track. There is one big exception with video, however. Beginning with Android SDK 1.6, recording video requires that you preview the camera images onto a `Surface` object. In basic applications this is not much of an issue, since the user probably wants to be viewing what the camera sees, anyway. For more sophisticated applications this could be a problem. If your application doesn't need to show the video feed to the user as it happens, you still need to provide a `Surface` object so the `camera` can preview the video. We expect this requirement will be relaxed in future versions of the Android SDK, so that applications could work directly with the video buffers without having to copy to a UI component as well. For now, though, we'll have to work with a `Surface` and we'll show you how to do this (Listing 9–6).

Listing 9–6. *Using the MediaRecorder Class to Capture Video*

```xml
<?xml version="1.0" encoding="utf-8"?>
<!-- This file is /res/layout/main.xml -->
<LinearLayout xmlns:android="http://schemas.android.com/apk/res/android"
    android:orientation="vertical" android:layout_width="fill_parent"
    android:layout_height="fill_parent">

    <Button android:id="@+id/bgnBtn" android:layout_width="fill_parent"
        android:layout_height="wrap_content" android:text="Begin Recording"
        android:enabled="false" />

    <Button android:id="@+id/stpBtn" android:layout_width="fill_parent"
        android:layout_height="wrap_content" android:text="Stop Recording" />

    <Button android:id="@+id/playRecordingBtn" android:layout_width="fill_parent"
        android:layout_height="wrap_content" android:text="Play Recording" />

    <Button android:id="@+id/stpPlayingRecordingBtn"
        android:layout_width="fill_parent" android:layout_height="wrap_content"
        android:text="Stop Playing Recording" />

    <RelativeLayout android:layout_width="fill_parent"
        android:layout_height="fill_parent"
        android:gravity="center">

        <VideoView android:id="@+id/videoView" android:layout_width="176px"
            android:layout_height="144px" />

    </RelativeLayout>
</LinearLayout>


import java.io.File;
import android.app.Activity;
import android.media.MediaRecorder;
import android.os.Bundle;
import android.util.Log;
import android.view.SurfaceHolder;
import android.view.View;
import android.view.View.OnClickListener;
import android.widget.Button;
import android.widget.MediaController;
import android.widget.VideoView;

public class MainActivity extends Activity implements SurfaceHolder.Callback {

    private MediaRecorder recorder = null;
    private static final String OUTPUT_FILE = "/sdcard/videooutput.mp4";
    private static final String TAG = "RecordVideo";
    private VideoView videoView = null;
    private Button startBtn = null;

    /** Called when the activity is first created. */
    @Override
    public void onCreate(Bundle savedInstanceState) {
        super.onCreate(savedInstanceState);
        setContentView(R.layout.main);
```

```java
        startBtn = (Button) findViewById(R.id.bgnBtn);

        Button endBtn = (Button) findViewById(R.id.stpBtn);

        Button playRecordingBtn = (Button) findViewById(R.id.playRecordingBtn);

        Button stpPlayingRecordingBtn =
(Button) findViewById(R.id.stpPlayingRecordingBtn);

        videoView = (VideoView)this.findViewById(R.id.videoView);

        final SurfaceHolder holder = videoView.getHolder();
        holder.addCallback(this);
        holder.setType(SurfaceHolder.SURFACE_TYPE_PUSH_BUFFERS);

        startBtn.setOnClickListener(new OnClickListener() {

            @Override
            public void onClick(View view) {
                try {
                    beginRecording(holder);
                } catch (Exception e) {
                    Log.e(TAG, e.toString());
                    e.printStackTrace();
                }
            }
        });

        endBtn.setOnClickListener(new OnClickListener() {

            @Override
            public void onClick(View view) {
                try {
                    stopRecording();
                } catch (Exception e) {
                    Log.e(TAG, e.toString());
                    e.printStackTrace();
                }
            }
        });

        playRecordingBtn.setOnClickListener(new OnClickListener() {

            @Override
            public void onClick(View view) {
                try {
                    playRecording();
                } catch (Exception e) {
                    Log.e(TAG, e.toString());
                    e.printStackTrace();
                }
            }
        });

        stpPlayingRecordingBtn.setOnClickListener(new OnClickListener() {
```

```java
        @Override
        public void onClick(View view) {
            try {
                stopPlayingRecording();
            } catch (Exception e) {
                Log.e(TAG, e.toString());
                e.printStackTrace();
            }
        }
    });
}

@Override
public void surfaceCreated(SurfaceHolder holder) {
    startBtn.setEnabled(true);
}

@Override
public void surfaceDestroyed(SurfaceHolder holder) {
}

@Override
public void surfaceChanged(SurfaceHolder holder, int format, int width,
    int height) {
    Log.v(TAG, "Width x Height = " + width + "x" + height);
}

private void playRecording() {
    MediaController mc = new MediaController(this);
    videoView.setMediaController(mc);
    videoView.setVideoPath(OUTPUT_FILE);
    videoView.start();
}

private void stopPlayingRecording() {
    videoView.stopPlayback();
}

private void stopRecording() throws Exception {
    if (recorder != null) {
        recorder.stop();
    }
}

@Override
protected void onDestroy() {
    super.onDestroy();
    if (recorder != null) {
        recorder.release();
    }
}

private void beginRecording(SurfaceHolder holder) throws Exception {
    if(recorder!=null)
    {
        recorder.stop();
        recorder.release();
```

```
        }

        File outFile = new File(OUTPUT_FILE);
        if(outFile.exists())
        {
            outFile.delete();
        }

        try {
            recorder = new MediaRecorder();
            recorder.setVideoSource(MediaRecorder.VideoSource.CAMERA);
            recorder.setAudioSource(MediaRecorder.AudioSource.MIC);
            recorder.setOutputFormat(MediaRecorder.OutputFormat.MPEG_4);
            recorder.setVideoSize(176, 144);
            recorder.setVideoFrameRate(15);
            recorder.setVideoEncoder(MediaRecorder.VideoEncoder.MPEG_4_SP);
            recorder.setAudioEncoder(MediaRecorder.AudioEncoder.AMR_NB);
            recorder.setMaxDuration(30000); // limit to 30 seconds
            recorder.setPreviewDisplay(holder.getSurface());
            recorder.setOutputFile(OUTPUT_FILE);
            recorder.prepare();
            recorder.start();
        }
        catch(Exception e) {
            Log.e(TAG, e.toString());
            e.printStackTrace();
        }
    }
}
```

As before when recording audio, we need to set the same permissions for audio (android.permission.RECORD_AUDIO) and the SD card (android.permission.WRITE_EXTERNAL_STORAGE), and now we need to add permission to the camera (android.permission.CAMERA). Listing 9–6 shows an activity class that provides a beginRecording() method to record video content from the device's camera to the SD card. Recall from the audio example earlier that the MediaRecorder requires you to set the recorder properties before calling prepare(). As shown, we set the MediaRecorder's video source to the device's camera, the audio source to the microphone, the output format to MPEG_4, and so on. We also set the audio and video encoders and a path to the output file on the SD card before calling the prepare() and start() methods. One of the last things we do before calling prepare() is to set a preview display for the MediaRecorder. This is where the Surface comes in. Our layout has a VideoView and this can act as a Surface for the preview. This allows the user to see what is being recorded from the camera. We set up the holder from the VideoView and then use it here. Note also that we only enable the Begin Recording button once the Surface has been created.

Listing 9–6 will capture video content from the camera and output it to the SD card in a file named videooutput.mp4. Note that currently you cannot manipulate the content from the camera before encoding and saving it—this may come in a future release of Android. One of the other features of this application is that we use the very same VideoView object to play back the video we just recorded. In fact, if you have previously recorded some video to the SD card using this application, then launched the application again, you will be able to immediately play back the previous video since it still exists as a file on your SD card, and this application is written to play back the video from that file.

Exploring the MediaStore Class

So far, we've dealt with media by directly instantiating classes to play and record media within our own application. One of the great things about Android is that you can access other applications to do work for you. The MediaStore class provides an interface to the media that is stored on the device (in both internal and external storage). MediaStore also provides APIs for you to act on the media. These include mechanisms for you to search the device for specific types of media, intents for you to record audio and video to the store, ways for you to establish playlists, and more. Note that this class was part of the older SDKs, but it has been greatly improved since the 1.5 release.

Because the MediaStore class supports intents for you to record audio and video, and the MediaRecorder class does also, an obvious question is, when do you use MediaStore vs. MediaRecorder? As you saw with the preceding video-capture example and the audio-recording examples, MediaRecorder allows you to set various options on the source of the recording. These options include the audio/video input source, video frame rate, video frame size, output formats, and so on. MediaStore does not provide this level of granularity, but you are not coupled directly to the MediaRecorder if you go through the MediaStore's intents. More important, content created with the MediaRecorder is not available to other applications that are looking at the media store. If you use MediaRecorder, you might want to add the recording to the media store using the MediaStore APIs, so it might be simpler just to use MediaStore in the first place. Another significant difference is that calling MediaStore through an intent does not require your application to request permissions to record audio, or access the camera, or to write to the SD card. Your application is invoking a separate activity, and that other activity must have permission to record audio, access the camera, and write to the SD card. The MediaStore activities already have these permissions. Therefore, your application doesn't have to. So, let's see how we can leverage the MediaStore APIs.

As we've seen, recording audio was easy, but its gets much easier if you use an intent from the MediaStore. Listing 9–7 demonstrates how to use an intent to record audio.

Listing 9–7. *Using an Intent to Record Audio*

```
<?xml version="1.0" encoding="utf-8"?>
<!-- This file is /res/layout/main.xml -->
<LinearLayout xmlns:android="http://schemas.android.com/apk/res/android"
    android:orientation="vertical"
    android:layout_width="fill_parent"
    android:layout_height="fill_parent"
    >
 <Button android:id="@+id/recordBtn"
            android:text="Record Audio"
            android:layout_width="wrap_content"
            android:layout_height="wrap_content" />
</LinearLayout>
```

```java
import android.app.Activity;
import android.content.Intent;
import android.net.Uri;
import android.os.Bundle;
import android.view.View;
import android.view.View.OnClickListener;
import android.widget.Button;

public class UsingMediaStoreActivity extends Activity {
    @Override
    protected void onCreate(Bundle savedInstanceState) {
        super.onCreate(savedInstanceState);

        setContentView(R.layout.main);

        Button btn = (Button)findViewById(R.id.recordBtn);
        btn.setOnClickListener(new OnClickListener(){

            @Override
            public void onClick(View view) {

                startRecording();

            }});
    }

    public void startRecording() {
        Intent intt = new Intent("android.provider.MediaStore.RECORD_SOUND");
        startActivityForResult(intt, 0);
    }

    @Override
    protected void onActivityResult(int requestCode, int resultCode, Intent data) {

        switch (requestCode) {
        case 0:
            if (resultCode == RESULT_OK) {
                Uri recordedAudioPath = data.getData();
            }
        }
    }
}
```

Listing 9–7 creates an intent requesting the system to begin recording audio. The code launches the intent against an activity by calling startActivityForResult(), passing the intent and the requestCode. When the requested activity completes, onActivityResult() is called with the requestCode. As shown in onActivityResult(), we look for a requestCode that matches the code that was passed to startActivityForResult() and then retrieve the URI of the saved media by calling data.getData(). You could then feed the URI to an intent to listen to the recording if you wanted to. The UI for Listing 9–7 is shown in Figure 9–6.

Figure 9–6. *Built-in audio recorder before and after a recording*

Figure 9–6 contains two screenshots. The image on the left displays the audio recorder during recording, and the image on the right shows the activity UI after the recording has been stopped.

Similar to the way it provides an intent for audio recording, the MediaStore also provides an intent for you to take a picture. Listing 9–8 demonstrates this.

Listing 9–8. *Launching an Intent to Take a Picture*

```xml
<?xml version="1.0" encoding="utf-8"?>
<!-- This file is /res/layout/main.xml -->
<LinearLayout xmlns:android="http://schemas.android.com/apk/res/android"
    android:orientation="vertical"
    android:layout_width="fill_parent"
    android:layout_height="fill_parent"
    >
  <Button android:id="@+id/btn"
            android:text="Take Picture"
            android:layout_width="wrap_content"
            android:layout_height="wrap_content"
            android:onClick="captureImage" />

</LinearLayout>
```

```java
import android.app.Activity;
import android.content.ContentValues;
import android.content.Intent;
import android.net.Uri;
import android.os.Bundle;
import android.provider.MediaStore;
import android.provider.MediaStore.Images.Media;
```

```java
import android.view.View;
import android.view.View.OnClickListener;
import android.widget.Button;

public class MainActivity extends Activity {

    Uri myPicture = null;

    @Override
    public void onCreate(Bundle savedInstanceState) {
        super.onCreate(savedInstanceState);
        setContentView(R.layout.main);

        setRequestedOrientation(ActivityInfo.SCREEN_ORIENTATION_LANDSCAPE);
    }

    public void captureImage(View view)
    {
        ContentValues values = new ContentValues();
        values.put(Media.TITLE, "My demo image");
        values.put(Media.DESCRIPTION, "Image Captured by Camera via an Intent");

        myPicture = getContentResolver().insert(Media.EXTERNAL_CONTENT_URI, values);

        Intent i = new Intent(MediaStore.ACTION_IMAGE_CAPTURE);
        i.putExtra(MediaStore.EXTRA_OUTPUT, myPicture);

        startActivityForResult(i, 0);
    }

    @Override
    protected void onActivityResult(int requestCode, int resultCode, Intent data) {
        if(requestCode==0 && resultCode==Activity.RESULT_OK)
        {
            // Now we know that our myPicture URI refers to the image just taken
        }
    }
}
```

The activity class shown in Listing 9–8 defines the captureImage() method. In this method, an intent is created where the action name of the intent is set to MediaStore.ACTION_IMAGE_CAPTURE. When this intent is launched, the camera application is brought to the foreground and the user takes a picture. Because we created the URI in advance, we can add additional details about the picture before the camera takes it. This is what the ContentValues class does for us. Additional attributes can be added to values besides TITLE and DESCRIPTION. Look up MediaStore.Images.ImageColumns in the Android reference for a complete list. After the picture is taken, our onActivityResult() callback is called. In our example, we've used the media content provider to create a new file. We could also have created a new URI from a new file on the SD card, as shown here:

```java
myPicture = Uri.fromFile(new File("/sdcard/DCIM/100ANDRO/imageCaptureIntent.jpg"));
```

However, creating a URI this way does not so easily allow us to set attributes about the image, such as TITLE and DESCRIPTION. There is another way to invoke the camera intent in order to take a picture. If we do not pass any URI at all with the intent, we will get a bitmap object returned to us in the intent argument for onActivityResult(). The problem with this approach is that by default, the bitmap will be scaled down from the original size, apparently because the Android team does not want you to receive a large amount of data from the camera activity back to your activity. The bitmap will have a size of 50k. To get the Bitmap object, you'd do something like this inside of onActivityResult():

```
Bitmap myBitmap = (Bitmap) data.getExtras().get("data");
```

MediaStore also has a video-capture intent that behaves similarly. You can use MediaStore.ACTION_VIDEO_CAPTURE to capture video.

Adding Media Content to the Media Store

One of the other features provided by Android's media framework is the ability to add information about content to the media store via the MediaScannerConnection class. In other words, if the media store doesn't know about some new content, we use a MediaScannerConnection to tell the media store about the new content. Then that content can be served up to others. Let's see how this works (see Listing 9–9).

Listing 9–9. *Adding a File to the MediaStore*

```xml
<?xml version="1.0" encoding="utf-8"?>
<!-- This file is /res/layout/main.xml -->
<LinearLayout
    xmlns:android="http://schemas.android.com/apk/res/android"
    android:orientation="vertical"
    android:layout_width="fill_parent"
    android:layout_height="wrap_content">

    <EditText android:id="@+id/fileName"
        android:hint="Enter new filename"
        android:layout_width="fill_parent"
        android:layout_height="wrap_content" />

    <Button android:id="@+id/scanBtn"
        android:text="Add file"
        android:layout_width="wrap_content"
        android:layout_height="wrap_content"
        android:onClick="startScan" />

</LinearLayout>


import java.io.File;
import android.app.Activity;
import android.content.Intent;
import android.media.MediaScannerConnection;
import android.media.MediaScannerConnection.MediaScannerConnectionClient;
import android.net.Uri;
import android.os.Bundle;
import android.util.Log;
import android.view.View;
```

```java
import android.widget.EditText;
import android.widget.Toast;

public class MediaScannerActivity extends Activity implements
MediaScannerConnectionClient
{
    private EditText editText = null;
    private String filename = null;
    private MediaScannerConnection conn;

    @Override
    protected void onCreate(Bundle savedInstanceState) {
        super.onCreate(savedInstanceState);
        setContentView(R.layout.main);

        editText = (EditText)findViewById(R.id.fileName);
    }

    public void startScan(View view)
    {
        if(conn!=null)
        {
            conn.disconnect();
        }

        filename = editText.getText().toString();

        File fileCheck = new File(filename);
        if(fileCheck.isFile()) {
            conn = new MediaScannerConnection(this, this);
            conn.connect();
        }
        else {
            Toast.makeText(this,
                "That file does not exist",
                Toast.LENGTH_SHORT).show();
        }
    }

    @Override
    public void onMediaScannerConnected() {
        conn.scanFile(filename, null);
    }

    @Override
    public void onScanCompleted(String path, Uri uri) {
        try {
            if (uri != null) {
                Intent intent = new Intent(Intent.ACTION_VIEW);
                intent.setData(uri);
                startActivity(intent);
            }
            else {
                Log.e("MediaScannerDemo", "That file is no good");
            }
        } finally {
            conn.disconnect();
```

```
                conn = null;
            }
        }
}
```

Listing 9–9 shows an activity class that adds a file to the `MediaStore`. If the add is successful, the added file is displayed to the user via an intent. What happens behind the scenes is that the file is inspected by the `MediaScanner` to determine what type of file it is and other relevant details about it. Of course, we could have given the `MediaScanner` the MIME type as the second argument to `scanFile()`. If `MediaScanner` can't determine what the type of the file is by the extension, it won't get added. If the file belongs in the `MediaStore`, a database entry is made into the media provider database. The file itself doesn't move. But now the media provider knows about this file. If you added an image file, you can now open the Gallery application and see it. If you added a music file, it will now show up in the Music application.

If you want to see inside the media provider's database, open a tools window, launch `adb shell` then navigate on the device to `/data/data/com.android.providers.media/databases`. There you will find databases, one of which is `internal.db`. There could be external database files there also, corresponding to one or more SD cards. Since you can use multiple SD cards with an Android phone, there could also be multiple external database files there. You can use the sqlite3 utility to inspect the tables in these databases. There are tables for audio, images, and video. See Chapter 3 for more information on using sqlite3.

This concludes our discussion of the media APIs. We hope you'll agree that playing and recording media content is simple with Android. Now we'll move on to the telephony APIs.

Using the Telephony APIs

In this section, we are going to explore Android's telephony APIs. Specifically, we will show you how to send and receive SMS messages, after which we'll explore making and receiving phone calls. We'll start with SMS.

Working with SMS

SMS stands for Short Message Service, as we mentioned earlier, but it's commonly called *text messaging*. The Android SDK supports sending and receiving text messages. We'll start by discussing various ways to send SMS messages with the SDK.

Sending SMS Messages

To send a text message from your application, you will add the `<uses-permission android:name="android.permission.SEND_SMS" />` permission to your manifest file and then use the `android.telephony.SmsManager` class (see Listing 9–10).

Listing 9–10. *Sending SMS (Text) Messages*

```xml
<?xml version="1.0" encoding="utf-8"?>
<!-- This file is /res/layout/main.xml -->
<LinearLayout xmlns:android="http://schemas.android.com/apk/res/android"
    android:orientation="vertical" android:layout_width="fill_parent"
    android:layout_height="fill_parent">

    <LinearLayout xmlns:android="http://schemas.android.com/apk/res/android"
        android:orientation="horizontal" android:layout_width="fill_parent"
        android:layout_height="wrap_content">

        <TextView android:layout_width="wrap_content"
            android:layout_height="wrap_content" android:text="Destination Address:" />

        <EditText android:id="@+id/addrEditText"
            android:layout_width="fill_parent" android:layout_height="wrap_content"
            android:phoneNumber="true" android:text="9045551212" />

    </LinearLayout>

    <LinearLayout xmlns:android="http://schemas.android.com/apk/res/android"
        android:orientation="vertical" android:layout_width="fill_parent"
        android:layout_height="wrap_content">

        <TextView android:layout_width="wrap_content"
            android:layout_height="wrap_content" android:text="Text Message:" />

        <EditText android:id="@+id/msgEditText" android:layout_width="fill_parent"
            android:layout_height="wrap_content" android:text="hello sms" />

    </LinearLayout>

    <Button android:id="@+id/sendSmsBtn" android:layout_width="wrap_content"
        android:layout_height="wrap_content" android:text="Send Text Message" />

</LinearLayout>


import android.app.Activity;
import android.os.Bundle;
import android.telephony.SmsManager;
import android.view.View;
import android.view.View.OnClickListener;
import android.widget.Button;
import android.widget.EditText;
import android.widget.Toast;

public class TelephonyDemo extends Activity
{
    @Override
    protected void onCreate(Bundle savedInstanceState) {
        super.onCreate(savedInstanceState);

        setContentView(R.layout.main);

        Button sendBtn = (Button)findViewById(R.id.sendSmsBtn);
```

```
        sendBtn.setOnClickListener(new OnClickListener(){

            @Override
            public void onClick(View view) {
                EditText addrTxt =
                    (EditText)TelephonyDemo.this.findViewById(R.id.addrEditText);

                EditText msgTxt =
                    (EditText)TelephonyDemo.this.findViewById(R.id.msgEditText);

                try {
                    sendSmsMessage(
                        addrTxt.getText().toString(),msgTxt.getText().toString());
                    Toast.makeText(TelephonyDemo.this, "SMS Sent",
                        Toast.LENGTH_LONG).show();
                } catch (Exception e) {
                    Toast.makeText(TelephonyDemo.this, "Failed to send SMS",
                        Toast.LENGTH_LONG).show();
                    e.printStackTrace();
                }
            }
        }});
    }

    @Override
    protected void onDestroy() {
        super.onDestroy();
    }

    private void sendSmsMessage(String address,String message)throws Exception
    {
        SmsManager smsMgr = SmsManager.getDefault();
        smsMgr.sendTextMessage(address, null, message, null, null);
    }
}
```

The example in Listing 9–10 demonstrates sending SMS text messages using the Android SDK. Looking at the layout snippet first, you can see that the user interface has two EditText fields: one to capture the SMS recipient's destination address (the phone number), and another to hold the text message. The user interface also has a button to send the SMS message, as shown in Figure 9–7.

Figure 9–7. *The UI for the SMS example*

The interesting part of the sample is the sendSmsMessage() method. The method uses the SmsManager class's sendTextMessage() method to send the SMS message. Here's the signature of SmsManager.sendTextMessage():

```
sendTextMessage(String destinationAddress, String smscAddress, String textMsg,
PendingIntent sentIntent, PendingIntent deliveryIntent);
```

In this example, you populate only the destination address and the text-message parameters. You can, however, customize the method so it doesn't use the default SMS center (the address of the server on the cellular network that will dispatch the SMS message). You can also implement a customization in which pending intents are called when the message is sent and a delivery notification has been received.

All in all, sending an SMS message is about as simple as it gets with Android. Realize that, with the emulator, your SMS messages are not actually sent to their destinations. You can, however, assume success if the sendTextMessage() method returns without an exception. As shown in Listing 9–10, you use the Toast class to display a message in the UI to indicate whether the SMS message was sent successfully.

Sending SMS messages is only half the story. Now we'll show you how to monitor incoming SMS messages.

Monitoring Incoming SMS Messages

The first step in monitoring incoming SMS messages is to request permission to receive them. Using the same application that you just created to send SMS messages, add the `<uses-permission android:name="android.permission.RECEIVE_SMS" />` permission to your manifest file. Next, you'll need to implement a monitor to listen for SMS messages. You accomplish this by implementing a BroadcastReceiver for the action `<action android:value="android.provider.Telephony.SMS_RECEIVED" />`. To implement the receiver, write a class that extends android.content.BroadcastReceiver and then register the receiver in your manifest file (within the `<application>`). Listing 9–11 demonstrates this.

Listing 9–11. *Monitoring SMS Messages*

```
<receiver android:name="MySMSMonitor">
    <intent-filter>
        <action android:name="android.provider.Telephony.SMS_RECEIVED"/>
    </intent-filter>
</receiver>


public class MySMSMonitor extends BroadcastReceiver
{
    private static final String ACTION = "android.provider.Telephony.SMS_RECEIVED";
    @Override
    public void onReceive(Context context, Intent intent)
    {
        if(intent!=null && intent.getAction()!=null &&
ACTION.compareToIgnoreCase(intent.getAction())==0)
        {
            Object[]pduArray= (Object[]) intent.getExtras().get("pdus");
```

```
        SmsMessage[] messages = new SmsMessage[pduArray.length];
        for (int i = 0; i<pduArray.length; i++) {
                messages[i] = SmsMessage.createFromPdu ((byte[])pduArray [i]);
        }
        Log.d("MySMSMonitor","SMS Message Received.");
    }
  }
}
```

The top portion of Listing 9–11 is the manifest definition for the BroadcastReceiver to intercept SMS messages. The SMS monitor class is MySMSMonitor. The class implements the abstract onReceive() method, which is called by the system when an SMS message arrives. One way to test the application is to use the Emulator Control view in Eclipse. Run the application in the emulator and then go to Window ➤ Show View ➤ Other ➤ Android ➤ Emulator Control. The user interface allows you to send data to the emulator to emulate receiving an SMS message or phone call. As shown in Figure 9–8, you can send an SMS message to the emulator by populating the "Incoming number" field and then selecting the SMS radio button. Then type some text in the Message field and click the Send button. Doing this sends an SMS message to the emulator and invokes your BroadcastReceiver's onReceive() method.

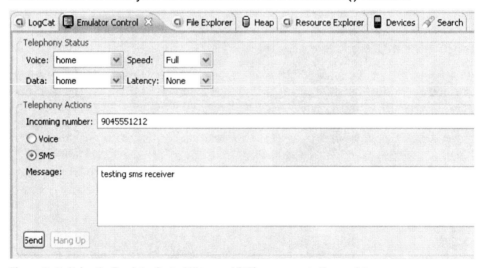

Figure 9–8. *Using the Emulator Control UI to send SMS messages to the emulator*

The onReceive() method will have the broadcast intent, which will contain the SmsMessage in the bundle property. You can extract the SmsMessage by calling intent.getExtras().get("pdus"). This call returns an array of objects defined in Protocol Description Unit (PDU) mode—an industry-standard way of representing an SMS message. You can then convert the PDUs to Android SmsMessage objects, as shown in Listing 9–11. As you can see, you get the PDUs as an object array from the intent. You then construct an array of SmsMessage objects, equal to the size of the PDU array. Finally, you iterate over the PDU array, and create SmsMessage objects from the PDUs by calling SmsMessage.createFromPdu(). What you do after reading the incoming message must be quick. A broadcast receiver gets high priority in the system, but must be done quickly and does not get put into the foreground for the user to see. Therefore, your options are limited. You should not do any direct UI work. Issuing a Notification is fine, as is starting a service to continue work there. Once the onReceive() method completes, the hosting process of the onReceive() method could get killed at any time. Starting a service is okay but binding to one is not, since that would mean your process needs to exist for a while, which might not happen.

Now let's continue our discussion about SMS by looking at how you can work with various SMS folders.

Working with SMS Folders

Accessing the SMS inbox is another common requirement. To get started, you need to add read-SMS permission (`<uses-permission android:name="android.permission.READ_SMS"/>`) to the manifest file. Adding this permission gives you the ability to read from the SMS inbox.

To read SMS messages, you need to execute a query on the SMS inbox, as shown in Listing 9–12.

Listing 9–12. *Displaying the Messages from the SMS Inbox*

```
<?xml version="1.0" encoding="utf-8"?>
<!-- This file is /res/layout/sms_inbox.xml -->
<LinearLayout xmlns:android="http://schemas.android.com/apk/res/android"
    android:orientation="vertical"
    android:layout_width="fill_parent"
    android:layout_height="fill_parent"
    >
    <TextView android:id="@+id/row"
    android:layout_width="fill_parent"
    android:layout_height="fill_parent"/>

</LinearLayout>


import android.app.ListActivity;
import android.database.Cursor;
import android.net.Uri;
import android.os.Bundle;
import android.widget.ListAdapter;
import android.widget.SimpleCursorAdapter;

public class SMSInboxDemo extends ListActivity {

    private ListAdapter adapter;
    private static final Uri SMS_INBOX = Uri.parse("content://sms/inbox");

    @Override
    public void onCreate(Bundle bundle) {
        super.onCreate(bundle);
        Cursor c = getContentResolver()
                .query(SMS_INBOX, null, null, null, null);
        startManagingCursor(c);
```

```
        String[] columns = new String[] { "body" };
        int[] names = new int[] { R.id.row };
        adapter = new SimpleCursorAdapter(this, R.layout.sms_inbox, c, columns,
                names);

        setListAdapter(adapter);
    }
}
```

Listing 9–12 opens the SMS inbox and creates a list in which each item contains the body portion of an SMS message. The layout portion of Listing 9–12 contains a simple TextView that will hold the body of each message in a list item. To get the list of SMS messages, you create a URI pointing to the SMS inbox (content://sms/inbox) and then execute a simple query. You then filter on the body of the SMS message and set the list adapter of the ListActivity. After executing the code from Listing 9–12, you'll see a list of SMS messages in the inbox. Make sure you generate a few SMS messages using the Emulator Control before running the code on the emulator.

Because you can access the SMS inbox, you would expect to be able to access other SMS-related folders such as the sent folder or the draft folder. The only difference between accessing the inbox and accessing the other folders is the URI you specify. For example, you can access the sent folder by executing a query against content://sms/sent. Following is the complete list of SMS folders and the URI for each folder:

- *All*: content://sms/all
- *Inbox*: content://sms/inbox
- *Sent*: content://sms/sent
- *Draft*: content://sms/draft
- *Outbox*: content://sms/outbox
- *Failed*: content://sms/failed
- *Queued*: content://sms/queued
- *Undelivered*: content://sms/undelivered
- *Conversations*: content://sms/conversations

Android combines MMS and SMS and allows you to access content providers for both at the same time, using an AUTHORITY of mms-sms. Therefore, you can access a URI such as this:

content://mms-sms/conversations

Sending E-mail

Now that you've seen how to send SMS messages in Android, you might assume that you can access similar APIs to send e-mail. Unfortunately, Android does not provide APIs for you to send e-mail. The general consensus is that users don't want an application to start sending e-mail on their behalf. Instead, to send e-mail, you have to go through the registered e-mail application. For example, you could use ACTION_SEND to launch the e-mail application:

```
Intent emailIntent=new Intent(Intent.ACTION_SEND);

String subject = "Hi!";
String body = "hello from android....";

String[] extra = new String[]{"aaa@bbb.com"};
emailIntent.putExtra(Intent.EXTRA_EMAIL, extra);

emailIntent.putExtra(Intent.EXTRA_SUBJECT, subject);
emailIntent.putExtra(Intent.EXTRA_TEXT, body);
emailIntent.setType("message/rfc822");

startActivity(emailIntent);
```

This code launches the default e-mail application and allows the user to decide whether to send the e-mail or not. Other "extras" that you can add to an email intent include EXTRA_CC and EXTRA_BCC.

Now let's talk about the telephony manager.

Working with the Telephony Manager

The telephony APIs also include the telephony manager (android.telephony.TelephonyManager), which you can use to obtain information about the telephony services on the device, get subscriber information, and register for telephony state changes. A common telephony use case requires that an application execute business logic upon incoming phone calls. For example, a music player might pause itself for an incoming call, and resume when the call has been completed. So in this section, we are going to show you how to register for telephony state changes and how to detect incoming phone calls. Listing 9–13 shows the details.

Listing 9–13. *Using the Telephony Manager*

```
public class TelephonyServiceDemo extends Activity
{
    private static final String TAG="TelephonyServiceDemo";
    @Override
    protected void onCreate(Bundle savedInstanceState)
    {
        super.onCreate(savedInstanceState);

        TelephonyManager teleMgr =
(TelephonyManager)getSystemService(Context.TELEPHONY_SERVICE);
        teleMgr.listen(new MyPhoneStateListener(),
PhoneStateListener.LISTEN_CALL_STATE);
    }

    class MyPhoneStateListener extends PhoneStateListener
    {
```

```
        @Override
        public void onCallStateChanged(int state, String incomingNumber) {
            super.onCallStateChanged(state, incomingNumber);

            switch(state)
            {
                case TelephonyManager.CALL_STATE_IDLE:
                    Log.d(TAG, "call state idle...incoming number is["+
incomingNumber+"]");break;
                case TelephonyManager.CALL_STATE_RINGING:
                    Log.d(TAG, "call state ringing...incoming number is["+
incomingNumber+"]");break;
                case TelephonyManager.CALL_STATE_OFFHOOK:
                    Log.d(TAG, "call state Offhook...incoming number is["+
incomingNumber+"]");break;
                default:
                    Log.d(TAG, "call state ["+state+"]incoming number is["+
incomingNumber+"]");break;
            }
        }
    }
}
```

When working with the telephony manager, be sure to add the <uses-permission android:name="android.permission.READ_PHONE_STATE" /> permission to your manifest file so you can access phone-state information. As shown in Listing 9–13, you get notified about phone-state changes by implementing a PhoneStateListener and calling the listen() method of the TelephonyManager. When a phone call arrives, or the phone state changes, the system will call your PhoneStateListener's onCallStateChanged() method with the new state and the incoming phone number. In the case of an incoming call, you look for the CALL_STATE_RINGING state. You write a debug message to the log file in this example, but your application could implement custom business logic in its place. To emulate incoming phone calls, you can use Eclipse's Emulator Control UI, as you did with SMS messages (see Figure 9–8).

When dealing with phone-state changes, you might also need to get the subscriber's (user's) phone number. TelephonyManager.getLine1Number() will return that for you.

Summary

In this chapter, we talked about the Android media framework and the telephony APIs. With respect to media, we showed you how to play audio and video. We also showed you how to record audio and video, both directly and via intents.

In the second part of the chapter, we talked about telephony services in Android. Specifically, we showed you how to send text messages and how to monitor incoming text messages. We also showed you how to access the various SMS folders on the device. We concluded with a discussion of the TelephonyManager class.

In the next chapter, we are going to turn our attention to 3D graphics by discussing how to use OpenGL with your Android applications.

Chapter 10

Programming 3D Graphics with OpenGL

In this chapter, we will talk extensively about working with the OpenGL ES graphics API on the Android Platform.

OpenGL ES is a version of OpenGL that is optimized for embedded systems and other low-powered devices such as mobile phones. The Android Platform supports OpenGL ES 1.0. The Android SDK distribution comes with a number of OpenGL ES samples. However, the documentation on how to get started with OpenGL ES is minimal to nonexistent in the SDK. The underlying assumption is that OpenGL ES is an open standard and that programmers can learn it from sources outside of Android. A side effect of this assumption is that the few Android online resources or the Android code samples that address using OpenGL with Android assume you're already familiar with OpenGL.

In this chapter, we will help you with these minor roadblocks. With few OpenGL prerequisites, by the end of this chapter, you'll be comfortable to program in OpenGL. We will do this by introducing almost no mathematics (unlike many OpenGL books).

In the first section of the chapter, we'll provide an overview of OpenGL, OpenGL ES, and some competing standards.

In the second section, we will explain the theory behind OpenGL. This is a critical section to read if you are new to OpenGL. In this section, we will cover OpenGL coordinates, its idea of a camera, and the essential OpenGL ES drawing APIs.

In the third section, we will explain how you interact with the OpenGL ES API on Android. This section covers `GLSurfaceView` and the `Renderer` interface and how they work together to draw using OpenGL. We will show you some simple examples in this section where we draw a simple triangle and show how that drawing is impacted by changing the OpenGL scene setup APIs.

> **NOTE:** The OpenGL camera concept is similar but distinct from the Camera class in Android's graphics package, which you learned about in Chapter 6. Whereas Android's Camera object from the graphics package simulates 3D-like viewing capabilities by projecting a 2D view moving in 3D space, the OpenGL camera is a paradigm that represents a virtual viewing point. In other words, it models a real-world scene through the viewing perspective of an observer looking through a camera. You'll learn more in the subsection "Understanding the Camera and Coordinates" under "Using OpenGL ES." Both cameras are still separate from the handheld device's physical camera that you use to take pictures or shoot video.

In the fourth section, we will take you a bit deeper into OpenGL ES and introduce the idea of shapes. We will also cover textures in this section as well as show you how to draw multiple figures during a single draw method.

We will then conclude the chapter with a list of resources that we have used as we researched material for this chapter.

With that let us look into the history and background of OpenGL.

Understanding the History and Background of OpenGL

OpenGL (originally called Open Graphics Library) is a 2D and 3D graphics API that was developed by Silicon Graphics, Inc. (SGI) for its Unix workstations. Although SGI's version of OpenGL has been around for a long time, the first standardized spec of OpenGL emerged in 1992. Now widely adopted on all operating systems, the OpenGL standard forms the basis of much of the gaming, computer-aided design (CAD), and even virtual reality (VR) industries.

The OpenGL standard is currently being managed by an industry consortium called The Khronos Group (http://www.khronos.org), founded in 2000 by companies such as NVIDIA, Sun Microsystems, ATI Technologies, and SGI. You can learn more about the OpenGL spec at the consortium's web site:

http://www.khronos.org/opengl/

The official documentation page for OpenGL is available here:

http://www.opengl.org/documentation/

As you can see from this documentation page, you have access to books and online resources dedicated to OpenGL. Of these, the gold standard is *OpenGL Programming Guide: The Official Guide to Learning OpenGL, Version 1.1*, also known as the "red book" of OpenGL. You can find an online version of this book here:

http://www.glprogramming.com/red/

This book is quite good and quite readable. We did have some difficulty, however, unraveling the nature of *units and coordinates* that are used to draw. We'll try to clarify these important ideas regarding what you draw and what you see in OpenGL. These ideas center on setting up the OpenGL camera and setting up a *viewing box*, also known as a *viewing volume* or *frustum*.

While we are on the subject of OpenGL, we should talk a little bit about Direct3D, which is part of Microsoft's DirectX API. It's likely that Direct3D will be the standard on Windows-based mobile devices. Moreover, because OpenGL and Direct3D are similar, you could even read books about Direct3D to get an understanding of how 3D drawing works.

This Direct3D standard, which emerged from Microsoft in 1996, is programmed using COM (Component Object Model) interfaces. In the Windows world, you use COM interfaces to communicate between different components of an application. When a component is developed and exposed through a COM interface, any development language on the Windows platform can access it, both from inside and outside the application. In the Unix world, CORBA (Common Object Request Broker Architecture) plays the role that COM plays for Windows.

OpenGL, on the other hand, uses language bindings that look similar to their C-language counterparts. A language binding allows a common library to be used from many different languages such as C, C++, Visual Basic, Java, and so on.

Let us now turn our attention to OpenGL ES, the version of OpenGL geared for the mobile platform.

OpenGL ES

The Khronos Group is also responsible for two additional standards that are tied to OpenGL: OpenGL ES, and the EGL Native Platform Graphics Interface (known simply as EGL). As we mentioned, OpenGL ES is a smaller version of OpenGL intended for embedded systems.

> **NOTE:** Java Community Process is also developing an object-oriented abstraction for OpenGL for mobile devices called Mobile 3D Graphics API (M3G). We will briefly give you an introduction to M3G in the subsection "M3G: Another Java ME 3D Graphics Standard."

The EGL standard is essentially an enabling interface between the underlying operating system and the rendering APIs offered by OpenGL ES. Because OpenGL and OpenGL ES are general-purpose interfaces for drawing, each operating system needs to provide a standard hosting environment for OpenGL and OpenGL ES to interact with. Android SDK, starting with its 1.5 release, hides these platform specifics quite well. We will learn about this in the second section titled "Interfacing OpenGL ES with Android."

The target devices for OpenGL ES include cell phones, appliances, and even vehicles. Because OpenGL ES has to be much smaller than OpenGL, many convenient functions have been removed. For example, drawing rectangles is not directly supported in OpenGL ES; you have to draw two triangles to make a rectangle.

As you start exploring Android's support for OpenGL, you'll focus primarily on OpenGL ES and its bindings to the Android OS through Java and EGL. You can find the documentation (man pages) for OpenGL ES here:

http://www.khronos.org/opengles/documentation/opengles1_0/html/index.html

We kept returning to this reference as we developed this chapter, because it identifies and explains each OpenGL ES API and describe the arguments for each. You'll find these APIs similar to Java APIs, and we'll introduce you to the key ones in this chapter.

OpenGL ES and Java ME

OpenGL ES, like OpenGL, is a C-based, flat API. Because the Android SDK is a Java-based programming API, you need a Java binding to OpenGL ES. Java ME has already defined this binding through JSR 239: Java Binding for the OpenGL ES API. JSR 239 itself is based on JSR 231, which is a Java binding for OpenGL 1.5. JSR 239 could have been strictly a subset of JSR 231, but that's not the case because it must accommodate some extensions to OpenGL ES that are not in OpenGL 1.5.

You can find the documentation for JSR 239 here:

http://java.sun.com/javame/reference/apis/jsr239/

This reference will give you a sense of the APIs available in OpenGL ES. It also provides valuable information about the following packages:

- javax.microedition.khronos.egl
- javax.microedition.khronos.opengles
- java.nio

The nio package is necessary because the OpenGL ES implementations take only byte streams as inputs for efficiency reasons. This nio package defines a lot of utilities to prepare native buffers for use in OpenGL. You will see some of these APIs in action in the "glVertexPointer and Specifying Drawing Vertices" subsection under "Using OpenGL ES."

You can find documentation (although quite minimal) of the Android SDK's support for OpenGL at the following URL:

http://developer.android.com/guide/topics/graphics/opengl.html

On this page, the documentation indicates that the Android implementation mostly parallels JSR 239 but warns that it might diverge from it in a few places.

M3G: Another Java ME 3D Graphics Standard

JSR 239 is merely a Java binding on a native OpenGL ES standard. As we mentioned briefly in the "OpenGL ES" subsection, Java provides another API to work with 3D graphics on mobile devices: M3G. This object-oriented standard is defined in JSR 184 and JSR 297, the latter being more recent. As per JSR 184, M3G serves as a lightweight, object-oriented, interactive 3D graphics API for mobile devices.

The object-oriented nature of M3G separates it from OpenGL ES. For details, visit the home page for JSR 184:

http://www.jcp.org/en/jsr/detail?id=184

The APIs for M3G are available in the Java package

javax.microedition.m3g.*;

M3G is a higher-level API compared to OpenGL ES, so it should be easier to learn. However, the jury is still out on how well it will perform on handhelds. As of now, Android does not support M3G.

So far, we have laid out the options available in the OpenGL space for handheld devices. We have talked about OpenGL ES and also briefly about the M3G standard. We will now focus on understanding the fundamentals of OpenGL ES.

Fundamentals of OpenGL

This section will help you understand the concepts behind OpenGL and the OpenGL ES API. We'll explain all the key APIs. To supplement the information from this chapter, you might want to refer to the "Resources" section towards the end of this chapter. The indicated resources there include the Red book, JSR 239 documentation, and the Khronps Group API reference.

> **NOTE:** As you start using the OpenGL resources, you'll notice that some of the APIs are not available in OpenGL ES. This is where The Khronos Group's OpenGL ES Reference Manual comes in handy.

We will cover the following APIs in a fair amount of detail because they're central to understanding OpenGL and OpenGL ES:

- glVertexPointer
- glDrawElements
- glColor
- glClear
- gluLookAt

- glFrustum
- glViewport

As we cover these APIs, you'll learn how to

- Use the essential OpenGL ES drawing APIs
- Clear the palette
- Specify colors
- Understand the OpenGL camera and coordinates

Essential Drawing with OpenGL ES

In OpenGL, you draw in 3D space. You start out by specifying a series of points, also called vertices. Each of these points will have three values: one for the x coordinate, one for the y coordinate, and one for the z coordinate.

These points are then joined together to form a shape. You can join these points into a variety of shapes called *primitive shapes*, which include points, lines, and triangles in OpenGL ES. Note that in OpenGL, primitive shapes also include rectangles and polygons. As you work with OpenGL and OpenGL ES, you will continue to see differences whereby the latter has fewer features than the former. Here's another example: OpenGL allows you to specify each point separately, whereas OpenGL ES allows you to specify them only as a series of points in one fell swoop. However, you can often simulate OpenGL ES's missing features through other, more primitive features. For instance, you can draw a rectangle by combining two triangles.

OpenGL ES offers two primary methods to facilitate drawing:

- glVertexPointer
- glDrawElements

> **NOTE**: We'll use the terms "API" and "method" interchangeably when we talk about the OpenGL ES APIs.

You use glVertexPointer to specify a series of points or vertices, and you use glDrawElements to draw them using one of the primitive shapes that we pointed out earlier. We'll describe these methods in more detail, but first let's go over some nomenclature around the OpenGL API names.

The names of OpenGL APIs all begin with gl. Following gl is the method name. The method name is followed by an optional number such as 3, which points to either the number of dimensions—such as (x,y,z)—or the number of arguments. The method name is then followed by a data type such as f for float. (You can refer to any of the OpenGL online resources to learn the various data types and their corresponding letters.)

We'll tell you about one more convention. If a method takes an argument either as a byte (b) or a float (f), then the method will have two names: one ending with b, and one ending with f.

Let's now look at each of the two drawing-related methods, starting with glVertexPointer.

glVertexPointer and Specifying Drawing Vertices

The glVertexPointer method is responsible for specifying an array of points to be drawn. Each point is specified in three dimensions, so each point will have three values: x, y, and z. Listing 10–1 shows how to specify three points in an array:

Listing 10–1. *Vertex Coordinates Example for an OpenGL Triangle*

```
float[] coords = {
    -0.5f, -0.5f, 0,    //p1: (x1,y1,z1)
     0.5f, -0.5f, 0,    //p2: (x1,y1,z1)
     0.0f,  0.5f, 0     //p3: (x1,y1,z1)
};
```

This structure in Listing 10–1 is a contiguous set of floats kept in a Java-based float array. Don't worry about typing or compiling this code anywhere yet—our goal at this point is just to give you an idea of how these OpenGL ES methods work. We will give you the working examples and code when we develop a test harness later to draw simple figures.

In Listing 10–1, you might be wondering what units are used for the coordinates in points p1, p2, and p3. The short answer is, as you model your 3D space, these coordinate units can be anything you'd like. But subsequently, you will need to specify something called a *bounding volume* (or *bounding box*) that quantifies these coordinates.

For example, you can specify the bounding box as a cube with 5-inch sides or a cube with 2-inch sides. These coordinates are also known as *world coordinates* because you are conceptualizing your world independent of the physical device's limitations. We will further explain these coordinates in the subsection "Understanding the Camera and Coordinates." For now, assume that you are using a cube that is 2 units across all its sides and centered at (x=0,y=0,z=0).

> **NOTE**: The terms *bounding volume*, *bounding box*, *viewing volume*, *viewing box*, and *frustum* all refer to the same concept: the pyramid-shaped 3D volume that determines what is visible onscreen. You'll learn more in the "glFrustum and the Viewing Volume" subsection under "Understanding the Camera and Coordinates."

You can also assume that the origin is at the center of the visual display. The z axis will be negative going into the display (away from you) and positive coming out of the display (toward you). x will go positive as you move right and negative as you move left.

However, these coordinates will also depend on the direction from which you are viewing the scene.

To draw these points in Listing 10–1, you need to pass them to OpenGL ES through the glVertexPointer method. For efficiency reasons, however, glVertexPointer takes a native buffer that is language-agnostic rather than an array of floats. For this, you need to convert the Java-based array of floats to an acceptable C-like native buffer. You'll need to use the java.nio classes to convert the float array into the native buffer. Listing 10–2 shows an example of using nio buffers:

Listing 10–2. *Creating NIO Float Buffers*

```
jva.nio.ByteBuffer vbb = java.nio.ByteBuffer.allocateDirect(3 * 3 * 4);
vbb.order(ByteOrder.nativeOrder());
java.nio.FloatBuffer mFVertexBuffer = vbb.asFloatBuffer();
```

In Listing 10–2, the byte buffer is a buffer of memory ordered into bytes. Each point has three floats because of the three axes, and each float is 4 bytes. So together you get 3 * 4 bytes for each point. Plus, a triangle has three points. So you need 3 * 3 * 4 bytes to hold all three float points of a triangle.

Once you have the points gathered into a native buffer, you can call glVertexPointer as shown in Listing 10–3.

Listing 10–3. *glVertexPointer API Definition*

```
glVertexPointer(
        // Are we using (x,y) or (x,y,z) in each point
        3,
        // each value is a float value in the buffer
        GL10.GL_FLOAT,
        // Between two points there is no space
        0,
        // pointer to the start of the buffer
        mFVertexBuffer);
```

In this listing, let's talk about the arguments of glVertexPointer method. The first argument tells OpenGL ES how many dimensions there are in a point or a vertex. In this case, we specified 3 for x, y, and z. You could also specify 2 for just x and y. In that case, z would be zero. Note that this first argument is not the number of points in the buffer, but the number of dimensions used. So if you pass 20 points to draw a number of triangles, you will not pass 20 as the first argument; you would pass 2 or 3, depending on the number of dimensions used.

The second argument indicates that the coordinates need to be interpreted as floats. The third argument, called a stride, points to the number of bytes separating each point. In this case, it is zero because one point immediately follows the other. Sometimes you can add color attributes as part of the buffer after each point. If you want to do that, you'd use a stride to skip those as part of the vertex specification. The last argument is the pointer to the buffer containing the points.

Now you know how to set up the array of points to be drawn, let's see how to draw this array of points using the glDrawElements method.

glDrawElements

Once you specify the series of points through glVertexPointer, you use the
glDrawElements method to draw those points with one of the primitive shapes that
OpenGL ES allows. Note that OpenGL is a state machine. It remembers the values set
by one method when it invokes the next method in a cumulative manner. So you don't
need to explicitly pass the points set by glVertexPointer to glDrawElements.
glDrawElements will implicitly use those points. Listing 10–4 shows an example of this
method with possible arguments.

Listing 10–4. *Example of glDrawElements*

```
glDrawElements(
        // type of shape
        GL10.GL_TRIANGLE_STRIP,
        // Number of indices
        3,
        // How big each index is
        GL10.GL_UNSIGNED_SHORT,
        // buffer containing the 3 indices
        mIndexBuffer);
```

The first argument indicates the type of geometrical shape to draw: GL_TRIANGLE_STRIP
signifies a triangle strip. Other possible options for this argument are points only
(GL_POINTS), line strips (GL_LINE_STRIP), lines only (GL_LINES), line loops (GL_LINE_LOOP),
triangles only (GL_TRIANGLES), and triangle fans (GL_TRIANGLE_FAN).

The concept of a STRIP in GL_LINE_STRIP and GL_TRIANGLE_STRIP is to add new points
while making use of the old ones. This way, you can avoid specifying all the points for
each new object. For example, if you specify four points in an array, you can use strips
to draw the first triangle out of (1,2,3) and the second one out of (2,3,4). Each new point
will add a new triangle. (You can refer to the OpenGL red book for more details.) You
can also vary these parameters to see how the triangles are drawn as you add new
points.

The idea of a FAN in GL_TRIANGLE_FAN applies to triangles where the first point is used as
a starting point for all subsequent triangles. So you're essentially making a FAN- or circle-
like object with the first vertex in the middle. Suppose you have six points in your array:
(1,2,3,4,5,6). With a FAN, the triangles will be drawn at (1,2,3), (1,3,4), (1,4,5), and (1,5,6).
Every new point adds an extra triangle, similar to the process of extending a fan or
unfolding a pack of cards.

The rest of the arguments of glDrawElements involve the method's ability to let you reuse
point specification. For example, a square contains four points. Each square can be
drawn as a combination of two triangles. If you want to draw two triangles to make up
the square, do you have to specify six points? No. You can specify only four points and
refer to them six times to draw two triangles. This process is called *indexing into the
point buffer*.

Here is an example:

```
Points: (p1, p2, p3, p4)
Draw indices (p1, p2, p3,    p2,p3,p4)
```

Notice how the first triangle comprises p1,p2,p3 and the second one comprises p2,p3,p4. With this knowledge, the second argument of glDrawElements identifies how many indices there are in the index buffer.

The third argument to glDrawElements (see Listing 10–4) points to the type of values in the index array, whether they are unsigned shorts (GL_UNSIGNED_SHORT) or unsigned bytes (GL_UNSIGNED_BYTE).

The last argument of glDrawElements points to the index buffer. To fill up the index buffer, you need to do something similar to what you did with the vertex buffer. Start with a Java array and use the java.nio package to convert that array into a native buffer.

Listing 10–5 shows some sample code that converts a short array of {0,1,2} into a native buffer suitable to be passed to glDrawElements:

Listing 10–5. *Converting Java Array to NIO Buffers*

```
//Figure out how you want to arrange your points
short[] myIndecesArray = {0,1,2};

//get a short buffer
java.nio.ShortBuffer mIndexBuffer;

//Allocate 2 bytes each for each index value
ByteBuffer ibb = ByteBuffer.allocateDirect(3 * 2);
ibb.order(ByteOrder.nativeOrder());
mIndexBuffer = ibb.asShortBuffer();

//stuff that into the buffer
for (int i=0;i<3;i++)
{
    mIndexBuffer.put(myIndecesArray[i]);
}
```

Now that you've seen mIndexBuffer at work in the preceding snippet (Listing 10–5), you can revisit Listing 10–4 and better understand how the index buffer is created and manipulated.

> **NOTE:** Rather than create any new points, the index buffer merely indexes into the array of points indicated through the glVertexPointer. This is possible because OpenGL remembers the assets set by the previous calls in a stateful fashion.

Now we'll look at two commonly used OpenGL ES methods: glClear and glColor. We'll use each of these in our upcoming test harness example.

glClear

You use the glClear method to erase the drawing surface. Using this method, you can reset not only the color, but also the depth and the type of stencils used. You specify which element to reset by the constant that you pass in: GL_COLOR_BUFFER_BIT, GL_DEPTH_BUFFER_BIT, or GL_STENCIL_BUFFER_BIT.

The color buffer is responsible for the pixels that are visible, so clearing it is equivalent to erasing the surface of any colors. The depth buffer refers to all the pixels that are visible in a 3D scene, depending on how far or close the object is.

The stencil buffer is a bit advanced to cover here, except to say this: you use it to create visual effects based on some dynamic criteria, and you use glClear to erase it.

> **NOTE**: A stencil is a drawing template that you can use to replicate a drawing many times. For example, if you are using Microsoft Office Visio, all the drawing templates that you save as *.vss files are stencils. In the noncomputer drawing world, you create a stencil by cutting out a pattern in a sheet of paper or some other flat material. Then you can paint over that sheet and remove it, creating the impression that results in a replication of that drawing.

For our purposes, you can use this code to clear the color buffer:

```
//Clear the surface of any color
gl.glClear(gl.GL_COLOR_BUFFER_BIT);
```

Now let's talk about attaching a default color to what gets drawn.

glColor

You use glColor to set the default color for the subsequent drawing that takes place. In the following code segment, the method glColor4f sets the color to red:

```
//Set the current color
glColor4f(1.0f, 0, 0, 0.5f);
```

Recall the discussion about method nomenclature: 4f refers to the four arguments that the method takes, each of which is a float. The four arguments are components of red, green, blue, and alpha (color gradient). The starting values for each are (1,1,1,1). In this case, we have set the color to red with half a gradient (specified by the last alpha argument).

Although we have covered the basic drawing APIs, we still need to address a few things regarding the coordinates of the points that you specify in 3D space. The next subsection explains how OpenGL models a real-world scene through the viewing perspective of an observer looking through a camera.

Understanding OpenGL Camera and Coordinates

As you draw in 3D space, you ultimately must project the 3D view onto a 2D screen—much like capturing a 3D scene using a camera in the real world. This symbolism is formally recognized in OpenGL, so many concepts in OpenGL are explained in terms of a camera.

As you will see in this section, the part of your drawing that becomes visible depends on the location of the camera, the direction of the camera lens, the orientation of the camera (such as upside down), the zoom level, and the size of the capturing "film."

These aspects of projecting a 3D picture onto a 2D screen are controlled by three methods in OpenGL:

- gluLookAt: Controls the direction of the camera
- glFrustum: Controls the viewing volume or zoom
- glViewport: Controls the size of the screen or the size of the camera's "film"

You won't be able to program anything in OpenGL unless you understand the implications of these three APIs. Let us elaborate on the camera symbolism further to explain how these three APIs affect what you see on an OpenGL screen. We will start with gluLookAt.

gluLookAt and the Camera Symbolism

Imagine you go on a trip to take pictures of a landscape involving flowers, trees, streams, and mountains. You arrive at a meadow; the scene that lies before you is equivalent to what you would draw in OpenGL. You can make these drawings big, like the mountains, or small, like the flowers—as long as they are all proportional to one another. The coordinates you'll use for these drawings, as we hinted at earlier, are called *world coordinates*. Under these coordinates, you can establish a line to be 4 units long on the x axis by setting your points as (0,0,0) to (4,0,0).

As you are getting ready to take a picture, you find a spot to place your tripod. Then you hook up the camera to the tripod. The location of your camera—not the tripod, but the camera itself—becomes the origin of your camera in the world. So you will need to take a piece of paper and write down this location, which is called the *eye point*. If you don't specify an eye point, the camera is located at (0,0,0), which is the exact center of your screen. Usually you want to step away from the origin so that you can see the (x,y) plane that is sitting at the origin of z=0. For argument's sake, suppose you position the camera at (0,0,5). This would move the camera off your screen toward you by 5 units.

You can refer to Figure 10–1 to visualize how the camera is placed.

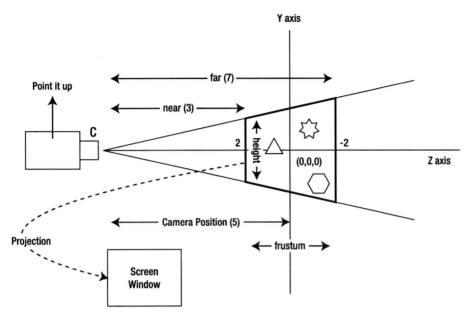

Figure 10–1. *OpenGL viewing concepts using the camera analogy*

Once you place the camera, you start looking ahead or forward to see which portion of the scene you want to capture. You will position the camera in the direction you are looking. This far-off point that you are looking at is called a *view point* or a *look-at point*. This point specification is really a specification of the direction. So if you specify your view point as (0,0,0), then the camera is looking along the z axis toward the origin from a distance of 5 units, assuming the camera is positioned at (0,0,5). You can see this in Figure 10–1, where the camera is looking down the z axis.

Imagine further that there is a rectangular building at the origin. You want to look at it not in a portrait fashion, but in a landscape fashion. What do you have to do? You obviously can leave the camera in the same location and still point it toward the origin, but now you need to turn the camera by 90 degrees. This is the *orientation* of the camera, as the camera is fixed at a given eye point and looking at a specific look-at point or direction. This orientation is called the *up vector*.

The up vector simply identifies the orientation of the camera such as up, down, left, right, or at an angle. This orientation of the camera is specified using a point as well. Imagine a line from the origin—not the camera origin, but the world-coordinate origin—to this point. Whatever angle this line subtends in three dimensions at the origin is the orientation of camera.

For example, an up vector for a camera might look like (0,1,0) or even (0,15,0), both of which would have the same effect. The point (0,1,0) is a point away from the origin along the y axis going up. This means you position the camera upright. If you use (0,-1,0), you would position the camera upside down. Still, in both cases, the camera is still at the same point (0,0,5) and looking at the same origin (0,0,0). You can summarize these three coordinates like this:

    ■ (0,0,5): Eye point (location of the camera)

    ■ (0,0,0): Look-at point (direction the camera is pointing)

    ■ (0,1,0): Up vector (whether the camera is up, down, or slanted)

You will use the gluLookAt method to specify these three points—the eye point, the look-at point, and the up vector:

```
gluLookAt(gl, 0,0,5,    0,0,0,    0,1,0);
```

The arguments are as follows: the first set of coordinates belongs to the eye point, the second set of coordinates belongs to the look-at point, and the third set of coordinates belongs to the up vector with respect to the origin.

Now we will turn our attention to the viewing volume.

glFrustum and the Viewing Volume

You might have noticed that none of the points describing the camera position using gluLookAt deal with size. They deal only with positioning, direction, and orientation. How can you tell the camera where to focus? How far away is the subject you are trying to capture? How wide and how tall is the subject area? You use the OpenGL method glFrustum to specify the area of the scene that you are interested in.

Think of the scene area as bounded by a box, also called the *frustum* or *viewing volume* (see the area marked by the bold border in the middle of Figure 10–1). Anything inside the box is captured, and anything outside the box is clipped and ignored. So how do you specify this viewing box? You first decide on the *near point*, or the distance between the camera and the beginning of the box. Then you can choose a *far point*, which is the distance between the camera and the end of the box. The distance between the near and far points along the z axis is the depth of the box. If you specify a near point of 50 and a far point of 200, then you will capture everything between those points and your box depth will be 150. You will also need to specify the left side of the box, the right side of the box, the top of the box, and the bottom of the box along the imaginary *ray* that joins the camera to the look-at point.

In OpenGL, you can imagine this box in one of two ways. One is called a *perspective projection*, which involves the frustum we've been talking about. This view, which simulates a natural camera-like function, involves a pyramidal structure in which the far plane serves as the base and the camera serves as the apex. The near plane cuts off the "top" of the pyramid, forming the frustum between the near plane and the far plane.

The other way to imagine the box involves thinking of it as a cube. This second scenario is called *orthographic projection*, which is suited for geometrical drawings that need to preserve sizes despite the distance from the camera.

Let's see, in Listing 10–6, how to specify the frustum for our example.

Listing 10–6. *Specifying a Frustum through glFrustum*

```
//calculate aspect ratio first
float ratio = (float) w / h;

//indicate that we want a perspective projection
glMatrixMode(GL10.GL_PROJECTION);

//Specify the frustum: the viewing volume
gl.glFrustumf(
    -ratio,    // Left side of the viewing box
    ratio,     // right side of the viewing box
    1,         // top of the viewing box
    -1,        // bottom of the viewing box
    3,         // how far is the front of the box from the camera
    7);        // how far is the back of the box from the camera
```

Because we set the top to 1 and bottom to -1 in the preceding code (Listing 10–6), we have set the front height of the box to 2 units. You specify the sizes for the left and right sides of the frustum by using proportional numbers, taking into account the window's aspect ratio. This is why this code uses the window height and width to figure out the proportion. The code also assumes the area of action to be between 3 and 7 units along the z axis. Anything drawn outside these coordinates, relative to the camera, won't be visible.

Because we set the camera at (0,0,5) and pointing toward (0,0,0), 3 units from the camera toward the origin will be (0,0,2) and 7 units from the camera will be (0,0,-2). This leaves the origin plane right in the middle of your 3D box.

So now you've identified how big your viewing volume is. You need to understand one more API to map these sizes to the screen: glViewport.

glViewport and Screen Size

glViewport is responsible for specifying the rectangular area on the screen onto which the viewing volume will be projected. This method takes four arguments to specify the rectangular box: the x and y coordinates of the lower-left corner, followed by the width and height. Listing 10–7 is an example of specifying a view as the target for this projection.

Listing 10–7. *Defining a ViewPort through glViewPort*

```
glViewport(0,              // lower left "x" of the rectangle on the screen
           0,              // lower left "y" of the rectangle on the screen
           width,          // width of the rectangle on the screen
           height);        // height of the rectangle on the screen
```

If your window or view size is 100 pixels in height and the frustum height is 10 units, then every logical unit of 1 in the world coordinates translates to 10 pixels in screen coordinates.

So far we have covered some important introductory concepts in OpenGL—material that can take many chapters to cover in books on the subject. Understanding these OpenGL fundamentals is useful for learning how to write Android OpenGL code. With these prerequisites behind us, we'll now discuss what is needed to call the OpenGL ES APIs that we have learned in this section.

Interfacing OpenGL ES with Android

OpenGL ES, as indicated, is a standard which is supported by a number of platforms. At the core it is a C-like API that addresses all of the OpenGL drawing chores. However, each platform and OS is different in the way it implements displays, screen buffers, and the like. These OS-specific aspects are left to each operating system to figure out and document. Android is no different.

Starting with its 1.5 SDK, Android simplified this interaction and initialization process necessary to start drawing in OpenGL. This support is provided in the package android.opengl. The primary class that provides much of this functionality is GLSurfaceView. GLSurfaceView has an internal interface called GLSurfaceView.Renderer. Knowing these two entities is sufficient to make a substantial headway with OpenGL on Android.

The other classes in the package include

- **GLU**: This utility class contains utilities that wrap the underlying OpenGL ES API in order to aggregate some common functionality. One of the primary GLU APIs that we have already covered is gluLookAt. Refer to the OpenGL SDK API documentation to discover other similar utilities.

- **GLUtils**: This utility class contains Android-specific utilities that are built to make interacting with the OpenGL ES easier. The key method that we use from this class is the texImage2D that takes a bitmap and makes it available to OpenGL ES for texturing.

- **Matrix**: This is the transformation matrix that is essential for transformations such as scaling, moving, etc.

- **Visibility:** Another utility class that we haven't used at all in this chapter. It deals with the visibility aspects of OpenGL such as what triangle meshes are visible on the screen.

- **GLDebugHelper**: A static utility class that allows you to wrap the "GL" and "EGL" interfaces so that you can control logging, errors, additional checks, etc.

These OpenGL packages sport the following interfaces:

- **GLSurfaceView.Renderer**: This interface allows for derived classes to draw. It allows GLSurfaceView to call draw when the surface has changed, etc. This is the primary interface that programmers normally work with. It is an example of how Android is trying to separate true OpenGL drawing (which is generic) from the OpenGL setup (which is Android specific).

- **GLSurfaceView.EGLConfigChooser**: This interface is there so that GLSurfaceView can choose the right EGLConfig object for initializing the OpenGL. An EGL Config tells the OpenGL the type of display characteristics. In SDKs prior to 1.5, you will have to orchestrate these classes yourself. For SDKs 1.5 and later the defaults are automatically configured and you don't have to specify these explicitly.

- **GLSurfaceView.GLWrapper**: This interface allows you to wrap the "gl" interface so that you can intercept the OpenGL calls across the entire system.

Using GLSurfaceView and Related Classes

Starting with 1.5 of the SDK the common usage pattern for using OpenGL is quite simplified. (Refer to the first edition of this book to see the Android 1.0–approach to address this.) Here are the steps you typically use to draw using these classes:

1. Implement the Renderer interface.

2. Provide the Camera settings needed for your drawing in the implementation of the renderer.

3. Provide the drawing code in the onDrawFrame method of the implementation.

4. Construct a GLSurfaceView.

5. Set the renderer you have implemented in the GLSurfaceView.

6. Indicate whether you want animation or not to the GLSurfaceView.

7. Set the GLSurfaceView in an Activity as the content view. You can also use this view wherever you can use a regular view.

Listing 10–8 shows a typical activity that uses some of these steps.

Listing 10–8. *A Simple OpenGLTestHarnessActivity*

```
public class OpenGLTestHarnessActivity extends Activity {
    private GLSurfaceView mTestHarness;
    @Override
    protected void onCreate(Bundle savedInstanceState) {
        super.onCreate(savedInstanceState);
        mTestHarness = new GLSurfaceView(this);
        mTestHarness.setEGLConfigChooser(false);
        mTestHarness.setRenderer(new SimpleTriangleRenderer(this));
        mTestHarness.setRenderMode(GLSurfaceView.RENDERMODE_WHEN_DIRTY);
        //mTestHarness.setRenderMode(GLSurfaceView.RENDERMODE_CONTINUOUSLY);
        setContentView(mTestHarness);
    }
    @Override
    protected void onResume()     {
        super.onResume();
        mTestHarness.onResume();
```

```
    }
    @Override
    protected void onPause() {
        super.onPause();
        mTestHarness.onPause();
    }
}
```

Let us explain the key elements of this source code. Here is the code that instantiates the GLSurfaceView:

```
    mTestHarness = new GLSurfaceView(this);
```

You then tell the view that you don't need a special EGL config chooser and the default will work by doing the following:

```
    mTestHarness.setEGLConfigChooser(false);
```

Then you set your renderer as follows:

```
    mTestHarness.setRenderer(new SimpleTriangleRenderer(this));
```

We haven't shown you the SimpleTriangleRenderer yet, but this is an instance of the Renderer interface that knows how to draw a simple triangle. (We will cover this very soon.)

Next you use one of these two methods to allow for animation or not:

```
mTestHarness.setRenderMode(GLSurfaceView.RENDERMODE_WHEN_DIRTY);
//mTestHarness.setRenderMode(GLSurfaceView.RENDERMODE_CONTINUOUSLY);
```

If you choose the first line, the drawing is going to be called only once or, more accurately, whenever it needs to be drawn. If you choose the second option, your drawing code will be called repeatedly so that you can animate your drawings.

That is all there is to interfacing with OpenGL on Android. Next, we'll explain the SimpleTriangleRender and show you a simple test harness to test it.

Simple Test Harness That Draws a Triangle

As we discussed earlier, drawing in OpenGL involves implementing the Renderer interface. The signature of this interface is shown in Listing 10–9.

Listing 10–9. *The Renderer Interface*

```
public static interface GLSurfaceView.Renderer
{
    void onDrawFrame(GL10 gl);
    void onSuraceChanged(GL10 gl, int width, int height);
    void onSurfaceCreated(GL10 gl, EGLConfig config);
}
```

The main drawing happens in the onDrawFrame() method. Whenever a new surface is created for this view, the onSurfaceCreated() method is called and we can call a number of OpenGL APIs such as dithering, depth control, or any others that can be called outside of the immediate onDrawFrame() method.

Similarly, when a surface changes, such as the width and height of the window, the onSurfaceChanged() method is called. You can set up your camera and viewing volume here.

Even in the onDrawFrame() method there are lot of things that may be common for your specific drawing context. You can take advantage of this commonality and abstract these methods in another level of abstraction called an AbstractRenderer which will have only one method that is left unimplemented called draw().

Listing 10–10 shows the code for the AbstractRenderer:

Listing 10–10. *The AbstractRenderer*

```
//filename: AbstractRenderer.java
public abstract class AbstractRenderer
implements GLSurfaceView.Renderer
{
    public void onSurfaceCreated(GL10 gl, EGLConfig eglConfig) {
        gl.glDisable(GL10.GL_DITHER);
        gl.glHint(GL10.GL_PERSPECTIVE_CORRECTION_HINT,
                GL10.GL_FASTEST);
        gl.glClearColor(.5f, .5f, .5f, 1);
        gl.glShadeModel(GL10.GL_SMOOTH);
        gl.glEnable(GL10.GL_DEPTH_TEST);
    }

    public void onSurfaceChanged(GL10 gl, int w, int h) {
        gl.glViewport(0, 0, w, h);
        float ratio = (float) w / h;
        gl.glMatrixMode(GL10.GL_PROJECTION);
        gl.glLoadIdentity();
        gl.glFrustumf(-ratio, ratio, -1, 1, 3, 7);
    }

    public void onDrawFrame(GL10 gl)
    {
        gl.glDisable(GL10.GL_DITHER);
        gl.glClear(GL10.GL_COLOR_BUFFER_BIT | GL10.GL_DEPTH_BUFFER_BIT);
        gl.glMatrixMode(GL10.GL_MODELVIEW);
        gl.glLoadIdentity();
        GLU.gluLookAt(gl, 0, 0, -5, 0f, 0f, 0f, 0f, 1.0f, 0.0f);
        gl.glEnableClientState(GL10.GL_VERTEX_ARRAY);
        draw(gl);
    }
    protected abstract void draw(GL10 gl);
}
```

Having this abstract class is very useful, as it allows us to focus on just the drawing methods. We'll use this class to create our SimpleTriangleRenderer class; Listing 10–11 shows the source code for this SimpleTriangleRenderer.

Listing 10–11. *SimpleTriangleRenderer*

```
//filename: SimpleTriangleRenderer.java
public class SimpleTriangleRenderer extends AbstractRenderer
{
    //Number of points or vertices we want to use
```

```
    private final static int VERTS = 3;

    //A raw native buffer to hold the point coordinates
    private FloatBuffer mFVertexBuffer;

    //A raw native buffer to hold indices
    //allowing a reuse of points.
    private ShortBuffer mIndexBuffer;

    public SimpleTriangleRenderer(Context context)
    {
        ByteBuffer vbb = ByteBuffer.allocateDirect(VERTS * 3 * 4);
        vbb.order(ByteOrder.nativeOrder());
        mFVertexBuffer = vbb.asFloatBuffer();

        ByteBuffer ibb = ByteBuffer.allocateDirect(VERTS * 2);
        ibb.order(ByteOrder.nativeOrder());
        mIndexBuffer = ibb.asShortBuffer();

        float[] coords = {
                -0.5f, -0.5f, 0, // (x1,y1,z1)
                 0.5f, -0.5f, 0,
                 0.0f,  0.5f, 0
        };
        for (int i = 0; i < VERTS; i++) {
            for(int j = 0; j < 3; j++) {
                mFVertexBuffer.put(coords[i*3+j]);
            }
        }
        short[] myIndecesArray = {0,1,2};
        for (int i=0;i<3;i++)
        {
            mIndexBuffer.put(myIndecesArray[i]);
        }
        mFVertexBuffer.position(0);
        mIndexBuffer.position(0);
    }

    //overriden method
    protected void draw(GL10 gl)
    {
        gl.glColor4f(1.0f, 0, 0, 0.5f);
        gl.glVertexPointer(3, GL10.GL_FLOAT, 0, mFVertexBuffer);
        gl.glDrawElements(GL10.GL_TRIANGLES, VERTS,
                GL10.GL_UNSIGNED_SHORT, mIndexBuffer);
    }
}
```

Although there seems to be a lot of code here, most of it is used to define the vertices and then translate them to NIO buffers from Java buffers. Otherwise, the draw method is just three lines: set the color, set the vertices, and draw.

> **NOTE**: Although we are allocating memory for NIO buffers, we never release them in our code. So who releases these buffers? How does this memory affect OpenGL?
>
> According to our research, the java.nio package allocates memory space outside of the Java heap that can be directly used by such systems as OpenGL, File I/O, etc. The nio buffers are actually Java objects that eventually point to the native buffer. These nio objects are garbage collected. When they are garbage collected they go ahead and delete the native memory. Java programs don't have to do anything special to free the memory.
>
> However the gc won't get fired unless there is memory needed in the Java heap. This means you can run out of native memory and gc may not realize it. There are examples on the internet on this subject where an out of memory exception will trigger a gc and that you would go try again to see if memory is available now due to gc having been invoked.
>
> Under ordinary circumstances—and this is important for OpenGL—you can allocate the native buffers and not worry about releasing allocated memory explicitly as that is done by the gc.

Now we have all the pieces necessary to test this drawing. We have the activity in Listing 10–8; we have the abstract renderer in Listing 10–10, and the SimpleTriangleRenderer (Listing 10–11) itself. All you have to do is invoke the Activity class through any of your menu items using the following:

```
private void invokeSimpleTriangle()
{
    Intent intent = new Intent(this,OpenGLTestHarnessActivity.class);
    startActivity(intent);
}
```

Of course, you will have to register the activity in the Android manifest file:

```
<activity android:name=".OpenGLTestHarnessActivity"
            android:label="OpenGL 15 Test Harness"/>
```

When you run this code, you will see the triangle like the one in Figure 10–2.

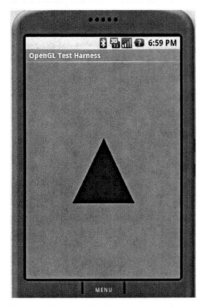

Figure 10–2. *A simple OpenGL triangle*

Changing Camera Settings

To understand the OpenGL coordinates better, let us experiment with the camera-related methods and see how they affect the triangle that we drew in Figure 10–2. Remember that these are the points of our triangle: (-0.5,-0.5,0 0.5,-0.5,0 0,0.5,0). With these points, the following three camera-related methods as used in AbstractRenderer (Listing 10–10) yielded the triangle as it appears in Figure 10–2:

```
//Look at the screen (origin) from 5 units away from the front of the screen
GLU.gluLookAt(gl, 0,0,5,    0,0,0,    0,1,0);
```

```
//Set the height to 2 units and depth to 4 units
gl.glFrustumf(-ratio, ratio, -1, 1, 3, 7);
```

```
//normal window stuff
gl.glViewport(0, 0, w, h);
```

Now suppose you change the camera's up vector toward the negative y direction, like this:

```
GLU.gluLookAt(gl, 0,0,5,    0,0,0,    0,-1,0);
```

If you do that, you'll see an upside-down triangle as in Figure 10–3. If you want to make this change, you can find the method to change in the AbstractRenderer.java file (Listing 10–10).

Figure 10–3. *A triangle with the camera upside down*

Now let's see what happens if we change the frustum, (also called the viewing volume or box). The following code increases the viewing box's height and width by a factor of 4 (see Figure 10–1 to understand these dimensions). If you recall, the first four arguments of glFrustum points to the front rectangle of the viewing box. By multiplying each value by 4 we have scaled the viewing box four times.

```
gl.glFrustumf(-ratio * 4, ratio * 4, -1 * 4, 1 *4, 3, 7);
```

With this code, the triangle you see shrinks because the triangle stays at the same units while our viewing box has grown. This method call appears in the AbstractRenderer.java class (see Listing 10–10). What you see after this change is shown in Figure 10–4.

Figure 10–4. *A triangle with a viewing box that's four times bigger*

Using Indices to Add Another Triangle

We'll conclude these simple triangle examples by inheriting from the AbstractRenderer class and creating another triangle simply by adding an additional point and using indices. Conceptually, you'll define the four points as (-1,-1,   1,-1,   0,1, 1,1). And you will ask OpenGL to draw these as (0,1,2   0,2,3). Listing 10–12 shows the code to do this. (Notice that we changed the dimensions of the triangle.)

Listing 10–12. *The SimpleTriangleRenderer2 Class*

```
//filename: SimpleTriangleRenderer2.java
public class SimpleTriangleRenderer2 extends AbstractRenderer
{
    private final static int VERTS = 4;
    private FloatBuffer mFVertexBuffer;
    private ShortBuffer mIndexBuffer;

    public SimpleTriangleRenderer2(Context context)
    {
        ByteBuffer vbb = ByteBuffer.allocateDirect(VERTS * 3 * 4);
        vbb.order(ByteOrder.nativeOrder());
        mFVertexBuffer = vbb.asFloatBuffer();

        ByteBuffer ibb = ByteBuffer.allocateDirect(6 * 2);
        ibb.order(ByteOrder.nativeOrder());
        mIndexBuffer = ibb.asShortBuffer();

        float[] coords = {
                -1.0f, -1.0f, 0, // (x1,y1,z1)
                 1.0f, -1.0f, 0,
                 0.0f,  1.0f, 0,
                 1.0f,  1.0f, 0
        };
        for (int i = 0; i < VERTS; i++) {
            for(int j = 0; j < 3; j++) {
                mFVertexBuffer.put(coords[i*3+j]);
            }
        }
        short[] myIndecesArray = {0,1,2,     0,2,3};
        for (int i=0;i<6;i++)
        {
            mIndexBuffer.put(myIndecesArray[i]);
        }
        mFVertexBuffer.position(0);
        mIndexBuffer.position(0);
    }

    protected void draw(GL10 gl)
    {
        gl.glColor4f(1.0f, 0, 0, 0.5f);
        gl.glVertexPointer(3, GL10.GL_FLOAT, 0, mFVertexBuffer);
        gl.glDrawElements(GL10.GL_TRIANGLES, 6, GL10.GL_UNSIGNED_SHORT,
                                                 mIndexBuffer);
    }
}
```

Once this SimpleTriangleRenderer2 class is in place, you can change the code in the
OpenGLTestHarnessActivity (see Listing 10–8) to invoke this renderer instead of the
SimpleTriangleRenderer:

```
mTestHarness = new OpenGLTestHarness(this);
mTestHarness.setRenderer(new SimpleTriangleRenderer2(this));
```

The changed portion is highlighted. After you change this code, you can run the
OpenGLTestHarnessActivity again to see the two triangles drawn out (see Figure 10–5).

Figure 10–5. *Two triangles with four points*

Animating the Simple OpenGL Triangle

You can easily accommodate OpenGL animation by changing the rendering mode on
the GLSurfaceView object. Listing 10–13 shows the sample code.

Listing 10–13. *Specifying Continuous-Rendering Mode*

```
//get a GLSurfaceView
GLSurfaceView openGLView;

//Set the mode to continuous draw mode
openGLView.setRenderingMode(GLSurfaceView.RENDERMODE_CONTINUOUSLY);
```

Note that we're showing you how to change the rendering mode here because we had
specified RENDERMODE_WHEN_DIRTY in the previous section. As we mentioned,
RENDERMODE_CONTINUOUSLY is, in fact, the default setting, so animation is enabled by
default. Once the rendering mode is continuous, it is up to the renderer's onDraw method
to do what's necessary to affect animation. To demonstrate this, we will show you an
example where the triangle drawn in the previous example (see Listing 10–11 and Figure
10–2) is rotated in a circular fashion. This example has the following two files:

■ AnimatedTriangleActivity.java, which is a simple activity to host the GLSurfaceView

■ AnimatedSimpleTriangleRenderer.java, which is responsible for animated drawing

Let us consider each of these files.

AnimatedTriangleActivity.java

The AnimatedTriangleActivity (as shown in Listing 10–14) resembles the simple unanimated triangle activity in Listing 10–8 that tests a simple triangle drawing. The goal of this activity is to provide a surface to draw on and then show it on the Android screen. Listing 10–14 shows the source code.

Listing 10–14. *AnimatedTriangleActivity Source Code*

```
//filename: AnimatedTriangleActivity.java
public class AnimatedTriangleActivity extends Activity {
    private GLSurfaceView mTestHarness;
    @Override
    protected void onCreate(Bundle savedInstanceState) {
        super.onCreate(savedInstanceState);

        mTestHarness = new GLSurfaceView(this);
        mTestHarness.setEGLConfigChooser(false);
        mTestHarness.setRenderer(new AnimatedSimpleTriangleRenderer(this));
        //mTestHarness.setRenderMode(GLSurfaceView.RENDERMODE_WHEN_DIRTY);
        setContentView(mTestHarness);
    }
    @Override
    protected void onResume()      {
        super.onResume();
        mTestHarness.onResume();
    }
    @Override
    protected void onPause() {
        super.onPause();
        mTestHarness.onPause();
    }
}
```

The key line of code in this activity is highlighted in bold font. We took the previous activity that we used for a simple drawing (see Listing 10–8) and commented out the rendering mode. This lets the GLSurfaceView default to continuous-rendering mode, which accommodates repeated calls to the onDraw method of the renderer, in this case AnimatedSimpleTriangleRenderer.

Now let's look into the AnimatedSimpleTriangleRenderer class, which appears in Listing 10–15. It's responsible for drawing the rectangle at frequent intervals to simulate animation.

AnimatedSimpleTriangleRenderer

The AnimatedSimpleTriangleRenderer class is very similar to the
SimpleTriangleRenderer (see Listing 10–11), except for what happens in the onDraw
method. In this method, we set a new rotation angle every four seconds. As the image
gets drawn repeatedly, you will see the triangle spinning slowly. Listing 10–15 contains
the complete implementation of the AnimatedSimpleTriangleRenderer class.

Listing 10–15. *AnimatedSimpleTriangleRenderer Source Code*

```java
//filename: AnimatedSimpleTriangleRenderer.java
public class AnimatedSimpleTriangleRenderer extends AbstractRenderer
{
   private int scale = 1;
   //Number of points or vertices we want to use
    private final static int VERTS = 3;

   //A raw native buffer to hold the point coordinates
   private FloatBuffer mFVertexBuffer;

   //A raw native buffer to hold indices
   //allowing a reuse of points.
   private ShortBuffer mIndexBuffer;

   public AnimatedSimpleTriangleRenderer(Context context)
   {
        ByteBuffer vbb = ByteBuffer.allocateDirect(VERTS * 3 * 4);
        vbb.order(ByteOrder.nativeOrder());
        mFVertexBuffer = vbb.asFloatBuffer();

        ByteBuffer ibb = ByteBuffer.allocateDirect(VERTS * 2);
        ibb.order(ByteOrder.nativeOrder());
        mIndexBuffer = ibb.asShortBuffer();

        float[] coords = {
                -0.5f, -0.5f, 0, // (x1,y1,z1)
                 0.5f, -0.5f, 0,
                 0.0f,  0.5f, 0
        };
        for (int i = 0; i < VERTS; i++) {
            for(int j = 0; j < 3; j++) {
                mFVertexBuffer.put(coords[i*3+j]);
            }
        }
        short[] myIndecesArray = {0,1,2};
        for (int i=0;i<3;i++)
        {
            mIndexBuffer.put(myIndecesArray[i]);
        }
        mFVertexBuffer.position(0);
        mIndexBuffer.position(0);
   }

   //overridden method
    protected void draw(GL10 gl)
    {
```

```
       long time = SystemClock.uptimeMillis() % 4000L;
       float angle = 0.090f * ((int) time);

       gl.glRotatef(angle, 0, 0, 1.0f);

       gl.glColor4f(1.0f, 0, 0, 0.5f);
       gl.glVertexPointer(3, GL10.GL_FLOAT, 0, mFVertexBuffer);
        gl.glDrawElements(GL10.GL_TRIANGLES, VERTS,
                GL10.GL_UNSIGNED_SHORT, mIndexBuffer);
    }
}
```

Now that you have both the AnimatedTriangleActivity.java and
AnimatedSimpleTriangleRenderer.java files, you can invoke this animated activity from
any menu item by calling the method identified in Listing 10–16.

Listing 10–16. *Invoking the Animated Activity*

```
private void invoke15SimpleTriangle()
{
    Intent intent = new Intent(this,AnimatedTriangleActivity.class);
    startActivity(intent);
}
```

Don't forget to register the activity in the AndroidManifest.xml file (see Listing 10–17).

Listing 10–17. *Registering the New Activity in the AndroidManifest.xml File*

```
<activity android:name=".AnimatedTriangleActivity"
                android:label="OpenGL Animated Test Harness"/>
```

Braving OpenGL: Shapes and Textures

We have covered a lot of ground in OpenGL already. We showed you how to draw a
simple triangle, and in the process, we explained the drawing primitives. We explained
the coordinate system through a camera analogy, and we discussed the importance of
three crtical APIs: gluLookAt (setting the camera), gluFrustum (setting the viewing
volume), and glViewPort (mapping the viewing volume to the screen).

Using these basics we have introduced you to the OpenGL starter framework on
Android. We have shown you how you can define base abstract classes to encapsulate
often repeated settings. Using these abstract classes, you have seen how to draw a
simple triangle and animate it using translation matrices.

In the rest of this chapter, we will bring you to the next level of OpenGL. In the examples
we have shown so far we have specified the vertices of a triangle explicitly. This
approach becomes inconvenient as soon as you start drawing squares, pentagons,
hexagons, and the like. We will show you that you will need higher-level object
abstractions such as shapes and even scene graphs, where the shapes decide what
their coordinates are. Using this approach, we will show you how to draw any polygon
with any number of sides, anywhere in your geometry.

We will then move on to OpenGL textures. Textures allow you to attach bitmaps and other
pictures to surfaces in your drawing. We will take the polygons that we know how to draw

now and attach some pictures to them. We will follow this up with another critical need in OpenGL: drawing multiple figures or shapes using the OpenGL drawing pipeline.

These fundamentals should take you a bit closer to starting to create workable 3D figures and scenes.

A Simple Menu Trick for Your Demos

So far we have created a separate activity for every example we have shown. This implies that we have to create an activity for each demo and that once something is an activity, you have to register it in the manifest XML file. We are going to show you a trick whereby you can design just one activity which, depending on the menu item clicked, can either change the view that it binds to, or in the case of a GLSurfaceView, use a different renderer for each menu item.

To understand this, we'll start with a set of menu items that describe the many demos we may have, shown in Listing 10–18. We have highlighted key parts of the listing in bold to show you what we are going draw as a result of each menu item from the set of menu items.

Listing 10–18. *Menu Structure for OpenGL Demos*

```xml
<menu xmlns:android="http://schemas.android.com/apk/res/android">
    <!-- This group uses the default category. -->
    <group android:id="@+id/menuGroup_Main">

        <item android:id="@+id/mid_OpenGL_SimpleTriangle"
            android:title="Simple Triangle" />

        <item android:id="@+id/mid_OpenGL_AnimatedTriangle15"
            android:title="Animated Triangle" />

        <item android:id="@+id/mid_rectangle"
            android:title="rectangle" />

        <item android:id="@+id/mid_square_polygon"
            android:title="square polygon" />

        <item android:id="@+id/mid_polygon"
            android:title="polygon" />

        <item android:id="@+id/mid_textured_square"
            android:title="textured square" />

        <item android:id="@+id/mid_textured_polygon"
            android:title="textured polygon" />

        <item android:id="@+id/mid_OpenGL_Current"
            android:title="Current" />

        <item android:id="@+id/menu_clear"
            android:title="clear" />
    </group>
</menu>
```

There is no mystery here. These menus indicate that we want to draw many types of figures. The prefix mid stands for menu item ID. This is just a convention that you can use to quickly identify menu IDs in the Eclipse ADT. Each menu item draws a separate OpenGL scene. The simple triangle menu item draws a simple triangle based on explicitly specified vertices. The animated triangle takes that simple triangle and spins it in time. The rectangle menu item draws a rectangle using two triangles whose vertices are explicitly specified. The polygon example shows how to define a polygon abstractly using its radius and number of sides and then have it generate the vertices. The textured square takes a square polygon and sticks a bitmap on it. The textured polygon actually draws two textured polygons using OpenGL drawing pipeline where a given figure is transformed twice to different positions to see two instances of the same figure.

Let us see how we will orchestrate these menu items into a single activity. Remember Listing 10–8 where we have seen one of these dedicated activities. Now contrast that activity with the following activity in Listing 10–19.

Here is the complete code listing for MultiViewTestHarnessActivity.

Listing 10–19. *MultiViewTestHarnessActivity*

```
public class MultiViewTestHarnessActivity extends Activity {
   private GLSurfaceView mTestHarness;
   @Override
   protected void onCreate(Bundle savedInstanceState) {
       super.onCreate(savedInstanceState);

       mTestHarness = new GLSurfaceView(this);
       mTestHarness.setEGLConfigChooser(false);

       Intent intent = getIntent();
       int mid = intent.getIntExtra("com.ai.menuid", R.id.MenuId_OpenGL15_Current);
       if (mid == R.id.MenuId_OpenGL15_Current)
       {
           mTestHarness.setRenderer(new TexturedPolygonRenderer(this));
           mTestHarness.setRenderMode(GLSurfaceView.RENDERMODE_CONTINUOUSLY);
           setContentView(mTestHarness);
           return;
       }

       if (mid == R.id.mid_OpenGL15_SimpleTriangle)
       {
           mTestHarness.setRenderer(new SimpleTriangleRenderer(this));
           mTestHarness.setRenderMode(GLSurfaceView.RENDERMODE_WHEN_DIRTY);
           setContentView(mTestHarness);
           return;
       }
       if (mid == R.id.mid_OpenGL15_AnimatedTriangle15)
       {
           mTestHarness.setRenderer(new AnimatedSimpleTriangleRenderer(this));
           setContentView(mTestHarness);
           return;
       }
       if (mid == R.id.mid_rectangle)
       {
           mTestHarness.setRenderer(new SimpleRectRenderer(this));
```

```
        mTestHarness.setRenderMode(GLSurfaceView.RENDERMODE_WHEN_DIRTY);
        setContentView(mTestHarness);
        return;
    }
    if (mid == R.id.mid_square_polygon)
    {
        mTestHarness.setRenderer(new SquareRenderer(this));
        mTestHarness.setRenderMode(GLSurfaceView.RENDERMODE_WHEN_DIRTY);
        setContentView(mTestHarness);
        return;
    }
    if (mid == R.id.mid_polygon)
    {
        mTestHarness.setRenderer(new PolygonRenderer(this));
        setContentView(mTestHarness);
        return;
    }
    if (mid == R.id.mid_textured_square)
    {
        mTestHarness.setRenderer(new TexturedSquareRenderer(this));
        mTestHarness.setRenderMode(GLSurfaceView.RENDERMODE_WHEN_DIRTY);
        setContentView(mTestHarness);
        return;
    }
    //otherwise do this
    mTestHarness.setRenderer(new TexturedPolygonRenderer(this));
    mTestHarness.setRenderMode(GLSurfaceView.RENDERMODE_CONTINUOUSLY);
    setContentView(mTestHarness);
    return;
}
@Override
protected void onResume()    {
    super.onResume();
    mTestHarness.onResume();
}
@Override
protected void onPause() {
    super.onPause();
    mTestHarness.onPause();
}
}
```

The first thing to notice in Listing 10–19 is the name of the activity. We have identified this as a `MultiViewTestHarnessActivity`, indicating that this activity, when invoked, can host multiple views depending on the menu invoking it. How does this activity know how it is invoked? This is shown in the following code segment (Listing 10–20).

Listing 10–20. *Reading Menu ID from an Intent*

```
Intent intent = getIntent();
int mid = intent.getIntExtra("com.ai.menuid", R.id.mid_OpenGL_Current);
if (mid == R.id.MenuId_OpenGL15_Current)
{
    ....
}
```

The first call tells the activity how it is invoked. The invoker is responsible for passing the menu ID through an intent extra data. The second line is retrieving this extra, and if it is not passed, the menu ID is assumed to be mid_OpenGL_Current, indicating that you should just execute the default view for which you haven't designated a particular menu item, since you are still experimenting with that menu item.

Listing 10–21 shows how this MultiViewTestHarnessActivity is invoked by another main activity that might be your true driver. That main activity will then own the menu and pass the menu invocations to the MultiViewTestHarnessActivity.

Listing 10–21. *Transferring Menu ID through an Intent*

```
@Override
public boolean onOptionsItemSelected(MenuItem item)
{
    if (item.getItemId() == R.id.mid_OpenGL10_SimpleTriangle)
    {
        //..Direct this menu item locally to the main activity
        //..which you may be using for other purposes
            return true;
    }
    //These menu items, direct them to the multiview
    this.invokeMultiView(item.getItemId());
        return true;
}

//here is invoking the multiview through a loaded intent
//carrying the menu id
//mid: menu id
    private void invokeMultiView(int mid)
    {
        Intent intent = new Intent(this,MultiViewTestHarnessActivity.class);
        intent.putExtra("com.ai.menuid", mid);
        startActivity(intent);
    }
```

We will not provide the code for the main activity here, as it will only make this chapter longer, without enhancing your understanding of Android or OpenGL. The code above should give you an idea of how to plug the activity here into any test activity you may already have.

The main activity used in this chapter look like that shown in Figure 10–6.

You can see that this is a simple activity with a bunch of menus in it. When you invoke the menus, each menu is directed to the MultiViewTestHarnessActivity (shown in Listing 10–19).

Using this approach, we can see how to re-implement the simple triangle through this multiview activity:

```
if (mid == R.id.mid_OpenGL15_SimpleTriangle)
{
    mTestHarness.setRenderer(new SimpleTriangleRenderer(this));
    mTestHarness.setRenderMode(GLSurfaceView.RENDERMODE_WHEN_DIRTY);
```

```
        setContentView(mTestHarness);
        return;
    }
```

Notice that we have used the same rendering object in the same manner as in the
SimpleTriangleActivity in Listing 10–8, but now it is sitting along with the other demos
(where we draw more than one figure and not just one triangle) in Listing 10–19. This
pattern also demonstrates the use of intent extras.

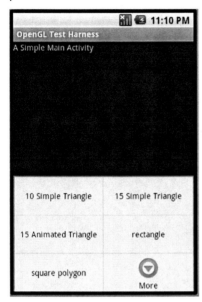

Figure 10–6. *OpenGL Test Harness Driver*

Drawing a Rectangle

Before going on to the idea of shapes, let's strengthen our understanding of drawing
with explicit vertices by drawing a rectangle using two triangles. This will also lay out the
groundwork for extending a triangle to any polygon.

You already have enough background to understand the basic triangle, so now we'll
show you the code for drawing a rectangle (Listing 10–22), followed by some brief
commentary.

Listing 10–22. *Simple Rectangle Renderer*

```
public class SimpleRectangleRenderer extends AbstractRenderer
{
    //Number of points or vertices we want to use
    private final static int VERTS = 4;

    //A raw native buffer to hold the point coordinates
    private FloatBuffer mFVertexBuffer;

    //A raw native buffer to hold indices
    //allowing a reuse of points.
```

```
    private ShortBuffer mIndexBuffer;

    public SimpleRectRenderer(Context context)
    {
        ByteBuffer vbb = ByteBuffer.allocateDirect(VERTS * 3 * 4);
        vbb.order(ByteOrder.nativeOrder());
        mFVertexBuffer = vbb.asFloatBuffer();

        ByteBuffer ibb = ByteBuffer.allocateDirect(6 * 2);
        ibb.order(ByteOrder.nativeOrder());
        mIndexBuffer = ibb.asShortBuffer();

        float[] coords = {
                -0.5f, -0.5f, 0, // (x1,y1,z1)
                 0.5f, -0.5f, 0,
                 0.5f,  0.5f, 0,
                -0.5f,  0.5f, 0,
        };

        for (int i = 0; i < VERTS; i++) {
            for(int j = 0; j < 3; j++) {
                mFVertexBuffer.put(coords[i*3+j]);
            }
        }
        short[] myIndecesArray = {0,1,2,0,2,3};
        for (int i=0;i<6;i++)
        {
            mIndexBuffer.put(myIndecesArray[i]);
        }
        mFVertexBuffer.position(0);
        mIndexBuffer.position(0);
    }

    //overriden method
    protected void draw(GL10 gl)
    {
        RegularPolygon.test();
        gl.glColor4f(1.0f, 0, 0, 0.5f);
        gl.glVertexPointer(3, GL10.GL_FLOAT, 0, mFVertexBuffer);
        gl.glDrawElements(GL10.GL_TRIANGLES, 6,
                GL10.GL_UNSIGNED_SHORT, mIndexBuffer);
    }
}
```

Notice that the approach for drawing a rectangle is quite similar to that for a triangle. We have specified four vertices instead of three. Then we have used indices as here:

```
    short[] myIndecesArray = {0,1,2,0,2,3};
```

We have reused the numbered vertices (0 through 3) twice so that each three vertices make up a triangle. So (0,1,2) makes up the first triangle and (0,2,3) makes up the second triangle. Drawing these two triangles using the GL_TRIANGLES primitives will draw the necessary rectangle.

You can see the image of the drawn rectangle in Figure 10–7.

Figure 10–7. *OpenGL rectangle drawn with two triangles*

Working with Shapes

This method of explicitly specifying vertices to draw can be tedious. For example, if you want to draw a polygon of 20 sides, then you need to specify 20 vertices, with each vertex requiring up to three values, for a total of 60 values. It is just not workable.

A Regular Polygon As a Shape

A better approach to draw such figures as a triangle or a square is to define an abstract polygon by defining some aspects of it such as the origin and radius and then have that polygon give us the vertex array, and possibly the index array (so that we can draw individual triangles), in return. The key then is to construct the abstract polygon that does this. We called this class RegularPolygon. Once we have this kind of an object we can use it as shown in Listing 10–23 to render various regular polygons.

Listing 10–23. *Using a RegularPolygon Object*

```
//A polygon with 4 sides and a radious of 0.5
//and located at (x,y,z) of (0,0,0)
 RegularPolygon square = new RegularPolygon(0,0,0,0.5f,4);

//Let the polygon return the vertices
 mFVertexBuffer = square.getVertexBuffer();

//Let the polygon return the triangles
 mIndexBuffer = square.getIndexBuffer();

//you will need this for glDrawElements
```

```
numOfIndices = square.getNumberOfIndices();

//set the buffers to the start
   this.mFVertexBuffer.position(0);
   this.mIndexBuffer.position(0);

//set the vertex pointer
   gl.glVertexPointer(3, GL10.GL_FLOAT, 0, mFVertexBuffer);

//draw it with the given number of Indices
   gl.glDrawElements(GL10.GL_TRIANGLES, numOfIndices,
           GL10.GL_UNSIGNED_SHORT, mIndexBuffer);
```

Notice how we have gotten the necessary vertices and indices from the shape of square. Although we haven't abstracted this idea of getting vertices and indices to a basic shape, it is possible that RegularPolygon could be deriving from such a basic shape that defines an interface for this basic contract. Here is an example:

```
public interface Shape
{
   FloatBuffer          getVertexBuffer();
   ShortBuffer          getIndexBuffer();
   int                  getNumberofIndices();
}
```

We will leave this idea of defining a base interface for a shape as food for thought for your own work. For now, we have built these methods out directly into the RegularPolygon.

Implementing the RegularPolygon Shape

As indicated, this RegularPolygon has the responsibility of returning what is needed to draw that regular polygon using OpenGL: vertices. First we need a mechanism to define what this shape is and where it is in the geometry.

For a regular polygon, there may be a number of ways of doing this. In our approach, we have defined the regular polygon using the number of sides and the distance from the center of the regular polygon to one of its vertices. We called this distance the radius, because the vertices of a regular polygon fall on the perimeter of a circle whose center is also the center of the regular polygon. So the radius of such a circle and the number of sides will tell us the polygon we want. By specifying the coordinates of the center we also know where to draw the polygon in our geometry.

The responsibility of this RegularPolygon class is to give us the coordinates of all the vertices of the polygon given its center and radius. Again, there may be a number of ways of doing this. Whatever mathematical method you choose to employ (based on middle school or high school math), in the end, as long as you return the vertices, you are good to go.

Here is the approach we have used. We started with the assumption that the radius is 1 unit. We figured out the angles for each line connecting the center to each vertex of the polygon. We kept these angles in an array. For each angle we calculated the x-axis projection and called this the "x multiplier array". (We used "multiplier array" because we started out with a unit of radius.) When we know the real radius we will multiply these values with the real radius to get the real x coordinate. These real x coordinates are then stored in an array called "x array". We do the same for the y-axis projections.

Now that you have an idea of what needs to happen in the implementation of the RegularPolygon, we'll give you the source code that addresses these responsibilities. Listing 10–24 shows all the code for the RegularPolygon in one place. (Please note that the source code is a few pages long.) To make the process of going through it less cumbersome, we have highlighted the function names and provided inline comments at the beginning of each function.

We define the key functions in a list which follows Listing 10–24. The important thing here is to figure out the vertices and return. If this is too cryptic, it shouldn't be hard to write your own code to get the vertices.

You will also note that this code also has functions that deal with texturing. We'll explain these texture functions in the "Working with Textures" section.

Listing 10–24. *Implementing a RegularPolygon Shape*

```
public class RegularPolygon
{
    //Space to hold (x,y,z) of the center: cx,cy,cz
    //and the radius "r"
    private float      cx, cy, cz, r;
    private int           sides;

    //coordinate array: (x,y) vertex points
    private float[] xarray = null;
    private float[] yarray = null;

    //texture arrray: (x,y) also called (s,t) points
    //where the figure is going to be mapped to a texture bitmap
    private float[] sarray = null;
    private float[] tarray = null;

    //*********************************************
    // Constructor
    //*********************************************
    public RegularPolygon(float incx, float incy, float incz, // (x,y,z) center
                     float inr, // radius
                     int insides) // number of sides
    {
        cx = incx;
        cy = incy;
        cz = incz;
        r = inr;
        sides = insides;

        //allocate memory for the arrays
        xarray = new float[sides];
        yarray = new float[sides];

        //allocate memory for texture point arrays
```

```
        sarray = new float[sides];
        tarray = new float[sides];

        //calculate vertex points
        calcArrays();

       //calculate texture points
        calcTextureArrays();
    }

//************************************************
//Get and convert the vertex coordinates
//based on origin and radius.
//Real logic of angles happen inside getMultiplierArray() functions
//************************************************
private void calcArrays()
{
    //Get the vertex points assuming a circle
    //with a radius of "1" and located at "origin" zero
    float[] xmarray = this.getXMultiplierArray();
    float[] ymarray = this.getYMultiplierArray();

    //calc xarray: get the vertex
    //by adding the "x" portion of the origin
    //multiply the coordinate with radius (scale)
    for(int i=0;i<sides;i++)
    {
        float curm = xmarray[i];
        float xcoord = cx + r * curm;
        xarray[i] = xcoord;
    }
    this.printArray(xarray, "xarray");

    //calc yarray: do the same for y coordinates
    for(int i=0;i<sides;i++)
    {
        float curm = ymarray[i];
        float ycoord = cy + r * curm;
        yarray[i] = ycoord;
    }
    this.printArray(yarray, "yarray");

}
//************************************************
//Calculate texture arrays
//See Texture subsection for more discussion on this
//Very similar approach.
//In this case the polygon has to map into a space
//that is a square
//************************************************
private void calcTextureArrays()
{
    float[] xmarray = this.getXMultiplierArray();
    float[] ymarray = this.getYMultiplierArray();

    //calc xarray
    for(int i=0;i<sides;i++)
```

```
    {
        float curm = xmarray[i];
        float xcoord = 0.5f + 0.5f * curm;
        sarray[i] = xcoord;
    }
    this.printArray(sarray, "sarray");

    //calc yarray
    for(int i=0;i<sides;i++)
    {
        float curm = ymarray[i];
        float ycoord = 0.5f +  0.5f * curm;
        tarray[i] = ycoord;
    }
    this.printArray(tarray, "tarray");
}

//*********************************************
//Convert the java array of vertices
//into an nio float buffer
//*********************************************
public FloatBuffer getVertexBuffer()
{
    int vertices = sides + 1;
    int coordinates = 3;
    int floatsize = 4;
    int spacePerVertex = coordinates * floatsize;

    ByteBuffer vbb = ByteBuffer.allocateDirect(spacePerVertex * vertices);
    vbb.order(ByteOrder.nativeOrder());
    FloatBuffer mFVertexBuffer = vbb.asFloatBuffer();

    //Put the first coordinate (x,y,z:0,0,0)
    mFVertexBuffer.put(cx); //x
    mFVertexBuffer.put(cy); //y
    mFVertexBuffer.put(0.0f); //z

    int totalPuts = 3;
    for (int i=0;i<sides;i++)
    {
        mFVertexBuffer.put(xarray[i]); //x
        mFVertexBuffer.put(yarray[i]); //y
        mFVertexBuffer.put(0.0f); //z
        totalPuts += 3;
    }
    Log.d("total puts:",Integer.toString(totalPuts));
    return mFVertexBuffer;
}

//*********************************************
//Convert texture buffer to an nio buffer
//*********************************************
public FloatBuffer getTextureBuffer()
{
    int vertices = sides + 1;
    int coordinates = 2;
    int floatsize = 4;
```

```
        int spacePerVertex = coordinates * floatsize;

        ByteBuffer vbb = ByteBuffer.allocateDirect(spacePerVertex * vertices);
        vbb.order(ByteOrder.nativeOrder());
        FloatBuffer mFTextureBuffer = vbb.asFloatBuffer();

        //Put the first coordinate (x,y (s,t):0,0)
        mFTextureBuffer.put(0.5f); //x or s
        mFTextureBuffer.put(0.5f); //y or t

        int totalPuts = 2;
        for (int i=0;i<sides;i++)
        {
            mFTextureBuffer.put(sarray[i]); //x
            mFTextureBuffer.put(tarray[i]); //y
             totalPuts += 2;
        }
        Log.d("total texture puts:",Integer.toString(totalPuts));
    return mFTextureBuffer;
}

//*********************************************
//Calculate indices forming multiple triangles.
//Start with the center vertex which is at 0
//Then count them in a clockwise direction such as
//0,1,2,  0,2,3, 0,3,4..etc
//*********************************************
public ShortBuffer getIndexBuffer()
{
    short[] iarray = new short[sides * 3];
    ByteBuffer ibb = ByteBuffer.allocateDirect(sides * 3 * 2);
    ibb.order(ByteOrder.nativeOrder());
    ShortBuffer mIndexBuffer = ibb.asShortBuffer();
    for (int i=0;i<sides;i++)
    {
        short index1 = 0;
        short index2 = (short)(i+1);
        short index3 = (short)(i+2);
        if (index3 == sides+1)
        {
            index3 = 1;
        }
        mIndexBuffer.put(index1);
        mIndexBuffer.put(index2);
        mIndexBuffer.put(index3);

        iarray[i*3 + 0]=index1;
        iarray[i*3 + 1]=index2;
        iarray[i*3 + 2]=index3;
    }
    this.printShortArray(iarray, "index array");
    return mIndexBuffer;
}
//*********************************************
//This is where you take the angle array
//for each vertex and calculate their projection multiplier
//on the x axis
```

```java
//***********************************************
private float[] getXMultiplierArray()
{
    float[] angleArray = getAngleArrays();
    float[] xmultiplierArray = new float[sides];
    for(int i=0;i<angleArray.length;i++)
    {
        float curAngle = angleArray[i];
        float sinvalue = (float)Math.cos(Math.toRadians(curAngle));
        float absSinValue = Math.abs(sinvalue);
        if (isXPositiveQuadrant(curAngle))
        {
            sinvalue = absSinValue;
        }
        else
        {
            sinvalue = -absSinValue;
        }
        xmultiplierArray[i] = this.getApproxValue(sinvalue);
    }
    this.printArray(xmultiplierArray, "xmultiplierArray");
    return xmultiplierArray;
}

//***********************************************
//This is where you take the angle array
//for each vertex and calculate their projection multiplier
//on the y axis
//***********************************************
private float[] getYMultiplierArray() {
    float[] angleArray = getAngleArrays();
    float[] ymultiplierArray = new float[sides];
    for(int i=0;i<angleArray.length;i++) {
        float curAngle = angleArray[i];
        float sinvalue = (float)Math.sin(Math.toRadians(curAngle));
        float absSinValue = Math.abs(sinvalue);
        if (isYPositiveQuadrant(curAngle)) {
            sinvalue = absSinValue;
        }
        else {
            sinvalue = -absSinValue;
        }
        ymultiplierArray[i] = this.getApproxValue(sinvalue);
    }
    this.printArray(ymultiplierArray, "ymultiplierArray");
    return ymultiplierArray;
}

//***********************************************
//This function may not be needed
//Test it yourself and discard it if you dont need
//***********************************************
private boolean isXPositiveQuadrant(float angle) {
    if ((0 <= angle) && (angle <= 90))  { return true;    }
    if ((angle < 0) && (angle >= -90))   { return true;    }
    return false;
}
```

```
//*********************************************
//This function may not be needed
//Test it yourself and discard it if you dont need
//*********************************************
private boolean isYPositiveQuadrant(float angle) {
   if ((0 <= angle) && (angle <= 90)) { return true; }
   if ((angle < 180) && (angle >= 90)) {return true;}
   return false;
}
//*********************************************
//This is where you calculate angles
//for each line going from center to each vertex
//*********************************************
private float[] getAngleArrays() {
   float[] angleArray = new float[sides];
   float commonAngle = 360.0f/sides;
   float halfAngle = commonAngle/2.0f;
   float firstAngle = 360.0f - (90+halfAngle);
   angleArray[0] = firstAngle;

   float curAngle = firstAngle;
   for(int i=1;i<sides;i++)
   {
      float newAngle = curAngle - commonAngle;
      angleArray[i] = newAngle;
      curAngle = newAngle;
   }
   printArray(angleArray, "angleArray");
   return angleArray;
}


//*********************************************
//Some rounding if needed
//*********************************************
private float getApproxValue(float f) {
   return (Math.abs(f) < 0.001) ? 0 : f;
}
//*********************************************
//Return how many Indices you will need
//given the number of sides
//This is the count of number of triangles needed
//to make the polygon multiplied by 3
//It just happens that the number of triangles is
// same as the number of sides
//*********************************************
public int getNumberOfIndices() {
   return sides * 3;
}
public static void test() {
   RegularPolygon triangle = new RegularPolygon(0,0,0,1,3);
}
private void printArray(float array[], String tag) {
   StringBuilder sb = new StringBuilder(tag);
   for(int i=0;i<array.length;i++) {
      sb.append(";").append(array[i]);
   }
   Log.d("hh",sb.toString());
```

```
    }
    private void printShortArray(short array[], String tag) {
        StringBuilder sb = new StringBuilder(tag);
        for(int i=0;i<array.length;i++) {
            sb.append(";").append(array[i]);
        }
        Log.d(tag,sb.toString());
    }
}
```

Here are the key elements in the code.

- *Constructor*: The constructor of a RegularPolygon takes as input the coordinates of the center, the radius, and the number of sides.

- *getAngleArrays*: This method is a key method that is responsible for calculating the angles of each spine of the regular polygon with the assumption that one of the sides of the polygon is parallel to the x-axis.

- *getXMultiplierArray and getYMultiplierArray*: These methods take the angles from getAngleArrays and project them to the x-axis and y-axis to get the corresponding coordinates, assuming the spine is a unit in length.

- *calcArrays*: This method uses the getXMultiplierArray and the getYMultiplierArray to take each vertex and scale them to match the specified radius and specified origin. At the end of this method the RegularPolygon will have the right coordinates, albeit in Java float arrays.

- *getVertexBuffer*: This method then takes the Java float coordinate arrays and populates NIO-based buffers that are needed by the OpenGL draw methods.

- *getIndexBuffer*: This method takes the vertices that are gathered and orders them such that each triangle will contribute to the final polygon.

The other methods that deal with textures follow a very similar pattern and will make more sense when we explain the textures in the next section. We have also included some print functions to print the arrays for debugging purposes.

Rendering a Square Using RegularPolygon

Now that we have looked at the basic building blocks, let's see how we could draw a square using a RegularPolygon of four sides. Listing 10–25 shows the code for the SquareRenderer mentioned in Listing 10–21, where we drew a square through a menu option.

Listing 10–25. *SquareRenderer*

```java
public class SquareRenderer extends AbstractRenderer
{
    //A raw native buffer to hold the point coordinates
    private FloatBuffer mFVertexBuffer;

    //A raw native buffer to hold indices
    //allowing a reuse of points.
    private ShortBuffer mIndexBuffer;

    private int numOfIndices = 0;

    private int sides = 4;

    public SquareRenderer(Context context)
    {
        prepareBuffers(sides);
    }

    private void prepareBuffers(int sides)
    {
        RegularPolygon t = new RegularPolygon(0,0,0,0.5f,sides);
        //RegularPolygon t = new RegularPolygon(1,1,0,1,sides);
        this.mFVertexBuffer = t.getVertexBuffer();
        this.mIndexBuffer = t.getIndexBuffer();
        this.numOfIndices = t.getNumberOfIndices();
        this.mFVertexBuffer.position(0);
        this.mIndexBuffer.position(0);
    }

    //overriden method
    protected void draw(GL10 gl)
    {
        prepareBuffers(sides);
        gl.glVertexPointer(3, GL10.GL_FLOAT, 0, mFVertexBuffer);
        gl.glDrawElements(GL10.GL_TRIANGLES, this.numOfIndices,
                GL10.GL_UNSIGNED_SHORT, mIndexBuffer);
    }
}
```

This code should be fairly obvious. We have derived it from the AbstractRenderer (see Listing 10–10) and overrode the draw method and used the RegularPolygon to draw out a square. When you choose the right menu option from Listing 10–21 you will see the following painted on the emulator screen (Figure 10–8).

Figure 10–8. *A square drawn as a regular polygon*

Animating RegularPolygons

Now that we have explored the basic idea of drawing a shape generically through the idea of a RegularPoygon, let's get a bit sophisticated and see if we can use animation where we start with a triangle and then end up with a circle by using a polygon whose sides increase every four seconds or so (Listing 10–26).

Listing 10–26. *PolygonRenderer*

```
public class PolygonRenderer extends AbstractRenderer
{
    //Number of points or vertices we want to use
    private final static int VERTS = 4;

    //A raw native buffer to hold the point coordinates
    private FloatBuffer mFVertexBuffer;

    //A raw native buffer to hold indices
    //allowing a reuse of points.
    private ShortBuffer mIndexBuffer;

    private int numOfIndices = 0;

    private long prevtime = SystemClock.uptimeMillis();

    private int sides = 3;

    public PolygonRenderer(Context context)
    {
        //EvenPolygon t = new EvenPolygon(0,0,0,1,3);
        //EvenPolygon t = new EvenPolygon(0,0,0,1,4);
```

```
        prepareBuffers(sides);
    }

    private void prepareBuffers(int sides)
    {
        RegularPolygon t = new RegularPolygon(0,0,0,1,sides);
        //RegularPolygon t = new RegularPolygon(1,1,0,1,sides);
        this.mFVertexBuffer = t.getVertexBuffer();
        this.mIndexBuffer = t.getIndexBuffer();
        this.numOfIndices = t.getNumberOfIndices();
        this.mFVertexBuffer.position(0);
        this.mIndexBuffer.position(0);
    }

    //overriden method
    protected void draw(GL10 gl)
    {
        long curtime = SystemClock.uptimeMillis();
        if ((curtime - prevtime) > 2000)
        {
            prevtime = curtime;
            sides += 1;
            if (sides > 20)
            {
                sides = 3;
            }
            this.prepareBuffers(sides);
        }
        //EvenPolygon.test();
        gl.glColor4f(1.0f, 0, 0, 0.5f);
        gl.glVertexPointer(3, GL10.GL_FLOAT, 0, mFVertexBuffer);
        gl.glDrawElements(GL10.GL_TRIANGLES, this.numOfIndices,
                GL10.GL_UNSIGNED_SHORT, mIndexBuffer);
    }
}
```

All we are doing in this code is changing the sides variable every four seconds. The animation comes from the way the Renderer is registered in Listing 10–21 where we registered this PolygonRenderer against the corresponding menu item.

It is instructive, however, to see the progress of the polygons over time. Figure 10–9 shows a hexagon toward the beginning of the cycle.

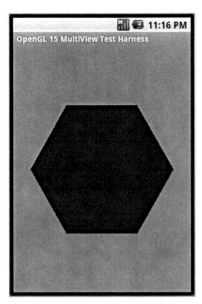

Figure 10–9. *Hexagon at the beginning of the polygon drawing cycle*

And here it is toward the end of the cycle (Figure 10–10).

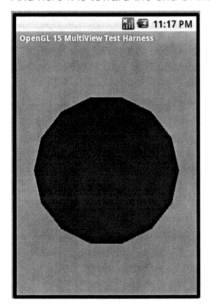

Figure 10–10. *A circle drawn as a regular polygon*

You can extend this idea of abstract shapes to more complex shapes and even to a scene graph where it consists of a number of other objects that are defined through some type of XML and then render them in OpenGL using those instantiated objects.

Let us now move on to textures to see how we can integrate the idea of sticking wallpapers to the surfaces we have drawn so far, such as squares and polygons.

Working with Textures

Textures is another important core topic in OpenGL. OpenGL textures have a number of nuances. We will cover only the fundamentals in this chapter so that you can get started with OpenGL textures. You can use the resources provided at the end of this chapter to dig deeper into textures.

Understanding Textures

An OpenGL Texture is a bitmap that you paste on a surface in OpenGL. (In this chapter we will cover only surfaces.) For example, you can take the image of a postage stamp and stick it on a square so that the square looks like a postage stamp. Or you can take the bitmap of a brick and paste it on a rectangle and repeat the brick image so that the rectangle looks like a wall of bricks.

The process of attaching a texture bitmap to an OpenGL surface is similar to the process of pasting a piece of wallpaper (in the shape of a square) on the side of a regularly or irregularly shaped object. The shape of the surface doesn't matter as long as you choose a paper that is large enough to cover the surface.

However to align the paper in a proper orientation so that the image is properly lined up you have to take each vertex of the shape and exactly mark it on the wallpaper so that the wallpaper and the object's shape are in lock step. If the shape is odd and has a number of vertices, each vertex needs to be marked on your paper as well.

Another way of looking at this is to envision that you lay the object on the ground face up and put the wallpaper on top of it and rotate the paper until the image is aligned in the right direction. Now poke holes in the paper at each vertex of the shape. Remove the paper and see where the holes are and note their coordinates on the paper, assuming the paper is calibrated. These coordinates are called texture coordinates.

Normalized Texture Coordinates

One unresolved or unstated detail is how big the object is and how big the paper. OpenGL uses a normalized approach to resolve this. OpenGL assumes that the paper is always a 1×1 square with it's origin at $(0,0)$ and the top right corner is at $(1,1)$. Then OpenGL wants you to shrink your object surface so that it fits within these 1×1 boundaries. So the burden is on the programmer to figure out the vertices of the object surface in a 1×1 square.

If you recall the design of our `RegularPolygon` from Listing 10–24, you know the way we drew a polygon using a similar approach where we assumed it is a circle of 1 unit radius. Then we figured out where each vertex is. If we assumed that that circle is inside a 1×1 square then that square could be our paper. So figuring out texture coordinates is very similar to figuring out the polygon vertex coordinates. This is why Listing 10–24 has the following function to calculate the texture coordinates:

```
calcTextureArray()
getTextureBuffer()
```

If you notice, every other function is common between calcTextureArrays and calcArrays methods. This commonality between vertex coordinates and texture coordinates is important to note when you are learning OpenGL.

Abstracting Common Texture Handling

Once you understand this mapping between texture coordinates and vertex coordinates and figure out the coordinates for the texture map, the rest is quite simple. Subsequent work involves loading the texture bitmap into memory and giving it a texture ID so that you can reuse this texture again. Then to allow for multiple textures loaded at the same time, you have a mechanism to set the current texture by specifying an ID. During a drawing pipeline you will specify the texture coordinates along with the drawing coordinates. Then you draw.

Because the process of loading textures is fairly common, we have abstracted out this process by inventing an abstract class called SingleAbstractTextureRenderer which inherits from AbstractRenderer.

Listing 10–27 shows the source code that abstracts out all the set-up code for textures.

Listing 10–27. *Abstracting Single Texturing Support*

```
public abstract class AbstractSingleTexturedRenderer
extends AbstractRenderer
{
    int mTextureID;
    int mImageResourceId;
    Context mContext;
    public AbstractSingleTexturedRenderer(Context ctx,
                                     int imageResourceId) {
        mImageResourceId = imageResourceId;
        mContext = ctx;
    }

    public void onSurfaceCreated(GL10 gl, EGLConfig eglConfig) {
        super.onSurfaceCreated(gl, eglConfig);
        gl.glEnable(GL10.GL_TEXTURE_2D);
        prepareTexture(gl);
    }
    private void prepareTexture(GL10 gl)
    {
        int[] textures = new int[1];
        gl.glGenTextures(1, textures, 0);

        mTextureID = textures[0];
        gl.glBindTexture(GL10.GL_TEXTURE_2D, mTextureID);

        gl.glTexParameterf(GL10.GL_TEXTURE_2D, GL10.GL_TEXTURE_MIN_FILTER,
                GL10.GL_NEAREST);
```

```java
        gl.glTexParameterf(GL10.GL_TEXTURE_2D,
                GL10.GL_TEXTURE_MAG_FILTER,
                GL10.GL_LINEAR);

        gl.glTexParameterf(GL10.GL_TEXTURE_2D, GL10.GL_TEXTURE_WRAP_S,
                GL10.GL_CLAMP_TO_EDGE);
        gl.glTexParameterf(GL10.GL_TEXTURE_2D, GL10.GL_TEXTURE_WRAP_T,
                GL10.GL_CLAMP_TO_EDGE);

        gl.glTexEnvf(GL10.GL_TEXTURE_ENV, GL10.GL_TEXTURE_ENV_MODE,
                GL10.GL_REPLACE);

        InputStream is = mContext.getResources()
                .openRawResource(this.mImageResourceId);
        Bitmap bitmap;
        try {
            bitmap = BitmapFactory.decodeStream(is);
        } finally {
            try {
                is.close();
            } catch(IOException e) {
                // Ignore.
            }
        }

        GLUtils.texImage2D(GL10.GL_TEXTURE_2D, 0, bitmap, 0);
        bitmap.recycle();
    }

    public void onDrawFrame(GL10 gl)
    {
        gl.glDisable(GL10.GL_DITHER);
        gl.glTexEnvx(GL10.GL_TEXTURE_ENV, GL10.GL_TEXTURE_ENV_MODE,
                GL10.GL_MODULATE);

        gl.glClear(GL10.GL_COLOR_BUFFER_BIT | GL10.GL_DEPTH_BUFFER_BIT);
        gl.glMatrixMode(GL10.GL_MODELVIEW);
        gl.glLoadIdentity();
        GLU.gluLookAt(gl, 0, 0, -5, 0f, 0f, 0f, 0f, 1.0f, 0.0f);

        gl.glEnableClientState(GL10.GL_VERTEX_ARRAY);

        gl.glEnableClientState(GL10.GL_TEXTURE_COORD_ARRAY);

        gl.glActiveTexture(GL10.GL_TEXTURE0);
        gl.glBindTexture(GL10.GL_TEXTURE_2D, mTextureID);
        gl.glTexParameterx(GL10.GL_TEXTURE_2D, GL10.GL_TEXTURE_WRAP_S,
                GL10.GL_REPEAT);
        gl.glTexParameterx(GL10.GL_TEXTURE_2D, GL10.GL_TEXTURE_WRAP_T,
                GL10.GL_REPEAT);

        draw(gl);
    }
}
```

In this code the single texture (a bitmap) is loaded and prepared in the onSurfaceCreated method. The code for onDrawFrame, just like the AbstractRenderer, sets up the dimensions of your drawing space so that your coordinates make sense. Depending on your situation, you may want to change this code to figure out your own optimal viewing volume.

Also notice how the constructor takes a texture bitmap which it prepares for later use. Depending on how many textures you have, you can craft your abstract classes accordingly.

As you went through Listing 10–27, you would have seen that you need the following APIs that revolve around textures. These are as follows:

- *glGenTextures*: This OpenGL method is responsible for generating unique IDs for textures so that those textures can be referenced later. Once you load the texture bitmap through GLUtils.texImage2D you will then bind that texture to a specific ID. Until a texture is bound to an ID generated by glGenTextures, the ID is just an ID. The OpenGL literature refers to these integer IDs as texture names.

- *glBindTexture*: You will use this OpenGL method to bind the currently loaded texture to a texture ID obtained from glGenTextures.

- *glTexParameter*: There are very many optional parameters you can set when you apply texture. This API allows you define what these options are. Some examples include GL_REPEAT, GL_CLAMP etc. For example, GL_REPEAT allows you to repeat the bitmap many times if the size of the object is larger. You can get a more complete list of these parameters from the following khronos OpenGL ES URL:
  http://www.khronos.org/opengles/documentation/opengles1_0/html/glTexParameter.html.

- *glTexEnv*: Some of the other texture-related options are specified through the glTexEnv method. Some example values include GL_DECAL, GL_MODULATE, GL_BLEND, GL_REPLACE, etc. For example, in the case of GL_DECAL, texture covers the underlying object. GL_MODULATE, as the name indicates, modulates the underlying colors instead of replacing them. Refer to the following URL for a complete list of the options for this API:
  http://www.khronos.org/opengles/documentation/opengles1_0/html/glTexEnv.html.

- *GLUtils.texImage2D*: This is an Android API that allows you to load the bitmap for texturing purposes. Internally this API calls the glTexImage2D of the OpenGL.

- *glActiveTexture*: This sets a given texture ID as the active structure.

- *glTexCoordpointer*: This OpenGL method is used to specify the texture coordinates. Each coordinate must match the coordinate specified in the glVertexPointer.

You can read up on most of these APIs from the OpenGL ES reference available at

`http://www.khronos.org/opengles/documentation/opengles1_0/html/index.html`

Drawing Using Textures

Once the bitmap is loaded and set up as a texture we should be able to utilize the RegularPolygon and use the texture coordinates and vertex coordinates to draw a regular polygon along with the texture. Listing 10–28 shows the actual drawing class that draws a textured square.

Listing 10–28. *TexturedSquareRenderer*

```
public class TexturedSquareRenderer extends AbstractSingleTexturedRenderer
{
    //Number of points or vertices we want to use
    private final static int VERTS = 4;

    //A raw native buffer to hold the point coordinates
    private FloatBuffer mFVertexBuffer;

    //A raw native buffer to hold the point coordinates
    private FloatBuffer mFTextureBuffer;

    //A raw native buffer to hold indices
    //allowing a reuse of points.
    private ShortBuffer mIndexBuffer;

    private int numOfIndices = 0;

    private int sides = 4;

    public TexturedSquareRenderer(Context context)
    {
        super(context,com.ai.android.OpenGL.R.drawable.robot);
        prepareBuffers(sides);
    }

    private void prepareBuffers(int sides)
    {
        RegularPolygon t = new RegularPolygon(0,0,0,0.5f,sides);
        this.mFVertexBuffer = t.getVertexBuffer();
        this.mFTextureBuffer = t.getTextureBuffer();
        this.mIndexBuffer = t.getIndexBuffer();
        this.numOfIndices = t.getNumberOfIndices();
        this.mFVertexBuffer.position(0);
        this.mIndexBuffer.position(0);
        this.mFTextureBuffer.position(0);

    }

    //overriden method
    protected void draw(GL10 gl)
    {
        prepareBuffers(sides);
        gl.glEnable(GL10.GL_TEXTURE_2D);
```

```
        gl.glVertexPointer(3, GL10.GL_FLOAT, 0, mFVertexBuffer);
        gl.glTexCoordPointer(2, GL10.GL_FLOAT, 0, mFTextureBuffer);
        gl.glDrawElements(GL10.GL_TRIANGLES, this.numOfIndices,
                GL10.GL_UNSIGNED_SHORT, mIndexBuffer);
    }
}
```

As you can see, most of the heavy lifting is carried out the by abstract textured renderer class and the `RegularPolygon` (calculated the texture mapping vertices. See Listing 10–24). With this code in place, if you pick the menu in Listing 10–21, you will see the textured square shown in Figure 10–11.

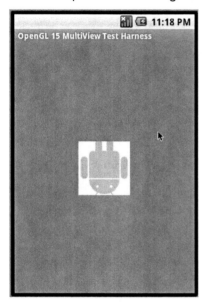

Figure 10–11. *A textured square*

Drawing Multiple Figures

Every example in this chapter so far has involved drawing a simple figure following a standard pattern. The pattern is: set up the vertices, load the texture, set up texture coordinates, and draw a single figure. What happens if you want to draw two figures? What if you want to draw a triangle using traditional means of specifying vertices and then a polygon using shapes such as the `RegularPolygon`? How do you need to specify combined vertices? Do you have to specify the vertices one time for both objects and then call the draw method? We will explore these critical question in this last section.

As it turns out, between two `draw()` calls of the Android OpenGL Renderer interface, OpenGL allows you to issue multiple `glDraw` methods. Between these multiple `glDraw` methods, you can set up fresh vertices and textures. All of these drawing methods will then go to the screen once the `draw()` method completes.

There is another trick you can use to draw multiple figures with OpenGL. Consider the polygons we have created so far. These polygons have the capability to render themselves at any origin by taking the origin as an input. As it turns out, OpenGL can do this natively where it allows you to specify a RegularPolygon always at (0,0,0) and have the "translate" mechanism of OpenGL move it off of the origin to the desired position. You can do the same again with another polygon and translate it to a different position, in the end drawing two polygons at two different places on the screen.

Listing 10–29 demonstrates these ideas by drawing the textured polygon multiple times.

Listing 10–29. *Textured Polygon Renderer*

```
public class TexturedPolygonRenderer extends AbstractSingleTexturedRenderer
{
    //Number of points or vertices we want to use
    private final static int VERTS = 4;

    //A raw native buffer to hold the point coordinates
    private FloatBuffer mFVertexBuffer;

    //A raw native buffer to hold the point coordinates
    private FloatBuffer mFTextureBuffer;

    //A raw native buffer to hold indices
    //allowing a reuse of points.
    private ShortBuffer mIndexBuffer;

    private int numOfIndices = 0;

    private long prevtime = SystemClock.uptimeMillis();
    private int sides = 3;

    public TexturedPolygonRenderer(Context context)
    {
        super(context,com.ai.android.OpenGL.R.drawable.robot);
        //EvenPolygon t = new EvenPolygon(0,0,0,1,3);
        //EvenPolygon t = new EvenPolygon(0,0,0,1,4);
        prepareBuffers(sides);
    }

    private void prepareBuffers(int sides)
    {
    RegularPolygon t = new RegularPolygon(0,0,0,0.5f,sides);
    //RegularPolygon t = new RegularPolygon(1,1,0,1,sides);
    this.mFVertexBuffer = t.getVertexBuffer();
    this.mFTextureBuffer = t.getTextureBuffer();
    this.mIndexBuffer = t.getIndexBuffer();
    this.numOfIndices = t.getNumberOfIndices();
    this.mFVertexBuffer.position(0);
    this.mIndexBuffer.position(0);
    this.mFTextureBuffer.position(0);
    }

    //overriden method
    protected void draw(GL10 gl)
    {
        long curtime = SystemClock.uptimeMillis();
        if ((curtime - prevtime) > 2000)
        {
```

```
        prevtime = curtime;
        sides += 1;
        if (sides > 20)
        {
            sides = 3;
        }
         this.prepareBuffers(sides);
    }
    gl.glEnable(GL10.GL_TEXTURE_2D);

    //Draw once to the left
    gl.glVertexPointer(3, GL10.GL_FLOAT, 0, mFVertexBuffer);
    gl.glTexCoordPointer(2, GL10.GL_FLOAT, 0, mFTextureBuffer);

    gl.glPushMatrix();
    gl.glScalef(0.5f, 0.5f, 1.0f);
    gl.glTranslatef(0.5f,0, 0);
    gl.glDrawElements(GL10.GL_TRIANGLES, this.numOfIndices,
            GL10.GL_UNSIGNED_SHORT, mIndexBuffer);

    //Draw again to the right
    gl.glPopMatrix();
    gl.glPushMatrix();
    gl.glScalef(0.5f, 0.5f, 1.0f);
    gl.glTranslatef(-0.5f,0, 0);
    gl.glDrawElements(GL10.GL_TRIANGLES, this.numOfIndices,
            GL10.GL_UNSIGNED_SHORT, mIndexBuffer);
    gl.glPopMatrix();
  }
}
```

This example demonstrates a number of concepts together:

- Drawing using shapes

- Drawing multiple shapes using transformation matrices

- Providing textures

- Providing animation

The main code in Listing 10–29 responsible for drawing multiple times is in the method draw(). We have highlighted corresponding lines in that method. You will notice that inside one draw() invocation we have called glDrawElements twice. Each of these times we set up the drawing primitives independent of the other time.

One more point to clarify is the use of transformation matrices. Every time glDrawElements() is called it uses a specific transformation matrix. If we were to change this to alter the position of the figure (or any other aspect of the figure) we would have to set it back to the original so that the next drawing could correctly draw. You accomplish this through push and pop operations provided on the OpenGL matrices.

Figure 10–12 shows the end result of this drawing exercise (this snapshot was taken toward the beginning of the animation).

Figure 10–12. *A pair of textured polygons*

Figure 10–13 shows the same exercise toward the middle of the animation.

Figure 10–13. *A pair of textured circles*

This concludes another important concept in OpenGL. This section showed how you can accumulate a number of different figures or scenes and draw them in tandem so that the end result forms a fairly complex OpenGL scene.

In the next section, we list some critical OpenGL resources which you can use for further explorations into OpenGL.

OpenGL Resources

We have found the following resources useful in understanding and working with OpenGL:

- Android's `android.opengl` package reference URL:
  `http://developer.android.com/reference/android/opengl/GLSurface View.html`.

- The Khronos Group's OpenGL ES Reference Manual:
  `http://www.khronos.org/opengles/documentation/opengles1_0/html/ index.html`.

- OpenGL Programming Guide (the "red book"):
  `http://www.glprogramming.com/red/`.

- Here is a very good article on texture mapping from Microsoft:
  `http://msdn.microsoft.com/en-us/library/ms970772(printer).aspx`.

- You can find very insightful course material on OpenGL from Wayne O. Cochran from Washington State University at this URL:
  `http://ezekiel.vancouver.wsu.edu/~cs442/`.

- Documentation for JSR 239 (Java Binding for the OpenGL ES API) is at
  `http://java.sun.com/javame/reference/apis/jsr239/`.

- You can find one of the authors of this book's research on OpenGL here:
  `http://www.satyakomatineni.com/akc/display?url=NotesIMPTitlesUR L&ownerUserId=satya&folderName=OpenGL&order_by_format=news`.

- You can find one of the authors of this book's research on OpenGL textures here:
  `http://www.satyakomatineni.com/akc/display?url=DisplayNoteIMPUR L&reportId=3190&ownerUserId=satya`.

Summary

We have covered a lot of ground in OpenGL—especially if you are new to OpenGL programming. We would like to think that this is a great introductory chapter on OpenGL, not only for Android but any other OpenGL system.

In this chapter you learned the fundamentals of OpenGL. You learned the Android-specific API that allows you to work with OpenGL standard APIs. We discussed shapes and textures, and we showed you how to use the drawing pipeline to draw multiple figures.

With this introduction, we encourage you to further hone your skills in OpenGL using the additional resources listed above. With increasing sophistication of mobile chips, OpenGL on mobile platforms should be ripe for development in the next few release cycles.

Chapter 11

Managing and Organizing Preferences

Like many other SDKs, Android supports preferences. Generally speaking, it tracks preferences for users of an application as well as the application itself. For example, a user of Microsoft Outlook might set a preference to view e-mail messages a certain way, and Microsoft Outlook itself has some default preferences that are configurable by users. But even though Android theoretically tracks preferences for both users and the application, it does not differentiate between the two. The reason for this is that Android applications run on a device that is generally not shared among several users; people don't share cell phones. So Android refers to preferences with the term *application preferences*, which encompasses both the user's preferences and the application's default preferences.

When you see Android's preferences support for the first time, you'll likely be impressed. Android offers a robust and flexible framework for dealing with preferences. It provides simple APIs that hide the reading and persisting of preferences, as well as prebuilt user interfaces that you can use to let the user make preference selections. We will explore all of these features in the sections that follow.

Exploring the Preferences Framework

Before we dig into Android's preferences framework, let's establish a scenario that would require the use of preferences and then explore how we would go about addressing it. Suppose you are writing an application that provides a facility to search for airline flights. Moreover, suppose that the application's default setting is to display flights based on the lowest cost, but that the user can set a preference to always sort flights by the least number of stops or by a specific airline. How would you go about doing that?

Understanding ListPreference

Obviously, you would have to provide a UI for the user to view the list of sort options. The list would contain radio buttons for each option, and the default (or current) selection would be preselected. To solve this problem with the Android preferences framework requires very little work. First, you would create a preferences XML file to describe the preference and then use a prebuilt activity class that knows how to show and persist preferences. Listing 11–1 shows the details.

Listing 11–1. *The Flight-Options Preferences XML File and Associated Activity Class*

```
<?xml version="1.0" encoding="utf-8"?>
<!-- This file is /res/xml/flightoptions.xml -->
<PreferenceScreen
        xmlns:android="http://schemas.android.com/apk/res/android"
    android:key="flight_option_preference"
    android:title="@string/prefTitle"
    android:summary="@string/prefSummary">

  <ListPreference
    android:key="@string/selected_flight_sort_option"
    android:title="@string/listTitle"
    android:summary="@string/listSummary"
    android:entries="@array/flight_sort_options"
    android:entryValues="@array/flight_sort_options_values"
    android:dialogTitle="@string/dialogTitle"
    android:defaultValue="@string/flight_sort_option_default_value" />

</PreferenceScreen>


package com.syh;

import android.os.Bundle;
import android.preference.PreferenceActivity;

public class FlightPreferenceActivity extends PreferenceActivity
{
    @Override
    protected void onCreate(Bundle savedInstanceState) {
        super.onCreate(savedInstanceState);
        addPreferencesFromResource(R.xml.flightoptions);
    }
}
```

Listing 11–1 contains an XML fragment that represents the flight-option preference setting. The listing also contains an activity class that loads the preferences XML file. Let's start with the XML. Android provides an end-to-end preferences framework. This means that the framework lets you define your preferences, display the setting(s) to the user, and persist the user's selection to the data store. You define your preferences in XML under /res/xml/. To show preferences to the user, you write an activity class that extends a predefined Android class called android.preference.PreferenceActivity, and then use the addPreferencesFromResource() method to add the resource to the activity's resource collection. The framework takes care of the rest (displaying and persisting).

In this flight scenario, you create a file called `flightoptions.xml` at `/res/xml/flightoptions.xml`. You then create an activity class called `FlightPreferenceActivity` that extends the `android.preference.PreferenceActivity` class. Next, you call `addPreferencesFromResource()`, passing in `R.xml.flightoptions`. Note that the preference resource XML points to several string resources. To ensure compilation, you need to add several string resources to your project. We will show you how to do that shortly. For now, have a look at the UI generated by Listing 11–1 (see Figure 11–1).

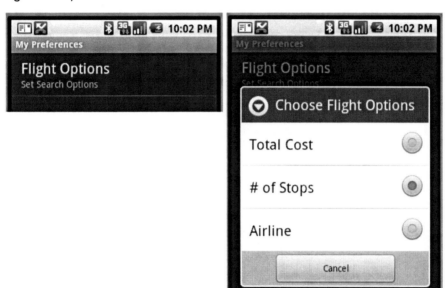

Figure 11–1. *The flight-options preference UI*

Figure 11–1 contains two views. The view on the left is called a *preference screen* and the UI on the right is a *list preference*. When the user selects Flight Options, the Choose Flight Options view appears as a modal dialog with radio buttons for each option. The user selects an option which immediately saves that option and closes the view. When the user returns to the options screen, the view reflects the saved selection from before.

As we discussed, the preferences XML file and associated activity class is shown in Listing 11–1. The code in that listing defines a `PreferenceScreen` and then creates a `ListPreference` as a child. For the `PreferenceScreen`, you set three properties: key, title, and summary. key is a string you can use to refer to the item programmatically (similar to how you use `android:id`); title is the screen's title (Flight Options); and summary is a description of the screen's purpose, shown below the title in a smaller font (Set Search Options, in this case). For the list preference, you set the key, title, and summary, as well as attributes for `entries, entryValues, dialogTitle,` and `defaultValue`. Table 11–1 summarizes these attributes.

Table 11–1. *A Few Attributes of android.preference.ListPreference*

Attribute	Description
android:key	A name or key for the option (such as `selected_flight_sort_option`).
android:title	The title of the option.
android:summary	A short summary of the option.
android:entries	The text of the items in the list that the option can be set to.
android:entryValues	Defines the key, or value, for each item. Note that each item has some text and a value. The text is defined by `entries` and the values are defined by `entryValues`.
android:dialogTitle	The title of the dialog—used if the view is shown as a modal dialog.
android:defaultValue	The default value of the option from the list of items.

To finish getting our example to work, add or modify the files as indicated in Listing 11–2.

Listing 11–2. *Setting Up the Rest of the Project for Our Example*

```xml
<?xml version="1.0" encoding="utf-8"?>
<!-- This file is /res/values/arrays.xml -->
<resources>
<string-array name="flight_sort_options">
    <item>Total Cost</item>
    <item># of Stops</item>
    <item>Airline</item>
</string-array>
<string-array name="flight_sort_options_values">
    <item>0</item>
    <item>1</item>
    <item>2</item>
</string-array>
</resources>


<?xml version="1.0" encoding="utf-8"?>
<!-- This file is /res/values/strings.xml -->
<resources>
    <string name="app_name">Preferences Demo</string>
    <string name="prefTitle">My Preferences</string>
    <string name="prefSummary">Set Flight Option Preferences</string>
    <string name="flight_sort_option_default_value">1</string>
    <string name="dialogTitle">Choose Flight Options</string>
    <string name="listSummary">Set Search Options</string>
    <string name="listTitle">Flight Options</string>
    <string name="selected_flight_sort_option">selected_flight_sort_option</string>
    <string name="menu_prefs_title">Settings</string>
    <string name="menu_quit_title">Quit</string>
</resources>
```

```xml
<?xml version="1.0" encoding="utf-8"?>
<!-- This file is /res/menu/mainmenu.xml -->
<menu xmlns:android="http://schemas.android.com/apk/res/android">
<item android:id="@+id/menu_prefs"
    android:title="@string/menu_prefs_title"
    />
<item android:id="@+id/menu_quit"
    android:title="@string/menu_quit_title"
    />
</menu>
```

```xml
<?xml version="1.0" encoding="utf-8"?>
<!-- This file is /res/layout/main.xml -->
<LinearLayout xmlns:android="http://schemas.android.com/apk/res/android"
    android:orientation="vertical"
    android:layout_width="fill_parent"
    android:layout_height="fill_parent"
    >

<TextView android:text="" android:id="@+id/text1"
    android:layout_width="fill_parent"
    android:layout_height="wrap_content"
    />

</LinearLayout>
```

```java
// This file is MainActivity.java
import android.app.Activity;
import android.content.Intent;
import android.content.SharedPreferences;
import android.os.Bundle;
import android.view.Menu;
import android.view.MenuInflater;
import android.view.MenuItem;
import android.widget.TextView;

public class MainActivity extends Activity {
    private TextView tv = null;

    /** Called when the activity is first created. */
    @Override
    public void onCreate(Bundle savedInstanceState) {
        super.onCreate(savedInstanceState);
        setContentView(R.layout.main);

        tv = (TextView)findViewById(R.id.text1);

        setOptionText();
    }

    @Override
    public boolean onCreateOptionsMenu(Menu menu)
    {
```

```java
        MenuInflater inflater = getMenuInflater();
        inflater.inflate(R.menu.mainmenu, menu);
        return true;
    }

    @Override
    public boolean onOptionsItemSelected (MenuItem item)
    {
        if (item.getItemId() == R.id.menu_prefs)
        {
            Intent intent = new Intent()
                    .setClass(this, com.syh.FlightPreferenceActivity.class);
            this.startActivityForResult(intent, 0);
        }
        else if (item.getItemId() == R.id.menu_quit)
        {
            finish();
        }
        return true;
    }

    @Override
    public void onActivityResult(int reqCode, int resCode, Intent data)
    {
        super.onActivityResult(reqCode, resCode, data);
        setOptionText();
    }

    private void setOptionText()
    {
        SharedPreferences prefs = getSharedPreferences("com.syh_preferences", 0);
        String option = prefs.getString(
                this.getResources().getString(R.string.selected_flight_sort_option),
this.getResources().getString(R.string.flight_sort_option_default_value));
        String[] optionText =
this.getResources().getStringArray(R.array.flight_sort_options);

        tv.setText("option value is " + option + " (" +
                optionText[Integer.parseInt(option)] + ")");
    }
}


<?xml version="1.0" encoding="utf-8"?>
<!-- This file is AndroidManifest.xml -->
<manifest xmlns:android="http://schemas.android.com/apk/res/android"
    package="com.syh"
    android:versionCode="1"
    android:versionName="1.0">
    <application android:icon="@drawable/icon" android:label="@string/app_name">
        <activity android:name=".MainActivity"
                android:label="@string/app_name">
            <intent-filter>
                <action android:name="android.intent.action.MAIN" />
                <category android:name="android.intent.category.LAUNCHER" />
            </intent-filter>
```

```
        </activity>

        <activity android:name=".FlightPreferenceActivity"
                android:label="@string/prefTitle">
            <intent-filter>
                <action android:name="com.syh.intent.action.FlightPreferences" />
                <category android:name="android.intent.category.PREFERENCE" />
            </intent-filter>
        </activity>

    </application>
    <uses-sdk android:minSdkVersion="3" />

</manifest>
```

After making these changes and running this app, you will first see a simple text message that says "option value is 1 (# of Stops)". Click on the Menu button and then on Settings to get to the `PreferenceActivity`. Click on the back arrow when done and you will see any changes to the option text immediately.

The first file we added was `/res/values/arrays.xml`. This file contains the two string arrays that we need to implement the option choices. The first array holds the text to be displayed and the second holds the values that we'll get back in our method calls, plus the value that gets stored in the preferences XML file. For our purposes, we chose to use array index values 0, 1, and 2 for `flight_sort_options_values`. We could use any value that helps us run the application. If our option was numeric in nature (for example a countdown timer starting value), then we could have used values such as 60, 120, 300, and so on. The values don't need to be numeric at all as long as they make sense to the developer; the user doesn't see these values unless you choose to expose them. The user only sees the text from the first string array `flight_sort_options`.

As we said earlier, the Android framework also takes care of persisting preferences. For example, when the user selects a sort option, Android stores the selection in an XML file within the application's `/data` directory (see Figure 11–2).

⊞ 🗁 com.google.android.googleapps	2008-09-27	03:37	drwxr-xr-x
⊞ 🗁 com.google.android.street	2008-09-27	03:37	drwxr-xr-x
⊞ 🗁 com.my.client	2008-12-22	19:51	drwxr-xr-x
⊞ 🗁 com.my.services	2008-12-22	19:36	drwxr-xr-x
⊞ 🗁 com.sayed	2008-12-15	02:16	drwxr-xr-x
⊞ 🗁 com.sayedhashimi	2008-12-03	02:22	drwxr-xr-x
⊟ 🗁 com.syh	2008-12-12	02:30	drwxr-xr-x
⊞ 🗁 lib	2008-12-12	02:30	drwxr-xr-x
⊟ 🗁 shared_prefs	2009-01-18	01:26	drwxrwx--x
📄 com.syh_preferences.xml	671 2009-03-12	01:44	-rw-rw----

Figure 11–2. *Path to an application's saved preferences*

The actual file path is `/data/data/[PACKAGE_NAME]/shared_prefs/[PACKAGE_NAME]_preferences.xml`. Listing 11–3 shows the `com.syh_preferences.xml` file for our example.

Listing 11–3. *Saved Preferences for Our Example*

```
<?xml version='1.0' encoding='utf-8' standalone='yes' ?>
<map>
    <string name="selected_flight_sort_option">1</string>
</map>
```

You can see that for a list preference, the preferences framework persists the selected item's value using the list's key attribute. Note also that the selected item's *value* is stored—not the text. A word of caution here: because the preferences XML file is only storing the value and not the text, should you ever upgrade your application and change the text of the options, or add items to the string arrays, any value stored in the preferences XML file should still line up with the appropriate text after the upgrade. The preferences XML file is kept during the application upgrade. If the preferences XML file had a "1" in it, and that meant "# of Stops" before the upgrade, it should still mean "# of Stops" after the upgrade.

The next file we touched was /res/values/strings.xml. We added several strings for our titles, summaries and menu items. There are two strings to pay particular attention to. The first is flight_sort_option_default_value. We set the default value to 1 to represent "# of Stops" in our example. It is usually a good idea to choose a default value for each option. If you don't choose a default value and no value has yet been chosen, the methods that return the value of the option will return null. Your code would have to deal with null values in this case. The other interesting string is selected_flight_sort_option. Strictly speaking, the user is not going to see this string. So we don't need to put it inside of strings.xml in order to provide alternate text for other languages. However, because this string value is a key used in the method call to retrieve the value, by creating an ID out of it, we can ensure at compile time that we didn't make a typo on the key's name.

The third file we added was /res/menu/mainmenu.xml. We're assuming that you'd like to access the preferences view through a menu and not through a button. This file represents our application's menu.

The fourth file we touched was /res/layout/main.xml. This is our main UI for this application. So far we've covered how to maintain the preferences, through the use of a special activity class PreferenceActivity. But you want to use preferences in your main activity, not a PreferenceActivity. Therefore, we need a way to get to the preferences from another activity. For this example, the layout is a simple TextView to display the current value of our flight preferences option.

Next up is the source code for our MainActivity. This is a basic activity that gets a handle to the TextView, then calls a method to read the current value of our option to set it into the TextView. We set up our menu, and the menu callback. Within the menu callback we launch an Intent for the FlightPreferenceActivity. When the preferences Intent returns to us, we call the setOptionText() method to update our TextView.

The setOptionText() method is where the fun is. The first step is to get a handle to the preferences, by referring to the appropriate preferences XML file name. Obviously you need to know what the file name will be using the pattern described above. The second option refers to whether or not you're going to only read the values, or write them. We'll discuss this a little more later. With a reference to the preferences, you call the appropriate methods to retrieve the values. In our example, we call `getString()`, since we know we're retrieving a string value from the preferences. The first argument is the string value of the option key. We noted before that using an ID ensures that we haven't made any typos while building our application. We could also have simply used the string `selected_flight_sort_option` for the first argument, which you might want to do because we want to keep applications as small and fast as possible. For the second argument, you specify a default value in case the value can't be found in the preferences XML file. When your application runs for the very first time, you don't have a preferences XML file, so without specifying a value for the second argument you'll always get null the first time. This is true even though you've specified a default value for the option in the `ListPreference` specification in `flightoptions.xml`. In our example we've set a default value, so the code in `setOptionText()` can be used to read what it is. Note that if we had not used an ID for the default value it would be a lot tougher to read it directly from the `ListPreference`. In addition to displaying the value of the preference, we also display the text of the preference. We're taking a shortcut in our example, since we used array indices for the values in `flight_sort_options_values`. By simply converting the value to an int we know which string to read from `flight_sort_options`. Had we used some other set of values for `flight_sort_options_values`, we would need to determine the index of the element that is our preference, then turn around and use that index to grab the text of our preference from `flight_sort_options`.

The final file to be touched for our example is `AndroidManifest.xml`. Because we now have two activities in our application, we need two activity tags. The first one is a standard activity of category `LAUNCHER`. The second one is for a `PreferenceActivity` so we set the action name according to convention for intents, and we set the category to `PREFERENCE`. We probably don't want the `PreferenceActivity` showing up with all our other applications, which is why we chose not to use `LAUNCHER` for it.

From an activity that extends `PreferenceActivity`, it's slightly easier to obtain a reference to the preferences. Instead of calling getPreferences() you would use this:

```
SharedPreferences prefs = getPreferenceManager().getDefaultSharedPreferences(this);
```

Manipulating Preferences Programmatically

It goes without saying that you might need to access the actual preference controls programmatically. For example, what if you need to provide the `entries` and `entryValues` for the `ListPreference` at runtime? You can define and access preference controls similar to the way you define and access controls in layout files and activities. For example, to access the list preference defined in Listing 11–1, you would call the `findPreference()` method of `PreferenceActivity`, passing the preference's key (note the similarity to `findViewById()`). You would then cast the control to `ListPreference` and then go about manipulating the control. For example, if you want to set the entries of the `ListPreference`, call the `setEntries()` method, and so on.

You can also use code to create Preferences or to perform other operations on them. Chapter 13 will show you how to do this.

So now you know how preferences work in Android. You know that Android provides prebuilt UIs to show preferences and also takes care of persisting them. In addition, Android provides the `android.preference.PreferenceActivity` class that you extend when implementing preferences within your application. This class provides APIs for you to load preferences and allows you to tie into and extend the preferences framework.

We showed you how to use the `ListPreference` view; now let's examine the other UI elements within the Android preferences framework. Namely, let's talk about the `CheckBoxPreference` view, the `EditTextPreference` view, and the RingtonePreference view.

Understanding CheckBoxPreference

You saw that the `ListPreference` preference displays a list as its UI element. Similarly, the `CheckBoxPreference` preference displays a check-box widget as its UI element.

To extend the flight-search example application, suppose you want to let the user set the list of columns he wants to see with the result set. This preference displays the available columns and allows the user to choose the desired columns by marking the corresponding check boxes. The user interface for this example is shown in Figure 11–3 and the preferences XML file is shown in Listing 11–4.

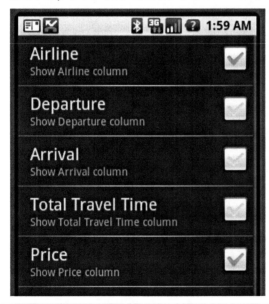

Figure 11–3. *The user interface for the check-box preference*

Listing 11–4. *Using a CheckBoxPreference*

```xml
<?xml version="1.0" encoding="utf-8"?>
<!-- This file is /res/xml/chkbox.xml -->
    <PreferenceScreen
        xmlns:android="http://schemas.android.com/apk/res/android"
                android:key="flight_columns_pref"
```

```
                android:title="Flight Search Preferences"
                android:summary="Set Columns for Search Results">
        <CheckBoxPreference
                android:key="show_airline_column_pref"
                android:title="Airline"
                android:summary="Show Airline column" />
        <CheckBoxPreference
                android:key="show_departure_column_pref"
                android:title="Departure"
                android:summary="Show Departure column" />
        <CheckBoxPreference
                android:key="show_arrival_column_pref"
                android:title="Arrival"
                android:summary="Show Arrival column" />
         <CheckBoxPreference
                android:key="show_total_travel_time_column_pref"
                android:title="Total Travel Time"
                android:summary="Show Total Travel Time column" />
        <CheckBoxPreference
                android:key="show_price_column_pref"
                android:title="Price"
                android:summary="Show Price column" />

</PreferenceScreen>

// CheckBoxPreferenceActivity.java

import android.os.Bundle;
import android.preference.PreferenceActivity;

public class CheckBoxPreferenceActivity extends PreferenceActivity
{
    @Override
    protected void onCreate(Bundle savedInstanceState) {
        super.onCreate(savedInstanceState);
        addPreferencesFromResource(R.xml.chkbox);
    }
}
```

Listing 11–4 shows the preferences XML file, chkbox.xml, and a simple activity class that loads it using addPreferencesFromResource(). As you can see, the UI has five check boxes, each of which is represented by a CheckBoxPreference node in the preferences XML file. Each of the check boxes also has a key, which—as you would expect—is ultimately used to persist the state of the UI element when it comes time to save the selected preference. With the CheckBoxPreference, the state of the preference is saved when the user sets the state. In other words, when the user checks or unchecks the preference control, its state is saved. Listing 11–5 shows the preference data store for this example.

Listing 11–5. *The Preferences Data Store for the Check-Box Preference*

```
<?xml version='1.0' encoding='utf-8' standalone='yes' ?>
<map>
    <boolean name="show_total_travel_time_column_pref" value="false" />
    <boolean name="show_price_column_pref" value="true" />
    <boolean name="show_arrival_column_pref" value="false" />
```

```
    <boolean name="show_airline_column_pref" value="true" />
    <boolean name="show_departure_column_pref" value="false" />
</map>
```

Again, you can see that each preference is saved through its key attribute. The data type of the CheckBoxPreference is a boolean, which contains a value of either true or false: true to indicate the preference is selected, and false to indicate otherwise. To read the value of one of the check-box preferences, you would get access to the shared preference and then call the getBoolean() method, passing the key of the preference:

```
Boolean option = prefs.getBoolean("show_price_column_pref", false);
```

One other useful feature of a CheckBoxPreference is that you can set different summary text depending on whether it's checked or not. The attributes are summaryOn and summaryOff. Now let's have a look at the EditTextPreference.

Understanding EditTextPreference

The preferences framework also provides a free-form text preference called EditTextPreference. This preference allows you to capture raw text rather than ask the user to make a selection. To demonstrate this, let's assume you have an application that generates Java code for the user. One of the preference settings of this application might be the default package name to use for the generated classes. So here, you want to display a text field to the user and allow her to set the package name for the generated classes. Figure 11–4 shows the UI and Listing 11–6 shows the XML.

Figure 11–4. *Using the EditTextPreference*

Listing 11–6. *An Example of an EditTextPreference*

```
<?xml version="1.0" encoding="utf-8"?>
<!-- This file is /res/xml/packagepref.xml -->
<PreferenceScreen
        xmlns:android="http://schemas.android.com/apk/res/android"
```

```
        android:key="package_name_screen"
        android:title="Package Name"
        android:summary="Set package name">

    <EditTextPreference
            android:key="package_name_preference"
            android:title="Set Package Name"
            android:summary="Set the package name for generated code"
            android:dialogTitle="Package Name" />

</PreferenceScreen>

// EditTextPreferenceActivity.java

import android.os.Bundle;
import android.preference.PreferenceActivity;

public class EditTextPreferenceActivity extends PreferenceActivity{

    @Override
    protected void onCreate(Bundle savedInstanceState) {
        super.onCreate(savedInstanceState);

        addPreferencesFromResource(R.xml.packagepref);
    }

}
```

You can see that Listing 11–6 defines a PreferenceScreen with a single EditTextPreference as a child. The generated UI for the listing features the PreferenceScreen on the left and the EditTextPreference on the right (see Figure 11–4). When the user selects Set Package Name, she is presented with a dialog to input the package name. When she clicks the OK button, the preference is saved to the preference store.

As with the other preferences, you can obtain the EditTextPreference from your activity class by using the preference's key. Once you have the EditTextPreference, you can manipulate the actual EditText by calling getEditText()—if, for example, you want to apply validation, preprocessing, or postprocessing on the value that the user types in the text field. To get the text of the EditTextPreference, just use the getText() method.

Now let's look at the preferences framework's RingtonePreference.

Understanding RingtonePreference

RingtonePreference deals specifically with ringtones. You'd use it in an application that gives the user an option to select a ringtone as a preference. Figure 11–5 shows the UI of the RingtonePreference example and Listing 11–7 shows the XML.

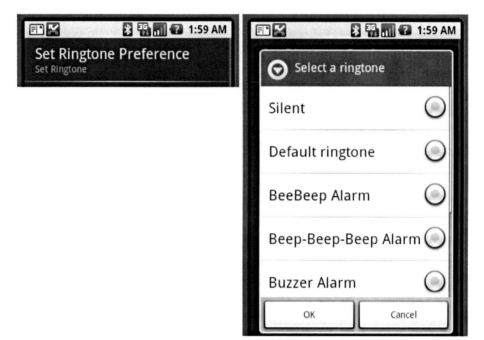

Figure 11–5. *The RingtonePreference example UI*

Listing 11–7. *Defining a RingtonePreference Preference*

```xml
<?xml version="1.0" encoding="utf-8"?>
<!-- This file is /res/xml/ringtone.xml -->
<PreferenceScreen
        xmlns:android="http://schemas.android.com/apk/res/android"
                android:key="ringtone_option_preference"
                android:title="My Preferences"
                android:summary="Set Ring Tone Preferences">
    <RingtonePreference
        android:key="ring_tone_pref"
        android:title="Set Ringtone Preference"
        android:showSilent="true"
        android:ringtoneType="alarm"
        android:summary="Set Ringtone" />
</PreferenceScreen>
```

```java
// RingtonePreferenceActivity.java

import android.os.Bundle;
import android.preference.PreferenceActivity;

public class RingtonePreferenceActivity extends PreferenceActivity
{
    @Override
    protected void onCreate(Bundle savedInstanceState) {
        super.onCreate(savedInstanceState);
        addPreferencesFromResource(R.xml.ringtone);
    }
}
```

When the user selects Set Ringtone Preference, the preferences framework displays a ListPreference containing the ringtones on the device (see Figure 11–5). The user can select a ringtone and then choose OK or Cancel. If he clicks OK, the selection is persisted to the preference store. Note that with the ringtones, the value stored in the preference store is the URI of the selected ringtone—unless he selects Silent, in which case the stored value is an empty string. An example URI looks like this:

```
<string name="ring_tone_pref">content://media/internal/audio/media/26</string>
```

> **NOTE:** If the emulator is short on ringtones, you can add some yourself. Copy music files to your SD card (this was covered in Chapter 9), go to the Android Music Player app, choose the music file, click on the Menu button, and click "Use as ringtone".

Finally, the RingtonePreference shown in Listing 11–7 follows the same pattern as the other preferences you've defined thus far. The difference here is that you set a few different attributes, including showSilent and ringtoneType. You can use showSilent to include the silent ringtone in the ringtone list, and ringtoneType to restrict the types of ringtones displayed in the list. Possible values for this property include ringtone, notification, alarm, and all.

Organizing Preferences

The preferences framework provides some support for you to organize your preferences into categories. If you have a lot of preferences, for example, you can build a view that shows high-level categories of preferences. Users could then drill down into each category to view and manage preferences specific to that group.

You can implement something like this in one of two ways. You can introduce nested PreferenceScreen elements within the root PreferenceScreen, or you can use PreferenceCategory elements to get a similar result. Figure 11–6 and Listing 11–8 show how to implement the first technique, grouping preferences by using nested PreferenceScreen elements.

The view on the left of Figure 11–6 displays two preference screens, one with the title Meats and the other with the title Vegetables. Clicking a group takes you to the preferences within that group. Listing 11–8 shows how to create nested screens.

Figure 11–6. *Creating groups of preferences by nesting PreferenceScreen elements*

Listing 11–8. *Nesting PreferenceScreen Elements to Organize Preferences*

```
<?xml version="1.0" encoding="utf-8"?>
<PreferenceScreen
        xmlns:android="http://schemas.android.com/apk/res/android"
                android:key="using_categories_in_root_screen"
                android:title="Categories"
                android:summary="Using Preference Categories">

    <PreferenceScreen
        xmlns:android="http://schemas.android.com/apk/res/android"
                android:key="meats_screen"
                android:title="Meats"
                android:summary="Preferences related to Meats">

        <CheckBoxPreference
                android:key="fish_selection_pref"
                android:title="Fish"
                android:summary="Fish is great for the healthy" />
        <CheckBoxPreference
                android:key="chicken_selection_pref"
                android:title="Chicken"
                android:summary="A common type of poultry" />
        <CheckBoxPreference
                android:key="lamb_selection_pref"
                android:title="Lamb"
                android:summary="Lamb is a young sheep" />

    </PreferenceScreen>
    <PreferenceScreen
```

```
            xmlns:android="http://schemas.android.com/apk/res/android"
                android:key="vegi_screen"
                android:title="Vegetables"
                android:summary="Preferences related to vegetable">
        <CheckBoxPreference
                android:key="tomato_selection_pref"
                android:title="Tomato "
                android:summary="It's actually a fruit" />
        <CheckBoxPreference
                android:key="potato_selection_pref"
                android:title="Potato"
                android:summary="My favorite vegetable" />

    </PreferenceScreen>

</PreferenceScreen>
```

You create the groups in Figure 11–6 by nesting PreferenceScreen elements within the root PreferenceScreen. Organizing preferences this way is useful if you have a lot of preferences and you're concerned about having the user scroll to find the preference he is looking for. If you don't have a lot of preferences but still want to provide high-level categories for your preferences, you can use PreferenceCategory, which is the second technique we mentioned. Figure 11–7 and Listing 11–9 show the details.

Figure 11–7. *Using PreferenceCategory to organize preferences*

Figure 11–7 shows the same groups we used in our previous example, but now organized with preference categories. The only difference between the XML in Listing 11–9 and the XML in Listing 11–8 is that you create a PreferenceCategory for the nested screens rather than nest PreferenceScreen elements.

Listing 11–9. *Creating Categories of Preferences*

```xml
<?xml version="1.0" encoding="utf-8"?>
<PreferenceScreen
        xmlns:android="http://schemas.android.com/apk/res/android"
                android:key="using_categories_in_root_screen"
                android:title="Categories"
                android:summary="Using Preference Categories">

    <PreferenceCategory
        xmlns:android="http://schemas.android.com/apk/res/android"
                android:key="meats_category"
                android:title="Meats"
                android:summary="Preferences related to Meats">

        <CheckBoxPreference
                android:key="fish_selection_pref"
                android:title="Fish"
                android:summary="Fish is great for the healthy" />
        <CheckBoxPreference
                android:key="chicken_selection_pref"
                android:title="Chicken"
                android:summary="A common type of poultry" />
        <CheckBoxPreference
                android:key="lamb_selection_pref"
                android:title="Lamb"
                android:summary="Lamb is a young sheep" />

    </PreferenceCategory>
    <PreferenceCategory
        xmlns:android="http://schemas.android.com/apk/res/android"
                android:key="vegi_category"
                android:title="Vegetables"
                android:summary="Preferences related to vegetable">
        <CheckBoxPreference
                android:key="tomato_selection_pref"
                android:title="Tomato "
                android:summary="It's actually a fruit" />
        <CheckBoxPreference
                android:key="potato_selection_pref"
                android:title="Potato"
                android:summary="My favorite vegetable" />

    </PreferenceCategory>

</PreferenceScreen>
```

Summary

In this chapter, we talked about managing preferences in Android. We showed you how to use ListPreference, CheckBoxPreference, EditTextPreference, and RingtonePreference. We also talked about programmatically manipulating preferences, and then showed you how to organize preferences into groups.

Chapter 12

Exploring Live Folders

In Chapter 10, we covered the OpenGL interface on Android in great detail. In Chapter 11, we covered how you manage preferences for your applications on the Android platform. In this chapter, we would like to welcome you to another advanced topic on the Android platform: live folders.

Live folders, introduced in SDK 1.5, allow developers to expose content providers such as contacts, notes, and media on the device's default opening screen (which we will refer to as the device's *home page*). When a content provider such as Android's `contacts` content provider is exposed as a live folder on the home page, this live folder will be able to refresh itself as contacts are added, deleted, or modified in the contacts database. We will explain what these live folders are, how to implement them, and how to make them "live."

Exploring Live Folders

A live folder in Android is to a content provider what an RSS reader is to a publishing web site. We said in Chapter 3 that content providers are similar to web sites that provide information based on URIs. As web sites proliferated, each publishing its information in a unique way, there arose a need to aggregate information from multiple sites so that a user could follow the developments through a single reader. To this end RSS was designed. RSS forced us to see a common pattern among disparate sets of information. Having a common pattern lets you design a reader once and use it to read any content, as long as the content has a uniform structure.

Live folders are not that different in concept. As an RSS reader provides a common interface to published web-site content, a live folder defines a common interface to a content provider in Android. As long as the content provider can satisfy this protocol, Android can create a live folder icon on the device's home page to represent that content provider. When a user clicks this live folder icon, the system will contact the content provider. The content provider is then expected to return a cursor. According to the live-folder contract, this cursor must have a predefined set of columns. This cursor is then visually presented through a `ListView` or a `GridView`.

Based on this common-format idea, live folders work like this:

1. First you create an icon on the home page representing a collection of rows coming from a content provider. You make this connection by specifying a URI along with the icon.

2. When a user clicks that icon, the system takes the URI and uses it to call the content provider. The content provider returns a collection of rows through a cursor.

3. As long as this cursor has columns expected by the live folder (such as name, description, and the program to invoke when that row is clicked), the system will present these rows as a `ListView` or a `GridView`.

4. Because the `ListViews` and `GridViews` are capable of updating their data when the underlying data store changes, these views are called "live"—hence the name "live folders."

Two key principles are at work in live folders. The first principle is that the column names are common across cursors. This principle allows Android to treat all cursors targeted for live folders the same way. The second principle is that the Android views know how to look for any updates in the underlying cursor data and change themselves accordingly. This second principle is not unique to live folders, but natural to all views in the Android UI, especially those views that rely on cursors.

Now that we have presented the idea of what live folders are, we'll systematically explore the live-folder framework. We will do that in two main sections. In the first main section, we will examine the overall end-user experience of a live folder. This should further clarify live folders.

In the second main section, we will show you how to build a live folder correctly so that it is actually live. It does take some extra work to make a live folder "live," so we will explore this not-so-obvious aspect of live folders.

How a User Experiences Live Folders

Live folders are exposed to end users through the device's home page. Users make use of live folders using a sequence like this:

1. Access the device's home page.

2. Go to the context menu of the home page. You can see the context menu by long-clicking on an empty space on the home page.

3. Locate a context-menu option called Folders and click it to see live folders that might be available.

4. From the list, choose and click the live folder name you want to expose on the home page. This creates an icon on the home page representing the chosen live folder.

5. Click the live-folder icon setup in step 4 to bring up the rows of information (the data represented by that live folder) in a `ListView` or a `GridView`.

6. Click one of the rows to invoke the application that knows how to display that row of data.

7. Use further menu options displayed by that application to view or manipulate a desired item. You can also use that application's menu options to create any new items allowed by that application.

8. Note that the live-folder display automatically reflects any changes to the item or set of items.

We'll walk you through these steps, illustrating them with screenshots. We will start with step 1: a typical Android home page (see Figure 12–1). Note that this home page may look a bit different depending on the Android release you are using.

Figure 12–1. *Android home page*

If you long-click this home page, you will see its context menu (see Figure 12–2).

Figure 12–2. *Context menu on the Android home page*

If you click the `Folders` sub-option, Android will open another menu showing live folders that are available (see Figure 12–3). We will build a live folder in the next section, but for now, assume that the live folder we want has already been built and is called "New live folder" (see Figure 12–3).

Figure 12–3. *Viewing the list of available live folders*

If you click this "New live folder," Android creates an icon on the home page representing the live folder. In our example, the name of this folder will be "Contacts LF," short for "Contacts Live Folder" (see Figure 12–4). This live folder will display contacts from the contacts database. (We'll discuss how to name this folder later, when we describe the `AllContactsLiveFolderCreatorActivity` class shown in Listing 12–2.)

Figure 12–4. *Live-folder icon on the home page*

You will see in the next section that an activity is responsible for creating the Contacts LF folder. For now, as far as the user experience is concerned, you can click the Contacts LF icon to see a list of contacts displayed in a ListView (see Figure 12–5).

Figure 12–5. *Showing live-folder contacts*

Depending on the number of contacts you have, this list might look different. You can click one of the contacts to display its details (see Figure 12–6).

Figure 12–6. *Opening a live-folder contact*

You can click the Menu button at the bottom to see how you can manipulate that individual contact (see Figure 12–7).

Figure 12–7. *Menu options for an individual contact*

If you choose to edit the contact, you will see the screen shown in Figure 12–8.

Figure 12–8. *Editing contact details*

To see the "live" aspect of this live folder, you can delete this contact or create a new one. Then when you go back to the live-folder view of Contacts LF, you will see those changes reflected. You can do this by clicking the Back button repeatedly until you see the Contacts LF folder.

Building a Live Folder

Now that you know what live folders are, we will show you how to build one. Once a live folder is built, you can use it to create an icon on the home page for that live folder. We will also show you how the "live" part of a live folder works.

To build a live folder, you need two things: an activity and a dedicated content provider. Android uses the "label" of this activity to populate the list of available live folders, as in Figure 12–3. Android also invokes this activity to get a URI that will be invoked to get a list of rows to display.

The URI supplied by the activity should point to the dedicated content provider that is responsible for returning the rows. The content provider returns these rows through a well-defined cursor. We call the cursor "well defined" because the cursor is expected to have a known predefined set of column names.

Typically, you package these two entities in an application and then deploy that application onto the device. You will also need some supporting files to make all this work. We will explain and demonstrate these ideas using a sample, which contains the following files:

- AndroidManifest.xml: This file defines which activity needs to be called to create the definition for a live folder.

- `AllContactsLiveFolderCreatorActivity.java`: This activity is responsible for supplying the definition for a live folder that can display all contacts in the contacts database.

- `MyContactsProvider.java`: This content provider will respond to the live-folder URI that will return a cursor of contacts. This provider internally uses the contacts content provider that ships with Android.

- `MyCursor.java`: This is a specialized cursor that knows how to perform a requery when underlying data changes.

- `BetterCursorWrapper.java`: This file is needed by `MyCursor` to orchestrate the requery.

- `SimpleActivity.java`: This simple activity is an optional file that you can use to test your project as you develop it. You will not need this file in your final deployment.

We'll describe each of these files to give you a detailed understanding of how live folders work.

AndroidManifest.xml

You're already familiar with `AndroidManifest.xml`; it's the same file that is needed for all Android applications. The live-folders section of the file, which is demarcated with a comment, indicates that we have an activity called `AllContactsLiveFolderCreatorActivity` that is responsible for creating the live folder (see Listing 12–1). This fact is expressed through the declaration of an intent whose action is `android.intent.action.CREATE_LIVE_FOLDER`.

The label of this activity, "New live folder," will show up in the context menu of the home page (see Figure 12–3). As we explained in the "How a User Experiences Live Folders" section, you can get to the context menu of the home page by long-clicking the home page.

Listing 12–1. *AndroidManifest.xml File for a Live-Folder Definition*

```
<?xml version="1.0" encoding="utf-8"?>
<manifest xmlns:android="http://schemas.android.com/apk/res/android"
     package="com.ai.android.livefolders"
     android:versionCode="1"
     android:versionName="1.0">
  <application android:icon="@drawable/icon" android:label="@string/app_name">
     <activity android:name=".SimpleActivity"
             android:label="@string/app_name">
        <intent-filter>
            <action android:name="android.intent.action.MAIN" />
            <category android:name="android.intent.category.LAUNCHER" />
        </intent-filter>
     </activity>

     <!-- LIVE FOLDERS -->
     <activity
```

```
    android:name=".AllContactsLiveFolderCreatorActivity"
    android:label="New live folder "
    android:icon="@drawable/icon">

    <intent-filter>
        <action android:name="android.intent.action.CREATE_LIVE_FOLDER" />
        <category android:name="android.intent.category.DEFAULT" />
    </intent-filter>
  </activity>

  <provider android:authorities="com.ai.livefolders.contacts"
    android:multiprocess="true"
        android:name=".MyContactsProvider" />

 </application>
 <uses-sdk android:minSdkVersion="3" />
<uses-permission android:name="android.permission.READ_CONTACTS"></uses-permission>
</manifest>
```

Another notable point of the code in Listing 12–1 is the provider declaration, which is anchored at the URI content://com.ai.livefolders.contacts and serviced by the provider class MyContactsProvider. This provider is responsible for providing a cursor to populate the ListView that opens when the corresponding live-folder icon is clicked (see Figure 12–5). The live folder activity AllContactsLiveFolderCreatorActivity needs to know what this URI is and return it to Android when it is invoked. Android invokes this activity when the live folder name is chosen to create a live folder icon on the home page.

According to the live-folder protocol, the CREATE_LIVE_FOLDER intent will allow the home page's context menu to show the AllContactsLiveFolderCreatorActivity as an option titled "New live folder" (see Figure 12–3). Clicking this menu option will create an icon on the home page, as shown in Figure 12–4.

It is the responsibility of AllContactsLiveFolderCreatorActivity to define this icon, which will consist of an image and a label. In our case, the code in AllContactsLiveFolderCreatorActivity specifies this label as Contacts LF (see Listing 12–2). So let's take a look at the source code for this live-folder creator.

AllContactsLiveFolderCreatorActivity.java

The AllContactsLiveFolderCreatorActivity class has one responsibility: to serve as the generator or creator of a live folder (see Listing 12–2). Think of it as a template for the live folder. Every time this activity is clicked (through the Folders option in the home page's context menu), it will generate a live folder on the home page.

This activity accomplishes its task by telling the invoker—the home page or live-folder framework, in this case—the name of the live folder, the image to use for the live-folder icon, the URI where the data is available, and the display mode (list or grid). The framework, in turn, is responsible for creating the live-folder icon on the home page.

> **NOTE:** For all the contracts needed by a live folder, see the Android SDK documentation for the
> `android.provider.LiveFolders` class.

Listing 12–2. *AllContactsLiveFolderCreatorActivity Source Code*

```
public class AllContactsLiveFolderCreatorActivity extends Activity
{
    @Override
    protected void onCreate(Bundle savedInstanceState)
    {
        super.onCreate(savedInstanceState);

        final Intent intent = getIntent();
        final String action = intent.getAction();

        if (LiveFolders.ACTION_CREATE_LIVE_FOLDER.equals(action))   {
            setResult(RESULT_OK,
                createLiveFolder(MyContactsProvider.CONTACTS_URI,
                        "Contacts LF",
                        R.drawable.icon)
                );
        }
        else   {
            setResult(RESULT_CANCELED);
        }
        finish();
    }

    private Intent createLiveFolder(Uri uri, String name, int icon)
    {
        final Intent intent = new Intent();
        intent.setData(uri);
        intent.putExtra(LiveFolders.EXTRA_LIVE_FOLDER_NAME, name);
        intent.putExtra(LiveFolders.EXTRA_LIVE_FOLDER_ICON,
                Intent.ShortcutIconResource.fromContext(this, icon));
        intent.putExtra(LiveFolders.EXTRA_LIVE_FOLDER_DISPLAY_MODE,
                LiveFolders.DISPLAY_MODE_LIST);
        return intent;
    }
}
```

The `createLiveFolder` method essentially sets values on the intent that invoked it. When
this intent is returned to the caller, the caller will know the following:

- The live-folder name

- The image to use for the live-folder icon

- The display mode: list or grid

- The data or content URI to invoke for data

This information is sufficient to create the live-folder icon as shown in Figure 12–4. When a user clicks this icon, the system will call the URI to retrieve data. It is up to the content provider identified by this URI to provide the standardized cursor. We'll now show you the code for that content provider: the MyContactsProvider class.

MyContactsProvider.java

MyContactsProvider has the following responsibilities:

1. Identify the incoming URI that looks like
   content://com.ai.livefolders.contacts/contacts.

2. Make an internal call to the Android-supplied contacts content provider identified by content://contacts/people/.

3. Read every row from the cursor and map it back to a cursor like MatrixCursor with proper column names required by the live-folder framework.

4. Wrap the MatrixCursor in another cursor so that the requery on this wrapped cursor will make calls to the contacts content provider when needed.

The code for MyContactsProvider is shown in Listing 12–3. Significant items are highlighted.

Listing 12–3. *MyContactsProvider Source Code*

```java
public class MyContactsProvider extends ContentProvider {

    public static final String AUTHORITY = "com.ai.livefolders.contacts";

    //Uri that goes as input to the live-folder creation
    public static final Uri CONTACTS_URI = Uri.parse("content://" +
            AUTHORITY + "/contacts"   );

    //To distinguish this URI
    private static final int TYPE_MY_URI = 0;
    private static final UriMatcher URI_MATCHER;
    static{
      URI_MATCHER = new UriMatcher(UriMatcher.NO_MATCH);
      URI_MATCHER.addURI(AUTHORITY, "contacts", TYPE_MY_URI);
    }

    @Override
    public boolean onCreate() {
        return true;
    }

    @Override
    public int bulkInsert(Uri arg0, ContentValues[] values) {
      return 0; //nothing to insert
    }
```

```java
//Set of columns needed by a live folder
//This is the live-folder contract
private static final String[] CURSOR_COLUMNS = new String[]
{
  BaseColumns._ID,
  LiveFolders.NAME,
  LiveFolders.DESCRIPTION,
  LiveFolders.INTENT,
  LiveFolders.ICON_PACKAGE,
  LiveFolders.ICON_RESOURCE
};

//In case there are no rows
//use this stand-in as an error message
//Notice it has the same set of columns of a live folder
private static final String[] CURSOR_ERROR_COLUMNS = new String[]
{
  BaseColumns._ID,
  LiveFolders.NAME,
  LiveFolders.DESCRIPTION
};


//The error message row
private static final Object[] ERROR_MESSAGE_ROW =
    new Object[]
    {
     -1,                                    //id
     "No contacts found",                   //name
     "Check your contacts database"         //description
    };

//The error cursor to use
private static MatrixCursor      sErrorCursor = new ⏎
               MatrixCursor(CURSOR_ERROR_COLUMNS);
static
{
  sErrorCursor.addRow(ERROR_MESSAGE_ROW);
}

//Columns to be retrieved from the contacts database
private static final String[] CONTACTS_COLUMN_NAMES = new String[]
{
  People._ID,
  People.DISPLAY_NAME,
  People.TIMES_CONTACTED,
  People.STARRED
};

public Cursor query(Uri uri, String[] projection, String selection,
                              String[] selectionArgs, String sortOrder)
{
   //Figure out the uri and return error if not matching
   int type = URI_MATCHER.match(uri);
   if(type == UriMatcher.NO_MATCH)
   {
     return sErrorCursor;
```

```java
    }

  Log.i("ss", "query called");

  try
  {
    MatrixCursor mc = loadNewData(this);
    mc.setNotificationUri(getContext().getContentResolver(),
                          Uri.parse("content://contacts/people/"));
    MyCursor wmc = new MyCursor(mc,this);
    return wmc;
  }
  catch (Throwable e)
  {
    return sErrorCursor;
  }
}

public static MatrixCursor loadNewData(ContentProvider cp)
{
  MatrixCursor mc = new MatrixCursor(CURSOR_COLUMNS);
  Cursor allContacts = null;
  try
  {
    allContacts = cp.getContext().getContentResolver().query(
      People.CONTENT_URI,
      CONTACTS_COLUMN_NAMES,
      null, //row filter
      null,
      People.DISPLAY_NAME); //order by

    while(allContacts.moveToNext())
    {
      String timesContacted = "Times contacted: "+allContacts.getInt(2);

      Object[] rowObject = new Object[]
      {
        allContacts.getLong(0),                         //id
        allContacts.getString(1),                       //name
        timesContacted,                                 //description
        Uri.parse("content://contacts/people/"
                          +allContacts.getLong(0)),     //intent uri
        cp.getContext().getPackageName(),               //package
        R.drawable.icon                                 //icon
      };
      mc.addRow(rowObject);
    }
    return mc;
  }
  finally
  {
    allContacts.close();
  }
}

@Override
public String getType(Uri uri)
```

```
    {
        //indicates the MIME type for a given URI
        //targeted for this wrapper provider
        //This usually looks like
        // "vnd.android.cursor.dir/vnd.google.note"
        return People.CONTENT_TYPE;
    }

    public Uri insert(Uri uri, ContentValues initialValues) {
        throw new UnsupportedOperationException(
                "no insert as this is just a wrapper");
    }

    @Override
    public int delete(Uri uri, String selection, String[] selectionArgs) {
        throw new UnsupportedOperationException(
            "no delete as this is just a wrapper");
    }

    public int update(Uri uri, ContentValues values,
            String selection, String[] selectionArgs)
    {
        throw new UnsupportedOperationException(
            "no update as this is just a wrapper");
    }
}
```

The set of columns shown in Listing 12–4 includes the standard columns that a live folder needs.

Listing 12–4. *Columns Needed to Fulfill the Live-Folder Contract*

```
    private static final String[] CURSOR_COLUMNS = new String[]
    {
      BaseColumns._ID,
      LiveFolders.NAME,
      LiveFolders.DESCRIPTION,
      LiveFolders.INTENT,
      LiveFolders.ICON_PACKAGE,
      LiveFolders.ICON_RESOURCE
    };
```

Most of these fields are self-explanatory, except for the INTENT item. If you look at Figure 12–5, you will see that NAME relates to the title of the item in the list. The DESCRIPTION will be underneath the NAME in the same list item.

The INTENT field is actually a string field pointing to the URI of the item in the content provider. Android will use a VIEW action by using this URI when a user clicks on that item. That is why this string field is called an INTENT field, because internally Android will derive the INTENT from the string URI.

The last two fields relate to the ICON that is displayed as part of the list. Again, refer to Figure 12–5 to see the icons. Study Listing 12–3 to see how these columns are provided values from the contacts database.

Also note that the `MyContactsContentProvider` above (the wrapper content provider) executes the code from Listing 12–5 to tell the underlying cursor that it needs to watch for any data changes.

Listing 12–5. *Registering a URI with a Cursor*

```
MatrixCursor mc = loadNewData(this);
mc.setNotificationUri(getContext().getContentResolver(),
                Uri.parse("content://contacts/people/"));
```

The function `loadNewData()` retrieves a set of contacts from the contact provider and creates `MatrixCursor`, which has the columns shown in Listing 12–4. The code then instructs the `MatrixCursor` to register itself with the `ContentResolver` so that the `ContentResolver` can alert the cursor when the data pointed to by the URI (`content://contacts/people`) changes in any manner.

You should find it interesting that the URI to watch is not the URI of our `MyContactsProvider` content provider, but the URI of the Android-supplied content provider for contacts. This is because `MyContactsProvider` is just a wrapper for the "real" content provider. So this cursor needs to watch the underlying content provider instead of the wrapper.

It is also important that we wrap the `MatrixCursor` in our own cursor, as shown in Listing 12–6.

Listing 12–6. *Wrapping a Cursor*

```
MatrixCursor mc = loadNewData(this);
mc.setNotificationUri(getContext().getContentResolver(),
            Uri.parse("content://contacts/people/"));
MyCursor wmc = new MyCursor(mc,this);
```

To understand why you need to wrap the cursor, you must examine how views operate to update changed content. A content provider, like the Contacts, typically tells a cursor that it needs to watch for changes by registering a URI as part of implementing the query method. This is done through `cursor.setNotificationUri`. The cursor then will register this URI and all its children URIs with the content provider. Then when an insert or delete happens on the content provider, the code for the insert and delete operations needs to raise an event signifying a change to the data in the rows identified by a particular URI.

This will trigger the cursor to get updated via `requery`, and the view will update accordingly. Unfortunately, the `MatrixCursor` is not geared for this `requery`. `SQLiteCursor` is geared for it, but we can't use `SQLiteCursor` here because we're mapping the columns to a new set of columns.

To accommodate this restriction, we have wrapped the `MatrixCursor` in a cursor wrapper and overridden the `requery` method to drop the internal `MatrixCursor` and create a new one with the updated data. To elaborate further, every time data changes we want to get a new `MatrixCursor`. However, to the Android LiveFolder framework we return only the wrapped outer cursor. This will tell the live folder framework that there is only one cursor, but underneath we are coming up with new cursors as data changes.

This is illustrated in the following two classes.

MyCursor.java

Notice how MyCursor is initialized with a MatrixCursor in the beginning (see Listing 12–7). On requery, MyCursor will call back the provider to return a MatrixCursor. Then the new MatrixCursor will replace the old one by using the set method.

> **NOTE:** We could have done this by overriding the requery of the MatrixCursor, but that class does not provide a way to clear the data and start all over again. So this is a reasonable workaround. (Note that MyCursor extends BetterCursorWrapper, which we'll discuss next.)

Listing 12–7. *MyCursor Source Code*

```
public class MyCursor extends BetterCursorWrapper
{
    private ContentProvider mcp = null;

    public MyCursor(MatrixCursor mc, ContentProvider inCp)
    {
        super(mc);
        mcp = inCp;
    }
    public boolean requery()
    {
        MatrixCursor mc = MyContactsProvider.loadNewData(mcp);
        this.setInternalCursor(mc);
        return super.requery();
    }
}
```

Now you'll look at the BetterCursorWrapper class to get an idea of how to wrap a cursor.

BetterCursorWrapper.java

The BetterCursorWrapper class (see Listing 12–8) is very similar to the CursorWrapper class in the Android database framework. But we need two additional things that CursorWrapper lacks. First, it doesn't have a set method to replace the internal cursor from the requery method. Second, CursorWrapper is not a CrossProcessCursor. Live folders need a CrossProcessCursor as opposed to a plain cursor because live folders work across process boundaries.

Listing 12–8. *BetterCursorWrapper Source Code*

```
public class BetterCursorWrapper implements CrossProcessCursor
{
    //Holds the internal cursor to delegate methods to
    protected CrossProcessCursor internalCursor;

    //Constructor takes a crossprocesscursor as an input
```

```
public BetterCursorWrapper(CrossProcessCursor inCursor)
{
    this.setInternalCursor(inCursor);
}

//You can reset in one of the derived class's methods
public void setInternalCursor(CrossProcessCursor inCursor)
{
    internalCursor = inCursor;
}

//All delegated methods follow
public void fillWindow(int arg0, CursorWindow arg1) {
    internalCursor.fillWindow(arg0, arg1);
}
// ..... other delegated methods
}
```

We haven't shown you the entire class, but you can easily use Eclipse to generate the rest of it. Once you have this partial class loaded into Eclipse, place your cursor on the variable named internalCursor. Right-click and choose Source ➤ Generate Delegated Methods. Eclipse will then populate the rest of the class for you. Let us now show you the simple activity you need to complete this sample project.

SimpleActivity.java

SimpleActivity.java (see Listing 12–9) is not an essential class for live folders, but its inclusion in the project gives you a common pattern for all your projects. Plus, it allows you to deploy the application and see it onscreen when you are debugging through Eclipse.

Listing 12–9. *SimpleActivity Source Code*

```
public class SimpleActivity extends Activity
{
    @Override
    public void onCreate(Bundle savedInstanceState)
    {
        super.onCreate(savedInstanceState);
        setContentView(R.layout.main);
    }
}
```

You can use any simple XML layout that you would like for the main.xml identified by R.layout.main. Listing 12–10 shows an example.

Listing 12–10. *Simple XML Layout File*

```
<?xml version="1.0" encoding="utf-8"?>
<LinearLayout xmlns:android="http://schemas.android.com/apk/res/android"
    android:orientation="vertical"
    android:layout_width="fill_parent"
    android:layout_height="fill_parent"
    >
<TextView
    android:layout_width="fill_parent"
```

```
        android:layout_height="wrap_content"
        android:text="Live Folder Example"
        />
</LinearLayout>
```

Now you have all the classes you need to build, deploy, and run the sample live-folder project through Eclipse. Let us conclude this section on live folders by showing you what happens when you access the live folder.

Exercising Live Folders

Once you have all these files for the live-folder project ready, you can build them and deploy them to the emulator. When you deploy this application through Eclipse, you will see the simple activity show up on the emulator. You are now ready to make use of the live folder that we have constructed.

Navigate to the device's home page; it should look like the screen in Figure 12–1. Follow the steps outlined at the beginning of the section, "How a User Experiences Live Folders." Specifically, locate the live folder you created and create the live-folder icon as shown in Figure 12–4. Click the Contacts LF live-folder icon, and you will see the contact list populated with contacts, as shown in Figure 12–5.

Summary

Live Folders provide an innovative single-click mechanism to display changing data on the home page. The data can be virtually anything as long as it can be laid out as a set of rows displayed in a list. All the data needs to have is a sense of how to identify and describe itself through name and description. Almost any data element will meet this requirement since most data can be named and described in some manner. It also helps if there is an activity that can display that data when clicked for further details through the live folder. This data can be local, such as contacts, or even net based, such as a summary of blogs.

In this chapter, we have also showed you how Android relies on an activity to obtain the content URI for a Live Folder. Android in turn uses this URI as the basis for obtaining a collection of rows that will be displayed as contents of that live folder. We have shown you how to implement a content provider that can supply data to the live folder based on the previous URI.

In this chapter we have also explained the nuances of live folder cursors and what mechanisms you will need to use if you wish to expose already-existing content providers as sources for live folders. We explained the need for cursor wrappers and showed you how to register with a ContentResolver to receive data updates.

In the next chapter we will introduce you to another home page innovation called Home Widgets.

Chapter 13

Home Screen Widgets

In this chapter, we will cover Android's home screen widgets in detail. Home screen widgets, like live folders, offer one more way of presenting frequently changing information on the home screen of Android. From a high-level perspective, home screen widgets are disconnected views (albeit populated with data) that are displayed on the home screen. The data content of these views is updated at regular intervals by background processes.

For example, an e-mail home screen widget might alert you to the number of outstanding e-mails to be read. However, please note that the widget will just show you the "count" of the e-mails and not the e-mails themselves. Clicking on the e-mail count will then take you to the activity that displays actual e-mails. These could even be external e-mail sources such as Yahoo, Gmail, or Hotmail, as long as the device has a way to access the counts through HTTP or other connectivity mechanisms.

We will divide this chapter into three sections. In the first section, we will introduce home screen widgets and their architecture. We will describe how Android uses `RemoteViews` for showing widgets, and co-opts broadcast receivers to update those `RemoteViews`. You will learn how to create activities to configure widgets on the home screen and discover the relationship between services and widgets. At the end of this section, you will have a clear understanding of the lifecycle of home screen widgets.

In the second section, we will show you how to design and develop a home widget through annotated code. You will learn how to define widgets to Android and how to write broadcast receivers to update these widgets. We will show you how to manage widget state through shared preferences and how to write an activity to configure widgets.

In the third section, we will talk about suitability, limitations, and broader guidelines for working with widgets. In this section, we will discuss the scope and applicability of widgets. In this section we will also offer design suggestions to write widgets that require far more frequent updates.

We will conclude the chapter with a collection of widget related programming resources.

Architecture of Home Screen Widgets

Let's start our discussion of home screen widgets architecture by considering what home screen widgets are in greater detail.

What Are Home Screen Widgets?

As indicated in the introduction, home screen widgets are views that can be displayed on a home page and updated frequently.

As a view, a widget's look and feel is defined through a layout xml file. For a widget, in addition to the layout of the view, you will need to define how much space the view of the widget will need on the home screen.

A widget definition also includes a couple of Java classes that are responsible for initializing the view and updating it frequently. These Java classes are responsible for managing the lifecycle of the widget on the home screen. These classes respond when the widget is dragged onto the home page and when the widget is uninstalled by dragging it to the trash can.

> **NOTE:** The view and the corresponding Java classes are architected in such a way that they are disconnected from each other. For example, any Android service or activity can retrieve the view using its layout ID and populate that view with data (just like populating a template) and send it to the home screen. Once the view is sent to the home screen it is dislodged from any underlying Java code.

At a minimum, a widget definition contains the following:

- A view layout to be displayed on the home screen, along with how big it should be to fit on a home page. Keep in mind that this is just the view without any data. It will be the responsibility of a Java class to update the view.

- A timer that specifies the frequency of updates.

- A Java class called a "widget provider" that can respond to timer updates in order to alter the view in some fashion by populating it with some data.

Once a widget is defined and the Java classes are provided, the widget will be available for use. We'll give you an overview of this user experience first.

User Experience with Home Screen Widgets

Home screen widget functionality in Android allows you to choose a widget to be placed on the home screen. When placed, the widget will allow you to configure it using an activity, if necessary. Let's start by locating the widget we want and creating an instance of it on the home screen.

Creating a Widget Instance on the Home Screen

To access the available widget list you need to long-click on the home page. This will bring up the home screen context menu as shown in Figure 13–1.

Figure 13–1. *Home screen context menu*

If you choose widgets from this list, you will be shown another screen that is a pick list of available widgets as shown in Figure 13–2.

Figure 13–2. *Home screen widget pick list*

Most of these widgets come as part of Android. Depending on the release of Android you are looking at, these may vary. In this list, the widget named Birthday Widget is a widget that we designed for this exercise. If you choose that widget, it will create a corresponding widget instance on the home screen that looks like the example Birthday Widget shown in Figure 13–3.

Figure 13–3. *An example birthday widget*

This widget is a birthday widget. It will indicate in its header the name of a person, how many days away this person's birthday is, the date of the birthday, and a link to buy gifts.

> **NOTE:** The view that is created on the home page for this widget definition is called a widget instance. The implication is that you can create more than one instance of this widget definition.

Understanding Widget Configurator

At this point we should introduce the previously mentioned *widget configurator*. A widget definition optionally includes a specification of an activity called a widget configurator activity. When you choose a widget from the home page widget pick list to create the widget instance, Android invokes the corresponding widget configuration activity. This activity is something you need to write, which is then responsible for configuring the widget instance.

In the case of our birthday widget, this configuration activity will prompt you for the name of the person and the upcoming birth date as shown in Figure 13–4. It is the responsibility of the configurator to save this information in a persistent place so that when an update is called on the widget provider, the widget provider will be able to locate this information and update the view with proper values which are set by the configurator.

Figure 13–4. *Birthday widget configurator activity*

NOTE: When a user chooses to create two birthday widget instances on the home screen, the configurator activity will be called twice (once for each widget instance).

Internally, Android keeps track of the widget instances by allocating them an ID. This ID is passed to the Java callbacks and also to the configurator Java class so that updates can be directed to the right instance. In Figure 13–3, in the later part of the string satya:3, the 3 is the widget ID—or, more accurately, the widget instance ID. The widget itself is identified by its component name (which is itself the class name and the package that the widget class is in; "Widget ID" and "widget instance ID" are interchangeably used in this chapter.) We have included the widget instance ID in Figure 13–3 to illustrate the point.

With this overview of a widget behind us, we will examine the lifecycle of a widget in greater detail next.

Lifecycle of a Widget

We have mentioned the widget definition a few times so far. We have also briefly talked about the role of Java classes. In this section, we will lay out both these ideas in a lot more detail and examine the lifecycle of a widget. The lifecycle of a widget has the following phases:

1. Widget definition
2. Widget instance creation
3. onUpdate() (when the time interval expires)
4. Responding to clicks (on the widget view on the home screen)
5. Widget deletion (from the home screen)
6. Uninstall

We will go through each of these phases in detail now.

Widget Definition Phase

The lifecycle of a widget starts with the definition of the widget view. This definition tells Android to show the widget name in the widget pick list (Figure 13–2) invoked from the home page. You will need two things to complete this definition. You will need a java class that implements the AppWidgetProvider and a layout view for the widget. Once you have these two you can define the widget to Android.

You start off this widget definition with the following entry in the android manifest file where you specify the AppWidgetProvider (Listing 13–1).

Listing 13–1. *Widget Definition in Android Manifest File*

```
<manifest..>
<application>
....
    <receiver android:name=".BDayWidgetProvider">
        <meta-data android:name="android.appwidget.provider"
            android:resource="@xml/bday_appwidget_provider" />
        <intent-filter>
            <action android:name="android.appwidget.action.APPWIDGET_UPDATE" />
        </intent-filter>
    </receiver>
    ...
    <activity>
        .....
    </activity>
<application>
</manifest>
```

This definition indicates that there is a broadcast receiver Java class called BDayWidgetProvider (as you will see, this inherits from the Android core class AppWidgetProvider from the widget package) that receives broadcast messages intended for application widget updates.

> **NOTE:** Android delivers the update messages as broadcast messages based on the frequency of the time interval.

The widget definition in Listing 13–1 also points to an xml file in the "/res/xml" directory that in turn specifies the widget view and the update frequency, as shown in Listing 13–2.

Listing 13–2. *Widget View Definition in Widget Provider Information XML File*

```
<appwidget-provider xmlns:android="http://schemas.android.com/apk/res/android"
    android:minWidth="150dp"
    android:minHeight="120dp"
    android:updatePeriodMillis="43200000"
    android:initialLayout="@layout/bday_widget"
    android:configure="com.ai.android.BDayWidget.ConfigureBDayWidgetActivity"
    >
</appwidget-provider>
```

This XML file is called the App widget provider information file. Internally, this gets translated to AppWidgetProviderInfo Java class. This file identifies the width and height of the layout to be 150dp and 120dp respectively. This definition file also indicates the update frequency to be 12 hours translated to milliseconds. The definition also points to a layout file (Listing 13–7) that describes what the widget view looks like (see Figure 13–5).

However, note that the layout for these widget views is restricted to contain only certain types of view elements. The combined view of a widget falls under a class of views called RemoteViews, Only certain types of child views are allowed for these remote views. The allowed sub-view elements are shown in Listing 13–3.

Listing 13–3. *Allowed View Controls in RemoteViews*

```
FrameLayout
LinearLayout
RelativeLayout

AnalogClock
Button
Chronometer
ImageButton
ImageView
ProgressBar
TextView
```

This list may also vary for each release. The primary reason for restricting what is allowed in a remote view is that these views are disconnected from the processes that actually control them. These widget views are hosted by an application like the Home application. The controllers for these views are background processes that get invoked by timers. For this reason, these views are called remote views. There is a corresponding Java class called RemoteViews that allows access to these views. In other words, programmers do not have direct access to these views to call methods on them. You have access to these views only through the RemoteViews (like a gatekeeper).

We will cover the relevant methods of a RemoteViews class when we explore the example in the next main section. For now, remember that only a limited set of views are allowed in the widget layout file (see Listing 13–3).

The widget definition (Listing 13–2) also includes a specification of the configuration activity that needs to be invoked when the user creates a widget instance. This configuration activity in Listing 13–2 is the ConfigureBDayWidgetActivity. This activity is like any other Android activity with a number of form fields. The form fields are used to collect the information needed by a widget instance.

Widget Instance Creation Phase

Once all the XML pieces needed by a widget definition are in place and all the widget Java classes are available, let's see what happens when a user chooses the widget name in the widget pick list (Figure 13–2) to create a widget instance. Android invokes the configurator activity (Figure 13–3) and expects that configurator activity to do the following:

1. Receive the widget instance ID from the invoking intent that started the configurator

2. Prompt the user through a set of form fields to collect the widget instance–specific information

3. Persist the widget instance information so that subsequent calls to widget update have access to this information

4. Prepare to display the widget view for the first time by retrieving the widget view layout and create a RemoteViews object with it

5. Call methods on the `RemoteViews` object to set values on individual view objects such as text, image, etc.

6. Also use the `RemoteViews` object to register any `onClick` events on any of the subviews of the widget

7. Tell the `AppWidgetManager` to paint the `RemoteViews` on the home screen using the instance ID of that widget

8. Return the widget ID and close.

On return from this activity, Android will paint the widget view as indicated by the configurator. Notice that the first painting in this case is done by the configurator and not the `AppWidgetProvider`'s `onUpdate()` method.

> **NOTE:** The configurator activity is optional. If the configurator activity is not specified, the call goes directly to the `onUpdate()`, even the first time. It is up to `onUpdate()` to update the view.

Android will repeat this process for each widget instance that the user creates. Also note that there is no direct documented support for restricting the user to a single widget instance.

Besides invoking the configurator activity, Android also invokes the `onEnabled` callback of the `AppWidgetProvider`. Let us briefly consider the callbacks on an `AppWidgetProvider` class by taking a look at the shell of our `BDayWidgetProvider`. (See Listing 13–4). We will examine the complete listing of this file later in Listing 13–9.

Listing 13–4. *A Widget Provider Shell*

```
public class BDayWidgetProvider extends AppWidgetProvider
{
    public void onUpdate(Context context,
                         AppWidgetManager appWidgetManager,
                         int[] appWidgetIds){}

    public void onDeleted(Context context, int[] appWidgetIds){}
    public void onEnabled(Context context){}
    public void onDisabled(Context context) {}
}
```

The `onEnabled()` callback method indicates that there is at least one instance of the widget up and running on the home screen. This means a user must have dropped the widget on the home page at least once. In this call, you will need to enable receiving messages for this component. (You will see this in Listing 13–9). In Android, classes are sometimes referred to as components, especially when they form a reusable unit such as an Activity, a Service, or a BroadcastReceiver. In this case, the base class `AppWidgetProvider` is a broadcast receiver component; we can enable or disable it to receive broadcast messages.

The `onDeleted()` callback method is called when a user drags the widget instance view to the trash can. This is where you will need to delete any persistence values you are holding for that widget instance.

The `onDisabled()` callback method is called after the last widget instance is removed from the home screen. This happens when a user drags the last instance of a widget to the trash. You should use this method to unregister your interest in receiving any broadcast messages intended for this component. (You will see this in Listing 13–9.)

The `onUpdate()` callback method is called every time the timer specified in Listing 13–2 expires. This method is also called the very first time the widget instance is created if there is no configurator activity. If there is a configurator activity then this method is not called at the creation of a widget instance. This method will subsequently be called when the timer expires at the frequency indicated.

onUpdate Phase

Once the widget instance shows up on the home screen, the next significant event is the expiration of the timer. As indicated, Android will call the `onUpdate()` in response to that timer. The way `onUpdate()` is called is through a broadcast receiver. This means the corresponding Java process in which the `onUpdate()` is defined will be loaded and will remain alive until the end of that call. Once the call returns the process will be ready to be taken down.

It is also recommended that if your response is going to take time to work, you should start a local service and have the service do the work. This allows the broadcast thread to return. The service will be running on a separate thread that is dedicated to that service process.

Either way, once you have the data available in `onUpdate()` method you can invoke the `AppWidgetManager` to paint the remote view that needs to be updated with the data that you have. The implication is that if you were to invoke a service to do the update instead, you would need to pass the widget ID as extra data to the intent that starts the service.

This goes to show that the `AppWidgetProvider` class is stateless and may even be incapable of maintaining static variables between invocations. This is because the Java process containing this broadcast receiver class could be taken down and reconstructed between two invocations resulting in re-initialization of static variables.

As a result, you will need to come up with a scheme to remember state if that is required. When the updates are not too frequent, such as every few seconds, it is quite reasonable to save the state of the widget instance in a persistent store such as a file, shared preferences, or a `sqllite` database. In the next example we will use shared preferences as the persistence API.

> **WARNING:** To save power, Android strongly recommends that the duration of the updates be more than an hour so that the device won't wake up too often. They also warn that in future releases this restriction of 30 minutes or more may be enforced.

For durations that are shorter, such as only seconds, you need to call this onUpdate() method yourself by using the facilities in the AlarmManager class. When you use the AlarmManager you also have the option not to call onUpdate(), but instead do the work of onUpdate() in alarm callbacks.

This is what you typically need to do in an onUpdate() method:

1. Make sure the configurator has finished its work, otherwise just return. This should not be problem in releases 2.0 and above, where the duration is expected to be longer. Otherwise it is possible that the onUpdate() will be called before the configurator has finished.

2. Retrieve the persisted data for that widget instance.

3. Retrieve the widget view layout and create a RemoteViews object with it.

4. Call methods on the RemoteViews to set values on individual view objects such as text, image, etc.

5. Register any onClick events on any of the views by using pending intents.

6. Tell the AppWidgetManager to paint the RemoteViews using the instance ID.

As you can see, there is a lot of overlap between what a configurator does and what the onUpdate() method does. You may want to reuse this functionality between the two.

Widget View Mouse Click Event Callbacks Phase

As stated, the onUpdate() method keeps the widget views up to date. The widget view and subelements in that view could have callbacks registered when there is a mouse click. Typically the onUpdate() method uses a pending intent to register an action for an event like a mouse click. This action could then start a service or start an activity such as opening up a browser.

This invoked service or activity can then communicate back with the view, if needed, using the widget instance ID and the AppWidgetManager. Hence it is important that the pending intent carries with it the widget instance ID.

Deleting a Widget Instance

Another distinct event that can happen to a widget instance is that it can get deleted. To do this, a user has to press down on the widget on the home screen. This will enable the trash can to show at the bottom of the home screen. The user can then drag the widget instance to the trash can. This will delete the widget instance from the screen.

This also calls the onDelete() method of the widget provider. If you have saved any state information for this widget instance you will need to delete that data in this onDelete method.

Android also calls onDisable() if the widget instance that is just deleted is the last of the widget instances of this type. You will use this callback to clean up any persistence attributes that are stored for all widget instances and also unregister for callbacks from the widget onUpdate() broadcasts (see Listing 13–9).

Uninstalling Widget Packages

That is the complete lifecycle of a widget. We will move on to the next section by briefly mentioning the need to clean up the widgets if you are planning to uninstall and install a new release of your .apk file containing these widgets.

It is recommended that you remove or delete all widget instances before trying to uninstall the package. Follow the directions in the "Deleting a Widget Instance" section to delete each widget instance until none remains.

Then you can uninstall and install the new release. This is especially important if you are using the Eclipse ADT to develop your widgets, because during the development time ADT tries to do this every time you run the application. So, between runs, make sure you remove the widget instances.

A Sample Widget Application

So far, we have covered the theory and approach behind widgets. Let us use that knowledge to create a sample widget that we can develop, test, and deploy.

The goal of the next exercise is to create a birthday reminder widget. Each widget instance will show a name, the date of the next birthday, and how many days from today until the birthday. It will also create an onClick area where you can click to buy gifts. This click will open up a browser and take you to http://www.google.com.

The layout of the finished widget should look like Figure 13–5.

Figure 13–5. *Birthday widget look and feel*

The implementation of this widget consists of the following widget-related files. Depending on the source java package you would like to use, the java files will be under the src subdirectory followed by a directory structure that you would use for your Java packages. For brevity and space we have used "…" to indicate those subdirectories.

- AndroidManifest.xml //: Where the AppWidgetProvider is defined

- res/xml/bday_appwidget_provider.xml //: Widget dimensions and layout

- res/layout/bday_widget.xml //: The widget layout

- res/drawable/box1.xml //: Provides boxes for sections of the widget layout

- src/.../BDayWidgetProvider //: Implementation of the AppWidgetProvider class

The implementation also contains the following files to manage the state of a widget:

- src/.../IWidgetModelSaveContract //: Contract for saving a widget model

- src/.../APrefWidgetModel //: Abstract preference-based widget model

- src/.../BDayWidgetModel //: Widget model holding the data for a widget view

- src/.../Utils.java //: A few utility classes

In addtion, the implementation has the following files for the widget configuration activity:

- src/.../ConfigureBDayWidgetActivity.java //: Configuration activity

- layout/edit_bday_widget.xml //: Layout for taking the name and birthday

We will walk through each file and explain any additional concepts we may have left out. At the end of this section, you can also copy and paste these files to create and test the birthday widget in your own environment.

Defining the Widget Provider

Definition of a widget starts in the Android application manifest file. This is where you specify the widget provider, widget configuration activity, and a pointer to another xml file that further defines the widget layout.

For the birthday widget, you can see all of these highlighted in the following Android manifest file (Listing 13–5). Notice the definition of BDayAppWidgetProvider as a broadcast receiver and also the definition for the configuration activity ConfigureBDayWidgetActivity.

Listing 13–5. *Android Manifest File for BDayWidget Sample Application*

```xml
<?xml version="1.0" encoding="utf-8"?>
<manifest xmlns:android="http://schemas.android.com/apk/res/android"
     package="com.ai.android.BDayWidget"
     android:versionCode="1"
     android:versionName="1.0.0">
    <application android:icon="@drawable/icon" android:label="Birthday Widget">
<!--
**********************************************************************
*  Birthday Widget Provider Receiver
**********************************************************************
 -->
   <receiver android:name=".BDayWidgetProvider">
      <meta-data android:name="android.appwidget.provider"
             android:resource="@xml/bday_appwidget_provider" />
      <intent-filter>
          <action android:name="android.appwidget.action.APPWIDGET_UPDATE" />
      </intent-filter>
   </receiver>
<!--
**********************************************************************
*  Birthday Provider Confiurator Activity
**********************************************************************
 -->
   <activity android:name=".ConfigureBDayWidgetActivity"
                 android:label="Configure Birthday Widget">
      <intent-filter>
          <action android:name="android.appwidget.action.APPWIDGET_CONFIGURE" />
      </intent-filter>
   </activity>

   </application>
   <uses-sdk android:minSdkVersion="3" />
</manifest>
```

> **NOTE:** The receiver node is a sibling node to the activity node, if you are familiar with the manifest file. It is also the immediate child of the application node.

The application label identifief by "Birthday Widget" in the following line

```xml
<application android:icon="@drawable/icon" android:label="Birthday Widget">
```

is what shows up in the widget pick list (Figure 13–2) of the home page. If you are creating a widget definition for the first time, make sure the following line is replicated exactly:

```
<meta-data android:name="android.appwidget.provider"
```

The spec `"android.appwidget.provider"` is Android specific and should be mentioned as such, and so are the lines below:

```
<intent-filter>
    <action android:name="android.appwidget.action.APPWIDGET_UPDATE" />
</intent-filter>
```

Finally, the configuration activity definition is like any other normal activity, except that it needs to declare itself as capable of responding to `APPWIDGET_CONFIGURE` actions.

Defining Widget Size

Although the Android manifest file defines the widget provider, the additional details of the widget are provided in a separate xml file. The additional details include the size of the widget, the layout file name for the widget, the update time period, and the configuration activity component (or class) name.

This additional XML file is indicated by the `android:resource` node of the previous widget provider definition (Listing 13–5). Listing 13–6 shows that widget provider information file (`/res/xml/bday_appwidget_provider.xml`).

Listing 13–6. *Widget View Definition for BDayWidget*

```
<!-- res/xml/bday_appwidget_provider.xml -->
<appwidget-provider xmlns:android="http://schemas.android.com/apk/res/android"
    android:minWidth="150dp"
    android:minHeight="120dp"
    android:updatePeriodMillis="4320000"
    android:initialLayout="@layout/bday_widget"
    android:configure="com.ai.android.BDayWidget.ConfigureBDayWidgetActivity"
    >
</appwidget-provider>
```

This file indicates to Android the width and height that you want in pixels. However, Android will round them to the nearest cell. Android organizes its home screen area into a matrix of cells; each cell carries 74 density-independent pixels (dp) in width and height. Android recommends that you specify your width and height in multiples of these cells minus 2 pixels (to adjust for rounding, etc.).

This file also indicates how often the `onUpdate()` needs to be called. Android highly recommends that this value be no more than a few times a day. You can put a value of 0 to indicate never to call the update. This is useful when you want to control your own updates through the Alarm Manager class.

The initial layout attribute points to the actual layout of the widget (Listing 13–7). Finally, the configure attribute points to the configuration activity class. This class needs to be fully qualified in its definition.

Let us examine the actual layout for the widget now.

Widget Layout-Related Files

From the previous section and Listing 13–6 you can see that the layout of a widget is defined in a layout file. This layout file is just like any other layout file for a view in Android.

However, to guide standardization around widgets, Android published a set of widget design guidelines. You can access these guidelines at

`http://developer.android.com/guide/practices/ui_guidelines/widget_design.html`

In addition to the guidelines, this resource has a set of view backgrounds that you can use to improve the look and feel of your widgets. In this example we took a slightly different route and used the traditional approach of view layouts with background shapes instead.

Widget Layout File

Listing 13–7 shows the layout file we used to produce the widget layout shown in Figure 13–5.

Listing 13–7. *Widget View Layout Definition for BDayWidget*

```
<!-- res/layout/bday_widget.xml -->
<?xml version="1.0" encoding="utf-8"?>
<LinearLayout xmlns:android="http://schemas.android.com/apk/res/android"
    android:orientation="vertical"
    android:layout_width="150dp"
    android:layout_height="120dp"
    android:background="@drawable/box1"
    >
<TextView
    android:id="@+id/bdw_w_name"
    android:layout_width="fill_parent"
    android:layout_height="30dp"
    android:text="Anonymous"
    android:background="@drawable/box1"
    android:gravity="center"
    />
<LinearLayout xmlns:android="http://schemas.android.com/apk/res/android"
    android:orientation="horizontal"
    android:layout_width="fill_parent"
    android:layout_height="60dp"
    >
    <TextView
        android:id="@+id/bdw_w_days"
        android:layout_width="wrap_content"
        android:layout_height="fill_parent"
        android:text="0"
        android:gravity="center"
        android:textSize="30sp"
        android:layout_weight="50"
```

```
        />
    <TextView
        android:id="@+id/bdw_w_button_buy"
        android:layout_width="wrap_content"
        android:layout_height="fill_parent"
        android:textSize="20sp"
        android:text="Buy"
        android:layout_weight="50"
        android:background="#FF6633"
        android:gravity="center"
    />
</LinearLayout>
<TextView
    android:id="@+id/bdw_w_date"
    android:layout_width="fill_parent"
    android:layout_height="30dp"
    android:text="1/1/2000"
    android:background="@drawable/box1"
    android:gravity="center"
    />
</LinearLayout>
```

This layout uses nested LinearLayout nodes to get the desired effect. Some of the controls also use a shape definition file called "box1.xml" to define the borders.

Widget Background Shape File

The code for this shape definition is shown in Listing 13–8. (This file should be in the /res/drawable subdirectory.)

Listing 13–8. *A Boundary Box Shape Definition*

```
<!-- res/drawable/box1.xml -->
<shape xmlns:android="http://schemas.android.com/apk/res/android">
    <stroke android:width="4dp" android:color="#888888" />
    <padding android:left="2dp" android:top="2dp"
            android:right="2dp" android:bottom="2dp" />
    <corners android:radius="4dp" />
</shape>
```

We have used this layout approach as it is quite useful not only for widgets but also for your other layouts. You may want to build an activity and test these layouts separately before actually testing them with your widget (at least that is what we did). It took us a number of trials to get the look and feel right. It can be quite tedious to attempt to experiment directly with widgets; every time you run the application you have to delete the widgets, uninstall, install, and then drag them back to the home page.

The files discussed so far complete the XML definitions needed by a typical widget. Let us see now how we will respond to the lifecycle events of widgets by examining the widget provider class.

Implementing a Widget Provider

As part of widget architecture, we have talked about the responsibilities of a widget provider class. A widget provider needs to implement the following broadcast receiver callback methods.

- onUpdate()
- onDelete()
- onEnable()
- onDisable()

The Java code in Listing 13–9 demonstrates the implementation of each of these methods.

Listing 13–9. *Sample Widget Provider: BDayWidgetProvider*

```
///src/<your-package>/BDayWidgetProvider.java
public class BDayWidgetProvider extends AppWidgetProvider
{
    private static final String tag = "BDayWidgetProvider";
    public void onUpdate(Context context,
                         AppWidgetManager appWidgetManager,
                         int[] appWidgetIds)  {
        final int N = appWidgetIds.length;
        for (int i=0; i<N; i++)
        {
            int appWidgetId = appWidgetIds[i];
            updateAppWidget(context, appWidgetManager, appWidgetId);
        }
    }

public void onDeleted(Context context, int[] appWidgetIds)
{
    final int N = appWidgetIds.length;
    for (int i=0; i<N; i++)
    {
        BDayWidgetModel bwm =
              BDayWidgetModel.retrieveModel(context, appWidgetIds[i]);
        bwm.removePrefs(context);
    }
}
    @Override
    public void onReceive(Context context, Intent intent) {
        final String action = intent.getAction();
        if (AppWidgetManager.ACTION_APPWIDGET_DELETED.equals(action)) {
            Bundle extras = intent.getExtras();
            final int appWidgetId = extras.getInt
                        (AppWidgetManager.EXTRA_APPWIDGET_ID,
                         AppWidgetManager.INVALID_APPWIDGET_ID);

            if (appWidgetId != AppWidgetManager.INVALID_APPWIDGET_ID) {
                this.onDeleted(context, new int[] { appWidgetId });
            }
        }
        else {
```

```
                super.onReceive(context, intent);
        }
    }

    public void onEnabled(Context context) {
        BDayWidgetModel.clearAllPreferences(context);
        PackageManager pm = context.getPackageManager();
        pm.setComponentEnabledSetting(
                new ComponentName("com.ai.android.BDayWidget",
                        ".BDayWidgetProvider"),
                PackageManager.COMPONENT_ENABLED_STATE_ENABLED,
                PackageManager.DONT_KILL_APP);
    }

    public void onDisabled(Context context) {
        BDayWidgetModel.clearAllPreferences(context);
        PackageManager pm = context.getPackageManager();
        pm.setComponentEnabledSetting(
                new ComponentName("com.ai.android.BDayWidget",
                        ".BDayWidgetProvider"),
                PackageManager.COMPONENT_ENABLED_STATE_DISABLED,
                PackageManager.DONT_KILL_APP);
    }

    private void updateAppWidget(Context context,
                        AppWidgetManager appWidgetManager,
                        int appWidgetId) {
        BDayWidgetModel bwm = BDayWidgetModel.retrieveModel(context, appWidgetId);
        if (bwm == null) {
            return;
        }
        ConfigureBDayWidgetActivity
                    .updateAppWidget(context, appWidgetManager, bwm);
    }
}
```

Refer to the "Architecture of Home Screen Widgets" section to see what needs to happen in each of these methods. For the birthday widget all these methods in turn make use of methods from the BDayWidgetModel class. Some of these methods are removePrefs(), retrievePrefs(), and clearAllPreferences().

The BDayWidgetModel class is used to encapsulate the state of our birthday widget instances. (We will cover this class in the next section.) To understand this widget provider class, all you need to know is that we are using a model class to retrieve data needed for this widget instance. This data is kept in preferences. That is why the methods are named removePrefs(), retrievePrefs(), and clearAllPreferences(). (They might make more sense if we were to substitute Data for Prefs resulting in removeData(), retrieveData(), and clearAllData().) Anyway that translation is just to make a point and you will not find methods named with Data() suffix.

As indicated, the update method is called for all the widget instances. This method must update all the widget instances. The widget instances are passed in as an array of IDs. For each id the onUpdate() method will locate the corresponding widget instance model and call the same method that is used by the configurator activity (see Listing 13–14) to display the retrieved widget model.

In the `onDelete()` method we have instantiated a `BDayWidgetModel` and then asked it to remove itself from the preferences persistence store.

In the `onEnabled()` method, as it is called only once when the first instance comes into play, we have cleared all persistence of the widget models so that we start with a clean slate. We do the same in the `onDisabled()` method, as well, so that no memory of widget instances exists.

In the `onEnabled()` method we enable the widget provider component so that it can receive broadcast messages. In the `onDisabled()` method we disable the component so that it won't look for any broadcast messages.

> **NOTE:** The `onReceive()` method is a special case. Prior to release 1.6 there was a bug where the `onDelete()` was not being called. Android provided a workaround by explicitly providing an `onReceive()` method. In release 1.6 and up you will not need this method; the same method from the base class is sufficient.

By employing the idea of widget models, the code stays clean. We'll explore the widget models and their implementation next.

Implementing Widget Models

What is a widget model? This is not an Android concept. However, if you are familiar with traditional UI programming, you will recall the concept of MVC (Model-View-Controller). Here, the model holds data needed by a view; the view is responsible for display; and the controller is responsible for mediating between the view and the model.

Although Android SDK does not mandate a specific approach, we have used this idea in order to simplify widget programming. In this approach, for every widget instance view you will have an equivalent Java class that is called a widget model. This model will have all the methods that can supply the needed data for the view instances.

In addition to supplying the data, we have created some base classes for these models so that they know how to save and retrieve themselves from a persistent store such as "shared preferences". We will go through the model class hierarchy and show you how we use shared preferences to store and retrieve data.

Interface for a Widget Model

We will start this discussion with an interface that acts as a contract for a widget model so that the widget model can declare the fields to be saved in a persistent data base. The contract also defines how to set a field when that field is retrieved from a database. The interface in addition provides an `init()` callback so that it is called when a model is newly retrieved from the database and before being passed on to a requesting client.

Listing 13–10 shows the source code for the widget contract interface.

Listing 13–10. *Saving Widget State: The Contract*

```
//filename: src/…/IWidgetModelSaveContract.java
public interface IWidgetModelSaveContract
{
    public void setValueForPref(String key, String value);
    public String getPrefname();

    //return key value pairs you want to be saved
    public Map<String,String> getPrefsToSave();

    //gets called after restore
    public void init();
}
```

This interface is designed in such a way that a derived abstract class will provide an implementation using a specific persistence store. As mentioned before, we will use the shared preferences facility of Android as the persistence store. As the name of this interface indicates, it is purely a save contract. The clients such as the BDayWidgetProvider will still rely on the most-derived class of this interface for specific methods.

> **NOTE:** Please remember that in a real world application you would structure this inheritance a bit differently: you would probably use a delegation mechanism for reuse instead of inheritance. However, this inheritance hierarchy will work well for our test case to demonstrate widget models.

Let us consider now the abstract implementation that stores the data fields of a widget as shared preferences.

Abstract Implementation of a Widget Model

All the code that is responsible for interacting with a persistent store is implemented in this APrefWidgetModel class. The Pref in this class stands for Preference because this class uses the SharedPrferences facility of Android to store the widget model data.

In addition, this class represents the idea of a basic widget. The field iid represents the "instance id" of the widget. This class always needs a constructor that takes the widget instance id as an argument to accommodate the instance id requirement.

Let's take a look at the source code of this class in Listing 13–11. Key methods of this class are highlighted.

Listing 13–11. *Implementing Widget Saves Through Shared Preferences*

```
//filename: /src/…/APrefWidgetModel.java
public abstract class APrefWidgetModel
implements IWidgetModelSaveContract
{
    private static String tag = "AWidgetModel";

    public int iid;
```

```java
        public APrefWidgetModel(int instanceId) {
            iid = instanceId;
        }
    //abstract methods
    public abstract String getPrefname();
    public abstract void init();
    public Map<String,String> getPrefsToSave(){    return null;}

      public void savePreferences(Context context){
          Map<String,String> keyValuePairs = getPrefsToSave();
          if (keyValuePairs == null){
            return;
          }
          //going to save some values
          SharedPreferences.Editor prefs =
            context.getSharedPreferences(getPrefname(), 0).edit();

          for(String key: keyValuePairs.keySet()){
            String value = keyValuePairs.get(key);
            savePref(prefs,key,value);
          }
          //finally commit the values
          prefs.commit();
      }

      private void savePref(SharedPreferences.Editor prefs,
                           String key, String value) {
          String newkey = getStoredKeyForFieldName(key);
          prefs.putString(newkey, value);
      }
      private void removePref(SharedPreferences.Editor prefs, String key) {
          String newkey = getStoredKeyForFieldName(key);
          prefs.remove(newkey);
      }
      protected String getStoredKeyForFieldName(String fieldName){
          return fieldName + "_" + iid;
      }
      public static void clearAllPreferences(Context context, String prefname) {
          SharedPreferences prefs=context.getSharedPreferences(prefname, 0);
          SharedPreferences.Editor prefsEdit = prefs.edit();
          prefsEdit.clear();
          prefsEdit.commit();
      }

      public boolean retrievePrefs(Context ctx) {
          SharedPreferences prefs = ctx.getSharedPreferences(getPrefname(), 0);
          Map<String,?> keyValuePairs = prefs.getAll();
          boolean prefFound = false;
          for (String key: keyValuePairs.keySet()){
            if (isItMyPref(key) == true){
                String value = (String)keyValuePairs.get(key);
                setValueForPref(key,value);
                prefFound = true;
            }
          }
          return prefFound;
      }
```

```
    public void removePrefs(Context context) {
        Map<String,String> keyValuePairs = getPrefsToSave();
        if (keyValuePairs == null){
            return;
        }
        //going to save some values
         SharedPreferences.Editor prefs =
            context.getSharedPreferences(getPrefname(), 0).edit();

         for(String key: keyValuePairs.keySet()){
            removePref(prefs,key);
         }
         //finally commit the values
         prefs.commit();
    }
    private boolean isItMyPref(String keyname) {
        if (keyname.indexOf("_" + iid) > 0){
            return true;
        }
        return false;
    }
    public void setValueForPref(String key, String value) {
        return;
    }
}
```

Let us see how the key methods of this class are implemented. We'll start by saving the widget model attributes in a shared preferences file:

```
public void savePreferences(Context context)
{
    Map<String,String> keyValuePairs = getPrefsToSave();
    if (keyValuePairs == null){ return; }

    //going to save some values
    SharedPreferences.Editor prefs =
    context.getSharedPreferences(getPrefname(), 0).edit();

    for(String key: keyValuePairs.keySet()){
        String value = keyValuePairs.get(key);
         savePref(prefs,key,value);
    }
    //finally commit the values
    prefs.commit();
}
```

This method starts off by asking the derived classes to return a map of key/value pairs where the keys are the attributes of the model and values are string representations of those attribute values. It will then ask the android context to get hold of a SharedPreferences file through context.getSharedPreferences(). This API needs a unique name for this package. The derived model is responsible for supplying this.

Once we get the shared preferences, by following the Android docs, we will ask to get an editable version of the shared preferences. Then we update the preferences one by one. Once that is complete we commit() the preferences so that they are persisted.

Read the API references for the SharedPreferences class and the SharedPreferences.Editor class to get more details. The resources section of this chapter has URLs pointing out where this information is. It is also worth noting that these shared preference files are XML files and can be found in the data directory of the package.

Because we have used a single file to store data for all widget instances we need a way to distinguish field names between multiple widget instances. For example, if we have two widget instances named 1 and 2, then we will need two keys to store the Name attribute so that there is a name_1 and name_2. We do this translation in the following method:

```
protected String getStoredKeyForFieldName(String fieldName) {
    return fieldName + "_" + iid;
}
```

The derived class also uses this method to examine which field to update when it is called with a setValue() method.

Implementation of a Widget Model for Birthday Widget

Ultimately the most-derived class in this hierarchy of widget models is responsible for actually maintaining all the fields needed by the view. It relies on its base classes to store and retrieve. We have designed this most-derived class in such a way that the clients that are dealing with these models directly deal with the most-derived class, as this is the class that is most pertinent to them.

For example, when a widget instance is first created by the configurator activity, the configurator activity instantiates one of these classes and fills up its values and asks to save itself.

This class, because of the needs of the view, maintains three fields:

- name: name of the person
- bday: the date the next birthday falls on
- url: the url to go to, to buy gifts

The class then has a calculated attribute called howManyDays, which represents the number of days from today to the date of the next birthday.

You will also notice that this class is responsible for fulfilling the save contract. These methods are as follows:

```
public void setValueForPref(String key, String value);
public String getPrefname();
public Map<String,String> getPrefsToSave();
```

Listing 13–12 lays out the code that orchestrates all of this.

Listing 13–12. *BDayWidgetModel: Implementing a State Model*

```java
//filename: /src/…/BDayWidgetModel.java
public class BDayWidgetModel extends APrefWidgetModel
{
    private static String tag="BDayWidgetModel";

    // Provide a unique name to store date
    private static String BDAY_WIDGET_PROVIDER_NAME=
        "com.ai.android.BDayWidget.BDayWidgetProvider";

    // Variables to paitn the widget view
    private String name = "anon";
    private static String F_NAME = "name";

    private String bday = "1/1/2001";
    private static String F_BDAY = "bday";

    private String url="http://www.google.com";

    // Constructor/gets/sets
    public BDayWidgetModel(int instanceId){
        super(instanceId);
    }
    public BDayWidgetModel(int instanceId, String inName, String inBday){
        super(instanceId);
        name=inName;
        bday=inBday;
    }
     public void init(){}
     public void setName(String inname){name=inname;}
     public void setBday(String inbday){bday=inbday;}

     public String getName(){return name;}
     public String getBday(){return bday;}

     public long howManyDays(){
        try      {
            return Utils.howfarInDays(Utils.getDate(this.bday));
        }
        catch(ParseException x){
            return 20000;
        }
     }
}

//Implement save contract

    public void setValueForPref(String key, String value){
        if (key.equals(getStoredKeyForFieldName(BDayWidgetModel.F_NAME))){
            this.name = value;
            return;
        }
        if (key.equals(getStoredKeyForFieldName(BDayWidgetModel.F_BDAY))){
            this.bday = value;
            return;
        }
    }
```

```
   public String getPrefname()    {
      return BDayWidgetModel.BDAY_WIDGET_PROVIDER_NAME;
   }

   //return key value pairs you want to be saved
   public Map getPrefsToSave()    {
      Map map
      = new HashMap();
      map.put(BDayWidgetModel.F_NAME, this.name);
      map.put(BDayWidgetModel.F_BDAY, this.bday);
      return map;
   }
   public String toString()    {
      StringBuffer sbuf = new StringBuffer();
      sbuf.append("iid:" + iid);
      sbuf.append("name:" + name);
      sbuf.append("bday:" + bday);
      return sbuf.toString();
   }
   public static void clearAllPreferences(Context ctx){
      APrefWidgetModel.clearAllPreferences(ctx,
             BDayWidgetModel.BDAY_WIDGET_PROVIDER_NAME);
   }

   public static BDayWidgetModel retrieveModel(Context ctx, int widgetId){
      BDayWidgetModel m = new BDayWidgetModel(widgetId);
      boolean found = m.retrievePrefs(ctx);
      return found ? m:null;
   }
}
```

As you can see, this class uses a couple of date-related utilities. We will show you the source code for these utilities before moving on to explaining the widget configuration activity implementation.

A Few Date-Related Utilities

Following is a utility class that is used to work with dates. It takes a date string and validates if it is a valid date. It also calculates how far a date is from today. The code is self explanatory. We have included it here for completeness.

Listing 13–13. *Date Utilities*

```
public class Utils
{
   private static String tag = "Utils";
   public static Date getDate(String dateString)
   throws ParseException {
      DateFormat a = getDateFormat();
      Date date = a.parse(dateString);
      return date;
   }
   public static String test(String sdate){
      try {
         Date d = getDate(sdate);
         DateFormat a = getDateFormat();
```

```
            String s = a.format(d);
            return s;
        }
        catch(Exception x){
            return "problem with date:" + sdate;
        }
    }
    public static DateFormat getDateFormat(){
        SimpleDateFormat df = new SimpleDateFormat("MM/dd/yyyy");
        //DateFormat df = DateFormat.getDateInstance(DateFormat.SHORT);
        df.setLenient(false);
        return df;
    }

    //valid dates: 1/1/2009, 11/11/2009,
    //invalid dates: 13/1/2009, 1/32/2009
    public static boolean validateDate(String dateString){
        try {
            SimpleDateFormat df = new SimpleDateFormat("MM/dd/yyyy");
            df.setLenient(false);
            Date date = df.parse(dateString);
            return true;
        }
        catch(ParseException x) {
            return false;
        }
    }
    public static long howfarInDays(Date date){
        Calendar cal = Calendar.getInstance();
        Date today = cal.getTime();
        long today_ms = today.getTime();
        long target_ms = date.getTime();
        return (target_ms - today_ms)/(1000 * 60 * 60 * 24);
    }
}
```

Now let's look at the implementation of the configuration activity that we have talked about already.

Implementing Widget Configuration Activity

In the "Architecture of Home Screen Widgets" section, we explained the role of configuration activity and its responsibilities. For the birthday widget example, these responsibilities are implemented in an activity class called ConfigureBDayWidgetActivity. You can see the source code for this class in Listing 13–14.

This class collects the name of the person and the next birthday. It then creates a BDayWidgetModel and stores it in shared preferences. It also has a function that knows how to transfer the BDayWidgetModel to a corresponding widget view.

Listing 13–14. *Implementing a Configurator Activity*

```
public class ConfigureBDayWidgetActivity extends Activity
{
    private static String tag = "ConfigureBDayWidgetActivity";
```

```java
    private int mAppWidgetId = AppWidgetManager.INVALID_APPWIDGET_ID;

    /** Called when the activity is first created. */
    @Override
    public void onCreate(Bundle savedInstanceState) {
        super.onCreate(savedInstanceState);
        setContentView(R.layout.edit_bday_widget);
        setupButton();

        Intent intent = getIntent();
        Bundle extras = intent.getExtras();
        if (extras != null) {
            mAppWidgetId = extras.getInt(
                    AppWidgetManager.EXTRA_APPWIDGET_ID,
                    AppWidgetManager.INVALID_APPWIDGET_ID);
        }

    }

    private void setupButton(){
        Button b = (Button)this.findViewById(R.id.bdw_button_update_bday_widget);
        b.setOnClickListener(
            new Button.OnClickListener(){
                public void onClick(View v)
                {
                    parentButtonClicked(v);
                }
            });

    }
    private void parentButtonClicked(View v){
        String name = this.getName();
        String date = this.getDate();
        if (Utils.validateDate(date) == false){
            this.setDate("wrong date:" + date);
            return;
        }
        if (this.mAppWidgetId == AppWidgetManager.INVALID_APPWIDGET_ID){
            return;
        }
        updateAppWidgetLocal(name,date);
        Intent resultValue = new Intent();
        resultValue.putExtra(AppWidgetManager.EXTRA_APPWIDGET_ID, mAppWidgetId);
        setResult(RESULT_OK, resultValue);
        finish();
    }
    private String getName(){
        EditText nameEdit = (EditText)this.findViewById(R.id.bdw_bday_name_id);
        String name = nameEdit.getText().toString();
        return name;
    }
    private String getDate(){
        EditText dateEdit = (EditText)this.findViewById(R.id.bdw_bday_date_id);
        String dateString = dateEdit.getText().toString();
        return dateString;
    }
    private void setDate(String errorDate){
```

```
        EditText dateEdit = (EditText)this.findViewById(R.id.bdw_bday_date_id);
        dateEdit.setText("error");
        dateEdit.requestFocus();
    }
    private void updateAppWidgetLocal(String name, String dob){
        BDayWidgetModel m = new BDayWidgetModel(mAppWidgetId,name,dob);
        updateAppWidget(this,AppWidgetManager.getInstance(this),m);
        m.savePreferences(this);
    }

    public static void updateAppWidget(Context context,
            AppWidgetManager appWidgetManager,
            BDayWidgetModel widgetModel)
    {
        RemoteViews views = new RemoteViews(context.getPackageName(),
                    R.layout.bday_widget);

        views.setTextViewText(R.id.bdw_w_name
            , widgetModel.getName() + ":" + widgetModel.iid);

        views.setTextViewText(R.id.bdw_w_date
            , widgetModel.getBday());

        //update the name
        views.setTextViewText(R.id.bdw_w_days,Long.toString(widgetModel.howManyDays()));

        Intent defineIntent = new Intent(Intent.ACTION_VIEW,
            Uri.parse("http://www.google.com"));
        PendingIntent pendingIntent =
            PendingIntent.getActivity(context,
                    0 /* no requestCode */,
                    defineIntent,
                    0 /* no flags */);
        views.setOnClickPendingIntent(R.id.bdw_w_button_buy, pendingIntent);

        // Tell the widget manager
        appWidgetManager.updateAppWidget(widgetModel.iid, views);
    }
}
```

If you look at the code for the function updateAppWidgetLocal(), it is the function that creates the model and stores it. It then uses the function updateAppWidget() to display it. It is worth noting how this function updateAppWidget() uses a pending intent to register a callback. The pending intent takes a primary intent such as

```
        Intent defineIntent = new Intent(Intent.ACTION_VIEW,
            Uri.parse("http://www.google.com"));
```

and creates a pending intent in order to "start an activity". In contrast, a pending intent can be used to "start a service" as well. It is also noteworthy that this function works with RemoteViews and also the AppWidgetManager. Notice the following in this function:

- Obtaining RemoteViews from the layout

- Setting text values on the RemoteViews

- Registering a pending intent through RemoteViews

- Invoking the AppWidgetManager to send the RemoteViews to the widget

- Returning at the end with a result

> **NOTE:** The static function udpateAppWidget can be called from anywhere as long as you know the widget ID. This suggests that you can update a widget from anywhere on your device and from any process, both visual and nonvisual.

It is also important that you use the following code to end the activity:

```
Intent resultValue = new Intent();
resultValue.putExtra(AppWidgetManager.EXTRA_APPWIDGET_ID, mAppWidgetId);
setResult(RESULT_OK, resultValue);
finish();
```

Notice how we are passing the widget ID back to the caller. This is how AppWidgetManager knows that the configurator activity is completed for that widget instance.

Let us conclude this discussion of widget configuration by presenting the form layout for the widget configuration activity through Listing 13–15. This view is pretty straightforward: it has a couple of text boxes and edit controls with an update button. You can also see this visually in Figure 13–4.

Listing 13–15. *Layout Definition for Configurator Activity*

```
<!-- res/layout/edit_bday_widget.xml -->
<?xml version="1.0" encoding="utf-8"?>
<LinearLayout xmlns:android="http://schemas.android.com/apk/res/android"
    android:id="@+id/root_layout_id"
    android:orientation="vertical"
    android:layout_width="fill_parent"
    android:layout_height="fill_parent"
    >
<TextView
    android:id="@+id/bdw_text1"
    android:layout_width="fill_parent"
    android:layout_height="wrap_content"
    android:text="Name:"
    />
<EditText
    android:id="@+id/bdw_bday_name_id"
    android:layout_width="fill_parent"
    android:layout_height="wrap_content"
    android:text="Anonymous"
    />
<TextView
    android:id="@+id/bdw_text2"
    android:layout_width="fill_parent"
    android:layout_height="wrap_content"
    android:text="Birthday (9/1/2001):"
    />
<EditText
    android:id="@+id/bdw_bday_date_id"
```

```
        android:layout_width="fill_parent"
        android:layout_height="wrap_content"
        android:text="ex: 10/1/2009"
    />
    <Button
        android:id="@+id/bdw_button_update_bday_widget"
        android:layout_width="fill_parent"
        android:layout_height="wrap_content"
        android:text="update"
    />
</LinearLayout>
```

This concludes our discussion on implementing a sample widget. As part of this exercise we have demonstrated the following:

- Defining a widget
- Responding to widget callbacks
- Providing a configuration activity for the widget
- Showing the use of `RemoteViews`
- Providing a framework for state management
- Designing a pleasing layout for a widget

With that, we will proceed by offering a few guidelines for widgets.

Widget Limitations and Extensions

Android home widgets appear simple when you first look at them. However, they have many nuances that need to be looked at when you start writing widgets that are a bit off the beaten path.

If your widget doesn't require any state management and doesn't need to be invoked more than a few times a day, then you have a widget that is very simple to write.

The next level of widget is one where you will need to manage the state but it is invoked infrequently, like the one we have shown here. These types of widget can benefit from a state management framework. We have shown in this chapter a bare-bones state management framework. We assume that more sophisticated ones will be available or that you could write one that is more robust and flexible.

The next level of widgets must be invoked at the levels of seconds and milliseconds. For these widgets, you will need to rig your own update calls using the Alarm Manager. You will also likely need a service to manage state frequently and not rely on a persistent framework. For example, if you were to write a widget for a `StopWatch` you would need to have a timer that counts at least every second, and you would also need to keep track of your counters, which implies state.

Another factor to consider is that the `RemoteViews` on which the widget view framework relies have no mechanism to edit directly on a widget (at least none that is documented). `RemoteViews` also put restrictions on what kinds of views and layouts can be used. You don't have direct control of the views, only control through the methods supplied by the `RemoteViews` class.

Based on the current design and intentions of widgets, Google seem to expect that the widgets mostly fall under category 1 or 2. There is lot of opportunity to expand the widget framework in coming releases.

Resources

As we have prepared material for this chapter we have found the following resources to be useful. We have presented them here in the order of their importance and utility.

- The official Android SDK documentation on app widgets is available at
  `http://developer.android.com/guide/topics/appwidgets/index.html`

- You will need to understand the `SharedPreferences` API for managing state. The API URL for this class is at
  `http://developer.android.com/reference/android/content/SharedPr`
  `eferences.html`

- Related to shared preferences is the `SharedPreferences.Editor` API. This is available at
  `http://developer.android.com/reference/android/content/SharedPr`
  `eferences.Editor.html`

- Use the following link from Android to design pleasing widget layouts:
  `http://developer.android.com/guide/practices/ui_guidelines/widg`
  `et_design.html`

- You will need to understand the `RemoteViews` API to paint and manipulate widget views. This API is available at
  `http://developer.android.com/reference/android/widget/RemoteVie`
  `ws.html`

- The widgets themselves are managed by a widget manager class. You can discover the API for this class at
  `http://developer.android.com/reference/android/appwidget/AppWid`
  `getManager.html`

- If you are in a hurry to borrow some code to get started on widgets you can use one of our co-authors' link where he gathers useful code snippets:
  `http://www.satyakomatineni.com/akc/display?url=DisplayNoteIMPUR`
  `L&reportId=3300&ownerUserId=satya`

- You can also find at the following link the research notes that were used in writing this chapter:
  `http://www.satyakomatineni.com/akc/display?url=DisplayNoteIMPUR`
  `L&reportId=3299&ownerUserId=satya`

Summary

We had fun in this chapter exploring the possibilities provided by Android Home Screen Widgets. These home screen widgets are simple ideas that could benefit user experience considerably.

We have covered the theory behind widgets and given you a working example to understand the nuances. We have elaborated the need for widget models and widget state management. We hope that the state management code we have presented can be used for your own widgets. Finally, we have touched upon the design issues and limitations of widgets.

Chapter 14

Android Search

In the last two chapters we introduced two home page–based Android innovations. In Chapter 12, we explained how live folders can reside on the home page and provide quick access to changing data in content providers. In Chapter 13, we explored home screen widgets that provide snapshots of relevant information right on the home page.

Continuing with this theme of *information at your fingertips*, in this chapter we will cover the Android search framework. The Android search framework is extensive. Although Android search appears to be available only on the home screen of the device, its influence can be extended to activities in your application.

We will start by giving a tour of the Android search facility. We will demonstrate global search, search suggestions, suggestion rewriting, and searching the Web. We will show you how to include and exclude local applications from participating in global search. In this usability tour we will also show you how suggestion providers interact with global search.

Following the usability tour, we will explore how activities in your applications integrate with the search key. We will work with activities that are not explicitly programmed for search and we will examine an activity that disables search. We will explore a topic called type-to-search that can be used by activities in applications to invoke search. We will also show you how an activity can explicitly invoke search through a menu.

The key to Android search extensibility is a concept called a *suggestion provider*. We will explore this concept and write a simple suggestion provider by inheriting from a base provider available in Android.

Often you will need to write a custom suggestions provider from scratch, however. We will discuss this next, which will take us to the core of the Android search architecture.

Finally, we will cover two advanced topics and show how you can use action keys available on a device to invoke custom actions using search suggestions. We will also describe how you can pass application-specific data to search when it is invoked. We will conclude the chapter with a set of resource URLs you can use as reference.

Android Search Experience

Search capabilities in Android extend the familiar web-based Google search bar to search both device-based local content and Internet-based external content. You can also use this search mechanism to invoke applications directly from the search bar on the home page. Android accomplishes this by providing a search framework that allows local applications to participate.

Android search protocol is simple. Android uses a single search box to let users enter search data. This is true whether you are using the global search box on the home page or searching through your own application. You use the same search box.

As the user enters text, Android takes the text and passes it to various applications that have registered to respond to search. Applications will respond by returning a collection of responses. Android aggregates these responses from multiple applications and presents them as a list of possible *suggestions*.

When the user clicks on one of these responses, Android invokes the application that presented the suggestion. In this sense, Android search is a federated search among a set of participating applications.

Although the overall idea is simple, the details of the protocol are extensive. We will cover these details through working samples later in this chapter. In this section, we will explore the search from a user's perspective.

Exploring Android Global Search

You can't miss search on Android; it is prominently displayed on the home page, as shown in Figure 14–1 (the search box is located on the top left-hand side of the screen and features the Google logo and a magnifying glass). This search box is also referred to as the *QSB* (Quick Search Box).

You can directly type into the QSB to start your search. You can also invoke the search by clicking on the Search action key. Action keys are the set of buttons that are shown in the figure on the right-hand side. The search key in the set is indicated by the magnifying glass. In this chapter, we refer to this key as the *search key*. We refer to the magnifying glass in the QSB as the *search icon*.

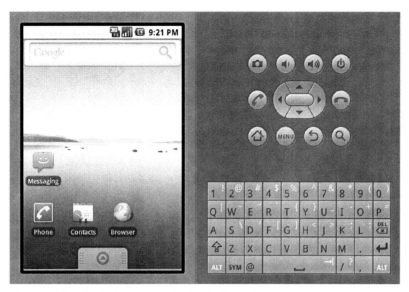

Figure 14–1. *Android home page with QSB and search key*

Much like the HOME key, you can click the search key any time, irrespective of the application that is visible. However, when an application is in focus there is an opportunity for the application to specialize the search, which we will go into later. This customized search is called a *local search.* The more general, common, and non-customized search is called a *global search.*

Let's look at how we could put the QSB to use. You give focus to QSB either by directly clicking on the QSB or by clicking on the search key. Do not type anything in the QSB yet. At this point, Android will display a screen that may look like Figure 14–2.

Figure 14–2. *QSB—zero suggestions mode*

Depending on what you have done on your device in the past, the image shown in Figure 14–2 may vary, since Android guesses what you are searching for based on past actions. This search mode, when there is no text entered in the QSB, is called *zero suggestions mode*. Depending on the search text that is entered, Android will provide a number of suggestions to the user. These suggestions show up below the QSB as a list. These are often called *search suggestions*. As you type each letter, Android will dynamically replace the search suggestions. When there is no search text, Android will display what are called *zero suggestions*. In Figure 14–2, Android has determined that Spare Parts is an application the user has used before and that it is a suitable suggestion to present even though no search text has been entered. Although we haven't typed anything in the QSB, Android also shows the "soft keyboard" in anticipation of an entry. This soft keyboard is also shown in Figure 14–2.

Let's see what happens when we start typing (Figure 14–3). When we type **a** in the QSB, Android looks for suggestions that start with "a" or are somehow related to "a". You will see that Android has already searched for local installed applications that start with "a" and also offered to search the Web.

Now we'll use the down arrow button to highlight the first suggestion. Figure 14–3 shows the view.

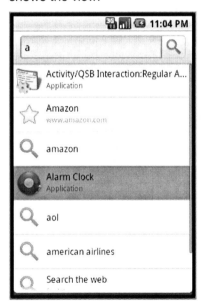

Figure 14–3. *Search suggestions*

Notice that the first suggestion is highlighted and the focus has shifted from QSB to the first highlighted suggestion. Android also expanded the screen to full screen by removing the soft keyboard, since you will not be typing when you navigate. The expanded screen size shows you more suggestions as well.

But let's look at suggestions one more time. Android takes the search text that has been typed so far and looks for what are called *suggestion providers.* Android calls each suggestion provider in an asynchronous manner to retrieve a set of matching suggestions as a set of rows. Android expects that these rows (called *search suggestions*) confirm to a set of predefined columns (*suggestion columns*). By exploring these well-known columns, Android will paint the suggestion list. When the search text changes, Android repeats the process all over again.

> **NOTE:** The set of search suggestions is also called the *suggestions cursor.* This is because the content provider representing the suggestion provider returns a `cursor` object.

At this point, if you were to navigate back to the QSB, Android would bring back the soft keyboard. Another thing to notice in Figure 14–3 is the relationship between the highlighted suggestion and the search text in the QSB. The search text remains "a" even though the highlighted suggestion is pointing to a specific item such as the Alarm Clock application. This is not always the case, however, as you can see in Figure 14–4, where we have navigated to a suggestion entry pointing to Wikipedia.

Figure 14–4. *Suggestion rewriting*

Notice how the search text "a" is replaced by a whole URL that would talk about "a" in Wikipedia. Now you can either click on the search icon in the QSB to go to Wikipedia, or simply click on the highlighted suggestion. Both will result in the same outcome.

NOTE: This process of modifying the search text based on the highlighted suggestion is called *suggestion rewriting.*

We will talk about suggestion rewriting in greater detail a bit later, but briefly, Android uses one of the columns in the suggestion cursor to look for this text. If that column exists, it will rewrite the search text, otherwise it will leave the entered search text as it is.

When a suggestion is not rewritten, there are two possibilities. If you click the search icon in the QSB it will search Google for that search text irrespective of what is highlighted. If you click the suggestion item directly it will call an activity called a *search activity* in the application that put up the suggestion to begin with. This search activity is then responsible for displaying the results of the search.

Figure 14–5 is an example of directly invoking a suggestion. In this example, the suggestion is an application called APIDemos. When you click it, Android will invoke that application directly. How this actually happens is a bit involved and we will go through later in this chapter (see the section "Implementing a Custom Suggestions Provider").

Figure 14–5. *Invoking an application through search*

Figure 14–6 shows what happens if you click the QSB search icon when your search text is "a."

Figure 14–6. *Searching the Web*

Now that you are familiar with using the QSB for your searching needs, in the next part of our tour we will explain how to enable or disable specific applications from participating in global search.

Enabling Suggestion Providers for Global Search

As we have already pointed out, applications use suggestion providers to respond to searches. Because your application has the infrastructure necessary to respond to searches doesn't mean your suggestions will show up in the QSB automatically. A user will need to allow your suggestion provider to participate. The following screens will walk you through the process of enabling or disabling available suggestion providers.

Let's start with the screen that will take us to the Android settings (Figure 14–7).

Figure 14–7. *Locating the settings application*

You can reach this view by clicking on the Show Applications arrow at the bottom of the device screen (see Figure 14–1 for the home screen). Use your arrow down key to navigate to the application that is named Settings, as shown in Figure 14–7. This will take you to the Android settings page which looks like Figure 14–8.

Figure 14–8. *Getting to the settings of the "Search" application*

Among the many Android settings, choose the Search (Manage search settings and history) option. This will bring you to the Search settings application shown in Figure 14–9.

Figure 14–9. *Search settings application*

In this activity, look for the tab called Quick Search Box and choose Searchable items (Choose what to search on the phone). This will show a list of available suggestion providers, as shown in Figure 14–10.

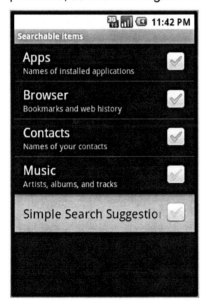

Figure 14–10. *Disabled search suggestion provider application*

Simple Search Suggestions Provider is one of the suggestion providers we have. (We will code this suggestion provider later as one of the examples.) By default, a new suggestion provider is not highlighted. Click on this line item to enable it for search. When it is enabled, your view of this page will change to the following where the item is check-marked. (See Figure 14–11.)

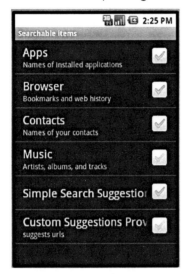

Figure 14–11. *An enabled search suggestions provider application*

QSB and Suggestions Provider Interaction

Now we'll explore how suggestions from a suggestions provider are used by QSB. Typically suggestions from your new provider show up as a "More results" icon in the suggestions list. (See Figure 14–12.)

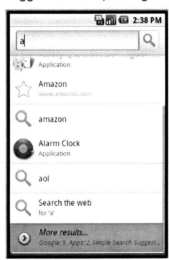

Figure 14–12. *More results from additional suggestions providers*

Notice how Android aggregates more suggestions from more applications into a summarized suggestion display item. When this is clicked, Android expands the results, as shown in Figure 14–13.

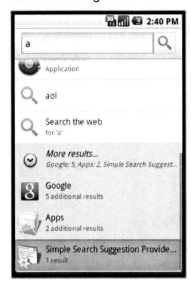

Figure 14–13. *More results from a specific suggestion provider*

Notice how suggestions from each application are still aggregated but at least broken down by each additional application. Now if you click on one of these applications, Android will take you to a specialized search with only suggestions from that application. You can see an example in Figure 14–14.

Figure 14–14. *Searching specifically through a suggestion provider*

At this point, this is no longer a global search but a local one that is dedicated to the application that provided the suggestion.

> **NOTE:** We will revisit these screens in greater detail later in the chapter in the "Implementing a Simple Suggestion Provider" and "Implementing a Custom Suggestion Provider" sections.

At this level of search (essentially local) if you click on the QSB search icon it will use the search text and take you to the search activity identified by this application, rather than search the Web for search text. And if you click on the suggestion in this local search mode it will still take you to the specialized search activity within your application.

So far, we've given you a high-level view of how search works in Android. Next we will explore these ideas further and show you how all this works through examples. We'll start by exploring how simple activities interact with search.

Activities and Search Key Interaction

What happens when a user clicks on the search key when an activity is in focus? The answer depends on the type of activity that is in focus. We will explore behavior for the following types of activities:

- A regular activity that is unaware of search
- An activity that explicitly disables search
- An activity that invokes global search explicitly
- An activity that specifies a local search

We will explore these options through a working sample containing the following files (after going through each of them we will show you the screens from this application to demonstrate the concepts).

The primary Java files are

- `RegularActivity.java`
- `NoSearchActivity.java`
- `SearchInvokerActivity.java`
- `LocalSearchEnabledActivity.java`
- `SearchActivity.java`

Each of these files, except the last one (`SearchActivity.java`), represents each type of activity that we want to examine as mentioned above. The last file, `SearchActivity.java`, is needed by the `LocalSearchEnabledActivity`. Each of these activities, including the `SearchActivity` has a simple layout with a text view in it. Each is supported by the following layout files:

- `res/layout/main.xml` (for the RegularActivity)

- res/layout/no_search_activity.xml
- res/layout/search_invoker_activity.xml
- res/layout/local_search_enabled_activity.xml
- res/layout/search_activity.xml

The following two files define these activities to Android and also search metadata for the one local search activity.

- manifest.xml
- xml/searchable.xml

The following file contains the text commentary for each of the layouts:

- res/values/strings.xml

The following two menu files provide menus needed to invoke the activities and also global search where needed:

- res/menu/main_menu.xml
- res/menu/search_invoker_menu.xml

We will now explore the interaction between activities and the search key by methodically walking through the source code of these files by each activity type. Let us start with the behavior of search key in the presence of a regular Android activity.

Behavior of Search Key on a Regular Activity

To test what happens when an activity that is unaware of search is in focus we'll show you an example of a regular activity. Listing 14–1 shows the java source code representing this `RegularActivity`.

Listing 14–1. *Regular Activity Source Code*

```java
//filename: RegularActivity.java
public class RegularActivity extends Activity
{
    private final String tag = "RegularActivity";

    @Override
     public void onCreate(Bundle savedInstanceState) {
        super.onCreate(savedInstanceState);
        setContentView(R.layout.main);
    }

    @Override
    public boolean onCreateOptionsMenu(Menu menu)
    {
        //call the parent to attach any system level menus
        super.onCreateOptionsMenu(menu);
        MenuInflater inflater = getMenuInflater(); //from activity
        inflater.inflate(R.menu.main_menu, menu);
        return true;
    }
```

```java
    @Override
    public boolean onOptionsItemSelected(MenuItem item)
    {
        appendMenuItemText(item);
        if (item.getItemId() == R.id.menu_clear) {
            this.emptyText();
            return true;
        }

        if (item.getItemId() == R.id.mid_no_search) {
            this.invokeNoSearchActivity();
            return true;
        }
        if (item.getItemId() == R.id.mid_local_search) {
            this.invokeLocalSearchActivity();
            return true;
        }
        if (item.getItemId() == R.id.mid_invoke_search) {
            this.invokeSearchInvokerActivity();
                return true;
        }
        return true;
    }

    private TextView getTextView()
    {
        return (TextView)this.findViewById(R.id.text1);
    }

    private void appendMenuItemText(MenuItem menuItem)
    {
        String title = menuItem.getTitle().toString();
        TextView tv = getTextView();
        tv.setText(tv.getText() + "\n" + title);
    }
    private void emptyText()
    {
        TextView tv = getTextView();
        tv.setText("");
    }
    private void invokeNoSearchActivity()
    {
        Intent intent = new Intent(this,NoSearchActivity.class);
        startActivity(intent);
    }
    private void invokeSearchInvokerActivity()
    {
        Intent intent = new Intent(this,SearchInvokerActivity.class);
        startActivity(intent);
    }
    private void invokeLocalSearchActivity()
    {
        Intent intent = new Intent(this,LocalSearchEnabledActivity.class);
        startActivity(intent);
    }
}
```

The goal of this activity is to play the role of a simple activity that is unaware of search. In this example, however, this activity also works as the driver to invoke other activity types that we would like to test. This is why you see some menu items being introduced to represent these additional activities. Each function that starts with invoke... has code to start the other type of activities that we want to test.

Let us take a look at the manifest file to see how this activity is defined (see Listing 14–2). You can also see the definition of other activities here, although they will not be explained until later.

Listing 14–2. *Activity/Search Key Interaction: Manifest File*

```xml
//filename: manifest.xml
<manifest xmlns:android="http://schemas.android.com/apk/res/android"
      package="com.ai.android.search.nosearch">
<application android:icon="@drawable/icon"
      android:label="Test Activity QSB Interaction">
    <activity android:name=".RegularActivity"
            android:label="Activity/QSB Interaction:Regular Activity">
            <intent-filter>
                <action android:name="android.intent.action.MAIN" />
                <category android:name="android.intent.category.LAUNCHER" />
            </intent-filter>
    </activity>

    <activity android:name=".NoSearchActivity"
            android:label="Activity/QSB Interaction::Disabled Search">
    </activity>

     <activity android:name=".SearchInvokerActivity"
              android:label="Activity/QSB Interaction::Search Invoker">
    </activity>

    <activity android:name=".LocalSearchEnabledActivity"
            android:label="Activity/QSB Interaction::Local Search">
            <meta-data android:name="android.app.default_searchable"
                android:value=".SearchActivity" />
    </activity>

    <activity android:name=".SearchActivity"
            android:label="Activity/QSB Interaction::Search Results">
            <intent-filter>
                <action android:name="android.intent.action.SEARCH" />
                <category android:name="android.intent.category.DEFAULT" />
            </intent-filter>
            <meta-data android:name="android.app.searchable"
                    android:resource="@xml/searchable" />
    </activity>
<!--
   <meta-data android:name="android.app.default_searchable"
            android:value="*" />
 -->
</application>
<uses-sdk android:minSdkVersion="4" />
</manifest>
```

Notice that the `RegularActivity` is defined as the main activity for this project and has no other characteristics that are related to search.

The layout file for this activity is shown in Listing 14–3.

Listing 14–3. *Regular Activity Layout File*

```
//filename: layout/main.xml
<?xml version="1.0" encoding="utf-8"?>
<LinearLayout xmlns:android="http://schemas.android.com/apk/res/android"
    android:orientation="vertical"
    android:layout_width="fill_parent"
    android:layout_height="fill_parent"
    >
<TextView
    android:id="@+id/text1"
    android:layout_width="fill_parent"
    android:layout_height="wrap_content"
    android:text="@string/regular_activity_prompt"
    />
</LinearLayout>
```

When this activity is displayed, it will look like the layout shown in Figure 14–15.

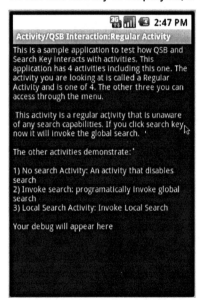

Figure 14–15. *Regular Activity/Search interaction*

Listing 14–4 shows the `strings.xml` that is responsible for the text you see on this activity's display.

Listing 14–4. *Activity/Search Key Interaction: strings.xml*

```
//filename: /res/values/strings.xml
<?xml version="1.0" encoding="utf-8"?>
<resources>
<!--
```

```
*************************************************
* regular_activity_prompt
*************************************************
-->
    <string name="regular_activity_prompt">
    This is a sample application to test how QSB and Search Key
    interacts with activities. This application has 4 activities
    including this one. The activity you are looking at is
    called a Regular Activity and is one of 4. The other three
    you can access through the menu.
    \n\n
    This activity is a regular activity that is unaware of
    any search capabilities. If you click search key now
    it will invoke the global search.
    \n
    \nThe other activities demonstrate:`
    \n\n1) No search Activity: An activity that disables search
    \n2) Invoke search: programatically invoke global search
    \n3) Local Search Activity: Invoke Local Search
    \n
    \nYour debug will appear here
    </string>

<!--
*************************************************
* no_search_activity_prompt
*************************************************
-->
    <string name="no_search_activity_prompt">
    In this activity the onSearchRequested
    returns a false. The search button
    should be ignored now.
    \n
    \nYou can click back now to access the
    previous activity and use the menus again
    to choose other activities.
    </string>
<!--
*************************************************
* search_activity_prompt
*************************************************
-->
    <string name="search_activity_prompt">
This is called a search activity or search results activity. This activity
is invoked by clicking on the search key when
some other activity uses this activity as its
search results activity.
\n\n
Typically you can retrieve the query string
from the intent to see what the query is.
    </string>
<!--
*************************************************
* search_invoker_activity_prompt
*************************************************
-->
    <string name="search_invoker_activity_prompt">
```

```
In this activity a search menu item is used
to invoke the default search. In this case
as there is no local search for this activity
specified global search is invoked. Use the
menu button to see the "search" menu. when you
click on that search menu you will see the
global search.
    </string>
<!--
**************************************************
* local_search_enabled_activity_prompt
**************************************************
-->
    <string name="local_search_enabled_activity_prompt">
This is a very simple activity that has indicated through
the manifest file that there is a an associated search
activity. With this association when the search key is
pressed the local search is presented instead of global.
\n\n
You can see the local nature of it by looking at the
label of the QSB and also the hint in the QSB. Both
came from the search metadata.
\n\n
Once you click on the query icon, it will transfer
you to the local search activity.
    </string>
<!--
**************************************************
* Other values
**************************************************
    <string name="app_name">Sample Search Application</string>
-->
    <string name="search_label">Local Search Demo</string>
    <string name="search_hint">Local Search Demo Hint</string>
</resources>
```

Like the Android manifest, this single `strings.xml` is serving all of the activities in this project. You can see that the string constant named `regular_activity` in the `strings.xml` is pointing to the text you see on the regular activity.

Listing 14–5 shows the menu XML file that is used for the regular activity. You can see this menu in action in Figure 14–16 above.

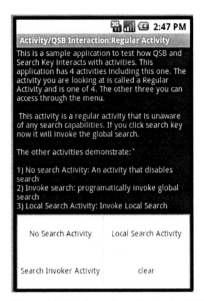

Figure 14–16. *Accessing other test activities*

Listing 14–5. *Regular Activity Menu File*

```
//filename: /res/menu/main_menu.xml
<menu xmlns:android="http://schemas.android.com/apk/res/android">
    <!-- This group uses the default category. -->
    <group android:id="@+id/menuGroup_Main">
        <item android:id="@+id/mid_no_search"
            android:title="No Search Activity" />

        <item android:id="@+id/mid_local_search"
            android:title="Local Search Activity" />

        <item android:id="@+id/mid_invoke_search"
            android:title="Search Invoker Activity" />

        <item android:id="@+id/menu_clear"
            android:title="clear" />
    </group>
</menu>
```

With these files in place you should be able to compile and test this activity (or you can wait until we have looked at all the activities for this project). If you would like to compile now, you will need to comment out the rest of the activities from the manifest file (you may not have source code for them at the moment).

Now, when you have this activity running (as in Figure 14–15) click the search key (see Figure 14–1 to locate the search key). The search key will bring the global search in response. This global search will look just like the global search in Figure 14–2.

TIP: When there is an activity that is unaware of search, clicking on the search key invokes the global search.

Behavior of an Activity That Disables Search

As described in the previous section, if an activity does nothing with regards to search, then search key will invoke the global search. However, an activity has an option to disable the search by returning false from the onSearchRequested() callback method of the activity class. Listing 14–6 shows the source code for such an activity.

Listing 14–6. *Activity Disabling Search*

```
//filename: NoSearchActivity.java
public class NoSearchActivity extends Activity
{
    @Override
    protected void onCreate(Bundle savedInstanceState) {
        super.onCreate(savedInstanceState);
        setContentView(R.layout.no_search_activity);
        return;
    }
    @Override
    public boolean onSearchRequested()
    {
    return false;
    }
}
```

Listing 14–7 shows the corresponding layout file for this activity.

Listing 14–7. *NoSearchActivity XML File*

```
//filename: layout/no_search_activity.xml
<?xml version="1.0" encoding="utf-8"?>
<LinearLayout xmlns:android="http://schemas.android.com/apk/res/android"
    android:orientation="vertical"
    android:layout_width="fill_parent"
    android:layout_height="fill_parent"
    >
<TextView
    android:id="@+id/text1"
    android:layout_width="fill_parent"
    android:layout_height="wrap_content"
    android:text="@string/no_search_activity_prompt"
    />
</LinearLayout>
```

You can invoke this NoSearchActivity by clicking the menu item No Search Activity in Figure 14–16. When displayed, this activity will look like that shown in Figure 14–17. Now if you press the search key (see Figure 14–1 for reference) it will not have any impact and you will not see anything happen. It is as if the search key had not been pressed.

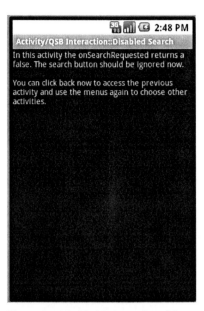

Figure 14–17. *Disabled search activity*

TIP: When there is an activity that disables search, clicking the search key disables invocation of search including global search.

Invoking Search Through a Menu

In addition to being able to respond to the search key, an activity can also choose to explicitly invoke search through a search menu item. Listing 14–8 shows the source code for an example activity that does this.

Listing 14–8. *SearchInvokerActivity*

```
//filename: SearchInvokerActivity.java
public class SearchInvokerActivity extends Activity
{
    @Override
    public void onCreate(Bundle savedInstanceState) {
        super.onCreate(savedInstanceState);
        setContentView(R.layout.search_invoker_activity);
    }

    @Override
    public boolean onCreateOptionsMenu(Menu menu)
    {
        super.onCreateOptionsMenu(menu);
        MenuInflater inflater = getMenuInflater();
        inflater.inflate(R.menu.search_invoker_menu, menu);
        return true;
    }
```

```
    @Override
    public boolean onOptionsItemSelected(MenuItem item)
    {
        appendMenuItemText(item);
        if (item.getItemId() == R.id.mid_si_clear)
        {
            this.emptyText();
            return true;
        }
        if (item.getItemId() == R.id.mid_si_search)
        {
            this.invokeSearch();
            return true;
        }
        return true;
    }

    private TextView getTextView()
    {
        return (TextView)this.findViewById(R.id.text1);
    }

    private void appendMenuItemText(MenuItem menuItem)
    {
        String title = menuItem.getTitle().toString();
        TextView tv = getTextView();
        tv.setText(tv.getText() + "\n" + title);
    }
    private void emptyText()
    {
        TextView tv = getTextView();
        tv.setText("");
    }
    private void invokeSearch()
    {
        this.onSearchRequested();
    }
}
```

Key portions of source code are highlighted in bold. Notice how a menu ID
(R.id.mid_si_search) is calling the function invokeSearch which will in turn call the
onSearchRequested(). This method, onSearchRequested(), invokes the search.

Listing 14–9 shows the layout for this activity.

Listing 14–9. *SearchInvokerActivity XML*

```
//filename: layout/search_invoker_activity.xml
<?xml version="1.0" encoding="utf-8"?>
<LinearLayout xmlns:android="http://schemas.android.com/apk/res/android"
    android:orientation="vertical"
    android:layout_width="fill_parent"
    android:layout_height="fill_parent"
    >
<TextView
    android:id="@+id/text1"
    android:layout_width="fill_parent"
```

```
    android:layout_height="wrap_content"
    android:text="@string/search_invoker_activity_prompt"
    />
</LinearLayout>
```

Listing 14–10 shows the corresponding menu XML for this activity.

Listing 14–10. *SearchInvokerActivity Menu XML*

```
//filename:menu/search_invoker_menu.xml
<menu xmlns:android="http://schemas.android.com/apk/res/android">
    <!-- This group uses the default category. -->
    <group android:id="@+id/menuGroup_Main">
        <item android:id="@+id/mid_si_search"
            android:title="Search" />

        <item android:id="@+id/mid_si_clear"
            android:title="clear" />
    </group>
</menu>
```

With the layout and menu in place, Figure 14–18 shows how this activity looks when invoked from the main menu on the RegularActivity (see Figure 14–16 for the menu item that invokes this).

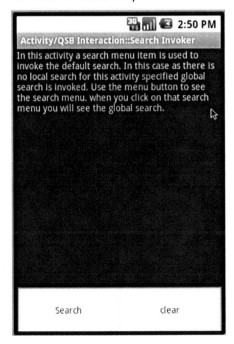

Figure 14–18. *Search invoker activity*

From this activity, if you click the Search menu option it will invoke the global search as shown in Figure 14–2.

Understanding Local Search and Related Activities

Now let's look at the circumstances under which the search key will *not* invoke a global search but instead invokes a local search. To do this, we have to understand local search a bit better.

A local search has three components. The first component is a search box that is very similar to the global search QSB. A QSB, whether local or global, provides text control to enter text and then click a search icon. A local QSB is typically invoked instead of the global one when an activity declares in the manifest file that it wants a local search. You can distinguish the invoked local QSB from the global one by looking at the heading of the QSB (see the title of Figure 14–14) and the hint (the text inside the search box) in the QSB. These two values, as you will see, come from a search metadata XML file.

The second component of local search is an activity that can receive a search string from the local QSB and show a set of results or any output that is related to the search text. Often this activity is called the search activity or search results activity.

The optional third component of local search is an activity that is allowed to invoke the search results activity just described (the second component). This invoking activity is often called search invoker or search invoking activity. This search invoker activity is optional because it is possible to have the global search directly invoke the local search activity (the second component) through a suggestion.

You can see these three components and how they interact with each other in context in Figure 14–19.

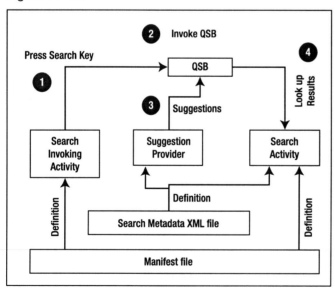

Figure 14–19. *Local search activity interaction*

In Figure 14–19 important interactions are shown as annotated (circled numbers) arrows. This figure is explained in detail below.

- A `SearchActivity` needs to be defined in the manifest file as an activity that is capable of receiving search requests. `SearchActivity` also uses a mandatory XML file to declare how the local QSB should be presented (such as with a title, hint, etc.) and if there is an associated suggestion provider. (See Listing 14–12). In Figure 14–19 you can see this as a couple of "Definition" lines that go between the `SearchActivity` and the two XML files (manifest file and the search metadata file).

- Once the `SearchActivity` is defined in the manifest file (see Listing 14–2), the `Search InvokingActivity` indicates in the manifest file that it is associated with the `SearchActivity`.

- With the definitions for both activities in place, when the `SearchInvokingActivity` is in focus, the press of the search key will invoke the local QSB. You can see this in Figure 14–19 through the circles numbered 1 and 2. You can tell that the invoked QSB is a local QSB by looking at the caption and hint of the QSB. These two values are set up in the mandatory search metadata XML definition. Once QSB is invoked through the search key, you will be able to type query text in the QSB. This local QSB, similar to the global QSB, is capable of suggestions. You can see this in Figure 14–19 in circle 3.

- Once the query text is entered and the search icon is clicked, the local QSB will transfer the search to the `SearchActivity` which is responsible for doing something with it, such as displaying a set of results. This is shown in Figure 14–19, circle 4.

We will examine each of these interactions by looking at the source code. We will start with Listing 14–11, the source code for `SearchActivity`, (which, again, is responsible for receiving the query and displaying search results).

Listing 14–11. *SearchActivity*

```
//filename: SearchActivity.java
public class SearchActivity extends Activity
{
    @Override
    protected void onCreate(Bundle savedInstanceState) {
        super.onCreate(savedInstanceState);
        setContentView(R.layout.search_activity);
        return;
    }
}
```

Notice how simple this search activity is. Later you'll see how queries are retrieved by this activity. For now we will show how this activity ends up being invoked. Here is how it is defined as a search activity responsible for results in the manifest file (see Listing 14–2):

```
<activity android:name=".SearchActivity"
            android:label="Activity/QSB Interaction::Search Results">
    <intent-filter>
```

```
        <action android:name="android.intent.action.SEARCH" />
        <category android:name="android.intent.category.DEFAULT" />
    </intent-filter>
    <meta-data android:name="android.app.searchable"
                    android:resource="@xml/searchable" />
</activity>
```

> **NOTE:** There are two things that need to be specified for a search activity. The activity needs to indicate that it can respond to SEARCH actions. It also needs to specify an xml file that describes the metadata that is required to interact with this search activity.

Listing 14–12 shows the search metadata XML file for this SearchActivity.

Listing 14–12. *Searchable.xml: Search Metadata*

```
///res/xml/searchable.xml
<searchable xmlns:android="http://schemas.android.com/apk/res/android"
    android:label="@string/search_label"
    android:hint="@string/search_hint"
    android:searchMode="showSearchLabelAsBadge"
/>
```

> **TIP:** The various options available in this XML are available at
> http://developer.android.com/reference/android/app/SearchManager.html.

We will cover more of these attributes later in the chapter. For now, the attribute android:label is used to label the search box. The attribute android:hint is used to place the text in the search box, similar to what's shown in Figure 14–14 or Figure 14–21.

Now let's examine how any activity can specify this SearchActivity as its search targetby looking at an activity that intends to use the SearchActivity as its target. We will call this the LocalSearchEnabledActivity. Listing 14–13 shows the source code for this activity.

Listing 14–13. *LocalSearchEnabledActivity*

```
//filename: LocalSearchEnabledActivity.java
public class LocalSearchEnabledActivity extends Activity
{
    @Override
    protected void onCreate(Bundle savedInstanceState) {
        super.onCreate(savedInstanceState);
        setContentView(R.layout.local_search_enabled_activity);
        return;
    }
}
```

Listing 14–14 shows the corresponding layout xml file for this activity.

Listing 14–14. *LocalSearchEnabledActivity Layout File*

```
//filename:local_search_enabled_activity
<?xml version="1.0" encoding="utf-8"?>
```

```
<LinearLayout xmlns:android="http://schemas.android.com/apk/res/android"
    android:orientation="vertical"
    android:layout_width="fill_parent"
    android:layout_height="fill_parent"
    >
<TextView
    android:id="@+id/text1"
    android:layout_width="fill_parent"
    android:layout_height="wrap_content"
    android:text="@string/local_search_enabled_activity_prompt"
    />
</LinearLayout>
```

You can invoke this activity from the main `RegularActivity` by clicking the Local Search Activity menu item (see Figure 14–16 to locate the menus). When invoked, this activity looks like Figure 14–20.

Figure 14–20. *Local search-enabled activity*

With this activity in focus, if you click on the device search key (originally shown in Figure 14–1), it will invoke a local search box (local QSB), as shown in Figure 14–21.

Figure 14–21. *Local Search QSB*

Notice the label of this search box and the hint of this search box. See how they differ from the global search (see Figure 14–2). The label and hint came from the search metadata specified for the SearchActivity (see Listing 14–12). Now if you type some text in the QSB and click the search icon you will end up invoking the SearchActivity (see Listing 14–11). Here is what this SearchActivity looks like (Figure 14–22).

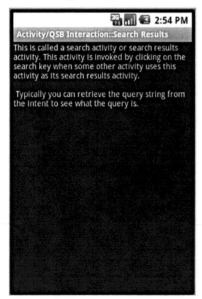

Figure 14–22. *Search results in response to the local search QSB*

Although this activity does not make use of any query search text to pull up results, it demonstrates how a search activity is defined and how it gets invoked. Later in the chapter we'll show how this SearchActivity makes use of search queries and the various search-related actions it needs to respond to.

Enabling Type-to-Search

So far we have explored a few ways of invoking search, both local and global. We have showed you how to search using QSB on the home page of the device. We have told you how to invoke global search from any activity as long as the activity doesn't prevent such a search. This is done through the search key. We have also showed you how an activity can specify local search. We will close this topic by showing one more way of invoking search called type-to-search.

When you are looking at an activity such as the RegularActivity shown in Figure 14–15 or the LocalSearchActivity in Figure 14–20, there is a way to invoke a search by typing a random letter (such as "t", for example). This mode is called *type-to-search* because any key you type that is not handled by the activity will invoke search.

The intention of type-to-search is simple. On any given activity you can tell Android that any key press can invoke search—except for the keys that the activity explicitly handles. For example, if an activity handles "x" and "y" but doesn't care about any other keys, the activity can choose to invoke the search for any other keys such as "z" or "a". This mode is useful for an activity that is already displaying search results. Such an activity can interpret a key press as a cue to start search again.

Here is the code you will use in your onCreate() method of the activity to enable this behavior (the first is used to invoke the global search and the second is used to invoke the local search):

```
this.setDefaultKeyMode(Activity.DEFAULT_KEYS_SEARCH_GLOBAL);
```

or

```
this.setDefaultKeyMode(Activity.DEFAULT_KEYS_SEARCH_LOCAL);
```

This concludes our discussion of the various ways in which Android search interacts with activities. Through a number of examples, we have shown a few ways in which local and global search can be invoked, and we have briefly touched upon search activities and suggestion providers.

Next, we will continue our exploration by implementing a simple suggestion provider application.

Implementing a Simple Suggestion Provider

We have already indicated how suggestion providers are used to allow applications to participate in global search. Now we will demonstrate it.

We will start by explaining how a simple suggestion provider application is expected to work. We will give you the list of files that are used in the implementation, which should give you a general idea of the application and what is involved in implementing it.

When you are writing a suggestion provider there are two main components. One is a suggestion provider that is responsible for returning suggestions to Android search. The second is a search activity that takes a query or a suggestion and turns it into search results.We will describe the responsibilities of each of these components and show how they are implemented through source code.

We will also show you how you can create a simple suggestion provider using only a few lines by deriving from a prefabricated provider called SearchRecentSuggestionsProvider, which is available in the Android SDK. We will then show you how our simple suggestion provider is defined in the manifest file. Finally, we will show you what methods of the SearchRecentSuggestionsProvider are used.

We will give you the full source code for the search activity and show how it is defined in the manifest file. We will also show you how this search activity stores recent suggestions so that they are available to the simple suggestion provider.

We will also talk about the search metadata that ties the search activity and the suggestion provider together, and we'll include in the application a simple search invoker activity that facilitates a local mechanism to invoke the search.

We will conclude this discussion with a tour of the application. This will prepare us for next section, in which we will implement a custom suggestions provider that does not use the SearchRecentSuggestionsProvider, from scratch.

But first, let us first plan our simple suggestions provider application.

Planning the Simple Suggestions Provider

Because we are planning on inheriting from the SearchRecentSuggestionsProvider, the functionality of the resulting suggestion provider is pretty fixed.

The SearchRecentSuggestionsProvider allows you to save the queries as they are presented to the search activity from the QSB. Once they are saved, they will be prompted back to the QSB through the suggestion provider.

In the derived suggestion provider we simply initialize the base provider. There is nothing else we need to do there. We will also go with a minimal search activity that is just a text view, to show that the search activity has been invoked. Inside the search activity we will show you the methods that are used to save the queries.

Once the application is complete, our goal is to see the previous queries prompted as suggestions in the QSB.

Now we'll show you the list of files that are used in the implementation of this project.

Simple Suggestions Provider Implementation Files

As indicated, the two primary files that take part in the implementation of a suggestion provider application are SearchActivity.java and SimpleSuggestionProvider.java. However, you will need a number of supporting files to complete the project. We will list all of these files and briefly mention what each one does. We include the source code for all of the files as we explain the solution.

Let's start with java files first:

- ▨ SimpleSuggestionProvider.java: Implements the suggestion provider that we are talking about

- ▨ SearchActivity.java: A mandatory file to work with the suggestion provider

- ▨ SimpleMainActivity.java: An optional activity to demonstrate local suggestions

Here are the corresponding layout files:

- ▨ main.xml: A layout file for the SimpleMainActivity

- ▨ search_activity.xml: A layout file for the SearchActivity

Here is the search metadata file.

- ▨ /xml/searchable.xml: This file is where the search activity is connected to the suggestion provider.

Of course we need the manifest file as well:

- ▨ manifest.xml: This is where all application components are defined to Android.

Let us explore these starting with the implementation of the SimpleSuggestionProvider class.

Implementing the SimpleSuggestionProvider class

In this simple suggestion provider project, the SimpleSuggestionProvider class acts as a suggestion provider by inheriting from the SearchRecentSuggestionsProvider. First let's look at the responsibilities of this simple suggestion provider.

Responsibilities of a Simple Suggestion Provider

Because our simple suggestion provider is derived from the
SearchRecentSuggestionsProvider most of the responsibilities are handled by the base
class. Our derived suggestion provider needs to initialize the base class with an
authority that is unique. This is because Android search invokes a suggestion provider
based on a unique content provider URI.

Once the suggestion provider is available it needs to be configured in the manifest file as
a regular content provider with an authority and also as a suggestion provider in the
search metadata XML file. In the search metadata the suggestion provider also gets tied
to a search activity.

Let's examine the source code of this provider and see how these responsibilities are met.

Complete Source Code of SimpleSuggestionProvider

Again, because we are inheriting from the SearchRecentSuggestionsProvider, the source
code for the simple suggestions provider is going to be quite simple, as shown in Listing
14–15.

Listing 14–15. *SimpleSuggestionProvider.java*

```
//SimpleSuggestionProvider.java
public class SimpleSuggestionProvider
extends SearchRecentSuggestionsProvider {

    final static String AUTHORITY =
      "com.ai.android.search.simplesp.SimpleSuggestionProvider";
    final static int MODE = DATABASE_MODE_QUERIES;

    public SimpleSuggestionProvider() {
        super();
        setupSuggestions(AUTHORITY, MODE);
    }
}
```

There are three things that are significant in this implementation. The first one is the
authority string. This is the same content provider identifying authority that we discussed
in Chapter 3. This authority string needs to be unique and the same as its definition in
the manifest file. (See the manifest file in Listing 14–16.)

The code also initializes the parent class by calling the setupSuggestions() method.
This method takes two arguments. One is the authority and the second is what is called
a database mode.

Let us talk about this database mode.

Understanding SearchRecentSuggestionsProvider Database Modes

The key functionality of Android-supplied SearchRecentSuggestionsProvider is to store
queries in the database so that they are available as future suggestions. A suggestion

has two text strings with it (see Figure 14–3). Only the first string is mandatory. As you use `SearchRecentSuggestionsProvider` to save these strings you need to tell it whether you want to store one string or two strings.

To accommodate this, there are two modes supported by this base suggestion provider. Both modes use the following prefix:

```
DATABASE_MODE_ ...
```

Here are both modes:

```
DATABASE_MODE_QUERIES
DATABASE_MODE_2LINES
```

The first mode indicates that just a single query string needs to be stored and replayed when needed. The second mode indicates that there are two strings that the suggestion provider can save. One string is the query and the other is the description line that shows up in the suggestion display item.

The `SearchActivity` is responsible for saving these when it is called to respond to queries. The `SearchActivity` would call the following method to store these items (we will cover this in greater detail when we discuss the search activity):

```
public void saveRecentQuery (String queryString, String line2);
```

The `queryString` is the string as typed by the user. This string will be displayed as the suggestion, and if the user clicks on the suggestion, this string will be sent to your searchable activity (as a new search query).

Here is what the Android docs say about the `line2` argument:

> *If you have configured your recent suggestions provider with DATABASE_MODE_2LINES, you can pass a second line of text here. It will be shown in a smaller font, below the primary suggestion. When typing, matches in either line of text will be displayed in the list. If you did not configure two-line mode, or if a given suggestion does not have any additional text to display, you can pass null here.*

TIP: You can learn more about this prefabricated suggestions provider at `http://developer.android.com/reference/android/provider/SearchRecentSugg estions.html`.

Now that we have the source code for our simple suggestions provider let us see how we register this provider in the manifest file.

Declaring the Suggestion Provider in the Manifest File

Because our `SimpleSuggestionProvider` is essentially a content provider it is registered in the manifest file like any other content provider. Listing 14–16 below shows the manifest file. Note that key sections of this file are highlighted.

Listing 14–16. *SimpleSuggestionProvider Manifest File*

```
//filename: manifest.xml
<?xml version="1.0" encoding="utf-8"?>
<manifest xmlns:android="http://schemas.android.com/apk/res/android"
      package="com.ai.android.search.simplesp"
      android:versionCode="1"
      android:versionName="1.0.0">
   <application android:icon="@drawable/icon"
             android:label="Simple Search Suggestion Provider:SSSP">
      <activity android:name=".SimpleMainActivity"
                android:label="SSSP:Simple Main Activity">
         <intent-filter>
            <action android:name="android.intent.action.MAIN" />
            <category android:name="android.intent.category.LAUNCHER" />
         </intent-filter>
      </activity>

<!--
*************************************************************
* Search related code: search activity
*************************************************************
  -->
   <activity android:name=".SearchActivity"
                android:label="SSSP: Search Activity"
                android:launchMode="singleTop">
      <intent-filter>
         <action android:name="android.intent.action.SEARCH" />
         <category android:name="android.intent.category.DEFAULT" />
      </intent-filter>
      <meta-data android:name="android.app.searchable"
                                 android:resource="@xml/searchable" />
   </activity>

   <meta-data android:name="android.app.default_searchable"
                           android:value=".SearchActivity" />

   <provider android:name=".SimpleSuggestionProvider"
         android:authorities
            ="com.ai.android.search.simplesp.SimpleSuggestionProvider" />
</application>
   <uses-sdk android:minSdkVersion="4" />
</manifest>
```

Notice how the authority of the simple suggestions provider matches in the source code (Listing 14–15) and the manifest files (Listing 14–16). In both cases the value of this authority is

`com.ai.android.search.simplesp.SimpleSuggestionProvider`

We will talk about the other sections of this manifest file when we cover the other aspects of this Simple Suggestions Provider.

Understanding Simple Suggestions Provider Search Activity

As we have already pointed out, the implementation of a suggestion provider has two parts: the suggestion provider itself and a search activity that can respond to the suggestions produced by a suggestion provider. We have already described the suggestion provider implementation. We will cover the corresponding Search activity next.

We will follow a track similar to the previous section. We will start by discussing the general responsibilities of a search activity. We will then present the complete source code to give you a bird's-eye view of how those responsibilities are fulfilled.

Responsibilities of a Simple Search Activity

A search activity is invoked by Android search with a query string. A search activity in turn needs to read this query string from the intent and do what is necessary.

Because a search activity is an activity, it is possible that it can be invoked by other intents and other actions. For this reason, it is a good practice to check the intent action that invoked it. In our case, when the Android search invokes this activity this action is ACTION_SEARCH.

Under some circumstances a search activity can invoke itself. When this is likely to happen, you should define the search activity launch mode as a `singleTop`. The activity will also need to deal with firing of `onNewIntent()`. We will cover this as well in the section "Understanding onCreate and onNewIntent."

When it comes to doing something with the query string, we will just log it. Once the query is logged we will need to save it in the `SearchRecentSuggestionsProvider` so that it is available as a suggestion for future searches.

Now let us look at the source code of the search activity class.

Complete Source Code of a Search Activity

Listing 14–17 presents the source code for this `SearchActivity` class.

Listing 14–17. *SimpleSuggestionProvider Search Activity*

```
//filename: SearchActivity.java
public class SearchActivity extends Activity
{
    private final static String tag ="SearchActivity";
    @Override
    protected void onCreate(Bundle savedInstanceState) {
        super.onCreate(savedInstanceState);
```

```
        Log.d(tag,"I am being created");
        //otherwise do this
        setContentView(R.layout.layout_test_search_activity);
    //this.setDefaultKeyMode(Activity.DEFAULT_KEYS_SEARCH_GLOBAL);
        this.setDefaultKeyMode(Activity.DEFAULT_KEYS_SEARCH_LOCAL);

        // get and process search query here
        final Intent queryIntent = getIntent();
        final String queryAction = queryIntent.getAction();
        if (Intent.ACTION_SEARCH.equals(queryAction))
        {
            Log.d(tag,"new intent for search");
            this.doSearchQuery(queryIntent);
        }
        else {
            Log.d(tag,"new intent NOT for search");
        }
        return;
    }

    @Override
    public void onNewIntent(final Intent newIntent)
    {
        super.onNewIntent(newIntent);
        Log.d(tag,"new intent calling me");

        // get and process search query here
        final Intent queryIntent = getIntent();
        final String queryAction = queryIntent.getAction();
        if (Intent.ACTION_SEARCH.equals(queryAction))
        {
            this.doSearchQuery(queryIntent);
            Log.d(tag,"new intent for search");
        }
        else {
            Log.d(tag,"new intent NOT for search");
        }
    }
    private void doSearchQuery(final Intent queryIntent)
    {
        final String queryString =
            queryIntent.getStringExtra(SearchManager.QUERY);

        // Record the query string in the recent queries suggestions provider.
        SearchRecentSuggestions suggestions = new SearchRecentSuggestions(this,
            SimpleSuggestionProvider.AUTHORITY,
            SimpleSuggestionProvider.MODE);
        suggestions.saveRecentQuery(queryString, null);
    }
}
```

Let us examine now how the search activity checks the action and retrieves the query string.

Checking the Action and Retrieving the Query

The search activity code checks for the invoking action by looking at the invoking intent and comparing it to the `constant intent.ACTION_SEARCH`. If the action matches then it invokes the `doSearchQuery()` function.

In the `doSearchQuery()` function, search activity retrieves the query string using an intent extra. Here is the code:

```
final String queryString =
    queryIntent.getStringExtra(SearchManager.QUERY);
```

Notice that intent extra is defined as `SearchManager.QUERY`. As you go through this chapter you will see a number of these extras defined in the `SearchManager` API reference. (We have included a URL to this reference in the "Resources" section.)

Understanding onCreate() and onNewIntent()

A search activity is kicked off by Android when a user enters text into a search box and clicks either a suggestion or the search icon. This creates the search activity and calls its `onCreate()` method. The intent that is passed to this `onCreate()` will have the action set to `ACTION_SEARCH`.

There are times when the activity is not created but instead passed the new search criteria through the `onNewIntent()` method. How does this happen? The callback `onNewIntent()` is closely related to the launching mode of an activity. If you look at Listing 14–16 you will notice that the search activity is set up as a `singleTop` in the manifest file.

When an activity is set up as a `singleTop`, it instructs Android not to create a new activity when that activity is already on top of the stack. In that case Android calls `onNewIntent()` instead of `onCreate()`. This is why in the activity source in Listing 14–17 we have two places where we examine the intent.

How to Test for onNewIntent()

Once you have `onNewIntent()` implemented you will start noticing that it doesn't get invoked in the normal flow of things. This begs a question. When will the search activity be on top of the stack? This usually doesn't happen.

Here is why it doesn't happen. Say a search invoker Activity A invokes search and that causes a search Activity B to come up. Activity B then displays the results and the user uses a back button to go back, at which time the Activity B, which is our search activity, is no longer on top of the stack, Activity A is. Or the user may click home key and use the global search on the home screen in which case home activity is the activity on top.

One way the search activity can be on top is this: say Activity A results in Activity B due to search. If Activity B defines a type-to-search then when you are focused on Activity B a search will invoke Activity B again with the new criteria. Listing 14–17 shows how we have set up the type-to-search to demonstrate. Here is the code again:

```
this.setDefaultKeyMode(Activity.DEFAULT_KEYS_SEARCH_LOCAL);
```

Saving the Query Using SearchRecentSuggestionsProvider

We have talked about how the search activity needs to save the queries that it has encountered so that they can be played back as suggestions. Here is the code segment that does this:

```
final String queryString =
    queryIntent.getStringExtra(SearchManager.QUERY);

// Record the query string in the recent queries suggestions provider.
SearchRecentSuggestions suggestions = new SearchRecentSuggestions(this,
        SimpleSuggestionProvider.AUTHORITY,
        SimpleSuggestionProvider.MODE);
suggestions.saveRecentQuery(queryString, null);
```

From this code you will see that, as indicated earlier, Android passes the query information as EXTRA through the intent.

Once you have the query available you can ask the underlying SearchRecentSuggestionsProvider to save it by instantiating a new suggestions object and asking it to save. Because we have used the single line mode, the second argument to the saveRecentQuery is null.

Now we'll look at the search metadata definition where we tie the search activity with the search suggestion provider.

Search Metadata

The definition of Search in Android starts with the search activity. You first define this in the manifest file. As part of this definition you will tell Android where to find the search metadata XML file. (See Listing 14–16).

Listing 14–18 shows the search metadata file for our application.

Listing 14–18. *SimpleSuggestionProvider Search Metadata*

```
//filename: searchable.xml
<searchable xmlns:android="http://schemas.android.com/apk/res/android"
    android:label="@string/search_label"
    android:hint="@string/search_hint"
    android:searchMode="showSearchLabelAsBadge"

    android:includeInGlobalSearch="true"
    android:searchSuggestAuthority=
         "com.ai.android.search.simplesp.SimpleSuggestionProvider"
    android:searchSuggestSelection=" ? "
/>
```

There are three attributes in this listing that are relevant to a suggestion provider. Let us work through them one by one.

The first attribute includeInGlobalSearch tells Android to use this suggestion provider as one of the sources in global QSB.

The second attribute, searchSuggestAuthority, points to the authority of the suggestion provider as defined in the manifest file (see Listing 14–16).

The third attribute, searchSuggestSelection, is always ? if you are deriving from the recent search suggestions provider. This string is passed to the suggestion provider as the selection string of the content provider query method. Typically, this would represent the where clause that goes into a select statement. Android then passes the query as the first entry in the select arguments array of the content provider query method. Because the code to respond to these nuances is hidden in the recent search suggestions provider, we won't be able to show you how these arguments are used in the query method of the content provider. We will go into this in more detail in the next section..

This concludes our discussion of writing a search activity for a simple suggestion provider. Now that you have seen the search suggestion provider and the search activity, let us talk about a search invoker activity that we will use as the main entry point for this application and that allows us to test local search.

Search Invoker Activity

Although we don't need this activity for completing the suggestion provider, this activity will let us invoke the local search when it is in focus. Listing 14–19 shows the source code for this search invoker activity.

Listing 14–19. *SimpleSuggestionProvider: Main Activity*

```
public class SimpleMainActivity extends Activity
{
    @Override
    public void onCreate(Bundle savedInstanceState) {
        super.onCreate(savedInstanceState);
        setContentView(R.layout.main);
    }
}
```

If you see the activity definition for this activity in the manifest file (Listing 14–16) you will notice that it doesn't explicitly say that it uses the SearchActivity as its default local search. This is because we have used that specification at the application level as opposed to at the activity level by introducing the following lines in the manifest file:

```
<meta-data android:name="android.app.default_searchable"
                        android:value=".SearchActivity" />
```

Notice how these lines are outside any activity in the manifest file (Listing 14–16). This specification tells Android that all activities in this application use SearchActivity as their default activity, including SearchActivity itself. You can take advantage of this later fact to invoke onNewIntent() by clicking on the search key when you are examining the results on the SearchActivity. This won't be the case if you were to define the default search only for the search invoker activity and not the whole application.

Here is the simple layout we are using for this main search invoker activity:

```
//filename: /res/layout/main.xml
<?xml version="1.0" encoding="utf-8"?>
```

```
<LinearLayout xmlns:android="http://schemas.android.com/apk/res/android"
    android:orientation="vertical"
    android:layout_width="fill_parent"
    android:layout_height="fill_parent"
    >
<TextView
    android:id="@+id/text1"
    android:layout_width="fill_parent"
    android:layout_height="wrap_content"
    android:text="@string/main_activity_text"
    />
</LinearLayout>
```

Here is the strings.xml to go with this layout file and the rest of the application:

```
<?xml version="1.0" encoding="utf-8"?>
<resources>
    <string name="main_activity_text">
    This is a simple activity. Click on the search key
    to invoke the local search.
    \n\n
    The suggestion provider will also participate
    in the global search. when you come to this
    application through the global search you will
    not see this view but instead be directly
    taken to the searchactivity view.
    </string>

    <string name="search_activity_text">
    If you are seeing this activity you are directed
    here either through the global search or through
    the local search.
    \n\n
    This activit also enables type-to-search. It also
    demonstrates the singletop/new intent concepts.
    </string>

    <string name="app_name">Simple Suggestion Provider</string>
    <string name="search_label">Local Search Demo</string>
    <string name="search_hint">Local Search Hint</string>
</resources>
```

Simple Suggestion Provider User Experience

If you run this application you will see a home screen that looks like the one shown in Figure 14–23 (this is our search invoker activity).

Figure 14–23. *Simple suggestion provider: main activity (enabled for local search)*

If you click the search key while this activity is in focus, you will see the local search invoked as in Figure 14–24.

Figure 14–24. *Simple suggestion provider: local search QSB*

As you can see, there are no suggestions in Figure 14–24 because we haven't searched for any so far. You can also see that this is a local search; the label and hint of the search are as we specified in the search metadata XML file.

Let us go ahead and search for string test1. This will take you to the Search Activity screen as shown in Figure 14–25.

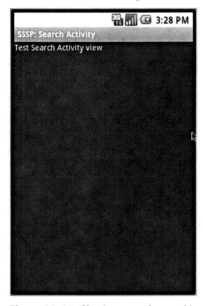

Figure 14–25. *Simple suggestion provider: local search results activity*

As you can see from the SearchActivity source in Listing 14–17, SearchActivity does nothing spectacular on the screen, but behind the scenes it is saving the query strings in the database. Now if you navigate back to the main screen (by pressing the back button) and invoke search again you will see the following screen (as shown in Figure 14–26) where the search suggestions are populated with the previous query text.

This is a good moment to see how we can invoke onNewIntent(). When you are on the search activity (Figure 14–24) you can type a letter like **t** and it will invoke the search again using type-to-search and you will see onNewIntent() called in the debug log.

Let us see what we need to do to see these suggestions show up in the global QSB. Because we have enabled includeInGlobalSearch you should be able to see these suggestions in the global QSB as well. However, before you can do that you need to enable this application for global QSB suggestions as shown in Figure 14–27.

Figure 14–26. *Simple suggestion provider: retrieved local suggestion*

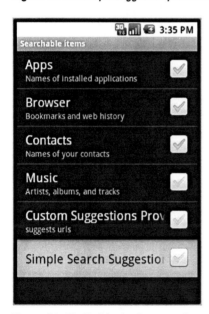

Figure 14–27. *Enable simple suggestion provider*

We showed you how to reach this screen at the beginning of the chapter. With this in place you can see the global search shown in Figure 14–28 working with our suggestion provider.

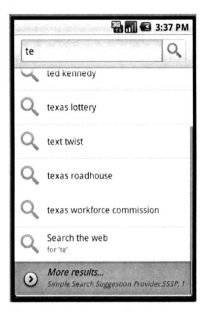

Figure 14–28. *More results: simple suggestion provider*

When you navigate through the global search to the specific item (as laid out in the "Simple Suggestion Provider User Experience" section) you will see the local search box show up, as in Figure 14–29.

Figure 14–29. *Transfering to local search: simple suggestion provider*

This concludes our discussion of the simple suggestion provider. You have learned about using the built-in `RecentSearchSuggestionProvider` to remember searches that are specific to your application. Using this approach, with minimal code you should be able to take local searches and make them available as suggestions even in a global context.

However, this simple exercise hasn't shown you how to write suggestion providers from scratch. More important, we haven't given you the slightest clue as to how a suggestion provider returns a set of suggestions and what columns are available in this suggestion set. To understand this and more, we need to implement a custom suggestions provider from scratch.

Implementing a Custom Suggestion Provider

Android search is too flexible not to customize. Because we used a pre-built suggestion provider in the last section, many features of a suggestion provider were hidden in the `SearchRecentSuggestionsProvider` and not discussed. We will explore these details next by implementing a custom suggestion provider called a `SuggestUrlProvider`.

We will start by explaining how this `SuggestUrlProvider` is expected work. We will then give you the file list in the implementation. These files should give you a general idea of how to build a custom suggestion provider.

As already mentioned, when you write a suggestion provider you implement two main components: the suggestion provider and a corresponding search activity. As before when we implemented the simple suggestion provider, we will discuss these two components in terms of their responsibilities and how those responsibilities are implemented.

In the suggestion provider implementation we will look at the type of URLs used in invoking the suggestion provider, how partial text is passed to the suggestion provider, the list of columns returned by the suggestion provider, and how the suggestion provider can pass information to the search activity.

In the search activity implementation we will look at how the activity is invoked and what search-related actions are passed in. We will show you how the search activity can retrieve the values from the intent that is used to invoke the activity.

Finally, we will show you how the completed application is used. Let's get started.

Planning the Custom Suggestion Provider

We are going to call our custom suggestion provider a `SuggestURLProvider`. The object of this provider is to monitor what is being typed in the QSB. If the search query has text that looks something like like "great.m" (the suffix .m is chosen to represent meaning) the provider will interpret the first part of the query as a word and suggest an Internet-based URL that can be invoked.

For every word, this provider suggests two URLs. The first is a URL that allows the user to search for the word using `http://www.thefreedictionary.com` and a second URL using http://www.google.com. Choosing one of these suggestions takes the user to one of these sites directly. If the user clicks on the search icon of the QSB then the search activity will simply log the query text on a simple layout of this activity. You will see this more clearly when we show you the screen images of this interaction.

Let us see the list of files that make up this solution or project .

SuggestURLProvider Project Implementation Files

As indicated, the two primary files are SearchActivity.java and SuggestUrlProvider.java. However, you will need a number of supporting files to complete the project. Here is a list of these files and a brief description of what each one does. We have included the source code for all of thefiles with the solution.

- SuggestUrlProvider.java: This file implements the protocol of a custom suggestion provider. In this case the custom suggestion provider interprets query strings as words and returns a couple of suggestions using a suggestion cursor

- SearchActivity.java: This activity is responsible for receiving the queries or suggestions provided by the suggestion provider. SearchActivity definition is also responsible for tying up the suggestion provider with this activity.

- layout/layout_search_activity.xml: This layout file is optionally used by the SearchActivity. In our example, we use this layout to log the query that is sent in.

- values/strings.xml: Contains string definitions for the layout, local search title, local search hint, and the like.

- xml/searchable.xml: Search metadata XML file that ties the SearchActivity, suggestion provider, and the QSB.

- manifest.xml: application manifest file when the search activity and suggestion provider are defined. This is also where you declare that the SearchActivity is to be invoked as a local search for this application.

Among all these files SuggestUrlProvider and SearchActivity are key files. We will start by exploring SuggestUrlProvider first.

Implementing the SuggestUrlProvider Class

In our custom suggestion provider project, the SuggestUrlProvider class is the one that implements the protocol of the suggestion provider. We will explore the implementation of SuggestUrlProvider beginning with its responsibilities.

Responsibilities of a Suggestion Provider

A suggestion provider is invoked by Android search using a URI that identifies the provider and an additional argument passing the query.

Android search uses two types of URIs to invoke the provider. The first is called the search URI, which is used to collect the set of suggestions. The response needs to be one or more rows, with each row containing a set of well-known columns.

The second URI is called a suggest URI which is used to update a suggestion that is previously cached. The response needs to be a single row containing a set of well-known columns.

A suggestion provider also needs to specify in the search metadata how it wants to receive the partial search query. This can be done through the `select` argument of the query method or the last path segment of the URI itself (which is also passed as one of the arguments to the query method of the provider).

For a suggestion provider there are a number of columns that are available, each enabling a certain search behavior. A provider first needs to decide on the set of columns it wants to return:

- Use one of the columns to control how you want to cache the suggestions that are returned to the Android search.

- Use the columns to decide and control if you want the suggestions to rewrite the text in the query box.

- Use the columns if you need to invoke an action directly instead of showing a set of search results when the user clicks on the suggestion.

Overall Source Code for SuggestUrlProvider

Listing 14–20 shows the source code for the `SuggestUrlProvider class`. Sections of this code are also examined in greater detail later in the chapter as we explain each of these responsibilities in greater detail.

Listing 14–20. *CustomSuggestionProvider Source Code*

```
public class SuggestUrlProvider extends ContentProvider
{
    private static final String tag = "SuggestUrlProvider";
    public static String AUTHORITY =
        "com.ai.android.search.custom.suggesturlprovider";

    private static final int SEARCH_SUGGEST = 0;
    private static final int SHORTCUT_REFRESH = 1;
    private static final UriMatcher sURIMatcher = buildUriMatcher();

    private static final String[] COLUMNS = {
            "_id",  // must include this column
            SearchManager.SUGGEST_COLUMN_TEXT_1,
```

```java
            SearchManager.SUGGEST_COLUMN_TEXT_2,
            SearchManager.SUGGEST_COLUMN_INTENT_DATA,
            SearchManager.SUGGEST_COLUMN_INTENT_ACTION,
            SearchManager.SUGGEST_COLUMN_SHORTCUT_ID
            };

    private static UriMatcher buildUriMatcher()
    {
        UriMatcher matcher =  new UriMatcher(UriMatcher.NO_MATCH);
        matcher.addURI(AUTHORITY,
            SearchManager.SUGGEST_URI_PATH_QUERY,
            SEARCH_SUGGEST);
        matcher.addURI(AUTHORITY,
            SearchManager.SUGGEST_URI_PATH_QUERY +
            "/*",
            SEARCH_SUGGEST);
        matcher.addURI(AUTHORITY,
            SearchManager.SUGGEST_URI_PATH_SHORTCUT,
            SHORTCUT_REFRESH);
        matcher.addURI(AUTHORITY,
            SearchManager.SUGGEST_URI_PATH_SHORTCUT +
            "/*",
            SHORTCUT_REFRESH);
        return matcher;
    }

    @Override
    public boolean onCreate() {
        //lets not do anything in particular
        Log.d(tag,"onCreate called");
        return true;
    }

    @Override
    public Cursor query(Uri uri, String[] projection, String selection,
            String[] selectionArgs, String sortOrder)
    {
        Log.d(tag,"query called with uri:" + uri);
        Log.d(tag,"selection:" + selection);

        String query = selectionArgs[0];
        Log.d(tag,"query:" + query);

        switch (sURIMatcher.match(uri)) {
            case SEARCH_SUGGEST:
                Log.d(tag,"search suggest called");
                return getSuggestions(query);
            case SHORTCUT_REFRESH:
                Log.d(tag,"shortcut refresh called");
                return null;
            default:
                throw new IllegalArgumentException("Unknown URL " + uri);
        }
    }

    private Cursor getSuggestions(String query)
    {
```

```
   if (query == null) return null;
   String word = getWord(query);
   if (word == null)
      return null;

   Log.d(tag,"query is longer than 3 letters");

        MatrixCursor cursor = new MatrixCursor(COLUMNS);
        //cursor.addRow(createRow(query,"row1"));
        cursor.addRow(createRow1(word));
        cursor.addRow(createRow2(word));
      return cursor;
}
private Object[] createRow1(String query)
{
    return columnValuesOfQuery(query,
         "android.intent.action.VIEW",
         "http://www.thefreedictionary.com/" + query,
         "Look up in freedictionary.com for",
         query);
}

private Object[] createRow2(String query)
{
    return columnValuesOfQuery(query,
         "android.intent.action.VIEW",
         "http://www.google.com/search?hl=en&source=hp&q=define%3A/"
      + query,
         "Look up in google.com for",
         query);
}
private Object[] columnValuesOfQuery(String query,
      String intentAction,
      String url,
      String text1,
      String text2)
{
    return new String[] {
            query,      // _id
            text1,      // text1
            text2,      // text2
            url,        // intent_data (included when clicking on item)
            intentAction, //action
            SearchManager.SUGGEST_NEVER_MAKE_SHORTCUT
    };
}

private Cursor refreshShortcut(String shortcutId, String[] projection) {
    return null;
}

public String getType(Uri uri) {
    switch (sURIMatcher.match(uri)) {
        case SEARCH_SUGGEST:
            return SearchManager.SUGGEST_MIME_TYPE;
        case SHORTCUT_REFRESH:
            return SearchManager.SHORTCUT_MIME_TYPE;
```

```
                    default:
                        throw new IllegalArgumentException("Unknown URL " + uri);
                }
        }

        public Uri insert(Uri uri, ContentValues values) {
            throw new UnsupportedOperationException();
        }

        public int delete(Uri uri, String selection, String[] selectionArgs) {
            throw new UnsupportedOperationException();
        }

        public int update(Uri uri, ContentValues values, String selection,
                String[] selectionArgs) {
            throw new UnsupportedOperationException();
        }

        private String getWord(String query)
        {
            int dotIndex = query.indexOf('.');
            if (dotIndex < 0)
                return null;
            return query.substring(0,dotIndex);
        }
}
```

Understanding Suggestion Provider URIs

Now that you have seen the complete source code of a custom suggestion provider,
let's look at how portions of this source code fulfills the URI responsibilities.

First let's look at the format of the URI that Android uses to invoke the suggestion
provider. If our suggestion provider has an authority of

`com.ai.android.search.custom.suggesturlprovider`

then Android will send in two possible URIs. The first type of URI is called a search URI.
It looks like one of the following:

`content://com.ai.android.search.suggesturlprovider/search_suggest_query`

or

`content://com.ai.android.search.suggesturlprovider/search_suggest_query/<your-query>`

This URI is issued when the user has started typing some text in the QSB. In one
variation of this, the query is passed as an additional element at the end of the URI as a
path segment. Whether to pass the query as a path segment or not is specified in the
search metadata file `searchable.xml`. We will discuss that specification when we cover
the search metadata in more detail.

The second type of URI that is targeted for a suggestion provider relates to Android
search shortcuts. Android search shortcuts are suggestions (see Figure 14–3) that
Android decides to cache, instead of calling the suggestion provider for fresh content.

We will talk about Android search shortcuts more when we discuss the suggestion columns. For now, this second URI looks like the following:

```
content://com.ai.android.search.suggesturlprovider/search_suggest_shortcut
```

or

```
content://com.ai.android.search.suggesturlprovider/search_suggest_shortcut/<shortcut-id>
```

This URI is issued by Android when it tries to determine if the shortcuts that it had cached are still valid. This type of URI is called the shortcut URI. If the provider returns a single row it will replace the current shortcut with the new one. If the provider sends a null then Android assumes this suggestion is no longer valid.

The SearchManager class in Android defines two constants to represent these URI segments that distinguish them (search_suggest_search and search_suggest_shortcut). They are respectively

```
SearchManager.SUGGEST_URI_PATH_QUERY
SearchManager.SUGGEST_URI_PATH_SHORTCUT
```

It is the responsibility of the provider to recognize these incoming URIs in its query() method. See Listing 14–20 to see how the UriMatcher is used to accomplish this. (You can refer to Chapter 3 on how to use UriMatcher in greater detail.)

Implementing getType() and Specifying MIME Types

Because a suggestion provider is ultimately a content provider it has the responsibility of implementing a content provider contract which includes defining an implementation for the getType() method.

You can consult Listing 14–20 again to see how getType() is implemented in this case. Android search framework through its SearchManager class provides a couple of constants to help with these MIME types. These MIME types are

```
SearchManager.SUGGEST_MIME_TYPE
SearchManager.SHORTCUT_MIME_TYPE
```

These translate to

```
vnd.android.cursor.dir/vnd.android.search.suggest
vnd.android.cursor.item/vnd.android.search.suggest
```

Passing Query to the Suggestion Provider: The Selection Argument

When Android uses one of the above URIs to call the provider, Android ends up calling the query() method of the suggestion provider to receive a suggestion cursor. If you see the implementation of the query() method in Listing 14–20 you will notice that we are using the selection argument and the selectionArgs argument in order to formulate and return the cursor.

To understand what is passed to through these two arguments you will need to see the searchable.xml, the search metadata file. Listing 14–21 shows the code for this metadata file.

Listing 14–21. *CustomSuggestionProvider Search Metadata*

```
//xml/searchable.xml
<searchable xmlns:android="http://schemas.android.com/apk/res/android"
    android:label="@string/search_label"
    android:hint="@string/search_hint"
    android:searchMode="showSearchLabelAsBadge"
    android:searchSettingsDescription="suggests urls"
    android:includeInGlobalSearch="true"

    android:searchSuggestAuthority="com.ai.android.search.custom.suggesturlprovider"
    android:searchSuggestIntentAction="android.intent.action.VIEW"
    android:searchSuggestSelection=" ? "
/>
```

Notice the searchSuggestSelection attribute in the search metadata definition file listing above. It directly corresponds to the selection argument of the content provider's query() method. If you revisit Chapter3 you will know that this argument is typically used to pass the where clause with substitutable ? symbols. The array of substitutable values are then passed through the selectionArgs array argument. That indeed is the case here. When you specify searchSuggestSelection Android assumes that you don't want to receive the search text through the URI but instead through the selection argument of the query() method. In that case Android search will send the ? (notice the empty space before and after the ? mark) as the value of the selection argument and passes the query text as the first element of the selection arguments array.

If you don't specify the searchSuggestSelection then it will pass the search text as the last path segment of the URI. You can choose one or the other. In our example, we have chosen the selection approach and not the URI approach.

Exploring Search Metadata for Custom Suggestion Providers

While we are on this topic of search metadata attributes let us explore what other attribute are available. We will mainly cover those attributes that are often used or relevant to suggestion providers. For a complete list you can refer to the SearchManager API URL:

http://developer.android.com/reference/android/app/SearchManager.html

The searchSuggestIntentAction attribute is used to pass or specify the intent action when the SearchActivity is invoked through an intent. This allows the SearchActivity to do something other than the default search. You can see this in Listing 14–23 where the searchActivity is looking for either a VIEW action or the SEARCH action by examining the action value of the intent.

Another attribute that we are not using here, but which is available to suggestion providers, is called searchSuggestPath. If specified, this string value is appended to the URI (one that invokes the suggestion provider) after the SUGGEST_URI_PATH_QUERY.

This allows a single custom suggestion provider to respond to two different search activities. Each SearchActivity will use a different URI suffix.

Just as with the Intent action, you can also specify intent data using the searchSuggestIntentData attribute. This is a data URI that can be passed along the action to the search activity, as part of the intent, when invoked.

Another attribute called searchSuggestThreshold indicates the number of characters that have to be typed in QSB before invoking this suggestion provider. The default threshold value is zero.

The attribute queryAfterZeroResults (true or false) indicates if the provider should be contacted if the current set of characters returned zero set of results for the next set of characters.

Now that we have looked at the URIs, selection arguments, and search metadata, let's move on now to the most important aspect of a suggestion provider: the suggestion cursor.

Suggestion Cursor Columns

A suggestion cursor is, after all, a cursor. It is no different from the database cursors we discussed at length in Chapter 3. The suggestion cursor acts as the contract between the Android search facility and a suggestion provider. This means the names and types of the columns that the cursor returns are fixed and known to both parties.

To provide flexibility to search, Android search offers a large number of columns, most of which are optional. A suggestion provider does not need to return all these columns; it can ignore sending in the columns that are not relevant to this suggestion provider. In this section we will cover the meaning and significance of most of the columns (for the rest, you can refer to the SearchManager API URL, which we have mentioned a few times already).

First, we'll talk about the columns that are available for a suggestion provider to return, what each column means, and how it affects search.

Like all cursors, a suggestion cursor also has to have an _id column. This is a mandatory column. Every other column starts with a SUGGEST_COLUMN_ prefix. These constants are defined as part of the SearchManager API reference. We will talk about the most frequently used columns below. For the complete list use the API references indicated at the end of this chapter.

- text_1: This is the first line of text in your suggestion (see Figure 14–3).

- text_2: This is the second line of text in your suggestion (see Figure 14–3).

- icon_1: This is the icon on the left side in a suggestion and is typically a resource ID

- icon_2: This is the icon on the right side in a suggestion and is typically a resource ID

- intent_action: This is what is passed to the SearchActivity when it is invoked as the intent action. This will override the corresponding intent action when available in the search metadata (see Listing 14–21).

- intent_data: This is what is passed to the SearchActivity when it is invoked as the intent data. This will override the corresponding intent action when available in the search metadata (see Listing 14–21). This is a data URI.

- intent_data_id: This gets appended to the data URI. It is especially useful if you want to mention the root part of the data in the metadata one time and then change this for each suggestion. It is a bit more efficient that way.

- query: The query string to be used to send to the search activity.

- shortcut_id: As indicated earlier, Android search caches suggestions provided by a suggestion provider. These cached suggestions are called shortcuts. If this column is not present, Android will cache the suggestion and will never ask for an update. If this contains a value equivalent to SUGGEST_NEVER_MAKE_SHORTCUT, then Android will not cache this suggestion. If it contains any other value, this ID is passed as the last path segment of the shortcut URI. (See the section "Understanding Suggestion Provider URIs.")

- spinner_while_refreshing: This Boolean value will tell Android if it should use a spinner when it is in the process of updating the shortcuts.

There are a variable set of additional columns for responding to action keys. We will cover that in the action keys section later. Let us see how our custom suggestion provider returns these columns.

Populating and Returning the List of Columns

Each custom suggestion provider is not required to return all these columns. For our suggestion provider we will return only a subset of the columns based on the functionality indicated in the "Planning the Custom Suggestion Provider" section.

By looking at Listing 14–20 you can see that out list of columns is as follows (extracted and reproduced in Listing 14–22):

Listing 14–22. *Defining Suggestion Cursor Columns*

```
private static final String[] COLUMNS = {
        "_id",  // must include this column
        SearchManager.SUGGEST_COLUMN_TEXT_1,
        SearchManager.SUGGEST_COLUMN_TEXT_2,
        SearchManager.SUGGEST_COLUMN_INTENT_DATA,
```

```
SearchManager.SUGGEST_COLUMN_INTENT_ACTION,
SearchManager.SUGGEST_COLUMN_SHORTCUT_ID
};
```

These columns are chosen so that the following functionality is met:

The user enters a word with a hint like "great.m" in the QSB, our suggestion provider will not respond until there is a "." in the search text. Once it is recognized, the suggestion provider will extract the word from it (in this case, "great") and then provide two suggestions back.

The first suggestion is to invoke the thefreewebdictionary.com with this word and a second suggestion is to search Google with a pattern of define:great.

To accomplish this, the provider loads up the column intent_action as intent.action.view and the intent data containing the entire URI. The hope is that Android will launch the browser when it sees the data URI starting with http://.

We will populate the text1 column with search some-website with: and text2 with the word itself (again, great, in this case). We will also set the shortcut ID to SUGGEST_NEVER_MAKE_SHORTCUT to simplify things. This setting disables caching and also prevents the suggest URI being fired.

This completes our analysis of custom suggestion provider class source code. We have learned about URIs, suggestion cursors, and suggestion provider–specific search metadata. We also know how to populate suggestion columns.

Now let's look into implementing the search activity for our custom suggestion provider.

Implementing a Search Activity for a Custom Suggestion Provider

As we have pointed out, implementation of a custom suggestions provider has two components: a custom suggestions provider and a search activity that can respond to suggestions. In the previous section we covered the custom suggestions provider implementation. We will look at the corresponding Search activity next.

Just as we did in the previous section, we'll start by discussing the general responsibilities of a search activity. We will then present the source code to give you a bird's-eye view of how those responsibilities are fulfilled.

Responsibilities of a Search Activity

During the simple suggestion provider implementation we covered only some of the responsibilities of a search activity. Now let's look at the aspects we overlooked.

Android search invokes a search activity in order to respond to search actions from one of two ways. This can happen either when a search icon is clicked from the QSB or when the user directly clicks on a suggestion.

When invoked, a search activity needs to examine why it is invoked. This information is available in the intent action. The search activity needs to examine intent action to do the right thing. In many cases, this action is ACTION_SEARCH. However, a suggestion provider has the option of overriding it by specifying an explicit action either through search metadata or through a suggestion cursor column. This type of action can be anything. In our case, we are going to be using a VIEW action.

As we pointed out in our discussion of the simple suggestion provider, it is also possible to set up the launch mode of the search activity as a `singleTop`. In this case, the search activity has the added responsibility of responding to `onNewIntent()` in addition to `onCreate()`. We will cover both these cases and show how similar they are.

We will use both `onNewIntent()` and `onCreate()` to examine both ACTION_SEARCH and also ACTION_VIEW. In case of search action we will simply display the query text back to the user. In case of view action we will transfer control to a browser and finish the current activity so that the user has the impression of invoking the browser by directly clicking on the suggestion.

With that, let us examine the source code of `SearchActivity.java`.

Source Code of SearchActivity for a Custom Suggestion Provider

Now that we know the responsibilities of a search activity and, specifically, which ones are applicable for our example, we can show you the source code of this search activity (Listing 14–23).

Listing 14–23. *SearchActivity*

```java
//file: SearchActivity.java
public class SearchActivity extends Activity
{
    private final static String tag ="SearchActivity";
    @Override
    protected void onCreate(Bundle savedInstanceState) {
        super.onCreate(savedInstanceState);

        Log.d(tag,"I am being created");
        setContentView(R.layout.layout_test_search_activity);

        // get and process search query here
        final Intent queryIntent = getIntent();

        //query action
        final String queryAction = queryIntent.getAction();
        Log.d(tag,"Create Intent action:"+queryAction);

        final String queryString =
            queryIntent.getStringExtra(SearchManager.QUERY);
        Log.d(tag,"Create Intent query:"+queryString);

        if (Intent.ACTION_SEARCH.equals(queryAction))
        {
            this.doSearchQuery(queryIntent);
```

```
    }
    else if (Intent.ACTION_VIEW.equals(queryAction))
    {
        this.doView(queryIntent);
    }
    else {
        Log.d(tag,"Create intent NOT from search");
    }
    return;
}

@Override
public void onNewIntent(final Intent newIntent)
{
    super.onNewIntent(newIntent);
    Log.d(tag,"new intent calling me");

    // get and process search query here
    final Intent queryIntent = newIntent;

    //query action
    final String queryAction = queryIntent.getAction();
    Log.d(tag,"New Intent action:"+queryAction);

    final String queryString =
        queryIntent.getStringExtra(SearchManager.QUERY);
    Log.d(tag,"New Intent query:"+queryString);

    if (Intent.ACTION_SEARCH.equals(queryAction))
    {
        this.doSearchQuery(queryIntent);
    }
    else if (Intent.ACTION_VIEW.equals(queryAction))
    {
        this.doView(queryIntent);
    }
    else {
        Log.d(tag,"New intent NOT from search");
    }
    return;
}
private void doSearchQuery(final Intent queryIntent)
{
    final String queryString =
        queryIntent.getStringExtra(SearchManager.QUERY);
    appendText("You are searching for:" + queryString);
}
private void appendText(String msg)
{
    TextView tv = (TextView)this.findViewById(R.id.text1);
    tv.setText(tv.getText() + "\n" + msg);
}
private void doView(final Intent queryIntent)
{
    Uri uri = queryIntent.getData();
    String action = queryIntent.getAction();
    Intent i = new Intent(action);
```

```
            i.setData(uri);
            startActivity(i);
            this.finish();
        }
    }
}
```

We'll start our analysis of this source code by examining first how this search activity is invoked.

Details of SearchActivity Invocation

Like all activities, we know that a search activity must have been invoked through an intent. However, it would be wrong to assume that it is always the action of the intent that is responsible for this. As it turns out, the search activity is invoked explicitly through its component name specification.

You might ask why this is important. Well, we know that in our suggestion provider we are explicitly specifying an intent action in the suggestion row. If this intent action is VIEW and the intent data is an HTTP URL, then an unsuspecting programmer would think that a browser will be launched in response, and not the search activity. That would certainly be desirable. But because the ultimate intent is also loaded with the component name of search activity in addition to the intent action and data, the component name will take precedence.

We are not sure why this restriction is there or how to overcome it. But the fact is, irrespective of the intent action that your suggestion provider specifies, search activity is the one that is going to be invoked. In our case, we will simply launch the browser from the search activity and close the search activity.

To demonstrate this, here is the intent that Android fires off to invoke our search activity when we click on a suggestion:

```
launching Intent {
act=android.intent.action.VIEW
dat=http://www.google.com
flg=0x10000000
cmp=com.ai.android.search.custom/.SearchActivity (has extras)
}
```

Notice the component spec of the intent. It is directly pointing to the search activity. So no matter what intent action you indicate, Android will always invoke search activity. As a result, it becomes the responsibility of the search activity to invoke the browser.

Let us look at what we do with these intents in the search activity.

Responding to ACTION_SEARCH and ACTION_VIEW

We know that a search activity is explicitly invoked by name by Android search. However, the invoking intent also carries with it the action that is specified. When QSB invokes this activity through the search icon this action is ACTION_SEARCH.

This action could be different if it was invoked by a search suggestion. It depends on how the suggestion provider set up the suggestion. In our case, the suggestion provider set this up as an ACTION_VIEW.

As a result, a search activity needs to examine the type of action. Here is how we examine this code to see whether to call a search query method or the view method. (This code segment is extracted from Listing 14–23)

```
if (Intent.ACTION_SEARCH.equals(queryAction))
{
    this.doSearchQuery(queryIntent);
}
else if (Intent.ACTION_VIEW.equals(queryAction))
{
    this.doView(queryIntent);
}
```

From the code you can see that we invoke doView() for a view action and doSearchQuery() in the case of a search action.

In the doView() function we will retrieve the action and the data URI and populate a new intent with them and then invoke the activity. This will invoke the browser. We will finish the activity so that the back button takes you back to whatever search invoked it.

In the doSearchQuery() we are just logging the search query text to the view. Let us take a look at the layout that is used to support doSearchQuery()

Search Activity Layout

Listing 14–24 shows a simple layout that is used by a search activity in case of doSearchQuery().The only important element is highlighted in bold.

Listing 14–24. *SearchActivity Layout XML*

```
//file: layout_search_activity.xml
<?xml version="1.0" encoding="utf-8"?>
<LinearLayout xmlns:android="http://schemas.android.com/apk/res/android"
    android:orientation="vertical"
    android:layout_width="fill_parent"
    android:layout_height="fill_parent"
    >
<TextView
    android:id="@+id/text1"
    android:layout_width="fill_parent"
    android:layout_height="wrap_content"
    android:text="@string/search_activity_main_text"
    />
```

It is appropriate at this point to show you the strings.xml that is responsible for some of the text needs of this application.

Corresponding strings.xml

This `strings.xml` as shown in Listing 14–25 defines text strings for the layout and also such things as the name of the application, some strings for configuring the local search, and the like.

Listing 14–25. *strings.xml*

```xml
<?xml version="1.0" encoding="utf-8"?>
<resources>
    <string name="search_activity_main_text">
    This is the search activity.
    \n\n
    This will be invoked if action_search
    is used as opposed to action_view.
    \n\n
    action_search happens if you press the search icon.
    \n\n
    action_view happens if you press on the suggestion
    </string>
    <string name="app_name">Custom Suggest Application</string>
    <string name="search_label">Custom Suggest Demo</string>
    <string name="search_hint">Custom Suggest Demo Hint</string>
</resources>
```

Responding to onCreate() and onNewIntent()

If you examine Listing 14–23 again, you will see that the code in `onCreate()` and `onNewIntent()` is almost identical. This is not an uncommon pattern.

When a search activity is invoked, depending on the launch mode of the search activity, either `onCreate()` or a `onNewIntent()` is called. If you don't respond to one of these you may miss a search invocation.

NOTE: For a useful reference on launch modes and `onNewIntent()` see the "References" section at the end of this chapter.

Notes on Finishing a Search Activity

Earlier in this discussion we briefly mentioned how to respond to `doView()`. Listing 14–26 shows you the code for this function now (excerpted from Listing 14–26).

Listing 14–26. *Finishing the Search Activity*

```java
private void doView(final Intent queryIntent)
{
    Uri uri = queryIntent.getData();
    String action = queryIntent.getAction();
    Intent i = new Intent(action);
    i.setData(uri);
    startActivity(i);
    this.finish();
}
```

The goal of this function is to invoke the browser. If we were not doing the `finish()` at the end, the user would be taken back to the search activity from the browser after clicking the back button, instead of back to the search screen where they came from, as expected.

Ideally, to give the best user experience the control should never pass through the search activity. Finishing this activity solves that problem. The preceding code segment also gives us an opportunity to examine how we transfer the intent action and intent data from the original intent (which are set by the suggestion provider) and then pass them on to a new browser intent.

This concludes several discussions. We have shown you a detailed suggestion provider implementation and a search activity implementation. In the process, we have also shown you the search metadata file and the `strings.xml`. We will conclude our examination of the files needed for implementing this chapter's project with a look at the application level manifest file.

Custom Suggestions Provider Manifest File

The manifest file is where you bring together many components of your application. For our custom suggestions provider application as in other examples, this is where you declare its components, such as the search activity and the suggestion provider. You also use the manifest file to declare that this application is enabled for local search by declaring the "search activity" as the default search.

These details are highlighted bold in the manifest file code (Listing 14–27).

Listing 14–27. *Custom Suggestion Provider Manifest File*

```
//file:manifest.xml
<?xml version="1.0" encoding="utf-8"?>
<manifest xmlns:android="http://schemas.android.com/apk/res/android"
     package="com.ai.android.search.custom"
     android:versionCode="1"
     android:versionName="1.0.0">
    <application android:icon="@drawable/icon"
                    android:label="Custom Suggestions Provider">
<!--
*************************************************************
* Search related code: search activity
*************************************************************
 -->
    <activity android:name=".SearchActivity"
                    android:label="Search Activity Label"
                    android:launchMode="singleTop">
       <intent-filter>
          <action android:name="android.intent.action.SEARCH" />
          <category android:name="android.intent.category.DEFAULT" />
       </intent-filter>

       <meta-data android:name="android.app.searchable"
                       android:resource="@xml/searchable" />
    </activity>
```

```
<!-- Declare default search -->
    <meta-data android:name="android.app.default_searchable"
                        android:value=".SearchActivity" />

<!-- Declare Suggestion Provider -->
    <provider android:name="SuggestUrlProvider"
                android:authorities="com.ai.android.search.custom.suggesturlprovider"
/>
</application>
    <uses-sdk android:minSdkVersion="4" />
</manifest>
```

As you can see, we have highlighted three things:

■ Defining the search activity along with its search metadata XML file

■ Defining the search activity as the default search for the application

■ Defining the suggestion provider and its authority

With all of the source code in place, it is time to take a tour of the application and see how it looks in the emulator.

Custom Suggestion User Experience

Once you build and deploy this app through ADT you will not see any activity pop-up because there is no activity to start. Instead, you will see that the application is successfully installed in the Eclipse console.

This means that the suggestion provider is ready to respond to the global QSB. But before that can take place, you will need to enable this suggestion provider to participate in global search.

Earlier in this chapter we showed you how to reach the search settings application. Here is a shortcut which uses the very search facility we have learned so far.

Open the global QSB and type **sett** in the QSB. This will bring up the settings application as one of the suggestions to be invoked.

Figure 14–30. *Invoking settings through search*

Notice how we are using what we have learned about QSB to invoke the settings application. Follow the approach specified at the beginning of this chapter to enable this application for suggestions. Once this is done, type the text in the QSB shown in Figure 14–31.

Figure 14–31. *More results from the custom suggestions provider*

Notice how search suggestions from the custom suggestions provider are presented. Now if you navigate to one of the suggestions provided by our custom suggestions provider and click the QSB search icon, Android will take you to the search activity directly without invoking any browser, as shown in Figure 14–32.

Figure 14–32. *Query search invoking search results*

This example demonstrates the ACTION_SEARCH vs. the ACTION_VIEW.

Once you have used this suggestion provider a few times, Android will present the suggestions as part of the main choice and not "more...". Figure 14–33 shows an example in which we have typed **chiaroscuro.m** in the global QSB.

Figure 14–33. *Suggestion provider precedence*

Notice how the suggestions are directly presented without a further "more..." prompt. Now if you click on the free dictionary suggestion you will see the invoked browser as in Figure 14–34.

Figure 14–34. *Free dictionary*

If you click on the Google suggestion item, you will see the browser shown in Figure 14–35.

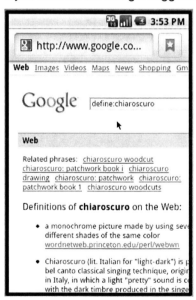

Figure 14–35. *Searching Google for a definition*

Here is an example of what happens if you don't type the suffix **.m**

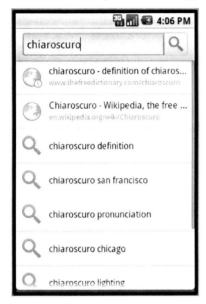

Figure 14–36. *Custom provider without a hint*

Notice how the suggestion provider hasn't provided anything back.

This concludes our discussion of building a functional custom suggestions provider from scratch. Although we've covered any aspects of search, there are still a couple of topics that we haven't talked about. These are action keys and Application-Specific search data. We will cover these next.

Using Action Keys and Application-Specific Search Data

Action keys and application-specific search data add further flexibility to Android search.

Action keys allow us to employ specialized device keys for search-related functionality. Application-specific search data allow an activity to pass additional data to the search activity.

Let's begin with action keys.

Using Action Keys in Android Search

So far we've shown a number of ways to invoke search:

- The search icon available in the QSB
- The search key that is part of a set of action keys (shown on the right side of Figure 14–1)
- An explicit icon or button that is displayed by an activity
- Any key press based on a type-to-search declaration

In this section we will look at another way of invoking search through action keys. Action keys are a set of keys available on the device which are tied to specific actions. Some examples of these action keys are shown in Listing 14–28.

Listing 14–28. *List of Action Key Codes*

```
keycode_dpad_up
keycode_dpad_down
keycode_dpad_left
keycode_dpad_right
keycode_dpad_center
keycode_back
keycode_call
keycode_camera
keycode_clear
kecode_endcall
keycode_home
keycode_menu
keycode_mute
keycode_power
keycode_search
keycode_volume_up
keycode_volume_down
```

You can see these action keys defined in the API for `KeyEvent` which is available at the following URL:

```
http://developer.android.com/reference/android/view/KeyEvent.html
```

> **NOTE:** Not all of these action keys can be co-opted for search, but some can, such as keycode_call. You will have to try each and see which is suitable for your need.

Once you know which action key you want to use you can tell Android that you are interested in this key by dropping it in the metadata using the XML segment in Listing 14–29.

Listing 14–29. *Action Key Definition Example*

```xml
<searchable xmlns:android="http://schemas.android.com/apk/res/android"
    android:label="@string/search_label"
    android:hint="@string/search_hint"
```

```
        android:searchMode="showSearchLabelAsBadge"

        android:includeInGlobalSearch="true"

android:searchSuggestAuthority="com.ai.android.search.simplesp.SimpleSuggestionProvider"
        android:searchSuggestSelection=" ? "
>
    <actionkey
        android:keycode="KEYCODE_CALL"
        android:queryActionMsg="call"
        android:suggestActionMsg="call"
        android:suggestActionMsgColumn="call_column" />

    <actionkey
        android:keycode="KEYCODE_DPAD_CENTER"
        android:queryActionMsg="doquery"
        android:suggestActionMsg="dosuggest"
        android:suggestActionMsgColumn="my_column" />
    .....
</searchable>
```

You can also have multiple action keys for the same search context. Here is what each attribute of the `actionKey` element stands for and how it is used to respond to an action key press.

- *keycode*: This is the key code as defined in the `KeyEvent` API class that should be used to invoke the search activity. There are two times when this key identified by the keycode can be pressed. The first is when the user enters query text in the QSB but hasn't navigated to any suggestions. Typically the user, without an action key implementation, will have pressed the search icon of the QSB. With an action key specified in the metadata of the search, Android allows the user to click the action key instead of the QSB search icon. The second is when the user navigates to a specific suggestion and then clicks the action key. In both cases the search activity is invoked with an action of `ACTION_SEARCH`. To know that this action is invoked through an action key, look for an extra string called `SearchManager.ACTION_KEY`. If you see a value here, you know that you are being called in response to an action key press.

- *queryActionMsg*: Any text you enter in this element is passed to the search activity invoking intent as an extra string called `SearchManager.ACTION_MSG`. If you retrieve this message from the intent and it is the same as what you have specified in the metadata then you know that you are being called directly from the QSB as a result of clicking on the action key. Without this test you will not know if the `ACTION_SEARCH` is called due to an action key click on the suggestion directly.

- *suggestActionMsg*: Any text you enter in this element is passed to the search activity invoking intent as an extra string called `SearchManager.ACTION_MSG`. The extra keys for this and the `queryActionMsg` are the same. If you give the same value for both of these fields, such as `call`, then you will not know in what way user has invoked the action key. In many cases, this is irrelevant so you can just give the same value for both. But if you have a need to distinguish one from the other, you will need to specify a value that is different from the `queryActionMsg`.

- *suggestActionMsgColumn*: The values `queryActionMsg` and `suggestActionMsg` apply globally to this search activity and the suggestion provider. There isn't a way to alter the action meaning based on the suggestion. If you would like to do that then you will need to tell the metadata that there is an extra column in the suggestion cursor. This will allow Android to pick up the text from that extra column and send it to the activity as part of the invoking `ACTION_SEARCH` intent. Interestingly, the value of this additional column is sent through the same extra key in the intent, namely `SearchManager.ACTION_MSG`.

Among these attributes the key code is mandatory. In addition to this there needs to be at least one of the additional three attributes present for the action key to fire.

If you were to use the `suggestActionMsgColumn`, you would need to populate this column in the suggestion provider class. In Listing 14–29 if you were to use both these keys then you would need to have two additional string columns defined in the suggest cursor (see Listing 14–22), namely `call_column` and `my_column`. In that case, your cursor column array would be as shown in Listing 14–30.

Listing 14–30. *Example of Action Key Columns in the Suggestion Cursor*

```
private static final String[] COLUMNS = {
        "_id",  // must include this column
        SearchManager.SUGGEST_COLUMN_TEXT_1,
        SearchManager.SUGGEST_COLUMN_TEXT_2,
        SearchManager.SUGGEST_COLUMN_INTENT_DATA,
        SearchManager.SUGGEST_COLUMN_INTENT_ACTION,
        SearchManager.SUGGEST_COLUMN_SHORTCUT_ID,
    "call_column",
    "my_column"
        };
```

Working with Application-Specific Search Context

Android search allows an activity to pass additional search data to the search activity when it is invoked. We will walk through the details of this now.

As we have shown, an activity in your application can override the `onSearchRequested()` method to disable search by returning false. Interestingly, the same method can be used instead to pass additional application-specific data to the search activity. Listing 14–31 shows an example.

Listing 14–31. *Passing Additional Context*

```
public boolean onSearchRequested()
{
    Bundle applicationData = new Bundle();
    applicationData.putString("string_key","some string value");
    applicationData.putLong("long_key",290904);
    applicationData.putFloat("float_key",2.0f);

    startSearch(null,          // Initial Search search query string
        false,          //don't "select initial query"
        applicationData,        // extra data
        false           // don't force a global search
        );

    return true;
}
```

> **NOTE:** You can use the following Bundle API reference to see the various functions available on the bundle object:
> `http://developer.android.com/reference/android/os/Bundle.html`.

Once the search has started this way, the activity can use the extra called `SearchManager.APP_DATA` to retrieve the application data bundle. Listing 14–32 shows how you can retrieve each of the above fields.

Listing 14–32. *Retrieving Additional Context*

```
Bundle applicationData =
    queryIntent.getBundleExtra(SearchManager.APP_DATA);
if (applicationData != null)
{
    String s = applicationData.getString("string_key");
    long   l = applicationData.getLong("long_key");
    float  f = applicationData.getFloat("float_key");
}
```

Let us talk about the `startSearch()` method. You can find this method at the following URL as part of the Activity API:

`http://developer.android.com/reference/android/app/Activity.html`

This takes the following four arguments

- `initialQuery // a string argument`
- `selectInitialQuery // boolean`
- `applicationDataBundle //Bundle`
- `globalSearchOnly //boolean`

The first argument, if available, will populate the query text in the QSB.

The second Boolean argument will highlight the text if true. Doing so will enable the user to replace all of the selected query text with what is typed over. If this is false, then the cursor will be at the end of the query text.

The third argument is, of course, the bundle that we are preparing.

The fourth argument, if true, will always invoke a global search. If it is false, then the local search is invoked first, if available; otherwise, it will use the global search.

Resources

As we come to the end of this chapter, we would like to give you a list of resources that we found valuable in writing it.

You can use the following to find the main documentation on Android search from Google. The same URL also works as the API reference for the main Android search facility, namely SearchManager:

```
http://developer.android.com/reference/android/app/SearchManager.html
```

As you design your own search activities, it is sometimes advantageous to set them up as singleTop resulting in the generation of a onNewIntent(). You can find more about this method at

```
http://developer.android.com/reference/android/app/Activity.html#onNewIntent↵
(android.content.Intent)
```

You can refer to the following Google sample online to see how an example suggestion provider is implemented. This link points primarily to the source code of the implementation.

```
http://developer.android.com/guide/samples/SearchableDictionary/index.html
```

You can read about the Search Recent Suggestions API at

```
http://developer.android.com/reference/android/provider/SearchRecentSuggestions.html
```

Read the material at the following URL to understand activities, tasks and launch modes, especially the singleTop launch mode, which is used often as a search activity:

```
http://developer.android.com/guide/topics/fundamentals.html
```

You can use the following Bundle API reference to see the various functions available on the bundle object. This is useful for application-specific search data:

```
http://developer.android.com/reference/android/os/Bundle.html
```

You can find the authors' research on Android search at the following URL. We will continue to update the content even after this book is published. You will also find additional links that will point to a location where you can download the projects described in this chapter.

```
http://www.satyakomatineni.com/akc/display?url=NotesIMPTitlesURL&ownerUserId=↵
satya&folderName=Android%20Search
```

Summary

In this chapter we laid out in a fair amount of detail the internal workings of Android search. You have learned how activities and suggestion providers interact with Android search. We have showed you how to use the `SearchRecentSuggestionsProvider`.

We coded from scratch a custom suggestions provider and, in the process, demonstrated the suggestion cursor and its columns in detail. We explored the URIs that are responsible for getting data from suggestion providers. We have presented a lot of sample code that should make it easy to devise and implement your creative search strategies.

Based on the flexibility of the suggestion cursor alone, Android search transcends a simple search to become a true conduit for information at your fingertips.

Chapter 15

Exploring Text to Speech and Translate APIs

Android 1.6 and later features a multilingual speech synthesis engine called Pico. It allows any Android application to speak a string of text with an accent that matches the language. Text to speech allows applications to interact with users without users having to look at the screen. This can be extremely important for a mobile platform. How many people have accidentally walked into traffic when they were reading a text message? What if you could simply listen to your text messages instead? What if you could listen to a walking tour instead of reading while walking? There are countless applications where the inclusion of voice would improve an application's usefulness. In this chapter, we'll explore the TextToSpeech class of Android and learn what it takes to get our text spoken to us. We'll also learn how to manage the locales, languages, and voices available.

This chapter will also describe how to interface to the online Google Translate API for translating text from one language to another. This capability has been available for a while now.

The Basics of Text to Speech in Android

Before we begin to integrate Text to Speech (TTS) into an application, let's hear it in action. In the emulator or device (Android SDK 1.6 or above), go to the main Settings screen, and then choose Text-to-speech (or "Speech synthesis", depending on which version of Android you're running). There is an option called "Listen to an example". Click this and you should hear the words "This is an example of speech synthesis in English." Notice the other options in this list (see Figure 15–1).

Figure 15–1. *Settings screen for Text to Speech*

You can change the language of the voice, and the speech rate. The language option changes both the words that are spoken as well as the accent of the voice doing the speaking, although the translation is still "This is an example of speech synthesis" in whatever language you've chosen. The text being read is translated, and the accent also changes according to the setting of the Language option. Be aware that the Text to Speech capability is really only the voice part. The translation part is being handled by Google Translate, which we cover in the second half of this chapter. Later, when we're actually implementing TTS in our application, we'll want to match the voice with the language, so the French text is spoken with a French voice. The speech rate value goes from "Very slow" to "Very fast". Pay careful attention to the option "Always use my settings". If this is set by you or by the user here in system settings, it's possible that your application will not behave as you expect since the settings here could override what you want to do in your application.

Let's understand what is happening when we play with these TTS settings. Behind the scenes, Android has fired up Pico, a multilingual speech synthesis engine. The preferences activity we're in has initialized the engine for our current language and speech rate. When we click "Listen to an example", the preferences activity sends text to the engine, and the engine speaks it to our audio output. Pico has broken down the text into pieces it knows how to say, and it has stitched those pieces of audio together in a way that sounds fairly natural. The logic inside the engine is actually much more complex than that, but for our purposes, we can pretend it's magic. Fortunately for us, this magic takes up very little room in terms of disk space and memory, so Pico is an ideal addition to a phone.

There is only one TTS engine on the device. The TTS engine is shared across all activities on the device, so we must be aware that we are not the only ones that might be using the TTS engine. It also means that we cannot be sure when our text will be spoken, or even if it will be spoken at all. The interface to the TTS engine provides us with callbacks, however, so we have some idea of what is going on with the text we've sent to be spoken.

In this example, we're going to create an application that will read our typed text back to us. It is fairly simple, but it's designed to show you how easy it can be to set up Text to Speech. To begin, create a new Android Project using the artifacts from Listing 15–1.

Listing 15–1. *XML and Java Code for Simple TTS Demo*

```xml
<?xml version="1.0" encoding="utf-8"?>
<!-- This file is /res/layout/main.xml -->
<LinearLayout xmlns:android="http://schemas.android.com/apk/res/android"
              android:orientation="vertical"
              android:layout_width="fill_parent"
              android:layout_height="fill_parent">

  <EditText android:id="@+id/wordsToSpeak"
    android:hint="Type words to speak here"
    android:layout_width="fill_parent"
    android:layout_height="wrap_content"/>

  <Button android:id="@+id/speak"
    android:text="Speak"
    android:layout_width="wrap_content"
    android:layout_height="wrap_content"
    android:enabled="false" />

</LinearLayout>
```

```java
import android.app.Activity;
import android.content.Intent;
import android.os.Bundle;
import android.speech.tts.TextToSpeech;
import android.speech.tts.TextToSpeech.OnInitListener;
import android.util.Log;
import android.view.View;
import android.view.View.OnClickListener;
import android.widget.Button;
import android.widget.EditText;

public class MainActivity extends Activity implements OnInitListener {
    private EditText words = null;
    private Button speakBtn = null;
    private static final int REQ_TTS_STATUS_CHECK = 0;
    private static final String TAG = "TTS Demo";
    private TextToSpeech mTts;

    /** Called when the activity is first created. */
    @Override
    public void onCreate(Bundle savedInstanceState) {
        super.onCreate(savedInstanceState);
        setContentView(R.layout.main);

        words = (EditText)findViewById(R.id.wordsToSpeak);
```

```java
        speakBtn = (Button)findViewById(R.id.speak);
        speakBtn.setOnClickListener(new OnClickListener() {
            @Override
            public void onClick(View view) {
                mTts.speak(words.getText().toString(), TextToSpeech.QUEUE_ADD, null);
            }});

        // Check to be sure that TTS exists and is okay to use
        Intent checkIntent = new Intent();
        checkIntent.setAction(TextToSpeech.Engine.ACTION_CHECK_TTS_DATA);
        startActivityForResult(checkIntent, REQ_TTS_STATUS_CHECK);
    }

    protected void onActivityResult(int requestCode, int resultCode, Intent data) {
        if (requestCode == REQ_TTS_STATUS_CHECK) {
            switch (resultCode) {
            case TextToSpeech.Engine.CHECK_VOICE_DATA_PASS:
                // TTS is up and running
                mTts = new TextToSpeech(this, this);
                Log.v(TAG, "Pico is installed okay");
                break;
            case TextToSpeech.Engine.CHECK_VOICE_DATA_BAD_DATA:
            case TextToSpeech.Engine.CHECK_VOICE_DATA_MISSING_DATA:
            case TextToSpeech.Engine.CHECK_VOICE_DATA_MISSING_VOLUME:
                // missing data, install it
                Log.v(TAG, "Need language stuff: " + resultCode);
                Intent installIntent = new Intent();
                installIntent.setAction(
                    TextToSpeech.Engine.ACTION_INSTALL_TTS_DATA);
                startActivity(installIntent);
                break;
            case TextToSpeech.Engine.CHECK_VOICE_DATA_FAIL:
            default:
                Log.e(TAG, "Got a failure. TTS apparently not available");
            }
        }
        else {
            // Got something else
        }
    }

    @Override
    public void onInit(int status) {
        // Now that the TTS engine is ready, we enable the button
        if( status == TextToSpeech.SUCCESS) {
            speakBtn.setEnabled(true);
        }
    }

    @Override
    public void onPause()
    {
        super.onPause();
        // if we're losing focus, stop talking
        if( mTts != null)
            mTts.stop();
    }
```

```
    @Override
    public void onDestroy()
    {
        super.onDestroy();
        mTts.shutdown();
    }
}
```

Our UI for this example is a simple EditText view to allow us to type in the words to be spoken, plus a button to initiate the speaking. (See Figure 15–2.) Our button has an onClick() method which grabs the text string from the EditText view, and queues it for the TTS engine using speak() with QUEUE_ADD. Remember that the TTS engine is being shared, so in this case we queue up our text for speaking behind whatever else might be there (which is most likely nothing). The other option is QUEUE_FLUSH, which will throw away the other text in the queue and immediately play ours instead. At the end of our onCreate() method, we initiate an Intent which requests the TTS engine to let us know if everything is okay for text to be spoken. Because we want the answer back, we use startActivityForResult() and pass a request code. We get the response in onActivityResult() where we look for CHECK_VOICE_DATA_PASS. Because the TTS engine can return more than one type of resultCode meaning OK, we cannot look for RESULT_OK. See the other values we can get by reviewing the switch statement.

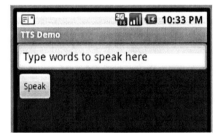

Figure 15–2. *User interface of TTS demo*

If we get CHECK_VOICE_DATA_PASS back, we instantiate a TextToSpeech object. Notice that our MainActivity implements OnInitListener. This allows us to receive a callback when the TTS engine interface has been created and is available, which we receive with the onInit() method. If we get SUCCESS inside of onInit(), then we know we're ready to speak text and we enable our button in the UI. Two more things to note are the call to stop() in onPause(), and the call to shutdown() in onDestroy(). We call stop() because if something goes in front of our application, we've lost focus and should stop talking. We don't want to interrupt something audio-based in another activity that has jumped in front. We call shutdown() to notify Android that we're through with the TTS engine and the resources can be released.

Go ahead and experiment with this example. Try different sentences or phrases. Now give it a large block of text to hear it go on and on. Now consider what would happen if our application were interrupted while the large block of text was being read, perhaps if some other application made a call to the TTS engine with QUEUE_FLUSH, or we simply lost focus. In fact, go ahead and hit the Home button while a large block of text is being spoken. Because of our call to stop() in onPause(), the speaking stops, even though our application is still running in the background. If our application regains focus, how can we know where we were? It would be nice if we had some way to know where we left off so we could begin speaking again, at least close to where we left off. There's a way, but it takes a bit of work.

Using Utterances to Keep Track of Our Speech

The TTS engine can invoke a callback in your application when it has completed speaking a piece of text, called an "utterance" in the TTS world. We set the callback using the setOnUtteranceCompletedListener() method on the TTS instance, mTts in our example above. When calling speak(), we can add a name-value pair to tell the TTS engine to let us know when that utterance is finished being played. By sending unique utterance IDs to the TTS engine, we can keep track of which utterances have been spoken and which have not. If we regain focus after an interruption, we could resume speaking with the next utterance after the last completed utterance. Building upon our previous example, change the code as shown in Listing 15–2 (changes are in bold).

Listing 15–2. *Changes to MainActivity to Illustrate Utterance Tracking*

```
import java.util.HashMap;
import java.util.StringTokenizer;

public class MainActivity extends Activity implements OnInitListener, ↵
OnUtteranceCompletedListener

    private int uttCount = 0;
    private int lastUtterance = -1;
    private HashMap<String, String> params = new HashMap<String, String>();

        @Override
        public void onClick(View view) {
            StringTokenizer st = new StringTokenizer(words.getText().toString(),",.");
            while (st.hasMoreTokens()) {
                params.put(TextToSpeech.Engine.KEY_PARAM_UTTERANCE_ID,
                        String.valueOf(uttCount++));
                mTts.speak(st.nextToken(), TextToSpeech.QUEUE_ADD, params);;
            }
        }

        @Override
        public void onInit(int status) {
            // Now that the TTS engine is ready, we enable the button
            if( status == TextToSpeech.SUCCESS) {
                speakBtn.setEnabled(true);
                mTts.setOnUtteranceCompletedListener(this);
            }
        }

        @Override
        public void onUtteranceCompleted(String uttId) {
            Log.v(TAG, "Got completed message for uttId: " + uttId);
            lastUtterance = Integer.parseInt(uttId);
        }
```

The first thing we need to do is make sure our `MainActivity` also implements the `OnUtteranceCompletedListener` interface. This will allow us to get the callback from the TTS engine when the utterances finish being spoken. We also need to modify our button `onClick()` method to pass the extra information to associate an utterance ID to each piece of text we send. For this new version of our example we're going to break up our text into utterances using the comma and period characters as separators. We then loop through our utterances passing each with `QUEUE_ADD` and not `QUEUE_FLUSH` (we don't want to interrupt ourselves!) and a unique utterance ID, which is a simple incrementing counter, converted to a `String`, of course. We can use any unique text for an utterance ID, since it's a `String`; we're not limited to numbers. In fact, we could use the string itself as the utterance ID, although if the strings get very long we might not want to for performance reasons. We need to modify the `onInit()` method to register ourselves for receiving the utterance completed callbacks and, finally, we need to provide the callback method `onUtteranceCompleted()` for the TTS engine to invoke when an utterance completes. For this example, we're simply going to log a message to `LogCat` for each completed utterance.

When you run this new example, type in some text that contains commas and periods, and then click the Speak button. Watch the `LogCat` window as you listen to the voice reading your text. You will notice that the text is queued up immediately, and as each utterance completes, our callback is invoked and a message is logged for each utterance. If you interrupt this example, for example, by clicking Home while the text is being read, you will see that the voice stops and the callbacks stop. We now know what the last utterance was, and we can pick up where we left off later when we regain control.

Using Audio Files for Your Voice

The TTS engine provides a way to properly pronounce words or utterances that by default come out wrong. For example, if you type in "Don Quixote" as the text to be spoken, you will hear a pronunciation of the name that is not correct. To be fair, the TTS engine is able to make a good guess at how words should sound, and cannot be expected to know every exception to all the rules. So how can this be fixed? One way is to record a snippet of audio to be played back instead of the default audio. In order to get the same voice as everything else, we want to use the TTS engine to make the sound, record the result, then tell the TTS engine to use our recorded sound in place of what it would normally do. The trick is to provide text that sounds like what we want. Let's get started.

Create a new Android project in Eclipse. Use the XML from Listing 15–3 to create the main layout. We're going to make this simpler by putting text directly into our layout file instead of using references to strings. Normally, you would want to use string resource IDs in your layout file. The layout will look like Figure 15–3.

Listing 15–3. *A Layout XML file to Demonstrate Saved Audio for Text*

```
<?xml version="1.0" encoding="utf-8"?>
<!-- This file is /res/layout/main.xml -->
```

```xml
<LinearLayout xmlns:android="http://schemas.android.com/apk/res/android"
    android:orientation="vertical" android:layout_width="fill_parent"
    android:layout_height="fill_parent">

  <EditText android:id="@+id/wordsToSpeak"
    android:text="Dohn Keyhotay"
    android:layout_width="fill_parent"
    android:layout_height="wrap_content"/>

  <Button android:id="@+id/speakBtn"
    android:text="Speak"
    android:layout_width="wrap_content"
    android:layout_height="wrap_content"
    android:enabled="false" />

  <TextView android:id="@+id/filenameLabel"
    android:text="Filename:"
    android:layout_width="wrap_content"
    android:layout_height="wrap_content"/>

  <EditText android:id="@+id/filename"
    android:text="/sdcard/donquixote.wav"
    android:layout_width="fill_parent"
    android:layout_height="wrap_content"/>

  <Button android:id="@+id/recordBtn"
    android:text="Record"
    android:layout_width="wrap_content"
    android:layout_height="wrap_content"
    android:enabled="false" />

  <Button android:id="@+id/playBtn"
    android:text="Play"
    android:layout_width="wrap_content"
    android:layout_height="wrap_content"
    android:enabled="false" />

  <TextView android:id="@+id/useWithLabel"
    android:text="Use with:"
    android:layout_width="wrap_content"
    android:layout_height="wrap_content"/>

  <EditText android:id="@+id/realText"
    android:text="Don Quixote"
    android:layout_width="fill_parent"
    android:layout_height="wrap_content"/>

  <Button android:id="@+id/assocBtn"
    android:text="Associate"
    android:layout_width="wrap_content"
    android:layout_height="wrap_content"
    android:enabled="false" />

</LinearLayout>
```

Figure 15–3. *User interface of TTS demo that associates a sound file to text*

We need a field to hold the special text that we'll record with the TTS engine into a sound file. We supply the file name in the layout as well. Finally, we need to associate our sound file to the actual string we want the sound file to play for.

Now let's look at the Java code for our `MainActivity` (see Listing 15–4). In the `onCreate()` method, we set up button click handlers for the Speak, Play, Record, and Associate buttons, then we initiate the TTS engine using an intent. The rest of the code consists of callbacks to handle the result from the intent that checks for a properly set up TTS engine, to handle the initialization result from the TTS engine, and the normal callbacks for pausing and shutting down our activity.

Listing 15–4. *Java Code to Demonstrate Saved Audio for Text*

```java
import java.io.File;
import android.app.Activity;
import android.content.Intent;
import android.media.MediaPlayer;
import android.os.Bundle;
import android.speech.tts.TextToSpeech;
import android.speech.tts.TextToSpeech.OnInitListener;
import android.util.Log;
import android.view.View;
import android.view.View.OnClickListener;
import android.widget.Button;
import android.widget.EditText;
import android.widget.Toast;

public class MainActivity extends Activity implements OnInitListener {
    private EditText words = null;
    private Button speakBtn = null;
    private EditText filename = null;
```

```java
    private Button recordBtn = null;
    private Button playBtn = null;
    private EditText useWith = null;
    private Button assocBtn = null;
    private String soundFilename = null;
    private File soundFile = null;
    private static final int REQ_TTS_STATUS_CHECK = 0;
    private static final String TAG = "TTS Demo";
    private TextToSpeech mTts = null;
    private MediaPlayer player = null;

    /** Called when the activity is first created. */
    @Override
    public void onCreate(Bundle savedInstanceState) {
        super.onCreate(savedInstanceState);
        setContentView(R.layout.main);

        words = (EditText)findViewById(R.id.wordsToSpeak);
        filename = (EditText)findViewById(R.id.filename);
        useWith = (EditText)findViewById(R.id.realText);

        speakBtn = (Button)findViewById(R.id.speakBtn);
        speakBtn.setOnClickListener(new OnClickListener() {
            @Override
            public void onClick(View view) {
                mTts.speak(words.getText().toString(), TextToSpeech.QUEUE_ADD, null);
            }});

        recordBtn = (Button)findViewById(R.id.recordBtn);
        recordBtn.setOnClickListener(new OnClickListener() {
            @Override
            public void onClick(View view) {
                soundFilename = filename.getText().toString();
                soundFile = new File(soundFilename);
                if (soundFile.exists())
                    soundFile.delete();

                if(mTts.synthesizeToFile(words.getText().toString(), null,
soundFilename)
                        == TextToSpeech.SUCCESS) {
                    Toast.makeText(getBaseContext(),
                            "Sound file created",
                            Toast.LENGTH_SHORT).show();
                    playBtn.setEnabled(true);
                    assocBtn.setEnabled(true);
                }
                else {
                    Toast.makeText(getBaseContext(),
                            "Oops! Sound file not created",
                            Toast.LENGTH_SHORT).show();
                }
            }});

        playBtn = (Button)findViewById(R.id.playBtn);
        playBtn.setOnClickListener(new OnClickListener() {
            @Override
            public void onClick(View view) {
```

```java
        try {
            player = new MediaPlayer();
            player.setDataSource(soundFilename);
            player.prepare();
            player.start();
        }
        catch(Exception e) {
            Toast.makeText(getBaseContext(),
                    "Hmmmmm. Can't play file",
                    Toast.LENGTH_SHORT).show();
            e.printStackTrace();
        }
    }});

    assocBtn = (Button)findViewById(R.id.assocBtn);
    assocBtn.setOnClickListener(new OnClickListener() {
        @Override
        public void onClick(View view) {
            mTts.addSpeech(useWith.getText().toString(), soundFilename);
            Toast.makeText(getBaseContext(),
                    "Associated!",
                    Toast.LENGTH_SHORT).show();
    }});

    // Check to be sure that TTS exists and is okay to use
    Intent checkIntent = new Intent();
    checkIntent.setAction(TextToSpeech.Engine.ACTION_CHECK_TTS_DATA);
    startActivityForResult(checkIntent, REQ_TTS_STATUS_CHECK);
}

protected void onActivityResult(int requestCode, int resultCode, Intent data) {
    if (requestCode == REQ_TTS_STATUS_CHECK) {
        switch (resultCode) {
        case TextToSpeech.Engine.CHECK_VOICE_DATA_PASS:
            // TTS is up and running
            mTts = new TextToSpeech(this, this);
            Log.v(TAG, "Pico is installed okay");
            break;
        case TextToSpeech.Engine.CHECK_VOICE_DATA_BAD_DATA:
        case TextToSpeech.Engine.CHECK_VOICE_DATA_MISSING_DATA:
        case TextToSpeech.Engine.CHECK_VOICE_DATA_MISSING_VOLUME:
            // missing data, install it
            Log.v(TAG, "Need language stuff: " + resultCode);
            Intent installIntent = new Intent();
            installIntent.setAction(
                TextToSpeech.Engine.ACTION_INSTALL_TTS_DATA);
            startActivity(installIntent);
            break;
        case TextToSpeech.Engine.CHECK_VOICE_DATA_FAIL:
        default:
            Log.e(TAG, "Got a failure. TTS apparently not available");
        }
    }
    else {
        // Got something else
    }
}
```

```
    @Override
    public void onInit(int status) {
        // Now that the TTS engine is ready, we enable buttons
        if( status == TextToSpeech.SUCCESS) {
            speakBtn.setEnabled(true);
            recordBtn.setEnabled(true);
        }
    }

    @Override
    public void onPause()
    {
        super.onPause();
        // if we're losing focus, stop playing
        if(player != null) {
            player.stop();
        }
        // if we're losing focus, stop talking
        if( mTts != null)
            mTts.stop();
    }

    @Override
    public void onDestroy()
    {
        super.onDestroy();
        if(player != null) {
            player.release();
        }
        if( mTts != null) {
            mTts.shutdown();
        }
    }
}
```

For this example to work, we need to add a permission in our AndroidManifest.xml file for android.permission.WRITE_EXTERNAL_STORAGE. When you run this example, you should see the UI as displayed in Figure 15–3.

We're going to record some text that sounds like what we want "Don Quixote" to sound like, except we can't use the real words. We need to make up text to get the sounds we want. Click the Speak button to hear how the fake words sound. Not too bad! Then click Record to write the audio to a WAV file. When the record is successful, the Play and Associate buttons get enabled. Click the Play button to hear the WAV file directly using a MediaPlayer. If you like how this sounds, click the Associate button. This invokes the addSpeech() method on the TTS engine which then ties our new sound file to the string in the "Use with" field. If this is successful, go back up to the top EditText view and type in "Don Quixote" and click Speak. Now it sounds like it's supposed to. Note that the synthesizeToFile() method only saves to the WAV file format, regardless of the file name extension, but you can associate other formatted sound files using addSpeech() — for example, MP3 files. The MP3 files will have to be created some way other than by using the synthesizeToFile() method of the TTS engine.

The uses of this method for speaking are very limited. In a scenario with unbounded words—that is, when you don't know in advance which words will be presented for speech—it is impossible to have at the ready all of the audio files you would need to fix the words that do not get pronounced correctly by Pico. In scenarios with a bounded domain of words—for example, reading the weather forecast—you could go through an exercise of testing all of the words in your application to find those that don't sound right and fixing them. Even in an unbounded situation, you could prepare some word sounds in advance so that critical words you expect will sound correct. You might, for instance, want to have a sound file at the ready for your company name, or your own name!

There's a dark side to the use of this method, however: the text you pass to `speak()` must match exactly the text you used in the call to `addSpeech()`. Unfortunately, you cannot provide an audio file for a single word and then expect the TTS engine to use the audio file for that word when you pass that word as part of a sentence to `speak()`. To hear your audio file you must present the exact text that the audio file represents. Anything more, or less, and Pico kicks in and does the best it can. One way around this is to break up our text into words, and pass each word separately to the TTS engine. While this could result in our audio file being played (of course we'd need to record "Quixote" separately from "Don"), the overall result will be choppy speech, as if each word were its own sentence. In some applications this might be acceptable. The ideal use case for audio files occurs when we need to speak predetermined canned words or phrases, where we know exactly in advance the text we'll need to have spoken.

So what are we to do when we know we'll get words in sentences that cannot be properly spoken by Pico? One method might be to scan our text for known "trouble" words, and to replace those words with "fake" words that we know Pico can speak properly. We don't need to show the text to the user that we give to the `speak()` method. So perhaps we could replace "Quixote" in our text with "Keyhotay" before we call `speak()`. The outcome is that it sounds right and the user is none the wiser. In terms of resource usage, storing the fake string is much more efficient than storing an audio file, even though we're still calling Pico. We had to call Pico for the rest of our text, so it's not much of a loss at all. On the other hand, we don't want to do too much second-guessing of Pico. That is, Pico has a lot of intelligence on how to pronounce things, and if we try to do Pico's job for it, we could run into trouble quickly.

In our last example, we recorded a sound file for a piece of text, so that when the TTS engine read it back to us later, it accessed the sound file instead of generating the speech using Pico. As you might expect, playing a small sound file takes fewer device resources than running a TTS engine and interfacing with it. Therefore, if you have a manageable set of words or phrases to provide sound for, you might want to create sound files in advance, even if the Pico engine pronounces them correctly. This will help your application run faster. If you have a small number of sound files, you will probably use less overall memory too. If you take this approach, you will want to use the following method call:

```
TextToSpeech.addSpeech(String text, String packagename, int soundFileResourceId)
```

This is a very simple way of adding sound files to the TTS engine. The text argument is the string to play the sound file for, `packagename` is the application package name where the resource file is stored, and soundFileResourceId is the resource ID of the sound file. Store your sound files under your application's /res/raw directory. When your application starts up, add your prerecorded sound files to the TTS engine by referring to their resource ID (e.g., R.raw.quixote). Of course you'll need some sort of database, or a predefined list, to know which text each sound file is for. If you are internationalizing your application, you can store the alternate sound files under the appropriate /res/raw directory; for example /res/raw-fr for French sound files.

Advanced Features of the TTS Engine

Now that you've learned the basics of Text to Speech, let's explore some advanced features of the TTS engine. We'll start with setting audio streams, which help you direct the spoken voice to the proper audio output channel. Next, we'll cover playing earcons (audible icons) and silence. Then we'll cover setting language options, and finish with a few miscellaneous method calls.

Setting Audio Streams

Earlier, we used a params HashMap to pass extra arguments to the TTS engine. One of the arguments we can pass (KEY_PARAM_STREAM) tells the TTS engine which audio stream to use for the text we want to hear spoken. See Table 15–1 for a list of the available audio streams.

Table 15–1. *Available Audio Streams*

Audio Stream	Description
STREAM_ALARM	The audio stream for alarms
STREAM_MUSIC	The audio stream for music playback
STREAM_NOTIFICATION	The audio stream for notifications
STREAM_RING	The audio stream for the phone ring
STREAM_SYSTEM	The audio stream for system sounds
STREAM_VOICE_CALL	The audio stream for phone calls

If the text we want spoken is related to an alarm, then we want to tell the TTS engine to play the audio over the audio stream for alarms. Therefore, we'd want to make a call like this prior to calling the speak() method:

```
params.put(TextToSpeech.Engine.KEY_PARAM_STREAM,
                String.valueOf(AudioManager.STREAM_ALARM));
```

Review Listing 15–2 to recall how we set up and passed a params HashMap to the speak() method call. You can put utterance IDs into the same params HashMap as the one you use to specify the audio stream.

Using Earcons

There is another type of sound that the TTS engine can play for us called earcons. An earcon is like an audible icon. It's not supposed to represent text, but rather provide an audible cue to some sort of event, or to the presence of something in the text that is not textual. An earcon could be a sound to indicate that we're now reading bullet points from a presentation, or that we've just flipped to the next page. Maybe your application is for a walking tour and the earcon tells the listener to move on to the next location on the tour.

To set up an earcon for playback, you need to invoke the addEarcon() method, which takes two or three arguments, similar to how addSpeech() works. The first argument is the name of the earcon, similar to the text field of addSpeech(). Convention says that you should enclose your earcon name in square brackets (e.g., "[boing]"). In the two-argument case, the second argument is a file-name string. In the three-argument case, the second argument is the package name, and the third argument is a resource ID, where the resource ID refers to an audio file most likely stored under /res/raw. To get an earcon played, use the playEarcon() method, which looks just like the speak() method with its three arguments.

The reason we use earcons instead of simply playing audio files using MediaPlayer is due to the queuing mechanism of the TTS engine. Instead of having to determine the opportune moment to play an audible cue, relying on callbacks to get the timing right, we can instead queue up our earcons among the text we send to the TTS engine. We then know that our earcons will be played at the appropriate time, and we can use the same pathway to get our sounds to the user, including the onUtteranceCompleted() callbacks to let us know where we are.

Playing Silence

The TTS engine has yet one more play method that we can use: playSilence(). This method also has three arguments like speak() and playEarcon(), where the second argument is the queue mode and the third is the optional params HashMap. The first argument to playSilence() is a long which represents the number of milliseconds to play silence for. You'd most likely use this method with the QUEUE_ADD mode in order to separate two different strings of text in time. That is, you could insert a period of silence in between two strings of text without having to manage the wait time in your application. You'd simply call speak(), and then playSilence(), and then another call to speak() to get the desired effect.

Using Language Methods

We haven't yet addressed the question of language, so we'll turn to that now. The Text to Speech capability reads text using a voice that corresponds to the language it was created for. The Italian voice is expecting to see text in the Italian language. It recognizes features of the text in order to pronounce it correctly. For this reason, it doesn't make sense to use the wrong language voice with the text sent to the TTS engine. Speaking French text with an Italian voice is likely to cause problems. It is best to match up the locale of the text with the locale of the voice.

The TTS engine provides some methods for languages, both to find out what languages are available, and to set the language for speaking. The TTS engine only has a certain number of language packs available, although it will be able to reach out to the Android Market to get more if they are available. We saw some code for this in Listing 15–1 within the onActivityResult() callback, where an Intent was created to get a missing language. Of course it is possible that the desired language pack has not been made available yet, but more and more will be available over time.

The method to check on a language is isLanguageAvailable(Locale locale). Since locales can represent both country and a language, and sometimes a variant, the answer back is not a simple true or false. The answer could be one of the following: TextToSpeech.LANG_COUNTRY_AVAILABLE which means that both country and language are supported, TextToSpeech.LANG_AVAILABLE which means that the language is supported but not the country, and TextToSpeech.LANG_NOT_SUPPORTED which means that nothing is supported. If you get back TextToSpeech.LANG_MISSING_DATA it means that the language is supported but the data files were not found by the TTS engine. Your application should direct the user to the Android Market, or suitable source, to find the missing data files. For example, the French language might be supported, but not French Canadian. If that were the case, if Locale.CANADA_FRENCH was passed to the TTS engine, the response would be TextToSpeech.LANG_AVAILABLE and not TextToSpeech.LANG_COUNTRY_AVAILABLE. The other possible return value is a special case where the Locale might include a variant, in which case the response could be TextToSpeech.LANG_COUNTRY_VAR_AVAILABLE, which means everything is supported.

The method to set a language is setLanguage(Locale locale). This returns the same result codes as does isLanguageAvailable(). To get the current default locale of the device, use the Locale.getDefault() method, which will return a locale value such as en_US or the appropriate value for where you are. Use the getLanguage() method of the TextToSpeech class to find out the current locale of the TTS engine. It would have been quite acceptable for us to use something like this in our example above to set the language for the TTS engine:

```
switch(mTts.setLanguage(Locale.getDefault())) {
case TextToSpeech.LANG_COUNTRY_AVAILABLE: …
```

Finally, to wrap up this discussion of Text to Speech, we'll cover a few other methods you can use. The setPitch(float pitch) method will change the voice to be higher or lower pitched, without changing the speed of the speaking. The normal value for pitch is 1.0. The lowest meaningful value appears to be 0.5 and the highest 2.0. You can set values lower and higher, but they don't appear to change the pitch any more after crossing these thresholds. The same thresholds appear to hold for the `setSpeechRate(float rate)` method. That is, you pass this method a float argument with a value between 0.5 and 2.0, where 1.0 would be a normal speech rate. A number higher than 1.0 means faster speaking, and lower than 1.0 means slower speaking. Another method you might want to use is `isSpeaking()`. This method returns `true` or `false` to indicate whether or not the TTS engine is currently speaking anything (including silence from `playSilence()`). If you need to be notified when the TTS engine has completed saying everything from its queue, you could implement a `BroadcastReceiver` for the `ACTION_TTS_QUEUE_PROCESSING_COMPLETED` broadcast.

Translating Text to a Different Language

In the first half of this chapter we showed you how to get text spoken audibly to the user. We were able to specify the accent of the voice using the TextToSpeech engine. In this section we will show you how to translate text from one language to another. Coupled with TextToSpeech, you will be able to take text from one language and speak it to your users in another language, complete with a proper voice.

Translating from one language to another is not something that will fit very well on a mobile device. The number of words in English alone is hundreds of thousands, even possibly more than a million (depending on how you define "English"). Loading languages and rules onto a mobile device to allow translation between arbitrary pairs of languages is just not feasible, yet.

Google has supplied an API on the Internet that does translations. It takes a string of text, and a pair of language specifications, one for the source and one for the destination, and it converts the text from the source language to the destination language. There is a catch though. The original intent of this service was to be called from web sites, not mobile devices. The Terms of Use for the Google AJAX Language API (as it is formally known) does not have a version for Android devices, like the Google Maps API Terms of Use does. To read the Terms of Use for the AJAX Language API, go here:

`http://code.google.com/apis/ajaxlanguage/terms.html`

While it is not entirely clear that Google intends Android developers to use this API, in fact, a demonstration of this API was given at Google I/O in May 2009 using an Android application! Perhaps by the time you read this, Google will have a separate Terms of Use for Android for the AJAX Language API, or perhaps the existing Terms will have been updated to make it clearer how they intend for it to be used with Android. In the meantime, you have a couple of options. First, you could go ahead and use the AJAX Language API directly from your Android application, as we will show you next. Second, you could access the AJAX Language API using a web server that you control, like a proxy to the AJAX Language API. Your application would interface with your web server, and your web server would make the calls to the AJAX Language API. With your own web server in the middle, it becomes much easier to disable the access to the AJAX Language API from your application, since you control a chokepoint between them. Of course, there may not be much you can do to allow your application to continue to work if you can't use the Google service anymore. At a minimum, you could build in some sort of response to your application that indicates that the service is no longer available from Google, in order to provide a suitable message to the user. In the former case, if Google asks that you stop using the AJAX Language API, you really won't be able to do much about it; your application has been distributed to devices and unless you've built in some way to make them stop using the API, they will continue to try to do so.

Google has the right to disable your access, but this could be somewhat difficult for them to do. Google did not state in the Terms of Use that you need to use an API key to use the AJAX Language API, although in the Developer Documentation (http://code.google.com/apis/ajaxlanguage/documentation/) it states that you *must* use a REFERER and you *should* use an API key. Without these, your requests will appear anonymously from the users' devices, and Google will have no way of contacting you if there is some problem with your use of the API. We've chosen to set the REFERER header value in our example below (see the Translator.java code) but we skipped the API key part. If you want to send an API key value to the AJAX Language API, you will first need to acquire one from Google. There are several API keys to choose from but, as of this writing, there is no way to get an API key specifically for the AJAX Language API. API keys for other AJAX APIs come with their own Terms of Use that you must agree to prior to getting a new API key. Note that you should not reuse your Maps API key for the AJAX APIs. To register for an AJAX API key, you only need submit the URL of your web site (the same one you used as your REFERER) and agree to the Terms of Use. With the new API key in hand, you would add it to the AJAX API URL with the following snippet:

```
&key=Your_API_key_goes_here_with_no_quotation_marks
```

If you decide to pass an API key to an AJAX API, the REFERER must be set to the same URL that you used to create the API key, or some sub-page of that URL. Otherwise, you will not get results back.

For the rest of this section, we will help you build an application that calls the Google AJAX Language API directly. Up to this point in the book, we've shown you all the individual components you need to get translations into your application. Now we'll bring them all together. For this example, we're going to create an application with an EditText for the input, use spinners to select the languages to translate to and from, a read-only EditText for the translated output, invoke a service over the Internet, and use a service to isolate the UI from logic that might take a while to succeed. One of the extras we need to include in this application is the Jakarta Commons Lang project, specifically to unescape XML entity codes into Unicodes for display. We'll cover how to do that too. Refer to Listing 15–5 for the XML layout, and Figure 15–4 to see what it looks like. Other listings will follow to flesh out the entire application. While it may seem like a lot of code here in this chapter, it's really not that much if you consider the functionality you are getting. (Also, you've seen everything in this example before in earlier chapters, from setting up a service to using spinners as drop-down menus.)

Listing 15–5. *XML Layout to Implement a Translation Demonstration*

```xml
<?xml version="1.0" encoding="utf-8"?>
<!-- This file is /res/layout/main.xml -->
<RelativeLayout xmlns:android="http://schemas.android.com/apk/res/android"
    android:orientation="vertical"
    android:layout_height="fill_parent"
    android:layout_width="fill_parent">

    <EditText android:id="@+id/input"
        android:hint="@string/input"
        android:layout_height="wrap_content"
        android:layout_width="fill_parent" />

    <Spinner android:id="@+id/from"
        android:layout_weight="1"
        android:layout_width="wrap_content"
        android:layout_height="wrap_content"
        android:layout_below="@id/input"
        android:prompt="@string/prompt" />

    <Button android:id="@+id/translateBtn"
        android:text="@string/translateBtn"
        android:layout_weight="1"
        android:layout_width="wrap_content"
        android:layout_height="wrap_content"
        android:layout_below="@id/input"
        android:layout_toRightOf="@id/from"
        android:enabled="false" />

    <Spinner android:id="@+id/to"
        android:layout_weight="1"
        android:layout_width="wrap_content"
        android:layout_height="wrap_content"
        android:layout_below="@id/input"
        android:layout_toRightOf="@id/translateBtn"
        android:prompt="@string/prompt" />

    <EditText android:id="@+id/translation"
        android:hint="@string/translation"
        android:layout_height="wrap_content"
        android:layout_width="fill_parent"
        android:editable="false"
        android:layout_below="@id/from" />

    <TextView android:id="@+id/poweredBy"
        android:text="powered by Google"
        android:layout_width="wrap_content"
        android:layout_height="wrap_content"
        android:layout_alignParentBottom="true" />

</RelativeLayout>
```

Figure 15–4. *The Translate demo UI*

Our layout is fairly straightforward. We set up fields for the text, what we're translating from and what we're translating to. We also set up spinners as drop-down menus for the language choices from and to. We of course need a button to initiate the translation and, finally, we need the "powered by Google" string which we anchor to the bottom of the screen (more on why we need to show this string later). Listing 15–6 shows the strings.xml and the arrays.xml files which are used to set up the strings in our user interface and menus.

Listing 15–6. *strings.xml and arrays.xml*

```xml
<?xml version="1.0" encoding="utf-8"?>
<!-- This file is /res/values/strings.xml -->
<resources>
    <string name="translateBtn">> Translate ></string>
    <string name="input">Enter the text to translate</string>
    <string name="translation">The translation will appear here</string>
    <string name="prompt">Choose a language</string>
</resources>


<?xml version="1.0" encoding="utf-8"?>
<!-- This file is /res/values/arrays.xml -->
<resources>
<string-array name="languages">
    <item>Chinese</item>
    <item>English</item>
    <item>French</item>
    <item>German</item>
    <item>Japanese</item>
    <item>Spanish</item>
</string-array>
<string-array name="language_values">
    <item>zh</item>
    <item>en</item>
    <item>fr</item>
    <item>de</item>
    <item>ja</item>
    <item>es</item>
</string-array>
</resources>
```

Now that our user interface is basically done, let's turn our attention to the service we're going to create that will interact with the Google AJAX Language API. Listing 15–7 contains the files to define the service interface.

Listing 15–7. *The Service Interface Files for Our Translate Application*

```
// This file is ITranslate.aidl under /src
interface ITranslate {
    String translate(in String text, in String from, in String to);
}


// This file is TranslateService.java
import android.app.Service;
import android.content.Intent;
import android.os.IBinder;
import android.util.Log;

public class TranslateService extends Service {
    public static final String TAG = "TranslateService";

    private final ITranslate.Stub mBinder = new ITranslate.Stub() {
        public String translate(String text, String from, String to) {
            try {
                return Translator.translate(text, from, to);
            } catch (Exception e) {
                Log.e(TAG, "Failed to translate: " + e.getMessage());
                return null;
            }
        }
    };

    @Override
    public IBinder onBind(Intent intent) {
        return mBinder;
    }
}
```

Remember that Eclipse will automatically generate Java code from our .aidl file once we save it in Eclipse. Our new service needs to invoke the static `Translator.translate()` method, which is provided as part of Listing 15–8.

Listing 15–8. *Java Code to Interface with the Google AJAX Language API*

```
// This file is Translator.java
import java.io.BufferedReader;
import java.io.InputStream;
import java.io.InputStreamReader;
import java.net.HttpURLConnection;
import java.net.URL;
import java.net.URLEncoder;

import org.apache.commons.lang.StringEscapeUtils;
import org.json.JSONObject;
import android.util.Log;


public class Translator {
```

```java
    private static final String ENCODING = "UTF-8";
    private static final String URL_BASE = ↵
"http://ajax.googleapis.com/ajax/services/language/translate?v=1.0&langpair=";
    private static final String INPUT_TEXT = "&q=";
    private static final String MY_SITE = "http://my.website.com";
    private static final String TAG = "Translator";

    public static String translate(String text, String from, String to) throws Exception
    {
        try {
            StringBuilder url = new StringBuilder();
            url.append(URL_BASE).append(from).append("%7C").append(to);
            url.append(INPUT_TEXT).append(URLEncoder.encode(text, ENCODING));

            HttpURLConnection conn = (HttpURLConnection) new URL(url.toString())
                                .openConnection();
            conn.setRequestProperty("REFERER", MY_SITE);
            conn.setDoInput(true);
            conn.setDoOutput(true);
            try {
                InputStream is= conn.getInputStream();
                String rawResult = makeResult(is);

                JSONObject json = new JSONObject(rawResult);
                String result = ((JSONObject)json.get("responseData"))
                                        .getString("translatedText");
                return (StringEscapeUtils.unescapeXml(result));
            } finally {
                conn.getInputStream().close();
                if(conn.getErrorStream() != null)
                    conn.getErrorStream().close();
            }
        } catch (Exception ex) {
            throw ex;
        }
    }

    private static String makeResult(InputStream inputStream) throws Exception {
        StringBuilder outputString = new StringBuilder();
        try {
            String string;
            if (inputStream != null) {
                BufferedReader reader =
                        new BufferedReader(new InputStreamReader(inputStream,
ENCODING));
                while (null != (string = reader.readLine())) {
                    outputString.append(string).append('\n');
                }
            }
        } catch (Exception ex) {
            Log.e(TAG, "Error reading translation stream.", ex);
        }
        return outputString.toString();
    }
}
```

The Translator class is where the meat is in this sample application. Basically, it creates an HTTP call to the Google AJAX Language API service, then reads the response. We'll get into the details a little later, but first, let's finish creating our sample application so you can try it out. Next up in Listing 15–9 is the Java code for our MainActivity.

Listing 15–9. *Java Code for our MainActivity*

```java
// This file is MainActivity.java
import android.app.Activity;
import android.content.ComponentName;
import android.content.Context;
import android.content.Intent;
import android.content.ServiceConnection;
import android.os.Bundle;
import android.os.Handler;
import android.os.IBinder;
import android.util.Log;
import android.view.View;
import android.view.View.OnClickListener;
import android.widget.ArrayAdapter;
import android.widget.Button;
import android.widget.EditText;
import android.widget.Spinner;
import android.widget.TextView;

public class MainActivity extends Activity implements OnClickListener {
    static final String TAG = "Translator";
    private EditText inputText = null;
    private TextView outputText = null;
    private Spinner fromLang = null;
    private Spinner toLang = null;
    private Button translateBtn = null;
    private String[] langShortNames = null;
    private Handler mHandler = new Handler();

    private ITranslate mTranslateService;

    private ServiceConnection mTranslateConn = new ServiceConnection() {
        public void onServiceConnected(ComponentName name, IBinder service) {
            mTranslateService = ITranslate.Stub.asInterface(service);
            if (mTranslateService != null) {
                translateBtn.setEnabled(true);
            } else {
                translateBtn.setEnabled(false);
                Log.e(TAG, "Unable to acquire TranslateService");
            }
        }

        public void onServiceDisconnected(ComponentName name) {
            translateBtn.setEnabled(false);
            mTranslateService = null;
        }
    };

    @Override
    protected void onCreate(Bundle icicle) {
        super.onCreate(icicle);
```

```
        setContentView(R.layout.main);
        inputText = (EditText) findViewById(R.id.input);
        outputText = (EditText) findViewById(R.id.translation);
        fromLang = (Spinner) findViewById(R.id.from);
        toLang = (Spinner) findViewById(R.id.to);

        langShortNames = getResources().getStringArray(R.array.language_values);

        translateBtn = (Button) findViewById(R.id.translateBtn);
        translateBtn.setOnClickListener(this);

        ArrayAdapter<?> fromAdapter = ArrayAdapter.createFromResource(this,
                R.array.languages, android.R.layout.simple_spinner_item);

fromAdapter.setDropDownViewResource(android.R.layout.simple_dropdown_item_1line);
        fromLang.setAdapter(fromAdapter);
        fromLang.setSelection(1); // English

        ArrayAdapter<?> toAdapter = ArrayAdapter.createFromResource(this,
                R.array.languages,android.R.layout.simple_spinner_item);
        toAdapter.setDropDownViewResource(android.R.layout.simple_dropdown_item_1line);
        toLang.setAdapter(toAdapter);
        toLang.setSelection(3); // German

        inputText.selectAll();

        Intent intent = new Intent(Intent.ACTION_VIEW);
        bindService(intent, mTranslateConn, Context.BIND_AUTO_CREATE);
    }

    @Override
    protected void onDestroy() {
        super.onDestroy();
        unbindService(mTranslateConn);
    }

    public void onClick(View v) {
        if (inputText.getText().length() > 0) {
            doTranslate();
        }
    }

    private void doTranslate() {
        mHandler.post(new Runnable() {
            public void run() {
                String result = "";
                try {
                    int fromPosition = fromLang.getSelectedItemPosition();
                    int toPosition = toLang.getSelectedItemPosition();
                    String input = inputText.getText().toString();
                    if(input.length() > 5000)
                        input = input.substring(0,5000);
                    Log.v(TAG,"Translating from " + langShortNames[fromPosition] + " to
" +
                                langShortNames[toPosition]);
                    result = mTranslateService.translate(input,
```

```
                                langShortNames[fromPosition],
                                langShortNames[toPosition]);
                    if (result == null) {
                        throw new Exception("Failed to get a translation");
                    }
                    outputText.setText(result);
                    inputText.selectAll();
                } catch (Exception e) {
                    Log.e(TAG, "Error: " + e.getMessage());
                }
            }
        });
    }
}
```

Our MainActivity sets up the user interface and the service, then provides a method to call for translation when the button is pressed. There's only one thing left to do and that's configure our AndroidManifest.xml file, which is shown in Listing 15–10. Notice that we need to get permission to access the Internet in order to invoke the Google AJAX Language API.

Listing 15–10. *The AndroidManifest.xml file*

```xml
<?xml version="1.0" encoding="utf-8"?>
<!-- This file is AndroidManifest.xml -->
<manifest xmlns:android="http://schemas.android.com/apk/res/android"
    package="com.androidbook.translation"
    android:versionName="1.0"
    android:versionCode="1" >

    <application android:label="Translate"
        android:icon="@drawable/icon">

        <activity android:name="MainActivity" android:label="Translate">
            <intent-filter>
                <action android:name="android.intent.action.MAIN" />
                <category android:name="android.intent.category.DEFAULT" />
                <category android:name="android.intent.category.LAUNCHER" />
            </intent-filter>
        </activity>

        <service android:name="TranslateService" android:label="Translate">
            <intent-filter>
                <action android:name="android.intent.action.VIEW" />
                <category android:name="android.intent.category.DEFAULT" />
            </intent-filter>
        </service>
    </application>
    <uses-permission android:name="android.permission.INTERNET" />
</manifest>
```

Before this example will build properly, we need to provide a helper class. The Jakarta Commons Lang project has a class called StringEscapeUtils that we would like to use to convert the result string from the AJAX Language API into something human-readable. The AJAX Language API can give us back XML entities representing certain special characters. For example, an apostrophe would come back as '. We want to display those special characters properly to the user. That's where the Jakarta Commons Lang project comes in. You will find it here:

```
http://commons.apache.org/lang/
```

Go to the Jakarta Commons Lang web site, then find and download the appropriate .zip file (for Windows) or .tar file (for Mac OS X or Linux) that contains the jar file. Unpack it so you can get to the jar file for the next step. Within Eclipse, you're going to select the project, right-click and choose Build Path ➤ Configure Build Path. Click the Libraries tab, then Add External JARs. Navigate to the commons-lang jar file and add it. Now click OK to finish adding the jar file to the project. Your application should build to completion. Go ahead and try it out. If the application doesn't fit too well in portrait mode, try using the Ctrl-F12 trick to switch the emulator to landscape mode. If you doubt any of the results you get back, go to this site to compare your results with Google's:

```
http://www.google.com/uds/samples/language/translate.html
```

There are several items we'd like to draw your attention to. Due to the Terms of Use, this example includes a "powered by Google" string on the UI. Also in the Terms of Use, the strings you pass must not exceed 5000 characters, so we cut them off if that happens. You'd likely want to do something a little different there, such as breaking the text into manageable chunks of text to pass to the API so you don't lose anything. We've intentionally kept the list of languages short just to make this application manageable, but feel free to add additional languages to the string arrays to do more translations. However, be aware that the Droid fonts may not have every character for every language that the translator can translate. Droid fonts were created especially for Android but they do not cover all characters for all languages. If you see strangeness in the results, you might suspect that you've got a font problem. It is possible to acquire additional fonts to alleviate this, but we won't be covering fonts in this chapter. The response from the API is structured using JSON. Therefore we use JSON to parse the response into our result string. (Note that JSON is provided as part of Android so we didn't need to grab it from the Internet to include it as an external jar file.)

One of the features of the AJAX Language API is that you don't have to tell it what the input language is. The API will make an attempt at guessing the input language. If you want to take this approach, you can choose to leave off the input language in the URL that you pass, and instead immediately follow the langpair= with %7C. This would be handy if you're not sure what language will be provided to you; however, without a sufficient amount of text passed to it, the API may not guess correctly.

Summary

In this chapter, we've shown you how to get your Android application to talk to the user. Android has incorporated a very nice TTS engine to facilitate this functionality. For a developer, there's not much to figure out. The Pico engine takes care of most of the work for us. When Pico runs into trouble there are ways to get to the desired effect, as we've demonstrated. The advanced features make life pretty easy too. The thing to keep in mind when working with Text to Speech is you must be a good mobile citizen: conserve resources, share the TTS engine responsibly, and use your voice appropriately.

We also showed you how to call a Google API over the Internet. For this particular case, we used the Google AJAX Language API, but you can use the same technique to access other Google APIs as well. When you need to perform on-the-fly translations of text from one language to another, this is a great way to do it.

Chapter 16

Touchscreens

Many Android devices incorporate touchscreens. When a device does not have a physical keyboard, much of the user input *must* come through the touchscreen. Therefore your applications will often need to be able to deal with touch input from the user. You've most likely already seen the virtual keyboard that displays on the screen when text input is required from the user. We used touch with mapping applications in Chapter 7 to pan the maps sideways. These implementations of the touchscreen interface have been hidden from you so far, but now we'll show you how to take advantage of the touchscreen.

This chapter is made up of four major parts. The first section will deal with MotionEvent objects, which is how Android tells an application that the user is touching a touchscreen. We'll also cover the VelocityTracker and drag and drop. The second section will deal with multi-touch, where a user can have more than one finger at a time on the touchscreen. The third section covers touches with maps, since there are some special classes and methods to help us with maps and touchscreens. Finally, we will include a section on gestures, a specialized type of capability in which touch sequences can be interpreted as commands.

Understanding MotionEvents

In this section we're going to cover how Android tells applications about touch events from the user. For now, we will only be concerned with one-finger-at-a-time touching the touchscreen. (We'll cover multi-touch in a later section.)

At the hardware level, a touchscreen is made up of special materials that can pick up pressure and convert that to screen coordinates. The information about the touch is turned into data, and that data is passed to the software to deal with it.

When a user touches the touchscreen of an Android device, a MotionEvent object is created. The MotionEvent contains information about where and when the touch took place, as well as other details of the touch event. The MotionEvent object gets passed to an appropriate method in your application. This could be the onTouchEvent() method of a View object. Remember that the View class is the parent of quite a few classes in

Android, including Layouts, Buttons, Lists, Surfaces, Clocks and more. This means we can interact with all of these different types of View objects using touch events. When the method is called, it can inspect the MotionEvent object to decide what to do. For example, a MapView could use touch events to move the map sideways to allow the user to pan the map to other points of interest. Or a virtual keyboard object could receive touch events to activate the virtual keys to provide text input to some other part of the user interface (UI).

A MotionEvent object is one of a sequence of events related to a touch by the user. The sequence starts when the user first touches the touchscreen, continues through any movements of the finger across the surface of the touchscreen, and ends when the finger is lifted from the touchscreen. The initial touch (an ACTION_DOWN action), the movements sideways (ACTION_MOVE actions) and the up event (an ACTION_UP action) of the finger all create MotionEvent objects. For ACTION_MOVE events, you could receive quite a few as the finger moves across the surface before you receive the final ACTION_UP event. Each MotionEvent object contains information about what action is being performed, where the touch is taking place, how much pressure was applied, how big the touch was, when the action occurred, and when the initial ACTION_DOWN occurred. There is a fourth possible action, which is ACTION_CANCEL. This action is used to indicate that a touch sequence is ending without actually doing anything. Finally, there is ACTION_OUTSIDE, which is set in a special case where a touch occurs outside of our window but we still get to find out about it.

There is another way to receive touch events, and that is to register a callback handler for touch events on a View object. The class to receive the events must implement the View.OnTouchListener interface, and the View object's setOnTouchListener() method must be called to setup the handler for that View. The implementing class of the View.OnTouchListener must implement the onTouch() method. Whereas the onTouchEvent() method takes just a MotionEvent object as a parameter, onTouch() takes both a View and a MotionEvent object as parameters. This is because the OnTouchListener could receive MotionEvent objects for multiple views. This will become clearer with our next example application.

If a MotionEvent handler (either through the onTouchEvent() or onTouch() method) consumes the event and no one else needs to know about it, the method should return true. This tells Android that the event does not need to be passed to any other views. If the View object is not interested in this event *nor any future events related to this touch sequence*, it returns false. The onTouchEvent() method of the base class View doesn't do anything and returns false. Subclasses of View may or may not do the same. For example, a Button object will consume a touch event since a touch is equivalent to a click, and therefore returns true from the onTouchEvent() method. Upon receiving an ACTION_DOWN event, the Button will change its color to indicate that it is in the process of being clicked, and the Button also wants to receive the ACTION_UP event to know when the user has let go so it can initiate the logic of clicking the button. If a Button object returned false from onTouchEvent(), it would not receive any more MotionEvent objects to tell it when the user lifted their finger from the touchscreen.

When we want touch events to do something new with a particular View object, we can extend the class, override the onTouchEvent() method, and put our logic there. We can also implement the View.OnTouchListener interface and set up a callback handler on the View object. By setting up a callback handler with onTouch(), MotionEvents will be delivered there first before they go to the View's onTouchEvent() method. Only if the onTouch() method returned false would our View's onTouchEvent() method get called. Let's get to our example application where this should be easier to see.

Listing 16–1 shows the XML of a layout file. Create a new Android project in Eclipse starting with this layout.

Listing 16–1. *XML Layout File for TouchDemo1*

```xml
<?xml version="1.0" encoding="utf-8"?>
<!-- This file is res/layout/main.xml -->
<LinearLayout xmlns:android="http://schemas.android.com/apk/res/android"
    android:layout_width="fill_parent"
    android:layout_height="fill_parent"
    android:orientation="vertical" >

  <RelativeLayout
    android:id="@+id/layout1"
    android:tag="trueLayoutTop"
    android:orientation="vertical"
    android:layout_width="fill_parent"
    android:layout_height="wrap_content"
    android:layout_weight="1"
    >

      <com.androidbook.touch.demo1.TrueButton android:text="returns true"
      android:id="@+id/trueBtn1"
      android:tag="trueBtnTop"
      android:layout_width="wrap_content"
      android:layout_height="wrap_content" />

      <com.androidbook.touch.demo1.FalseButton android:text="returns false"
      android:id="@+id/falseBtn1"
      android:tag="falseBtnTop"
      android:layout_width="wrap_content"
      android:layout_height="wrap_content"
      android:layout_below="@id/trueBtn1" />

  </RelativeLayout>
  <RelativeLayout
    android:id="@+id/layout2"
    android:tag="falseLayoutBottom"
    android:orientation="vertical"
    android:layout_width="fill_parent"
    android:layout_height="wrap_content"
    android:layout_weight="1"
    android:background="#FF00FF"
    >

      <com.androidbook.touch.demo1.TrueButton android:text="returns true"
      android:id="@+id/trueBtn2"
      android:tag="trueBtnBottom"
```

```
android:layout_width="wrap_content"
android:layout_height="wrap_content" />

<com.androidbook.touch.demo1.FalseButton android:text="returns false"
android:id="@+id/falseBtn2"
android:tag="falseBtnBottom"
android:layout_width="wrap_content"
android:layout_height="wrap_content"
android:layout_below="@id/trueBtn2" />

    </RelativeLayout>
</LinearLayout>
```

A couple of things to point out about this layout. We've incorporated tags on our UI objects. We'll be able to refer to these tags in our code as events occur on them. We've also used RelativeLayouts to position our objects. Also notice how we've used custom objects (TrueButton and FalseButton). You'll see in the Java code that these are classes extended from the Button class. Figure 16–1 shows what this layout looks like and Listing 16–2 shows our button Java code.

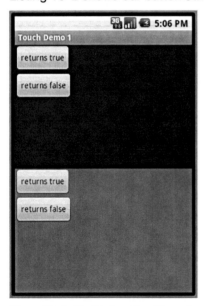

Figure 16–1. *The UI of our TouchDemo1 application*

Listing 16–2. *Java Code for the Button Classes for TouchDemo1*

```java
// This file is BooleanButton.java
import android.content.Context;
import android.util.AttributeSet;
import android.util.Log;
import android.view.MotionEvent;
import android.widget.Button;

public abstract class BooleanButton extends Button {
    protected boolean myValue() {
        return false;
```

```
    }

    public BooleanButton(Context context, AttributeSet attrs) {
        super(context, attrs);
    }

    @Override
    public boolean onTouchEvent(MotionEvent event) {
        String myTag = this.getTag().toString();
        Log.v(myTag, "----------------------------------");
        Log.v(myTag, MainActivity.describeEvent(this, event));
        Log.v(myTag, "super onTouchEvent() returns " + super.onTouchEvent(event));
        Log.v(myTag, "and I'm returning " + myValue());
        event.recycle();
        return(myValue());
    }
}
```

```
// This file is TrueButton.java
import android.content.Context;
import android.util.AttributeSet;

public class TrueButton extends BooleanButton {
    protected boolean myValue() {
        return true;
    }

    public TrueButton(Context context, AttributeSet attrs) {
        super(context, attrs);
    }
}
```

```
// This file is FalseButton.java
import android.content.Context;
import android.util.AttributeSet;

public class FalseButton extends BooleanButton {

    public FalseButton(Context context, AttributeSet attrs) {
        super(context, attrs);
    }
}
```

The BooleanButton class was built so we can reuse the onTouchEvent() method, which we've customized by adding the logging. Then we created TrueButton and FalseButton, which will respond differently to the MotionEvents passed to them. This will be made clearer when you look at the main activity code which is shown in Listing 16–3.

Listing 16–3. *Java Code for Our Main Activity*

```
// This file is MainActivity.java
import android.app.Activity;
import android.os.Bundle;
import android.util.Log;
import android.view.MotionEvent;
import android.view.View;
```

```java
import android.view.View.OnTouchListener;
import android.widget.Button;
import android.widget.RelativeLayout;

public class MainActivity extends Activity implements OnTouchListener {
    /** Called when the activity is first created. */
    @Override
    public void onCreate(Bundle savedInstanceState) {
        super.onCreate(savedInstanceState);
        setContentView(R.layout.main);

        RelativeLayout layout1 = (RelativeLayout) findViewById(R.id.layout1);
        layout1.setOnTouchListener(this);
        Button trueBtn1 = (Button)findViewById(R.id.trueBtn1);
        trueBtn1.setOnTouchListener(this);
        Button falseBtn1 = (Button)findViewById(R.id.falseBtn1);
        falseBtn1.setOnTouchListener(this);

        RelativeLayout layout2 = (RelativeLayout) findViewById(R.id.layout2);
        layout2.setOnTouchListener(this);
        Button trueBtn2 = (Button)findViewById(R.id.trueBtn2);
        trueBtn2.setOnTouchListener(this);
        Button falseBtn2 = (Button)findViewById(R.id.falseBtn2);
        falseBtn2.setOnTouchListener(this);
    }

    @Override
    public boolean onTouch(View v, MotionEvent event) {
        String myTag = v.getTag().toString();
        Log.v(myTag, "----------------------------");
        Log.v(myTag, "Got view " + myTag + " in onTouch");
        Log.v(myTag, describeEvent(v, event));
        if( "true".equals(myTag.substring(0, 4))) {
            Log.v(myTag, "and I'm returning true");
            return true;
        }
        else {
            Log.v(myTag, "and I'm returning false");
            return false;
        }
    }

    protected static String describeEvent(View view, MotionEvent event) {
        StringBuilder result = new StringBuilder(300);
        result.append("Action: ").append(event.getAction()).append("\n");
        result.append("Location: ").append(event.getX()).append(" x ")
.append(event.getY()).append("\n");
        if(    event.getX() < 0 || event.getX() > view.getWidth() ||
                event.getY() < 0 || event.getY() > view.getHeight()) {
            result.append(">>> Touch has left the view <<<\n");
        }
        result.append("Edge flags: ").append(event.getEdgeFlags()).append("\n");
        result.append("Pressure: ").append(event.getPressure()).append("   ");
        result.append("Size: ").append(event.getSize()).append("\n");
        result.append("Down time: ").append(event.getDownTime()).append("ms\n");
        result.append("Event time: ").append(event.getEventTime()).append("ms");
        result.append("  Elapsed: ").append(event.getEventTime()-event.getDownTime());
```

```
        result.append(" ms\n");
        return result.toString();
    }
}
```

Our main activity code sets up callbacks on our buttons and the layouts so we can process the touch events (i.e., the MotionEvent objects) for everything in our UI. We've added lots of logging so you'll be able to tell exactly what's going on as touch events occur. When you compile and run this application, you should see a screen that looks like Figure 16–1.

To get the most out of this application, you need to open up LogCat in Eclipse to watch the messages fly by as you touch the touchscreen. This works in the emulator as well as on a real device. We also advise you to maximize the LogCat window so you can more easily scroll up and down to see all of the generated events from this application. To maximize the LogCat window just double-click on the LogCat tab. Now go to the application UI and touch and release on the top-most button marked "returns true". If you're using the emulator, use your mouse to click and release the "returns true" button. You should see at least two events logged in LogCat. The messages are tagged as coming from trueBtnTop and were logged from the onTouch() method in MainActivity. See MainActivity.java for the onTouch() method's code. As you view the LogCat output, see which method calls are producing the values. For example, the value displayed after "Action:" comes from the getAction() method. Listing 16–4 shows a sample of what you might see in LogCat from the emulator, and Listing 16–5 shows a sample of what you might see from a real device.

Listing 16–4. *Sample LogCat Messages from TouchDemo1 from the Emulator*

```
trueBtnTop        ----------------------------
trueBtnTop        Got view trueBtnTop in onTouch
trueBtnTop        Action: 0
trueBtnTop        Location: 52.0 x 20.0
trueBtnTop        Edge flags: 0
trueBtnTop        Pressure: 0.0   Size: 0.0
trueBtnTop        Down time: 163669ms
trueBtnTop        Event time: 163669ms  Elapsed: 0 ms
trueBtnTop        and I'm returning true
trueBtnTop        ----------------------------
trueBtnTop        Got view trueBtnTop in onTouch
trueBtnTop        Action: 1
trueBtnTop        Location: 52.0 x 20.0
trueBtnTop        Edge flags: 0
trueBtnTop        Pressure: 0.0   Size: 0.0
trueBtnTop        Down time: 163669ms
trueBtnTop        Event time: 163831ms  Elapsed: 162 ms
trueBtnTop        and I'm returning true
```

Listing 16–5. *Sample LogCat Messages from TouchDemo1 from a Real Device*

```
trueBtnTop        ----------------------------
trueBtnTop        Got view trueBtnTop in onTouch
trueBtnTop        Action: 0
trueBtnTop        Location: 42.8374 x 25.293747
trueBtnTop        Edge flags: 0
trueBtnTop        Pressure: 0.05490196   Size: 0.2
```

```
trueBtnTop          Down time: 24959412ms
trueBtnTop          Event time: 24959412ms   Elapsed: 0 ms
trueBtnTop          and I'm returning true
trueBtnTop          ----------------------------
trueBtnTop          Got view trueBtnTop in onTouch
trueBtnTop          Action: 2
trueBtnTop          Location: 42.8374 x 25.293747
trueBtnTop          Edge flags: 0
trueBtnTop          Pressure: 0.05490196   Size: 0.2
trueBtnTop          Down time: 24959412ms
trueBtnTop          Event time: 24959530ms   Elapsed: 118 ms
trueBtnTop          and I'm returning true
trueBtnTop          ----------------------------
trueBtnTop          Got view trueBtnTop in onTouch
trueBtnTop          Action: 1
trueBtnTop          Location: 42.8374 x 25.293747
trueBtnTop          Edge flags: 0
trueBtnTop          Pressure: 0.05490196   Size: 0.2
trueBtnTop          Down time: 24959412ms
trueBtnTop          Event time: 24959567ms   Elapsed: 155 ms
trueBtnTop          and I'm returning true
```

The first event has an action of 0 which is ACTION_DOWN. The last event has an action of 1 which is ACTION_UP. If you used a real device you might see more than two events. Any events in between ACTION_DOWN and ACTION_UP will most likely have an action of 2 which is ACTION_MOVE. The other possibilities are an action of 3 which is ACTION_CANCEL and 4 which is ACTION_OUTSIDE. When using real fingers on a real touchscreen you can't always touch and release without a slight movement on the surface, so some ACTION_MOVE events are not unexpected.

There are some other differences between the emulator and a real device. Notice that the precision of the location within the emulator is to whole numbers (52 by 20), whereas on a real device you see fractions (42.8374 by 25.293747). The location for a MotionEvent has an X and Y component, where X represents the distance from the left-hand side of the View object to the point touched, and Y represents the distance from the top of the View object to the point touched.

You should also notice that the pressure in the emulator is zero, as is the size. For a real device, the pressure represents how hard the finger pressed down, and size represents how large the touch is. If you touch lightly with the tip of your pinky finger the values for pressure and size will be small. If you press hard with your thumb both pressure and size will be larger. The documentation says that the values of pressure and size will be between 0 and 1. However, due to differences in hardware, it may be very difficult to use any absolute numbers in your application for making decisions about pressure and size. It would be fine to compare pressure and size between MotionEvents as they occur in your application, but you may run into trouble if you decide that pressure must exceed a value such as 0.8 to be considered a hard press. On that particular device you might never get a value above 0.8. You might not even get a value above 0.2.

NOTE: In Listing 16–5, you may have noticed that the pressure and size values did not change during the touch sequence on a real device. This is actually due to a bug in the Android code for the Motorola Droid device (Android 2.0) which will be fixed. Normally, a real device would show changing values for pressure and size as a touch sequence progresses from the `ACTION_DOWN` event, through `ACTION_MOVE` events, and finally to the `ACTION_UP` event.

The down time and event time values operate in the same way between the emulator and a real device, the only difference being that the real device has much larger values. The elapsed times work the same.

The edge flags are for detecting when a touch has reached the edge of the physical screen. The Android SDK documentation says that the flags are set to indicate that a touch has intersected with an edge of the display (top, bottom, left or right). However, the `getEdgeFlags()` method may always return zero, depending on what device or emulator it is used on. With some hardware, it is too difficult to actually detect a touch at the edge of the display, so Android is supposed to pin the location to the edge and set the appropriate edge flag for you. This doesn't always happen, so you should not rely on the edge flags being set properly. The `MotionEvent` class provides a `setEdgeFlags()` method so you could set the flags yourself if you wanted to.

The last thing to notice is that our `onTouch()` method returns `true` because our `TrueButton` is coded to return `true`. Returning `true` tells Android that the `MotionEvent` object has been consumed and there is no reason to give it to someone else. It also tells Android to keep sending touch events from this touch sequence to this method. That's why we got the `ACTION_UP` event, as well as the `ACTION_MOVE` event in the case of the real device.

Now touch the "returns false" button near the top of the screen. For the remainder of this section we will show only sample `LogCat` output from a real device. The differences have been explained, so if you are working with the emulator you should understand why you are seeing what you are seeing. Listing 16–6 shows a sample `LogCat` output for your "returns false" touch.

Listing 16–6. *Sample LogCat from Touching the Top "returns false" Button*

```
falseBtnTop        ------------------------------
falseBtnTop        Got view falseBtnTop in onTouch
falseBtnTop        Action: 0
falseBtnTop        Location: 61.309372 x 44.281494
falseBtnTop        Edge flags: 0
falseBtnTop        Pressure: 0.0627451   Size: 0.26666668
falseBtnTop        Downtime: 28612178ms
falseBtnTop        Event time: 28612178ms  Elapsed: 0 ms
falseBtnTop        and I'm returning false
falseBtnTop        ------------------------------
falseBtnTop        Action: 0
falseBtnTop        Location: 61.309372 x 44.281494
falseBtnTop        Edge flags: 0
falseBtnTop        Pressure: 0.0627451   Size: 0.26666668
falseBtnTop        Downtime: 28612178ms
```

```
falseBtnTop        Event time: 28612178ms  Elapsed: 0 ms
falseBtnTop        super onTouchEvent() returns true
falseBtnTop        and I'm returning false
trueLayoutTop      ----------------------------
trueLayoutTop      Got view trueLayoutTop in onTouch
trueLayoutTop      Action: 0
trueLayoutTop      Location: 61.309372 x 116.281494
trueLayoutTop      Edge flags: 0
trueLayoutTop      Pressure: 0.0627451   Size: 0.26666668
trueLayoutTop      Downtime: 28612178ms
trueLayoutTop      Event time: 28612178ms  Elapsed: 0 ms
trueLayoutTop      and I'm returning true
trueLayoutTop      ----------------------------
trueLayoutTop      Got view trueLayoutTop in onTouch
trueLayoutTop      Action: 2
trueLayoutTop      Location: 61.309372 x 111.90039
trueLayoutTop      Edge flags: 0
trueLayoutTop      Pressure: 0.0627451   Size: 0.26666668
trueLayoutTop      Downtime: 28612178ms
trueLayoutTop      Event time: 28612217ms  Elapsed: 39 ms
trueLayoutTop      and I'm returning true
trueLayoutTop      ----------------------------
trueLayoutTop      Got view trueLayoutTop in onTouch
trueLayoutTop      Action: 1
trueLayoutTop      Location: 55.08958 x 115.30792
trueLayoutTop      Edge flags: 0
trueLayoutTop      Pressure: 0.0627451   Size: 0.26666668
trueLayoutTop      Downtime: 28612178ms
trueLayoutTop      Event time: 28612361ms  Elapsed: 183 ms
trueLayoutTop      and I'm returning true
```

Now we're seeing very different behavior so let's explain what happened. Android receives the ACTION_DOWN event in a MotionEvent object, and passes it to our onTouch() method in the MainActivity class. Our onTouch() method records the information in LogCat and returns false. This tells Android that our onTouch() method did not consume the event, so Android looks to the next method to call, which in our case is the overridden onTouchEvent() method of our FalseButton class. Since FalseButton is an extension of the BooleanButton class, refer to the onTouchEvent() method in BooleanButton.java to see the code. In the onTouchEvent() method, we again write information to LogCat, we call the parent class's onTouchEvent() method, and then we also return false. Notice that the location information in LogCat is exactly the same as before. This should be expected because we're still in the same View object, the FalseButton. We see that our parent class wants to return true from onTouchEvent() and we can see why. If you look at the button in the UI it should be a different color from the "returns true" button. Our "returns false" button now looks like it's partway through being pressed. That is, it looks like a button looks when it has been pressed but has not been released. Our custom method returned false instead of true. Because we again told Android that we did not consume this event, by returning false, Android never sends the ACTION_UP event to our button so our button doesn't know that the finger ever lifted from the touchscreen. Therefore, our button is still in the pressed state. If we had returned true like our parent wanted to, we would eventually have received the ACTION_UP event so we could change the color back to the normal button color. To recap, every time we return false from a UI object for a received MotionEvent object,

Android stops sending MotionEvent objects to that UI object, and Android keeps looking for another UI object to consume our MotionEvent object.

You might have realized that when we touched our "returns true" button, we didn't get a color change in the button. Why is that? Well, because onTouch() was called before any button methods got called, and because onTouch() returned true, Android never bothered to call the "returns true" button's onTouchEvent() method. If you add a v.onTouchEvent(event); line to the onTouch() method just before returning true, you will see the button change color. You will also see more log lines in LogCat since our onTouchEvent() method is also writing information to LogCat.

Let's keep going through the LogCat output. Now that Android has tried twice to find a consumer for the ACTION_DOWN event and failed, it goes to the next View in the application that could possibly receive the event, which in our case is the layout underneath the button. We called our top layout trueLayoutTop and we can see that it received the ACTION_DOWN event.

Notice that our onTouch() method got called again, although now with the layout view and not the button view. Everything about the MotionEvent object passed to onTouch() for trueLayoutTop is the same as before, including the times, except for the Y coordinate of the location. The Y coordinate changed from 44.281494 for the button to 116.281494 for the layout. This makes sense because the button is not in the upper left corner of the layout, it's below the "returns true" button. Therefore the Y coordinate of the touch relative to the layout is larger than the Y coordinate of the same touch relative to the button; the touch is further away from the top edge of the layout than it is from the top edge of the button. Because onTouch() for the trueLayoutTop returns true, Android sends the rest of the touch events to the layout and we see the log records corresponding to the ACTION_MOVE and the ACTION_UP events. Go ahead and touch the top "returns false" button again and notice that the same set of log records occurs. That is, onTouch() is called for the falseBtnTop, onTouchEvent() is called for falseBtnTop, then onTouch() is called for trueLayoutTop for the rest of the events. Android only stops sending the events to the button for one touch sequence at a time. For a new sequence of touch events, Android will send to the button unless it gets another return of false from the called method, which it still does in our sample application.

Now touch your finger on the top layout but not on either button, then drag your finger around a bit and lift it off the touchscreen. (If you're using the emulator, just use your mouse to do a similar motion.) Notice a stream of log messages in LogCat where the first record has an action of ACTION_DOWN, and then there are many ACTION_MOVE events followed by an ACTION_UP event.

Now touch the top "returns true" button, but before lifting off of the button, drag your finger around the screen, then lift your finger off of the screen. Listing 16–7 shows some new information in LogCat.

Listing 16–7. *LogCat Records Showing a Touch Outside of Our View*

```
[ … log messages of an ACTION_DOWN event followed by some ACTION_MOVE events … ]

trueBtnTop      Got view trueBtnTop in onTouch
trueBtnTop      Action: 2
```

```
trueBtnTop          Location: 150.41768 x 22.628128
trueBtnTop          >>> Touch has left the view <<<
trueBtnTop          Edge flags: 0
trueBtnTop          Pressure: 0.047058824   Size: 0.13333334
trueBtnTop          Downtime: 31690859ms
trueBtnTop          Event time: 31691344ms  Elapsed: 485 ms
trueBtnTop          and I'm returning true

[ … more ACTION_MOVE events logged … ]

trueBtnTop          Got view trueBtnTop in onTouch
trueBtnTop          Action: 1
trueBtnTop          Location: 291.5864 x 223.43854
trueBtnTop          >>> Touch has left the view <<<
trueBtnTop          Edge flags: 0
trueBtnTop          Pressure: 0.047058824   Size: 0.13333334
trueBtnTop          Downtime: 31690859ms
trueBtnTop          Event time: 31692493ms  Elapsed: 1634 ms
trueBtnTop          and I'm returning true
```

Even after your finger drags itself off of the button, we continue to get notified of touch events related to the button. The first record in Listing 16–7 shows an event record where we're no longer on the button. In this case, the X coordinate of the touch event is to the right of the edge of our button object. But we keep getting called with MotionEvent objects until we get an ACTION_UP event. This is because we continue to return true from the onTouch() method. Even when we finally lift our finger off of the touchscreen, and even if our finger isn't on the button, our onTouch() method still gets called to give us the ACTION_UP event because we keep returning true. This is something to keep in mind when dealing with MotionEvents. When the finger has moved off of the view, we could decide to cancel whatever operation might have been performed, and return false from the onTouch() method so we don't get notified of further events. Or we could choose to continue to receive events (by returning true from the onTouch() method) and only perform the logic if the finger returns to our view before lifting off.

The touch sequence of events got associated to our top "returns true" button when we returned true from onTouch(). This told Android that it could stop looking for an object to receive the MotionEvent objects, and just send all future MotionEvent objects for this touch sequence to us. Even if we encounter another view when dragging our finger, we're still tied to the original view for this sequence.

Let's see what happens with the lower half of our application. Go ahead and touch the "returns true" button in the bottom half. We see the same thing as happened with the top "returns true" button. Because onTouch() returns true, Android sends us the rest of the events in the touch sequence until the finger is lifted from the touchscreen. Now touch the bottom "returns false" button. Once again, the onTouch() method returns false and the onTouchEvent() method returns false (both associated with the falseBtnBottom view object). But this time, the next view to receive the MotionEvent object is the falseLayoutBottom object, and it also returns false. Now we're done. Because the onTouchEvent() method called the super's onTouchEvent() method, the button has changed color to indicate it's half-way through being pressed. But again, the button will stay this way because we never get the ACTION_UP event in this touch sequence, due to our methods returning `false` all the time. Unlike before, even the layout is not interested in this event. If you were to touch the bottom "returns false" button and hold it down, then drag your finger around the display, you would not see any more records in `LogCat` because we don't get any more `MotionEvent` objects sent to us. We always returned `false` so Android isn't going to bother us with any more events for this touch sequence. Again, if we start a new touch sequence, we can see new `LogCat` records showing up. If you initiate a touch sequence in the bottom layout and not on a button, you will see a single event in `LogCat` for `falseLayoutBottom` that returns `false` and then nothing after that (until you start a new touch sequence).

So far, we've used buttons to show you the effects of `MotionEvent` events from touchscreens. It's worth pointing out that normally you would implement logic on buttons using the `onClick()` method. We used buttons for this sample application because they're easy to create and because they are subclasses of `View` and therefore can receive touch events just like any other view. Remember that these techniques apply to any `View` object in your application, be it a standard view class or a customized view class.

Using VelocityTracker

Android provides a class to help handle touchscreen sequences, and that class is `VelocityTracker`. When a finger is in motion on a touchscreen, it might be nice to know how fast it is moving across the surface. For example, if the user is dragging a finger quickly across the screen, this could indicate a flinging motion, for which your application may wish to perform flinging logic. Android provides `VelocityTracker` to help with the math involved.

To use `VelocityTracker`, you first get an instance of a `VelocityTracker` by calling the static method `VelocityTracker.obtain()`. You can then add `MotionEvent` objects to it with the `addMovement(MotionEvent ev)` method. You would call this method in your handler that receives `MotionEvent` objects, from a handler method such as `onTouch()` or from a view's `onTouchEvent()`. The `VelocityTracker` uses the `MotionEvent` objects to figure out what is going on with the user's touch sequence. Once `VelocityTracker` has at least two `MotionEvent` objects in it, we can use the other methods to find out what is going on.

The two `VelocityTracker` methods `getXVelocity()` and `getYVelocity()` return the corresponding velocity of the finger in the X and Y directions respectively. The value returned from these two methods will represent pixels per time period. This could be pixels per millisecond or pixels per second or really anything you want. To tell the `VelocityTracker` what time period to use, and before you can call these two getter methods, you need to invoke the `VelocityTracker`'s `computeCurrentVelocity(int units)` method. The value of `units` represents how many milliseconds are in the time period for measuring the velocity. If you want pixels per millisecond, use a units value of 1; if you want pixels per second, use a units value of 1000. The value returned by the `getXVelocity()` and `getYVelocity()` methods will be positive if the velocity is toward the right (for X) or down (for Y). The value returned will be negative if the velocity is toward the left (for X) or up (for Y).

When you are done with the VelocityTracker object you got with the obtain() method, call the VelocityTracker object's recycle() method. Listing 16–8 shows a sample onTouchEvent() handler for a view.

Listing 16–8. *Sample Handler That Uses VelocityTracker*

```
private VelocityTracker vTracker = null;

@Override
public boolean onTouchEvent(MotionEvent event) {
    int action = event.getAction();
    switch(action) {
        case MotionEvent.ACTION_DOWN:
            if(vTracker == null) {
                vTracker = VelocityTracker.obtain();
            }
            else {
                vTracker.clear();
            }
            vTracker.addMovement(event);
            break;
        case MotionEvent.ACTION_MOVE:
            vTracker.addMovement(event);
            vTracker.computeCurrentVelocity(1000);
            Log.v(TAG, "X velocity is " + vTracker.getXVelocity() +
                    " pixels per second");
            Log.v(TAG, "Y velocity is " + vTracker.getYVelocity() +
                    " pixels per second");
            break;
        case MotionEvent.ACTION_UP:
        case MotionEvent.ACTION_CANCEL:
            vTracker.recycle();
            break;
    }
    event.recycle();
    return true;
}
```

A few notes about VelocityTracker. Obviously when you've only added one MotionEvent to a VelocityTracker (i.e., the ACTION_DOWN event) the velocities cannot be computed as anything other than zero. But we need to add the starting point so that the subsequent ACTION_MOVE events can calculate velocities then. It turns out that the velocities reported after ACTION_UP is added to our VelocityTracker are also zero. Therefore, do not read the X and Y velocities after adding ACTION_UP expecting to get motion. If you're writing a gaming application in which the user is throwing an object on the screen, use the velocities after adding the last ACTION_MOVE event to calculate the object's trajectory across the game view. VelocityTracker is somewhat costly in terms of performance so use it sparingly. Also, make sure that you recycle it as soon as you are done with it in case someone else wants to use one. There can be more than one VelocityTracker in use in Android, but they can take up a lot of memory, so give yours back if you're not going to continue to use it. In Listing 16–8, we also use the clear()

method if we're starting a new touch sequence (i.e., if we get an ACTION_DOWN event and our VelocityTracker object already exists) instead of recycling this one and obtaining a new one.

Exploring Drag and Drop

Now that we've seen how to receive MotionEvent objects in code, let's do something interesting with them. We're going to explain how to implement drag and drop. To start, let's do some dragging. In this next sample application, we're going to take a white dot and drag it to a new location in our layout. Using Listing 16–9, create a new Android project and setup the layout XML file as indicated, and add a new class called Dot using the Java code. Note that the package name in the layout XML file for the Dot element must match the package name you use for your application. Also note that we can leave the main Activity class alone since it is fine as-is. The UI for this application is shown in Figure 16–2.

Listing 16–9. *Sample Layout XML and Java Code for Our Drag Example*

```
<?xml version="1.0" encoding="utf-8"?>
<!-- This file is res/layout/main.xml -->
<LinearLayout xmlns:android="http://schemas.android.com/apk/res/android"
    android:orientation="vertical"
    android:layout_width="fill_parent"
    android:layout_height="fill_parent"
    >

  <com.androidbook.touch.dragdemo1.Dot
    android:id="@+id/dot"
    android:tag="trueDot"
    android:layout_width="wrap_content"
    android:layout_height="wrap_content" />

</LinearLayout>


import android.content.Context;
import android.graphics.Canvas;
import android.graphics.Color;
import android.graphics.Paint;
import android.util.AttributeSet;
import android.view.MotionEvent;
import android.view.View;

public class Dot extends View {
    private static final float RADIUS = 20;
    private float x = 30;
    private float y = 30;
    private float initialX;
    private float initialY;
    private float offsetX;
    private float offsetY;
    private Paint backgroundPaint;
    private Paint myPaint;
```

```java
    public Dot(Context context, AttributeSet attrs) {
        super(context, attrs);

        backgroundPaint = new Paint();
        backgroundPaint.setColor(Color.BLUE);

        myPaint = new Paint();
        myPaint.setColor(Color.WHITE);
        myPaint.setAntiAlias(true);
    }

    @Override
    public boolean onTouchEvent(MotionEvent event) {
        int action = event.getAction();
        switch(action) {
        case MotionEvent.ACTION_DOWN:
            // Need to remember where the initial starting point
            // center is of our Dot and where our touch starts from
            initialX = x;
            initialY = y;
            offsetX = event.getX();
            offsetY = event.getY();
            break;
        case MotionEvent.ACTION_MOVE:
        case MotionEvent.ACTION_UP:
        case MotionEvent.ACTION_CANCEL:
            x = initialX + event.getX() - offsetX;
            y = initialY + event.getY() - offsetY;
            break;
        }
        event.recycle();
        return(true);
    }

    @Override
    public void draw(Canvas canvas) {
        int width = canvas.getWidth();
        int height = canvas.getHeight();
        canvas.drawRect(0, 0, width, height, backgroundPaint);

        canvas.drawCircle(x, y, RADIUS, myPaint);
        invalidate();
    }
}
```

Figure 16–2. *User interface for our Drag Demo application*

When you run this application, you will see a white dot on a blue background. You can touch the dot then drag it around the screen. When you lift off, the dot stays where it is until you touch it again and drag it somewhere else. We've really simplified this to show you just the basics of how to move an object on the screen. The draw() method puts the dot at its current location of X and Y. By receiving MotionEvent objects in the onTouchEvent() method, we can modify the X and Y values by the movement of our touch. We record the starting position of the dot in the ACTION_DOWN method, as well as the starting touch location. Because we don't always touch the object in the very center, the touch coordinates will not be the same as the location coordinates of the object. Also, if our object's reference point is not the center but the upper-left corner, we must be sure we take that into account as well. When our finger starts moving across the screen, we adjust the location of the object by the deltas in x and y based on the MotionEvents that we get. When we stop moving (i.e., ACTION_UP), we finalize our location using the last coordinates of our touch. We're doing a little cheating here because our Dot view is positioned on the screen relative to (0,0). That means that we can simply draw the circle relative to (0,0) as opposed to some other reference point. If our object is not positioned relative to (0,0) we might need to provide additional offsets for the location of our object. We also don't have to worry about scrollbars in this example, which could complicate the calculation of the position of our object on the screen. But the basic principle is still the same. By knowing the starting location of the object to be moved, and keeping track of the delta values of our touch from ACTION_DOWN through to ACTION_UP, we can adjust the location of the object on the screen.

Dropping an object onto another object on the screen has much less to do with touch than it does with knowing where things are on the screen. We're not going to provide an example here of dropping but we will explain the principles. As you saw earlier, as we drag an object around the screen, we are aware of its position relative to one or more reference points. We can also interrogate objects on the screen for their locations and sizes. We can then determine if our dragged object is "over" another object. The typical process of figuring out a drop target for a dragged object is to iterate through the available objects that we can drop on, and determine if our current position overlaps with that object. Each object's size and position (and sometimes shape) can be used to make this determination. If we get an ACTION_UP event, meaning that the user has let go of our dragged object, and the object is over something we can drop onto, then we can fire the logic to process the drop action. This might be the action of dragging something to the trash can, where the object being dragged should be deleted. Or it could be dragging a file to a folder for the purposes of moving or copying it.

Multi-Touch

Now that you've seen single touches in action, let's move on to multi-touch. Multi-touch has gained a lot of interest ever since the TED conference in 2006 at which Jeff Han demonstrated a multi-touch surface for a computer user interface. Using multiple fingers on a screen opens up a lot of possibilities for manipulating what's on the screen. For example, by putting two fingers on an image and moving them apart, that action could zoom in on the image. By placing multiple fingers on an image and turning clockwise you could rotate the image on the screen. Android introduced support for multi-touch with Android SDK 2.0. In that release you were able to use up to three fingers on a screen at the same time to perform actions such as zoom, rotate, or whatever else you could imagine doing with multiple touches. If you think about it, though, there is no magic to this. If the screen hardware can detect multiple touches as they initiate on the screen, and can notify your application as those touches move in time across the surface of the screen, then notify you when those touches lift off of the screen, your application can figure out what the user is trying to do with those touches. While it's not magic, it isn't easy either. We're going to help you understand multi-touch in this section.

The basics of multi-touch are exactly the same as for single touch. MotionEvent objects get created for touches, and these MotionEvent objects are passed to your methods just like before. Your code can read the data about the touches and decide what to do. At a basic level, the methods of MotionEvent are the same; that is, we call getAction(), getDownTime(), getX() and so on. However, when more than one finger is touching the screen, the MotionEvent object must include information from all fingers, with some caveats. The action value from getAction() is for one finger, not all. The down time value is for the very first finger down, and stays the same for as long as there is at least one finger down. The location values getX() and getY(), as well as getPressure() and getSize(), can take an argument for the finger; therefore, you need to use some sort of index value to request the information for the finger you're interested in. There are method calls that we used above that did not take any argument to specify a finger (e.g., getX(), getY()), so which finger would the values be for if we used those methods? You can figure it out, but it takes some work. Therefore, if you don't take into account multiple fingers all of the time, you might end up with some strange results. But let's dig into this to figure out what to do.

The first method of MotionEvent you need to know about for multi-touch is getPointerCount(). This tells you how many fingers are represented in the MotionEvent object. This doesn't necessarily tell you how many fingers are actually touching the screen, since that depends on the hardware and on Android. You may find that on certain devices getPointerCount() does not report all fingers that are touching, just some. But let's press on. As soon as you've got more than one finger being reported in MotionEvent objects, you need to start dealing with the pointer index and the pointer Ids.

The MotionEvent object contains information for pointers starting at index 0 and going up to the number of fingers being reported in that object. The pointer index always starts at 0. If there are three fingers being reported, pointer indexes will be 0, 1, and 2. Calls to methods such as getX() must include the pointer index for the finger you want information about. Pointer Ids are integer values representing which finger is being tracked. Pointer Ids start at 0 for the first finger down, but don't always start at 0 once fingers are coming and going on the screen. Think of a pointer Id as the name of that finger while it is being tracked by Android. For example, imagine a pair of touch sequences for two fingers, starting with finger 1 down, then finger 2 down, then finger 1 up, then finger 2 up. The first finger down will get pointer Id 0. The second finger down will get pointer Id 1. Once the first finger goes up, finger 2 will still be associated with pointer Id 1. Whereas the pointer index for finger 2 becomes 0, because the pointer index always starts at 0. In this example, pointer Id 1 starts as pointer index 1 when it goes down, and then shifts to pointer index 0 once finger 1 leaves the screen. Your applications will use pointer Ids to link together the events associated to a particular finger even as other fingers are involved. Let's look at an example.

Listing 16–10 shows our new XML layout plus our Java code for a multi-touch application. Create a new application using Listing 16–10 then run it. Figure 16–3 shows what it should look like.

Listing 16–10. *XML Layout and Java for a Multi-Touch Demo*

```
<?xml version="1.0" encoding="utf-8"?>
<!-- This file is /res/layout/main.xml -->
<RelativeLayout  xmlns:android="http://schemas.android.com/apk/res/android"
    android:id="@+id/layout1"
    android:tag="trueLayout"
    android:orientation="vertical"
    android:layout_width="fill_parent"
    android:layout_height="wrap_content"
    android:layout_weight="1"
    >

    <TextView android:text="Touch fingers on the screen and look at LogCat"
    android:id="@+id/message"
    android:tag="trueText"
    android:layout_width="wrap_content"
    android:layout_height="wrap_content"
    android:layout_alignParentBottom="true" />

</RelativeLayout>


// This file is MainActivity.java
import android.app.Activity;
```

```java
import android.os.Bundle;
import android.util.Log;
import android.view.MotionEvent;
import android.view.View;
import android.view.View.OnTouchListener;
import android.widget.RelativeLayout;

public class MainActivity extends Activity implements OnTouchListener {
    /** Called when the activity is first created. */
    @Override
    public void onCreate(Bundle savedInstanceState) {
        super.onCreate(savedInstanceState);
        setContentView(R.layout.main);

        RelativeLayout layout1 = (RelativeLayout) findViewById(R.id.layout1);
        layout1.setOnTouchListener(this);
    }

    @Override
    public boolean onTouch(View v, MotionEvent event) {
        String myTag = v.getTag().toString();
        Log.v(myTag, "-----------------------------");
        Log.v(myTag, "Got view " + myTag + " in onTouch");
        Log.v(myTag, describeEvent(event));
        if( "true".equals(myTag.substring(0, 4))) {
            Log.v(myTag, "and I'm returning true");
            return true;
        }
        else {
            Log.v(myTag, "and I'm returning false");
            return false;
        }
    }

    protected static String describeEvent(MotionEvent event) {
        StringBuilder result = new StringBuilder(500);
        result.append("Action: ").append(event.getAction()).append("\n");
        int numPointers = event.getPointerCount();
        result.append("Number of pointers: ").append(numPointers).append("\n");
        int ptrIdx = 0;
        while (ptrIdx < numPointers) {
            int ptrId = event.getPointerId(ptrIdx);
            result.append("Pointer Index: ").append(ptrIdx);
            result.append(", Pointer Id: ").append(ptrId).append("\n");
            result.append("    Location: ").append(event.getX(ptrIdx));
            result.append(" x ").append(event.getY(ptrIdx)).append("\n");
            result.append("    Pressure: ").append(event.getPressure(ptrIdx));
            result.append("    Size: ").append(event.getSize(ptrIdx)).append("\n");

            ptrIdx++;
        }
        result.append("Downtime: ").append(event.getDownTime()).append("ms\n");
        result.append("Event time: ").append(event.getEventTime()).append("ms");
        result.append("  Elapsed: ").append(event.getEventTime()-event.getDownTime());
        result.append(" ms\n");
        return result.toString();
    }
}
```

Figure 16–3. *Our multi-touch demo application*

If you only have the emulator, this application will still work, but you won't be able to get multiple fingers simultaneously on the screen. You'll see output similar to what we saw in the previous application. Listing 16–11 shows sample LogCat messages for a touch sequence like we described earlier. That is, finger 1 presses on the screen, then finger 2 presses, then finger 1 leaves the screen, and then finger 2 leaves the screen.

Listing 16–11. *Sample LogCat Output for a Multi-Touch Application*

```
trueLayoutTop      ----------------------------
trueLayoutTop      Got view trueLayoutTop in onTouch
trueLayoutTop      Action: 0
trueLayoutTop      Number of pointers: 1
trueLayoutTop      Pointer Index: 0, Pointer Id: 0
trueLayoutTop         Location: 722.3844 x 94.37604
trueLayoutTop          Pressure: 0.07450981      Size: 0.2
trueLayoutTop      Downtime: 15778221ms
trueLayoutTop      Event time: 15778221ms   Elapsed: 0 ms
trueLayoutTop      and I'm returning true

trueLayoutTop      ----------------------------
trueLayoutTop      Got view trueLayoutTop in onTouch
trueLayoutTop      Action: 2
trueLayoutTop      Number of pointers: 1
trueLayoutTop      Pointer Index: 0, Pointer Id: 0
trueLayoutTop         Location: 722.3844 x 97.29675
trueLayoutTop          Pressure: 0.07450981      Size: 0.2
trueLayoutTop      Downtime: 15778221ms
trueLayoutTop      Event time: 15778470ms   Elapsed: 249 ms
trueLayoutTop      and I'm returning true
trueLayoutTop      ----------------------------
trueLayoutTop      Got view trueLayoutTop in onTouch
trueLayoutTop      Action: 261
```

```
trueLayoutTop        Number of pointers: 2
trueLayoutTop        Pointer Index: 0, Pointer Id: 0
trueLayoutTop           Location: 722.3844 x 98.75711
trueLayoutTop           Pressure: 0.07450981     Size: 0.2
trueLayoutTop        Pointer Index: 1, Pointer Id: 1
trueLayoutTop           Location: 343.8656 x 103.625
trueLayoutTop           Pressure: 0.06666667     Size: 0.2
trueLayoutTop        Downtime: 15778221ms
trueLayoutTop        Event time: 15778499ms  Elapsed: 278 ms
trueLayoutTop        and I'm returning true

trueLayoutTop        ----------------------------
trueLayoutTop        Got view trueLayoutTop in onTouch
trueLayoutTop        Action: 2
trueLayoutTop        Number of pointers: 2
trueLayoutTop        Pointer Index: 0, Pointer Id: 0
trueLayoutTop           Location: 702.8365 x 100.704285
trueLayoutTop           Pressure: 0.07450981     Size: 0.2
trueLayoutTop        Pointer Index: 1, Pointer Id: 1
trueLayoutTop           Location: 343.8656 x 95.836395
trueLayoutTop           Pressure: 0.06666667     Size: 0.2
trueLayoutTop        Downtime: 15778221ms
trueLayoutTop        Event time: 15778785ms  Elapsed: 564 ms
trueLayoutTop        and I'm returning true
trueLayoutTop        ----------------------------
trueLayoutTop        Got view trueLayoutTop in onTouch
trueLayoutTop        Action: 6
trueLayoutTop        Number of pointers: 2
trueLayoutTop        Pointer Index: 0, Pointer Id: 0
trueLayoutTop           Location: 702.8365 x 100.704285
trueLayoutTop           Pressure: 0.07450981     Size: 0.2
trueLayoutTop        Pointer Index: 1, Pointer Id: 1
trueLayoutTop           Location: 343.8656 x 95.34961
trueLayoutTop           Pressure: 0.06666667     Size: 0.2
trueLayoutTop        Downtime: 15778221ms
trueLayoutTop        Event time: 15778812ms  Elapsed: 591 ms
trueLayoutTop        and I'm returning true

trueLayoutTop        ----------------------------
trueLayoutTop        Got view trueLayoutTop in onTouch
trueLayoutTop        Action: 2
trueLayoutTop        Number of pointers: 1
trueLayoutTop        Pointer Index: 0, Pointer Id: 1
trueLayoutTop           Location: 343.8656 x 94.86282
trueLayoutTop           Pressure: 0.07450981     Size: 0.2
trueLayoutTop        Downtime: 15778221ms
trueLayoutTop        Event time: 15778825ms  Elapsed: 604 ms
trueLayoutTop        and I'm returning true

trueLayoutTop        ----------------------------
trueLayoutTop        Got view trueLayoutTop in onTouch
trueLayoutTop        Action: 1
trueLayoutTop        Number of pointers: 1
trueLayoutTop        Pointer Index: 0, Pointer Id: 1
trueLayoutTop           Location: 323.42917 x 92.42886
trueLayoutTop           Pressure: 0.07450981     Size: 0.2
trueLayoutTop        Downtime: 15778221ms
```

```
trueLayoutTop        Event time: 15779138ms  Elapsed: 917 ms
trueLayoutTop        and I'm returning true
```

We'll now discuss what is going on with this application. The first event we see is the ACTION_DOWN of the first finger. We learn about this using the getAction() method. Please refer to the describeEvent() method in MainActivity.java to follow along with which methods produce which output. We get one pointer with index 0 and pointer Id 0. After that we'll probably see several ACTION_MOVE events for this first finger. We still only have one pointer and the index and Id are still both 0. A little later we get the second finger touching the screen. The action is now a decimal value of 261. What does this mean? The action value is actually made up of two parts: an indicator of which pointer the action is for, and what action that pointer is doing. Converting decimal 261 to hexadecimal we get 0x00000105. The action is the smallest byte (5, in this case) and the pointer Id is the next byte over (1, in this case). Note that this tells us the pointer Id and not the pointer index. If we pressed a third finger onto the screen, the action would be 0x00000205 (or decimal 517). A fourth finger would be 0x00000305 (or decimal 773). And so on.

Now look at the next pair of records from LogCat in Listing 16–11. The first record is for an ACTION_MOVE event. Remember that it is difficult to keep fingers from moving on a real screen. When we lift finger 1 off of the screen, we get an action value that looks similar to the compound value for a down event, but the action is 6 instead of 5. Lifting the first finger in a multi-touch situation gives an action value of 0x00000006 (or decimal 6). If we had lifted the second finger in a multi-touch situation we would get an action value of 0x00000106 (or decimal 262). Notice how we still have information for two fingers when we get the ACTION_UP for one of them.

The last pair of records in Listing 16–11 show one more ACTION_MOVE event for finger 2, followed by an ACTION_UP for finger 2. This time we see an action value of 1 (ACTION_UP). We didn't get an action value of 262, but we'll explain that next. Also notice that in our ACTION_MOVE event, the pointer index has changed from 1 to 0, but the pointer Id has remained as 1.

Going back to the beginning of Listing 16–11, the first finger down is pointer Id 0, so why don't we get 0x00000005 (or decimal 5) for the action value when the first finger is pressed to the screen before any other fingers? This is a good question without a happy answer. We can get an action value of 5 in the following scenario. Press finger 1 to the screen, then finger 2, resulting in action values of 0 and 261 (ignoring the ACTION_MOVE values for the moment). Now lift finger 1 (action value of 6) and press it back down on the screen. The pointer Id of the second finger (finger 2) remained as 1. For the moment when finger 1 was in the air, our application knew about pointer Id 1 only. Once finger 1 pressed back down on the screen, Android assigned pointer Id 0 to finger 1, and since now we know there are multiple fingers involved, we get an action value of 5 (pointer Id of 0 and the action value of 5). The answer to the question is backward compatibility, but it is not a happy answer. In a scenario with two fingers, if the first finger touches the screen in a location, followed by a second finger in a different location on the screen, the up action of the first finger would not be recognized by an application not expecting multi-touch events. This is because the lifting of the first finger first would give an action value of 6, not 1. It's when the second finger is lifted that the application will receive an action value of 1.

When only one finger remains on the screen, Android treats it like a single-touch case. So we get the old ACTION_UP value of 1 instead of a multi-touch ACTION_UP value of 6 coupled with the pointer Id. But wait, the pointer Id of this last finger on the screen in our example above is still 1, so we really should have received an action value of 262. Our code will need to consider these cases carefully. A pointer Id of 0 could result in an ACTION_DOWN value of 0 or 5, depending on which pointers are in play. The last finger up will get an ACTION_UP value of 1 no matter which pointer Id it is.

The MotionEvent class comes with some helper constants to figure out what is going on. For example, MotionEvent.ACTION_POINTER_3_DOWN is 0x00000205 (or decimal 517) which we described earlier as the third finger down. These values may not be all that useful, however, since you'd be better off looking at the pointer Id in the second byte and the action in the first byte. In fact, though, it would be even better to use some other constants from the MotionEvent class to read the value returned by getAction(). Those constants are MotionEvent.ACTION_POINTER_ID_MASK, MotionEvent.ACTION_MASK, and MotionEvent.ACTION_POINTER_ID_SHIFT. By and'ing the returned value with each of these masks, and shifting the result for the pointer Id, you'd be able to reliably figure out what is going on, no matter how many fingers the device can support. Some sample code for this is provided in Listing 16–12.

Listing 16–12. *Sample Code for Figuring Out the Result from MotionEvent.getAction()*

```
int action = event.getAction();
int ptrId = event.getPointerId(0);
if(event.getPointerCount() > 1)
    ptrId = (action & MotionEvent.ACTION_POINTER_ID_MASK) >>>
                            MotionEvent.ACTION_POINTER_ID_SHIFT;
action = action & MotionEvent.ACTION_MASK;
if(action < 7 && action > 4)
    action = action - 5;
int ptrIndex = event.findPointerIndex(ptrId);
```

Note that this code is handling the strangeness that was explained above, where the pointer Id for the last finger left on the screen is not made part of the value returned from getAction(), and also where the action part of the value returned is 5 or 6 instead of 0 or 1. After these statements in Listing 16–12 have executed, ptrId will hold the pointer Id associated to the action, action will have a value between 0 and 4, and ptrIndex will have the pointer index value for use with getX() and similar methods of MotionEvent. One way to look at the values returned from getAction() is to realize that any value greater than 4 represents a value that relates to a pointer Id. Any value less than or equal to 4 represents a value that relates to the only finger we know about, regardless of what pointer Id it is.

Touches with Maps

Maps can receive touch events as well. We have already seen how touching a map can bring up a zoom control, or allow us to pan the map sideways. These are built-in functions of maps. But what if we want to do something different? We're going to show you how to implement some interesting functionality with maps, including the ability to click a location and get its latitude and longitude. From there, we can do lots of very useful things.

One of the main classes for maps is `MapView`. This class has an `onTouchEvent()` method just like the `Views` we covered earlier, and takes a `MotionEvent` object as its only argument. We can also use the `setOnTouchListener()` method to set up a callback handler for touch events on a `MapView`. Other main types of objects for maps are the set of `Overlays`, including `ItemizedOverlay` and `MyLocationOverlay`. These were all introduced in Chapter 7. These `Overlay` classes also have an `onTouchEvent()` method, although the signature is slightly different from the `onTouchEvent()` method on a regular `View`. For an `Overlay`, the method signature is

`onTouchEvent(android.view.MotionEvent e, MapView mapView)`

We can override the `onTouchEvent()` method if we want to do different things with maps. It is more common to override methods in an `Overlay` class than in `MapView`, so we will focus our attention there for this section. As before, the `onTouchEvent()` method for `Overlays` deals with `MotionEvent` objects. Even with maps, the `MotionEvent` object gives us X and Y coordinates of where the user has touched the touchscreen. This is only marginally useful when dealing with maps, since we often want to know the actual location on the map where the user touched. Fortunately, there are ways to figure this out.

`MapView` provides an interface called `Projection`, and `Projection` has methods to convert from a pixel to a `GeoPoint`, or from a `GeoPoint` to a pixel. To get a `Projection`, call the `MapView.getProjection()` method. Once you have the `Projection`, the methods `fromPixels()` and `toPixels()` can be used for the conversions. Keep in mind that the `Projection` is only good while the map doesn't change in the view. Within your `onTouchEvent()` method, you can convert the X and Y location values to a `GeoPoint` using `fromPixels()`.

An interesting and very useful method of `Overlay` is the `onTap()` method, which is similar to the `onTouch()` method we saw earlier in this chapter, but different in a key way. Map `Overlays` do not have an `onTouch()` method. The signature of the `onTap()` method is

`public boolean onTap(GeoPoint p, MapView mapView)`

This means that when a user touches on our `Overlay`, our `onTap()` method gets called with the `GeoPoint` of where the user touched. This will save us a lot of time trying to figure out where on the map they're touching. We no longer need to worry about converting from an X and Y coordinate location to a latitude and longitude coordinate. Android takes care of this for us.

We're now going to revisit the example from Chapter 7 in which we displayed a map with buttons for the different modes (Satellite, Street, Traffic, and Normal). We're going to add the ability to launch StreetView on a location from the map. To do this we need to add an `Overlay` object to our `MapView`, and when the `Overlay` object receives a touch event we'll convert that touch event to a location on the map. With the converted location, we'll launch an intent to invoke StreetView on that location. We'll start by making a copy in Eclipse of our MapsDemo from Chapter 7 (see Listings 7-12 and 7-13). Then we'll use Listing 16–13 to modify the onCreate() method of the main `Activity`, plus add a new class with the file `ClickReceiver.java`, also provided in this listing. The changes to the onCreate() method are shown in bold. The UI will still look just like it did in Figure 7-7.

Listing 16–13. *Adding Touch to Our Maps Demo*

```
@Override
protected void onCreate(Bundle savedInstanceState) {
    super.onCreate(savedInstanceState);
    setContentView(R.layout.mapview);

    mapView = (MapView)findViewById(R.id.mapview);

    ClickReceiver clickRecvr = new ClickReceiver(this);
    mapView.getOverlays().add(clickRecvr);
}


// This file is ClickReceiver.java
import android.content.Context;
import android.content.Intent;
import android.net.Uri;
import android.util.Log;

import com.google.android.maps.GeoPoint;
import com.google.android.maps.MapView;
import com.google.android.maps.Overlay;

public class ClickReceiver extends Overlay{
    private static final String TAG = "ClickReceiver";
    private Context context;

    public ClickReceiver(Context _context) {
        context = _context;
    }

    @Override
    public boolean onTap(GeoPoint p, MapView mapView) {
        Log.v(TAG, "Received a click at this point: " + p);

        if(mapView.isStreetView()) {
            Intent myIntent = new Intent(Intent.ACTION_VIEW, Uri.parse
                ("google.streetview:cbll=" +
                (float)p.getLatitudeE6() / 1000000f +
                "," + (float)p.getLongitudeE6() / 1000000f
                +"&cbp=1,180,,0,1.0"
                ));
```

```
            context.startActivity(myIntent);
              return true;
        }
        return false;
    }
}
```

That's all we need to do for this new example to work—unless of course you don't have StreetView available in your emulator or device. StreetView was included in the emulators for CupCake (1.5) and Donut (1.6) but was removed in the Éclair (2.0) emulator. One way around this is to get a real device, which should have StreetView installed, and test on there. If all you have is an emulator, you could try the following simple procedure:

1. Set up an AVD that is based on Google APIs version 1.6 or 1.5.

2. Use "adb pull /system/app/StreetView.apk" StreetView.apk to copy this application from your emulator to your workstation's hard drive.

3. Set up an AVD that is based on Google APIs for the version you want to run on.

4. Use "adb install StreetView.apk" using the .apk file you copied off in step 2 above.

This should install the StreetView application into your emulator and allow our example above to work.

When you run your newly-modified Maps Demo application, zoom in on a city so you can see the streets. Click the Street button to get the blue outlines on streets that support StreetView (i.e., they have pictures in the Google database). Now you can touch a street and the onTap() method of our ClickReceiver will be called, which in turn will contact the StreetView activity with the location from our touch event using an intent. If you touch an area of the map where StreetView does not have pictures, you will see an empty StreetView screen with an indication such as "Invalid panorama". This means Google can't find any images near enough to that location. Click the back arrow to return to our Maps application and try another location. If you look in LogCat you will see that we've logged the latitude and longitude of the map location that was touched. Notice that the GeoPoint object uses ints for the lat and long, while the StreetView URI requires floats.

For this sample application, we've chosen to send an intent with the lat/long of our touched location to the StreetView activity. But you can imagine the other possibilities open to you. With the lat/long of a location, we could use the Geocoder to find out what's around that location. We could use the location to navigate to it using turn-by-turn directions. We could measure how far away the location is from where we are. We can even store the location for later use.

Gestures

Gestures are a special case of a touchscreen event. Basically, a gesture is a pre-recorded touchscreen motion that your application can expect from the user. If the user performs the same gesture as the pre-recorded gesture when using your application, your application can invoke specific logic according to what that gesture means to your application. Gestures require an overlay that can detect a gesture by the user to pass it to the underlying activity. Using gestures can simplify a user interface by eliminating buttons or other controls in favor of finger swipes or drawing motions. They can also make for interesting game interfaces. In this section, we will explore how to record gestures and how to use them in your application.

Before we get into gesture code, let's play with the Gestures Builder application that comes with your emulator. This will help you understand what a gesture is. Gestures Builder creates and manages a gestures file that contains a library of gestures. Launch an emulator from Eclipse, unlock the emulator device, then go to your apps and choose Gestures Builder. Figure 16–4 shows the app icon.

Figure 16–4. *The Gestures Builder icon*

The Gestures Builder app will open to a mostly blank screen. Click the Add gesture button. You will be prompted for a Name. The name you give will be associated to the gesture you're about to record. This name will be used in your code to refer to the gesture, and will serve as a sort of command name. When the user performs the gesture to your application, the name will be passed to your methods so your application can do what the user is expecting it to do. The name you give could be a noun like "spiral" or "checkmark", or it could be like a command such as "fetch" or "stop". For now, let's call our first gesture "checkmark", so type in **checkmark** for the Name. Now draw a check mark in the big blank space underneath. If you don't like your first attempt, simply redraw a new check mark. The old one will erase as soon as you start drawing a new one. When you're happy with your check mark, click Done. You should see a screen like that shown in Figure 16–5.

Figure 16–5. *Our check mark gesture saved to the /sdcard*

Note that you could record different types of check marks and give them all the same name of "checkmark". Record at least one more check mark–like gesture and also name it checkmark; it could be smaller or bigger or in some way different than your first check mark while still retaining the basic shapeness of a check mark. Add some different gestures with different names using the "Add gesture" button. Each time you click Done you add another gesture to your library. You might try to use a multi-touch gesture, drawing two fingers across the screen at the same time, to make an equals sign. This doesn't work in Android 2.0 and you only get one line. Maybe in the future multi-touch gestures—that is, gestures where two or more fingers are touching the screen at the same time—will be supported.

Each gesture has a name and is made up of strokes. A gesture stroke is a touch sequence starting from when a finger touches down on the screen to when that finger lifts from the screen. As you learned earlier, a touch sequence is made up of MotionEvent objects. Similarly, a gesture stroke is made up of gesture points. Gestures get collected into a gesture store. A gesture library contains one gesture store. In Android, these are all classes that you can use in your code. See Figure 16–6 for a diagram that shows the relationships.

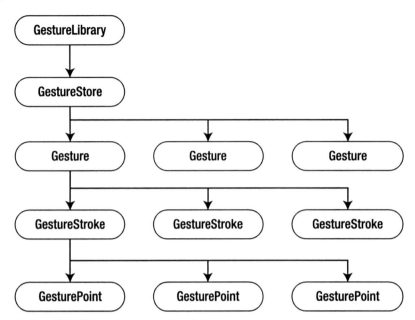

Figure 16–6. *The structure of gesture classes*

While we can't use multi-touch to create a gesture, there is an ability to have multiple gesture strokes in a single gesture. For example, to create a letter E gesture, you would need at least two gesture strokes; one gesture stroke could trace the top, back, and bottom sides of the E, then a second stroke could provide the center dash to complete the letter. You could also draw the back of the E with a vertical gesture stroke, followed by three separate horizontal gesture strokes to finish the letter. There are other ways you could draw an E, and fortunately, the gesture library allows you to give all of them the name "E" while recording different gestures. Go ahead and record E a few different ways, since your users might draw an E in different ways and you want your application to recognize an E, however the user decides to draw it. Figure 16–7 shows different ways of recording an E.

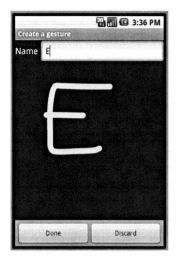  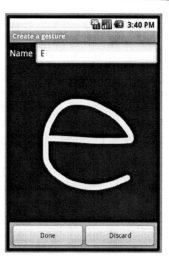

Figure 16–7. *Different ways to record an "E" gesture*

You may find it challenging to create a multi-stroke gesture in Gestures Builder in the emulator. As we noted earlier, you can simply redraw your gesture over the last one and the last one will be erased. So how does Android know when you're starting over, or when you're just adding another gesture stroke to the current gesture? Android uses a value called the `FadeOffset` which is a time value in milliseconds, and if you wait longer than this time value to start the next gesture stroke of your gesture, then Android assumes you're starting over, or starting a new gesture. By default the time value is 420 milliseconds. This means that if you are drawing a gesture on the screen, and you lift your finger for longer than 420 milliseconds before drawing the next gesture stroke in your gesture, Android will assume you've already finished, and will use what you've drawn so far as the entirety of your gesture. On a real device, the default value might be long enough to start the next stroke of a gesture. On the emulator, though, it might not be. It depends on how fast your workstation is.

If you're having trouble getting Gestures Builder in the emulator to accept a multi-stroke gesture, you can create your own version of Gestures Builder and modify the default value of `FadeOffset`. GestureBuilder is provided as a sample application under your Android SDK directory, in `platforms/android-2.0/samples/GestureBuilder`. You can create a new Android project in Eclipse using the "Create project from existing sample" option and choosing GestureBuilder from the drop-down menu. Then go into the project's `/res/layout/create_gesture.xml` file and add the attribute `android:fadeOffset="1000"` to the `GestureOverlayView` element. This will extend `FadeOffset` to 1 second (1000 milliseconds). You are free to choose a different value if you wish.

Let's investigate where these gestures went. The Toast message in Gestures Builder tells us the gestures are being saved to `/sdcard/gestures`. Use File Explorer in Eclipse, or `adb`, and navigate to the `/sdcard` folder of the emulator. There you will see a file called `gestures`. Notice that it is not very big. The `gestures` file is a binary file so you will not be able to edit it by hand. In order to modify the contents you will need to use the Gestures

Builder app. When building your gesture-enabled application, you will need to copy the gestures file to your application's /res/raw directory. For this, you will need to use the File Copy feature of File Explorer, or use adb pull to get the gestures file onto your workstation so you can copy it into your project.

Besides adding new gestures in Gestures Builder, you can long-click an existing gesture to bring up a menu. From the menu, you can change the gesture's name or delete it. You cannot re-record the gesture, so if you don't like the gesture itself, you'll need to delete it and re-add it. One thing you might want to do is record variations of gestures and give them the same name. The name does not have to be unique, although the gestures with the same name should be similar. This can account for user variation in inputting the gesture. For example, you could record several different check marks and give them all the same name ("checkmark"). When the user does a check mark–gesture in your application, as long as it matches one of the check mark–gestures you've recorded, your application will receive "checkmark" to know what the user did.

Now we're going to create a sample application that uses our new gestures file. Using Eclipse, create a new Android Project. Refer to Listing 16–14 for the XML of our layout file, and for the code of our Activity class.

Listing 16–14. *Java Code for Our Gesture Revealer Application*

```xml
<?xml version="1.0" encoding="utf-8"?>
<!-- This file is /res/layout/main.xml -->
<LinearLayout xmlns:android="http://schemas.android.com/apk/res/android"
    android:orientation="vertical"
    android:layout_width="fill_parent"
    android:layout_height="fill_parent"
    >
<TextView
    android:layout_width="fill_parent"
    android:layout_height="wrap_content"
    android:text="Draw gestures and I'll guess what they are"
    />

<android.gesture.GestureOverlayView
    android:id="@+id/gestureOverlay"
    android:layout_width="fill_parent"
    android:layout_height="fill_parent"
    android:gestureStrokeType="multiple"
    android:fadeOffset="1000" />

</LinearLayout>


import java.util.ArrayList;
import android.app.Activity;
import android.gesture.Gesture;
import android.gesture.GestureLibraries;
import android.gesture.GestureLibrary;
import android.gesture.GestureOverlayView;
import android.gesture.Prediction;
import android.gesture.GestureOverlayView.OnGesturePerformedListener;
import android.os.Bundle;
import android.util.Log;
```

```java
import android.widget.Toast;

public class MainActivity extends Activity implements OnGesturePerformedListener {
    private static final String TAG = "Gesture Revealer";
    GestureLibrary gestureLib = null;

    @Override
    public void onCreate(Bundle savedInstanceState) {
        super.onCreate(savedInstanceState);
        setContentView(R.layout.main);

//        gestureLib = GestureLibraries.fromRawResource(this, R.raw.gestures);
        gestureLib = GestureLibraries.fromFile("/sdcard/gestures");
        if (!gestureLib.load()) {
            Toast.makeText(this, "Could not load /sdcard/gestures",
                Toast.LENGTH_SHORT).show();
            finish();
        }

        // Let's take a look at the gesture library we have work with
        Log.v(TAG, "Library features:");
        Log.v(TAG, "  Orientation style: " + gestureLib.getOrientationStyle());
        Log.v(TAG, "  Sequence type: " + gestureLib.getSequenceType());
        for( String gestureName : gestureLib.getGestureEntries() ) {
            Log.v(TAG, "For gesture " + gestureName);
            int i = 1;
            for( Gesture gesture : gestureLib.getGestures(gestureName) ) {
                Log.v(TAG, "    " + i + ": ID: " + gesture.getID());
                Log.v(TAG, "    " + i + ": Strokes count: " +
gesture.getStrokesCount());
                Log.v(TAG, "    " + i + ": Stroke length: " + gesture.getLength());
                i++;
            }
        }

        GestureOverlayView gestureView =
            (GestureOverlayView) findViewById(R.id.gestureOverlay);
        gestureView.addOnGesturePerformedListener(this);
    }

    @Override
    public void onGesturePerformed(GestureOverlayView view, Gesture gesture) {
        ArrayList<Prediction> predictions = gestureLib.recognize(gesture);

        if (predictions.size() > 0) {
            Prediction prediction = (Prediction) predictions.get(0);
            if (prediction.score > 1.0) {
                Toast.makeText(this, prediction.name, Toast.LENGTH_SHORT).show();
                for(int i=0;i<predictions.size();i++)
                    Log.v(TAG, "prediction " + predictions.get(i).name +
                            " - score = " + predictions.get(i).score);
            }
        }
    }
}
```

In this example, we're going to simply access the exact same file that the Gestures Builder application wrote to. In our onCreate() method, we use the GestureLibraries.fromFile() method to do this. But we also show in the comments how you would access a gestures file that is part of your application. If you were to use the fromRawResource() method, you'd use an argument like our regular resource IDs, and you'd put the gestures file into the /res/raw directory.

Our application doesn't do a whole lot, but running it will give you a better understanding of what is going on inside Android as it processes gestures. At startup, our application loads the gestures file and logs what it finds. It also logs the results of trying to match a sample gesture drawn into the input screen of our application. Go ahead and run the Gesture Revealer application, assuming, of course, that you've run Gestures Builder already and have some gestures in the /sdcard/gestures file. See how each gesture is logged with the ID, the number of strokes, and the length.

Draw in gestures that you know exist in your gesture library. Then draw in some that you know do not exist. Watch the LogCat records to see what's happening. You may notice that sometimes what you draw is not recognized when you think it should be, or that what Android recognized was not what you had in mind, but most of the time it correctly recognizes what you drew. You may also have noticed that when Android recognizes your input gesture, you get scores for all gestures in your library, but when Android doesn't recognize your input gesture, you don't get anything at all in predictions.

Also note what happens if you have a multi-stroke gesture, such as the letter E, and you take too long between strokes. The application will take what you've drawn so far and use that to compare to your gesture library, which is likely to result in the wrong match, or no match at all. This time delay is controlled by FadeOffset. Here is where it gets tricky. We want Android to begin matching gestures as soon as we're done drawing our gesture, but we have no way to know if the user is done drawing the gesture unless we wait for some period of time and don't see the start of a new gesture stroke. Therefore, FadeOffset serves two purposes. One is to control how long to wait for a new gesture stroke as part of the current gesture, and the other is to control how long to wait to begin matching our gesture against the known gestures in our gesture library. Making FadeOffset very large means having to wait for a long time before the matching process begins. Making FadeOffset too small means not being able to draw a multi-stroke gesture because Android will think we're done before we get to the next gesture stroke. Whether 420 milliseconds is the right value to use is up to you. You might want to use a Preference value so users can adjust it for themselves.

While on the topic of multi-stroke gestures, note that the GestureOverlayView has a setting that controls whether or not multi-stroke gestures are expected. The attribute in XML is android:gestureStrokeType and the value is either single (the default) or multiple. If you want to be able to draw multi-stroke gestures, this attribute must be set. You can also set it programmatically using setGestureStrokeType(int type), using an argument of either GestureOverlayView.GESTURE_STROKE_TYPE_SINGLE or GestureOverlayView.GESTURE_STROKE_TYPE_MULTIPLE. GestureOverlayView also has XML attributes and methods for setting colors and line thicknesses.

To create your own gesture-aware application, you will need to decide what gestures your application will act on, create a library of those gestures, and then implement the onGesturePerformedListener interface, probably in your Activity, to recognize the gestures and take appropriate action.

What if you want your users to be able to record their own gestures? For example, if they would like to use a different gesture for an action in your application instead of the gesture that you provide? This is possible, but means that you need to have a gesture library file that can be written to. The logical place to put this is in /sdcard. And it's fairly simple to create a new gesture library file, read out the default gestures from the gesture library file that comes with your application, and then overwrite gestures that the user wants to replace with their own gestures. You can use the implementation of the Gestures Builder application as mentioned above, to see how to implement a gesture recorder. Or maybe someone will write a Gestures Builder application that responds to intents, so you could simply invoke that activity to add a new gesture. Alternatively, you could record just the user's gestures into a new writable gesture library file, then load two gesture libraries into your application, the user's and your original. Within the onGesturePerformed() method, you could first try recognize() on the user's library, then on your own. You could compare the top scores from any predictions from each library to decide which action to take.

Summary

In this chapter we showed you how to deal with touchscreens, starting first with single-touch applications, then moving on to multi-touch. We explained how touch works with maps and how Android provides some helpful classes and methods for dealing with touches and maps. Finally, we explored the Gesture mechanisms in Android that allow your applications to receive user input in a new and perhaps simpler way than using keyboards or other UI controls.

Titanium Mobile: A WebKit-Based Approach to Android Development

In this chapter, we are going to introduce a novel yet complementary approach to programming applications on the Android platform, inspired by the trend that began with RIA (Rich Internet Applications). Some of the key features of RIA are the ability to drag and drop, provide animation, and talk to servers without refreshing through HTML browsers. Although these activities have been traditionally accomplished through plug-ins such as Flash, recent advances in RIA accomplish them by taking advantage of the HTML DOM (Document Object Model).

Titanium Mobile is a product from Appcelerator Inc. (http://www.appcelerator.com) that brings the advances of RIA to mobile devices. In addition to bringing this new RIA model to the popular mobile platforms (Android and iPhone), Titanium Mobile is also open source and licensed under the Apache v2.0 license. In this chapter, we will introduce you to this new, yet familiar, paradigm and walk you through the architecture and mechanics of Titanium Mobile.

We've organized this chapter into three sections. We will start with an overview of Titanium Mobile and cover its history, architecture, and programming ecosystem. We'll show you how to sign up for and download Titanium Mobile. We'll introduce you to the components of the Titanium Developer, including its sandbox, where you will type and test a few lines of stand-alone javascript code which will say "Hello World".

In the second section, we will walk you through the lifecycle of a project using a simple "Hello World" project. Unlike the sandbox example, this project has a formal structure which you can build and distribute. In this second section we will create the project, test it on an emulator, package the project as an .apk file, and sign the .apk file so that it can be installed on other emulator instances and devices.

In the third section, we will cover what it takes to write client-side applications in JavaScript without help from a server-side UI framework such as JSP (Java Server

Pages) or ASP.NET. This topic will cover advanced JavaScript that you will need. We will also cover a critical JavaScript library called JQuery. We will also briefly enumerate a number of JavaScript API wrappers to the native Android platform provided by Titanium Mobile. We will conclude the chapter by drawing out the significance of this approach to Android development.

> **NOTE:** A Titanium-like approach to Android application development can supplement your development efforts by giving you a faster and prettier path to application development. The "prettier" path comes from the simplicity and flexibility of the HTML and CSS UI. This is not to mention the platform-independent abstraction provided by Titanium Mobile, which can also make your application run on multiple mobile platforms.

Before we start, we want to point out that this chapter offers an introduction to Titanium Mobile; we will not attempt to cover Titanium Mobile in depth. However, we will provide a clear roadmap to the maze of open source tools you will need to make this paradigm work. This is important, as the documentation on the Titanium Mobile web site assumes that the developer is already familiar with the Web 2.0 development paradigm.

Titanium Mobile Overview

If you are a web developer, you may already be familiar with some of the technologies and tools in the browser and RIA space such as Flash/Flex from Adobe, SilverLight from Microsoft, JavaFx from Sun, and Laszlo from Laszlo Systems.

These RIA tools provide rich interaction to the user by allowing such things as drag and drop, animation, tree controls, and richer tables.

Flash/Flex does this through the Flash browser plug-in. Silverlight does this through a Dotnet browser plug-in that provides the CLR (Common Language Runtime) environment. JavaFx does this through JRE (Java Runtime Engine). Laszlo does this by co-opting the Flash plug-in as well.

There is one technology in RIA space that doesn't use any plug-ins but uses native browser controls. In this alternative, JavaScript libraries, taking advantage of HTML DOM (Document Object Model), have allowed programming in RIA directly without any plug-ins. These JavaScript libraries provide a surprisingly capable architecture for building RIA through DOM and Ajax (Asynchronous JavaScript and XML).

> **NOTE:** If you are not familiar with DOM or Ajax, please refer to external sources to understand how they contribute to RIA.

This JavaScript/HTML-based RIA approach, which doesn't use any new plug-ins, allows for a development gradient where you can become sophisticated over time without having to commit to a steep learning curve up front.

This is all fine for web development, you may say, but what has this got to do with developing on Android when we are talking about native applications? As it turns out, the browser in Android is Chrome based, which in turn is based on the seemingly ubiquitous WebKit engine that powers web browsers such as Chrome and Safari.

Technologies are emerging that allow you to drive the WebKit natively using HTML and JavaScript files stored on the local device. This is where Titanium Mobile comes into play. Titanium Mobile exploits the WebKit to provide cross-platform solutions that locally run on Windows desktops, Mac desktops, iPhone, and the Android OS.

> **NOTE:** Appcelerator Inc. (originally called Hakano) is based in Mountain View, California, and was founded in 2006 by Jeff Haynie and Nolan Wright with product offerings developed around Web 2.0. In early 2008, they extended their product strategy to use a WebKit-based, cross-platform approach for desktops and mobile platforms. These efforts have resulted in the Titanium product suite.

Let's look now at the kind of architecture Titanium Mobile has under the hood to provide a rich user experience and also cross-platform compatibility.

Architecture

At the core, Titanium Mobile is a wrapper for working with WebKit, which is available on Android and other mobile devices such as iPhone. Titanium Mobile then supplements the WebKit capabilities by providing a set of JavaScript APIs that map to the native Android libraries such as file systems and media. This JavaScript-based API abstraction on a native device gives a uniform API to a seasoned web developer to write applications to the native OS interface. How Titanium accomplishes this at a high level is depicted in Figure 17–1.

The figure has three main sections or blocks: B1, B2, and B3. B1 is the project that you maintain for developing one of your applications. B2 is the Titanium Developer IDE. (We sometimes call this simply the Titanium IDE.) B3 represents the Android emulator or the device.

A Titanium project represented by B1 is just a directory on your hard drive where you keep your HTML resources. Other than some housekeeping files and build files, most of your source files are kept in a subdirectory called Resources. This project directory is known to the Titanium IDE (in Figure 17–1 this relationship is identified as line L1).

The JavaScript in this project has access to native JavaScript libraries provided by the Titanium Developer IDE. This native JavaScript comes with the Titanium IDE and is indicated inside the Titanium IDE box (B2). This relationship is indicated through line L2.

Titanium IDE will take the project and create an .apk file, which is then installed on the device (B3). This is indicated by Generate (L3) and Build (L4) lines.

NOTE: The IDE actually creates an intermediate project (line L3) resembling an Eclipse ADT project before building it. This is important to know because it is possible to take this intermediate project and actually debug it in the Eclipse IDE.

Once installed, this .apk file will drive the WebKit (line L6) through the available resource files. When the .apk is installed on the device, the files from Resources subdirectory (HTML, image, JavaScript, CSS, etc.) will be copied to the device as well. This is how WebKit is able to locate relative HTML files (line L7).

The JavaScript code from the HTML files (which themselves are part of the .apk) will also have access to the native Android platform through Native JavaScript APIs provided by the Titanium Developer (line L5).

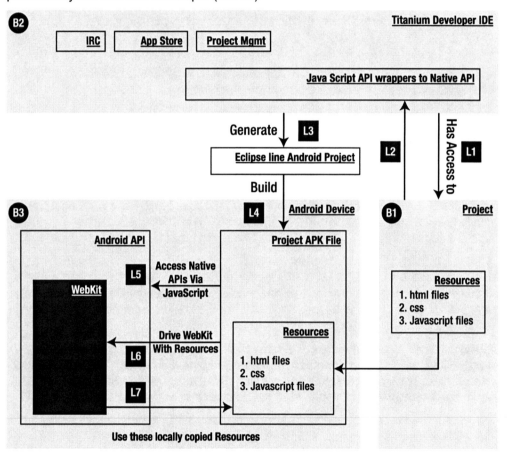

Figure 17–1. *Titanium Mobile high-level architecture*

Now that we have briefly explored the Titanium Mobile architecture diagram for Android, we'll explore each of the following architectural components in a bit more detail:

- A Titanium project containing resources

- The Titanium IDE

- How to build and deploy the project on a device

Nature of a Titanium Project

A Titanium Mobile project is very much like an HTML development project where you have an index.html and a series of subdirectories where you keep HTML files, CSS files, and other JavaScript libraries (both yours and third party's). Titanium calls this root directory a Resources directory and is represented in the diagram as a Resources box inside the B1 box.

This Resources subdirectory is created for you when you use the Titanium IDE and create a project. You will see in the examples that follow later in this chapter the exact directory structure for this project. Developers can choose to use any set of JavaScript libraries that they are familiar with. There is also a set of JavaScript APIs that Titanium makes available to your JavaScript code.

Components of the Titanium Developer IDE

Let's talk about the components of the Titanium Developer IDE (represented by box B1 in Figure 17–1). Strictly speaking, this is not an IDE in the sense of, say, Eclipse. It doesn't offer you any editors. However, it allows you to create project directories and \ compile, build, test, and deploy projects. It is more like a build and collaborative environment. For example, once you are satisfied with your edits, you can go to the Titanium IDE and test the program on the Android emulator. The Titanium Mobile team recommends that each developer choose their respective IDEs to edit and work with JavaScript and HTML.

This Titanium Developer IDE has the following key components:

- *Project management*: Creates, builds, packages, tests, and deploys projects (applications)

- *App Store*: An application store where a community of developers can upload and download their applications

- *IRC*: An internet relay chat where you can ask for help, which is directly integrated into your workspace(a real convenience)

In subsequent chapters you will get to know how each of these works.

Building and Deploying Projects through Titanium IDE

Now let's examine the build features of the Titanium IDE. Once you create and edit your files, as in any other project, you ask the Titanium Developer tool to build and test your application (which essentially is in the Resources directory). The IDE will then convert the files into an Android project, very similar in structure to an Eclipse ADT structure.

This intermediate Android project is then compiled to make an .apk file. The IDE will take this .apk file (just like the Eclipse ADT) and install it on the Android emulator. The Titanium Developer will also automatically invoke the emulator. All of these steps are components of the build-and-test step. At the end of this option you will see your application show up in the emulator.

You can repeat this process of editing and testing until you are satisfied, and then proceed to get a final copy of the signed .apk file that is ready for distribution. (When you are testing the application you will not need a signed .apk file.) The Titanium Developer IDE does this automatically. However, to deploy it with an external device, you will need to explicitly sign the .apk file through the Titanium IDE.

In the process of creating the .apk file, the Titanium Developer copies the Resources directory to the assets subdirectory so that the native WebKit can access these files during execution. Also the JavaScript APIs will end up calling the native versions of the Java API on Android.

You can see that the magic of Titanium is quite rational after all. Now, let's look at what is possible with WebKit-like architecture.

The Titanium Ecosystem

The thin veneer of Titanium Mobile could be misleading for a traditional developer who is used to complete solutions like Microsoft's ASP.NET or Adobe's Flash/Flex. In contrast, Titanium Mobile relies on an open source ecosystem to draw its strength from.

Although Titanium Mobile is only a wrapper, it relies on proven technologies such as AJAX, JQuery, DOJO, Mootools, JSON, Aptana, and Microsoft Web Express. Depending on your taste, you can choose any of these technologies. Titanium Mobile will provide a pathway to use them on Android. Of course, Titanium Mobile, also enriches the JavaScript APIs through its set of wrappers to the underlying Android API.

When you are working with Titanium, you will need to choose some of these tools for your programming needs. You may choose one tool for the UI and another tool for server-side access, or one more tool for persistence.

We have chosen JQuery as a good candidate for UI development since it is simple to learn, well documented, yet sufficient for the programming complexities, and is expected to grow in the Open source community.

> **NOTE:** Due to space restrictions, we will not cover the persistence aspect or the server-side aspect of Titanium Mobile applications in this book. We will leave those areas to you for further exploration. By covering JQuery and the UI, we hope we have explained the primary pattern of Titanium development. The aspects that we have not covered here follow standard patterns and are easier to figure out on your own.

Now it's time to embark on our brief journey into Titanium development by downloading Titanium Developer.

Downloading and Installing Titanium Developer

In this section, we will show you how to install Titanium Mobile and introduce you to its feature set. We will cover the menus and screens available in the IDE. This will help you to get a feel for what is possible with the IDE and how you can use it to develop your own applications.

> **NOTE:** As in the rest of this book (except for Chapter 2), we use Windows XP as the operating system for the projects in this chapter. Note that the discussion also applies to Mac OS X at a high level.

You will need to sign up for Titanium Mobile before you can install it. The sigup and install process works best if you are connected to the Internet. (You can also download a zip file and install it, if you'd rather not be connected.) The system is designed to work well in a connected mode, both during installation and development. (Note: A newer release, 0.8.1, seems to help with proxy setup, but we haven't tested that version.)

You can sign up for Titanium Mobile at `http://www.appcelerator.com`. If you don't see the button that lets you sign up you can access it directly by typing

`http://www.appcelerator.com/products/request-titanium-mobile/`

Once signup is complete, you will receive an e-mail with the file to download and install Titanium Mobile (it is about 40MB). (We had to go back to the server a few times to get the full package during the installation process when we tried.) Once installed, it will create an icon on your desktop. It is also important to note that there is no uninstall utility at this time. You will have to manually remove the directories yourself. Under Windows XP you can do the following (shown in Listing 17–1) to completely remove the Titanium Developer.

Listing 17–1. *Directories to Remove for Uninstalling Titanium*

```
\documents and settings\all users\application data\Titanium
\documents and settings\\application data\Titanium
\Program Files\Titanium (your install directory)
```

Here are some additional instructions on uninstalling and reinstalling the Titanium Developer. The link has a similar set of instructions for Mac OS X.

`http://support.appcelerator.net/faqs/titanium-installation/reinstalling-titanium-developer`

Once installed, you will see an icon that looks like Figure 17–2.

Figure 17–2. *Titanium Developer Icon*

If you click this icon, it will start the Titanium Developer IDE. With no projects, the Titanium Developer IDE looks like Figure 17–3. At this point, there are two ways to create a project. You can either choose the Create button or use the New Project icon at the top. We will discuss creating new projects in detail later in the section "Creating a Project."

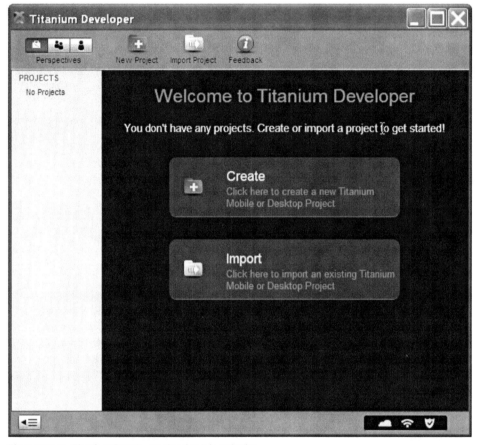

Figure 17–3. *Titanium Developer after fresh installation*

WARNING: Please be aware of the differences in version numbers as you test this chapter. Titanium Developer is a fast-moving target. The version that is available when you try it out may not match the one we have tested with. The goal of this chapter is to give you a feel for the nature of development using Titanium. You will need to adjust material depending on the latest version of Titanium at the point of your development. At the time of this writing the version is 0.5.0.

In this section, we also want to familiarize you with the complete scope of the Titanium Developer IDE. However, in Figure 17–3, as we don't have any projects yet, some of the menus are not available for us to describe the IDE fully. For now we are going to show you a screenshot of what the IDE will look like when you have one of these projects. This will allow us to introduce the IDE in a comprehensive manner. With at least one project in place, the IDE will look like Figure 17–4. This view is called the Project Perspective.

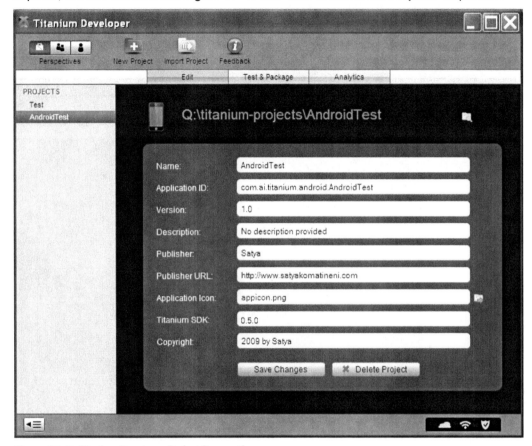

Figure 17–4. *Titanium Developer Project Perspective*

This Titanium Developer Project Perspective (Figure 17–4) has two project examples. You see the project names on the left-hand side. One is called Test and one is called AndroidTest. Test is a desktop application and AndroidTest is an Android Mobile application. You can use the same Titanium Developer IDE to develop both desktop and mobile applications.

An application (or project) like AndroidTest is essentially a directory on your local drive. For example, AndroidTest which is highlighted in Figure 17–4 is residing at c:\work\AndroidTest. The other parameters you see for this highlighted application are just attributes. One key attribute is the application ID which is going to be used for creating the root package for the Android Package file (.apk file).

NOTE: On some releases of Titanium Developer, "Desktop" is the default option. You won't see "Mobile" as one of the options because the options are not in an option box but in an edit control. But if you click on the edit control that shows the application type as "Desktop" it will then open up the option dropdown that shows "Mobile". But again, this may be corrected in your downloaded release of Titanium.

Once you have a project available, one option that you will use often is the Test & Package tab shown in Figure 17–5.

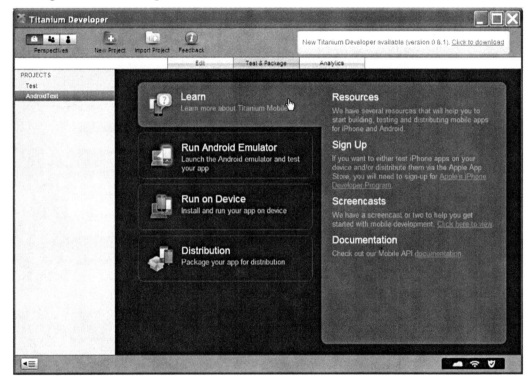

Figure 17–5. *Titanium Developer Test & Package tab*

This tab is responsible for taking your project resources and deploying them to the Android emulator for testing purposes. It also allows you to run on the device as well as prepare the Android application package for distribution purposes. This includes taking the package and installing it on a different emulator on a different development box or moving it to the Android marketplace or moving it to the Titanium App store. We will cover some of these later in the chapter.

Another nifty feature of the Titanium Developer tool is the Application store that you can browse for working applications. Here is the screenshot of this face of the tool (Figure 17–6). You can reach this screen by clicking on the Community perspective (the middle button in the top left-hand collection of buttons called "perspectives"). Once you are in the community perspective you will need to select the Apps tab.

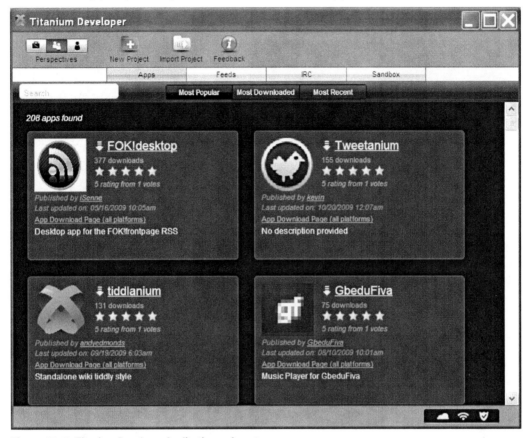

Figure 17–6. *Titanium Developer Application or App store*

The Titanium Developer also comes with a scratchpad (Figure 17–7) that you can quickly use to test sample code. You can reach this screen by going to the Community perspective again and choosing the Sandbox tab.

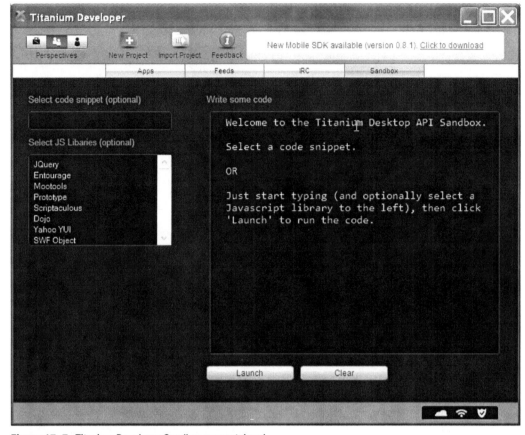

Figure 17-7. *Titanium Developer Sandbox or scratchpad*

A few things are evident in Figure 17-7. You can see that Titanium works in unison with a number of other tools such as JQuery and Mootools, which are displayed in the Select JS Libraries list box.

> **NOTE:** These tools are also available as options when you create a new project. When you pick these tools, Titanium will copy the necessary JavaScript files to your Resource directory. Or you can download the necessary files yourself from these tools' respective home pages.

The launch window of the Sandbox allows you to type any valid HTML or JavaScript and executes it. As an example, type the following HTML (Listing 17-2) and click on the launch button (shown in Figure 17-7).

Listing 17-2. *Hello World for the Titanium IDE Scratchpad*

```
<html><head></head>
<body>
<h2>Hello World</h2>
</body></html>
```

Listing 17–3 will show you a screen on your desktop with "Hello World" in it. You can then try adding some script to it as follows.

Listing 17–3. *Hello World with JavaScript for the Titanium IDE Scratchpad*

```
<html><head></head>
<body>
        <h2>Hello World</h2>
<script>
        alert('hello there');
</script>
</body></html>
```

When you launch using this HTML file, you will see the JavaScript alert "hello there" on your desktop HTML page. These examples are presented here to give you a feel for the underlying architecture of how HTML and JavaScript are orchestrated by Titanium Mobile.

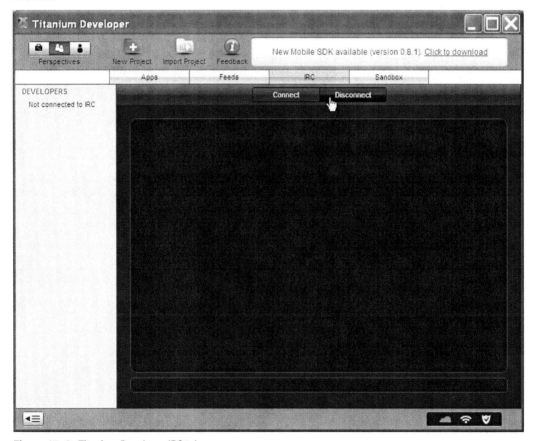

Figure 17–8. *Titanium Developer IRC tab*

Let us conclude this installation section by showing the IRC tab where you can interactively work with other online Titanium developers (see Figure 17–8). You can reach this screen by going to the Community perspective (middle button in the top-left corner) and then accessing the IRC tab. When you click the Connect button in this view you will see all the developers that are online in the left-hand portion of the screen.

Before moving on to the next section, let's quickly review what we have covered so far. We have elaborated the architecture of Titanium Mobile, and showed you how Titanium Mobile allows you to program on a local device using HTML-related technologies, especially JavaScript. You learned how to download and install Titanium Mobile. We have also introduced the Titanium Mobile IDE and its features. This is fantastic background for the next section.

Getting to Know the Ropes: The First Project

Next, we will focus on the lifecycle of a typical Titanium Mobile project. We will show you how to create a project with default options and test that project on the emulator. We will then take this default project and change it, to introduce your own HTML content by displaying a "Hello World" application.

We will then walk you through a couple of techniques for provisioning your project for debugging purposes. You will then learn how to package this project as an .apk file. Finally you will see how to sign and deploy this .apk file in other emulator instances.

We'll start with the first one of these: creating a simple project.

Creating a Titanium Mobile Project

You can create a new Titanium Mobile project by clicking the New Project icon (Figure 17–3) in the top row of the Titanium Mobile IDE. To create the project, you can use the properties shown in Figure 17–4. This will create a project on your local drive as shown in Listing 17–4.

Listing 17–4. *Titanium Mobile Project Structure*

```
c:\work\AndroidTest1
   \build
      \android\<eclipse like project structure>
   \Resources
      \android\appicon.png
            \default.png
      \<your files and sub directories go here>
      \index.html
      \index.css
      \about.html
   \manifest
   \tiapp.xml
```

Depending on the release, you may have some additional files or fewer files. But you get the general idea of the project structure here. The key directory, as indicated in the "Architecture" section, is the Resources subdirectory. This is where you need to create the HTML files, CSS files, JavaScript files, and so forth. You can have as many subdirectories as you want from here underneath (from the resources subdirectory onward) to realize your application. This directory is very similar to a directory that you would use to manage a web site.

Outside of this directory, under the root, the key file is `tiapp.xml`. This file acts as the configuration file for the Titanium project that is created. In Listing 17–5 we'll take a look at the `tiapp.xml` that gets generated by default when you create this project.

Listing 17–5. *Example tiapp.xml*

```xml
<?xml version="1.0" encoding="UTF-8"?>
<ti:app xmlns:ti="http://ti.appcelerator.org">
    <id>com.ai.titanium.android.AndroidTest1</id>
    <name>AndroidTest1</name>
    <version>1.0</version>
    <icon>appicon.png</icon>
    <persistent-wifi>false</persistent-wifi>
    <prerendered-icon>false</prerendered-icon>
    <statusbar-style>opaque</statusbar-style>
    <windows>
        <window>
            <id>initial</id>
            <url>index.html</url>
            <backgroundColor>#111</backgroundColor>
          <icon>ti://featured</icon>
          <barColor>#000</barColor>
          <fullscreen>false</fullscreen>
        </window>
        <window>
            <id>about</id>
            <url>about.html</url>
            <backgroundColor>#111</backgroundColor>
          <icon>ti://top rated</icon>
            <barColor>#000</barColor>
          <fullscreen>false</fullscreen>
        </window>
    </windows>
</ti:app>
```

We're primarily concerned with giving you a general introduction to Titanium development, so we won't go into each of the xml tags in `tiapp.xml`. You can read more about them by visiting the appcelerator community web site at

`http://www.appcelerator.com/community/`

The following URL is also useful for getting started:

`http://www.codestrong.com/timobile/guides/get_started/`

We have highlighted the nodes that we intend to discuss here, however. The highlighted window tag defines how many HTML files we want the app to display in multiple tabs. In Listing 17–5 we have two windows, one pointing to `index.html`, and the second pointing to `about.html`.

With these files which the new project automatically created in place, you can turn to the Test&Package tab of the Titanium Developer (see Figure 17–5) and choose to run the project in the emulator.

When you run this newly created application it looks like the following in the emulator (Figure 17–9). You should see this application started on the emulator without explicitly starting it, just like the Eclipse ADT. If it doesn't for some reason you can go to the Android menu and explicitly start it.

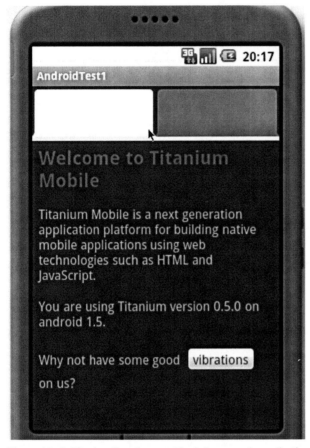

Figure 17–9. *Titanium Developer multi-window sample application*

If you take a look at the index.html and about.html you will see that index.html is populated into the first tab.

Crafting "Hello World"

Now let's see how we can simplify this initial project by getting rid of the tabs and provide just one window. We'll also change the background color to white so that the first page will look like the one shown in Figure 17–10.

We will need to do the following to make this happen:

1. Provide a new index.html or change the existing index.html so that it looks like the page in Figure 17–10.

2. Change `tiapp.xml` so that there is only one window and the url of the window is pointing to the index.html in step. Change the background color of the window to a light color.

We will walk through these steps now.

Figure 17–10. *A Sample Android "Hello World"*

The index.html that you will need to make this web page is shown in Listing 17–6. You can replace the index.html that was created for you by the IDE with this file.

Listing 17–6. *Stand-alone "Hello World" Example*

```
<html><body>
<h2>Hello World</h2>

<p><a href="javascript:alert('hello')">
Click here to execute JavaScript
</a></p>
</body></html>
```

This index.html is simple enough. The goal of this page is to call the JavaScript alert function to say hello when you click on the link that says `click here to execute JavaScript`.

Once this modified index.html is in place, let us see what you will need to change in the tiapp.xml. Here is the updated tiapp.xml. (Listing 17–7)

Listing 17–7. *tiapp.xml with a Single Window*

```
<?xml version="1.0" encoding="UTF-8"?>
<ti:app xmlns:ti="http://ti.appcelerator.org">
    <id>com.ai.titanium.android.AndroidTest2</id>
    <name>AndroidTest</name>
    <version>1.0</version>
    <icon>appicon.png</icon>
    <persistent-wifi>false</persistent-wifi>
    <prerendered-icon>false</prerendered-icon>
    <statusbar-style>opaque</statusbar-style>
    <windows>
        <window>
            <id>initial</id>
            <url>index.html</url>
            <backgroundColor>white</backgroundColor>
          <icon>ti://featured</icon>
          <barColor>#000</barColor>
          <fullscreen>false</fullscreen>
        </window>
    </windows>
</ti:app>
```

The important elements are highlighted. Notice that there is only one window now pointing to the index.html and that its background color is stated as white.

> **NOTE:** As you go through these examples, notice that we are incrementing the application title as AndroidTest1, AndroidTest2, etc. You don't have to do it this way. We are doing this because we want to make it easier to get screenshots in a repeatable fashion. Otherwise, once we change the code we will lose the old test case. Hopefully, that is a minor distraction that you can follow.

With index.html and tiapp.xml in place, you can package and test this application in the emulator. When you run this application now through the Titanium Mobile IDE, you will see the Figure 17–10 in the Android emulator.

Provisioning the Application for Debugging

One of the reasons we have used an "alert" in the JavaScript in our index.html (Listing 17–6) is to test JavaScript to see if it is running. An alert is a good way to do this. In fact, many programmers use JavaScript alerts as a debugging tool.

However, you will notice that the JavaScript from the index.html (Listing 17–6) will just not say "hello" from the Android emulator. Yet, the same project, if you were to create it on the desktop, will readily say "hello." What gives?

Apparently Appcelerator Inc. overrode this function to write the message to an internal debug console. As it turns out, WebKit, being the host of a web page (in this case the index.html) allows a client to configure what "alert" really means. On the Android platform Appcelerator chose to divert the message to a log stream instead of directing it to the console. We can only guess as to the motivations.

There are two possible motivations. In the JavaScript space, developers are increasingly using alert just as a way to debug. The argument goes that if an alert is used primarily as a debug tool, why not just log the message and not have the message show up on the screen as well? This unnecessary message will only distract the users from the real application. The second reason is the nature of Android. Dialogs in Android are asynchronous. So it will be pretty round-about to make that alert dialog wait, as that is what is expected by JavaScript.

There are two workarounds to this problem. The first is to use the Titanium UI API for creating a native Android alert dialog with an OK button. The second option is to use the Titanium Debug API. We will cover both here.

Listing 17–8 gives the example index.html rewritten to use both these options.

Listing 17–8. *index.html That Uses Alternative Debug Options*

```
<html><head>
<script>
function myalert(message)
{
    var a = Titanium.UI.createAlertDialog();
    a.setMessage(message);
    a.setTitle('My Alert');
    a.setButtonNames(["OK"]);
    a.show();
}

function dalert(message)
{
    Titanium.API.info(message);
    alert(message);
    //var a = prompt(message);
    myalert(message);
}
</script>

</head>

<body>
<h2>Hello World</h2>

<p><a href="javascript:dalert('hello')">
Click here to execute JavaScript
</a></p>

</body></html>
```

The function myalert uses the Android dialog option. When this function is called, the screen will look like Figure 17–11. This works well, but you must be aware that native alert dialogs in Android are asynchronous and also need to be reference-counted for efficiency. So you may want to use them sparingly.

Figure 17–11. *Titanium native alert window*

The second option is to use the Titanium Debug API to log debug messages instead of alerts. This is demonstrated in the function `dalert`. These messages will go to the Titanium Mobile Console window. The console window is the window that gets shown when you use the launch tab. You will need to do the following to activate the launch tab.

1. Choose the project name by clicking it in the project list.

2. Click the Test & Package tab.

3. Click the vertical Android emulator tab. This will show the console window on the right inside the IDE with two buttons at the bottom to "launch" and "stop emulator."

4. Click Launch App to run the app. When the app is running, the Titanium debug messages will show up in this right-hand console window.

Figure 17–12 shows an example.

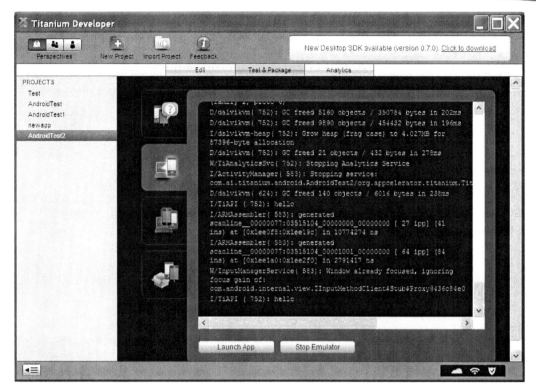

Figure 17–12. *Titanium Titanium mobile console window*

Notice the line in the middle of the screen that says I/TiApi: hello. This is the message we have sent through Titanium.API.info(message). (Interestingly, though, the "prompt" JavaScript function works fine.) If you are trying this for the first time, we want to mention this alert surprise which you may run into.

Now that we have an application and we know how to debug it, let us take this application and package it as an .apk file.

Packaging the Application

In Android, the unit of deployment is an Android package file called an .apk file. (You can refer to Chapter 7 for more details on how to work with .apk files.) You will need one of these .apk files to move your application to other places.

According to Android, an .apk file has to be signed in order to be deployed in an emulator or device or the marketplace. In fact, when you develop and test Android applications through the Eclipse ADT, the ADT is signing them (behind the scenes) with a built-in key that is only good for test deployment in the emulator. Android also treats the .apk files that are installed with the same signature a bit specially, where they share the process space.

> **NOTE:** When two .apk files share the same process space they are sharing the JVM that makes up the process space. They can share common variables, but problems in one .apk file can affect the other .apk file as well.

This may be good or bad, depending on how much isolation you would like. The signature is also important for installing updates to that application.

For more information on signing the application please see Chapter 7. You can also read more at

```
http://developer.android.com/guide/publishing/app-signing.html
```

As a side note, Android keeps the debug or development time key stores at the following locations:

- *For Mac OS X and Linux*: `~/.android/debug.keystore`

- *For Windows XP*: `C:\Documents and Settings\\.android\debug.keystore`

- *For Windows Vista*: `C:\Users\\.android\debug.keystore`

To sign an .apk file yourself you will need to understand the key infrastructure that is provided by the JDK (Java Development Kit). (We mentioned in Chapter 2 that to run Eclipse you will need to download a compatible JDK.) You will need to use the `keytool` from the JDK to create a key store with a password. (See Chapter 7, or consult `http://java.sun.com/javase/6/docs/technotes/tools/windows/keytool.html` for more information.) Listing 17–9 shows an example of creating a key store along with one key called `mykey` with `/jre/bin/keytool`:

Listing 17–9. *keytool Options*

```
keytool
  -genkey //generate a public/private key
  -alias mykey //name of the key
  -keystore c:\somekeystore.store //location of a store
  -storepass abc //password
  -keypass abc //password
  -keyalg RSA //key algorithm
  -validaty 14000 //how many days is it valid
```

Once you have the key store created you can use the Distribution tab (see Figure 17–4 under Test & Packaging) to create an .apk file. Titanium Developer will prompt you for a key name to sign the package with. You will need to know the path to the key store and the key store password. If you don't remember the key name (also called an alias) you can use the `keytool` to list the entries in the key store for you. But at a minimum you will need to write down and keep the key store location and password somewhere safe. Here is an example command that will list the contents of a key store:

```
keytool -list c:\somekeystore.store
```

Under the covers, Titanium uses `jarsigner` (covered in Chapter 7) to take the key alias you have specified and sign the .apk file. Titanium will then create the physical .apk file in the directory that you have specified.

It is worth noting here that the Eclipse ADT (also explained in Chapter 7) allows you to create an .apk file unsigned (you will then use the `keytool` and `jarsigner` to sign it yourself) but the Taninum Developer uses only the signed approach for creating .apk files that can be run outside its environment.

For testing the application on the emulator, both Eclipse ADT and Titanium IDE sign the .apk files with a built-in key that is only good for test deployment in the emulator. In fact, we indicated earlier where these default keys are kept in the case of the Eclipse ADT. Titanium IDE maintains a similar store. However, you rarely need to know where these development keys are stored.

Installing the .apk File on Your Own Emulator

With the signed .apk file in your hand, you can proceed to install that file in an Android emulator that you normally use (as opposed to the emulator that Titanium uses) to test your other Android applications. To do this you will need to start the emulator by doing the following:

```
\android\tools\emulator @avdname
```

Here avdname is the name of your Android Virtual Device (AVD). (See Chapter 2 for a description of AVDsand how to create them.) This is a mechanism that allows you to run multiple emulators, each with its own level of Android SDK and tools for testing purposes. Creating an AVD is a bit complicated, but here is a quick command for doing so:

```
android create avd -t 3 -c 32M -p ..\avds\avd3 -n avd 3
```

Here –t is target Android SDK level, -c is memory, -p is the path, and avd3 is the name of the avd.

Once the emulator is up and running, you can use the commands in Listing 17–10 to install and uninstall that package.

Listing 17–10. *adb Install and Uninstall Options*

```
adb install [-l] [-r]
- push this package file to the device and instal it
      ('-l' means forward-lock the app)
      ('-r' means reinstall the app, keeping its data)

adb uninstall [-k]
- remove this app package from the device
      ('-k' means keep the data and cache directorie)
```

Notice how during the install you are using the file name and during the uninstall you are using the fully qualified java-like package name. For our `AndroidTest2` application, the fully qualified package name will be

```
com.ai.android.titanium.AndroidTest2
```

You can also use the emulator or the device directly to uninstall any application. Here are the steps for that approach:

1. Start the Emulator.

2. From menu choose Dev Tools.

3. Go to Package Browser and locate your package.

4. Choose menu while highlighting the package name.

5. Choose Delete Package from the menu options.

Again, to start the emulator you need the avd name. You can use the following two commands to help with this. The first one will list the available avds and the second one will start the emulator for a given avd.

```
\tools\android list avd // lists avds available
\tools\emulator @avdname // start a specific avd
```

Of course, after going through all this you will finally be able to run your app in the emulator of your choice. When you run the app in your emulator, what you see in the emulator will be the same as shown in Figure 17–10.

We will leave this section with another nifty thing you can do with your Titanium project. As part of the build, Titanium actually creates a subdirectory called android under the build subdirectory. This directory is actually a full-fledged Eclipse ADT project. All you have to do on Windows is move the tiapp.xml and the Resources subdirectory into the build/android/assets. Then the build/android subdirectory is complete and now you can test or develop further in the Android native environment under the Eclipse ADT. You may have to delete R.java if you see build errors.

Planning for Real-World Applications

The proposition so far in this chapter has been that with HTML or JavaScript we can write all our applications. But how practical is that? In any application you will need mechanisms to program a flexible UI with forms, media, and so forth. You will need something to host your business logic and you will need something to read and persist state in a database.

Let us talk about simpler things first: middleware and data. JavaScript through AJAX and JSON can always request data through servers which can act as conduits for persistence and also some or all business logic. If the application were to access some local resources or local databases they could always use SQLite. But you would expect that cloud services and the threetier model are better for all but special cases. You would foresee no significant problems with this approach.

A UI framework is a different beast, however. Frameworks like Swing and WPF (Windows Presentation Framework) are complex frameworks. How far can plain HTML combined with JavaScript match these UI capabilities?

Although a number of hurdles remain, a tool like JQuery that is based on JavaScript gives a powerful model to dynamically alter the HTML DOM tree to address some of these questions.

JQuery is nimble, simple, and extensible. The "query" in JQuery comes from its ability to query any node in an HTML DOM through succinct syntax like CSS selectors and XSLT expressions. So the query in JQuery does not indicate its affinity to being a database tool. It is in fact a UI tool for HTML. We will go through a few examples in this chapter to show you how this works.

JQuery is just one of the tools in this genre that use HTML and JavaScript for extensive UI programming. You are free to investigate these alternatives and choose an appropriate one for your needs.

With that said, let us take a quick tour of JQuery.

Essential Primer on JQuery

You can find the home page for JQuery at http://jquery.com/. From there you will be able to download the single JavaScript file that makes up JQuery. This file is about 100K of JavaScript. Once you download it, you will be able to include it in your HTML pages using the code segment in Listing 17–11.

Listing 17–11. *Including JQuery in an HTML File*

```
<script src="../../js/jquery132-dev.js"></script>
```

Overall, the documentation at the site is very good. This makes it easy to quickly learn JQuery. And you can leverage this knowledge in your serverside HTML programming as well.

Let us see what we can do with it. One common thing you might want to do in HTML is to locate a div or a paragraph and replace the contents of that element with some text. You may also want to change the style of that div or hide that div. So let us do each of these (see Listing 17–12).

Listing 17–12. *JQuery Selection Examples*

```
function replaceAParagraph(newText)
{
    //locate the HTML element with an ID
    //it returns an array of matching elements
    var myParagraph = $("#MyParagraphID")[0];

    //read the old HTML from the element
    var oldText = myParagraph.html();

    //replace it with the new
    myParagraph.html(newText);

    //or simpler format
    $("#MyParagraphID").html(newText);

    //change the style of that element
```

```
    $("#MyParagraphID").css("color:red;");

    //hide the element
    $("#MyParagraphID").hide();
}
```

The $ is a function that belongs to JQuery and uses selectors to locate the needed element. Its syntax for getting at an element is elaborate and forms the core of JQuery. Listing 17–13 shows some of the many ways of using a selector.

Listing 17–13. *Various JQuery Selectors*

```
$("#MyElementID") // A specific id
$(".MyClass") //all elements matching this class
$("p") // all paragraphs
$("p.MyClass") //paragraphs with MyClass
$("div") // all divs
$(".MyClass1.MyClass2.MyClass3") // locate three classes
$("div,p,p.MyClass,#MyElementID") //matching all those

//Immediate children
$("#Main > *") // All children of Main
$("parent > child")

//Children and grand children
$("ancestor descendents")
$("form input") // all input fields in a form

$("label + input") // all inputs next to a label
$("prev + next")

//starting at myclass find siblings of type div
$(".myclass ~ div")
$("prev ~ next)
```

Once a certain set of elements is selected using these selectors, you can filter the output nodes further by using the following filter syntax:

```
$("selector:criteria")
```

Here is how you use this selector and criteria syntax:

```
$("tr:even").css("background-color", "#bbbbff");
```

This example selects every row of a table which is an even row and then sets its style. Some of the possible criteria are shown in Listing 17–14.

Listing 17–14. *JQuery Selection Criteria*

```
first
last
even
odd
eq(index)
lt(index)
gt(index)
header //(h1, h2 etc)
animated
```

Listing 17–15 presents a few more examples taken from the JQuery documentation site and slightly changed to better format them.

Listing 17–15. *Implementing hover over a Paragraph*

```
function hoverParagraph()
{
    $("p").hover(function () {
        $(this).css({'background-color' : 'yellow', 'font-weight' : 'bolder'});
    }, function () {
        var cssObj = {
          'background-color' : '#ddd',
          'font-weight' : '',
          'color' : 'rgb(0,40,244)'
        }
        $(this).css(cssObj);
    });
}
```

This is an example in which a paragraph is located and a set of callback functions are registered for a hover action. The first function changes the CSS of the paragraph to use ayellow background and the font weight of bold. The second function changes it to a different CSS when the hover is off.

Listing 17–16 is an example of working with a mouseover.

Listing 17–16. *Working with a Mouseover*

```
function paragraphMouseover()
{
    $("p").mouseover(function () {
        $(this).css("color","red");
    });
}
```

This is an example in which the CSS of a paragraph is changed with an anonymous function on a mouseover.

Essential Primer on Advanced JavaScript

As you start adapting JavaScript-centric technologies such as JQuery or Titanium (through its JavaScript API) you will start noticing JavaScript patterns that are quite unusual to someone that only uses JavaScript occasionally to supplement web pages.

The first of these surprises comes from the array and object equivalence. Let us lay this mystery out. We'll start with an object declaration or initialization in JavaScript.

```
var myobj = {};
```

The curly braces in this context define the start and end of an object initialization. In this example we have nothing inside the curly braces. This tells JavaScript that myobj is an object with no content or members in it. However, this defines an object. Let us extend this initialization pattern:

```
var myobj = {name:"phone-number1",value:"123456"};
```

This statement allows you to do the following:

```
alert(myobj.name());
or
alert(myobj["name"]);
```

This proves the equivalence of associative arrays and objects, and goes to show that an object's members are represented internally as an associative array. The converse is true too.

```
var myobj={};
myobj["name"] = "aaaa";
myobj["value"] = "bbbb";
```

The following two statements will be identical as well.

```
alert(myobj.name());
or
alert(myobj["name"]);
```

This sort of object initialization is pretty handy. Consider the following snippet, which we will use in a subsequent section (See isting 17–17.)

Listing 17–17. *JavaScript Array Definition Example*

```
var  itemArray = [
     {name: "Social", value: "12345678"},
     {name: "cell1", value: "12345678"},
     {name: "cell2", value: "12345678"}
];
```

This quickly defines an array of three objects, each holding a name/value pair as their fields. The object initialization pattern allows nested objects as well. Here is an example (Listing 17–18).

Listing 17–18. *Nested Object Initialization*

```
    var someobj = {field1:10,
    field2:"string",
    field3:{field1:10,field2:"string"));
```

This essentially forms the basis of JSON (JavaScript Object Notation). Data that is in the form of JSON is often used as a communication mechanism between clients and servers. If you are not familiar with the idea you may want to read up on JSON (http://json.org) as you will want to use something like this to communicate with web servers to retrieve or save data over HTTP.

Let us now talk briefly about anonymous functions. Consider the following example (Listing 17–19).

Listing 17–19. *Anonymous Functions*

```
function Person() {
  var age = 40; //init value
  this.setAge = function(howold) { age = howold };
  this.firstname = "First";
  this.lastname = "Last";
}
```

```
var me = new Person();
me.firstname = "aaaa";
me.lastname = "bbbb";
me.setAge(25);
//the following will be wrong
me.age=44;
```

In the example above, the member setAge is defined as an anonymous function with access to the private variable age, whereas the firstname and lastname are public variables.

We will conclude this section with a discussion of JavaScript namespaces, as they are used quite a bit in JavaScript-based libraries.

Consider the following pattern (Listing 17–20), which is often quoted as an approach to maintain namespaces in JavaScript.

Listing 17–20. *JavaScript Namespaces*

```
var MY_NAME_SPACE = function() {
    return {
        method_1 : function() {
            // do stuff here
        },
        method_2 : function() {
            // do stuff here
        }
    };
}();
```

It is quite revealing to understand this type of JavaScript coding pattern. At a high level the above code allows you to do the following:

```
MY_NAME_SPACE.method_1();
MY_NAME_SPACE.method_2();
```

The MY_NAME_SPACE prefix will prevent the author from conflicting with other libraries. But let us understand what is happening. We'll start with the returnstatement. If you see the pattern

```
var someobj = {method_1: function() {}, method_2: function2() {}}
```

this is essentially an object initialization where the object has two members, method_1 and method_2, and each is an anonymous function. So if this is an object, then the above statement is

```
var MY_NAME_SPACE = function() { return someobj; }();
```

where the someobj happens to be an object with functions method1 and method2. Now without the trailing (), MY_NAME_SPACE would have been a function and not an object like someobj with methods in it. And we need someobj so that we can do someobj.method1(). The trailing () essentially executes the anonymous function and makes MY_NAME_SPACE point to the someobj that is returned as a result. That is how we are able to do this:

```
MY_NAME_SPACE.method_1();
MY_NAME_SPACE.method_2();
```

Sometimes you will see this pattern written as follows:

```
var MY_NAME_SPACE = (function() {
   return {
      method_1 : function() {
         // do stuff here
      },
      method_2 : function() {
         // do stuff here
      }
   };
})();
```

Understanding the Microtemplating Engine

As soon as you start programming HTML as if it is a UI framework, you will quickly realize you could benefit from a templating engine used in technologies like JSP or ASP. Consider the following JavaScript array, for example:

```
var  itemAarray = [
      {name: "Social", value: "12345678"},
      {name: "cell1", value: "12345678"},
      {name: "cell2", value: "12345678"}
];
```

Say you want to create an HTML page that looks like this:

```
Social
12345678
Cell1
12345678
Cell2
12345678
```

It is really painful, even with the convenience of a Jquery, to create all those HTML nodes on the fly. Instead you would want to use a template that looks like a typical JSP page as shown in Listing 17–21:

Listing 17–21. *Example HTML Template*

```
<#
for(var i=0; i < itemArrayData.length; i++)
{
     var item = itemArrayData[i];
#>
   <p><#=item.name #>:<#=item.value #></p>
<# } #>
```

where the <%= of JSP is replaced with <#. To expand this template against the above JavaScript data set you will need some kind of a template engine that can be executed in JavaScript. John Resig, the author of JQuery, wrote one such templating engine. Due to its "tininess" it came to be called The JavaScript Microtemplating Engine.

Listing 17–22 shows the complete source code (as provided by John Resig, originally and subsequently altered on the Web by a number of folks), which you can save in a file for inclusion:

Listing 17–22. *John Resig's Code for Microtemplating Engine*

```
var _tmplCache = {}
this.parseTemplate = function(str, data) {
    /// <summary>
    /// Client side template parser that uses <#= #> and <# code #> expressions.
    /// and # # code blocks for template expansion.
    /// NOTE: chokes on single quotes in the document in some situations
    ///        use ' for literals in text and avoid any single quote
    ///        attribute delimiters.
    /// </summary>
    /// <param name="str" type="string">The text of the template to expand</param>
    /// <param name="data" type="var">
    /// Any data that is to be merged. Pass an object and
    /// that object's properties are visible as variables.
    /// </param>
    /// <returns type="string" />
    var err = "";
    try {
        var func = _tmplCache[str];
        if (!func) {
            var strFunc =
            "var p=[],print=function(){p.push.apply(p,arguments);};" +
                        "with(obj){p.push('" +
            //                    str
            //                        .replace(/[\r\t\n]/g, " ")
            //                        .split("<#").join("\t")
            //                        .replace(/((^|#>)[^\t]*)'/g, "$1\r")
            //                        .replace(/\t=(.*?)#>/g, "',$1,'")
            //                        .split("\t").join("');")
            //                        .split("#>").join("p.push('")
            //                        .split("\r").join("\\'") + "');}return p.join('');";

            str.replace(/[\r\t\n]/g, " ")
                .replace(/'(?=[^#]*#>)/g, "\t")
                .split("'").join("\\'")
                .split("\t").join("'")
                .replace(/<#=(.+?)#>/g, "',$1,'")
                .split("<#").join("');")
                .split("#>").join("p.push('")
                + "');}return p.join('');";

            //alert(strFunc);
            func = new Function("obj", strFunc);
            _tmplCache[str] = func;
        }
        return func(data);
    } catch (e) { err = e.message; }
    return "< # ERROR: " + err.htmlEncode() + " # >";
}
```

Let us now show you an index.html that uses the concepts discussed so far and takes that object array and generates an HTML representation (see Listing 17–23). You will need to either download and include the jquery.js from the Jquery web site or use the one that came with Titanium. If you want to use the one that came with Titanium you will need to choose it when you create the project for the list of tools. (We found it easier to download it from the Jquery site. If you miss that step during project creation, you won't have the option of choosing it later.) You will also need to create the `template-engine.js` using the code above and place it in an appropriate subdirectory of the `Resources`.

Listing 17–23. *HTML Utilizing Microtemplating Engine*

```
<html><head>
<script src="../../js/jquery132-dev.js"></script>
<script src="../../js/template-engine.js"></script>


<script>
//Data
var itemArray = [
                {name: "Social", value: "12345678"},
                {name: "cell1", value: "12345678"},
                {name: "cell2", value: "12345678"}
            ];

function onloadFunction()
{
   var s = $("#MyTemplate").html();
   var s1 = parseTemplate(s, {itemArrayData: itemArray});
   $("#target").html(s1);
}
</script>

<script id="MyTemplate" type="text/html">
 <#
 for(var i=0; i < itemArrayData.length; i++)
 {
     var item = itemArrayData[i];
 #>
     <p><#=item.name #>:<#=item.value #></p>
 <# } #>
</script>

</head>

<body onload="onloadFunction()">
<div id="target">
<p>target</p>
</div>
</body></html>
```

Here is what this code does. In the body of the HTML it defines a `div` with an ID of `target`. On document load the function `onLoadFunction()` runs the template against the data using the `parsetemplate()` method. It uses the jQuery selectors to first locate the template, which is anchored as a script element with the ID `MyTemplate`. The output from the parse template will be an expanded string. This string will then be inserted into the `div` as inner HTML. Again we use the jQuery selector to locate the target `div`.

If you make this the `index.html` in your previous project and test it, you will see a screen that looks like Figure 17–13 in your emulator.

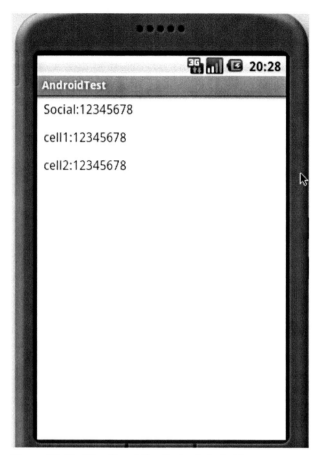

Figure 17-13. *Micro Templating Engine in Android*

That concludes our search for a tool that we can use effectively to craft complex HTML applications. JQuery has far more capabilities than this simple example demonstrates, but we have shown you some of the possibilities. There is also some additional work going on towards JQuery UI on the Internet which you may want to check out. A number of JavaScript programmers we have talked to also speak highly of Aptana Studio, which is based on Eclipse and offers many code development features for JavaScript.

Let us conclude this topic by briefly discussing Titanium-specific JavaScript API wrappers.

Additional Titanium Mobile APIs

Titanium Mobile supports a number of additional APIs to work with the native platform. You can discover these at http://www.codestrong.com/timobile/api/. We mention some of them briefly in Table 17-1.

Table 17–1. *Titanium APIs for Android*

Namespace	Contents
API	Has all the logging methods.
Accelerometer	Has the ability to listen and respond to accelerometer events.
App	You can get your project's properties here at runtime.
Database	Allows you to execute and work with SQLite database.
Filesystem	Has the ability to work with local files and directories.
Geolocation	Gets lat longs and watches for a certain location.
Gesture	Works with portrait, landscape views.
Media	Has the ability to work with images, sounds, videos.
Network	Basic networking stack around httpclient.
Platform	You can work with things such as phone number, model, name, version, etc.
UI	Includes dialogs, menus, tables.

Summary

We have covered a lot of ground and presented a very innovative approach to supplement your programming toolkit for Android. This WebKit-based approach can supplement the Android framework in a number of ways. It promotes quick development due to the easier layout semantics of HTML (for example, scrolling is so natural to HTML that you don't even need to think about it). The resulting UI can be easily styled with CSS. This approach also has a significant cross-platform appeal, which will open doors for web developers to be more productive on mobile platforms. Finally, the progress that is being made on the UI side for web frameworks is bound to spill over and enrich this programming experience further with the introduction of HTML5.

We have given you a lot of information in this chapter to understand the implications and architecture of WebKit-based technology and discover how suitable it is to your needs. This is a fun technology to program in. Tool sets involved are widely popular. Moreover, there's a lot of documentation available on the Internet. All these factors should make Titanium an attractive alternative to use on Android.

Chapter 18

Working with Android Market

Creating a great application that people will love also means you need an easy way for people to find it and download it. Google created Android Market to serve this purpose. From an icon right on the device, users can click straight into the Market to browse, search, review, and download applications. Many applications are free and some are not; the Market provides the payment mechanisms for easy purchasing. The Market is even accessible from intents inside of applications, making it easy for applications to reach out to the Market to guide the user into getting what they need for your application to be successful. For example, when a new version of your application becomes available, you can make it easy for the user to go straight to that Market page to get or buy the new version. Android Market is not the only way to get applications to devices, however, and other channels are popping up on the Internet.

While Android Market is normally available from a commercial handset device, it is not available over the Internet, nor is it available from within the emulator. This makes things a little more difficult for a developer. Ideally you will have a device of your own that you can use with Android Market. Android Market is available on the Android Developer Phone but will not show or download any paid applications. This is one of Google's ways of keeping paid apps from being pirated.

In this chapter, we'll explore how to get you set up for publishing applications to the Market, how to prepare your application for sale through the Market, how users will find, download and use your applications, and finally, alternative ways outside of Android Market to make your applications available.

Becoming a Publisher

Before you can upload an application to Android Market, you need to become a publisher. This is done by creating a Developer Account. Once that's done you will be able to upload your applications to the Market so they can be found and downloaded by users. Google has made the process to get a Developer Account relatively painless, and reasonably priced.

To publish anything, you first need to have a Google account—for example, a `gmail.com` e-mail account. Next, you establish an identity with the Android Market. You do this by going to this web page: `http://market.android.com/publish/signup`. You will need to provide a developer name, an e-mail address, a web site address, and a phone number where you can be contacted. All of these fields are required. You will be able to change these values later, once your account is set up. On the next screen in the process you will need to pay the registration fee. This is done via Google Checkout. In order to continue with the transaction, you will be required to log in with a Google account.

One of the choices during the payment process is called "Keep my email address confidential". This refers to the current transaction between you and Google Android Market to "purchase" publisher access. If you choose yes, you'll keep your e-mail address secret from Google Android Market. This has nothing to do with keeping your e-mail address secret from buyers of your application. Buyers' ability to see your e-mail address has nothing to do with this check box choice. More on that later.

After collecting the payment details, you're almost done. Next up is the Android Market Developer Distribution Agreement. This is the legal contract between Google and you. It spells out the rules for distributing apps, collecting payments, refunds, feedback, ratings, user rights, developer rights, and so on. There's more on these in the "Following the Rules" section of this chapter.

Upon accepting the Agreement, you will be taken to a page commonly called the Developer Console at `http://market.android.com/publish/Home`.

Following the Rules

The Android Market Developer Distribution Agreement contains a lot of rules. You might want legal counsel to review the contract before agreeing to it. This section describes some highlights you might be interested in.

- You have to be a developer in good standing to use the Android Market. This means you must go through the process as described above to get registered, you must accept the Agreement, and you must abide by the rules in the Agreement. Breaking the rules could get you barred and your products removed from the Market.

- You can distribute products for free or for a price. The Agreement applies either way. If selling products, you must have a payment processor such as Google Checkout. When Android 2.0 was introduced, Google Checkout was the only way to collect money through the Android Market. It is becoming possible for users to simply charge to their phone bill for downloading applications from Android Market, as announced by T-Mobile on November 4, 2009. It has not been possible to use PayPal or other payment processors to sell through the Android Market. This may change in a future release, however. Paid apps will incur a transaction fee, and possibly a fee from the device carrier, to be deducted from the sale price. As of January 2010, the transaction fee is 30 percent, so if the sale price is $10, Google collects $3 and you get $7 (assuming no carrier fees).

- It is your responsibility to remit appropriate taxes to your taxing authorities. When you set up your merchant account, you specify the appropriate tax rates to apply to purchases from people in other locations. Google Checkout will collect the appropriate taxes based on how you set up Google Checkout. This money will be provided to you, and you must remit it appropriately. For additional information on sales taxes in the US, try `http://biztaxlaw.about.com/od/businesstaxes/f/onlinesalestax.htm` and `http://www.thestc.com`.

- You are allowed to distribute a free demo version of your application, with an option to pay to unlock the application's full set of features; however, you must collect the payment via an authorized Android Market Payment Processor. You are not allowed to redirect users of your free application to some other payment processor to collect upgrade fees. You are also not allowed to charge a subscription fee for applications distributed through Android Market. Service fees are actually a good way to go if you can, since it helps prevent piracy of your application, and it can improve your overall cash flow. However, it means you can't sell that version of your application from within Android Market. This feature may be provided in Android Market in the future.

- Refunds are given to users who uninstall within 48 hours of purchasing an application. This can also serve as a sort of "free" trial. Dealing with a free application and an upgrade to a paid application can be troublesome, so going the refund-within-48-hours route is one way to keep it simple. (We'll show you some other ways later in this chapter.) Refunds are not given to users who can preview the product prior to download. This includes ringtones and wallpapers. You are required to provide adequate support for your product. If adequate support is not provided, users can request refunds and these will be charged back to you, possibly including handling fees.

- Users get unlimited reinstalls of applications downloaded from the Android Market. If a user does a factory reset of their device, this feature allows them to get all their apps back without having to repurchase.

- Developers agree to protect the privacy and legal rights of users. This includes protecting, (i.e., securing) any data that might be collected in the process of using the application. It is possible to change the rules regarding users' data protection, but only by displaying and having the user accept a separate agreement between you and the user.

- Your application must not compete with Android Market. Google does not want an application from within Android Market to sell Android products from outside of Android Market, thus bypassing the payment processor. This does not mean that you can't also sell your application through other channels, just that your application on Android Market cannot itself be doing the selling of Android products outside of the Android Market.

- Google will assign product ratings to your products. The ratings could be based on user feedback, install rates, uninstall rates, refund rates, and/or a Developer Composite Score. The Developer Composite Score is calculated by Google using past history across applications, and this could influence the rating of new applications. For this reason, it is important to release good quality applications associated to you, even the free ones. Earlier we mentioned that one way to do a free trial is to let users do a refund within the first 48 hours. Here we note that refunds can count against your score so this is a big reason why you wouldn't necessarily want to use refunds as a way to implement a free trial.

- By selling your application through Android Market you are granting the user a "non-exclusive, worldwide, perpetual license to perform, display and use the Product on the device". However, it is quite all right for you to write a separate End User License Agreement (EULA) that supersedes the statement above. Make this EULA available on your web site or otherwise provide a way for shoppers and users to be able to read it.

- Google requires that you abide by the branding rules for Android. Those rules include restrictions on the use of the word Android, as well as use of the robot graphic, logo, and custom typeface. For more details, go to this web site: `http://www.android.com/branding.html`.

Developer Console

From the Developer Console you can buy an Android Developer Phone (ADP), set up a merchant account (so you can charge for your applications), upload applications, and get information about your uploaded applications. You can also edit your account details including developer name, e-mail address, web address, and phone number.

The Android Developer Phone is a special device created specifically for Android developers. It is a full-featured device that is unlocked and not tied to any particular carrier. It will accept all SIM cards and comes with a 1GB SD card, a camera, a slider keyboard, and GPS. *Unlocked* means that you can do just about anything to it, including load a new version of the firmware and the Android platform, not just applications. While it might be tempting to get a device such as this to test out your applications, if all you want is a device for testing applications, you're better off buying a phone from a commercial carrier. The software that comes on the ADP is basic, whereas the software package from a carrier has more applications and more features. You can access a commercial phone from your workstation just like you can the ADP in order to do debugging. If you want to test out new versions of Android firmware, or the Android platform itself, then you'll need to get an ADP. Otherwise stick with a commercial Android phone.

If you do not set up a merchant account using Google Checkout, you will be unable to charge for your products in the Android Market. Setting up a merchant account is not difficult. Click the link from the Developer Console, fill out the application, agree to the Terms of Service and you're all set. You will need to provide a US Federal tax ID (EIN), a credit card number plus a US Social Security Number (SSN), or just a credit card number. The tax information is used to verify your credit status to ensure timely deposits. The credit card information is used to handle chargebacks due to buyer disputes when there are insufficient funds in your Google Checkout account. You can also supply bank account information to enable electronic funds transfers from the proceeds of your sales. Note that Google Checkout is a service for more than just Android Market. Therefore, do not get confused by the transaction fee information for Google Checkout for non-Android Market sales. The 30 percent mentioned above is the transaction fee rate for Android Market. There is also additional Google Checkout transaction fee information for non-Android Market sales and those do not apply to Android Market.

Uploading and monitoring your applications are probably the main functions of the Developer Console that you will use. (We'll discuss uploading applications later in this chapter.) For monitoring, the Market provides tools to see how your application is doing in terms of total downloads, and how many users still have it installed. You can see the overall rating of your apps in terms of 0 to 5 stars, and also how many people have submitted a rating. The Developer Console allows you to republish your application—for upgrades, for example—or to unpublish the application. Unpublishing does not remove it from devices, nor does it even necessarily remove it from the Google servers, especially if it's a paid app. A user who has paid for your application and who has uninstalled it, but not requested a refund, is allowed to reinstall it later even if you've unpublished it. The only way it is truly unavailable to users is if Google pulls it due to violation of the rules.

The way you see comments about your application is the same way that the users do, through Android Market. It is in your best interest to read the comments in order to address any problems quickly.

Preparing Your Application for Sale

There are quite a few things to think about and do to take an application from code complete to Android Market. This section will help you through those items.

Testing for Different Devices

With more and more Android devices becoming available, and each one potentially having some new hardware configuration, it is very important that you test for those devices you want to support. The ideal case would be to get access to one of each type of device to test your application on. The next best choice is to configure Android Virtual Devices (AVDs) for each type of device, specifying the appropriate hardware configuration, then testing with the emulator and each AVD. The Android SDK provides the Instrumentation class to assist with testing, as well as the UI/Application Exerciser Monkey. These tools will help you do automated testing so you don't spend forever testing your application. Before you begin testing, you probably want to remove any no-longer-needed testing artifacts from your code and from /res. You want your application to be as small as possible and to run as quickly as possible with the least amount of memory.

Supporting Different Screen Sizes

When Android SDK 1.6 came out, developers had to contend with new screen sizes, and in order to run on the new smaller size you must set a specific <supports-screens> element as a child element of <manifest> within the AndroidManifest.xml file. Without this new tag specifying that your application supports the small screen size, your application will not be visible in Market to devices that have a small screen. Of course this means that your application needs to be compiled against Android SDK 1.6 or newer. If you want your application to run on devices still using Android SDK 1.5, you'll need to be sure you don't take advantage of any new APIs that were introduced with Android SDK 1.6 or later. Then test against AVDs for older devices as well as newer devices. To support different screen sizes, you may need to create alternate resource files under /res. For example, for files in /res/layout, you may need to create corresponding files in /res/layout-small to support small screens. This does not mean you must also create corresponding files in /res/layout-large and /res/layout-normal, since Android will look in /res/layout if it can't find what it needs in a more specific resource directory such as /res/layout-large. Remember, too, that you can have combinations of qualifiers for these resource files; for example, /res/layout-small-land would contain layouts for small screens in landscape mode. Supporting small screens probably means creating alternate versions of drawables such as icons, too. For drawables, you may need to create alternate resource directories, taking into account screen resolution as well as screen size.

Preparing AndroidManifest.xml for Uploading

Your `AndroidManifest.xml` file probably needs to be tweaked a little bit before you can upload it to Android Market. By default, the ADT (Android Development Tools) in Eclipse does not add any attributes to the `<application>` tag within `AndroidManifest.xml`. However, before you can upload to Android Market, you need to make sure you've specified the `android:icon` attribute within the `<application>` tag. ADT normally puts the `android:icon` attribute in the `<activity>` tag, which is also needed. In fact, your application will work fine on devices and in the emulator with the `android:icon` specified in the `<activity>` tag, but when Android Market inspects your application's .apk file when uploading, it looks for the icon information in the `<application>` tag. To resolve this, simply copy the `android:icon` attribute from your `<activity>` tag to your `<application>` tag. Android Market also prevents uploading your application if the package name you've used starts with com.google, com.android, android, or com.example, but hopefully you didn't use one of those in your application.

There are many other compatibilities to consider as you test your application against device configurations. Some devices have cameras, some don't have physical keyboards, some have trackballs instead of directional pads. Use `<uses-configuration>` and `<uses-feature>` tags in your `AndroidManifest.xml` file as needed to define what hardware/platform requirements your application has. Android Market will enforce this and not let your application be downloaded to a device that won't support your application. Note that these tags are different and separate from the `<uses-permission>` tags of the `AndroidManifest.xml` file. While the user's device may come equipped with a camera, that doesn't mean the user wants to grant your application permission to use it. At the same time, declaring that your application needs permission to use the camera does not tell Android Market that your application requires a camera on the device. In most cases, you would end up with both tags in your `AndroidManifest.xml` file, for specifying that a camera is required, and for specifying that permission to use the camera is required.

Localizing Your Application

If your application will be used in other countries, you might want to consider localizing it. This is relatively easy to do technically. Finding someone to do the localizing is another matter. From the technical point of view, you simply create another folder under /res—for example, /res/values-fr to hold a French version of `strings.xml`. Take your existing `strings.xml` file, translate the string values to the new language, and save the new translated file under the new resource folder using the same file name as the original file. This same technique works for the other types of resource files—for example, drawables and menus. Images and colors may work better for your users if they are different for different countries or cultures. For this reason, it is a good idea to not use true color names for your resource names for colors. In the online documentation for colors, it is common to see something like this:

```
<color name="solid_red">#f00</color>
```

This means that in your code or other resource files, you're referring to the color by the actual name of the color, in this case, solid_red. In order to localize the color to some other color more appropriate for the other country or culture, it would be better to use a color name such as accent_color1 or alert_color. In English, red might be the appropriate color value to use while in Spanish it might be better to use a shade of yellow. Because a color name like alert_color does not reveal the actual color that you're using, it is less confusing when you want to change the actual color value to something else. At the same time, you can design a pleasing color scheme, with base colors and accent colors, and be more confident that you're using the correct colors in the correct places.

Menu choices might need to be changed in different countries, using fewer or more menu items, or organized differently, depending on where the application is being used. If you are faced with this situation, you are probably better off putting all your string text into strings.xml, or other files located under the /res/values directory, and using string IDs in the appropriate resource files everywhere else. This makes it much less likely that you will miss translating a string value in some obscure resource file. Your language translation work is then limited to the files under /res/values.

Preparing Your Application Icon

Shoppers and your users will see your application's icon and label prominently in both Android Market and on their device, once they've downloaded it. Please take special care to create a good icon and a good label for your application. Localize them as necessary or as desired. And remember that for different screen sizes, your icon may need to be tweaked to look good. Check out what other developers have done with their icons, especially those applications in the same category as your application. You want your application to get noticed, so it's better not to blend in with all the others. At the same time, you want your icon and label to work well on a device when surrounded by lots of other application icons that do other things. You don't want a user to be confused about what your application does because the icon has nothing to do with the functionality of your application.

Considerations for Paid Apps

Free applications don't need to worry much about software piracy, but paid apps do. If you are selling your application for a price, you have some other considerations to think about. Do you offer separate free and paid applications requiring you to build and manage two applications? Or do you keep one code base and use some sort of technique to tell if this application was paid for or not? No matter which approach is taken, how do you protect your application from being copied and installed on other devices for other people? Due to security vulnerabilities in phones, and due to the ability of certain people to get inside devices, fool-proof guarantees of copy-protection are extremely difficult to manage. One technique for maintaining a single code base, but allowing for separate free and paid modes is to take advantage of the `PackageManager`:

```
this.getPackageManager().checkSignatures(mainAppPkg, keyPkg)
```

This method compares the signatures of the two named packages and returns `PackageManager.SIGNATURE_MATCH` if they both exist and are the same. The package names must be different for each app to co-exist in Android Market, but that's fine. In your code, when you need to decide whether or not to allow functionality, you can call this method and provide the package name of your main application as well as the package name of your unlocking application. You then make the unlocking application a paid app in Android Market. If the user buys the unlocking application and downloads it to their device, the main application will then get a signature match and unlock the extra functionality. A less-clean way to deal with a single code base is to use source code versioning systems to configure appropriate sharing of common elements, and build scripts to handle creating the free and paid versions of your application.

Directing Users Back to the Market

Android has introduced a new URI scheme to help facilitate finding applications in Android Market: `market://`. For example, if you want to direct your users to the Market to locate a needed component, or to upsell to an additional app that unlocks features in your application, you would do something shown here, where `MY_PACKAGE_NAME` would be replaced by your real package name:

```
Intent intent = new Intent(Intent.ACTION_VIEW,
        Uri.parse("market://search?q=pname:MY_PACKAGE_NAME"));
startActivity(intent);
```

This will launch the Market app on the device and take the user to that package name. The user can then choose to download or buy the application. Note that this scheme does not work in a normal web browser. In addition to searching using package name (pname), you can search by developer name using `market://search?q=pub:"Fname Lname"` or against any of the public fields (application title, developer name, and application description) in Android Market using `market://search?q=<querystring>`.

Preparing Your .apk File for Uploading

To get your tested application ready for uploading—that is, to create the .apk file to upload— you need to do the following things (all covered in Chapter 7 in the section called "Signing Applications for Deployment"):

1. Create (if you haven't already) a production certificate to sign your application with.

2. If you're using maps, replace the MAP API key in `AndroidManifest.xml` with your production MAP API key. If you forget to do this, none of your users will be able to see maps.

3. Export your application by right-clicking on your project in Eclipse, choosing Android Tools ➤ Export Unsigned Application Package, and choosing an appropriate file name. It is convenient to give this file a temporary name because when you run zipalign in step 5, you need to provide an output file name and that should be your production .apk file name.

4. Run `jarsigner` on your new .apk file to sign it with the production certificate from step 1 above.

5. Run `zipalign` on your new .apk file to adjust any uncompressed data to the appropriate memory boundaries for better performance at runtime. This is where you will provide the final filename for your application's .apk file.

Uploading Your Application

Uploading is easy to do but takes some preparation. Before you begin an upload there are some things you will need to have ready and decisions to make. This section will go through that preparation and those decisions. Then when you've got everything you need, go to the Developer Console and choose Upload Application. You'll be prompted to supply lots of information about your application, the Market will run some processing of your application and the information, and then your application will show up in the Market!

The previous section in this chapter discussed preparing your application .apk file for uploading. Making your application attractive to shoppers requires some marketing on your part. You need good descriptions of what it is and does, and you need good images so shoppers understand what they might download.

One of the first items you'll be asked for when uploading an application is screenshots. The easiest way to capture screenshots of your application is to use DDMS. Fire up Eclipse, launch your application in the emulator or on a real device, and then switch Eclipse perspectives to DDMS and the Device view. From within the Device view, select the device where your application is running, and then click on the Screen Capture button (it looks like a little painting in the upper-right corner) or choose it from the View menu. If you have a choice when saving, choose 24-bit color. Android Market will convert your screenshots to compressed JPEG; starting with 24-bit will produce better results than starting with 8-bit color. Choose screenshots that will make your application stand out from the rest, but that also show the important functionality.

You can provide a promotional graphic as well, but its size is smaller than a screenshot. Although this graphic is optional, it is a good idea to include one. You never know when the graphic could be displayed; without one, you don't know what will be displayed in its place, if anything.

Android Market asks for textual information about your application to display to shoppers, including the title, descriptive text and promotional text. Promotional text can only be provided if you already provided a promotional graphic. Text can be provided in multiple languages, since you can choose to distribute your application to countries all over the world. The graphics mentioned above can only be supplied to Android Market once, so if your screenshots look different in different locales, you'll need to consider other ways to make those available to shoppers, perhaps on your own web site. This may change in the future. If you have written a separate EULA for your users, provide a link to it in your descriptive text so shoppers can view it prior to downloading your application. Consider that shoppers will likely use search to locate applications, so be sure to put appropriate words into your text to maximize your hit rate on searches related to your application's functionality. Finally, it's worthwhile to put a short comment in the text that says to e-mail you if the user runs into problems. Without this simple prompt, people are more likely to leave a negative comment, and a negative comment really limits your ability to troubleshoot and solve the problem, as compared to an e-mail exchange with the affected user.

One drawback to the user feedback mechanism described earlier is that it does not distinguish the version of your application. If negative reviews are received against version 1, and you release version 2 with everything fixed, the reviews from version 1 are still there and shoppers can't tell that those comments don't apply to the new version. When releasing a new version of an application, the application rating (number of stars) does not get reset, either. Keep this in mind when crafting your marketing text, or consider releasing the new version as a separate application.

One of your responsibilities when writing the text for your application is to disclose the permissions that are required. These are the same permissions as set in the `<uses-permission>` tags of your `AndroidManifest.xml` file within your application. When the user downloads your application to their device, Android will check the `AndroidManifest.xml` file and ask the user about all of the uses-permission requirements before completing the install. So you might as well disclose this up front. Otherwise you risk negative reviews from users surprised that an application requires some permission that they are not prepared to grant. Not to mention the refunds which also count against your Developer Composite Score. Similar to permissions, if your application requires a certain type of screen, or a camera, or other device feature, this should be disclosed in your text descriptions of your application.

When uploading your application, you will need to choose an application type and a category. As these values change with time we won't list them here, but it's easy to go to the Upload Application screen to see what they are.

Next is where you set the price of your application. By default the price is free, and you must have previously set up a Merchant Account in Google Checkout if you want to charge for your application. Setting the right price for an application is tricky, unless you've got some sophisticated market research capabilities, and even then it's still tricky. Prices set too high could turn people off, and you risk the effects of refunds if people don't feel the price was worth it. Prices set too low could also turn people off because they might think it's a cheap application.

Android Market provides an option to set copy protection on applications when you are uploading them. The copy protection will make your application use more device memory. It is also not fool-proof, and there are no guarantees that your application cannot be copied off of a device. For this reason, you may want to consider additional or alternative ways to prevent pirating of your application.

One of the last decisions to make before uploading your application is to choose the locations and carriers for your application to be visible to. By choosing All, your application will be available everywhere. However, you may want to restrict distribution geographically or by carrier. Depending on what functionality is in your application, you may need to restrict by location in order to comply with US export law. You may choose to restrict your application by carrier if your application has compatibility issues with certain carrier's devices or policies. To see carriers, click on a country link and the available carriers for that country will be displayed, allowing you to choose the ones you want. Choosing All also means that any new locations or carriers that Google adds will automatically see your application with no intervention from you.

Even though your developer profile contains your contact information, you can set different information when uploading each application. The Market asks for the web site, e-mail address, and phone number as contact information related to this application. You must supply at least one of these so buyers can get support, but you don't need to supply all three.

With all these decisions made, you must then attest that your application abides by Android's Content Guidelines (basically no nasty stuff), and make a second attestation that the software is okay for export from the United States. US export laws apply because Google's servers are located inside the US, even if you are outside of the US, and even if both you and your customer are outside of the US. Remember that you can always choose to distribute your application through other channels. You can then publish your application by clicking on the Publish button. Android Market will perform some checks on your application, for instance checking your application's certificate for the expiration date. If all goes well, your application will now be available for download. Congratulations!

User Experience on Android Market

Android Market is officially only available from devices, which means the user experience is via devices. Developers don't have any control over how Android Market works, other than to provide good text and graphics for their application's listing in the Market. Therefore, the user experience is pretty much up to Google. From a device, a user can search by keyword, look at top downloaded applications (both free and paid), featured applications, or new applications, or browse by categories. Once they find an application they want they simply select it, which pops up an item details screen allowing them to install it or buy it. Buying will take the user to Google Checkout to conduct the financial part of the transaction. Once downloaded, the new application shows up with all the other applications.

Android Market has an option to view downloaded applications in My Downloads. This area contains all installed apps, and any apps that you've purchased, even if you've removed them (perhaps you removed them just to make room for other applications).

This means you could delete a paid app from your phone, then reinstall it later without having to repurchase it. Of course, if you opted for a refund, the app will not show up in My Downloads. Also, free apps that you remove from your device will also not show up in My Downloads. The list of apps in My Downloads is tied to your Google Account used for the device. This means you could switch to a new physical device and still have access to all the apps you've paid for. But beware. Since you might have multiple identities with Google, you must use the exact same identity as before to get your apps on a new device. When viewing apps in My Downloads, any that have upgrades available will indicate this and allow you to get the upgrade.

Android Market filters applications available to users. It does this in a number of ways. Users in some countries can only see free applications because of the commerce legalities involved for Google in that country. Google is trying hard to overcome commerce hurdles so all paid apps will be available everywhere. Until that time comes, users in some countries will be unable to access paid apps. Users with devices running older versions of Android will not be able to see applications that require a newer version of the Android SDK. Users with device configurations that are not compatible with the requirements of the application (expressed via the `AndroidManifest.xml` file) will not be able to see those applications. For example, applications not specifically supporting small screens cannot be seen in Android Market by users on devices with small screens. This filtering is mostly intended to protect users from downloading applications that will not work on their device.

When purchasing apps in Android Market from other countries, your transaction may be subject to currency conversion, which can also carry an additional fee. You're really purchasing using the Google Checkout from the seller's country. Android Market will display an approximate amount but the actual charges could vary, depending on when the transaction is placed and with which payment processor. Buyers may notice a pending transaction against their account for a small amount (for example $1 US). This is done by Google to ensure that the payment information provided is correct, and this pending charge will not actually go through.

Unofficially, you can get to Android Market without using Android Market from a device. A few web sites are available that mirror Android Market. Shoppers can search, browse categories, and find out about Android Market applications over the Internet without having a device. This gets around the filtering that Android Market does based on your device configuration and location. However, this does not get apps onto your device. Android Market does not yet offer downloading via the Web, so even if you know an application exists in Android Market by using one of these sites, if it's not visible to your device you won't be able to get it through the Market. Examples of these mirror sites are `http://www.androlib.com` and `http://www.androidzoom.com`. There was another site called `http://www.cyrket.com` that performed this function, but it has apparently shut down.

Additionally, there are Android app stores completely separate from Android Market. Examples of these are `http://www.andappstore.com`, `http://slideme.org`, and `http://www.androidgear.com`. From these sites you can search, browse, find out about apps, and also download apps, either from a device or via a web browser. These sites don't have to abide by Google's rules, including the transaction fees for paid apps and methods of payment. PayPal and other payment processors can be used to purchase apps on these separate sites. These sites also don't restrict by location or device configuration. Some of them provide an Android client that can be installed, or in some cases may come pre-installed on a device. Users can simply launch a browser on their device and find the app they want to download via the web site; when the file is saved to the device, Android knows what to do with it. That is to say, a downloaded .apk file is treated as an Android application. If you click on it in the Download history of the browser (not to be confused with My Downloads, covered earlier) you will be prompted to see if you want to install it or not. This freedom means you can set up your own methods of downloading Android applications to users, even from your own web site and with your own payment methods. You must still deal with collecting any necessary sales tax and remitting those to the appropriate authorities.

While not restricted by Google's rules, these alternate methods of app distribution may not offer the same sort of buyer protections that are found in Android Market. It may be possible to purchase an application through an alternate market that will not work on the buyer's device. The buyer may also be responsible for creating backups, in case they lose the application from their device, or for transferring applications if they switch to a new device. Remember that Google does not restrict developers from selling their applications in multiple markets at the same time as they sell through Android Market. So consider all your options to make the most of your efforts.

Summary

You are now equipped to take on the world with your Android applications! We've shown you how to get yourself ready, how to get your application ready, how to publish, and how users will find, download and use your application.

Chapter 19

Outlook and Resources

In this last chapter of the book we would like to review the current progress of Android and its future outlook in the mobile marketplace.

To see how successful Android has been during 2009, we will first list the device manufacturers that have committed to building Android based devices. To see the progress in the capabilities of Android devices we will briefly examine the device specs for T-Mobile G1 (from 2008), Motorola Droid (late 2009) and the recently released Google's unlocked device NexusOne (early 2010). We have also seen the emergence of a number of Android application stores in 2009. We will list some of these online Android application stores.

To understand how Android will fare in the future, we will look at some of the Mobile OSs and contrast them to the Android OS and its framework and conclude the chapter with a set of useful resources covering Android development and Android news.

Current State of Android

Android has done really well in 2009. At the end of 2008 there is just one Android based device in the market, T-Mobile G1. In early 2009 there were reports that there could be as many as 18 device manufacturers that are expected to release devices by the end of 2009. It sounded too ambitious. There were also only a few thousand android based applications in early 2009. As 2009 has come to pass there are indeed over 18 device manufacturers that are already selling Android based devices ranging from Cell phones to Netbooks to eReaders. There are over 20,000 apps and counting in the various app stores. Hardly a week goes by without an article or two in the Wall Street Journal concerning Android.

Let us take a look at the range of devices that are available or announced in the market place.

Android Based Mobile Device Manufacturers

At the end of 2009 the list of manufacturers that make devices that run Android OS include

- Archos (An Internet tablet)
- Barnes and Noble (Nook book reader)
- Entourage (Dual faced eReader like a real book)
- General Mobile
- HTC (Maker of Magic, Hero, Droid Eris, Click/Tatoo)
- HKC (A clone platform for HTC)
- Huawei
- Lenovo
- LG Group
- Motorola
- Qigi
- Samsung
- Gini
- Ericson
- Acer
- Skytone (alpha-680 netbook)
- ICD Vega (tablet)

Most of these are mobile phone manufacturers and some manufacturers make Netbooks (Acer) and book readers (Barnes and Noble, Entourage). As you can see the avalanche of Android devices is here.

Let us consider a couple of these devices to see what kind of specs we could expect on these devices. Let us start with the more popular Motorola Droid

Motorola Droid

Motorola Droid comes with an ARM Cortex processor that clocks between 256 Mhz to 550Mhz (According to the Motorola spec site). It supports onboard RAM between 256M to 512MB. It has a WVGA capacitive touch screen, TFT (Thin Film Transistor) LCDs. Droid has a camera with 5 mega pixel resolution (Compare that to 12 Megapixels in more dedicated digital cameras). Droid supports GPS, Wifi, Bluetooth. Droid also comes with a USB 2.0 compliant micro USB. In addition to these Droid supports Acclerometer,

Proximity sensors, and can recognize ambient light. Droid also has a physical keyboard. You can see more of these specs at

```
http://www.motorola.com/Consumers/US-EN/Consumer-Product-and-Services/↵
Mobile-Phones/ci.Motorola-DROID-US-EN.alt
```

T-Mobile G1

Let's compare Motorola Droid to the T-Mobile G1 that came out last year. G1 has a Qualcomm processor that is at 528Mhz. It has an onboard RAM of 192Mb. It has an HVGA (320x480) TFT based flat touch sensitive screen. Its camera is 3.2 mega pixels. Its connectivity includes Bluetooth, GPS, and Wifi. It also supports USB 2.0 compatible micro USB. You can see more of these specs at

```
http://www.htc.com/www/product/g1/specification.html.
```

Nexus One

As we are considering a sampling of these devices let us also take a look at the latest addition from Google. In early 2010 Google has released an unlocked phone named "Nexus One" (`http://www.google.com/phone`) with the following specs. It will have a snapdragon processor (Qualcomm QSD 8250) running at 1GHz (Compare this to the current iPhone at 600MHz or Droid at 550Mhz). It will have a display WVGA (800X480) resolution and uses AMOLED (Active Matrix Organic Light Emitting Diodes) technology as opposed to TFTs. OLED technology allows for brighter, sharper and lighter displays. It will also have a 5 mega pixel camera. It will only have a virtual keyboard. It will be enabled for GSM and Wifi. The cost without a contract is $529.00 and the cost may vary if you were to sign up with a carrier such as T-Mobile. At the time of this writing only T-Mobile is available as a carrier but Verizon (US market) and Vodafone (European market) are announced to be carriers in Spring of 2010. You can see more of the technical specs at

```
http://www.google.com/phone/static/en_US-nexusone_tech_specs.html
```

As you can see things have progressed nicely for Android in 2009. Let us take a look at another growth aspect of Android, the Application Stores.

Android Application Stores

Another development in Android which may continue to advance is the number of application stores that sell android based applications online. At the time of this writing the list include

- Android Market (from Google)
- Slideme
- Andappstore
- Mplayit

- Androlib

- Storeoid (From General Mobile)

- Androidgear

- Handango

You may ask why these many stores? The often cited reasons seem to vary. We will list some of these here. As of today Google Market is not available in all countries nor does it have all payment methods. On another note some devices may be specialized requiring special attention such as dual sims (General Mobile's DSTL1 is an example). Some applications may be tailored for these special purpose devices. Another reason is that manufacturers like Motorola or Carriers like Verizon may want to control their applications to suit their needs. There is also some criticism that Google Market does not have the best browsing experience. Whatever the reasons may be, the application stores seem to mushroom.

Let us briefly cover each of the above listed stores and what they have to offer.

Android Market (`http://www.android.com/market/`), maintained by Google, is clearly the official Android store and continues to get better with each release. The chapter on Android Market has laid out its pros and cons.

Slideme (`http://slideme.org/applications`) is founded in 2008 and based in Seattle. Goal of `slideme` include niche markets, payment methods, apps that users can't find in traditional channels. Another stated goal of `slideme` is to sell and deliver applications globally.

At **Andappstore** (`http://andappstore.com/`) the goal seem to be to support both approved and unapproved android devices. The site seem basic, however. Compared to this site even `Slideme` site seems reasonably sophisticated.

mplayit (`http://mplayit.com`) is a site where you can browse apps not only for Android but also for iphone, and blackberry. `Mplayit` is a Facebook application that promises better browsing and buying experience. This site is quite well done and has an opportunity to build a user community around the buying experience. This site falls under the category of a directory service to the underlying Android Market data points.

AndroLib (`http://www.androlib.com/`), like `mplayit`, is another directory site exposing the underlying Android Market apps. However, unlike `mplayit`, it is not a Facebook application.

Storeoid is from General Mobile (`http://www.generalmobile.com/`), the maker of dual-sim android phones. To provide unique applications for their handsets, especially in Europe, General Mobile is planning to open Storeoid soon.

Androidgear (`http://www.androidgear.com`), related to PocketGear, seem to be an established company that has a good web based platform for selling. They have opened Androidgear to sell android based apps. The site looks well organized.

Handango (http://www.handango.com) seem like a seasoned online outlet for all types of gadgets and mobile applications. They sell not only for android but for many other mobile devices.

Among all these stores the number of Android application at the end of 2009 are expected to be around 20,000. As you can see the Android market place is transforming quickly towards a critical mass. To compare, iPhone is supposed to have around 80,000 apps at this time.

Outlook For Android

Android has more than met its expectations during 2009. Let us see in this section the competition for Android by looking at various Mobile efforts in the market place. We will also see how nimble is Android by looking at how it supports a quickly changing standard such as HTML 5.

This analysis will answer what is different about Android that garnered this much of success and will the success sustain going forward.

Quick Summary of Mobile Operating Systems

There has been much talk for over 10 years that mobile computing is the technology of the year. The reality has been that mobile computing has been on a more gradual trajectory. It is not until the advent of iPhone that revolutionary changes have taken place in the hardware or the software mobile space. 2009 and 2010 will probably be the years where the hardware will continue to accelerate in processing power and display clarity. We have already seen announcements that devices with processor speeds of 1GHz and on-board memory of 1 to 4GB to be released in 2010.

As we look at the Android OS, one obvious question is what other OSs exist for Mobile and how do they differ from Android. The number of Mobile OS efforts continue to increase. To list some, they are: Symbian, Blackberry (RIM - Research In Motion), iPhone OS (Apple), Moblin (intel), Maemo (Nokia), Windows Mobile (Microsoft), Palm OS, BREW (Qualcomm), and JavaFx Mobile/SavaJe (A java based OS from Sun). Let us see the primary characteristics of each of these.

Blackberry OS (http://na.blackberry.com/eng/developers/) from RIM (Research In Motion) is a very popular OS due to the penetration of Blackberry devices among corporations. This OS is a dedicated OS. Among other programmable interfaces Blackberry OS supports the Java programming language through Java ME. Notably its support include MIDP (Mobile Information Device Profile) and WAP (Wireless Application Protocol - primarily to support accessing mobile web from a mobile phone environment).

Symbian (http://www.symbian.org/) is one of the older OS's developed for ARM processors and specialized for mobile experience. Recently it is acquired by Nokia and is being used for their low end phones. Nokia has open sourced Symbian since its acquisition. The core languages to develop in Symbian are C++ and Java (through Java ME).

Moblin (http://moblin.org/about-moblin) is based on Linux and supported by Intel. This optimized Linux platform is open-source and is expected to support netbooks and mobile internet devices. The development environment is essentially a set of Linux development tools. Intel provides a set of "c" based libraries called Moblin Core that is optimized for mobile platforms. You can call these libraries from a variety of high level languages. The UI of Moblin is based on an open source effort called "clutter" (http://clutter-project.org) which itself is a wrapper on OpenGL. Bottom line with Moblin is that Intel is trying to bring together all mobile friendly efforts in the Linux space under a single umbrella.

Maemo (http://maemo.org/development/), like Moblin, is based on Linux. Maemo supports application development using c, c++, and python using Eclipse plugins. Maemo uses scratchbox (http://www.scratch-box.org) cross-compilation facility to develop programs that can run on other processors such as ARM . The Maemo platform has been developed by Nokia for its high end mobile devices. You will also use tools like GTK+, a popular windowing tool kit on Linux.

iPhone OS (http://developer.apple.com/iphone) is based on OS X but optimized for mobile needs. iPhone developers use the Mac OS X based XCode developer tools. The tools include an IDE, UI designer, debugger etc. Same set of tools are used to build both for Mac OS X and iPhone. The primary framework in this environment is called Cocoa, with a specialized version of it optimized for touch and mobile called Cocoa touch. Cocoa is developed in Objective-c, an object oriented language that is a superset of "c". It is also claimed to be dynamic similar to AppleScript, Python or Ruby. Apparently one can write applications in these scripting languages through the Cocoa Bridge.

Palm (http://www.palm.com/us) seem to be embracing both palm OS and windows mobile for their devices. Under Palm OS one would use Codewarior or Palm OS developer suite which includes the Eclipse IDE and the gcc compiler. Palm OS provides emulators that work with the eclipse IDE to test programs. Palm OS also allows programming through Java using the Java ME standard.

Windows Mobile (http://msdn.microsoft.com/en-us/windowsmobile/default.aspx) brings the complete windows programming experience to the mobile platform. Programming for windows mobile uses the same tool sets such as Visual Studio and the DotNet suite to the mobile platform. Any language that is built for the dotnet runtime will work. There are a number of languages including C# that fits this pattern.

BREW (https://brewmobileplatform.qualcomm.com/) is a mobile platform from Qualcomm. Programming in BREW is carried out through Visual Studio or Eclipse in "c" or "c++". The development platform of choice is windows although the code will run on ARM based devices. Development can also be done through FLASH based tools. BREW supports Java as well through Java ME.

JavaFX Mobile (http://www.sun.com/software/javafx/mobile/index.jsp) is an effort from Sun that is similar to Microsoft's Silverlight where a declarative approach is used to create rich UI experience. JavaFX mobile will run on any mobile platform that supports JavaME. A few years ago Sun bought SavaJe that has produced a Java based OS for mobile devices. These efforts from SavaJe have folded into JavaFX mobile. The development environment for JavaFX is essentially a java based development environment. This could be Netbeans environment from Sun or the open-sourc Eclipse IDE.

Given these efforts of the past and present what do they predict for Android? Does Android have advantages to fare well in the mobile space? Who will be its competitors?

Contrasting Android with other Mobile OSs

Let us see how each of these OSs that we have just outlined are geared for future.

Symbian's future seem a bit uncertain as Nokia, its sponsor, is already using `Maemo` for high-end mobile computing needs. Blackberry OS seem too proprietary and seem to be relying on Java ME for its widespread use. Java ME itself seems to be mired by the lengthy confusing standardization process. At least our quick analysis hasn't readily revealed compelling reasons that it would be an important force in the mobile computing space.

Moblin, based on Linux, is an odd player in the mix as Intel is espousing it as a platform for internet enabled tablets and mobile devices. Moblin's reliance on Linux and Linux based tools leave Apple and Windows developers outside the scope. Same is probably true of Maemo. They don't have the broad appeal needed by the larger programming community which would include Windows and Apple.

Palm seem to be taking a different route. The company has conceded that there are opportunities to make the device and not depend on the OS. By supporting multiple OSs on its device it may perhaps weather the storm better. It appears that it will tilt towards Windows Mobile. Under that argument they may even embrace Android at some time in the future.

That leaves really three strong players in the market. Windows Mobile, iPhone OS, and Android. Windows Mobile because Microsoft has lot of experience selling to device makers. The Dotnet based toolsets are formidable including its Silverlight suite. Although considered slow and buggy at the moment they will only get better and more appealing as the devices grow in processing power. The only question mark will be does the core windows code is amenable for optimization with the speed that is necessary in the market place. Apple has a formidable set of tools as well. But the reliance on Objective-C and the MacOS X platform as a prerequisite may continue to limit the number of developers although there are over 100,000 iPhone apps available. In short Apple continues to be an innovation engine.

Android has some advantages and some disadvantages in this space. Compared to the OSs that we have surveyed Android is one of the simplest and most comprehensive platforms with everything available as a single download. It is developer friendly to start programming. At the same time Android framework is fairly advanced. However as a complete set of tools Windows Mobile may have an edge. However Java brings a broader appeal and more programmers to the Android space. By choosing Java as the main language there is a performance compromise especially for games etc. Apple with its explicit memory management may be better suited in this need. Perhaps Android could fix this with non managed languages in the future.

Ultimately this race may be won by who is easy to work with for developers, and who is innovative and who is nimble. Speaking of being nimble let us take a look at an example and see how Android is responding to it.

Support for HTML 5 and What it Reveals

As we talk about development frameworks such as WPF (Windows Presentation Framework) or Cocoa Touch (Apples UI framework) or Android we tend to overlook another programmable work horse on the device. It is the browser. The days where browser is just a display of HTML content is getting behind us. The ability to run JavaScript and being able to manipulate the DOM has enabled a new paradigm for programming. We have outlined the scope of this ability in Chapter 17 when we have covered Titanium.

This trend is going to get some real teeth with HTML 5 as it supports the following features

- web workers
- video element
- canvas
- application caches and database
- geo location
- cross-document messaging
- content editable
- server sent events

Web workers allow browsers to start multiple threads to execute code. Previously one has to use `iframes` and AJAX to accomplish something like this. Now this is built into the browser. JavaScript provides new objects to facilitate these concepts.

The video element is used to play various video formats natively in the browser without the help of plugins such as `Flash` or `Silverlight`.

The "`canvas`" element is used to draw anything like a drawing surface using a scripting language like JavaScript. An open-source effort called "BeSpin" used this canvas approach to allow programming in the cloud using web pages.

The application cache allows offline storage to such things as email etc.

The geo location support allows for identifying the user locale both geographically where available and in-terms of ip addresses that are being used etc.

Cross document messaging allows sharing of data between two documents that are from two different domains in a secure way.

Content editable concept allows the browser to be able to change part of an html document by the user. This opens up WIKI like opportunities in a more direct manner.

Server-sent events allows for servers to push events to browsers. Together these features make the browser a standard programming framework controlled by many scripting languages. Many of these features are already supported by Chrome, Firefox, Opera and Safari. These are expected to be in the next version of `ie` when it is released. As far as Android is concerned, the following are stated to be explicitly supported

- Database API support, for client-side databases using SQL.
- Application cache support, for offline applications.
- Geolocation API support, to provide location information about the device.
- Video tag support in full screen mode.

The ability to support more of these features in a quicker way will enable exciting applications on Android. This level of agility might differentiate Android from others if Google could sustain it as the Android platform advances.

Let us conclude this chapter with set of useful Android related resources.

Android Resources

We will break the resources into two types. The first set will identify core resources which are useful for developers. The second set will include a list of resources to keep tabs on Android related news.

Core Android Resources

The resources in this section center around core Android support from Google.

Android Developers home page (`http://developer.android.com`): This is the main entry page for Android developers. As new SDKs are announced, this page will lead you to the right URLs.

The Developer's Guide (`http://developer.android.com/guide/index.html`): This is the Android Dev Guide for the most current release. Currently this documentation covers the Android 2.0 SDK.

Android 2.0 Features (`http://developer.android.com/sdk/android-2.0-highlights.html`): You can get a high level view of Android 2.0 features here.

Android 2.0 API level changes (`http://developer.android.com/sdk/android-2.0.html#api`): This URL lists a set of new APIs under 2.0

Android SDK downloads (`http://developer.android.com/sdk/index.html`): You can download the Android SDKs from this URL.

Android Open Source Project (http://source.android.com/): If you are looking for Android SDK source code, you will find it here.

Google I/O Developer Conference (http://code.google.com/events/io/): This site contains content from the Google I/O conference, including material from sessions about Android. You can look at conference material from previous years as well.

Git (http://git-scm.com/): To work with Android code, you need to use Git, an open source version-control system that accommodates large, distributed projects.

The Android Blog (http://android-developers.blogspot.com/): You will find in depth articles and commentary on the Android internals here.

Google Android Developers Group (http://groups.google.com/group/android-developers): This is the discussion group for android development issues

Android Issues List (http://code.google.com/p/android/issues/list): This is where bugs about android are reported and resolved. This site is helpful to see what are known issues with the android platform.

One of the co-authors site (http://www.satyakomatineni.com): Satya often keeps a running journal of his work, research, and code around android at this site. The links on the home page will direct you to various aspects of android.

Android News Related Resources

It may be worthwhile to check often what is happening with the Android platform by taking a peek at one or all of the following news sites dedicated to Android.

Anddev.org (http://www.anddev.org): This site has a number of forums addressing news, Android phone reviews, Android application reviews, Android coding problems, and Tutorials with source code. The idea seem sound with right contents, but coverage seem a bit spotty.

Androidandme (http://www.androidandme.com): This site seem more like a news magazine on Android. Its contents include phones, carriers, Applications, Games, Phone hacks, help for beginers, forums, and a store where you can buy phones and accessories. As anddev.org is organized around forums, this site is organized around blogs grouped into categories. It does have forums as well and seem to have a sizable user community.

Android guys (http://www.androidguys.com): This is a news site with an emphasis on podcasts. The main contents include News, A store to buy accessories and software, and a lot of podcasts. The store at this site is pretty elaborate. The site is also blog centric where each item is like an article or a blog post.

Androidauthority (http://www.androidauthority.com/): Another news site. It has news and reviews of android phone and applications. It has videos, store, and a section on netbooks. This looks like a basic blog site that has forums, categories and a store. But primarily, as the site says, this is a news and reviews site.

Androidcentral (http://www.androidcentral.com): This is news site seem to have articles, news, store, and forums

Summary

We have covered a lot of ground on Android in this book. We have covered all the topics in depth with working examples. In this last chapter we have analyzed the mobile market place and showed you how Android fits in to the future of mobile computing. We have listed a number of resources in the end to continue to keep in touch with Android.

Finally we thank you for allowing us to explain what we have learned about Android. Please don't hesitate to contact us if you have questions that we could help you with. You can contact any or all of us using the following emails

- Sayed Hashimi: hashimisayed@gmail.com
- Satya Komatineni: satya.komatineni@gmail.com
- Dave MacLean: davemac327@gmail.com

Index

■Special Characters

$ function, JQuery, 652
_data column, 94
_ID column, 47, 51, 89, 543

■Numerics

100ANDRO directory, 330
2D animation. *See* animation
3D graphics, 15

■A

AAPT (Android Asset Packaging Tool), 42, 65
about.html file, 641, 642
AbsoluteLayout layout manager, 149
Abstract Window Toolkit (AWT), Java SE, 2
abstracting common texture handling, 411–414
AbstractRenderer class, 381, 385, 386, 406
accelerateInterpolator tag, 232
Accelerometer, Titanium Mobile API, 660
Acclerometer sensor, 676
action keys, 492, 557–559
ACTION_CALL activity, 110
ACTION_CANCEL action, 592, 598
ACTION_DIAL activity, 109, 110
ACTION_DOWN event, 592, 599, 600, 601, 604, 605, 607, 613, 614
ACTION_GET_CONTENT intent, 119, 120
ACTION_KEY, SearchManager class, 558
ACTION_MASK constant, MotionEvent class, 614
ACTION_MOVE event, 592, 598, 599, 601, 604, 613
ACTION_MSG, SearchManager class, 558, 559
ACTION_OUTSIDE action, 592, 598
ACTION_PICK action, 117–119

ACTION_POINTER_3_DOWN constant, 614
ACTION_POINTER_ID_MASK constant, 614
ACTION_POINTER_ID_SHIFT constant, 614
ACTION_SEARCH action, 525, 527, 546, 548–549, 554, 558
ACTION_TTS_QUEUE_PROCESSING_COMPLETED, 579
ACTION_UP event, 592, 598, 599, 600, 601, 602, 604, 607, 608, 613, 614
ACTION_VIEW, 546, 548–549, 554
<action> tag, 312, 667
actionKey element, 558
Active Matrix Organic Light Emitting Diodes (AMOLED), 677
activities
    defined, 31
    directly invoking with components, 113–114
    regular, 503–509
    related to local search, 514–519
    simple suggestion provider search, 525–529
    simple suggestion provider search invoker, 529–530
    that disable search, 510
    widget configuration, 483–487
Activity class, 62, 93, 175, 177, 180, 182, 188, 189, 422, 423
activity node, 470
activity object, 70
activity windows, management of, 13
activity.onCreateContextMenu( ) method, 186
activity.registerForContextMenu( ) method, 186
AdapterContextMenuInfo class, 188
adapters
    ArrayAdapter, 165–166
    creating, 166–167
    SimpleCursorAdapter, 165
AdapterView class, 164

G

◼ J

Breinigsville, PA USA
16 November 2010
249414BV00016B/1/P